REVELATION
A COMMENTARY AND SURVEY SERIES

GOD'S FINAL WORD

HERE IS THE BOOK THAT CONCLUDES AND EXPANDS THE BOOK OF DANIEL

**Premillennial
Dispensational
King James Version**

Based on sound and Influential Bible Institute Material from a Past Generation

By
J. A. Moorman

> **Disclaimer**
>
> The author of this work has quoted the writers of many articles and books. This does not mean that the author endorses or recommends the works of others. If the author quotes someone, it does not mean that he agrees with all of the author's tenets, statements, concepts, or words, whether in the work quoted or any other work of the author. There has been no attempt to alter the meaning of the quotes; and therefore, some of the quotes are long in order to give the entire sense of the passage.

Copyright © 2018 by Jack A. Moorman
All Rights Reserved
Printed in the United States of America

ISBN 978-0-9993545-1-3

All Scripture quotes are from the King James Bible.

No part of this work may be reproduced without the expressed consent of the publisher, except for brief quotes, whether by electronic, photocopying, recording, or information storage and retrieval systems.

Address All Inquiries To:
THE OLD PATHS PUBLICATIONS, INC.
142 Gold Flume Way
Cleveland, Georgia, U.S.A.
Web: www.theoldpathspublications.com
E-mail: TOP@theoldpathspublications.com

DEDICATION

To the Godly teachers at Indiana Bible College and Tennessee Temple Bible College, who in the mid 1960's influenced the direction I would take on the Blessed Hope and the Fundamentals of the Faith.

Thank You very much,
Jack A. Moorman

TABLE OF CONTENTS

DEDICATION 3
TABLE OF CONTENTS 4
INTRODUCTION 11
   HERE IS THE BOOK THAT CONCLUDES AND EXPANDS 11
   THE BOOK OF DANIEL 11
   HERE IS THE BOOK THAT GATHERS 12
   THE PREVIOUS PROPHECIES AND QUOTATIONS OF SCRIPTURE 12
   HERE IS THE BOOK THAT DISPLAYS 12
   THE NAMES AND TITLES OF THE LORD JESUS CHRIST.. 12
   HERE IS THE BOOK THAT HEIGHTENS AND ILLUSTRATES 15
   THE LITERAL TRUTHS OF CHRIST'S RETURN WITH 15
   A STRIKING DISPLAY OF EMBLEMATIC LANGUAGE 15
   HERE IS A BOOK OF SPIRITUAL ARITHMETIC 16
   HERE IS THE BOOK THAT BRINGS THE FINAL WORD TO THE 17
   GREAT DOCTRINAL TRUTHS OF SCRIPTURE 17
      THE DOCTRINE OF CHRIST HIMSELF. 17
      THE DOCTRINE OF SCRIPTURE. 18
      THE DOCTRINE OF THE TRINITY. 18
      THE DOCTRINE OF MAN. 18
      THE DOCTRINE OF SALVATION. 18
      THE DOCTRINE OF THE CHURCH. 19
      THE DOCTRINE OF ANGELS. 19
      THE DOCTRINE OF THE SECOND COMING. 19
   HERE IS THE BOOK THAT CORRSPONDS TO 21
   AND FULFILLS ALL THAT BEGAN IN THE BOOK OF GENESIS 21
   THE KEY TO UNDERSTANDING THE STRUCTURE OF REVELATION 21
   OUTLINE 22
CHAPTER 1 25
   COMMENTARY 25
   A. THE PREFACE 25
   B. THE APOSTOLIC BENEDICTION 27
   FIFTEEN CATIGORICAL STATEMENTS CONCERNING 32
   WHAT THE BLOOD OF JESUS CHRIST *DOES*: 32
   JOHN MACARTHUR AND THE BLOOD OF CHRIST BY E. L. BYNUM 32
   RETURN TO: THE APOSTOLIC BENEDICTION 1:4-8 34
   C. THE GLORIOUS VISION OF THE LORD JESUS CHRIST 37
   REVIEW 46
   D. THE THREEFOLD DIVISION OF THE BOOK 48
   THE *SEVEN STARS* AND THE IMMENSE ROLE OF ANGELS 49
   THE HUMAN LEADER VIEW 49
   THE ANGEL - SUPERNATURAL BEING VIEW 50
   THE CONTEXT OF THE ANGELS IN REVELATION 1-3 51
   ANGELS AND STARS IN THE SCRIPTURES 51
   TWENTY-ONE INSTANCES OF HOLY ANGELS IN REVELATION 52
   ANGELS WITNESS THE CHURCHES NOW, AND WILL BEAR WITNESS AT THE JUDGEMENT SEAT OF CHRIST 55
   II THE THINGS WHICH ARE (1:19): THE CHURCH AGE – SEVEN KINDS (SEEN THROUGHOUT HISTORY) AND TIMES (DISTINCT PERIODS) OF CHURCHES 56

INDEX

THE SECOND COMING EMPHASIS GIVEN TO	56
THE SEVEN CHURCHES	56
THE ILLUSTRATIVE AND TYPICAL ASPECT OF	57
THE SEVEN CHURCHES	57
THE SEVEN AGE ASPECT OF THE CHURCHES	58
CHAPTER 2	**61**
A. EPHESUS:	61
EPHESUS, THE FOURTH LARGEST CITY OF THE ROMAN EMPIRE	61
B. SMYRNA:	67
FIVE CROWNS PROMISED TO BELIEVERS	71
C. PERGAMOS:	72
SATAN'S SEAT: BROUGHT FROM BABYLON TO PERGAMOS	73
D. THYATIRA:	79
A TIMELINE OF DOCUMENTED	82
ROMAN CATHOLIC PERSECUTION	82
"POPE FRANCIS SILENCE ON CATHOLIC PERSECUTION OF PROTESTANTS IN MEXICO"	84
1600 YEARS OF NON-BIBLICAL HERESY BROUGHT INTO THE CATHOLIC CHURCH,	85
CHAPTER 3	**89**
E. SARDIS: THE REFORMATION CHURCH	89
AUGUSTINE: THE FOUNDER OF THE *NON WATCHING CHURCH*	94
F. PHILADELPHIA:	98
KEPT FROM THE HOUR: EVIDENCE FOR	103
THE PRETRIBULATION RAPTURE	103
CHAPTER 4	**105**
THE TWOFOLD PURPOSE OF THE TRIBULATION:	105
THE CHURCH IS RAPTURED BEFORE	106
THE SEVEN YEARS OF WRATH	106
TEN BASIC REASONS FOR BELIEVING IN	107
THE PRETRIIBULATION RAPTURE	107
"FIFTY REASONS FOR THE PRETIBULATIONAL RAPTURE"	107
BY JOHN WALVOORD	107
FURTHER CONSIDERATIONS ON	111
THE PRETRIBULATIONAL RAPTURE	111
THE RAPTURE IS INTIMATED IN THE GOSPELS	111
THE RAPTURE AND THE LAST TRUMPET	112
THE RAPTURE AND *THE DAY OF CHRIST* IN II THESSALONIANS 2	114
THE RESTATED EVENTS OF II THESSALONIANS	116
A POST-TRIBULATION RAPTURE IS CONTRADICTORY	117
ARGUING FOR BUT NOT PREPARING FOR	117
A MID OR POST-TRIBULATIONAL RAPTURE	117
IT IS A GRIEVOUS ERROR TO SAY, "CHRIST CANNOT RETURN TODAY"!	118
THE FALL BACK POSITIONS USED TO AVOID	118
THE IMMINENT RAPTURE	118
CONCLUSION OF THE PHILADELPHIA LETTER	119
THE D,L. MOODY MEETINGS IN ENGLAND, SCOTLAND AND IRELAND	124
STRONG PREMILLENNIAL BIBLE INSTITUTES CHARACTERIZED THE PHILADELPHIA ERA	128
THE TROJAN HORSE: A WARNING NOT HEEDED IN THE PHILADELPHIA ERA	129
FACTS THAT WERE IGNORED IN THE RUSH TO THE VATICANUS, SINAITICUS TEXT:	
STRIKING DIFFERENCES FROM THE RECEIVED TEXT OF THE KJV	131
G. LAODICEA:	132

AN OVERRIDING CATALYST IN THE LAODECIAN ERA	135
THE POPULAR VIEW OF	138
THE BILLY GRAHAM CRUSADES (WIKIPEDIA)	138
THE OTHER VIEW: COMPLIANCE WITH	138
LIBERAL PROTESTANTISM AND CATHOLICISM	138
A FLEETING LOOK AT WHAT IT ONCE WAS BEFORE THE BILLY GRAHAM CRUSADES DESCENDED INTO LAODECIA	140
RETURN TO THE LAODICEA LETTER	141
LAODECIA IS WEALTHY BUT POOR: 38 RICH PREACHERS	142
CHAPTER 4 CONTINUED	**149**
THE THINGS WHICH MUST BE HEREAFTER	149
A. JOHN IS CAUGHT UP: THE SCENE IN HEAVEN BEFORE THE TRIBULATION: THE THRONE, THE SEALED BOOK	149
THE RAPTURE IN CHAPTER FOUR	151
JOHN HIMSELF IS IN HEAVEN	151
THE TWENTY-FOUR ELDERS ARE IN HEAVEN	151
THE SEVEN LAMPS ARE IN HEAVEN	152
FIVE-FOLD PRAISE TO THE ETERNAL GOD	162
CHAPTER 5	**165**
THE LAMB AND THE SEVEN-SEALED BOOK	165
THE OVERALL THEME OF CHAPTER FIVE	165
IS IT A SEVEN-SEALED *BOOK* OR *SCROLL*?	166
THE USE OF *BIBLION* AND *BIBLOS* IN THE KJV	167
CHAPTER 6	**177**
B. THE SEVEN YEAR TRIBULATION	177
THE SEAL JUDGEMENTS AND OTHER EVENTS	177
THE OLIVET DISCOURSE GIVES THE SAME ORDER AS REVELATION 6	178
THE FIRST FOUR SEALS: THE HORSEMEN	179
THE FIRST SEAL: DECEPTION 6:1,2	179
SIGNS OF THE COMING ANTICHRIST	181
THE SECOND SEAL: WAR 6:3,4	182
TEN WARS WITH HIGHEST DEATH TOLL, *EIGHT IN CHINA*	186
THE THIRD SEAL: FAMINE 6:5,6	188
WORLD POPULATION	190
THE FOURTH SEAL: GLOBAL DEATH 6:7,8	190
FROM THE PRESENT DAY TO THE BLACK DEATH:	192
EIGHT OF THE WORST PANDEMICS	192
THE FIRST HALF OF THE TRIBULATION: "*NOT SO BAD*"!!	194
THE FIFTH SEAL: MARTYRDOM	195
MARTYR TIMES WILL RETURN!	196
AN INTERMEDIATE BODY!	198
THE SIXTH SEAL: TERRESTIAL AND CELESTIAL UPHEAVE	199
THE WORLD DURING THE TRIBULATION SEES TRUTH REGARDING BIBLICAL COSMOLOGY	204
1. THEY WILL LEARN: THE EARTH WAS *FOUNDED* ON THE FIRST DAY OF THE CREATION WEEK	204
2. THEY WILL LEARN: THE FIRMAMENT WAS CREATED ON THE SECOND DAY	205
THEY WILL LEARN: THE SUN, MOON AND STARS WERE, (1) CREATED, (2) PLACED IN THE FIRMAMENT AND (3) STRETCHED OUT ON THE FOURTH DAY	205
3. THEY WILL LEARN: THE BIBLE NEVER SPEAKS OF THE EARTH MOVING, EXCEPT IN TIMES OF JUDGEMENT	206
4. THEY WILL LEARN: THE BIBLE *ALWAYS* SPEAKS OF THE SUN MOVING	206

INDEX

   B. THE SEVEN YEAR TRIBULATION 6-18 210
CHAPTER 7 211
   THE CHRONOLOGICAL KEY 211
   REGARDING THE SECOND HALF OF THE TRIBULATION, AND AFTER THESE THINGS 211
   THE THREE 3½ YEAR TIME DESIGNATIONS 211
   144,000 JEWISH EVANGELISTS SEALED 213
   THE ORDER OF BIRTH OF THE SONS OF JACOB 217
   WITH THEIR MOTHERS GENESIS 29,30,35 217
   DOES *ISRAEL* EVER MEAN ANYONE OTHER THAN *ISRAEL*? 218
CHAPTER 8 227
   THE TRUMPET JUDGEMENTS AND OTHER EVENTS 227
   THE PRELUDE TO THE SOUNDING OF THE TRUMPETS 227
   THE SIX TRUMPETS BLOWN: WOEFUL WRATH 230
   THE FIRST FOUR TRUMPETS: DESOLATIONS ON A GREATER SCALE 230
   THE FIRST TRUMPET: THE STRICKEN EARTH 231
   ONE OF THE WORST SUMMERS IN US HISTORY FOR WILDFIRES 231
   THE SECOND TRUMPET: THE STRICKEN SEAS 232
   CLEANING UP THE FUKUSHIMA NUCLEAR PLANT 232
   IS EXPECTED TO TAKE 30 TO 40 YEARS 232
   NASA REPORTS A MAJOR INCREASE IN ASTROID ACTIVITY 233
   THE THIRD TRUMPET: THE STRICKEN RIVERS 235
   THE FOUTH TRUMPET: THE STICKEN UNIVERSE 236
CHAPTER 9 239
   THE FIFTH AND SIXTH TRUMPETS: DESOLATIONS ON A WOEFUL SCALE 239
   THE FIFTH TRUMPET, FIRST WOE: *THE WORLD DESIRES TO DIE* ! 239
   ABUSSOS, THE BOTTOMLESS PIT 241
   THE LOCUST PLAGUE IN JOEL 241
   THE SIXTH TRUMPET, SECOND WOE: *A FURTHER THIRD OF THE WORLD DIES* ! 245
   THE TRUMPET JUDGEMENTS AND OTHER EVENTS 250
CHAPTER 10 251
   THE HERALD ANGEL ANNOUNCES THE SEVENTH TRUMPET 251
   GOD'S RAINBOW VERSUS THE LGBT RAINBOW, ... 252
   SEVEN STIPES VERSUS SIX 252
   THE APOSTLE EATS THE LITTLE BOOK 255
CHAPTER 11 257
   THE TWO WITNESSES 257
   THE MEASURING OF THE TRIBULATION TEMPLE 257
   THE MINISTRY OF THE WITNESSES 258
   THE 1260 DAY MINISTRY OF THE TWO WITNESSES WILL OPPOSE THE LATTER PART OF ANTICHRIST'S 2300 DAY "TELECAST" FROM THE TEMPLE MOUNT 259
   THE IDENTITY OF THE TWO WITNESSES 260
   AND THE COMING OF ELIJAH 260
   A FURTHER ANNOUNCEMENT OF THE SEVENTH TRUMPET 265
CHAPTER 12 269
   THE SUN-CLOTHED WOMAN, THE DRAGON, THE MANCHILD 269
   THE WOMAN, DRAGON AND MANCHILD INTRODUCED 269
   AN ALTERNATIVE AND LIKELY CORRECT VIEW OF THE SEVEN CROWNED HEADSAND THE TEN CROWNED HORNS 274
   THE DRAGON CAST OUT OF HEAVEN 276
   THE FLIGHT OF THE WOMAN 279

CHAPTER 13 283
THE BEAST 283
COMPARING BEAST'S DESCRIPTION IN REVELATION 12,13 AND DANIEL 7, 8: A DEVELOPING AND COMPLEMENTARY PICTURE OF THE SAME PERSON AND EMPIRE 286
THE FALSE PROPHET 288
666 WORDS DERIVED BY INCREASING EACH LETTER IN 292
THE ALPHABET BY SIX.. 292

CHAPTER 14 295
THE 144,000 JEWISH EVANGELISTS IN HEAVEN 295
THE SIX CALLS (THE FINAL CALL) 297
THE FIRST CALL: THE EVERLASTING GOSPEL 297
THE SECOND CALL: THE FALL OF BABLYON... 298
THE THIRD CALL: THE DOOM OF BEAST WORSHIPPERS 299
THE FOURTH CALL: THE BLESSED MARTYRS... 300
THE FIFTH CALL: THE REAPING OF THE EVIL HARVEST 301
THE SIXTH CALL: THE VINTAGE OF ARMAGEDDON 303

CHAPTER 15 307
THE PREPARATION FOR THE VIAL JUDGEMENTS 307

CHAPTER 16 311
THE SEVEN VIALS POURED OUT: UNMINGLED, FULL WRATH... 311
THE FIRST VIAL: THE MALIGNITY OF THE MARK 311
REVELATION SIXTEEN IS THE *GREAT* CHAPTER 311
THE SECOND VIAL: *OCEANS OF BLOOD* 312
THE THIRD VIAL: *RIVERS OF BLOOD*... 312
THE FOURTH VIAL: *THE SCORCHING SUN* 313
THE FIFTH VIAL: DARKNESS UPON THE BEAST'S COMMAND POST.............................. 313
THE SIXTH VIAL: THE STAMPEDE TO ARMAGEDDON 314
THE SEVENTH VIAL: WORLD WIDE DEVASTATION 317

CHAPTER 17 321
JUDGEMENT ON RELIGIOUS BABYLON 321
THE DESCRIPTION OF THE WOMAN AND THE BEAST 322
THE INTERPRETATION OF THE *BEAST* 324
HEREAFTER IN CHAPTER 17 THE EMPHASIS IS INCREASINGLY ON INDIVIDUAL LEADERS RATHER THAN THE NATIONS OVER WHICH THEY RULED 325
THE FINAL SEVEN NATIONS AND THE CURRENT.. 327
GROUP OF SEVEN (G 7) 327
THE INTERPRETATION OF THE *HORNS* 328
THE INTERPRETATION OF THE *WOMAN SITTING ON THE BEAST* 329

CHAPTER 18 331
JUDGEMENT ON POLITICAL-COMMERCIAL BABYLON... 331
BABYLON'S DESTRUCTION DECLARED 332
BABYLON'S DESTRUCTION LAMENTED.. 335
BABYLON'S DESTRUCTION EFFECTED 338
THE BABYLON AND ISRAEL PARALLELS IN JEREMIAH 50, 51....................................... 339
BABYLON: FIRST PROPHECY 340
BABYLON: SECOND PROPHECY 340
BABYLON: THIRD PROPHECY 340
BABYLON: FOURTH PROPHECY 341
BABYLON: FIFTH PROPHECY 342
BABYLON: SIXTH PROPHECY 342

INDEX

- BABYLON: SEVENTH PROPHECY 343
- BABYLON: EIGHTH PROPHECY 343
- BABYLON: CONCLUDING PROPHECY 344

CHAPTER 19 345
- C. THE SECOND COMING OF THE LORD JESUS CHRIST   19 345
- THE REJOICING 345
- CHRIST'S RETURN: PRECEDED BY REJOICING FOR THE FALL OF BABYLON 345
- CHRIST'S RETURN: PRECEDED BY REJOICING FOR 347
- THE MARRIAGE OF THE LAMB 347
- THE RETURN OF JESUS CHRIST 349
- ARMAGEDDON 352
- THE SUPPER OF THE GREAT GOD 19:17-21 352

CHAPTER 20 355
- THE THOUSAND YEAR REIGN OF JESUS CHRIST 355
- SATAN IS BOUND 355
- THE SAINTS REIGN 356
- THE CHARACTER OF THE MILLENNIAL KINGDOM 359
- SINNERS REBEL 361
- THE CATASTROPHIC SHOCK AT THE CLOSE OF THE MILLENNIUM 361
- SATAN IS DOOMED 365
- THE GREAT WHITE THRONE JUDGEMENT 365
- CREATION IN SEVEN DAYS POINTS TO EARTH'S HISTORY COMPLETED IN SEVEN THOUSAND YEARS 369
- ETERNAL GENERATIONS AS THE SAND OF THE SEA 369
- AND THE STARS OF HEAVEN ! 369

CHAPTER 21 & 22 373
- E. THE ETERNAL AGES   21,22 373
- ETERNITY: JOY OR SORROW FOREVER 373
- NEW JERUSALEM: ITS EXTERIOR 377
- THE VISTA OF THE CITY 377
- THE WALL, GATES AND FOUNDATIONS 378
- NUMBER TWELVE IN NEW JERUSALEM 378
- THE APPROACHES TO THE CITY 381
- NEW JERUSALEM: ITS INTERIOR 383
- THE FINAL CALL 385
- THE FIRST TESTIMONY 385
- THE FINAL CONFIRMATIONS 385
- THE SECOND TESTIMONY 386
- THE FINAL CHOICES 386
- THE THIRD TESTIMONY 388
- THE FINAL INVITATIONS 388
- THE FOURTH TESTIMONY 389
- THE FINAL WARNINGS 389
- THE SEVEN BEATITUDES OF THE BOOK OF REVELATION 390

ABOUT THE AUTHOR 391

The Book of Revelation
GOD'S FINAL WORD

The Isle of Patmos

Blessed is he that readeth, and they that hear the words of this prophecy, and keep those things which are written therein: for the time is at hand. 1:3.

Behold, I come quickly: blessed is he that keepeth the sayings of the prophecy of this book. 22:7.

And, behold, I come quickly; and my reward is with me, to give every man according as his work shall be. 22:12.

For I testify unto every man that heareth the words of the prophecy of this book, If any man shall add unto these things, God shall add unto him the plagues that are written in this book. 22:18.

And if any man shall take away from the words of the book of this prophecy, God shall take away his part out of the book of life, and out of the holy city, and from the things which are written in this book. 22:19.

He which testifieth these things saith, Surely I come quickly. Amen. Even so, come, Lord Jesus. 22:20.

INTRODUCTION

HERE IS THE BOOK THAT CONCLUDES AND EXPANDS THE BOOK OF DANIEL

All of the Bibles prophetic teaching regarding the Second Coming of Christ is interrelated and forms a wonderful harmonious unit. However at the heart of this vast body of revelation are the Books of Daniel and Revelation. Together they form an inter-linked foundation. It has long been the practice to study the Two Books together. Daniel introduces Revelation; Revelation greatly expands and magnifies this introduction. Sound Bible Institutes have generally taught both as a unit. Here are seven examples (among many) of the special linkage between Daniel and Revelation (adapted from Michael Hunt, *Agape Bible Study*).

THE VISION	DANIEL	REVELATION
1. Seven and 3 and ½ Year Time Periods	9:26,27; 12:7	11:3,7,9,11
2. 10 horns	7:8	12:3, 13:1; 17:3,8
3. The Leopard, Bear, Lion	7:4-6	13:2
4. The Beast speaking great blasphemies	7:8,11	13:5
5. War against Tribulation Believers	7:21	13:7
6. Worship of the Beast's Image	3:5-7, 15	13:15
7. The Son of Man coming in Clouds of Glory	7:13	1:7; 14:14

In addition, both the Prophet Daniel and the Apostle John had the unique and surpassing experience of seeing the Lord Jesus Christ in His Glory. To Daniel He appeared beside the great river Hiddekel (Tigris; Dan 10:5,6). He now appears to the Apostle John by the Mediterranean on the Isle of Patmos (Rev 1:13). The vision of *The Man* in Daniel 10 and Revelation 1 helps to show the unity of these Books.

Both are also uniquely designated as being blessed and beloved. *Daniel* as we have seen was *greatly beloved*, and with this unique statement he is the Old Testament counterpart to the Apostle John, *the disciple whom Jesus loved*. This is Heaven's singular honour for the men through whom the books composing the two primary pillars of Bible Prophecy were written.

THE PROPHET DANIEL
- *I am come to shew thee; for thou art **greatly beloved*** (Dan 9:23).
- *O Daniel, a man **greatly beloved*** (Dan 10:11).
- *O man **greatly beloved*** (Dan 10:19).

THE APOSTLE JOHN
- *one of his disciples, **whom Jesus loved*** (Jhn 13:23).
- *the other disciple, **whom Jesus loved*** (Jhn 20:2).

THE BOOK OF REVELATION

- *that disciple **whom Jesus loved*** (Jhn 21:7).
- *the disciple **whom Jesus loved*** (Jhn 21:20).

HERE IS THE BOOK THAT GATHERS
THE PREVIOUS PROPHECIES AND QUOTATIONS OF SCRIPTURE

The New Testament Books of Matthew, Hebrews and Revelation contain the largest number of quotations and allusions to the Old Testament; but whereas Matthew has 92, and Hebrews 102, the Book of Revelation contains 285 quotations and allusions from the Old Testament. With this Revelation is the mighty capstone and conclusion to the entire Bible. These quotations deal largely with the subject of the Lord's Return and of His Person and Work. In these quotations we see the Lord Jesus Christ as the Alpha and Omega *whose goings forth have been from of old, from everlasting past eternity* (Micah 5:2).

HERE IS THE BOOK THAT DISPLAYS
THE NAMES AND TITLES OF THE LORD JESUS CHRIST

The *Names* of Christ reveal His *Person*. It is proper therefore that the Bible concludes with a full display of that *NAME that is above every name* (Phil 2:9). No other Book of Scripture gives such a full display. The following list gives the first mention in Revelation of these Names and Titles.

- Jesus Christ 1:1
- Faithful Witness 1:5
- First Begotten of the Dead 1:5
- Prince of the Kings of the Earth 1:5
- Almighty 1:8
- Alpha and Omega 1:8
- First and Last 1:8
- Son of Man 1:13
- He that liveth and was dead 1:18
- He that holdeth the seven stars 2:1
- He who walketh midst the golden candlesticks 2:1
- He which hath the sharp sword with two edges 2:12
- Son of God 2:18
- He which searches the reins and hearts 2:23
- He that hath the seven Spirits of God 3:1
- He that hath the seven stars 3:1
- He that is Holy and True 3:7
- He that hath the key of David 3:7
- He that openeth and no man shutteth 3:7
- He that shutteth and no man openeth 3:7
- The Amen 3:14
- The Faithful and True Witness 3:14
- The Beginning of the Creation of God 3:14
- Lord 4:11
- Lion of the Tribe of Judah 5:5
- The Root of David 5:5
- A Lamb as it had been slain 5:6

INTRODUCTION

- The Lamb 5:8
- Lord of lords 17:14
- King of kings 17:14
- Faithful and True 19:11
- Rider of the white horse 19:11
- The Word of God 19:13
- Christ 20:4
- The Lord God of the holy prophets 22:6
- Beginning and the End 22:13
- The Bright and Morning Star 22:16

Drawn from http://avirtuouswoman.org/jesus-in-the-book-of-revelation/

Note that the Old Testament title, **Almighty** or **God Almighty** (*El Shaddai*) is applied to Christ (1:8). This occurs eight times in Revelation and only once elsewhere in the New Testament. In the passages below, *Almighty*, refers to both the Father or the Son.

- *I am Alpha and Omega, the beginning and the ending, saith the Lord, which is, and which was, and which is to come,* **the Almighty** (1:8).
- *And the four beasts had each of them six wings about him; and they were full of eyes within: and they rest not day and night, saying, Holy, holy, holy,* **Lord God Almighty**, *which was, and is, and is to come* (4:8).
- *Saying, We give thee thanks,* **O Lord God Almighty**, *which art, and wast, and art to come; because thou hast taken to thee thy great power, and hast reigned* (11:17).
- *And they sing the song of Moses the servant of God, and the song of the Lamb, saying, Great and marvellous are thy works,* **Lord God Almighty**; *just and true are thy ways, thou King of saints* (15:3).
- *And I heard another out of the altar say, Even so,* **Lord God Almighty**, *true and righteous are thy judgments* (16:7).
- *For they are the spirits of devils, working miracles, which go forth unto the kings of the earth and of the whole world, to gather them to the battle of that great day of* **God Almighty** (16:14).
- *And out of his mouth goeth a sharp sword, that with it he should smite the nations: and he shall rule them with a rod of iron: and he treadeth the winepress of the fierceness and wrath of* **Almighty God** (19:15).
- *And I saw no temple therein: for the* **Lord God Almighty** *and the Lamb are the temple of it* (21:22).

Consider also the Title **Son of Man** (Dan 7:13; Rev 14:14). This Title declares that as Glorified Man, Christ will restore all that the first man, Adam, lost. It is not once used in the Epistles of Paul; but occurs 84 times in the New Testament outside of those Epistles. Compare the *head* of Christ in the first and last New Testament occurrence.

- *And Jesus saith unto him, The foxes have holes, and the birds of the air have nests; but the Son of man* **hath not where to lay** <u>**his head**</u> (Matt 8:20).
- *And I looked, and behold a white cloud, and upon the cloud one sat like unto the Son of man,* **having on** <u>**his head**</u> **a golden crown**, *and in his hand a sharp sickle* (Rev 14:14).

Ponder further that while our Saviour is *KING OF KINGS AND LORD OF LORDS* in Revelation (and thus EMBOLDENED in our King James Bible;19:16); yet sight is never lost

THE BOOK OF REVELATION

that He is **the Lamb slain** for lost sinners. Christ is called the *Lamb* no fewer than 28 times in the Book of Revelation.

> *• And I beheld, and, lo, in the midst of the throne and of the four beasts, and in the midst of the elders, stood* **a Lamb as it had been slain**, *having seven horns and seven eyes, which are the seven Spirits of God sent forth into all the earth (5:6).*
>
> *• And when he had taken the book, the four beasts and four and twenty elders* **fell down before the Lamb**, *having every one of them harps, and golden vials full of odours, which are the prayers of saints (5:8).*
>
> *• Saying with a loud voice,* **Worthy is the Lamb** *that was slain to receive power, and riches, and wisdom, and strength, and honour, and glory, and blessing (5:12).*
>
> *• And every creature which is in heaven, and on the earth, and under the earth, and such as are in the sea, and all that are in them, heard I saying, Blessing, and honour, and glory, and power, be unto him that sitteth upon the throne, and* **unto the Lamb** *for ever and ever (5:13).*
>
> *• And I saw when* **the Lamb opened one of the seals**, *and I heard, as it were the noise of thunder, one of the four beasts saying, Come and see (6:1).*
>
> *• And said to the mountains and rocks, Fall on us, and hide us from the face of him that sitteth on the throne, and from* **the wrath of the Lamb** *(6:16).*
>
> *• After this I beheld, and, lo, a great multitude, which no man could number, of all nations, and kindreds, and people, and tongues, stood before the throne, and* **before the Lamb,** *clothed with white robes, and palms in their hands (7:9).*
>
> *• And cried with a loud voice, saying, Salvation to our God which sitteth upon the throne, and* **unto the Lamb** *(7:10).*
>
> *• And I said unto him, Sir, thou knowest. And he said to me, These are they which came out of great tribulation, and have washed their robes, and made them white in* **the blood of the Lamb** *(7:14).*
>
> *• For* **the Lamb which is in the midst of the throne** *shall feed them, and shall lead them unto living fountains of waters: and God shall wipe away all tears from their eyes (7:17).*
>
> *• And they overcame him by* **the blood of the Lamb**, *and by the word of their testimony; and they loved not their lives unto the death (12:11).*
>
> *• And all that dwell upon the earth shall worship him, whose names are not written in* **the book of life of the Lamb slain** *from the foundation of the world (13:8).*
>
> *• And I looked, and, lo,* **a Lamb stood** *on the mount Sion, and with him an hundred forty and four thousand, having his Father's name written in their foreheads (14:1).*
>
> *• These are they which were not defiled with women; for they are virgins. These are they which* **follow the Lamb** *whithersoever he goeth. These were redeemed from among men, being the firstfruits unto God and to the Lamb (14:4).*
>
> *• The same shall drink of the wine of the wrath of God, which is poured out without mixture into the cup of his indignation; and he shall be tormented with fire and brimstone in the presence of the holy angels, and* **in the presence of the Lamb** *(14:10).*
>
> *• And they sing the song of Moses the servant of God, and* **the song of the Lamb**, *saying, Great and marvellous are thy works, Lord God Almighty; just and true are thy ways, thou King of saints (15:3).*
>
> *• These shall* **make war with the Lamb, and the Lamb shall overcome them**: *for he is Lord of lords, and King of kings: and they that are with him are called, and chosen, and faithful (17:14).*
>
> *• Let us be glad and rejoice, and give honour to him: for* **the marriage of the Lamb** *is*

INTRODUCTION

come, and his wife hath made herself ready (19:7).

• *And he saith unto me, Write, Blessed are they which are called unto* **the marriage supper of the Lamb**. *And he saith unto me, These are the true sayings of God* (19:9).
• *And there came unto me one of the seven angels which had the seven vials full of the seven last plagues, and talked with me, saying, Come hither, I will shew thee* **the bride, the Lamb's wife** (21:9).
• *And the wall of the city had twelve foundations, and in them the names of* **the twelve apostles of the Lamb** (21:14).
• *And I saw no temple therein: for* **the Lord God Almighty and the Lamb are the temple** *of it* (21:22).
• *And the city had no need of the sun, neither of the moon, to shine in it: for the glory of God did lighten it, and* **the Lamb is the light** *thereof* (21:23).
• *And there shall in no wise enter into it any thing that defileth, neither whatsoever worketh abomination, or maketh a lie: but they which are written in* **the Lamb's book of life** (21:27).
• *And he shewed me a pure river of water of life, clear as crystal, proceeding out of* **the throne of God and of the Lamb**. (22:1).
• *And there shall be no more curse: but* **the throne of God and of the Lamb** *shall be in it; and his servants shall serve him* (22:3).

H. H. Snell writes:

> In the Revelation, THE LAMB is the **center** around which all else is clustered, the **foundation** on which everything lasting is built, the **nail** on which all hangs, the **object** to which all points, and the **spring** from which all blessing proceeds. THE LAMB is the light, the glory, the life, the Lord of Heaven and earth, from whose face all defilement must flee away, and in whose presence fulness of joy is known. Hence, we cannot go far in the study of the Revelation, without seeing THE LAMB, like direction-posts along the road, to remind us that He who did by Himself purge our sins is now highly exalted, and that to Him every knee must bow, and every tongue confess (*Notes on the Revelation*, in Walvoord).

HERE IS THE BOOK THAT HEIGHTENS AND ILLUSTRATES THE LITERAL TRUTHS OF CHRIST'S RETURN WITH A STRIKING DISPLAY OF EMBLEMATIC LANGUAGE

Imagery from almost every aspect of nature as well as grotesque non-natural forms are used by the Holy Spirit to emphasize the literal truth of this Book of Revelation.

From the animal world images appear: such as Christ as the *Lamb*; the *four horses* in Chapter 6, the *four creatures around the throne, locusts*, the *scorpions*, the *lion*, the *leopard*, the *bear*, *frogs*. There are unnatural beasts, such as those in Revelation 13.

From the natural world: *trees, grass. Earth, sky, sea, rivers. Sun, moon, stars, thunder, lightning, hail.*

Forms of humanity: *mother, child, wife, bride, harlot, man-child, saints, multitudes, witnesses, blasphemers.*

Images alluding to the Old Testament Temple: *the golden candlesticks of the churches, the heavenly Tabernacle, the altar, ark, and censer.*

Old Testament characters: *Balaam, Jezebel.*

Geographic descriptions: *the River Euphrates, Sodom, Armageddon, Jerusalem, the Great Sea.*

Christ, in this use of emblematic language is at the centre: He is the *Lamb* and *Lion* of the *tribe of Judah* and the *Root and Offspring of David*.

The emblem of Revelation are interpreted both in the book itself and other places in the Scriptures.

- The ***seven stars*** (1:16) represent seven angels (1:20).
- The ***seven candlesticks*** (1:13) represent seven churches (1:20).
- The ***hidden manna*** (2:17) speaks of Christ in glory (cp. Exod 16:33,34; Heb 9:4).
- The ***Morning Star*** (2:28) refers to Christ returning before the dawn, pointing to the Rapture of the Church before the establishment of the Kingdom (cp. Rev 22:16; 2 Pet 1:19).
- The ***key of David*** (3:7) represents the power to open and close doors (Is. 22:22).
- The ***seven lamps of fire*** represent the sevenfold Holy Spirit (4:5).
- The ***four beasts around the Throne*** (4:7) portray the attributes of God as reflected in His creatures.
- The ***seven eyes*** represent the sevenfold Holy Spirit (5:6).
- The ***odours*** of the golden vials symbolize the prayers of the saints (5:8).
- The ***four horses*** and their riders (6:1 ff.) represent successive events in the developing Tribulation.
- The ***fallen star*** (9:1) is the angel of the abyss, probably Satan (9:11).
- Many references are made to Jerusalem: ***the great city*** (11:8), **Sodom and Egypt** (11:8); and which stand in contrast to the ***new Jerusalem***, the heavenly city.
- The ***woman and the man-child*** (12:1,2) represent Israel and the 144,000 (12:5,6; Isa 66:7-9).
- ***Satan*** is described as the great dragon, the old serpent, and the devil (12:9; 20:2).
- The ***time, times, and half a time*** (12:14) are the same as 1,260 days (12:6).
- The ***beast out of the sea*** (13:1-10) is the future world ruler and his empire.
- The ***beast out of the earth*** (13:11-17) is the false prophet (19:20).
- The ***harlot*** (17:1) is Religious Babylon (17:5); she is the one who sits on seven hills (17:9), and is apostate Christendom headed by Rome.
- The ***waters*** (17:1) on which the woman sits represent the peoples of the world (17:15).
- The ***ten horns*** (17:12) are ten powerful nations associated with the Beast (13:1; 17:3,7, 8,11-17). They become the Antichrist's powerbase in his worldwide rule.
- The ***Lamb*** is Lord of lords and King of kings (17:14); yet the One who died.
- ***Fine linen*** represents the righteousness of the saints (19:8).
- ***The Root and Offspring of David*** (22:16) describe the deity and humanity of Christ.

HERE IS A BOOK OF SPIRITUAL ARITHMETIC

Very prominent in the book of Revelation is the use of numbers, namely, 2, 3, 3½, 4, 5, 6, 7, 10, 12, 24, 42, 144, 666, 1,000, 1,260, 1,600, 7,000, 12,000, 144,000, 100,000,000, and 200,000,000. These numbers are to be understood literally, but also with special spiritual significance.

The number *seven* is used 54 times, more than any other number in the book, and refers for example to seven literal churches in the opening chapter. Yet by the very use of this number (which speaks of completion) the concept is conveyed that these were representative churches which give a complete summary of the various conditions to be found in churches from John's day to the time of the Rapture. Note also:

INTRODUCTION

- Seven *candlesticks*
- Seven *stars*
- Seven *spirits of God*
- Seven *seals*
- Seven *angels* with seven *trumpets*
- Seven *vials* containing the seven *last plagues*
- Seven *thunders*
- Seven thousand *killed* in the earthquake in Chapter 12
- Seven *heads on the dragon* and *seven crowns,*
- Seven *heads* on the beast in Chapter 13
- Seven *mountains* in Chapter 17

Next in importance to the number seven and in the order of their frequency are the numbers *twelve*, *ten*, and *four*. For example:

- Twelve thousand *were sealed from each of the twelve tribes.*
- Twelve times two *elders*
- Twelve thousand *furlongs is the length, width and height of New Jerusalem*
- Twelve times twelve cubits is the height of the walls of New Jerusalem

From these indications it is clear that while the numbers are literal they also present a great deal more than that. Few numbers have attracted greater than the number of the Beast, 666 (13:18). While it may symbolize that no matter how many times repeated the number six will always fall short of the number seven and thus despite his great power the Antichrist will only be a man after all; yet beyond that there is a literal reality to 666 which as yet is not known to us. Also of special importance is the reference to forty-two months or 1,260 days, describing the precise length of the second half of the Tribulation and the number of days from the setting up of the image of the beast unto Christ's Return.

HERE IS THE BOOK THAT BRINGS THE FINAL WORD TO THE GREAT DOCTRINAL TRUTHS OF SCRIPTURE

The great emphasis of the Book of Revelation is the Second Coming of Christ and the events that occur in the immediate proximity of His Coming. Nevertheless few books of the Bible give a more complete overview of the great doctrines of Scripture.

THE DOCTRINE OF CHRIST HIMSELF.

The Book is as the first sentence declares: *The Revelation of Jesus Christ*. It reveals Jesus Christ as the glorified One in contrast to the Christ of the Gospels, who was seen in humiliation and suffering. The 37 Names and Titles given to Christ in Revelation declare Him to be the Eternal God, the Eternal Son of God. This Book declares Him *in respect to eternity*; that He is from eternity past to eternity future (1:8).

This Book also declares Him *in respect to time*. In His humanity He is *the root of David*, but also *the offspring of David* (22:16). He is *the beginning of the creation of God* (3:14). Though always God and always the Son of God, in past eternity He became the *prototype* of creation. He would be the first to take creature form. He would become the pattern for the creation of Adam, the head of God's creative work (cp. Col 1:15-18). His Death and Resurrection are declared (1:18). Special emphasis is placed on the shedding of His Blood (1:5; 7:14). Note further below.

THE BOOK OF REVELATION

THE DOCTRINE OF SCRIPTURE.

At its very beginning a special blessing is pronounced upon the reader and hearer of its Words. These Words are declared to be *the word of God, and of the testimony of Jesus Christ* (1:3). Therefore Divine and verbal inspiration are declared at the outset. Divine preservation of the Scriptures is also declared with the warning at the close.

- *For I testify unto every man that heareth the words of the prophecy of this book,* **If any man shall add** *unto these things, God shall add unto him the plagues that are written in this* book: And **if any man shall take away** *from the words of the book of this prophecy, God shall take away his part out of the book of life, and out of the holy city, and from the things which are written in this book* (22:18,19).

The Book of Revelation is a compendium of what was written by inspiration before. In its 404 verses of the Apocalypse, there are 285 quotations and allusions to the Old Testament. Quotations and allusions are drawn from nearly all of the books of the Old Testament. The fact that Revelation is so saturated with Scripture quotation makes it the fitting conclusion to the Bible.

THE DOCTRINE OF THE TRINITY.

The study of Revelation gives great insights to the truths concerning the Godhead: the Father, the Son, and the Holy Spirit. Here we see the holiness and justice of God; His majesty; His omnipotence; His omniscience; His omnipresence; His eternality. Here we see the righteousness of God and His divine judgment upon sin. This character of God is in keeping with his role as the divine Judge of men.

God the Father is seen on the Throne in 4:2,3 and 5:1,7. God the Holy Spirit, through whom John received the revelation (1:10), appears frequently and in various emblematic forms (*the seven-fold Spirit having seven horns and seven eyes*; 4:5; 5:6). Revelation concludes with the Holy Spirit giving an all-encompassing invitation (22:7). But, in keeping with the title and theme of the Book, the central revelation concerns Christ. He is seen in His coming into the world through the Tribe of Judah and of the House of David and His ultimate humiliation as the Slain Lamb. He is seen triumphant over death, He is seen as the Eternal One; as having infinite power and majesty; as the One who is worthy of all honour and adoration. Before His glorified humanity the apostle *falls as one dead* (1:17).

THE DOCTRINE OF MAN.

Man is revealed in Revelation in his most utter need of Divine grace. He is shown to be totally deserving of the judgement of God. Few books of the Bible describe man in greater depravity and as the object of more severe wrath. The summit of human blasphemy and wickedness is portrayed in the Beast and the False Prophet who are the supreme demonstration of Satan's handiwork in the human race.

THE DOCTRINE OF SALVATION.

The redemptive purpose of God is constantly in view in the Book of Revelation, beginning with the reference in 1:5 to Christ as the One *who loved us, and washed us from our sins in his own blood*. His crucifixion is mentioned in 1:7, and constant allusions follow as Christ is presented as the Slain Lamb, as the One who redeemed mankind *by His blood out of every kindred, tongue, and nation* (5:9); and the One whose Blood can make *white* the robes of the martyrs (7:14). It is because of His Finished Work in sacrifice that the invitation

INTRODUCTION

of the Spirit and bride (22:17) can be made to anyone who chooses to partake of *the water of life*. Salvation is ascribed to God three times (7:10; 12:10; 19:1). Emphasis is on the doctrine of redemption, and the saints are declared to be a redeemed people.

THE DOCTRINE OF THE CHURCH.

A major section dealing with the Church is found in the opening chapters of Revelation. Here are incisive letters to the seven churches. Here the emphasis is on practical truth and holy living, in keeping with their relationship to the Head of the church, Jesus Christ. Reference to the New Testament Church as the *ekklesia* (called out assembly) is not to be found in Chapters 4 through 18, but the Church as the Wife of the Lamb reappears in 19:7,8 and is included with the apostles in the description of the new Jerusalem, which the Church shares with saints of other ages.

It is to be carefully noted that the *ekklesia,* when used in the sense of believers in the Body of Christ, is nowhere found in Revelation from 3:14 to 22:16; but rather, the general word *hagios* (saint) is used. This supports the view that true believers are raptured before the Tribulation judgements take place (Chapters 6-19; cp. 3:10; 4:1) The true Church (1-3) is seen in contrast to the Harlot (ch. 17), and is also distinguished from the from those converted during the Tribulation (cp.7:14).

The churches described in Chapters 1-3 describe seven *categories* of churches that have existed for the past two thousand years. They are also a *prophecy* (cp. 1:3) of seven stages of Church History between the First and Second Comings of Christ.

THE DOCTRINE OF ANGELS.

No other book in the New Testament speaks more often of angels than the Book of Revelation. They are the principal vehicle of communication to John of the truths he is recording. The holy angels are seen in power and majesty in sharp contrast to the wicked or fallen angels also described in the Book. Angels are prominent in the scenes of Heaven in Chapters 4 and 5, and they reappear to sound the seven trumpets in Chapters 8 through 11. The truth of chapter 11 concerning the Two Witnesses is transmitted to John through an angel, and the warfare against the wicked angels is described dramatically in Chapter 12. The seven vials of the wrath of God are also administered by the angels in Chapters 15 and 16, and the judgment upon Babylon is related through angelic ministry. Angels accompany the Lord in His Second Coming in Chapter 19. The final message of the book recorded in Chapter 22 comes to John through the ministry of angels.

THE DOCTRINE OF THE SECOND COMING.

The Bible closes with a Book devoted *entirely* to the Second Coming of Christ and the events which occur in the times of His Coming. While a great deal is said in the previous sixty-five Books of Scripture nothing stated before prepares the reader for the *full force* of the Subject that is given in the Final Book!

With the Second Coming of Christ always imminent and likely to occur at any moment, Revelation begins with an account of the strengths and weaknesses of the churches, but especially with the emphasis that the Church is to watch for His Return (2:16,25; 3:3,10,11). *Hereafter* (4:1), is the tumultuous completion of the of the Times of Gentiles and the account Daniel's Seventieth Week for the Israel, both culminating in the Second Coming of Christ.

Nowhere else in Scripture is such a graphic description given of the seven year Tribulation. Here alone the great subject of the Old Testament prophets and of Christ

THE BOOK OF REVELATION

Himself when on earth – the Kingdom reign from the Throne of David - is declared to be a thousand years in length. Here, a clear distinction is made between the Millennium and that which follows, the New Heavens and New Earth. No book of Scripture more specifically sets before the believer in Christ his eternal hope and gives greater assurance of God's triumph over wickedness, rebellion, and unbelief.

In a word, the book of Revelation sees restored all that was lost in the Garden of Eden and infinitely more. Virtually every major theme of prophecy presented in the previous sixty-five Books of Scripture is dealt with, and that with special attention to completion and fulfilment. For this reason, Revelation is *the Bible in Miniature*.

(Sections of the above were drawn from *The Revelation of Jesus Christ* by John F. Walvoord).

The supreme revelation of Christ in this Book is that given in Chapter 19 where He is described as descending from heaven as King of kings and Lord of lords to slay the wicked, to deliver the righteous, and to accomplish His righteous purpose in the earth.

As Charles Wesley's great hymn describes:

INTRODUCTION

HERE IS THE BOOK THAT CORRSPONDS TO AND FULFILLS ALL THAT BEGAN IN THE BOOK OF GENESIS

GENESIS	REVELATION
The Beginning (Alpha)	The Consummation (Omega)
1:1 Heaven and Earth Created	21:1 Heaven and Earth passed away
1:16 Sun to govern the day	21:23 No need for the sun
1:5 Darkness called night	22:5 No night there
1:10 Waters He called seas	21:1 No more seas
2:10-14 A river in Eden	22:1,2 A river in New Jerusalem
37 Earth's government (Israel)	16:16 Earth's judgement (Israel)
1:26 Man in God's image	13 Man headed by Satan's image
3:1 Serpent	12:9; 20:2 Dragon
3:6 Entrance of sin	21:27 End of sin
3:14-17 Curse pronounced	22:3 No more curse
3:19 Death entered	21:4 No more death
3:24 Man driven out of Eden	22 Man restored
3:24 Tree of life guarded	22:14 Right to tree of life
3:17 Sorrow and suffering enter	22:4 No more sorrow
10:8-10 Nimrod founds Babylon	17; 18 Babylon falls
6-9 God's Flood to destroy evil generation	12:15 Satan's flood to destroy Israel
6-9 Rebels destroyed by flood	20:9 Rebels destroyed by fire
9:13 A rainbow: God's promise	4:3; 10:1 A rainbow for remembrance
13:19 Sodom & Egypt	11:8 Sodom & Egypt
14 A confederation vs. Abraham's people	12 A confederation vs. Abraham's Seed
24 A Bride for Isaac	21 A Bride for Christ
2:21 Bride paid for by a wound in his side	21 Bride paid for by a wound in His side
2:18-23 Marriage of First Adam	19 Marriage of Last Adam
3:21 Adam and Eve clothed in animal skins	3:4,5 Saints clothed in white raiment
3:24 Man's dominion ceases	22 Satan's domain ceases

THE KEY TO UNDERSTANDING THE STRUCTURE OF REVELATION

Chapter 1:19 gives the threefold outline of the Book.

Write the things
  (1) which thou <u>hast seen</u>,
  (2) and the things <u>which are</u>,
  (3) and the things <u>which shall be hereafter</u>.

The things which thou hast seen refer to Christ in His Glory, and as it relates to both the Church Age and His Second Coming. ***The things which are*** refer to the churches and the

Church Age (as shown by the immanency of Christ's Return). ***The things which shall be hereafter*** refer to seven year Tribulation (after the believing Church is removed). This will include also: the Return of Christ, the Millennial Reign of Christ, the New Heaven, New Earth and New Jerusalem.

The major portion of third section deals with the seven year Tribulation. Note that the *things which **shall be** hereafter* (1:19), change to *things which **must be** hereafter* (4:1). This section is based on three series of judgments: The Seven Seals, Seven Trumpets, and Seven Vials. The Seals cover the entire Tribulation; the Trumpets, the latter half; and the Vials, the last months or weeks of the Tribulation.

The Seventh Seal opens up into and includes the Seven Trumpets. The Seventh Trumpet opens up into and includes the Seven Vials. Thus all of the Trumpet and Vial judgments are contained within the Seventh Seal. The following notes will demonstrate that the Seventh Seal covers the second half of the Tribulation. *Everything* in Revelation from Chapter 7 unto the Return of Christ in Chapter 19 occurs in the second half.

OUTLINE

I THE THINGS WHICH THOU HAST SEEN (1:19): The Glorified Christ During the Present Age as Priest and soon to be King 1
   A. The Preface 1:1-3
   B. The Apostolic Benediction 1:4-8
   C. The Glorious Vision of the Lord Jesus Christ 1:9-18
   D. The Threefold Division of the Book 1:19,20

II THE THINGS WHICH ARE (1:19): The Church Age – Seven <u>Kinds</u> (seen throughout history) and <u>Times</u> (distinct periods) of Churches 2,3
   A. EPHESUS: The Post Apostolic Church – Sound in doctrine, busy, but love is waning 2:1-7.
   B. SMYRNA: Imperial Rome ***Persecutes*** the Church – Faithful to Christ, sorely persecuted, poor by the world's standards, but spiritually rich 2:8-11.
   C. PERGAMOS: Imperial Rome ***Accepts*** the Church – Persecution ceases, generally sound in its view of Christ, but false doctrine and worldly living are making inroads, intimidating power of bishops 2:12-17.
   D. THYATIRA: Ecclesiastical Rome ***Becomes*** the Church – Very busy, active, powerful, but in league with *the depths of Satan* (2:24) 2:18-29.
   E. SARDIS: The Reformation Church – ***Comes out*** but retains much of Rome's "deadness" (3:1), i.e. rituals, robes, infant baptism, state church, claims for itself God's promises to Israel, non-literal view of Bible prophecy 3:1-6.
   F. PHILADELPHIA: Seen mainly from 1850 to 1950 – Small but faithful, open door to world evangelization, interprets Bible prophecy literally 3:7-13.
   G. LAODICEA: Last Days Church – Big, wealthy, worldly, blind to Biblical truth. Its lifestyle, music etc., mixed in with that of the world 3:14-22.

III THE THINGS WHICH MUST BE HEREAFTER (1:19; 4;1): 4-22
   A. JOHN IS CAUGHT UP: THE SCENE IN HEAVEN BEFORE THE TRIBULATION Compare Daniel 7:9-14 4,5
      1. The Throne 4
      2. The Lamb and the Seven-Sealed Book 5
   B. THE SEVEN YEAR TRIBULATION 6-18
      <u>1. The Seal Judgements and Other Events 6,7</u>

INTRODUCTION

    a. Six Seals Opened: ***Wrath*** (6:17) 6
    b. 144,000 Jewish Men Sealed 7:1-8
    c. A Multitude of Gentiles Saved 7:9-17
   2. <u>The Trumpet Judgements and Other Events 8-14</u>
    a. The Seventh Seal Opened 8:1-6
    b. The Six Trumpets Blown: ***Woeful Wrath*** (8:13) 8:7-9:21
    c. The Herald Angel Announces the Seventh Trumpet (10:7) 10
    d. The Two Witnesses 11:1-13
    e. A Further Announcement of the Seventh Trumpet 11:14-19
    f. The Woman, The Dragon, The Manchild 12
    g. The Beast and the False Prophet 13
    h. The 144,000 Jewish Evangelists In Heaven 14:1-5
    i. The Six Calls (The Final Call) 14:6-20
   3. <u>The Vial Judgements and Other Events 15-18</u>
    a. The Preparation 15
    b. The Seven Vials Poured Out: ***Unmingled Full Wrath*** (14:10; 15:1) 16
    c. Judgement on Religious Babylon 17
    d. Judgement on Commercial-Political Babylon 18
 C. THE SECOND COMING OF THE LORD JESUS CHRIST 19
   1. The Rejoicing 1-10
   2. The Return of Jesus Christ 11-16
   3. Armageddon 17-21
 D. THE THOUSAND YEAR REIGN OF JESUS CHRIST 20
   1. Satan is Bound 1-3
   2. The Saints Reign 4-6
   3. Sinners Rebel 7-9
   4. Satan is Doomed 10
   5. The Great White Throne Judgement 11-15
 E. THE ETERNAL AGES 21,22
   1. Eternity: Joy or Sorrow Forever 21:1-8
   2. New Jerusalem: Its Exterior 21:9-27
   3. New Jerusalem: Its Interior 22:1-5
   4. The Bible's Final Call 22:6-21

CHAPTER 1

COMMENTARY

I THE THINGS WHICH THOU HAST SEEN (1:19): The Glorified Christ During the Present Age as Priest and soon to be King 1
A. The Preface 1:1-3
B. The Apostolic Benediction 1:4-8
C. The Glorious Vision of the Lord Jesus Christ 1:9-18
D. The Threefold Division of the Book 1:19,20

A. THE PREFACE 1:1-3

1:1) ***The Revelation of Jesus Christ, which God gave unto him, to shew unto his servants things which must shortly come to pass; and he sent and signified it by his angel unto his servant John:*** (1:2) ***Who bare record of the word of God, and of the testimony of Jesus Christ, and of all things that he saw.***
(1:3) ***Blessed is he that readeth, and they that hear the words of this prophecy, and keep those things which are written therein: for the time is at hand.***

1. THE CIRCUMSTANCES OF THE BOOK 1:1.

(1) THIS IS THE REVELATION OF JESUS CHRIST. ***The revelation of Jesus Christ*** The entire Bible is such; for all revelation comes through Christ and all centres in Him; and especially *in these last days God has spoken to us by his Son,* and concerning his Son (Heb 1:3). Christ is Prophet and Priest, but now He is fully revealed as King (11:15). The word *revelation* is the translation of *apokalypsis* (lit. "to take away the covering").

(2) THIS IS A REVELATION WHICH WAS GIVEN UNTO CHRIST: ***which God gave unto him.*** Though Christ is himself God, and as such has all light and life in Himself, yet, as He sustains the office of *Mediator between God and man* (1 Tim 2:5), He receives His instructions from the Father. Our Lord Jesus is the *Great Trustee* of divine revelation (Matt 24:35), and now especially of the great matters concerning His Return. The revelation of the Father to the Son is previously mentioned in John 3:34,35; 5:20-24; 7:16; 8:28; 12:49; 14:10, 24.

(3) THIS IS A REVELATION WHICH IS IMMINENT: ***which must shortly come to pass.*** It has been nearly two thousand years. To the weary believer it may seem long. To the mocker the promise is a cause of derision. To the Lord a thousand years is *but a day*.

> • Knowing this first, that **there shall come in the last days scoffers**, *walking after their own lusts, And saying,* **Where is the promise of his coming?** *for since the fathers fell asleep, all things continue as they were from the beginning of the creation* (2 Pet 3:3,4).
> • But, beloved, be not ignorant of this one thing, that **one day is with the Lord as a thousand years, and a thousand years as one day**. *The Lord is not slack concerning his promise, as some men count slackness; but is longsuffering to us-ward, not willing that any should perish, but that all should come to repentance.* **But the day of the Lord will come as a thief in the night**; *in the which the heavens shall pass away with a great*

noise, and the elements shall melt with fervent heat, the earth also and the works that are therein shall be burned up (2 Pet 3:8-10).

That which regards the Church began almost immediately (ch. 2,3). That which takes place *hereafter* (1:19; ch. 4-22) will not take place until the Coming of Christ. Note that the Tribulation (after the Rapture and before the Return of Christ) is described, as in 2 Peter, to be a time of *burning* (Isa 24:6; Mal 4:1).

That which Daniel declared would occur *in the latter days* (Dan 10:14) is here described as **shortly** (*en tachei*), that is, quickly, suddenly, at any moment and unexpectedly for most. It may be *long* (Matt 25:19, Mk 13:34), but the term *shortly* is the word used for the Lord's Return (cp. Lk 18:8; Acts 12:7; 22:18; Rom 16:20). A similar word, *tachys*, is translated *quickly* seven times in Revelation (2:5, 16; 3:11; 11:14; 22:7, 12, 20).

(4) THIS IS A REVELATION CHRIST INTRUSTED TO HIS ANGEL: **and he sent and signified it by his angel.** Here is the order followed in this Book: the Father gave it to Christ, and Christ employed an angel to communicate it to John. The angels are God's messengers; they are *ministering spirits to the heirs of salvation* (Heb 1:14). A previous occurrence of **signified** illustrates the meaning of the term here:

- *And I, if I be lifted up from the earth, will draw all men unto me. This he said,* **signifying** *what death he should die* (Jhn 12:32,33).

Emblematic or symbolic language is given by inspiration to impress and clarify literal truth. The angel enabled the Apostle to understand this form of revelation.

(5) THIS IS A REVELATION THAT WAS GIVEN TO THE APOSTLE JOHN: **unto his servant John.** As the angels are the messengers of Christ, the Apostles are the messengers of the churches. What they receive from heaven, they are to communicate on earth. John was the apostle chosen for this service.

John is declared to be the recipient of the revelation, his name occurring four other times in this Book (1:4, 9; 21:2; 22:8). That John should be called a **servant** (*doulos*) rather than an apostle is in common with the term being used of other Apostles in the New Testament (Rom 1:1; Phil. 1:1; Titus 1:1; Jms 1:1; 2 Pet 1:1; Jude 1). Some think that John was the only surviving apostle, the rest having sealed their testimony with their blood. This was to be the *last* Book of divine revelation; and notice of such was given to the churches by the *last* of the apostles.

John was, under the New Testament, as the prophet Daniel under the Old, *a man greatly beloved.* He was the *servant* of Christ; he was an Apostle, an Evangelist, and a Prophet; he served Christ in each of the three extraordinary offices of the early Church. Christ calls him in an eminent sense, His *servant John.*

2. THE ATTESTATION OF THE BOOK 1:2. *Who bare record of the word of God, and of the testimony of Jesus Christ, and of all things that he saw.* It is observable that the historical books of the Old Testament do not always have the name of the historian prefixed to them, for example *Judges, Kings, Chronicles;* but in the prophetical books the name is *always* prefixed, as *Isaiah, Jeremiah, Ezekiel* and all the others. So in the New Testament, though John's name is not prefixed to his First Epistle (nor is it directly prefixed *by name* to his Gospel or the two other Epistles), yet it is prefixed in this prophecy. Nothing recorded in this revelation was his own invention or imagination; but all was the record of God and the testimony of Jesus Christ; and, as he added nothing to it, so he kept back no part of the counsels of God.

CHAPTER 1

The expression *bare record* occurs three times in this chapter. It means "to bear witness to," or "to testify concerning." The book of Revelation is *the Word of God*, that is, its words originate from God, but John is careful to tell us that he bears witness of his reception of these Words. This is true of the entire Bible but especially so stated in its final Book. Note John's statements of *bearing witness* in his Gospel and Epistle (Jhn 1:15; 21:24; 1 Jhn 1: 1,2,3).

2. THE BLESSING OF THE BOOK 1:3.
(1) THE THREEFOLD BLESSING. This makes the preface of Revelation unique among the 66 Books of the Bible. ***Blessed is he that readeth, and they that hear the words of this prophecy, and keep those things which are written therein*** (1:3). It is a blessed privilege to *read* all of the Bible; but especially this Book! It is blessed to *listen* to the Bible; but especially this Book! And, it is a blessing to *keep* the Bible; but this Book especially.

The three words (***readeth, hear, keep***) are in the present tense, implying continued reading, hearing, and observing. The book of Revelation is the only book of Scripture containing such an opening promise of blessing. The blessing here pronounced is the first of *seven beatitudes* in the book (1:3; 14:13; 16:15; 19:9; 20:6; 22:7, 14).

This anticipates that many would neglect Revelation and refuse to take its prophecies literally. It is a sad fact that the one Book in the New Testament which invokes a special blessing on the reader should often be left unread. John Calvin wrote many commentaries, but none on Revelation. The events here described will occur literally and in proximity to Christ's Return. Calvinism, generally, has sought to discount this.

(2) THE DESCRIPTION OF THE BOOK OF REVELATION. It is described as ***the words of this prophecy***. Thus the Book as a whole is prophetic, especially with regard to events that will take place at the time of Christ's Return. It also demonstrates that the account of the Seven Churches are prophetic and describe churches from John's day unto the Second Coming, and likely stages of Church History.

(3) THE SPECIAL REASON FOR THE BLESSING: ***the time is at hand.*** Christ's Coming is imminent, and especially so now as we *see the day approaching* (Heb 10:25). Though the time may seem long (Matt 25:19; Mk 13:34) there is no prophesied event which prevents His Coming from taking place now.

The time (*kairos*) can refer to a space or period of time. Daniel mentions *the time of the end* five times (Dan 8:17; 11:35,40; 12:4,9). *The time* is also declared to be *at hand* at the close of the Book (22:10), and there are five other references to time, using *kairos* (11:18; 12:12 and three occurrences in 12:14). These occurrences generally refer to a *short time*. An even shorter time is indicated by *hour* (*hora*). Time in general is designated by the Greek word *chronos*.

B. THE APOSTOLIC BENEDICTION 1:4-8

(1:4) ***John to the seven churches which are in Asia: Grace be unto you, and peace, from him which is, and which was, and which is to come; and from the seven Spirits which are before his throne;***

(1:5) ***And from Jesus Christ, who is the faithful witness, and the first begotten of the dead, and the prince of the kings of the earth. Unto him that loved us, and washed us from our sins in his own blood,*** (1:6) ***And hath made us kings and priests unto God and his Father; to him be glory and dominion for ever and ever. Amen.***

(1:7) ***Behold, he cometh with clouds; and every eye shall see him, and they also which pierced him: and all kindreds of the earth shall wail because of him. Even so, Amen.***

(1:8) ***I am Alpha and Omega, the beginning and the ending, saith the Lord, which is, and which was, and which is to come, the Almighty.***

THE BOOK OF REVELATION

1. THE INTRODUCTION TO THE BENEDICTION 1:4.
(1) THE BENEDICTION IS DECLARED TO THE SEVEN CHURCHES OF ASIA. *John to the seven churches which are in Asia* (1:4). The Seven Churches are named in 1:11, and distinct messages are sent to each in Chapters 2 and 3. Each of the seven churches were located in the western half of Asia Minor. The apostolic blessing is more expressly directed to them because they were nearest to John, who was now "off-shore" from them in the isle of Patmos. John's ministry is said to have been associated with Ephesus and he would have had a first-hand knowledge of them and special care for them.

These are *seven* churches and with this number we are alerted to the fact that a statement of *completion* and *totality* is about to be made. The number *seven* is written on the face of the Scriptures. We will be given a complete summary of Church History from John's day to the time of the Rapture.

(2) THE BENEDICTION IS TWO-FOLD. *Grace be unto you, and peace*. This is the same greeting as bestowed in the Epistles of Paul. These two words express the essence of the believer's experience. *Grace* is God's attitude toward the believer on the basis of Christ's Sacrifice. It is coupled with *peace*. This word speaks of His relationship with the believer and as a result the believer may now have the peace of God. *Peace* speaks of relationship and here the *peace* of God that comes from that relationship. *Grace* is God's good will toward us and His good work in us; and *peace* is the comforting evidence and assurance of this grace. Grace represents standing; peace represents experience.

The Seven Churches of Asia and the Church Age

(3) THE BENEDICTION IS GIVEN BY THE HOLY TRINITY: *from him which is, and which was, and which is to come; and from the seven Spirits which are before his throne.* From where does such a great blessing come? In whose name does the Apostle bless the churches? It is in the Name of God; it is in the Name of the Father, the Son and the Holy Spirit; it is in the Name of the Godhead, the Holy Trinity. The First and Third Persons are mentioned in verse 4, while the body of the Benediction (1:5-8) is devoted entirely to the Second Person, the Son.

CHAPTER 1

[1] THE FATHER IS FIRST NAMED. He is described as Jehovah *who is, and who was, and who is to come.* He is eternal, unchangeable, the same to the Old-Testament believer *who was*, and to the New Testament church *who is*, and who will be the same, *who is to come*, to the believer at His Second Coming. This expression is used four other times and is also applied directly to Christ.

- *I am Alpha and Omega, the beginning and the ending, saith the Lord,* **which is, and which was, and which is to come***, the Almighty* (1:8).
- *And the four beasts had each of them six wings about him; and they were full of eyes within: and they rest not day and night, saying, Holy, holy, holy, LORD God Almighty,* **which was, and is, and is to come** (4:8).
- *Saying, We give thee thanks, O LORD God Almighty,* **which art, and wast, and art to come**; *because thou hast taken to thee thy great power, and hast reigned* (11:17).
- *And I heard the angel of the waters say, Thou art righteous, O Lord,* **which art, and wast, and shalt be***, because thou hast judged thus* (16:5).

This description of *past, present, and future* corresponds to the threefold chronological division of the book itself (1:19). The Holy Spirit is **before his**, for, all things are governed by His Spirit.

[2] THE HOLY SPIRIT IS NEXT NAMED: **and from the seven Spirits which are before his throne.** He is called *the seven Spirits*, not seven in number, nor in nature, but the infinite *perfect* Spirit of God in His workings and attributes.

- *And the* **(1)** *spirit of the LORD shall rest upon him,* **(2)** *the spirit of wisdom* **(3)** *and understanding,* **(4)** *the spirit of counsel* **(5)** *and might,* **(6)** *the spirit of knowledge* **(7)** *and of the fear of the LORD* (Isa 11:2).
- *And unto the angel of the church in Sardis write; These things saith he that hath* **the seven Spirits of God,** *and the seven stars; I know thy works, that thou hast a name that thou livest, and art dead* (Rev 3:1).
- *And out of the throne proceeded lightnings and thunderings and voices: and there were seven lamps of fire burning before the throne, which are* **the seven Spirits of God** (Rev 4:5).
- *And I beheld, and, lo, in the midst of the throne and of the four beasts, and in the midst of the elders, stood a Lamb as it had been slain, having seven horns and seven eyes, which are* **the seven Spirits** *of God sent forth into all the earth* (Rev 5:6).

2. THE SUBJECT OF THE BENEDICTION 1:5-8. After the mention of the First and Third Persons we now come to the Second Person who is the subject of the benediction and of the Book itself. He is *God manifest in the flesh* (1 Tim 3:16), whom John had seen as *the Word made flesh* (Jhn 1:14) and dwelling on the earth for a time. John now sees Him again, but in glorious form.

Here then we have the grand particulars of this One who is the Subject of this Last Book of the Bible and whose Name is added to that of the Father and the Holy Spirit in this magnificent benediction.

(1) AS TO CHRIST'S PERSON. *And from Jesus Christ, who is the faithful witness, and the first begotten of the dead, and the prince of the kings of the earth* (1:5).

[1] HIS TESTIMONY. He *is the faithful witness*. He was from eternity a witness to all the counsels of Godhead (Jhn 1:18), and He was in time a faithful witness to the revealed will of God. Concerning Him, the Father has now *spoken to us by his Son* (Heb 1:2). As the faithful Witness He fulfilled the role of Prophet in His First Coming (Jhn 18:37). *He is the Amen, the faithful and true witness* (3:14); and upon this witness we may safely rest.

[2] HIS RESURRECTION. He is the ***first-begotten of the dead***. He is the First Parent (*Matthew Henry*) and head of the resurrection, the only one who raised Himself by His own power (Jhn 10:17,18), and who will by the same power raise up His people from their graves to *everlasting life* (Jhn 14:19; cp. Dan 12:2). By this we are *begotten again unto a lively hope by the resurrection of Jesus Christ from the dead,* (1 Pet 1:3).

Christ's Resurrection was a discriminatory resurrection. His resurrection and that of his followers is *out of* the mass of men who died. This is indicated by the preposition *ek*, "out of (cp. Phil 3:11). As Christ is first (cp. *firstfrui*ts, 1 Cor 15:20) so the rising of all believers will follow. Christ and all the righteous dead are included in the *first resurrection* (Rev. 20:5,6), and this in stages. The wicked dead are raised last, after the Millennium (20:12,13).

[3] HIS KINGSHIP. He is ***the prince of the kings of the earth***; from Him they have their authority; by Him their power is limited and their wrath restrained; by Him their counsels are over-ruled, and to Him they are accountable.

If not outwardly seen now, it will be at His Second Coming when He returns as *KING OF KINGS AND LORD OF LORDS* (Rev 19:16). His witness as Prophet and His resurrection are now past. His fulfilment of the role of *Prince of the kings of the earth* is future, to be achieved after his victory over the Beast and the False Prophet (Rev 19), fulfilling Isaiah 9:6,7 and *many* other verses such as –

- *Yea, all kings shall fall down before him: all nations shall serve him* (Psa 72:11).
- *Behold, the days come, saith the LORD, that I will raise unto David a righteous Branch, and a King shall reign and prosper, and shall execute judgment and justice in the earth* (Jer 23:5).
- *And the LORD shall be king over all the earth: in that day shall there be one LORD, and his name one* (Zech 14:9).

(2) AS TO CHRIST'S WORKINGS. ***Unto him that loved us, and washed us from our sins in his own blood, And hath made us kings and priests unto God and his Father; to him be glory and dominion for ever and ever. Amen*** (1:5,6).

[1] HIS LOVE. ***Unto him that loved us.*** This is a wellspring whose depths cannot be plumbed. No merit or reason can be found for His love for poor lost sinners, *dead in trespasses and sins* (Eph 2:1).

- *We love him, because he first loved us* (1 Jhn 4:19).
- *For the love of Christ constraineth us; because we thus judge, that if one died for all, then were all dead* (2 Cor 5:14).

[2] HIS SACRIFICE: ***and washed us from our sins in his own blood.*** Sins leave a stain upon the soul, a stain of guilt and of pollution. Nothing can remove this but the Blood of Christ. As no other means was available to wash out the terrible stain, Christ was willing to shed his own Blood to provided cleansing and purchase pardon and purity. As the Book of Revelation gives the *Final Word* concerning the great doctrines of Scripture, when we come to the Blood of Christ we have the definitively wonderful statement that the Blood of Christ ***Washes*** (Rev 1:5; 7:14). Here are fifteen categorical statements, from among many, declaring what the Blood of Jesus Christ *DOES*.

- *For the life of the flesh is in **the blood: and I have given it to you upon the altar** to make an atonement for your souls: for **it is the blood that maketh an atonement for the soul*** (Lev 17:11).

CHAPTER 1

- *Take heed therefore unto yourselves, and to all the flock, over the which the Holy Ghost hath made you overseers, **to feed the church of God, which he hath purchased with his own blood** (Acts 20:28).*
- *Whom God hath set forth to be a **propitiation through faith in his blood**, to declare his righteousness for the remission of sins that are past, through the forbearance of God (Rom 3:25).*
- *Much more then, being now **justified by his blood**, we shall be saved from wrath through him (Rom 5:9).*
- *In whom we have **redemption through his blood, the forgiveness of sins**, according to the riches of his grace (Eph 1:7).*
- *But now in Christ Jesus ye who sometimes were far off are **made nigh by the blood of Christ** (Eph 2:13).*
- *And, having **made peace through the blood of his cross, by him to reconcile** all things unto himself; by him, I say, whether they be things in earth, or things in heaven (Col 1:20).*
- *Saying, This is the blood of the testament which God hath enjoined unto you. Moreover he sprinkled with blood both the tabernacle, and all the vessels of the ministry. And almost all things are by the law purged with blood; and **without shedding of blood is no remission** (Heb 9:20-22).*
- *Having therefore, brethren, **boldness to enter into the holiest by the blood of Jesus** (Heb 10:19).*
- *Wherefore Jesus also, **that he might sanctify the people with his own blood**, suffered without the gate (Heb 13:12).*
- *Forasmuch as ye know that ye were not **redeemed with** corruptible things, as silver and gold, from your vain conversation received by tradition from your fathers; But with **the precious blood of Christ**, as of a lamb without blemish and without spot (1 Pet 1:18,19).*
- *But if we walk in the light, as he is in the light, we have fellowship one with another, and **the blood of Jesus Christ his Son cleanseth us from all sin**. If we say that we have no sin, we deceive ourselves, and the truth is not in us. If we confess our sins, he is faithful and just to forgive us our sins, and to cleanse us from all unrighteousness (1 Jhn 1:7-9).*
- *And they sung a new song, saying, Thou art worthy to take the book, and to open the seals thereof: for thou wast slain, and hast **redeemed us to God by thy blood** out of every kindred, and tongue, and people, and nation (Rev 5:9).*
- *And I said unto him, Sir, thou knowest. And he said to me, These are they which came out of great tribulation, and **have washed their robes, and made them white in the blood of the Lamb** (Rev 7:14).*
- *And I heard a loud voice saying in heaven, Now is come salvation, and strength, and the kingdom of our God, and the power of his Christ: for the accuser of our brethren is cast down, which accused them before our God day and night. And **they overcame him by the blood of the Lamb**, and by the word of their testimony; and they loved not their lives unto the death (Rev 12:10,11).*
- *Of how much sorer punishment, suppose ye, shall he be thought worthy, who hath trodden under foot the Son of God, and hath **counted the blood of the covenant, wherewith he was sanctified, an unholy thing**, and hath done despite unto the Spirit of grace (Heb 10:29)?*

FIFTEEN CATIGORICAL STATEMENTS CONCERNING WHAT THE BLOOD OF JESUS CHRIST *DOES*:

makes atonement,
purchases,
propitiates,
justifies,
redeems,
provides forgiveness,
brings nigh,
makes peace,
reconciles,
remits,
gives entrance,
sanctifies,
washes,
overcomes Satan,
brings judgement to the denier

Here are fifteen resounding statements of what the Blood of Jesus Christ *DOES*! The Book of Revelation gives final emphasis to the Biblical imperative that **without shedding of blood is no remission** (Heb 9:22). Coupled with the intricate instructions in the Levitical Offerings concerning the Blood, it becomes absolutely certain that upon His Death had the Blood of Christ remained in His veins the sacrifice would not have sufficed for the lost sinner.

It is not surprising that in these last days the doctrine of Blood Atonement has been downgraded in the teaching, preaching and Christian music. Notable is the controversy that began in the 1970's over statements concerning the Blood of Christ by John MacArthur. Though MacArthur has often tried to "explain" and "clarify" and has had to do this regarding other areas of concern in his ministry (even to the point of retraction), yet regarding this subject he has fallen *woefully short* of the categorical declaration that Scripture makes concerning the Blood of Christ. Below are extracts from a paper written by E. L. Bynum, one of the earlier authors to raise the alarm.

John MacArthur and the Blood of Christ by E. L. Bynum

The following article is being reprinted from the Plains Baptist Challenger of August, 1986. After all these years, this information about John MacArthur's teaching, is still needed today. His teaching on the blood of Christ is dangerous, and people are still being led astray by it.

MacArthur Minimizes the Blood

The April 1986 edition of *Faith For The Family* quotes him as saying in a 1976 article entitled, ***Not His Bleeding But His Dying*** "It was His death that was efficacious. . not His blood. . . Christ did not bleed to death. The shedding of blood had nothing to do with bleeding. . . it simply means death. . . Nothing in His human blood saves...It is not His blood that I love. . . it is Him. It is not His bleeding that saved me, but His dying." It is incredible to me, that a Christian minister would make such statements.

CHAPTER 1

He Does Not Like Revelation 1:5 In The KJV

In *Not His Bleeding But His Dying*, MacArthur had this to say: "I may add a note on Revelation 1:5, a passage which is confusing in the King James Version. The word 'washed' is not correct. The Greek work is 'delivered.'

- *Unto him that loved us, and washed us from our sins in his own blood* (Rev. 1:5).

What could possibly be confusing about that? He says that "washed" is incorrect and that it should be "delivered." Like most "great" scholars today, MacArthur suffers from the Westcott and Hort syndrome. "Washed" is in the Textus Receptus... The word was changed by Lachmann, 1842-1850, Tischendorf, Eighth Edition, 1865-1872, and Tregelles, 1857-1872. These are three of the men that laid the groundwork for Westcott and Hort, so that they could make the alarming changes in their Revised Version. The American Standard Version, 1901, of course went along with the change, but they did put in a significant footnote. While rendering the word as "loosed," their footnote says, "Many authorities, some ancient, read washed."

John MacArthur's Subsequent Statements

A few months ago a pastor friend and I visited a John MacArthur meeting in Vancouver, and I purchased a copy of MacArthur's commentary on Hebrews with the desire to see exactly what he says about the Blood of Jesus Christ. This commentary was published in 1983 by Moody Press. There can be no mistake about MacArthur's position that the Blood itself does not save us, that the Blood is SYMBOLIC of death. Words could not be plainer. In a mere three pages of this book MacArthur uses the term "symbolic" no less than thirteen times [here are several examples]:

- "Blood is a SYMBOL of death, and therefore follows closely the idea of a testator's having to die in order for a will to become effective...
- "It is possible to become morbid about Christ's sacrificial death and preoccupied with His suffering and shedding of blood. It is especially possible to become unbiblically preoccupied with the physical aspects of His death. It was not Jesus' physical blood that saves us, but His dying on our behalf, which is SYMBOLIZED by the shedding of His physical blood ...
- "The purpose of the blood was to SYMBOLIZE sacrifice for sin, which brought cleansing from sin.
- "Again, however, we need to keep in mind that the blood was a SYMBOL. If Christ's own physical blood, in itself, does not cleanse from sin, how much less did the physical blood of animals...
- "Since the penalty for sin is death, nothing but death, SYMBOLIZED by shedding of blood, can atone for sin. ... the only way we can participate in the New Covenant, is through the atoning DEATH of Jesus Christ, made effective for us when we trust in Him as saving Lord" (John MacArthur, Hebrews, pp. 236-238).

Let me remind our readers that this book is still being published by Moody Press and is being sold by John MacArthur's ministry. I purchased it directly from his ministry in Canada this year. This is not something that MacArthur said off the cuff many years ago and which he has since corrected. This is precisely what the man believes today. MacArthur's position on the Blood of Christ is a great heresy. It is

precisely the same heresy promoted by the translator of the Today's English Version, who replaced the term "blood" with "death" in most key passages.
http://www.thewatchmanwakes.com/John-Macarthur-and-the-Blood-of-Christ.html

The reader is encouraged to read the entire paper by E.L. Bynum (written 1995), and also the longer work, *John MacArthur's Heresy on the Blood of Christ* (1995) by Dr. D.A. Waite.

Back 1986 I received a tape from MacArthur's ministry in which he sought to defend his statements. *Again*, the Blood of Christ is only a symbol of His Death, and does not in itself cleanse from sin. The tape went further than his original comments in exposing the depths of his heresy. In 1991 I listened to a radio broadcast: *Again*, the Blood is only a symbol of death and does not in itself save. He also referred to the sacred sacrificial system of the Old Testament as the "*whole rigmarole.*" In 2012 I perused a copy of the *MacArthur Bible Commentary* (2005). *Again*, the Blood is a symbol of death and is not in itself efficacious.

Recently (October 2016) I viewed a You Tube presentation (from a December 2008 interview with MacArthur). After saying he had been misrepresented, he proceeded to "explain" once again that the Blood is a metaphor and symbol of Christ's Death. "The actual blood, the fluid in his body, does not cleanse from sin". Many of those who commented were shocked at the heretical, bizarre and irreverent way in which he spoke. For example: "Christ did not bleed to death, he was asphyxiated, as were all who were crucified." (!!!).

John MacArthur and those who defend his statements on the Blood of Christ have as Hebrews 10:29 warned, **counted the blood of the covenant....an unholy thing.** The six minute video is not pleasant viewing. https://www.youtube.com/watch?v=9470k9b2iVg

We rejoice in Revelation 1:5: *Unto him that loved us, and washed us from our sins in his own blood.*

We can sing fervently: *WHAT CAN WAS AWAY MY SIN, NOTHING BUT THE BLOOD OF JESUS.*

Thus, the Apocalypse opens with the Blood of Christ for sin, and closes (21:8) with the Lake of Fire because the Blood has been rejected. There is no middle ground. The sinner must make his choice.

RETURN TO: THE APOSTOLIC BENEDICTION 1:4-8

1. THE INTRODUCTION TO THE BENEDICTION 1:4
2. THE SUBJECT OF THE BENEDICTION 1:5-8.

(1) AS TO CHRIST'S PERSON. *And from Jesus Christ, who is the faithful witness, and the first begotten of the dead, and the prince of the kings of the earth* (1:5).

[1] HIS TESTIMONY. He *is the faithful witness*.

[2] HIS RESURRECTION. He is the *first-begotten of the dead*.

[3] HIS KINGSHIP. He is *the prince of the kings of the earth*.

(2) AS TO CHRIST'S WORKINGS. *Unto him that loved us, and washed us from our sins in his own blood, And hath made us kings and priests unto God and his Father; to him be glory and dominion for ever and ever. Amen* (1:5,6).

[1] HIS LOVE. *Unto him that loved us.*

[2] HIS SACRIFICE: *and washed us from our sins in his own blood.*

[3] HIS BESTOWMENT. *And hath made us kings and priests to God and his Father* (1:6). Having justified and sanctified the believer, He makes them *kings* to his Father; that is, in his Father's account and for His glory. As kings, they will reign with His Son at His Return and with Him *judge the world*. He hath made them *priests*, given them

CHAPTER 1

access to His Throne, enabled them to enter into the holiest and to offer spiritual and acceptable sacrifices. He has given them an unction suitable to this office (1 Jhn 2:20,27).

Though Christ is not yet openly exercising His rights over the kings of the earth, He does now bestow these honours upon believers in anticipation of that *crowning day*.

> •*But ye are a chosen generation, a **royal priesthood**, an holy nation, a peculiar people; that ye should shew forth the praises of him who hath called you out of darkness into his marvellous light* (1 Pet 2:9).
>
> •*And hast made us unto our God **kings** and **priests**: and **we shall reign** on the earth* (Rev 5:10).

Because of His [1] Love, [2] Sacrifice, [3] Bestowment, **to him be glory and dominion for ever and ever. Amen** (1:6). To such a Saviour and Lord the right to everlasting glory and dominion is attributed.

> •*And there was given him **dominion**, and **glory**, and a kingdom, that all people, nations, and languages, should serve him: his dominion is an **everlasting** dominion, which shall not pass away, and his kingdom that which shall not be destroyed* (Dan 7:14).

[4] HIS COMING. **Behold, he cometh with clouds; and every eye shall see him, and they also which pierced him: and all kindreds of the earth shall wail because of him. Even so, Amen** (1:7). This *BOOK*, the Revelation, begins and ends with a declaration of the Second Coming of the Lord Jesus Christ. We should set ourselves to meditate frequently upon the Second Coming of Christ, and keep it in the eye of faith and expectation. John speaks as one who saw that day: **Behold, he cometh**, as sure as if you beheld Him with your eyes. **He cometh with clouds**, which are his chariot and pavilion. He will come publicly: **Every eye shall see him**, the eye of His people, the eye of His enemies, every eye, yours and mine. He shall come to Israel who **pierced him**; and the world at large who rejected Him. He will come to religious leaders who crucified Him afresh by their apostasy. He will come to the astonishment of the pagan world. For He comes to take vengeance on those who know not God (do not want to know Him) and obey not the Gospel of Christ.

This *EVENT* is introduced by the first of many instances of **Behold** in Revelation. Modern versions say *Look*; the AV translators rightly understood that is goes much deeper. It is something that we are *beholden of.* The words are emphatic! As Christ was received by a cloud in His ascension (Acts 1:9,11), so He will come in the clouds of heaven. His Second Coming back to earth will be an event *seen by every eye*.

> •*And then shall appear the sign of the Son of man in heaven: and then shall **all the tribes of the earth mourn, and they shall see** the Son of man coming in **the clouds of heaven** with power and great glory* (Matt 24:30).
>
> •*Jesus saith unto him, Thou hast said: nevertheless I say unto you, **Hereafter shall ye see** the Son of man sitting on the right hand of power, and coming in **the clouds of heaven*** (Matt 26:64).
>
> •*Men's hearts failing them for fear, and for looking after those things which are coming on the earth: for the powers of heaven shall be shaken. And **then shall they see** the Son of man coming in **a cloud** with power and great glory* (21:26,27).

There is no indication that the world as a whole will see Christ at the time of the Rapture of the church. At His coming to establish His kingdom, however, all will see Him. Especially distinguished will be those who *pierced Him*. While the sins of all the lost have pierced Him, this refers to Israel.

THE BOOK OF REVELATION

•*And I will pour upon **the house of David**, and upon the inhabitants of Jerusalem, the spirit of grace and of supplications: and **they shall look upon me whom they have pierced**, and they shall mourn for him, as one mourneth for his only son, and shall be in bitterness for him, as one that is in bitterness for his firstborn (Zech 12:10).*

To this declaration of the Return of Christ is added the affirmation, **Even so, Amen.** The Greek word for *Amen* is a transliteration of the Hebrew word of similar sound, meaning "truth" or "faithfulness", hence the meaning "be it true" or "so be it." An Old Testament illustration of its use is found in Isaiah 65:16 with the twice repeated phrase, *the God of truth*.

•*That he who blesseth himself in the earth shall bless himself in **the God of truth**; and he that sweareth in the earth shall swear by **the God of truth**; because the former troubles are forgotten, and because they are hid from mine eyes.*

Christ is called *the Amen* in Revelation 3:14, and with the added ascription, *the faithful and true witness*. In John 14:6 Christ said, *I am the way, the truth, and the life*. Thus in the main part of this benediction which concerns Christ, we have seen: *His Person, His Workings*, and now following on naturally we see *His Testimony*.

(3) AS TO CHRIST'S TESTIMONY. ***I am Alpha and Omega, the beginning and the ending, saith the Lord, which is, and which was, and which is to come, the Almighty*** (1:8). This is a threefold testimony concerning the Lord Jesus Christ and ETERNITY.

This account concerning Christ is ratified and confirmed by Himself. (1:8). Here our Lord Jesus justly claims the same honour and power that is ascribed to the Father (1:4). He is the ***Alpha and Omega, the beginning and the ending*** (1:8). All things are from him and for him. He is ***the Almighty***; He is the same eternal and unchangeable One. And surely whoever presumes to blot out one character of this name of Christ deserves to have their name blotted out of the book of life. Those that honour Him, He will honour; but those who despise Him *shall be lightly esteemed* (1 Sam 2:30). *Matthew Henry*.

As the Father, Christ is the Eternal One. The eternity, present power, and future glory of the Son of God are in are in view in this passage. As the Father, so the Son is ***the Almighty*** (Gr. *pantocrator*), a term found ten times in the New Testament, nine instances being in Revelation.

Christ is the ***Alpha and Omega*** and by this term His is the Eternal God as expressed elsewhere in Scripture.

•*And when I saw him, I fell at his feet as dead. And he laid his right hand upon me, saying unto me, Fear not; **I am the first and the last** (Rev 1:17).*

•*And he said unto me, It is done. **I am Alpha and Omega, the beginning and the end**. I will give unto him that is athirst of the fountain of the water of life freely (Rev 21:6).*

•*And, behold, I come quickly; and my reward is with me, to give every man according as his work shall be. **I am Alpha and Omega, the beginning and the end, the first and the last** (Rev 22:12,13).*

•*And God said unto Moses, **I AM THAT I AM**: and he said, Thus shalt thou say unto the children of Israel, **I AM** hath sent me unto you (Exod 3:14).*

•*Ye are my witnesses, saith the LORD, and my servant whom I have chosen: that ye may know and believe me, and understand that **I am he: before me there was no God formed, neither shall there be after me** (Isa 43:10).*

•*Thus saith the LORD the King of Israel, and his redeemer the LORD of hosts; **I am the first, and I am the last; and beside me there is no God** (Isa 44:6).*

CHAPTER 1

•*Hearken unto me, O Jacob and Israel, my called;* ***I am he; I am the first, I also am the last*** (Isa 48:12).

Here then in this Preface and Apostolic Benediction we have a summary of the Person and Work of the Lord Jesus Christ as found throughout Scripture.

C. THE GLORIOUS VISION OF THE LORD JESUS CHRIST 1:9-18

(1:9) ***I John, who also am your brother, and companion in tribulation, and in the kingdom and patience of Jesus Christ, was in the isle that is called Patmos, for the word of God, and for the testimony of Jesus Christ.*** (1:10) ***I was in the Spirit on the Lord's day, and heard behind me a great voice, as of a trumpet,*** (1:11) ***Saying, I am Alpha and Omega, the first and the last: and, What thou seest, write in a book, and send it unto the seven churches which are in Asia; unto Ephesus, and unto Smyrna, and unto Pergamos, and unto Thyatira, and unto Sardis, and unto Philadelphia, and unto Laodicea.***

(1:12) ***And I turned to see the voice that spake with me. And being turned, I saw seven golden candlesticks;*** (1:13) ***And in the midst of the seven candlesticks one like unto the Son of man, clothed with a garment down to the foot, and girt about the paps with a golden girdle.*** (1:14) ***His head and his hairs were white like wool, as white as snow; and his eyes were as a flame of fire;*** (1:15) ***And his feet like unto fine brass, as if they burned in a furnace; and his voice as the sound of many waters.*** (1:16) ***And he had in his right hand seven stars: and out of his mouth went a sharp twoedged sword: and his countenance was as the sun shineth in his strength.***

(1:17) ***And when I saw him, I fell at his feet as dead. And he laid his right hand upon me, saying unto me, Fear not; I am the first and the last:*** (1:18) ***I am he that liveth, and was dead; and, behold, I am alive for evermore, Amen; and have the keys of hell and of death.***

We have now come to that glorious vision which the apostle had of the Lord Jesus Christ, when He came to deliver this revelation to him
1. THE CIRCUMSTANCES OF THE VISION 1:9-11.

(1) THE RECIPIENT: JOHN. ***I John, who also am your brother, and companion in tribulation, and in the kingdom and patience of Jesus Christ*** (1:9).

[1] JOHN'S STATE AND CONDITION. He was as many believers have been, a persecuted man, banished, and perhaps imprisoned for his adherence to Christ. He was their ***brother***, though an apostle; he seems to value himself more for his relation to the churches, than his authority over them. He was their ***companion in tribulation***: the persecuted servants of God did not suffer alone, the same trials are accomplished in others. He was their companion in ***patience***. Not only was suffering experienced but grace to bear the suffering
(2 Cor 1:5). He was their *brother and companion* **in the kingdom and patience of Jesus Christ**, a sufferer for Christ's cause, for asserting His kingly rights and His coming kingly reign.

Though John mentions his name twice before (1:1,4), this is the first of three instances of the expression ***I John***; this at the beginning of the Book, and the other two at the end (21:2; 22:8). In the Gospel of John he refers to himself as *the disciple which testifieth of these things* (Jhn 21:24). In his Epistles John describes himself as an *elder* (2 Jhn 1; 3 Jhn 1). Here John describes himself only as a ***brother*** and ***companion*** of the seven churches in their trouble. He was well known to them and bound by ties of spiritual life and kinship. Compare *I Daniel* (Dan 7:28; 9:2; 10:).

THE BOOK OF REVELATION

The word *patience* (*hypomone*) denotes the hope and expectancy of faith which results in endurance. It is a word used in connection with the Second Coming of Christ.

- *And the Lord direct your hearts into the love of God, and into the **patient waiting for Christ*** (2 Thess 3:5).
- *Be **patient therefore, brethren, unto the coming of the Lord**. Behold, the husbandman waiteth for the precious fruit of the earth, and hath **long patience for it**, until he receive the early and latter rain. Be ye also **patient**; stablish your hearts: for the coming of the Lord draweth nigh* (Jms 5:7,8).

[2] JOHN'S LOCATION AND REASON FOR IT. John ***was in the isle that is called Patmos, for the word of God, and for the testimony of Jesus Christ*** (1:9). John himself is under persecution, being in exile on the Isle of Patmos because of his active preaching of the Word of God and his testimony concerning Jesus Christ (cp. 1 Pet 4:12-19).

Paul was placed in Arabia in order to receive the revelation made to him there, and John was placed in Patmos for a similar purpose. It is likely that he was banished there because of his fidelity to the Gospel.

- *But when it pleased God, who separated me from my mother's womb, and called me by his grace, **To reveal his Son in me**, that I might preach him among the heathen; immediately I conferred not with flesh and blood: Neither went I up to Jerusalem to them which were apostles before me; **but I went into Arabia**, and returned again unto Damascus* (Gal 1:15-17).

John was favoured with this revelation in ***the isle that is called Patmos***. He does not say who banished him there. It may often be better for a believer to speak sparingly about their sufferings.

The Isle of Patmos

CHAPTER 1

Of this John Walvoord writes:

> The exile of John to the Isle of Patmos is in itself a moving story of devotion to Christ crowned with suffering. This small island, rocky and forbidding in its terrain, about ten miles long and six miles wide, is located in the Aegean Sea southwest of Ephesus just beyond the Island of Samos. Early church fathers such as Irenaeus, Clement of Alexandria, and Eusebius state that John was sent to this island as an exile under the ruler Domitian. (See Introduction.) According to Victorinus, John, though aged, was forced to labor in the mines located at Patmos. Early sources also indicate that about A.D. 96, at Domitian's death, John was allowed to return to Ephesus when the Emperor Nerva was in power.
>
> It was in these bleak circumstances, shut off from friends and human fellowship, that John was given the most extensive revelation of future things shown to any writer of the New Testament. Though men could circumscribe his human activities, they could not bind the Spirit of God nor the testimony of Jesus Christ. John's experiences paralleled those of the Old Testament prophets. Moses wrote the Pentateuch in the wilderness. David wrote many psalms while being pursued by Saul. Isaiah lived in difficult days and died a martyr's death. Ezekiel wrote in exile. Jeremiah's life was one of trial and persecution. Peter wrote his two letters shortly before martyrdom. Thus in the will of God the final written revelation was given to John while suffering for Christ and the gospel (*The Revelation of Jesus Christ*).

The words concerning his reason for being there may have an opposite and twofold meaning; the Roman authorities placed John on Patmos *for the word of God, and for the testimony of Jesus Christ* (that is, because he preached it). But the Lord placed him there *for the word of God, and for the testimony of Jesus Christ* (that is, that he might receive this further revelation). God can turn things around!

[3] THE TIME JOHN BEGAN TO RECEIVE THE VISION. *I was in the Spirit on the Lord's day* (1:10). Note the frame that his soul was in at this time: *He was in the Spirit*. He was in the Holy Spirit. Only is such a state would he be able to receive the uncommon manifestations (both of glory and evil) that would now be revealed.

The Lord's day is commonly thought to mean Sunday, However, it is generally believed among premillennialists that this means John is being transported into the future day of the Lord (Christ's Return, the Tribulation and attendant events).

This is the position of John Walvoord:

> John's statement in verse 10 that he was in the Spirit refers to his experience of being carried beyond normal sense into a state where God could reveal supernaturally the contents of this book. Such was the experience of Ezekiel (Ezek. 2:2; 3:12,14; etc.), Peter (Acts 10:10,11; 11: 5), and Paul (Acts 22:17-18).
>
> The expression "on the Lord's day" has been taken by some to refer to the first day of the week, by others to the day of the Lord. The word *Lord* in this passage is actually an adjective, used in the sense of "lordian." Though today the expression is used commonly of the first day of the week, it is nowhere so used in the Bible. The day of Christ's resurrection is consistently referred to as "the first day of the week" and never as the Lord's day (Matt 28:1; Mk 16:2,9; Lk 24:1; Jhn 20:1,19; Acts 20:7; 1 Cor 16:2). It is true that the same adjective (Gr., *kyriakos*) is found in 1 Corinthians 11:20 referring to the Lord's Supper characteristically observed by the early church on the first day of the week. Moulton and Milligan also call attention to the fact that the word is frequently used outside the Bible in the sense of "imperial" and cite Deissmann: "that

the distinctive title 'Lord's Day' may have been connected with the conscious feelings of protest against the cult of the Emperor with its 'Emperor's Day.'"

There is no solid evidence, however, that the expression used by John was ever intended to refer to the first day of the week. It is rather a reference to the day of the Lord of the Old Testament, an extended period of time in which God deals in judgment and sovereign rule over the earth. The adjectival form can be explained on the ground that in the Old Testament there was no adjectival form for "Lord," and therefore the noun had to be used. The New Testament term is therefore the equivalent to the Old Testament expression "the day of the Lord." On the basis of the evidence, the interpretation is therefore preferred that John was projected forward to the future day of the Lord.

Nevertheless the Greek "the Lordian day" is distinct from *the day of the Lord* (*he hemera tou kyriou*, 1 Thess 5:2; 2 Thess 2:2; 2 Pet. 3:10). Further, the wording does not say nor convey the thought that John was carried by the Spirt **to** the Lord's Day. He was in the Spirt **on** the Lord's day. The statement is specific that it was **on** the Lord's day that this revelation took place.

In the chronology of the Book, Chapters 1-3 *do not* present the Day of the Lord. John is not transported to see the Day of the Lord (*the things which must be hereafter*) until Chapter 4:1. He is now to be given a prophecy concerning the Church Age, and Sunday, the day the church met, is the appropriate day for such a revelation.

As we serve Christ in our local church, that too should be our desire. May we be *in the Spirit on the Lord's Day*, the day of Christ's Resurrection (Lk 24:34; Acts 2:36).

[4] THE COMMISSION JOHN RECEIVED.

One. THE TRUMPET SUMMONS: **and heard behind me a great voice, as of a trumpet** (1:10). The apostle gives an account of what he heard when thus in the Spirit. A startling summons was given: **and heard behind me a great voice, as of a trumpet.** The voice of Christ applying to Himself His character just revealed as the *Alpha and Omega* (1:8), that is the *Word*, now declares in trumpet tones to John: **I am Alpha and Omega, the first and the last:** The Words of Scripture are a *great voice*; the Words of Scripture are a *trumpet* call; the Words of Scripture demand our closest attention; and now especially so in the Book of Revelation. Compare this summons with that given to Moses:

> •*And it came to pass on the third day in the morning, that there were thunders and lightnings, and a thick cloud upon the mount, and* **the voice of the trumpet** *exceeding loud; so that all the people that was in the camp trembled* (Exod 19:16).

> •*And when* **the voice of the trumpet sounded long**, *and waxed louder and louder, Moses spake, and God answered him by a voice. And the LORD came down upon mount Sinai, on the top of the mount: and the LORD called Moses up to the top of the mount; and Moses went up* (Exod 19:19,20).

Two. THE ETERNAL NAME. **I am Alpha and Omega, the first and the last** (1:11). Christ has just ratified the Apostolic Benediction (1:4-8) by pronouncing this great Name; He now uses it again in His commission to John.

> •*I am* **Alpha and Omega**, *the beginning and the ending, saith the Lord, which is, and which was, and which is to come, the Almighty* (1:8).
> •*And when I saw him, I fell at his feet as dead. And he laid his right hand upon me, saying unto me, Fear not; I am* **the first and the last** (1:17).

CHAPTER 1

As the *Alpha and Omega*, Christ is the Word, the source of all knowledge. Christ is before all time, for His *goings forth are from everlasting* (Micah 5:2), but with respect to time He is *the First and the Last* and the Lord of all time.

Three. THE CONSUMMATE INSTRUCTION: ***and, What thou seest, write in a book, and send it unto the seven churches which are in Asia; unto Ephesus, and unto Smyrna, and unto Pergamos, and unto Thyatira, and unto Sardis, and unto Philadelphia, and unto Laodicea*** (1:11). The command to write, found twelve times in the book, indicates that John was to write after seeing each vision, in contrast to 10:4, where he is told not to write. The message of the entire book is to be sent to each of the seven churches along with the particular message to the individual church. The seven churches are mentioned here in the order of the letters given in Chapters 2 and 3. Note: their order, beginning with Ephesus and ending with Laodicea, is based on their geographic location. We will see also that their order presents a *prophecy* (1:3) of seven stages of church history from the time of the Apostles to the time of the Rapture.

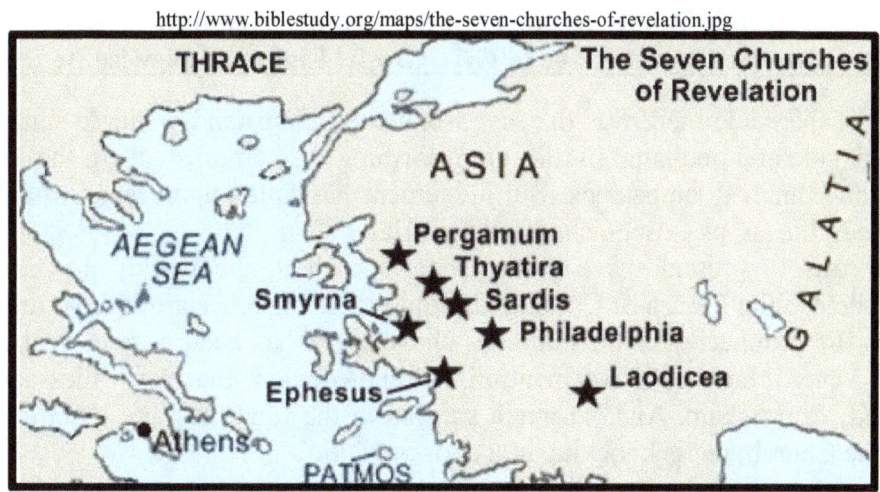

The Geographic Order of the Seven Churches

2. THE VISION OF THE LORD JESUS CHRIST 1:12-18.
    (1) CHRIST IN RELATION TO THE SEVEN CHURCHES 1:12-16.
        [1] HE SAW THE CHURCHES AS CANDLESTICKS. ***And I turned to see the voice that spake with me. And being turned, I saw seven golden candlesticks*** (1:12). As it is explained in the last verse of the Chapter (1:20), John saw the churches under the emblem of ***seven golden candlesticks***. The churches are compared to candlesticks, because their primary purpose is to hold forth the light of the Gospel. The churches are not candles: Christ only and the Scriptures is our light. We receive our light from Him and hold it forth to the world (Phil 2:16). They are ***golden*** candlesticks, for they should be precious and pure, comparable to fine gold. The last time John saw a *candlestick* was in the years before AD 70!

**Titus Arch in Rome: Removal of the Temple Menorah in A.D. 70
In the Present Age Churches are to Give Gospel Light or Likewise Be Removed**

In the Tabernacle there was the seven-branched lampstand, a single stand with three lamps on each side and one lamp in the centre forming the central shaft. In the Temple there were ten seven-branched lampstands. But judgement has fallen upon Israel, the Temple had been destroyed, the lamps extinguished and the priests slain.

Israel was to present the Light of the Messiah to the world; she failed! In this dispensation before the Return of Christ, individual local churches are to give out the Gospel Light, but as the prophecies of the churches show, there has been a great deal that has not been *light*. Many churches have neutralized and denied the very message they are commissioned to proclaim. And, so much so, that in the final message, *Laodicea*, Christ is not even in the Church, but is knocking at a door outside.

Thus before Revelation tells about the judgements upon the world during the Tribulation and ***the things which shall be hereafter*** (1:19; 4:1) it must tell us about ***the things which are***.

> • *For the time is come that **judgment must begin at the house of God**: and if it first begin at us, what shall the end be of them that obey not the gospel of God? And if the righteous scarcely be saved, where shall the ungodly and the sinner appear*
> (1 Pet 4:17,18)?

In the description here, instead of one lampstand with seven lamps there are seven separate lamp-stands each made of gold and arranged in a circle. Again, the principal function of a church is the giving forth of Biblical and Gospel Light. The golden metal, as in the Tabernacle and Solomon's Temple, represents the Deity and Glory of Christ, and symbolize Divine relationship and appointment. The implied olive oil is symbolic of the power of the Holy Spirit issuing forth in the witness of the churches. The voice was as of a trumpet, for judgment is the subject of the scene and of the entire Book. If there is no Gospel witness then the church merely *cumbered the ground* (Lk 13:7). This was the case with the first church described in Revelation, Ephesus.

CHAPTER 1

http://www.vipephesustours.com/wp-content/uploads/2016/01/sites-to-see-in-ephesus.jpg

<u>**Ephesus:**</u> ***...or else I will come unto thee quickly and will remove thy candlestick*** **(2:5)**

(1) CHRIST IN RELATION TO THE SEVEN CHURCHES 1:12-16.
    [1] HE SAW THE CHURCHES AS CANDLESTICKS (1:12).
    [2] HE SAW CHRIST IN PRIESTLY GLORY (1:13-16).
        One. HIS POSITION. **And in the midst of the seven candlesticks one like unto the Son of man** (1:13). The Churches form a *camp* and the Messiah is walking in the midst of them as He walked in the midst of the Tribes of Old Testament Israel.

> • *For the LORD thy God walketh* **in the midst of thy camp**, *to deliver thee, and to give up thine enemies before thee; therefore shall thy camp be holy: that he see no unclean thing in thee, and turn away from thee* (Deut 23:14).

If requirements were so of Israel in the Old Testament, how much more should it be of the local churches in the New Testament! John saw the Lord Jesus Christ in the midst of the golden candlesticks; for He has promised to be with his churches always to the end of the world, filling them with light, and life and if necessary as we will see, chastening them.

The Title assigned to Christ is that of *the Son of man*, the One who regains all that the first man Adam lost (1 Cor 15:21,22). This is a frequent Title in the Gospels, but infrequent in Revelation, being found only once more (14:14). As in Daniel it is a title that speaks of His Return and kingly rights. Thus He is seen here as Priest and King. Note how the Title is introduced: ***one like the Son of man***.

> • *I saw in the night visions, and, behold,* **one like the Son of man** *came with the clouds of heaven, and came to the Ancient of days, and they brought him near before him. And* ***there was given him dominion, and glory, and a kingdom***, *that all people, nations, and languages, should serve him: his dominion is an everlasting dominion, which shall not pass away, and his kingdom that which shall not be destroyed* (Dan 7:13,14).

* *And I looked, and behold a white cloud, and upon the cloud **one sat like unto the Son of man**, having on his head **a golden crown**, and in his hand a sharp sickle* (Rev 14:14).

<u>Two</u>. HIS GARMENTS: ***clothed with a garment down to the foot, and girt about the paps with a golden girdle*** (1:13). He is clothed in a princely and priestly robe, denoting righteousness and honour. It was *down to the foot*, for He is *all* righteous. As the Old Testament High Priest who had a wide band and a breast-plate on which the names of the tribes of Israel were engraved, so Christ is also likewise and far more so girded.

More specifically Walvoord says:

> Like Aaron's robe being designed *for glory and beauty* (Exod 28:2), the golden girdle corresponds to that used by the high priest to bind his garments higher on the body than at the loins. Josephus explains this as being in keeping with the dignity and majesty of the high priest and as being designed to allow greater freedom in movement. The golden girdle corresponds to the girdle of the high priest which has golden thread in it, but here it is made entirely of gold. The sombre presence of Christ in His role as judge and priest in the midst of the churches is a significant introduction to chapters 2 and 3.

<u>Three</u>. HIS FORM.

*1. **His head and his hairs were white like wool, as white as snow*** (1:14). This is likely the attribute directed to the faithful but suffering church at Smyrna (2:8). Christ as the Father, is *the Ancient of days* (cp. *the Ancient of days did sit, whose garment was white as snow, and the hair of his head like the pure wool*. Dan 7:9). Christ's hoary head was not a sign of decay, but was indeed *a crown of glory* (Prov 16:31). If Christ's people, as Smyrna, may live but a short time in this world, they may have comfort in One who is everlasting. (*These things saith the first and the last, which was dead, and is alive*. 2:8). In this attribute of Eternal Being, the Son shares the same Title as the Father.

* *For unto us a child is born, unto us a son is given: and the government shall be upon his shoulder: and his name shall be called Wonderful, Counsellor, The mighty God, **The everlasting Father**, The Prince of Peace* (Isa 9:6).

*2. **His eyes were as a flame of fire*** (1:14). This attribute was directed to the church at Thyatira (2:18). His eyes pierce and penetrate into the very hearts and reins of men; they scatter terrors among his adversaries. Thyatira had many good works, but these could not hide the Jezebel religion that had taken hold in the church. Our Lord's is a judgement that gets right to the heart and does not miss its mark. Here, before His Coming, we see His eyes as Priest; shortly His eyes will be as King.

* *And I saw heaven opened, and behold a white horse; and he that sat upon him was called Faithful and True, and in righteousness he doth judge and make war. **His eyes were as a flame of fire**, and on his head were many crowns; and he had a name written, that no man knew, but he himself* (Rev 19:11,12).

*3. **His feet like unto fine brass, as if they burned in a furnace*** (1:15). His feet are strong and steadfast, supporting his own interest, subduing his enemies, treading them to ashes. The metal described declares Divine judgment as embodied in the Old Testament types of the brazen altar and other items of brass used in connection with sacrifice for sin (cp. Exod 38:30). Both the fire and the brass give fair notice that *judgment must begin at the house of God* (1 Pet 4:17).

CHAPTER 1

*4. **His voice as the sound of many waters*** (1:15). He can and will make himself heard to those who are afar off as well as to those who are near. His Gospel is a mighty stream, fed by the upper springs of infinite wisdom and knowledge. *Matthew Henry.* Here is the thundering voice of the Son of God revealing the majesty and power before which human authority must bow. As now, but especially during the Tribulation, there will be opposing voices, and they will be brought to nothing.

- *I beheld then because of **the voice of the great words which the horn spake**: I beheld even till the beast was slain, and his body destroyed, and given to the burning flame* (Dan 7:11).
- *And **he shall speak great words against the most High**, and shall wear out the saints of the most High, and think to change times and laws: and they shall be given into his hand until a time and times and the dividing of time* (Dan 7:25).
- *And when **the seven thunders had uttered their voices**, I was about to write: and I heard a voice from heaven saying unto me, Seal up those things which the seven thunders uttered, and write them not* (Rev 10:4).
- *And men were scorched with great heat, and **blasphemed the name of God**, which hath power over these plagues: and they repented not to give him glory* (Rev 16:9).

*5. **And he had in his right hand seven stars*** (1:16). This declaration was given to the church at Sardis. Many think the seven stars refer to the leaders or pastors of the seven churches. They are in Christ's hand and under His direction. All of their light, influence and protection are from Him. As the churches were to emit light as *candlesticks*, the leaders of the churches were to project light as *stars*. They are responsible for the spiritual welfare of these seven churches. They are in Christ's Hand; if they are faithful none can pluck them out of Christ's Hand, if unfaithful none can deliver them from His Hand. Unfaithful leaders are said to be *wandering stars, to whom is reserved the blackness of darkness for ever* (Jude 13).

Yet as verse 20 shows, there is *mystery* here and the question arises and will be discussed as to whether they are real angels or *as the angels* (Matt 22:30). They are *angels*!

- *The **mystery of the seven stars** which thou sawest in my right hand, and the seven golden candlesticks. The seven stars are **the angels of the seven churches**: and the seven candlesticks which thou sawest are the seven churches* (1:20).

*6. **Out of his mouth went a sharp twoedged sword*** (1:16). This was the preface given to the church at Pergamos. Here there was a special kind of evil, *Satan's Seat* (2:13). His word, both wounds and heals. It strikes at sin and will inflict a mortal wound at His Return (Ch. 19). "For the Romans the sword was the principal weapon of offense. They were instructed to use it in such a way as not to expose themselves to a thrust from their enemy. The objective was to kill, not merely to wound. Hence, as used here in Revelation, it implies slaying the wicked. The particular word used for *sword* (*romphaia*) here refers to a long and heavy sword mentioned five other times in the book of Revelation. By contrast, a different word for sword is used in Hebrews 4:12. The sword mentioned in Revelation has the character of a sword of devastating judgment rather than a sword uncovering unbelief as in Hebrews 4:12, and indicates the omnipotence of the Son of God." *Walvoord.*

- *And take the helmet of salvation, and **the sword of the Spirit, which is the word of God*** (Eph 6:17).

THE BOOK OF REVELATION

• *For **the word of God is quick, and powerful, and sharper than any twoedged sword**, piercing even to the dividing asunder of soul and spirit, and of the joints and marrow, and is a discerner of the thoughts and intents of the heart* (Heb 4:12).

• *And **out of his mouth goeth a sharp sword**, that with it he should smite the nations* (Rev 19:15).

7. **His countenance was as the sun shineth in his strength** (1:16). The sight was too bright and dazzling for mortal eyes to behold. The seventh and concluding statement concerning John's view of the Son of God reveals the brilliant glory of His countenance, as the sun shining in its strength. The bright light which now attends His glory was that which blinded Paul on the road to Damascus and that which is the terror of the sinner as well as the assurance of the saint. In their glorified body, saints will be able to see the glory of God. The assurance is given in 1 John 3:2.

• *We know that, when he shall appear, we shall be like him; for **we shall see him as he is***.

• *But unto you that fear my name shall **the Sun of righteousness arise** with healing in his wings; and ye shall go forth, and grow up as calves of the stall* (Mal 4:2).

• *And the city had no need of the sun, neither of the moon, to shine in it: for the glory of God did lighten it, and **the Lamb is the light thereof*** (Rev 21:23).

In this revelation of the Son of Man are seen the attributes of omnipotence, righteousness, sovereignty, majesty, truth, and love.

REVIEW

I. THE THINGS WHICH THOU HAST SEEN (1:19): THE GLORIFIED CHRIST DURING THE PRESENT AGE AS PRIEST AND SOON TO BE KING 1:1-20
    A. THE PREFACE 1:1-3
    B. THE APOSTOLIC BENEDICTION 1:4-8
    C. THE GLORIOUS VISION OF THE LORD JESUS CHRIST 1:9-18
        1. THE CIRCUMSTANCES OF THE VISION 1:9-11.
        2. THE VISION OF THE LORD JESUS CHRIST 1:12-18.
            (1) CHRIST IN RELATION TO THE SEVEN CHURCHES 1:12-16.
                [1] HE SAW THE CHURCHES AS CANDLESTICKS (1:12).
                [2] HE SAW CHRIST IN PRIESTLY GLORY (1:13-16).

(2) CHRIST IN RELATION TO JOHN 1:17,18. *And when I saw him, I fell at his feet as dead. And he laid his right hand upon me, saying unto me, Fear not; I am the first and the last* (1:17): *I am he that liveth, and was dead; and, behold, I am alive for evermore, Amen; and have the keys of hell and of death* (1:18).

[1] THE EFFECT UPON JOHN. *And when I saw him, I fell at His feet as dead.* The apostle was overpowered with the greatness of the glory in which Christ appeared, though he had been so familiar with Him before during His three year ministry.

In contrast to those periods of intimate fellowship when frequently he laid His head upon the Lord, John now falls as dead before that same Presence, now glorified and whose power and majesty are no longer veiled and whose righteousness is revealed to be a consuming fire. The revelation of God and His glory on other occasions in the Bible had a similar overwhelming effect, as in the case of Abraham (Gen 17:3), Manoah (Jdg 13:20), Ezekiel (Ezek 3:23; 43:3; 44:4), Daniel (Dan 8:17; 10:8-9, 15-17), and the disciples on the Mount of Transfiguration (Matt 17:6). Those who do not fall down before God at the

CHAPTER 1

revelation of His glory and majesty are brought to immediate self-judgment and reverent fear as in the case of Gideon (Jdg 6:22,23), Job (Job 42:5,6), Isaiah (Isa 6:5), Zacharias (Lk 1:12), and Peter (Lk 5:8).

[2] THE GOODNESS OF THE LORD JESUS TO JOHN. *He laid his hand upon me* (1:17), He raised him up; *he did not plead against him with his great power, but he put strength into him* (Job 23:6), He spoke kind words to him.

One. WORDS OF COMFORT. *Fear not.* He commanded away the slavish fears of His disciple.

Two. WORDS OF INSTRUCTION. He reveals four things to John concerning His Person and Work.

1. HIS DIVINE NATURE. *I am the first and the last.* The Son of God is eternal and *before* all time (Micah 5:2; Jhn 1:1-3). He is the Creator of time and with regard to that is *the First and the Last.*

2. HIS FORMER SUFFERINGS. *I am he that liveth and was dead* (1:18); He is the very One that His disciples saw upon the Cross dying for the sins of world (Jhn 1:29).

3. HIS RESURRECTION AND LIFE: *and, behold. I am alive for evermore. Amen.* I have conquered death and opened the grave, and am partaker of an endless life.

4. HIS OFFICE AND AUTHORITY: *and have the keys of hell and of death,* He has sole dominion in and over the invisible world, opening and none can shut, shutting so that none can open. He brings men to the gates of death and hell, and that when He determines (Psa 22:29). He is the Judge of all and beyond His sentence there lies no appeal.

In His Death and Resurrection, Christ took from Satan any power he had over death through the sins he introduced (cp. Heb2:14,15).

> • *Forasmuch then as the children are partakers of flesh and blood, he also himself likewise took part of the same; that through death he might destroy him that had the power of death, that is, the devil; And deliver them who through fear of death were all their lifetime subject to bondage* (Heb 2:14,15).

No man can die apart from Christ's permission even though afflicted by Satan and in trial and trouble. As the One who has absolute authority over Hell, Christ is absolutely sovereign over Heaven and the life to come. The Greek word *hades* commonly translated "hell" refers to the intermediate state and is to be distinguished from the Lake of Fire or *Gehenna*, which refers to the eternal state. Christ is sovereign over the *first death* and the *second death*; therefore we must come to Him who is the *Life* (Jhn 14:19).

> • *He that hath an ear, let him hear what the Spirit saith unto the churches; He that overcometh shall not be hurt of* **the second death** *(Rev 2:11).*
>
> • *Blessed and holy is he that hath part in the first resurrection: on such* **the second death** *hath no power, but they shall be priests of God and of Christ, and shall reign with him a thousand years (Rev 20:6).*
>
> • *And death and hell were cast into the lake of fire. This is* **the second death**
> (Rev 20:14).
>
> • *But the fearful, and unbelieving, and the abominable, and murderers, and whoremongers, and sorcerers, and idolaters, and all liars, shall have their part in the lake which burneth with fire and brimstone: which is* **the second death** *(Rev 21:8).*

THE BOOK OF REVELATION

Christ is the Conqueror of death and the grave; thus as Man He obtained the victory over all that man was subjected to by sin and which fills him with terror (Heb 2:14,15).

D. THE THREEFOLD DIVISION OF THE BOOK 1:19,20

(1:19) *Write the things which thou hast seen, and the things which are, and the things which shall be hereafter;*

(1:20) *The mystery of the seven stars which thou sawest in my right hand, and the seven golden candlesticks. The seven stars are the angels of the seven churches: and the seven candlesticks which thou sawest are the seven churches.*

1. THE COMMISSION TO WRITE THE THREEFOLD DIVISION 1:19. *Write the things which thou hast seen* (Chapter 1), *and the things which are* (The Church Age: Chapters 2,3), *and which shall be hereafter* (The Tribulation, Millennium and Eternity: Chapters 4-22).

John having begun as a worshipper (1:17) and in the Spirit (1:10), is now commissioned to write. In this commission we have the threefold outline of the Book. *The things which thou hast seen*; that is, the subjects and scenes of Chapter 1 where John had his preliminary vision. Here, the main subject of the entire book has been introduced, Jesus Christ the glorious Coming King.

The second division, *the things which are*, clearly points to Chapters 2 and 3 with the seven messages to churches. Their contemporary situation provides the framework for a prophecy (1:3) of seven kinds of churches that will be seen throughout the age from John's day until the Rapture. They also present seven basic stages of Church History up to Christs Return.

The third division, *the things which shall be hereafter*, deals with the Book's major content, from Chapters 4 to 22. In these the Millennial Reign and the Eternal Ages are dealt with (Chs. 20-22), but the major focus is the seven year Tribulation, which after the Introduction (Chs. 4,5) is described fully in Chapters 6-19.

Concerning this threefold division based on verse 19, Walvoord writes:

> The advantage of this outline is that it deals in a natural way with the material rather than seizing on incidentals as some expositors have done or avoiding any outline at all, as is true of other expositors. It is not too much to claim that this outline is the only one which allows the book to speak for itself without artificial manipulation and which lays guidelines of sufficient importance so that expositors who follow this approach have been able to establish a system of interpretation of the book of Revelation, namely, the futurist school. It is significant that practically all other approaches to the book of Revelation yield widely differing interpretations in which there is little uniformity when one interpreter is compared to the next. The futurist school at least agrees on some of its main lines of interpretation.
>
> The decision to follow this outline is a major one and can only be supported by the self-consistency of the interpretation of the book as a whole to which it gives rise. Further support will also be found in the exposition of chapter 4 with its evidence for prophecy of future events.

2. THE INTERPRETATION (WITH MYSTERY) OF TWO SYMBOLS. *The mystery of the seven stars which thou sawest in my right hand, and the seven golden candlesticks. The seven stars are the angels of the seven churches: and the seven candlesticks which thou sawest are the seven churches* (1:20). It is significant as indicated in this verse that the symbolic revelation given in this Book serve a number of purposes:

CHAPTER 1

(1) They are meant to be understood.
(2) They are to be understood by reference to other Scriptures, whether in the immediate context or not.
(3) They test and exercise the fidelity of the reader.
(4) They refer to literal truth.
(5) They heighten the understanding of literal truth.

While other symbols have been set forth in this chapter, yet with the *stars* and *candlesticks* there is a twofold distinction. (1) We are told the interpretation in the immediate context, and (2) We are also told that that in the Biblical sense there is *mystery*. Thus something new is here revealed that we have not seen before.

We will show that regarding the *candlesticks*, they refer to much more than seven literal churches of that day, they in fact give a prophetic age-spanning revelation up to the Second Coming of Christ. This among premillennialists has been generally accepted. However, regarding the *seven stars* as actual **angels** has led to quite a lot of discussion with many accepting that this is one of the *very fe*w places in Scripture where the word for angel refers to a man, and that here it refers to the seven pastors or leaders of the seven churches.

Two obvious questions arise:

(1) How can a man be called an angel?
(2) How can an angel be given the warning that these "angels" are given?

The passage says they are angels and therefore that is what they are! We have stated in the introduction that the great truths and doctrines of Scripture are given their final word in Revelation. With this passage, we find how a final word is given concerning angels. The following is an edited and abridged summarization from the substantial study, *The Meaning of Angels in Revelation 2 and 3* by Dr. Robert Dean.

THE *SEVEN STARS* AND THE IMMENSE ROLE OF ANGELS

One of the hermeneutical challenges facing the student of the Apocalypse of Jesus Christ to John the Apostle, and one that has generated significant discussion is the identification of the "seven angels of the seven churches" in Revelation 2-3.
The two symbols are each identified: the stars are the angels of the churches; the lampstands are the seven churches. However, this still raises a number of questions. Who exactly are these angels? Why are these reports seemingly addressed to angels? If these are not angels, then to what could ἄγγελος refer? How does the star symbolism help identify them? What is the relationship between these ἄγγελοι and the churches?
Whether of the Human Leader View or the Superhuman Angel View, neither has garnered a majority support and difficulties are acknowledged regardless of which view is adopted.

THE HUMAN LEADER VIEW

The *angel* is the leader of the local church. Support for this view appeals to Malachi 2:7 and 3:1 where the angel/messenger describes the priest as the one who instructs the people (Mal. 2:7) and then describes the predecessor to the Messiah as "My messenger" (Mal. 3:1). The same Hebrew word is used elsewhere (Hag 1:13), as well as prophets in general (2 Chron 36:15,16). In each of these cases, ἄγγελος is used in the Septuagint translation. New Testament support is found in Matthew 11:10, Mark

1:2, Luke 7:27 (all of which quote Mal. 3:1 and use ἄγγελος). Since ἄγγελος is used of human messengers of God in the Old Testament, advocates of this view argue that the ἄγγελοι of Revelation 2-3 must also be human messengers of God.

The church leader option is sustainable since the Pastor (Bishop, Elder) as the leader of the local congregation is accountable for its successes and failures, so he can stand as the responsible representative of the local assembly. Further the final formula in each of the seven letters states, *He that hath an ear let him hear what the Spirit saith unto the churches*. This shows that each local congregation was the intended audience, and an earthly, not heavenly, messenger must therefore be in view. The most convincing aspect of this interpretation is that it avoids the difficulties associated with explaining why angels seem to be addressed as the corporate representatives responsible for the failures of these churches.

The most common objection to the human leader or pastor view is that ἄγγελος is never used of a pastor. If "pastor" were intended, why did John not use the word indicating pastor, bishop or elder? It is never used in the New Testament of a human being, and its overwhelming usage in the Old Testament is that of superhuman being, whether of angels generally or Christ as the Angel of the Lord. [It is to this latter that Malachi 3:1 refers].

The role of angels is a subject not so prominent in the Bible as are other themes of study, yet what is revealed shows that their power and influence is great beyond words and their numbers are *innumerable*.

- *And he said, The LORD came from Sinai, and rose up from Seir unto them; he shined forth from mount Paran, and he came with **ten thousands** of saints: from his right hand went a fiery law for them* (Deut 33:2).

- *The chariots of God are **twenty thousand, even thousands** of angels: the Lord is among them, as in Sinai, in the holy place* (Psa 68:17).

- *A fiery stream issued and came forth from before him: **thousand thousands** ministered unto him, and **ten thousand times ten thousand** stood before him: the judgment was set, and the books were opened* (Dan 7:10).

- *And I beheld, and I heard the voice of many angels round about the throne and the beasts and the elders: and the number of them was **ten thousand times ten thousand, and thousands of thousands*** (Rev 5:11).

- *But ye are come unto mount Sion, and unto the city of the living God, the heavenly Jerusalem, and to an **innumerable** company of angels* (Heb 12:22).

Against such a background the implication of the seven angels, seen as stars in in the right hand of the Lord Jesus Christ (1:16,20), and their relationship to the seven churches can be better understood if the role of angels throughout the Book of Revelation is observed. In short, it is a role which generally sees them as witnesses to judicial proceedings. We continue to draw from *The Meaning of Angels in Revelation 2 and 3* by Dr. Robert Dean. From the link that follows, the reader is encouraged to read the entire study, it is one of the most insightful and succinct available on the subject.

THE ANGEL - SUPERNATURAL BEING VIEW

Many view the angels of the churches as being guardian angels who guide and protect each congregation. Support for this is based on examples of heavenly representatives appointed to watch over earthly nations (Dan 10:13, 21; 12:1).

Additional support is derived from the role of angels as guardians to individuals (Dan 11:1; Matt 18:10; Acts 12:15; 1 Cor 11:10; Heb 1:14).

In general the angels-are-angels view has significant support. First, the term ἄγγελος is used consistently everywhere else in Revelation to describe supernatural beings. Second, the ἄγγελος are identified as stars in Revelation 1:20, a common metaphor for angels (cf., Rev. 12:4). However, the major flaw of this view is that none of the explanations for the role of these angels seems satisfactory. The guardian angel option merely affirms the role of angels as guardians but fails to show either how a "church guardian" role fits the context of local church practice and teaching in the rest of the New Testament.

The weaknesses with the angel interpretation is centered on why the letter to each church would be addressed to an actual angel. The idea of a guardian angel of an assembly may appeal but has little Scriptural support. It is argued, that as almost all of the rebukes in Chapters 2,3 use the second person singular pronoun and means that the angels themselves are being addressed. Since elect angels do not sin, why are they accused of sin and why would they need to repent? So despite strong lexical and contextual evidence for it, the problem of such an angel's relationship to the associated church seems to be the decisive reason for rejecting it. The next section, therefore, will re-examine the Scriptural data regarding angels and will search whether or not a role for angels has been left undiscussed in current commentaries.

THE CONTEXT OF THE ANGELS IN REVELATION 1-3

First, the vision of the Lord is the background out of which the seven letters of Revelation 2-3 come. Here our Lord is pictured not as sacrificed Lamb, nor as a Prophet or as a Priest, but as the Royal Judge. As Royal Judge, He holds the seven stars in his right hand, indicating the sovereignty exercised over these stars.

Second, the angels, represented as stars are distinct from the seven lampstands which represent the churches.

Third, the nature of each of these letters is to present the divine critique of the churches' behaviour; to rebuke them for failure, and to encourage them to and for obedience.

Fourth, the addressing of these seven evaluations to an angel as a singular individual is followed predominately by second person singular pronouns and verb forms (though with occasional third person plural forms included). Although the NT epistles are generally addressed to groups, and plural verbs and pronouns are used, it is not uncommon in Scripture elsewhere to address a group as if it were an individual and to use second person singular verbs and pronouns in a collective sense.

Fifth, the angel of each assembly may only appear to be addressed as if he is the church and the one responsible for this behaviour. We must note that the initial command to John was that he write to the seven churches (1:11). No mention of angels was made in verse ll. Further, in the letters themselves, each is said to be spoken by the Spirit *to the churches* (Rev 2:7, 11, 17, 29; 3:6, 13, 22). It is therefore likely that the address "to the angel" does not mean the angel is held responsible for their actions, but that the angel is being made aware of the performance assessment of each church.

ANGELS AND STARS IN THE SCRIPTURES

The vast majority of the mention of stars in Scripture refer to the literal orbs of light hung in space on that fourth creation day (Gen 1:16; 15:5; Isa 13:10). In a number of passages, however, a connection is made between the literal stars called *the host of heaven* (Deut 4:19) and the angelic hosts, also called the *host of heaven* (1 Kng 22:19). In two related passages the tribes of Israel are symbolically represented by stars (Gen. 37:9, Rev 12:1). The Old Testament speaks of a "mysterious" connection between the stars and the angels. Judges, Job, Isaiah, and Daniel all connect stars to heavenly beings that serve God.

In the New Testament the word ἀστήρ (star) appears twenty-four times. Of these, several refer to the literal heavenly luminaries (Matt 24:29; 1 Cor 15:41), four refer to the literal Star of Bethlehem (Matt. 2:2, 7, 9, 10), one is the figurative use for wandering false prophets (Jude 13), once as a symbol for the twelve tribes of Israel (Rev. 12:1), and Christ as the "Bright, Morning star" (Rev. 22:16). The remaining passages, all of which are in Revelation, use stars to refer to angels (Rev. 1:16, 20; 2:1; 3:1; 9:1; 12:4). Notable is the casting by the Dragon of *the third part of the stars of heaven to the earth* (Rev 12:4). Thus, stars are equated with angels in Scripture but not as prophets or pastors.

TWENTY-ONE INSTANCES OF HOLY ANGELS IN REVELATION

1. THE ANGEL SENT BY CHRIST TO JOHN (1:1, 19:9-10; 22:6, 8, 9, 16). The entire Book was communicated to John via an angel. Six times reference is made to this angel, who apparently remained with John and guided him through the revelatory process. This angel is first introduced in 1:1 as being uniquely assigned to the Lord Jesus Christ. He is called *His angel* (1:1) and *My* (Christ's) *angel* (22:6, 16)…The primary mission of this angel was to reveal the contents of this revelation to John. The theme of which is the completion of God's plan for judging the wicked, both human and demonic, and for blessing believers.

2. GENERAL REFERENCES TO THE HOLY ANGELS (3:5; 5:11-12; 7:11-12; 14:10). The number of these angels are described as *ten thousands times ten thousands and thousands of thousands* (Rev. 5:11). They join in praising God for His work among men. Perhaps the most significant for our purposes is the description of the unsaved being tormented in the presence of the holy angels (Rev14:10). As with their observance of the church (1 Cor 11:10; Eph 3:10; 1 Pet 1:12) they will oversee the judgements of the Tribulation. This is a judicial scene of the heavenly court room. The seven sealed book is itself is a judicial document that outlines the procedure by which the Lord Jesus Christ will take ownership of the earth. As sergeant at arms the vast host oversees this judicial process.

3. THE FOUR BEASTS (LIVING CREATURES (4:6-9; 5:6, 8, 11, 14; 6:1, 3, 5-7; 7:11; 14:3; 15:7; 19:4). They are mentioned in eight scenes in Revelation. They are also involved in overseeing the outworking of divine justice in the Tribulation. Each time the Lamb breaks one of the first four seals, one of the living creatures in successive order calls for John to come witness the execution of the judgment (6:1, 3, 5, 6, 7). In the final series of judgments, it is one of the four Living Beings who distributes the seven golden vials of the wrath of God to the seven angels.

4. THE FIRST *STRONG* ANGEL (5:2). Three angels in Revelation are described as strong (5:2; 10:1; 18:21). The first of these angels serves as court herald announcing a judicial question with a loud voice: *Who is worthy to open the book and to loose the seals thereof* (5:2)?

5. THE FOUR ANGELS AT THE FOUR CORNERS OF THE EARTH (7:1-2). In an interlude following the judgment of the sixth seal, John sees four angels at the four corners of the earth restraining the winds of the earth. The power angels have over

CHAPTER 1

the natural forces of the universe can also be observed in Revelation 14:18 and 16:5. These four winds depict God's judgment upon the earth dwellers through meteorological disaster. The Jewish concept was that the winds directly from the four points of the compass were favorable, but those in between (northwest, northeast, southwest, southeast) would be unfavorable and destructive. Thus, these angels are restraining winds which will bring destruction on the earth. Again, we discover angels as officials carrying out judicial decrees from the judgment throne of God.

6. THE ANGEL WITH THE SEAL OF THE LIVING GOD (7:2-8). At this juncture, John sees another angel rising from the east with a seal, crying to the four wind restraining angels to wait to release their winds until he seals the 144,000. The role of this angel is to forestall execution of the judgments of the four angels to provide time to seal the 144,000 from Israel. The act of sealing was a legally-recognized means for identifying property and protecting it. The angel is carrying out a mission related to the Judge of the earth.

7. THE SEVEN ANGELS WITH THE SEVEN TRUMPETS (8:2, 6-13; 9:1, 13-15; 10:7; 11:15). When the Lamb breaks the seventh seal, silence descends over the heavenly court awed by the finality of these judgments. This seventh seal is comprised of seven trumpet judgments, and each judgment is announced by an angel serving as an officer of the heavenly court. The final judgment will be revealed to hold seven final "Vial" judgments.

8. THE ANGEL WITH THE GOLDEN CENSER (8:3-5). The first angels sound the four trumpets initiating these judgments in Revelation 8:7-12. Following this another angel, not one of the seven, presents a golden censer at the altar. The incense burning in the censer represents the prayers of the Tribulation saints presented before the throne of God. These burning coals are then thrown upon the earth (cp. Ezek. 10:2). Again the throne here continues to be a throne of judgment. The prayers are a cry for judgement upon the earth-dwellers (cp. Rev 6:10). Here the angel representing the Tribulation saints corroborates that of angels representing believers, and confirms that angels of Revelation 2-3 can be corporate representatives of those assemblies.

9. THE ANGEL (*STAR*) WITH THE KEY TO THE BOTTOMLESS PIT (9:1). This star must be an unfallen angel dispatched on a divine mission to advance the next stage of God's punishment against the rebellious earth dwellers. Such an act of releasing those imprisoned is again that of a court official carrying out the decrees of the Judge.

Demonic creatures followed by an army of 200 million range out across the earth.

10. THE SECOND *STRONG* ANGEL CLOTHED WITH A CLOUD (10:1-11). The second *strong angel* descends in dramatic fashion. His visage shines like the sun, a reflection of the glory of God which invests the angel with heavenly authority. He is clothed with a cloud and rainbow, which mark him as an emissary from the court of Heaven. The cloud shows his mission to be related to judgment. Of the twenty other occurrences of νεφέλη in the NT, nine come in connection with scenes of judgment (Matt.24:30; 26:24; Mk 13:26; 14:62; Lk 21:27; Rev 1:7; 14:14-16).

11. MICHAEL AND HIS ANGELS (12:7). With this angelic warfare of the Tribulation the devil's angels are permanently ejected from any entrance into Heaven and with the devil are thrown down to the earth. While this scene is more military than judicial it does have judicial overtones and sets the stage for the final judgments on fallen angels and the wicked men upon the earth. Rather than remaining unseen, they become visible and their effects are visible seen from the release of those horrific demon armies in Revelation chapter 9. But at the end, even Babylon becomes inhabited by demons (Rev 18:2).

THE BOOK OF REVELATION

12. THE THREE ANGELS ANNOUNCING JUDGMENT (14:6-11). The first announcement is a reminder of God's grace before judgment. The second angel announces the certainty of divine judgment on Babylon and her final doom. The angel announcing the warning against worshipping the Beast (14:9-11). This third angel announces the certainty of divine judgment on anyone who worships the beast and receives his mark.

13. THE THREE ANGELS IN THE TEMPLE OF HEAVEN (14:15,17-20). Following the three angelic heralds, are three angels, each of whom comes out of the heavenly temple and each successively calls upon the Son of Man to begin His final judgment. The image compares judgment to reaping at the harvest. The first angel calls for Christ to begin reaping (14:15). The second angel then appears with a sharp sickle (14:17-20) but does not begin the reap until the third angel appears and calls for him to begin the final judgment (14:18). The harvest illustration depicts evil in its prime and fully ripe for judgment. The time for the harvest has come, and the time for the Reaper to judge evil has finally arrived.

14. THE SEVEN ANGELS WITH THE SEVEN LAST PLAGUES (15:1, 6-8; 16:1-6, 8-12, 17; 17:1-3, 7-18; 21:9-10, 15-17; 22:1,6). Like the seven angels who sounded the trumpets, these angels oversee the final judgments from the throne of God. Six bowls of wrath are poured out upon the earth. "Wrath" expresses the outworking of divine judgment throughout the Scriptures. Following the third of these unparalleled plagues, an angel not of the seven, speaks. Identified as only the "angel of the waters," this angel praises God, extolling Him as Holy and His judgments as righteous and true (Rev16:5,6). The seventh bowl brings the final judgment, the battle of Armageddon, the destruction of the kings of the earth and the civilizations of the earth dwellers. One of these seven angels then takes John to witness the final judgment of Babylon the Great (Rev. 17:1).

15. THE ANGEL HAVING GREAT AUTHORITY AND POWER (18:1-3). Unlike the two previous *strong* angels and the one following, this angel is identified as having great power in the sense of *authority* (Gr. *exousia*). The powerful authority relates to the gravity of God's announcement which he now delivers: *Babylon the great is fallen, is fallen*. His message is so weighty that it could only be delivered by one manifesting such power.

16. THE THIRD *STRONG* ANGEL CASTING A STONE INTO THE SEA (18:21-24). The action depicts the destruction of Babylon. It describes the totality of the destruction Babylon will not be found any longer; music, trades, crafts, industry, social and business life will all be finally destroyed.

17. THE ANGELIC GUIDE TO JOHN (19:10). As the Lord Jesus Christ prepares to descend to the earth in victory, John is overwhelmed by his vision of the bride making herself ready for the marriage of the Lamb. At the moment the angelic guide instructs him to write, John begins to fall down to worship the angel. The angel quickly admonished him saying that he is but a fellow servant of John and his brethren, i.e., church age believers. This is another example that some angels guide and serve church age saints.

18. THE ANGEL STANDING IN THE SUN (19:17-18). The description of the final military campaign against the forces of wickedness is interrupted by another announcement. The birds of the air are called to partake of a great supper, a meal of carrion, feasting on the carnage following the battle of Armageddon. Like the previous angels announcing the doom of Babylon, this angel reinforces the total judgment of God now falling upon the earth.

CHAPTER 1

19. THE ANGEL HAVING THE KEY AND GREAT CHAIN (20:1-3). This angel *comes down from heaven*, demonstrating that his origin is from the Supreme Court of Heaven. His role is that of an officer of the court, a bailiff, in conducting the condemned to his place of imprisonment. The one chained is the Dragon, Satan, and is bound in the bottomless pit for a thousand years.

20. THE TWELVE ANGELS AT THE TWELVE GATES OF NEW JERUSALEM (21:12). The gates around the city reinforce the idea of the security and power of the city. The twelve angels serve as guards, strengthening the impression of the city's might and security.

21. THE ANGEL WITH THE MEASURING REED (21:17). The measurements taken by the angel of the city convey the holiness, perfection, absolute conformity to God's standard and pattern in creation.

SUMMARY OF ANGELIC JUDICIAL ACTIVITY IN THE BOOK OF REVELATION. With the exception of the angels in the final two chapters, the role of the angels in Revelation is related to the outworking of divine justice. The throne room of Revelation 4-5 depicts a throne of judgment. The angels serve as legal witnesses to divine judgment, they carry out divine judgment, they serve warning of divine judgment. The seven letters to the seven churches also fit this theme. Here too angels give witnesses to judicial evaluation, consistent with the role of angels throughout The Book Revelation.

These seven ecclesiastical evaluation reports reveal that Church Age believers will not be exempt from future judgment, though the issue will not affect their eternal destiny. It does provide the basis of what believers will have to answer to at the Judgement Seat of Christ.

- *But why dost thou judge thy brother? or why dost thou set at nought thy brother? for* **we shall all stand before the judgment seat of Christ** (Rom 14:10).
- *Every man's work shall be made manifest: for the day shall declare it, because it shall be revealed by fire; and the fire shall try every man's work of what sort it is* (1 Cor 3:13).
- *For* **we must all appear before the judgment seat of Christ**; *that every one may receive the things done in his body, according to that he hath done, whether it be good or bad* (2 Cor 5:10).

ANGELS WITNESS THE CHURCHES NOW, AND WILL BEAR WITNESS AT THE JUDGEMENT SEAT OF CHRIST.

- *For I think that God hath set forth us the apostles last, as it were appointed to death: for we are made* **a spectacle unto the world, and to angels**, *and to men* (1 Cor 4:9).
- *For this cause ought the woman to have power on her head* **because of the angels** (1 Cor 11:10).
- *To the intent that now* **unto the principalities and powers in heavenly places might be known by the church** *the manifold wisdom of God* (Eph 3:10).

At Mount Sinai, angels are not mentioned in Moses' account, yet Galatians 3:19 affirms that the Law was *ordained by angels*. This, from what we have now seen indicates that they were legal witnesses to the giving of the Law and also to its reception by Israel. Moses calls *upon heaven and earth as a witness* (Deut 4:26; 30:19; 32:1). This is more than simple personification. As non-living entities, the heavens and earth cannot serve as legal witnesses. This phrase refers to the inhabitants of the heavens and the earth. And then, centuries later Isaiah brings lawsuit against Israel in the same fashion.

- *Give ear, O ye heavens, and I will speak; and hear, O earth, the words of my mouth* (Deut 32:1).
- *Hear, O heavens, and give ear, O earth: for the LORD hath spoken, I have nourished and brought up children, and they have rebelled against me* (Isa 1:2).

Therefore, just as Israel's writing prophets called upon angels to witness Israel's covenant violations, John is told to call upon angelic observers as witnesses to the fidelity and conduct of the seven churches.
http://www.pre-trib.org/articles/view/meaning-of-angels-in-revelation-2-and-3

The mystery of the seven stars which thou sawest in my right hand, and the seven golden candlesticks. The seven stars are the angels of the seven churches: and the seven candlesticks which thou sawest are the seven churches (1:20). The witness of the angels to the Seven Churches will extend across the centuries unto the Rapture.

II THE THINGS WHICH ARE (1:19): The Church Age – Seven Kinds (seen throughout history) and Times (distinct periods) of Churches 2,3

The apostle John, having in the foregoing chapter written *the things which he had seen*, now proceeds to write concerning *the things that are*. These are the things concerning the seven churches; they are the things that are and will continue to be unto the Second Coming of Christ. That this is so and that the letters are not limited to churches John addressed in the first century can be seen by the references to the Return of Christ (while in some cases He comes in judgement, but also His actual Second Coming is in view).

THE SECOND COMING EMPHASIS GIVEN TO THE SEVEN CHURCHES

- **To Ephesus**: *I will come unto thee quickly, and will remove thy candlestick out of his place, except thou repent* (2:5).
- **To Pergamos**: *Repent; or else **I will come unto thee quickly**, and will fight against them with the sword of my mouth* (2:16).
- **To Thyatira**: *Behold, **I will cast her** into a bed, and them that commit adultery with her **into great tribulation,** except they repent of their deeds* (2:22)…***Hold fast till I come*** (2:25)…*To him **will I give power over the nations**. And **he shall rule them with a rod of iron*** (2:26,27).
- **To Sardis**: *If therefore thou shalt not watch, **I will come on thee as a thief**, and thou shalt not know **what hour I will come upon thee*** (3:3).
- **To Philadelphia**: ***I also will keep thee from the hour of temptation, which shall come upon all the world, to try them that dwell upon the earth. Behold, I come quickly*** (3:10,11).

CHAPTER 1

The Geographical Aspect of the Seven Churches

The Road Connecting the Seven Churches

It may be wondered why these particular churches were addressed. There were many churches located in the area where these churches were found and some of which were larger, but God has selected seven and these seven only. As we have seen from the maps there is a geographical nearness with these seven. They form an arch and were located on a circular road connecting them to each other and to the most populous part of the province. Thus with the Book of Revelation being sent to these seven would enable its rapid dispersion much further afield. This was especially so as the order of presentation began at the great centre of Ephesus one the largest and most influential crossroads of the Roman Empire.

THE ILLUSTRATIVE AND TYPICAL ASPECT OF THE SEVEN CHURCHES

There are *seven* churches and by this number we are alerted to the fact that a statement of completion and conclusion is being made concerning them. There will be seven basic kinds and types of churches during the age between the First and Second Comings of Christ. Each church needed a particular message, and the spiritual state of each church corresponded precisely to the exhortation which was given. Each illustrated circumstances and problems that were common in churches at that time and would also be throughout the ages of church history. The messages to the seven churches therefore embody admonition suitable for churches in seven basic kinds of spiritual need.

Along with the messages to the churches were exhortations which are personal in character constituting instruction and warning to the individual Christian. Each of the messages as given to the churches therefore ends in a personal exhortation beginning with the phrase *He that hath an ear, let him hear.*

THE BOOK OF REVELATION

http://jimbomkamp.com/Revelation/seven%20churches.gif

THE SEVEN CHURCHES OF REVELATION

	Ephesus The Apostolic Church Rev. 2:1-7	Smyrna The Persecuted Church Rev. 2:8-11	Pergamum The Indulged Church Rev. 2:12-17	Thyatira The Pagan Church Rev. 2:18-29	Sardis The Dead Church Rev. 3:1-6	Philadelphia The Church Christ Loved Rev. 3:7-13	Laodicea The Lukewarm Church Rev. 3:14-22
	A.D. 30-100	A.D. 100-312	A.D. 312-606	A.D. 606-Tribulaiton	A.D. 1520-Tribulation Protestant Reformation	A.D. 1750-Rapture	A.D. 1900-Tribulation
Commendation I know your...	Good works, labor, patience. Hated Nicolaitians.	Works, tribulation, poverty.	Works. Held fast my name. Has not denied my faith.	Good works, love, service, faith, patience.	Works. A name that you live.	Works. Missions. Little strength. Kept my word. Not denied my name.	Not one word!
Condemnation	You have left your first love.	Not one word!	You have false teachers of Balaam and the Nicolaitans.	You allow Jezebel to teach idolatry and compromise.	You are dead. Works not complete.	Not one word!	You are lukewarm, wretched, miserable, poor, blind and naked.
Counsel I counsel you...	Remember from where you are fallen and repent.	Fear not. Be faithful.	Repent.	Hold fast what you have until I come.	Watch. Strengthen the things that remain. Remember, hold fast and repent.	Hold fast what you have.	Buy gold tried by fire and white raiment. Anoint your eyes. Be zealous and repent.
Challenge To him that overcomes...	Will give to eat of the tree of life	Will not be hurt by the second death.	Will give hidden manna and a white stone.	Will give millennial leadership and the Morning Star.	Will be clothed in white raiment. I will not blot his name out of the book of life.	Will make him a pillar and write upon him the name of God and My new name.	Will grant to sit with me on my throne.

The Comparative Aspect of the Seven Churches

THE SEVEN AGE ASPECT OF THE CHURCHES

Prophecy does not begin in Revelation with the events directly related to the Return of Christ, *the things which must be hereafter* (1:19,4:1), but rather with *the things which are* (Ch. 2,3), the Church Age before Christ's Rapture and Return. The *entire* Book is a prophecy (1:3). Here then is a prophecy of seven kinds of churches that will exist throughout the present age, but also in a broad outline there are here seven progressive stages of church history through that period.

While many deny the church age view, there is good reason to accept the principle, John Walvoord says.

> Many expositors believe that in addition to the obvious implication of these messages the seven churches represent the chronological development of church history viewed spiritually. They note that Ephesus seems to be characteristic of the Apostolic Period in general and that the progression of evil climaxing in Laodicea seems to indicate the final state of apostasy of the church. This point of view is postulated upon a providential arrangement of these churches not only in a geographical order but by divine purpose, presenting also a progress of Christian experience corresponding to church history. As in all scriptural illustrations, however, it is obvious that every detail of the messages addressed to these particular churches is not necessarily fulfilled in succeeding periods of church history. ...
>
> The prophetic interpretation of the messages to the seven churches, to be sure, should not be pressed beyond bounds, as it is a deduction from the content, not from the explicit statement of the passage.... The general trend indicated confirms other Scripture (1 Tim 4; 2 Tim 2,3) that, instead of progressive improvement and a trend

toward righteousness and peace in the church age, it may be expected that the age will end in failure as symbolized in the church of Laodicea. This is taught expressly in passages describing the growing apostasy in the professing church culminating in the apostate Christendom of the time of the great tribulation. Simultaneous with this development in the church as a whole there will be fulfilment of the divine plan of God in calling out a true church designed to be a holy bride for the Son of God and a promised translation from the earth before the final tragic scenes of the Tribulation are enacted.

C.I. Scofield wrote:

The messages to the seven churches have a fourfold application:
(1) Local, to the churches actually addressed;
(2) Admonitory, to all churches in all time as tests by which they may discern their true spiritual state in the sight of God;
(3) Personal, in the exhortations to him "that hath an ear," and in the promise "to him that overcometh";
(4) Prophetic, as disclosing seven phases of the spiritual history of the church from, say, A.D. 96 to the end. It is incredible that in a prophecy covering the church period, there should be no such foreview. These messages must contain that foreview if it is in the book at all, for the church does not appear after Revelation 3:22. Again, these messages by their very terms go beyond the local assemblies mentioned. Most conclusively of all, these messages do present an exact foreview of the spiritual history of the church, and in this precise order. **Ephesus** gives the general state at the date of the writing; **Smyrna**, the period of the great persecutions; **Pergamos**, the church settled down in the world, "where Satan's seat is," after the conversion of Constantine, say A.D. 316. **Thyatira** is the Papacy, developed out of the **Pergamos** state: Balaamism (worldliness) and Nicolaitanism (priestly assumption) having conquered. As Jezebel brought idolatry into Israel, so Romanism weds Christian doctrine to pagan ceremonies. **Sardis** is the Protestant Reformation, whose works were not *perfect*. **Philadelphia** is whatever bears clear testimony to the Word and the Name in the time of self-satisfied profession represented by **Laodicea**.

The following gives a further basic overview of these seven stages of Church History:

ONE. EPHESUS: The Post Apostolic Church – Sound in doctrine, busy, faithful in exposing error, but love is waning 2:1-7.
TWO. SMYRNA: **Imperial Rome <u>Persecutes</u> the Church** – Faithful to Christ, sorely persecuted, poor by the world's standards, but spiritually rich 2:8-11.
THREE. PERGAMOS: **Imperial Rome <u>Accepts</u> the Church** – Persecution ceases, generally sound in its view of Christ, but false doctrine and worldly living are making inroads, intimidating rise to power of bishops, compare, *Satan's Seat* (2:13), beginnings of Papal Rome 2:12-17.
FOUR. THYATIRA: **Ecclesiastical Rome <u>Becomes</u> the Church** – Very busy, active, powerful, but in league with the *depths of Satan* (2:24). Much of professing "Christendom" comes under Papal Rome, but groups like the Waldensians and others remain separate
2:18-29.
FIVE. SARDIS: The Reformation Church – **Comes out but retains much of Rome's "deadness"** (v. 1), rituals, robes, infant baptism, state church, claims for itself God's promises to Israel (replacement theology), non-literal view of Bible prophecy 3:1-6.

SIX. PHILADELPHIA: Seen mainly from 1850 to 1950 – Small but faithful, open door to world evangelization, small Bible Institute movement, interprets Bible prophecy literally, promotes worldwide missionary movement, Jewish evangelism, sees the return of the Jews to Israel as a fulfilment of Ezekiel 37:1-8 (a return in which their faith was not yet in the Messiah, 37:8) 3:7-13.

SEVEN. LAODICEA: Last Days Church – Big, wealthy, worldly, a social gathering, blind to Biblical truth. Its lifestyle, music etc. is mixed in with the world. Lowest common denominator kind of faith (Lk 18:8); a mixture of ecumenism, charismaticism, Catholicism. Christ is on the outside seeking entrance 3:14-22.

CHAPTER 2

A. EPHESUS: The Post Apostolic Church – Sound in doctrine, vigilant against error, busy, but love is waning   2:1-7

(2:1) Unto the angel of the church of Ephesus write; These things saith he that holdeth the seven stars in his right hand, who walketh in the midst of the seven golden candlesticks;

(2:2) I know thy works, and thy labour, and thy patience, and how thou canst not bear them which are evil: and thou hast tried them which say they are apostles, and are not, and hast found them liars: (2:3) And hast borne, and hast patience, and for my name's sake hast laboured, and hast not fainted.

(2:4) Nevertheless I have somewhat against thee, because thou hast left thy first love. (2:5) Remember therefore from whence thou art fallen, and repent, and do the first works; or else I will come unto thee quickly, and will remove thy candlestick out of his place, except thou repent.

(2:6) But this thou hast, that thou hatest the deeds of the Nicolaitans, which I also hate.

(2:7) He that hath an ear, let him hear what the Spirit saith unto the churches; To him that overcometh will I give to eat of the tree of life, which is in the midst of the paradise of God.

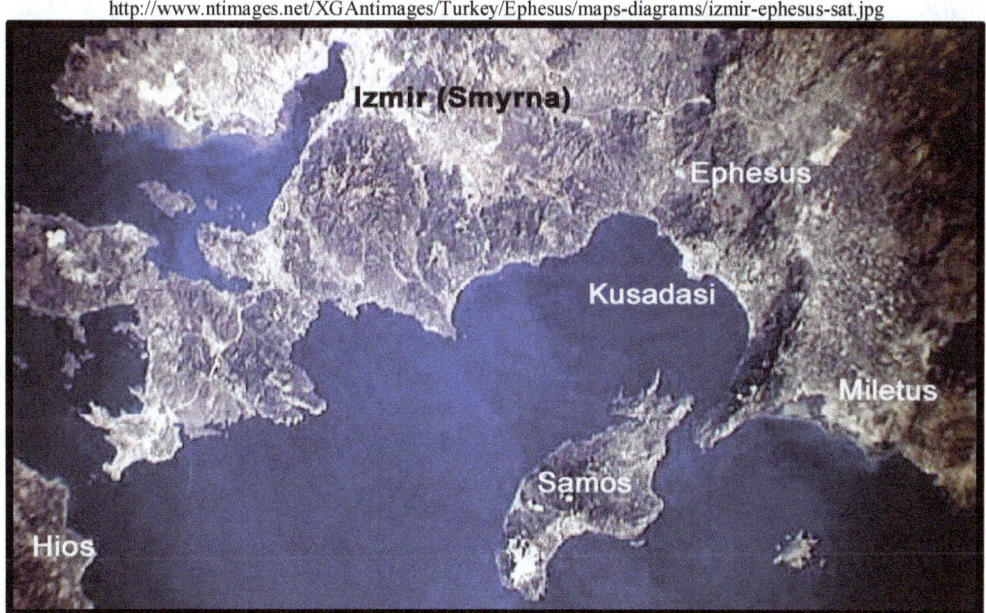

http://www.ntimages.net/XGAntimages/Turkey/Ephesus/maps-diagrams/izmir-ephesus-sat.jpg

Ephesus, The Fourth Largest City of the Roman Empire

1. THE INSCRIPTION OF THE LETTER.

(1) TO WHOM THE FIRST LETTER IS WRITTEN. *Unto the angel of the church of Ephesus write* (2:1). The churches are divided into three and four. In the first three promise follows injunction ; in the last four the order is reversed. In writing to the witnessing angel, the letter is also written to the church at Ephesus and also to the other churches. Note the added statement that is made in each letter:

- *He that hath an ear, let him hear **what the Spirit saith unto the churches*** (2:7).

The famous church planted by the apostle Paul (Acts 19), and afterwards according to early documents was overseen by the Apostle John. Paul had some thirty years before told Timothy to *remain in Ephesus* (1 Tim 1:3).

Ephesus with a population of a quarter million was the principle city in the Roman province of Asia and fourth city of the Empire behind Rome, Alexandria and Antioch. Paul had ministered there for three years as recorded in Acts 19. The effectiveness of his ministry is stated in Acts 19:10, *All they which dwelt in Asia heard the word of the Lord Jesus, both Jews and Greeks.* The preaching of the gospel had affected the worship of Diana, in whose temple was considered one of the seven wonders of the world.

The reduction in the sale of idols of Diana led to the riot recorded in Acts 19:23-41. Demetrius, a leader of the silversmiths called a meeting to reverse the fall in sales.

- *Sirs, ye know that by this craft we have our wealth. Moreover ye see and hear, that not alone at Ephesus, but almost throughout all Asia, this Paul hath persuaded and turned away much people, saying that they be no gods, which are made with hands: So that not only this our craft is in danger to be set at nought; but also that the temple of the great goddess Diana should be despised, and her magnificence should be destroyed, whom all Asia and the world worshippeth* (Acts 19:25-27).

The resulting riot forced Paul to leave, after which Timothy for many years led the church. The Apostle John is believed to have succeeded Timothy.

(2) FROM WHOM THE LETTER WAS SENT. **He that holdeth the seven stars in his right hand** (See 1:13,16,20). The stars, as we have seen are the witnessing angels (1:20). They are in Christ's hand and are responsible to give a sound and honest witness to the facts stated in the letters and to what they observe in the churches. They are *stars*, they will give a clear, precise, unambiguous witness whether good or bad. In court proceedings today reference is sometimes made to a *star witness*.

With these angelic-star-witnesses in hand, Christ is He **who walketh in the midst of the seven golden candlesticks.** This intimates Christ's relationship to His churches. He is present and conversant with them. He knows and observes their state. He takes pleasure in them, as a man does to walk in His garden. Though Christ is in heaven, He walks in the midst of his churches on earth. The churches are not arranged in a line that He walks along, but are here in a circle in which He is *in the midst*. Christ is often spoken of as being **in the midst**.

- *Where they crucified him, and two other with him, on either side one, and **Jesus in the midst*** (Jhn 19:18).
- *Then the same day at evening, being the first day of the week, when the doors were shut where the disciples were assembled for fear of the Jews, came **Jesus** and stood **in the midst**, and saith unto them, Peace be unto you* (Jhn 20:19).
- *And after eight days again his disciples were within, and Thomas with them: then came **Jesus**, the doors being shut, and stood **in the midst**, and said, Peace be unto you* (Jhn 20:26).
- *And I beheld, and, lo, **in the midst** of the throne and of the four beasts, and **in the midst** of the elders, stood a **Lamb** as it had been slain, having seven horns and seven eyes, which are the seven Spirits of God sent forth into all the earth* (Rev 5:6).
- *For **the Lamb** which is **in the midst** of the throne shall feed them, and shall lead them unto living fountains of waters: and God shall wipe away all tears from their eyes* (Rev 7:17).

CHAPTER 2

The churches are candlesticks. This is their purpose. Their primary function is to give out the Light of Christ (Jhn 1:9) and the Light of the Scriptures (Psa 119:130; cp. Matt 5:16).

2. THE CONTENTS OF THE LETTER.

(1) THE COMMENDATION. Christ tells Ephesus that which He always declares, *I know*. Therefore His commendation and rebuke is to be taken to heart. He does not "venture and opinion"; He *knows*. He commends them for three basic things:

[1] THEIR LABOUR. ***I know thy works, and thy labour, and thy patience*** (2:2). Grass was not growing under their feet; this was a working church. This was a church that illustrated the great Biblical truth that *faith without works is dead* (Jms 2:26). The Apostolic Church (and immediately after) was a working church. And, that work consisted primarily in the spread of the Gospel and the building up of believers in Biblical faith. This they did with nearly nothing we have today. No transport; no central heating, no printing presses, no computers, no supermarkets, no clothing shops. The Apostle Paul set an example:

- *For ye remember, brethren, our labour and travail: for labouring night and day, because we would not be chargeable unto any of you, we preached unto you the gospel of God* (1 Thess 2:9).

[2] THEIR VIGILANCE: ***and how thou canst not bear them which are evil: and thou hast tried them which say they are apostles, and are not, and hast found them liars*** (2:2). In *speaking the truth in love* (Eph 4:30), we must not compromise with error. We understand that there is a "learning curve" in understanding the truths of God's Word, but for the sake of peace we must not cover what the Bible clearly shows is error. If people want to twist, or add to, or take away from the Bible: if they claim they have apostolic or prophetic gifts, then as with the church at Ephesus, they should be put to the test.

- *Thus saith the LORD of hosts, Hearken not unto the words of the prophets that prophesy unto you: they make you vain:* ***they speak a vision of their own heart****, and not out of the mouth of the LORD* (Jer 23:16).
- *I have not sent these prophets, yet they ran:* ***I have not spoken to them, yet they prophesied*** (Jer 23:21).
- *Beloved, believe not every spirit, but* ***try the spirits whether they are of God****: because many false prophets are gone out into the world* (1Jhn 4:1).
- *For I testify unto every man that heareth the words of the prophecy of this book,* ***If any man shall add unto these things****, God shall add unto him the plagues that are written in this book: And* ***if any man shall take away from the words of the book*** *of this prophecy, God shall take away his part out of the book of life, and out of the holy city, and from the things which are written in this book* (Rev 22:18,19).

[3] THEIR ENDURANCE. ***And hast borne, and hast patience, and for my name's sake hast laboured, and hast not fainted*** (2:3). Christ keeps an account of every day's work. He watches over us as we set out and as we come home. He knows if we have fainted and He bears us up. Men may forget what you do for the Lord, but God does not. At Ephesus there was a tenacity in the work; *they did not faint*! Further, it is noted that their labour is motivated as work *for my name's sake*. It was not for their name or reputation for which they worked so hard, it was for Christ.

- *Thou therefore* ***endure hardness, as a good soldier*** *of Jesus Christ* (2 Tim 2:3).

THE BOOK OF REVELATION

> • *For God is not unrighteous to forget your **work** and labour of love, which ye have shewed toward his name, in that ye have ministered to the saints, and do minister* (Heb 6:10).

These remarkable characteristics establish the fact that the church at Ephesus had served the Lord well, and few modern churches could qualify for such a commendation.

(2) THE REBUKE. ***Nevertheless, I have somewhat against, because thou hast left thy first love*** (2:4). Those that have much good in them may have something that is wrong – *very wrong*. Our Lord Jesus, takes notice of both; though He first observes what is good, and is very ready to commend it.

But, there is a ***nevertheless*** here. The sin that Christ charged this church with was their decay and declension in holy love and zeal: *Thou hast left thy first love;* not left and forsaken Christ Himself, but lost the fervency of their love for Him that they once had. In the busyness of the routine affection can abate if care is not taken. Christ is grieved when His people become cool and distant toward Him.

(3) THE APPEAL. advice and counsel given them from Christ: ***Remember therefore from whence thou art fallen, and repent, and do the first works*** (2:5). They were to Remember, Repent and Return. They were to compare their present with their former. If there was a first love they would certainly remember it. What they had now for Christ, was only *a going through the motions* compared with the holy zeal they once knew. Believers can fall, and this is called a *fall*.

Their defect was a matter of heart rather than of the head or the will. The ardour which they once knew had grown cold. In the letter to the Ephesians, written some thirty years before, Paul commended them for their love. Note also the example given to Timothy, a pastor of the church at Ephesus, concerning a love for the Lord's Return

> • *Wherefore I also, after I heard of your faith in the Lord Jesus, and **love unto all the saints**, Cease not to give thanks for you, making mention of you in my prayers* (Eph. 1:15,16).
> • *Henceforth there is laid up for me a crown of righteousness, which the Lord, the righteous judge, shall give me at that day: and not to me only, but unto all them also that **love his appearing*** (2 Tim 4:8).

This state of affairs cannot be allowed to continue; they must repent. The firstworks must certainly mean fellowship with the Lord Himself; abiding in Him, prayer, confession of the fallen state, reading the Bible with a heart of faith, getting back to the primary calling.

> • *God is faithful, by whom ye were **called unto the fellowship of his Son Jesus Christ our Lord*** (I Cor 1:9).

The church at Ephesus was now in its second generation. Though they continued to labour faithfully as those who had preceded them, the love of God which characterized the first generation was missing. This cooling of heart which had overtaken them in relationship to God was a dangerous forerunner of spiritual apathy which later was to erase all Christian testimony at Ephesus. Thus it has ever been the history of the church: first a cooling of spiritual love, then the love of God replaced by a love for the things of the world. Note the following.

<u>Love of the World Generally</u>. ***Love not the world***, *neither the things that are in the world. If any man love the world, the love of the Father is not in him* (1 Jhn 2:15).

CHAPTER 2

Substituting Anything for Love of Christ is Called Idolatry. *Little children, keep yourselves from **idols*** (1 Jhn 5:21)

Love of Money. *For the **love of money** is the root of all evil: which while some coveted after, they have erred from the faith, and pierced themselves through with many sorrows* (1 Tim 6:10).

Even Love of Family. *He that loveth **father or mother** more than me is not worthy of me: and he that loveth **son or daughter** more than me is not worthy of me* (Matt 10:37; cp. 19:29; 1 Cor 7:34).

[1] A WARNING: *or else I will come unto thee quickly, and will remove thy candlestick out of his place, except thou repent* (2:5). There is no sharper warning to the other seven churches than this. No matter how much is being done in a church, a candlestick cannot burn if love for something else has replaced love for Christ. May it ever be: *The love of God is shed abroad in our hearts by the Holy Ghost which is given unto us* (Rom 5:5).

The downward spiral was not reversed. History records that the church at Ephesus retained its prominence and importance for several centuries. It was the seat of eastern bishops (*Nicolaitanism !*) and was the venue for an important gathering of the third General Council in 431. The ruins of the church of Saint Mary where this meeting took place can still be seen. Ephesus as a city declined after the fifth century, and the Turks deported its remaining inhabitants in the fourteenth century. Today, except as a tourist destination, it is uninhabited; only an important ruin in that area. It is seven miles from the sea due to accumulation of silt which has stopped up the harbour of this once important seaport.

http://1.bp.blogspot.com/-_jtz6F_Eghw/UbR4Sdg25FI/AAAAAAAAeE/uhxCTKwR1is/s1600/3+Ephesus+Church+of+Mary.jpg

Church of Saint Mary, Ephesus

Note that the prophecy states *I will come unto thee quickly*; as historic Ephesus declined gradually, this must refer primarily to judgement upon churches in these last days which while being relatively sound in doctrine show very little interest in and love for the Lord's imminent Return. The warning is similar to that given to the "reformed" church at Sardis.

• *Remember therefore how thou hast received and heard, and hold fast, and repent. If therefore thou shalt not watch, I will come on thee as a thief, and thou shalt not know what hour I will come upon thee* (Rev 3:3).

[2] AN ENCOURAGEMENT. **But this thou hast, that thou hatest the deeds of the Nicolaitans, which I also hate** (2:6). Indifference toward truth and error, good and evil, may be viewed as *charitable*, but it is not so with Christ. Having been given a strong warning the church is again on these points commended.

As a group "history has no record of the Nicolaitans" (*The Companion Bible*). It is nevertheless commonly stated that "the Nicolaitans were a licentious sect advocating complete freedom in Christian conduct including participation in heathen feasts and free love" (Walvoord). Henry Alford (*The Greek New Testament*) states, "The prevailing opinion among the fathers was, that they were a sect founded by Nicolaus the proselyte of Antioch, one of the seven deacons" (Acts 6:5). This is nevertheless an opinion without any clear evidence. Given the extent of the condemnation that this group receives (2:6,15), it is clearly not a small sect but something major.

There is a good reason why the *Fathers* (usually early bishops) to whom Alford refers would like to pin the blame for this group on Nicolaus or someone else. It seems clearly to refer to a *big* movement of which they were the prominent head. Rather than the autonomy of individual local churches, with *Nicolaitainism* we see the rise of the bishops ruling over groups and cities of local churches. Eventually the powerful bishops ceded their authority to the ultimate bishop, the Pope of Rome. The power that the bishops claimed for themselves was the first and biggest error in the early church. It was hated (at least in the beginning) by Ephesus; embraced by Pergamos (for it had become *doctrine*, 2:5); and most importantly it was hated by the Lord Himself; **which I also hate**. Note, that it is the sin, deeds and doctrine, that is hated and not the sinner that is hated.

Scofield writes concerning the Nicolaitans:

> From *nikao*, "to conquer," and *laos*, "the people," or "laity." There is no ancient authority for a sect of the Nicolaitanes. If the word is symbolic it refers to the earliest form of the notion of a priestly order, or "clergy," which later divided an equal brotherhood Matthew 23:8 into "priests" and "laity." What in Ephesus was *deeds* (2:6) had become in Pergamos a *doctrine* (2:15; cp.1 Pet 5:2,3; Matt 24:49).

- *Feed the flock of God which is among you, taking the oversight thereof, not by constraint, but willingly; not for filthy lucre, but of a ready mind; Neither as being lords over God's heritage, but being ensamples to the flock* (1 Pet 5:2,3).

3. THE CONCLUSION OF THE LETTER.

(1) TO THE HEARER. **He that hath an ear, let him hear what the Spirit saith unto the churches** (2:7). What is written in the Scriptures is spoken by the Spirit of God. And, what is said to one church concerns all the **churches**, in every place and every age. It may seem sufficient to say this only once, but there is a great need to stress the point, and thus it is repeated for each of the seven churches.

(2) TO THE OVERCOMER. **To him that overcometh will I give to eat of the tree of life, which is in the midst of the paradise of God** (2:7). The promises to the overcomer mount as the defection of the church descends. The ascent is from the Tree of Life to the Throne of Christ (3:21). Life is the first necessity and must precede kingship. The intervening steps mark the upward path of ever increasing glory.

The promise here mentioned for overcomers is not a message to a special group of Christians distinguished by their spirituality and power compared to other believers who lack these qualities; it is rather a general description of that which is normal and to be expected among all who are true followers of Christ. The First Epistle of John asks the question, *Who is he that overcometh the world* (1Jhn 5:5)? The question is answered, *He that believeth that*

CHAPTER 2

Jesus is the Son of God. In other words, those in the Ephesian church who were genuine Christians and by this token had overcome the unbelief and sin of the world are promised the *right to the tree of life* (22:14) which is *in the midst of the paradise of God* (2:7).

This tree, first mentioned in the Garden of Eden in Genesis 3:22, is later found in the midst of the street of the new Jerusalem, where it bears its fruit for the abundant health and life of the nations (Rev 22:2). Both the expanding nations (21:24) and those with glorified bodies will partake of this tree. For the former it will give *healing to the nations* (22:2; cp. Gen 3:22). For the latter to partake will be one of the delights of the New Jerusalem.

- *In the midst of the street of it, and on either side of the river, was there the tree of life, which bare twelve manner of fruits, and yielded her fruit every month: and **the leaves of the tree were for the healing of the nations*** (Rev 22:2).

B. SMYRNA: Imperial Rome Persecutes the Church – Faithful to Christ, sorely persecuted, poor by the world's standards, but spiritually rich 2:8-11

(2:8) ***And unto the angel of the church in Smyrna write; These things saith the first and the last, which was dead, and is alive;***
(2:9) ***I know thy works, and tribulation, and poverty, (but thou art rich) and I know the blasphemy of them which say they are Jews, and are not, but are the synagogue of Satan.***
(2:10) ***Fear none of those things which thou shalt suffer: behold, the devil shall cast some of you into prison, that ye may be tried; and ye shall have tribulation ten days: be thou faithful unto death, and I will give thee a crown of life.***
(2:11) ***He that hath an ear, let him hear what the Spirit saith unto the churches; He that overcometh shall not be hurt of the second death.***

We now proceed to the second epistle sent to another of the Asian churches, where as before we observe,

1. THE INSCRIPTION OF THE LETTER.

(1) TO WHOM THE LETTER IS WRITTEN. ***And unto the angel of the church in Smyrna write*** (2:8). Smyrna was a thriving city then and unlike Ephesus still is and still retains a Christian witness. It represents the faithful church and the church faced with great suffering. If one travelled from Ephesus to Smyrna (second in size in the area to Ephesus), he would cover a distance of about thirty-five miles to the north, entering Smyrna by what was called the "Ephesian Gate." Anciently it was called "The lovely—the crown of Ionia—the ornament of Asia." It was also in the first century noted for its wickedness and opposition to the Gospel. In this large and flourishing commercial centre was a little church that remained faithful.

Smyrna (Izmir)

(2) <u>FROM WHOM THE LETTER WAS SENT</u>. *These things saith the first and the last, which was dead, and is alive* (2:8; see 1:17,18).

[1] CHRIST AS IN CHAPTER ONE IS *THE FIRST AND THE LAST*. It is but a little wisp of time that is allowed to us in this world, but our Redeemer is *the first and the last*. He is **the first**, for *all things were created by him* (Col 1:16), and He was before all things with God and is the Eternal God Himself (Jhn 1:1-3). He is **the last**, for all things are *created for Him* (Col 1:16), and He will be the Judge of all and Restorer of all at His Second Coming and throughout eternity. This is the title of the Son of God, from *everlasting and to everlasting*, and it is the title of One that is the unchangeable *Mediator between God and man* (1 Tim 2:5); *Jesus, the same yesterday, to-day, and for ever* (Heb 13:8). He was *the first*, for in Him the foundation stone of all is laid. He is *the last*, for by Him the top-stone of His Millennial Kingdom and New Heavens and New Earth will be brought forth.

[2] <u>HE WAS DEAD AND IS ALIVE</u>. He died for our sins; *He is alive*, for *He rose again for our justification* (Rom 4:25), and *He ever lives to make intercession for us* (Heb 7:25). He was dead, and by dying purchased salvation for us; He is alive, and by his life applies this salvation to us. And *if, when we were enemies, we were reconciled by his death, much more, being reconciled, we shall be saved by his life* (Rom 5:10).

The church at Smyrna is told that the One who was eternal became incarnate and died, a reminder that even the eternal Son of God willingly became subject to the rejection and persecution of man. But as He rose victorious, so in Him they and all believers look forward to this glad victory.

The word Smyrna itself means "myrrh," a sweet perfume used in embalming the dead and was also included in the holy anointing oil used in the Tabernacle (Exod 30:23). It is a perfume and mentioned in Psalms with reference to Christ, the Heavenly Bridegroom. Thus, by this word, for the believer there is a sweetness in death.

- *All thy garments smell of myrrh, and aloes, and cassia, out of the ivory palaces, whereby they have made thee glad* (Psa 45:8).

CHAPTER 2

2. THE CONTENTS OF THE LETTER. As with the church at Ephesus there is a *Commendation*, but unlike that church and the other churches except Philadelphia, there is no *Rebuke*. In fact it is the shortest of the Letters (only four verses), and that because there was nothing in conduct or practice or doctrine with which the Lord must take issue. Also, like the others there is an *Appeal*, but at Smyrna both the commendation and the appeal have to do with the severe trial the church was then facing and would continue to face.

(1) THE COMMENDATION IN VIEW OF THEIR PRESENT TRIALS. *I know thy works, and tribulation, and poverty, (but thou art rich) and I know the blasphemy of them which say they are Jews, and are not, but are the synagogue of Satan* (2:9).

[1] HE KNEW THEIR *WORKS*. This is said about each of the churches, though in the case of Sardis and Laodicea there is an immediate clarification. At Sardis their works were *not found perfect* (3:2), and at Laodicea their works only served to demonstrate that they were *neither hot nor cold* (3:15). In the other churches the works were good, but except for Philadelphia are counter-balanced by "works" that were *bad*. Like Ephesus, Smyrna knew that *faith without works is dead* (Jms 2:26).

[2] HE KNEW THEIR *TRIBULATION*. This warfare between the Seed of the woman and the seed of the serpent, unites the first Book of the Bible with the last (Gen 3:15). It has been the story of the ages. *In the world ye shall have tribulation* (Jhn 16:33).

[3] HE KNEW THEIR *POVERTY*. The word used (*ptocheian*) means *abject poverty*. They were not just poor (*penia*). It may be that they were drawn from a poor class of people, but it is more probable that their extreme poverty is explained by the fact that they had been robbed of their goods in the process of their persecution and affliction and Imperial Rome did nothing to stop it (cp. Hab 1:4; Heb 10:34).

Suddenly the opposite is stated: **But thou art rich**. In the same spirit other Scripture speaks of *the poor of this world rich in faith* (Jms 2:5); and, *as poor, yet making many rich* (2 Cor. 6:10). They were poor in temporals, but rich in spirituals—poor in goods, and yet rich in grace. Their spiritual riches are set in stark contrast and demonstrated by their material poverty. Many who are rich in temporary and fleeting riches are poor in spiritual and eternal riches. Thus it was with the church of Laodicea. Neither Christ nor a Smyrna kind of church has any time for the "prosperity gospel" being preached today.

[4] HE KNEW THE SLANDER AGAINST THEM. *I know the blasphemy of them which say they are Jews, and are not, but are the synagogue of Satan* (2:9). Note: *the synagogue of Satan* (2:9), *Satan's seat* (2:13), and, *the depths of Satan* (2:24). The first is Jewish, the second and third are Gentile.

They of the *synagogue of Satan* were Jewish by race but not by *the faith of Abraham who saw Christ's day* (Jhn 8:56). In New Testament times the Jewish leaders and many among the common people who rejected the Gospel were the most vociferous enemies of the Gospel. They did all in their power to slander both Christ and the early church before the Roman authorities. This was the constant background to the spread of the Gospel in the Book of Acts (12:3,11; 13:50; 14:2,19; 17:5,13; 18:12; 22:30; 24:5; 25:2,7,15,24).

Many of the *Synagogue of Satan*, have as foretold in the letter to Philadelphia, become worshippers of the Messiah. The Philadelphia stage of Church History would see a great increase in Jewish evangelism.

> • *Behold, I will make them of the synagogue of Satan, which say they are Jews, and are not, but do lie; behold, I will make them to come and worship before thy feet, and to know that I have loved thee* (Rev 3:9).

It has always been true that false religion from whatever source has been the most zealous in opposing that which is true. The Smyrna Christians found few friends in the hostile world around them.

(2) THE APPEAL IN VIEW OF THEIR FUTURE TRIALS. *Fear none of those things which thou shalt suffer: behold, the devil shall cast some of you into prison, that ye may be tried; and ye shall have tribulation ten days: be thou faithful unto death, and I will give thee a crown of life* (2:10). Christ foreknows the future trials of His people, and forewarns them of them, and fore-arms them against them.

[1] CHRIST GIVES COMFORTING COUNSEL. *Fear none of those things which thou shalt suffer.* Note: it is assumed that God's people will suffer. He did not say, "Fear not because you *will not* suffer." Here is not only a command to *Fear Not*, but also an enablement. He does not ask us to do something that He does not enable us to do. *Fear none of those things*. They may be varied and many; in fact *manifold* (1 Pet 1:6), but fear *none* of them. Christ does not entice men to follow Him by promising them ease and pleasure, but plainly tells them that there will be suffering.

- *Yea, and all that will live godly in Christ Jesus shall suffer persecution* (2 Tim 3:12).

[2] CHRIST GIVES SPECIFIC WARNING: *behold, the devil shall cast some of you into prison, that ye may be tried; and ye shall have tribulation ten days*. The warning is tempered somewhat. He says *some* and *ten days*. It will not be *all* and it will not be *forever*. The *ten days* may refer to what believers have experienced throughout the church age and thus only a short time in comparison to the glory that lies ahead.

- *For I reckon that the sufferings of this present time are not worthy to be compared with the glory which shall be revealed in us (Rom 8:18).*

Many think the *ten days* refer in the first instance to the ten periods of severe persecution instituted by the caesars of Imperial Rome. Walvoord writes:

> The first under **Nero**, AD 54.
> The second under **Domitian**, AD 81.
> The third under **Trajan** AD 98.
> The fourth under **Adrian** [Hadrian], AD 117.
> The fifth under **Septimius Severus**, AD 193.
> The sixth under **Maximin**, AD 235.
> The seventh under **Decius**, AD 249.
> The eighth under **Valerian**, AD 254.
> The ninth under **Aurelian**, AD 270.
> The tenth under **Diocletian**, AD 284.

The date mentioned is the beginning of the reign of each emperor, not necessarily the beginning of the persecution. Some have applied the *ten days* to the ten years of persecution under Diocletian.

[3] CHRIST GIVES A STRENGTHENING PROMISE: *be thou faithful unto death, and I will give thee a crown of life.* For the true believer (and true believers, despite the valleys, continue to believe) there is here a sure and suitable promise. *First*. The Sureness of the Reward: *I will give thee*. He that has said it is the One that will do it. *Secondly*, The Suitableness of the Reward. *A crown*, to reward their poverty, their fidelity, and their conflict. *A crown of life*, to reward those who are faithful even unto death, who are faithful till they die, and who part with life itself in fidelity to Christ. The life so worn out in

his service, or laid down in his cause, shall be rewarded with another and a much better life and one that is eternal.

3. THE CONCLUSION OF THE LETTER.

(1) TO THE HEARER. *He that hath an ear, let him hear what the Spirit saith unto the churches* (2:11). All believers in all the churches must hear for they too and to some extent will experience *tribulation for ten days*. In fact given what is now mentioned (the second death), let all men and women in all the world hear what passes between Christ and His churches.

(2) TO THE OVERCOMER. *He that overcometh shall not be hurt of the second death.* There is a death after the body is dead. This second death is unspeakably worse than the first death, both in the dying pangs and agonies of it and in the duration; it is *eternal death,* dying the death, to die and to be always dying." *Matthew Henry*. The *second death* will have no power over those who are *partakers of the first resurrection.*

- But **the rest of the dead** *lived not again until the thousand years were finished. This is the first resurrection. Blessed and holy is he that hath part in* **the first resurrection**: *on such* **the second death** *hath no power, but they shall be priests of God and of Christ, and shall reign with him a thousand years (Rev 20:5,6).*
- *And the sea gave up the dead which were in it; and death and hell delivered up the dead which were in them: and they were judged every man according to their works. And death and hell were cast into the lake of fire. This is* **the second death** *(Rev 20:13,14).*

Smyrna was a martyr church. Death was in it very name. They were dying but their persecutors were also dying. How great a difference there was between the two *dyings*. Believers in the sorely tried and martyred church at Smyrna were promised a Crown of Life. Note the other crowns promised by the Lord.

FIVE CROWNS PROMISED TO BELIEVERS

The Crown of Life. The crown that is eternal life itself. The glories of life eternal stand in contrast to the trials of persecution and that even when they extend to martyrdom. *Fear none of those things which thou shalt suffer: behold, the devil shall cast some of you into prison, that ye may be tried; and ye shall have tribulation ten days: be thou faithful unto death, and I will give thee* ***a crown of life*** (Rev 2:10).

The Crown of Righteousness. Promised for a righteous life and love for the Lord's Return. *I have fought a good fight, I have finished my course, I have kept the faith: Henceforth there is laid up for me* ***a crown of righteousness****, which the Lord, the righteous judge, shall give me at that day: and not to me only, but unto all them also that love his appearing* (2 Tim 4:7,8).

The Crown of Glory. For faithful leaders. *Neither as being lords over God's heritage, but being ensamples to the flock. And when the chief Shepherd shall appear, ye shall receive* ***a crown of glory*** *that fadeth not away* (1 Pet 5:3,4).

The Crown of Rejoicing. Those won to Christ by faithful soul winners. *For what is our hope, or joy, or* ***crown of rejoicing****? Are not even ye in the presence of our Lord Jesus Christ at his coming* (1 Thess 2:19)?

The Incorruptible Crown. Discipline and self-control in the Christian race. *And every man that striveth for the mastery is temperate in all things. Now they do it to obtain a corruptible* ***crown****; but we* ***an incorruptible****. I therefore so run, not as uncertainly; so fight I, not as one that beateth the air: But I keep under my body, and*

THE BOOK OF REVELATION

bring it into subjection: lest that by any means, when I have preached to others, I myself should be a castaway (1 Cor 9:25-27).

C. PERGAMOS: Imperial Rome Accepts the Church – Held to Christ's Name, Bishops become powerful, Sin enters, Joined to Satan's Seat ! 2:12-17

(2:12) *And to the angel of the church in Pergamos write; These things saith he which hath the sharp sword with two edges;*
(2:13) *I know thy works, and where thou dwellest, even where Satan's seat is: and thou holdest fast my name, and hast not denied my faith, even in those days wherein Antipas was my faithful martyr, who was slain among you, where Satan dwelleth.*
(2:14) *But I have a few things against thee, because thou hast there them that hold the doctrine of Balaam, who taught Balac to cast a stumblingblock before the children of Israel, to eat things sacrificed unto idols, and to commit fornication.* (2:15) *So hast thou also them that hold the doctrine of the Nicolaitans, which thing I hate.* (2:16) *Repent; or else I will come unto thee quickly, and will fight against them with the sword of my mouth.*
(2:17) *He that hath an ear, let him hear what the Spirit saith unto the churches; To him that overcometh will I give to eat of the hidden manna, and will give him a white stone, and in the stone a new name written, which no man knoweth saving he that receiveth it.*

1. THE INSCRIPTION OF THE LETTER.
(1) TO WHOM THE LETTER IS WRITTEN. *And to the angel of the church in Pergamos write* (2:12). Pergamos was wealthy city located north of Smyrna, about twenty miles from the Mediterranean. Today a small village named Bergama is located below the hilltop ruins. A nominal Christian testimony has continued in the town to modern times.

http://www.greeceturkeytours.com/wp-content/uploads/2013/02/Pergamum-Temples.jpg

Pergamos

The city was legendary for its many temples and altars to idolatry; these included the *serpent god* of healing, Esculapius, and also Athena, Dionysus, and Zeus. The altar to Zeus can now be seen at the *Pergamum Museum* in Berlin. In this polluted atmosphere so completely opposed to the Gospel was situated the little church to which Christ now writes

There was something else at Pergamos that was for more deceptive than its brazen idolatry. Twice in verse 13 it is said that this was the city of **Satan's Seat**. With Satan's influence so blatantly obvious in the world, to single out Pergamos with such an epithet must indicate something unparalleled! There was! It represented the most basic and pervasive form of false religion – the ancient Babylonian worship of **the mother and child**. It combined with the two other "doctrines" at work in Pergamos, *the doctrine of the Nicolaitans* and *the doctrine of Balaam* (2:14,15). The name Pergamos means "married". At Pergamos a marriage began to take place between Christianity and the ancient pagan mystery of the *mother and child*.

SATAN'S SEAT: BROUGHT FROM BABYLON TO PERGAMOS

With his copious documentation, Alexander Hislop's *The Two Babylons* remains by far the foremost work on the ancient Babylonian cult. The following quotations from Hislop by Harry Ironside (*Lectures on the Book of Revelation*) have been used by many over the years as a valid summary of the subject. Referring to Revelation 17:5 and the emboldened words - ***MYSTERY BABYLON THE GREAT, THE MOTHER OF HARLOTS AND ABOMINTATIONS OF THE EARTH*** – Hislop writes:

> The woman is a religious system, who dominates the civil power, at least for a time. The name upon her forehead should easily enable us to identify her. But in order to do that we will do well to go back to our Old Testament, and see what is there revealed concerning literal Babylon, for the one will throw light upon the other . . .
>
> We learn that the founder of Bab-el, or Babylon, was Nimrod, of whose unholy achievements we read in the 10th chapter of Genesis. He was the arch-apostate of the patriarchal age . . . he persuaded his associates and followers to join together in *building a city and a tower which should reach unto heaven* . . . to be recognized as a temple or rallying centre for those who did not walk in obedience to the Word of the Lord . . . they called their city and tower Bab-El, the gate of God; but it was soon changed by divine judgment into Babel, *Confusion*. It bore the stamp of unreality from the first, for we are told *they had brick for stone, and slime had they for mortar*. An imitation of that which is real and true has ever since characterized Babylon, in all ages. Nimrod, or Nimroud-bar-Cush . . . was a grandson of Ham, the son of Noah . . .
>
> Ancient lore now comes to our assistance, and tells us that the wife of Nimroud-bar-Cush was the infamous Semiramis the First. She is reputed to have been the foundress of the Babylonian mysteries and the first high-priestess of idolatry. Thus Babylon became the fountainhead of idolatry, and the mother of every heathen and pagan system in the world. The mystery-religion that was there originated spread in various forms throughout the whole earth. . . and is with us today . . . and shall have its fullest development when the Holy Spirit has departed and the Babylon of the Apocalypse holds sway.
>
> Building on the primeval promise of the woman's Seed who was to come (Gen 3:15), Semiramis bore a son whom she declared was miraculously conceived! and when she presented him to the people, he was hailed as the promised deliverer. Thus was introduced **the mystery of the mother and the child**, a form of idolatry that is older than any other known to man. The rites of this worship were secret. Only the initiated were permitted to know its mysteries. It was Satan's effort to delude mankind with an imitation so like the truth of God that they would not know the true Seed of the woman when He came in the fullness of time. . . .

THE BOOK OF REVELATION

From Babylon this mystery-religion spread to all the surrounding nations . . . Everywhere the symbols were the same, and everywhere the cult of the ***mother and the child*** became the popular system; their worship was celebrated with the most disgusting and immoral practices. The image of ***the queen of heaven with the babe in her arms*** was seen everywhere, though the names might differ as languages differed. It became the mystery-religion of Phoenicia, and by the Phoenicians was carried to the ends of the earth. Astoreth and Tammuz, the mother and child of these hardy adventurers, became Isis and Horus in Egypt, Aphrodite and Eros in Greece, Venus and Cupid in Italy, and bore many other names in more distant places. Within 1000 years Babylonianism had become the religion of the world.

Linked with this central mystery were countless lesser mysteries. . . . Among these were the doctrines of ***purgatorial purification after death***, salvation by countless sacraments such as priestly absolution, ***sprinkling with holy water***, the ***offering of round cakes to the queen of heaven*** as mentioned in the book of Jeremiah, dedication of virgins to the gods, which was literally sanctified prostitution, weeping for Tammuz for a period of 40 days, prior to the great festival of Istar, who was said to have received her son back from the dead; for it was taught that Tammuz was slain by a wild boar and afterwards brought back to life. To him the egg was sacred, as depicting the mystery of his resurrection . . . the ***sign of the cross*** was sacred to Tammuz, as symbolizing the life-giving principle and as the first letter of his name. It is represented upon vast numbers of the most ancient altars and temples, and did not, as many have supposed, originate with Christianity.

From this mystery-religion, the patriarch Abraham was separated by divine call; and with this same evil cult the nation that sprang from him was in constant conflict, until under Jezebel, a Phoenician princess, it was grafted onto what was left of the religion of Israel in the northern kingdom in the day of Ahab, and was the cause of their captivity at last. Judah was polluted by it, for Baal-worship was but the Canaanitish form of the Babylonian mysteries, and only by being sent into captivity to Babylon itself did Judah become cured of her fondness for idolatry. Baal was the Sun-God, the Life-giving One, identical with Tammuz. . . .

Worship of the Mother and Child Across the Ages

CHAPTER 2

Though Babylon as a city had long been but a memory, her mysteries had not died with her. When the city and temples were destroyed, the high-priest fled with a company of initiates and their sacred vessels and images to Pergamos . . .From there, they afterwards crossed the sea and emigrated to Italy. . . . There the ancient cult was propagated under the name of the Etruscan Mysteries, and eventually Rome became the headquarters of Babylonianism. The chief priests wore **mitres shaped like the head of a fish**, in honour of Dagon, the fish-god, the Lord of life—another form of the Tammuz mystery, as developed among Israel's old enemies, the Philistines. The chief priest when established in Rome took the title **Pontifex Maximus**, and this was imprinted on his mitre. When Julius Caesar had become the head of the State, he was elected Pontifex Maximum, and this title was held henceforth by all the Roman emperors down to **Constantine the Great**, who was, at one and the same time, head of the church and high priest of the heathen! The title was afterwards conferred upon the bishops of Rome, and is borne by the Pope today, who is thus declared to be, not the successor of the fisherman-apostle Peter, but the direct successor of the high priest of the Babylonian mysteries, and the servant of the fish-god Dagon, for whom he wears, like his idolatrous predecessors, the fisherman's ring.

During the early centuries of the church's history, the mystery of iniquity had wrought with such astounding effect, and Babylonian practices and teachings had been so largely absorbed by that which bore the name of the church of Christ, that the truth of the Holy Scriptures was obscured, while idolatrous practices were foisted upon the people as Christian sacraments, and heathen philosophies took the place of gospel instruction. Thus was developed that amazing system which for a thousand years dominated Europe and trafficked in the bodies and souls of men, until the great Reformation of the 16th century brought in a measure of deliverance.

"It is not too much to say that the false doctrines and practices found within Romanism are directly attributable to the union of this paganism with Christianity when Constantine declared Rome to be a Christine empire and decreed an end to the persecution of Christians." (Ironside quoting Hislop, pp. 287-295).

(2) FROM WHOM THE LETTER WAS SENT. ***These things saith he which hath the sharp sword with two edges***. In the first chapter we read that *out of his mouth went a sharp two-edged sword* (1:16). Pergamos was infested with false teachers who were doing all in their power to corrupt the Biblical beliefs and conduct of the church. The sword that is to be applied is not a civil or military sword. Both the Roman Catholic and to a certain extent Calvin's Protestant Church have wielded that sword. (See our tract, *Calvin and Persecution*). It is not a sword made of steel for it comes from Christ's mouth. The Scriptures themselves are the sword given to the believer in the battle against error.

- *And take the helmet of salvation, and **the sword of the Spirit, which is the word of God*** (Eph 6:17).

The word of God is a ***sword***; it is a weapon both offensive and defensive. It is a ***sharp sword***. It had not dulled or lost its cutting edge across the centuries. God's preserved words (Matt 24:35) as found in the Masoretic Text of the Old Testament and the Received Text of the New Testament and which forms the basis of the King James Version and translations in other languages is a *sharp sword*. Few realize that 2900 words are missing from modern New Testaments. See *Missing in Modern Bibles*.

It is a ***sharp sword with two edges***; it cuts and defends in every direction. There is no escaping the *edge* of this sword; if you turn to the right hand, it has an *edge* on that side; if on the left, it will strike there also; it *turns every way* (cp. Gen 3:24). It is more than adequate for the errors that had entered Pergamos – *Satan's seat, the doctrine of Baalam* and *the doctrine of the Nicolaitans* (2:13-15). It can also cut *between*! *It pierces even to the dividing asunder of soul and spirit, and of the joints and marrow, and is a discerner of the thoughts and intents of the heart* (Heb 4:12).

2. THE CONTENTS OF THE LETTER.
(1) THE COMMENDATION. *I know thy works, and where thou dwellest, even where Satan's seat is: and thou holdest fast my name, and hast not denied my faith, even in those days wherein Antipas was my faithful martyr, who was slain among you, where Satan dwelleth* (2:13). Christ takes notice of the trials and difficulties this church encountered. The works of God's servants are best known when the circumstances under which they did those works are considered.

[1] THEY UPHELD CHRIST'S NAME DESPITE *SATAN'S SEAT*. Pergamos with all her other idolatry had taken the further leap and become the world centre of *Satan's Seat*. Yet against the background of it being the centre of the ancient Babylonian *mother and child* cult and now combining that with the worship of Mary and the Christ Child; there was a strong attempt at Pergamos to hold fast to the true Biblical faith in Christ.

Proper honour is shown to Mary in the Scriptures, but in the very few places we see Mary in the Bible, she is *never* worshiped. Prayers as in the Rosary are *never* offered to her. The Wise Men did not pray to her, they worshiped Christ (Matt 2:11). The Shepherds did not pray to her (Lk 2:16). Simeon and Anna did not pray to her (Lk 2:22-39). Those at the Cross or upper room did not pray to her (Jhn 19:25,26; Acts 1:14). She is *never* exalted on (or above) a level with Christ Himself. There is *nothing* in the Bible about her immaculate conception (without inherited sin), or her ascension into Heaven without dying. She is *never* seen in the Bible as a Co-mediatrix or Co-redemptrix with Christ. Yet before these falsehoods where established at Rome, they found a footing in Pergamos. What the Bible does say concerning Mary is clear - She acknowledged like all other lost sinners who come to salvation - She needed a *Saviour*!

• *And Mary said, My soul doth magnify the Lord, And **my spirit hath rejoiced in God my Saviour*** (Lk 1:46,47).

The *Large* Mary and *Small* Christ Seen in Roman Catholic Churches, The Church of Our Lady of the Rosary and St Dominic, Palermo, Sicily

CHAPTER 2

[2] THEY UPHELD THE FAITH DESPITE PERSECUTION: *and hast not denied my faith, even in those days wherein Antipas was my faithful martyr, who was slain among you, where Satan dwelleth* (2:13). They were faithful to the great Biblical truths even though it meant persecution and in the example given here - martyrdom. Who Antipas was, we have no certain account. It is lost from the pages of history but not from the inerrant page of Scripture. Perhaps as was often the case, the officials at Pergamos attempted to erase his name from all remembrance, but Christ remembered. The Lord says he was **MY FAITHFUL MARTYR**. He held his ground in the eye of the storm **where Satan dwelleth.** The name Antipas means, *Against All* !

The death of Antipas was like that of a soldier dying on the field of battle shortly before a peace treaty is signed. Soon after, Imperial Rome would put a stop to persecution.

> Constantine was the first emperor to stop Christian persecutions and to legalise Christianity along with all other religions and cults in the Roman Empire.
> In February 313 AD, Constantine met with Licinius in Milan, where they developed the Edict of Milan. The edict stated that Christians should be allowed to follow the faith without oppression. This also allowed the return of confiscated Church property.
>
> Scholars debate whether Constantine adopted his mother St. Helena's Christianity in his youth, or whether he adopted it gradually over the course of his life. Constantine possibly retained the title of *pontifex maximus* a title emperors bore as heads of the ancient Roman religion priesthood until Gratian (375–383) renounced the title. *Wikipedia.*

Imperial Rome rather than waging war against the Church had now received it with open arms. Persecution stopped but **Satan's seat** with its rapidly growing *mother and child* cult remained. The "heat was off" and Biblical faith was entering a subtle and dangerous phase.

(2) THE REBUKE. ***But I have a few things against thee, because thou hast there them that hold the doctrine of Balaam, who taught Balac to cast a stumblingblock before the children of Israel, to eat things sacrificed unto idols, and to commit fornication. So hast thou also them that hold the doctrine of the Nicolaitans, which thing I hate*** (2:14,15). A twofold *doctrine* had entered the Church. The word *doctrine* speaks of that which is formulated and official; thus it is entrenched.

The reference to Balaam refers to Numbers 22-25 when this strange prophet was hired by the kings of the Midianites and the Moabites to curse the children of Israel. Concerning Balaam Scofield writes:

> Balaam is the typical hireling prophet, seeking only to make a market of his gift. This is the *way of Balaam* (2 Pet 2:15) and characterizes false teachers. The *error of Balaam* (Jude11) was that he could see only the natural morality--a holy God, he reasoned, must curse such a people as Israel. Like all false teachers he was ignorant of the higher morality of vicarious atonement, by which God could be just and yet the justifier of believing sinners (Rom 3:26). The *doctrine of Balaam* here in Revelation 2:14 refers to his teaching Balak to corrupt the people whom he could not curse. This would be brought about by getting them to intermarry with idol worshippers (cp. Num 31:16 with Num 25:1-3; James 4:4). Spiritually, Balaamism in teaching never rises above natural reasoning; in practice, it is easy going world-conformity (cp. Rom 12:1,2).

The further error at Pergamos was that the *deeds of the Nicolaitans* which Ephesus hated (Rev 2:6) was now accepted as *doctrine*. The rise of powerful bishops continued unabated. The stage was now being set for the ultimate *Pontifex Maximus* in Rome.

With the so-called conversion of Constantine, the time of persecution which the church had previously endured was replaced by a period in which the church was favoured by the government. The edicts of persecution which had characterized the previous administration were repealed and Christians were allowed to worship according to the dictates of their conscience. Near the end of the fourth century, the Emperor Theodosius (reigned 379-395) issued a decree prohibiting paganism.

Under these circumstances it soon became popular to be a Christian, and the convictions of Christians were quickly blurred. It became increasingly difficult to maintain a clear distinction between the church and the world and to preserve the purity of Biblical doctrine. Though some benefit was secured by the successful defence of Biblical truth by the Council of Nicaea in AD 325 which thwarted the denial of the Deity of Christ by Arius and his followers, the history of the three centuries which followed is a record of increasing corruption and the attempt to combine Christian theology with pagan philosophy. Biblical simplicity was replaced by a complicated church organization which substituted human creeds, rituals and the worship of Mary for the true Biblical Faith. (See *Walvoord*).

(3) THE APPEAL. **Repent; or else I will come unto thee quickly, and will fight against them with the sword of my mouth** (2:16). Whether sooner or later, the sinner will be made to realize that no sword cuts so deep, nor inflicts so mortal a wound, as the sword of Christ's mouth. It will always come to pass; will always be fulfilled. If there is repentance it will bring the greatest balm of comfort. If it is unheeded its judgements will strike to the very quick of the soul.

Note again, that as with Ephesus, Christ warned ***I will come unto thee quickly*** (2:5). The "Christianised" form of the mother and child worship with it rituals and pontifex maximus rule developed in the early centuries of the Church and remains "rock solid" unto this day. And, this despite all of the reverses that the Roman Catholic church has experienced. Therefore as with Ephesus, this is a prophecy of what will befall Romanism after the Rapture and during the Tribulation.

> • *And the woman was arrayed in purple and scarlet colour, and decked with gold and precious stones and pearls, having a golden cup in her hand full of abominations and filthiness of her fornication: And upon her forehead was a name written, MYSTERY, BABYLON THE GREAT, THE MOTHER OF HARLOTS AND ABOMINATIONS OF THE EARTH. And I saw the woman drunken with the blood of the saints, and with the blood of the martyrs of Jesus: and when I saw her, I wondered with great admiration* (Rev 17:4-6).
>
> • *And the ten horns which thou sawest upon the beast, these shall hate the whore, and shall make her desolate and naked, and shall eat her flesh, and burn her with fire. For God hath put in their hearts to fulfil his will, and to agree, and give their kingdom unto the beast, until the words of God shall be fulfilled. And the woman which thou sawest is that great city, which reigneth over the kings of the earth* (Rev 17:16-18).

3. THE CONCLUSION OF THE LETTER.

(1) TO THE HEARER. **He that hath an ear, let him hear what the Spirit saith unto the churches** (2:17). All the churches must hear that that the overwhelming issue at Pergamos, that something so extraordinary that it could be called **Satan's seat** would be a matter that they too would have to face. Soon much of so-called Christendom would be

corrupted by the "Christianised" *mother and child worship*, and would be dominated by the *Pontifex Maximus* rule set up in Rome.

(2) TO THE OVERCOMER. ***To him that overcometh will I give to eat of the hidden manna, and will give him a white stone, and in the stone a new name written, which no man knoweth saving he that receiveth it.*** Not everyone was corrupted by the rapid spread of Catholicism. Though the name meant "universal" there were groups of believers that did not yield to it. They were persecuted, martyred, hunted, dispossessed, slandered, their records burned. Their names are varied: Waldensians, Cathars, Albigenses's, Donatists, and others. They were especially prominent in southern France and northern Italy. Their strength lay in their love of the Scriptures; they fed on the ***hidden manna***. It was *hidden* from their persecutors both in their attempts to exterminate the Scriptures and refusal to read the Scriptures. It was hidden in the hearts of these believers, as the Scriptures should be (Psa 119:11). It was fed upon, as the Scriptures should be (Jer 15:16). The Brook Cherith (1 Kng 17:4) and Jezebel's table (1 Kng 17:19) illustrate this contrast.

These were branded as heretics by Rome with every slander heaped upon the names they went by. By Christ they are given a ***white stone*** of absolution, acquittal and approval. Their records were destroy and their names blotted out on earth, but in Heaven they have ***a new name written***. It is a better name and unknowingly unique to them (cp. 3:12; 14:1,3).

D. THYATIRA: Ecclesiastical Rome Becomes the Church – Very busy, active, powerful, but in league with the depths of Satan (2:24). Much of professing "Christendom" comes under Papal Rome, but groups like the Waldensians and others remain separate 2:18-29

(2:18) *And unto the angel of the church in Thyatira write; These things saith the Son of God, who hath his eyes like unto a flame of fire, and his feet are like fine brass;*

(2:19) *I know thy works, and charity, and service, and faith, and thy patience, and thy works; and the last to be more than the first.*

(2:20) *Notwithstanding I have a few things against thee, because thou sufferest that woman Jezebel, which calleth herself a prophetess, to teach and to seduce my servants to commit fornication, and to eat things sacrificed unto idols.* (2:21) *And I gave her space to repent of her fornication; and she repented not.* (2:22) *Behold, I will cast her into a bed, and them that commit adultery with her into great tribulation, except they repent of their deeds.* (2:23) *And I will kill her children with death; and all the churches shall know that I am he which searcheth the reins and hearts: and I will give unto every one of you according to your works.*

(2:24) *But unto you I say, and unto the rest in Thyatira, as many as have not this doctrine, and which have not known the depths of Satan, as they speak; I will put upon you none other burden.* (2:25) *But that which ye have already hold fast till I come.*

(2:26) *And he that overcometh, and keepeth my works unto the end, to him will I give power over the nations:* (2:27) *And he shall rule them with a rod of iron; as the vessels of a potter shall they be broken to shivers: even as I received of my Father.* (2:28) *And I will give him the morning star.* (2:29) *He that hath an ear, let him hear what the Spirit saith unto the churches.*

What was begun in Pergamos reaches its full bloom in Thyatira. Here, as Jezebel did in Israel is the consummation of the attempt to wed paganism with (a little!) Biblical truth. The *eyes of fire* (2:18) read the thoughts and the affections (2:23). The *feet of blazing brass break the earthen vessels to shivers* (2:27). All is judgment. In the midst of the corruption a little group held fast to love and service and faith and patience; and their energy was progressive; it marked increasing devotedness; they toiled harder at the end than they did at the beginning.

1. THE INSCRIPTION OF THE LETTER.

(1) TO WHOM THE LETTER IS WRITTEN. *And unto the angel of the church in Thyatira write* (2:18). Thyatira was a small thriving town located about forty miles southeast of Pergamos. It had been established as a Macedonian colony by Alexander the Great after the destruction of the Persian empire. Located in a rich agricultural area, it was famous for the manufacture of purple dye and cloth.

The other mention of Thyatira in Scripture is found in Acts 16:14,15 where the conversion of Lydia is recorded: *And a certain woman named Lydia, a seller of purple, of the city of Thyatira, which worshipped God, heard us: whose heart the Lord opened, that she attended unto the things which were spoken of Paul.* Perhaps the Gospel was first brought to Thyatira through the witness of Lydia. By this time was likely already in Heaven and would not have to hear what had befallen the church.

Christ now directs the longest of the seven letters to this small Christian assembly. All was not well in Thyatira, and to this little church is addressed one of the most severe of the seven epistles. As Thyatira represents what was happening during this stage of Church History, there is likely a tacit connection here what we read about *purple* and *scarlet* in Religious Babylon.

> • *So he carried me away in the spirit into the wilderness: and I saw a woman sit upon a* **scarlet coloured** *beast, full of names of blasphemy, having seven heads and ten horns. And the woman was arrayed in* **purple and scarlet colour**…(Rev 17:3,4).

Ruins of Ancient Thyatira within Modern Akhisar

(2) FROM WHOM THE LETTER WAS SENT. *These things saith the Son of God, who hath his eyes like unto a flame of fire, and his feet are like fine brass* (2:18).

[1] THE DEITY OF CHRIST. The chief point of distinction in this description of Christ and that given in 1:13-16. is that He is named *the Son of God* in contrast to *the Son of Man*. His title here is in keeping with the character of the judgment pronounced upon

Thyatira. Their departure from the true worship of Jesus Christ the Son of God was so serious that it called for a reiteration of His Deity. He is the eternal and only-begotten Son of God, which denotes that He has the same nature as the Father. In *the mother and child worship* which became entrenched in the Thyatira stage of Church History, it declared that Christ does not share Deity with any but the Father (and the Holy Spirit). He does not share Deity with Mary.

[2] THE EYES OF CHRIST. The description of *His eyes like unto a flame of fire* speaks of burning indignation and purifying judgment. They are piercing eyes, penetrating, perfect in knowledge, with complete insight into all persons and all things.

[3] THE FEET OF CHRIST. In a similar way His feet are declared to be *like fine brass* (Gr. *chalkolibano*). This word is found only here in the Bible, and shows it to be something extraordinary, far beyond the normal word for *brass*. All is pure and holy. As He judges with perfect wisdom, so He acts with perfect might.

2. THE CONTENTS OF THE LETTER.

(1) THE COMMENDATION. *I know thy works, and charity, and service, and faith, and thy patience, and thy works; and the last to be more than the first* (2:19). It is remarkable that the church was commended first for its charity, or love, especially when neither Ephesus or Smyrna or Pergamos were commended for this quality. In fact, as patience is connected to hope in the New Testament we have in this commendation to Thyatira what we read in the famous Love Chapter.

- *But if we **hope** for that we see not, then do we with **patience** wait for it* (Rom 8:25; cp. Rom 15:4; 1 Thess 1:3).
- *And **now abideth faith, hope, charity**, these three; but the greatest of these is charity* (1 Cor 13:13).

Further, the fact that their *faith* is commended shows that it was a true Biblical and unmingled faith. It was not a faith that rested in Christ along with the *mother and child cult*. This shows that with this commendation (and likely elsewhere in these letters) it is the believing remnant that is being addressed. Thyatira represents the full development of Catholicism. The church at large had embraced *the mother and child worship;* there was a remnant that had not. While they had disobeyed the clear Biblical mandate to separate and join groups like the Waldensians, they had perhaps because of other pressures sought to maintain a witness within Catholicism. **Not a good decision!** In fact it can be strongly argued that it was a defective charity that allowed Jezebel to remain in this church.

- ***Be ye not unequally yoked together with unbelievers***: *for what fellowship hath righteousness with unrighteousness? and what communion hath light with darkness? And what concord hath Christ with Belial? or **what part hath he that believeth with an infidel? And what agreement hath the temple of God with idols?** for ye are the temple of the living God; as God hath said, I will dwell in them, and walk in them; and I will be their God, and they shall be my people. **Wherefore come out from among them, and be ye separate, saith the Lord**, and touch not the unclean thing; and I will receive you* (2 Cor 6:14-17).

(2) THE REBUKE.

[1] TOLERATION OF JEZEBEL: HER DEEDS. *Notwithstanding I have a few things against thee, because thou sufferest that woman Jezebel, which calleth herself a prophetess, to teach and to seduce my servants to commit fornication, and to eat things sacrificed unto idols* (2:20). There were a *few things* at Thyatira and as such they were

obvious and could not be missed. They were *few*, but they were *big*. Little room was left for anything else.

Toleration was the sin of Thyatira. Their "charity" let Jezebel alone. Loyalty to Christ demanded that she and what she represented be put out of the church. Note that *Balaam* at Pergamos represented more of a force from without the church; Jezebel who was Queen of Israel was more a force from within.

As Jezebel of old, an influential woman had marched into the church at Thyatira. She claimed like many today in the Charismatic Movement to have the gift of extra biblical revelation (the Bible by itself is supposed not to be enough). She was immoral and taught that to "win the world you must be like the world." She was a *real* Jezebel!

According to 1 Kings, the historic Jezebel was the wife of Ahab, king of Israel, and she was the daughter of Ethbaal, king of the Sidonians. She was one of the most evil characters of the Old Testament and attempted to combine the worship of Israel with the worship of Baal. The mother and child worship was at the centre of this. She did all she could to stamp out the true worship of Jehovah and influenced her weak husband to the extent that it is recorded in 1 Kings 16:33, *And Ahab made a grove; and Ahab did more to provoke the Lord God of Israel to anger than all the kings of Israel that were before him.*

The Baal worship that Jezebel introduced was the same mother and child cult was but the same manifestation of the mother and child cult. Walter J. Veith writes:

> Mother and child worship was the basis of the ancient religions. In the various religions of the world, the same system of worship was perpetuated under different names. In **Egypt**, the mother and child were worshiped as Isis and Osiris or Horus, in **India** as Isi and Iswara, in **China** and **Japan** as the mother goddess Shing-moo with child, in **Greece** as Ceres or Irene and Plutus, in **Rome** as Fortuna and Jupitor-puer, or Venus and Adurnis, and in **Scandinavia** as Frigga and Balder. The mother and child were worshiped in **Babylon** as Ishtar and Tammuz, and ***in Phoenicia, as Ashtoreth and Baal***. *Paganism and Catholicism: The Mother – Son Sun Worship System*

Jezebel had killed practically all the prophets of the Lord and sought to kill Elijah. (1 Kng 19:2). She attempted by every means to blot out every witness to Biblical Truth. This is precisely what Catholicism has done, but is seldom mentioned today.

A TIMELINE OF DOCUMENTED ROMAN CATHOLIC PERSECUTION

For detailed sources see: David A. Plaisted, *Estimates of the Number Killed by the Papacy in the Middle Ages and Later* http://www.cs.unc.edu/~plaisted/estimates.html

1096 Roman Catholic crusaders kill half the Jews in Worms, Germany.

1098 Roman Catholic crusaders kill almost all of the inhabitants of the city of Antioch.

1099 Roman Catholic crusaders kill 70,000 Muslims and Jews when they capture Jerusalem.

1208 – 1226 The Albigensian Crusades in southern France. Roman Catholic crusaders kill approximately 20,000 citizens of Beziers, France, on July 22, 1209. Albigensian Christians and Catholics were slain. By the time the Roman Catholic armies finished their "crusade," almost the entire population of southern France (mostly Albigensian Christians) has been exterminated. During the six centuries of papal Inquisition that began in the 13th century, up to 50 million people were killed. [See David A. Plaisted for this figure].

CHAPTER 2

1236 Roman Catholic crusaders kill Jews in the Anjou and Poitou regions of western France. The Catholic crusaders trample under their horses 3000 Jews who refuse baptism.
1243 Roman Catholic mobs burn alive all the Jews in Berlitz, Germany (near Berlin).
1298 Roman Catholic mobs burn alive all Jews in Rottingen, Germany.
April 26, 1349 Roman Catholic mobs burn to death all Jews in Germersheim, Germany.
1348 – 1349 The Jews are blamed for the bubonic plague. Author Dave Hunt tells us, "Accused of causing the 'Black Death' Jews were rounded up [by Roman Catholic mobs] and hanged, burned, and drowned by the thousands in revenge."
1389 Roman Catholic mobs kill 3000 Jews in Prague when they refuse to be baptized.
1481 – 1483 At the direction of the Roman Catholic inquisitors, authorities burn at the stake at least 2000 people during the first two years of the Spanish Inquisition.
1540 – 1570 Roman Catholic armies kill at least 900,000 Waldensian Christians of all ages during this 30-year period.
1550 – 1560 Roman Catholic troops kill at least 250,000 Dutch Protestants via torture, hanging, and burning during this ten-year period.
1553 – 1558 Roman Catholic Queen Mary I of England (aka "bloody Mary") attempts to bring England back under the yoke of papal tyranny. During her reign, approximately 200 men and woman are burned to death at the sake. Her victims include bishops, scholars, and other Protestant leaders.
1572 St. Bartholomew's Day Massacre. French Roman Catholic soldiers begin killing Protestants in Paris on the night of August 24, 1572. The soldiers killed at least 10,000 Protestants during the first three days. At least 8000 more Protestants are killed as the slaughter spreads to the countryside.
1618 – 1648 The Thirty Years' War. This religious war is planned, instigated, and orchestrated by the Roman Catholic Jesuit order and its agents in an attempt to exterminate all the Protestants in Europe. Many countries in central Europe lose up to half their population.
1641 – 1649 Eight years of Jesuit-instigated Roman Catholic persecution of Irish Protestants claims the lives of at least 100,000 Protestants.
1685 French Roman Catholic soldiers kill approximately 500,000 French Protestant Huguenots on the orders of Roman Catholic King Louis 14 of France.
Circa 1938 – 1945 As Adolf Hitler was Catholic (as were other leading Nazi's Himmler, Goebbels, Heydrich, Hess…..) and nearly all the Holocaust deaths took place in Roman Catholic countries, the question of complicity or inaction has long been debated. The conduct of the wartime Pope is also debated; see: *Pope Pius XII and the Holocaust* http://www.jewishvirtuallibrary.org/pope-pius-xii-and-the-holocaust
1941 – 1945 The Catholic Ustashi in Croatia killed very large numbers of Serbian Orthodox Christians. Killer squads were often led by priests. The numbers were such that it has been called the *Serbian Holocaust*.
http://www.nytimes.com/1994/05/12/opinion/l-world-war-ii-serb-holocaust-no-fiction-072370.html. See Darryl Eberhart, *The Bloody History of Papal Rome—A Timeline*.

Jezebel did not only bring false religion into Old Testament Israel (the mother and child cult), she slew those who would not conform. This fact and as she is mentioned here in Thyatira is a prophecy of what would happen in so-called Christendom. As the Jezebel religion became all pervasive in Israel and led to deportation, it also foretells the extent to which it would affect the professing Church and likewise lead to judgement.

Note further how that on the eve of their captivity *Queen of Heaven* and *Tammuz* religion had corrupted Judah:

- *The children gather wood, and the fathers kindle the fire, and the women knead their dough, to make cakes to **the queen of heaven**, and to pour out drink offerings unto other gods, that they may provoke me to anger (Jer 7:18).*
- *But we will certainly do whatsoever thing goeth forth out of our own mouth, to burn incense unto **the queen of heaven**, and to pour out drink offerings unto her, as we have done, we, and our fathers, our kings, and our princes, in the cities of Judah, and in the streets of Jerusalem: for then had we plenty of victuals, and were well, and saw no evil. But since we left off to burn incense to **the queen of heaven**, and to pour out drink offerings unto her, we have wanted all things, and have been consumed by the sword and by the famine. And when we burned incense to **the queen of heaven**, and poured out drink offerings unto her, did we make her cakes to worship her, and pour out drink offerings unto her, without our men (Jer 44:17-19)?*
- *Thus saith the LORD of hosts, the God of Israel, saying; Ye and your wives have both spoken with your mouths, and fulfilled with your hand, saying, We will surely perform our vows that we have vowed, to burn incense to **the queen of heaven**, and to pour out drink offerings unto her: ye will surely accomplish your vows, and surely perform your vows (Jer 44:25).*
- *Then he brought me to the door of the gate of the LORD'S house which was toward the north; and, behold, there sat women **weeping for Tammuz** (Ezek 8:14.*

[2] JEZEBEL'S IMPENITENCE. *And I gave her space to repent of her fornication; and she repented not* (2:21). God is never without a witness and the unconverted and unconverted religious leaders cannot claim they had no warning. That non Catholic Christians may still have a hard struggle in Catholic countries can be seen from the following
Associated Press report for 23 February 2016:

"POPE FRANCIS SILENCE ON CATHOLIC PERSECUTION OF PROTESTANTS IN MEXICO"

Four days after Pope Francis visited Chiapas, local officials **agreed to restore** water and electricity to 27 Protestant families. Two years ago, the utilities were **turned off** when the families refused to participate in or donate money to Catholic celebrations…But in another Chiapas village, Catholic officials refused last week to allow an elderly Protestant man to be buried there. The man was part of 12 Protestant families who were expelled from the village for their faith in 2012, and have been living in a homeless shelter in nearby San Cristóbal de las Casas. The city is where Francis led Mass and **denounced** Mexico's treatment of its indigenous peoples. John L. Allen Jr., associate editor of Crux, called the pope's silence on Catholic persecution of Protestants "a striking omission."…..

He didn't address the **persecution that indigenous Catholics have leveled against Protestants** in Chiapas…Chiapas Protestants have been **banished from their homes and land**. Sometimes after having their utilities cut off. Sometimes after threats of lynching. The day before Francis's visit, one evangelical church was **broken into and burned down**. The expulsions and occasional physical violence have largely been ignored by the state and federal government (emphasis theirs). http://www.christianitytoday.com/gleanings/2016/february/pope-francis-catholic-persecution-protestant-mexico-chiapas.html

CHAPTER 2

[3] **JEZEBEL'S DOOM.** *Behold, I will cast her into a bed, and them that commit adultery with her into great tribulation, except they repent of their deeds.* (2:23) *And I will kill her children with death; and all the churches shall know that I am he which searcheth the reins and hearts: and I will give unto every one of you according to your works* (2:22,23). Cast into a bed of pain, not of pleasure, into a bed of flames; and those who have sinned with her shall suffer with her. This will take place during the Tribulation.

The historic Jezebel was cast out of a window; the ecclesiastical Jezebel will be cast into a bed, a bed of anguish and death. As Jehu destroyed the one when painting her face and adorning herself so Antichrist will destroy the other at the moment of her greatest beauty and splendour (2 Kng 9:30-37; Rev 17:3-8;16-18).

(3) THE APPEAL. *But unto you I say, and unto the rest in Thyatira, as many as have not this doctrine, and which have not known the depths of Satan, as they speak; I will put upon you none other burden. But that which ye have already hold fast till I come* (2:24,25). Mariolatry with all of its attendant doctrines are the *depths of Satan* and must be acknowledged as such.

1600 YEARS OF NON-BIBLICAL HERESY BROUGHT INTO THE CATHOLIC CHURCH, A PARTIAL LIST

- **310** Prayers for the dead and the sign of the Cross.
- **375** Veneration of angels and dead saints.
- **394** The daily Mass, Christ crucified anew, not a Finished Work.
- **431** The worship of Mary; called "Mother of God"; Council of Ephesus.
- **500** Priests began to dress differently from the laity.
- **526** Extreme Unction for the dead.
- **593** Doctrine of Purgatory; Gregory the Great.
- **600** Latin Language imposed in services.
- **600** Prayers to dead saints as well as Mary.
- **610** Boniface III, first to assume the title "pope."
- **709** Kissing the Pope's feet.
- **750** Temporal power, city of Rome given to Pope Stephen II.
- **788** Worship of the cross, images and relics.
- **850** Holy Water mixed with a pinch of salt and blessed by a priest.
- **890** Veneration of St. Joseph.
- **995** Canonization of dead saints; Pope John XV.
- **998** Fasting on Fridays and during Lent.
- **11th Cent.** The Mass was developed gradually as a sacrifice; attendance made obligatory.
- **1079** Celibacy of the priesthood decreed, Pope Hildebrand, Boniface VII.
- **1090** The Rosary (prayer beads); Peter the Hermit. Copied from Hindus and Mohammedans.
- **1184** Inquisition of "heretics;" Council of Verona.
- **1190** Sale of Indulgences, a purchase of forgiveness for the dead and a "permit of the living to indulge in sin."
- **1215** Transubstantiation; Pope Innocent III. The priest pretends to change a wafer into the actual body of Christ, and then pretends to eat Him during the Mass.
- **1215** Confession of sins to a priest at least once a year; Innocent III, Lateran Council.
- **1220** Adoration of the wafer (Host); Pope Honorius.
- **1229** The Bible forbidden to laymen and placed in an Index of forbidden books by the Council of Valencia.

THE BOOK OF REVELATION

1287 The Scapular, invented by Simon Stock an English monk. It is a piece of brown cloth with a picture of Mary; when worn it is supposed to protect against dangers.
1439 Purgatory proclaimed as a dogma by Council of Florence.
1545 Tradition is of equal authority with the Bible; the Council of Trent.
1546 The apocryphal books added to the Bible; Council of Trent.
1560 The Creed of Pope Pius IV was imposed as the official creed.
1834 The Immaculate Conception of Mary; Pope Pius IX.
1870 Papal Infallibility; Pope Pius IX.
1950 Assumption (bodily ascension) of the Virgin Mary; Pope Pius XII. http://www.jesus-issavior.com/False%20Religions/Roman%20Catholicism/catholic_heresies-a_list.htm

Note: Tertullian in 220 AD refers to **infant baptism** and the practice has its roots in paganism. It was officially accepted by the Council of Carthage in 418 and became foundational to Catholic Doctrine. **Protestants frequently omit infant baptism from lists as the above because they themselves practice it!!!!**

After the commendation in verse 24 to those who had not known (experienced) the doctrines called the *depths of Satan*, and had kept themselves and their churches away from its clutches, they are told *to hold fast till I come*. All of God's people are called to hold firm to the Bible and shun non-Biblical heresy. All are called to do this in an attitude of watching for the Lord's Return. Yet sadly we know from other Scriptures that it will be otherwise.

- *Nevertheless when the Son of man cometh, shall he find faith on the earth (Lk 18:8)?*
- *Preach the word; be instant in season, out of season; reprove, rebuke, exhort with all longsuffering and doctrine. For **the time will come when they will not endure sound doctrine**; but after their own lusts shall they heap to themselves teachers, having itching ears; And they shall turn away their ears from the truth, and **shall be turned unto fables** (2 Tim 4:2-4).*

3. THE CONCLUSION OF THE LETTER.

(1) TO THE OVERCOMER. *And he that overcometh, and keepeth my works unto the end* (2:26). In the previous letters the call *to hear* comes before the promise to the overcomer, but from Thyatira onward the order is reversed. As the Church Age proceeds and draws to its perilous close there will be increasingly more to *overcome*;

Here the overcomer is described as one who *keeps to the work of God*. This implies that they knows what the Biblical work of God is. There is much that keeps people busy, but whether it is a Biblical work to which God calls is another matter.

- *For all seek their own, not the things which are Jesus Christ's* (Phil 2:21).

[1] DOMINION IS PROMISED: *to him will I give power over the nations: And he shall rule them with a rod of iron; as the vessels of a potter shall they be broken to shivers: even as I received of my Father* (2:26,27). This is precisely what Rome has sought to do and to no small extent has succeeded; but it was not in the power of Christ that such took place. Christ is coming back in power and glory and believers of the Church Age with Him. Here is a description of what will take place when He destroys all opposition at the Battle of Armageddon; when He sits upon David's Throne and when He reigns in perfect righteousness for a thousand years – and His saints with Him.

Satan in his temptation offered Christ the sceptre of world rule (Matt 4:8-10). It was immediately rejected and will only be received from His Father (Matt 7:13,14); but others have accepted that offer and governed accordingly. It has resulted in unimaginable darkness and suffering upon the earth. In this passage while the victory entirely belongs to Christ, the emphasis is upon those that reign with Him.

CHAPTER 2

[2] LIGHT IS PROMISED. **And I will give him the morning star** (2:28). The saints rule with Christ in His power and His light. Rarely except in OT Israel has there been rule upon this earth that had the clear rays of Divine Light. During the Thyatira period it was called the *Dark Ages*. Shortly Christ will receive the sceptre from His Father. After Armageddon, it will be light and life upon earth. Christ is the Morning Star, and as such He brings day with Him. *The Sun of righteousness shall arise* (Malachi 4:2).

- *Behold, a king shall reign in righteousness, and princes shall rule in judgment (Isa 32:1).*

(2) TO THE HEARER. **He that hath an ear, let him hear what the Spirit saith unto the churches** (2:29). In the *End Time* ecumenical *neither cold nor hot* (3:15) "churches together" age, believers must remain vigilant toward the inroads of Romanism.

CHAPTER 3

E. SARDIS: The Reformation Church – Comes out but retains much of Rome's deadness: rituals, robes, infant baptism, state church, claims for itself God's promises to Israel (replacement theology), non-literal view of Bible prophecy. Augustinian theology evolves into the deadness of Five Point Calvinism 3:1-6

(3:1) *And unto the angel of the church in Sardis write; These things saith he that hath the seven Spirits of God, and the seven stars; I know thy works, that thou hast a name that thou livest, and art dead.*

(3:2) *Be watchful, and strengthen the things which remain, that are ready to die: for I have not found thy works perfect before God.* (3:3) *Remember therefore how thou hast received and heard, and hold fast, and repent. If therefore thou shalt not watch, I will come on thee as a thief, and thou shalt not know what hour I will come upon thee.* (3:4) *Thou hast a few names even in Sardis which have not defiled their garments; and they shall walk with me in white: for they are worthy.*

(3:5) *He that overcometh, the same shall be clothed in white raiment; and I will not blot out his name out of the book of life, but I will confess his name before my Father, and before his angels.* (3:6) *He that hath an ear, let him hear what the Spirit saith unto the churches.*

http://www.padfield.com/turkey/sevenchurches/images/Sardis_04.jpg

Ruins in Sardis of a Pagan Temple and Nearby Church, *About all that is left*!

1. THE INSCRIPTION OF THE LETTER

(1) TO WHOM THE LETTER WAS SENT. *And unto the angel of the church in Sardis write* (3:1). The city of Sardis was fifty miles east of Smyrna and thirty miles southeast of Thyatira. Located on the commercial trade route running east and west through western Asia Minor it was an important and ancient city which came back into prominence during Roman times. Much of its wealth came from textile manufacturing and the jewellery

trade. Its prominent Temple of Artemis ruin dates from the fourth century BC. The remains of a Christian church building have been discovered immediately adjacent to the temple. This testifies of a Christian witness in this pagan city which was infamous for its loose living. The church to which the letter was addressed continued until the 14th century, but beyond the fact that at the time of writing (***thou hast a name that thou livest***) it was never thereafter known to be prominent. Today only a small village (Sart) exists near the ruins.

(2) FROM WHOM THE LETTER WAS SENT. ***These things saith he that hath the seven Spirits of God, and the seven stars*** (3:1). This aspect of Christ from Chapter 1 (1:4,16,20) must be seen in connection with what immediately follows and which as we will see is a truly astounding statement: ***I know thy works, that thou hast a name that thou livest, and art dead.*** Sardis has a WIDESPREAD REPUTATION for being a Live Church; but it is not so! Except for the ***few names*** (3:4), it is a DEAD CHURCH! As we will see, to many this is a fact *unimaginable* !

[1] THE HOLY SPIRIT BEARS WITNESS TO SARDIS' DEADNESS. The Holy Spirit is One, yet in the fullness of His graces and operations, like the seven branched candlestick. He is ***the seven Spirits of God*** (Isa 11:2-5; Rev 5:6). He illuminates as to the true nature of the case. He gives a true witness.

- *And it is the Spirit that beareth witness, because the Spirit is truth* (1 Jhn 5:6).

But also, where there is a languishing ministry, there is here assurance that Christ has the seven Spirits, *the Spirit without measure* (Jhn 3:34). To Him all may come for reviving and lifting up. Note that in Chapter 1, *the seven Spirits are before his throne* (1:4); here they are in Christ's Right Hand. The Holy Spirit does not operate independently of Christ.

[2] THE SEVEN ANGELS BEAR WITNESS TO SARDIS' DEADNESS. As we saw at the conclusion of Chapter 1, ***the seven stars*** are the *seven angels* of the *seven churches*. There we saw that angels throughout the Book of Revelation serve as legal witnesses to divine judgment, they carry out divine judgment, they serve warning of divine judgment. The seven angels of the seven churches fulfil this same remit in the sense that they give witness to judicial evaluation. The judicial verdict of the Lord Jesus Christ (despite all reports to the contrary) is that Sardis is a ***dead*** church; seven angels are now called to give witness to this fact.

2. THE CONTENTS OF THE LETTER. There is a marked change in our Lord's method of address to the church at Sardis. Hitherto He has commenced with words of commendation. Here, He begins with words of condemnation; and, except for ***the few*** (3:4) there is no word of commendation. In the previous churches (except for Smyrna), evil was coming into the church and gaining control, but had not yet taken over completely. Therefore those "pockets of good" and the work of the faithful remnant could be praised and mentioned first. Here the picture is that of a church totally mired in an evil system, and though seeking to come out, makes its exit not with the best reasons and brings much of the old with it. Compare Henry the XIII's divorce as the cause for establishing the Church of England.

(1) THE REBUKE. ***I know thy works, that thou hast a name that thou livest, and art dead*** (3:1). Here, *the* works, and regardless of what men may think of them (and they thought very highly), from the Lord all that issues forth is a *death sentence*! THOU ART DEAD. It is very likely that *the works* that brought forth such a verdict refers to the trappings, rituals and basic theology of Romanism that still clung to the Protestant Church at the time of the Reformation. In the providence of God, the Protestant Church began to publish the Bible and for this we are eternally grateful, but had they truly believed the Bible they would not have allowed so many of the vestiges of Rome to remain.

CHAPTER 3

These were *dead works* (Heb 9:14). They brought deadness, resulted in deadness, and for a very long time most of Protestantism has been dead to the Scriptures. German rationalism soon engulfed the seminaries of Europe. All of the mainline Protestant denominations are liberal and modernistic. The World Council of Churches is a primary example. The same Antisemitism that characterised Romanism before the Reformation became imbedded in the Protestant churches afterwards. Augustinian theology evolved into the deadness of philosophical Calvinism. For well over a century Protestantism has denied and undermined the Bible they so zealously propagated during the Reformation. **Thou hast a name that thou livest, and art dead.**

The following gives excerpts from the penetrating *Midnight Cry* study: "The Tragedy of the Reformation (AD 1500~Tribulation)." Some will say that the author has gone too far. Nevertheless one cannot deny the unpalatable point with which he begins - that the Lord gives more praise to the Thyatira and Pergamos period than to Sardis. This is likely because small groups like the Waldensians, Albigenses, Cathars, Donatists and others, remained more fervent for truth during the Pergamos and Thyatira eras than in the Sardis.

> Could it be that in the Lord's eyes this period of church history is less to be praised than the period of paganization, or the period led by "Jezebel?" Evidently, that is the case. And what a sad period of church history would this be?
>
> The name "Sardis" comes from the same root as the "sardine stone" (Rev. 4:3), which was a rich, blood-red gem. The picture here is one of bloodied men. Truly, the Reformers carried out their rebellion against the Roman Catholic church at great peril to their own lives, and many of them eventually lost their lives after cruel torture. Surely the Lord has something good to say about the brave defenders of the Truth that dared leave the Catholic church and begin their own spiritual communities. And yet we search in vain for any such praise in the letter before us. What does the Lord say about the Reformation? Simply this: you have a reputation (or name, see Prov 10:7; 22:1; Eccl 6:4; 7:1, etc.) for being a living thing, but you are a dead thing.
>
> Reputation wise, the Reformation is credited with restoring the vitality of the Christian faith after long centuries of Catholic demoralization. Martin Luther's assertions that Scripture alone, *sola scriptura*, is the only authority for the church, and that *the just shall live by faith* (that is, that salvation requires only faith in the Lord Jesus, not the Roman Catholic sacraments) all sound very good, very true, very orthodox.
>
> The Lord appears to acknowledge that while it is orthodox, it is "dead orthodoxy." The fact of the matter is, the Reformation produced much intellectual consent to the truths of Scripture, but no life flowed from it. This is true because the Reformation was in reality only a baby step towards true Christianity. While some of the grosser excesses and errors of the Catholic church were shed, the order and organization of Jezebel's religion were imported wholesale into the new churches that sprang from the Reformation.
>
> First of all, the Nicolaitan separation of clergy and laity was retained. The church continued to teach "sacraments" and insisted that these sacraments be performed only by specially ordained, professional "holy" men on behalf of the laity. The nature of "transubstantiation" in the Eucharist was debated, for example, but instead of standing tall for the truth, Martin Luther and other reformers settled for a compromise; the wine and bread do not become the Blood and Body of Christ, but the latter are somehow mystically present in the elements.
>
> Of all the compromises made to appease Jezebel, (and to not rattle the sensibilities of the masses who had been raised under that system in Germany,

Scotland, Geneva and other centers of the Reformation), perhaps the two most "deadening" aspects of the Reformation were the retention of infant baptism—which supposedly ushers noncomprehending souls into the kingdom of God through a rite or a ritual, rather than through faith in the Gospel; The second is amillennial theology—which denies the future return of the Lord Jesus to rule a literal, physical kingdom on this earth.

In effect, the Reformation replaced one militant, amillennial state church with another militant, amillennial state church. All it managed to remove from the mix was the Pope. But the leaders of the new churches were not always that much better. John Calvin has often been referred to as the "protestant pope" due to his severe control over the church in Geneva. The liturgy and the "church calendar" with its long list of pseudo–scriptural "holy days" and feasts was brought virtually intact into the new Reformed communions.

Another "deadening" factor was the introduction of full-blown predeterminism, which eventually became popularized by the term "Five-point Calvinism," even though there wasn't much difference between Calvin and Luther in their approach to this issue. This intellectual conceit, when taken consistently with its tenets, invariably quenches the fire of evangelism and brings a deadness of the spirit to every congregation that adopts it, or succumbs to a pastor who converts to it....

Then, underscoring the error of amillennialism, the Lord points out that this church is not looking for the Lord's return. Contrast the Lord's statement to the church at Sardis, *I shall come upon thee as a thief, and thou shalt not know what hour I come upon thee* with this statement by the Apostle Paul to a "premillennial" church:
For yourselves know perfectly that the day of the Lord so cometh as a thief in the night... But ye, brethren are not in darkness, that that day should overtake you as a thief (I Thess 5:2,4)...

So here we have the second church in this series of seven that has been given the dubious honor of a promise by the Lord Himself that they will miss the Rapture and continue into the Great Tribulation. This promise is to mainline, dead orthodox denominations that hold to "Reformed theology," that sprinkle infants into the kingdom with no scriptural authority for doing so, and maintain their amillennial theology to this day. In recent years it has been resurrected under the name "Dominion Theology," "Kingdom Now" theology and the like. Regardless of what it is called, it is the same old error that began with Augustine's City of God. It is to be shunned and avoided at all costs....http://www.midnightcry.net/Seven_Letters/church_at_sardis.htm

(2) THE APPEAL
[1] CONCERNING THE BIBLICAL TRUTHS THEY HAD. **Be watchful, and strengthen the things which remain, that are ready to die: for I have not found thy works perfect before God.** (3:2). The church at Sardis was classified as being *dead*, yet it is obvious from this verse that there were some who still had true spirituality and held to the truths of Scripture. Otherwise it would not have been possible to, *strengthen the things which remain*. There was now a far greater emphasis on justification by faith (though to no little extent undermined by the retention of infant baptism). Many became clear that it is Christ and not Mary who is the object of our faith and worship. The Pope was no longer seen as the head of the church. In the Reformation period there were also some who were not "beclouded" with the heavy mists of philosophical Calvinism that had been so immediately superimposed upon the minds and hearts of those that had left Romanism.

The Bible was there, and far more accessible than before. They could read it for themselves, rather than be told how to read it. When the common people began to study the

CHAPTER 3

Bible itself, and avoid reading it through the spectacles of one of the "learned doctors" of the Reformed church, it soon became apparent that the Reformation was a long way from being a *perfect work* of God. It had not gone far enough and had taken too much of the old system with it.

[2] CONCERNING THE BIBLE THEY RECEIVED. **Remember therefore how thou hast received and heard, and hold fast, and repent** (3:3). Sardis had *received and heard* the Bible. They had *received* much more of it than the previous churches. Printing had been invented. The mass manufacture of paper had now begun. The publishing of the Bible into the languages of Europe had brought great light to multitudes. For the first time in history, many of the common people had the Bible, or a portion of the Bible in their hands. No one had *received* like Sardis had! They had **received** the Bible. They had **heard** the Bible. Some were now determined to **hold fast** to the Bible. And, rather than the labourous works base penance system of Catholicism, the Bible itself would be the basis by which they would come to true *repentance*.

[3] CONCERNING THE SECOND COMING OF CHRIST. **If therefore thou shalt not watch, I will come on thee as a thief, and thou shalt not know what hour I will come upon thee** (3:3). Sardis pictures a kind of church that is not actively watching for the Lord's Return, and this with little exception has been the case of the Reformed Church. It does not take literally the vast prophetic portions of Scripture. **For the Reformed Church and the Catholic Church**:

- There is no Rapture.
- There is no literal Seven Year Tribulation on the earth.
- There is no literal reign of Christ on David's throne and on the earth, for 1000 year.
- The Biblical covenants with Abraham and David *will not* be fulfilled literally, and are replaced by extra-biblical philosophic covenants (*Covenant Theology*).
- The promises to Israel are promises to the Church. (*Replacement Theology*).
- There is no salvation for Israel *nationally* or literal return to the Land of Israel.
- The Book of Revelation does not present literal truth.

http://www.catholic.org/files/images/saints/ahippo.gif

Augustine, Bishop of Hippo in North Africa

THE BOOK OF REVELATION

AUGUSTINE: THE FOUNDER OF THE *NON WATCHING CHURCH*

What is the cause and reason for such a blanket denial of what (and if words mean anything) is so clearly taught in the Bible. The answer is simple! This is what the Roman Catholic Church taught and was brought in with little change into the newly formed Protestant churches. Where did the Catholic Church get it? Certainly, and among others, Origen (AD 184-253) with his allegorizing approach played a key role; but the chief influence came from Augustine, Bishop of Hippo (Algeria) and his book *The City of God*.

In his study, *Amillenniallism from Augustine to Modern Times,* John Walvoord writes:

> It is difficult to overestimate the importance of Augustine in the history of theology. Not only did his thinking crystallize the theology which preceded him, but to a large extent he laid the foundations for both Catholic and Protestant doctrine. B. B. Warfield, quoting Harnack, refers to Augustine as "incomparably the greatest man whom, between Paul the Apostle and Luther the Reformer, the Christian Church has possessed." While the contribution of Augustine is principally noted in the areas of the doctrine of the church, hamartiology, the doctrine of grace, and **predestination**, he is also the greatest landmark in the early history of **amillennialism** [no literal physical reign of Christ on David's Throne on the earth, as stated repeatedly in scripture].
>
> The importance of Augustine to the history of amillennialism is derived from two reasons. First, there are no acceptable exponents of amillennialism before Augustine...Prior to him, amillennialism was associated with the heresies produced by the allegorizing and spiritualizing school of theology at Alexandria which not only opposed premillennialism but subverted any literal exegesis of Scripture whatever... Augustine is, then, the first theologian of solid influence who adopted amillennialism.
>
> The second reason is that his viewpoint became the prevailing doctrine of the Roman Church, and it was adopted with variations by most of the Protestant Reformers along with many other teachings of Augustine. The writings of Augustine, in fact, occasioned the shelving of premillennialism by most of the organized church...The fact that Augustine was amillennial in his viewpoint is noted with pride by modern amillennialists to show that their position is historic and a part of the central teaching of the church. O.T. Allis, for instance, loses no time in his attack on premillennialism to point out in the second page of his volume that Augustinian amillennialism was the norm for the church of the middle ages...
>
> Augustine conceived of the present age as a conflict between the City of God and the City of Satan, or the conflict between the church and the world. This was viewed as moving on to the ultimate triumph of the church to be climaxed by a tremendous struggle in which the church would be apparently defeated, only to consummate in a tremendous triumph in the second coming of Christ to the earth. **Augustine held that the present age of conflict is the millennium**...
>
> Augustine's interpretation of Revelation 20 is not very specific. As in his entire discussion of this doctrine, the treatment is cursory and brief. He discusses Revelation 20 in three or four pages and dismisses without any real argument the literal view. In fact, Augustine, like many others, does not seem to grasp the principles involved....There is no future millennium in the ordinary meaning of the term. The present age is the millennium; **Satan is bound now**; when Christ returns the present millennium will close, the future millennium or eternity will begin...
>
> Augustine's doctrine that Satan is bound in this age—an essential of his system of interpretation—is a notable illustration of spiritualized and strained exegesis (cf. Luke 10:18 and Revelation 20:2-3). Nothing is clearer from Scripture, the history of

CHAPTER 3

the church, and Christian experience than that Satan is exceedingly active in this present age against both Christians and unbelievers.

It is no wonder that Warfield, though a disciple of Augustine, completely abandons this idea as far as earth is concerned and limits it to the idea that "saints described are removed from the sphere of Satan's assaults," i.e., Satan is bound in respect to heaven only [and further, that prophecies of the Millennium itself will be fulfilled in Heaven]. While Warfield's explanation is no more sensible than Augustine's as far as an exegesis of the Scriptures is concerned, it at least accords with the facts of church history…

It is clear that the great Protestant leaders such as **Calvin, Luther, and Melanchthon are properly classed as amillennial**. As far as millennial teaching was concerned, **they were content to follow the Roman Church** in a weakened Augustinian viewpoint. Calvin's discussion of the millennium is a fair sample of the attitude of the Reformers. They treated the doctrine superficially and arbitrarily, making the view ridiculous by misrepresentation…

https://bible.org/seriespage/4-amillenniallism-augustine-modern-times   (emphasis mine).

[4] CONCERNING THE *FEW* OF SARDIS. *Thou hast a few names even in Sardis which have not defiled their garments; and they shall walk with me in white: for they are worthy* (3:4). If for a professing Christian the doctrine of the imminent Return of Christ is abandoned, the result will be a lessening of purity in the life.

- *We know that, **when he shall appear**, we shall be like him; for we shall see him as he is. And **every man that hath this hope in him purifieth himself**, even as he is pure* (1 Jhn 3:2,3).

The clergy in the state churches soon become susceptible to declining standards both personal and doctrinal. The fact that all was not well in the *day to day* life of the Protestant Church can be seen in the rise of the Puritan and the Brethren movements.

Puritans sought both individual and corporate conformity to the teaching of the Bible, with moral purity pursued down to the smallest detail, as well as ecclesiastical purity to the highest level. They believed that man existed for the glory of God, that his first concern in life was to do God's will and so to receive future happiness. They believed that Jesus Christ was the center of public and personal affairs, and was to be exalted above all other names (*Wikipedia*).

The Puritans were Calvinistic and held varied millennial beliefs: some were premillennial. The Brethren, too, *came out* (often from the Church of England); they came out further and with less baggage and took a clear stand on the Biblical teaching of Israel, the premillennial Return of Christ, and usually the Pre Tribulational Rapture. It is primarily through the early Brethren movement that there was a return to the literal understanding of Bible Prophecy. First among them was a former Anglican priest, John Darby.

http://www.christianitytoday.com/history/people/pastorsandpreachers/john-nelson-darby.html

3. THE CONCLUSION OF THE LETTER.

(1) TO THE OVERCOMER. *He that overcometh, the same shall be clothed in white raiment; and I will not blot out his name out of the book of life, but I will confess his name before my Father, and before his angels* (3:5). This relates directly to those who had or were seeking *a name* at Sardis (3:1). Men may be enrolled in the registers of the church but in the rolls of Heaven that name may come to be blotted out when it appears that it was only a name, without evidence of spiritual life. There were many at Sardis that *had a name that they lived but were dead* (3:1). This verse indicates that when they lived on earth, their names were for a time recorded in the Book in Heaven (they could have been saved!), but when they died without receiving eternal life in Christ, their names were blotted out.

Relating this passage to true believers: the world may have ignored or misrepresented or even sought to blot out their names. While others were seeking a *name*, they simply went on their way serving Christ (cp. Jhn 3:30). Any notice of them many have been forgotten, but that will not be the case in Heaven. It will not happen in Christ's Book or in the day He declares their *name* before the angels.

The Sardis/Protestant church had also been very proud of its clerical robes. These are a carryover from the ostentatious robes of Catholicism. *In Heaven there is a better robe*.

Robes: The Archbishop, The Pope, and John Calvin
Beware of the scribes, which desire to walk in long robes (Lk 20:46).

(2) TO THE HEARER. *He that hath an ear, let him hear what the Spirit saith unto the churches* (3:6). The ears of God's people must not only be open to hear what our Lord says to Pergamos and Thyatira (Roman Catholicism), but also to Sardis (Calvinistic Protestantism).

In our study *THE TWO LINES: Whosoever Will - Chosen In Christ, 263 Scripture Passages*; the following summaries were given.

THE GENERAL CONCLUSION:
• These verses do not present God bringing people into the world with no hope of salvation and ultimately only to send them to hell (as Calvinism teaches).
• They do demonstrate that many will not believe (John 5:40) and then in judicial blindness, cannot believe (Matthew 13:13-15; John 12:39,40).
• They demonstrate that God's foreknowledge (1Peter 1:2) includes foreseen faith (John 6:64).

- They demonstrate that the extent of the Atonement can be Biblically summed up as follows: Christ died for many (Matt. 20:28); Christ died for the sheep (John 10:15); Christ died for the church (Eph. 5:25); Christ died for all (1 Tim. 2:6); Christ died for every man (Heb. 2:9); Christ died for the whole world (1 John 2:2).

CALVINISM RESTATES:
- *Whosoever will* (Rev 22:17) to mean: whosoever will among the elect.
- *The sins of the whole world* (1 Jhn 2:2) to mean: the whole world of the elect.
- *Will have all men to be saved* (1 Tim 2:4) to mean: all kinds of men.
- *Gave himself a ransom for all* (1 Tim 2:6) to mean: all of the elect.
- *Willing that none should perish* (2 Pet 3:9) to mean: none of the elect should perish.
- *Taste death for every man* (Heb 2:9) to mean: every kind of man.
- *Saviour of all men* (1 Tim 4:10) to mean: all among the elect.
- *Be ye saved, all the ends of the earth* (Isa 45:22) to mean: all of the elect in the ends of the earth.

CALVINISTS ARE OFTEN NOT SO ASSURED THAT THEY THEMSELVES ARE AMONG THE ELECT:
- They lack the confidence 1 John 5:13 affords.
- They are plagued with doubt as to their eternal wellbeing, and constantly ask the question: Do I truly have saving faith?

CALVINISM REPLACES TWO BIBLICAL TRUTHS:
- Israel with the Church (Replacement Theology: No national future for Israel).
- The Biblical Covenants (Abrahamic, Davidic) with their own philosophical covenants.

CALVINISM SHOWS VERY LITTLE DAY TO DAY, PRACTICAL INTEREST IN THE IMMINENT RETURN OF CHRIST:
- They take literally the Biblical prophecies of Christ's First Coming and yet interpret symbolically the events accompanying His Second Coming. This is a huge contradiction!
- They deny the Rapture.
- They deny the Seven year Tribulation.
- They deny Christ's literal millennial reign upon earth from Jerusalem.
- They deny Israel's right to inhabit its ancient land-grant promised to Abraham (Gen. 17:8).
- Calvinism denies Christ's right to literally and visibly reign upon the earth that He created and died for. This is the height of arrogance!

CALVINISTS GENERALLY SUPPRESS THE FACT:
- That their namesake, John Calvin was guilty of substantial persecution.
- That the minutes of the Geneva *Town Council Meetings* 1541–59 record many of the persecutions Calvin inflicted.
- That Calvin's own statements reveal his strong inclination toward persecution. See for sources: *Calvin and Persecution, Why the Silence!*

DO CALVINIST'S REALLY BELIEVE WHAT CALVIN ACTUALLY SAID?
"Predestination we call the decree of God, by which He has determined in Himself, what He would have to become of every individual of mankind. For they are not all created with a similar destiny: but **eternal life is foreordained for some, and eternal damnation for others**"(*Institutes of the Christian Religion*, Book III, chap. 21).
"**God devotes to destruction whom he pleases ... they are predestinated to eternal death** without any demerit of their own, merely by his sovereign will. ... He orders all things by his

counsel and decree in such a manner, that **some men are born devoted from the womb to certain death, that his name be glorified in their destruction**. ... God chooses whom he will as his children ... while he rejects and reprobates others" (*Institutes of the Christian Religion*, Book III, chap. 23).

In short, Calvinism is a philosophy that has been superimposed upon the Bible. It deflects adherents away from a simple and direct reading of the Scriptures. A natural reading of the Bible will not lead to the horrendous conclusion that God brings people into the world only for the ultimate purpose of damning them to hell.

F. PHILADELPHIA: Seen mainly from 1850 to 1950 – Small but faithful, open door to world evangelization, interprets Bible prophecy literally 3:7-13

(3:7) *And to the angel of the church in Philadelphia write; These things saith he that is holy, he that is true, he that hath the key of David, he that openeth, and no man shutteth; and shutteth, and no man openeth;*
(3:8) *I know thy works: behold, I have set before thee an open door, and no man can shut it: for thou hast a little strength, and hast kept my word, and hast not denied my name.* (3:9) *Behold, I will make them of the synagogue of Satan, which say they are Jews, and are not, but do lie; behold, I will make them to come and worship before thy feet, and to know that I have loved thee.* (3:10) *Because thou hast kept the word of my patience, I also will keep thee from the hour of temptation, which shall come upon all the world, to try them that dwell upon the earth.*
(3:11) *Behold, I come quickly: hold that fast which thou hast, that no man take thy crown.*
(3:12) *Him that overcometh will I make a pillar in the temple of my God, and he shall go no more out: and I will write upon him the name of my God, and the name of the city of my God, which is new Jerusalem, which cometh down out of heaven from my God: and I will write upon him my new name.*
(3:13) *He that hath an ear, let him hear what the Spirit saith unto the churches.*

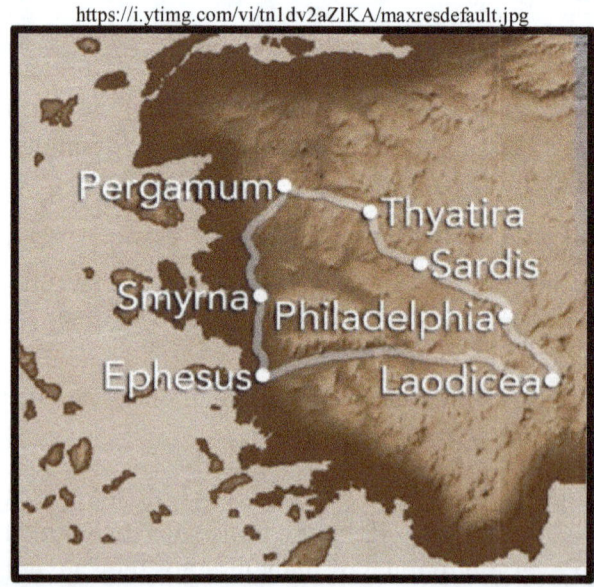

Philadelphia's Place on the Triangular Road Connecting the Churches

1. THE INSCRIPTION OF THE LETTER

CHAPTER 3

(1) TO WHOM THE LETTER WAS SENT. *And to the angel of the church in Philadelphia write* (3:7). Here is a church which was faithful to Christ and the Word of God. The city of Philadelphia today is known as Alasehir, and is some 28 miles southeast of Sardis. It was named after a king of Pergamos, Attalus Philadelphus, who built the city.

The Greek word Philadelphia means *brotherly love* or *kindness*, and is so translated six times in the NT (Rom 12:10; 1 Thess 4:9; Heb 13:1; 1 Pet 1:22; 2 Pet l:7, twice). Here the word occurs for the seventh and final time, but only here is it used of the city bearing this name.

The city of Philadelphia had a long history but also a history of natural disasters, and several times was almost completely destroyed by earthquakes. The promise of verse twelve: *Him that overcometh will I make a pillar in the temple of my God, and he shall go no more out*, would have brought special comfort to Philadelphia believers in John's day. In this respect Philadelphia pictures the faithful church of the last days that is looking for the Lord's return amid increasing turbulence in the world.

"Through the centuries, a nominal Christian testimony continued in Philadelphia and prospered even under Turkish rule. But all professing Christians left the city for Greece after World War I" (Walvoord).

Ruins of Philadelphia in Alasehir

Philadelphia represents the small and independent churches that *KEPT MY WORD* (Rev 3:10). This is the church that breaks loose from the shackles of Calvinistic Protestantism with its state church, heavy denominational overlord's, antisemitism and replacement theology. As an era, it can be seen in the period from about 1850 when the literal interpretation of Bible Prophecy began again to be firmly established (as it had been in the centuries before Augustine). It extends to about 1950 with the rise of neo-evangelicalism (a merger of fundamentalism with modernism), the ecumenical movement and the onset of the charismatic movement with its worldliness and extrabiblical revelations.

It was (and where it still remains) the church of the *open door* (Rev 3:8). Through this door has come world missions, evangelism, Jewish evangelism, Gospel literature distribution and sound Bible Institutes. Regarding Jewish evangelism, came the acceptance of what the Bible so clearly emphasises as to the national future of Israel. Philadelphia as an era ran concurrently with the return of the Jewish People to their Biblical Land (albeit as the Bible foretold, in unbelief, Ezek 37:8). With the *Blessed Hope* (Titus 2:13) at the forefront Philadelphia represents the doctrinally distinct church. All of this changed with the rise of the Laodecian era.

(2) FROM WHOM THE LETTER WAS SENT. *These things saith he that is holy, he that is true, he that hath the key of David, he that openeth, and no man shutteth; and shutteth, and no man openeth* (3:7).

[1] HERE IS CHRIST'S PERSONAL CHARACTER. *He that is holy, he that is true.* By the time you get to the Philadelphia stage of Church History there will have been self-imposed "heads" of churches that have not been *holy and true.* Christ is *holy* in His nature and therefore He cannot but be *true* to His Word, for He has spoken in His holiness. *But as he which hath called you is holy, so be ye holy in all manner of conversation* (1 Pet 1:15).

As the One who is true, Christ is the Author of truth in contrast to all error or false doctrine. In the midst of so much that is false and perverted, Jesus Christ stands alone as the One who is completely true. This brings out the great truth that right doctrine and right living go together. There can be no holiness without truth.

[2] HERE IS CHRIST'S GOVERNMENTAL CHARACTER. He **hath the key of David, he that openeth, and no man shutteth; and shutteth, and no man openeth.** He is declared in 1:18 to *have the keys of hell and of death.* Here are keys of a further nature. In Isaiah 22:22 where, speaking of Eliakim the son of Hilkiah, it is recorded that *the key of the house of David will I lay upon his shoulder; so he shall open, and none shall shut; and he shall shut, and none shall open.* Eliakim had the key to all the treasures of the king, and when he opened the door it was opened, and when he closed the door it was closed. Christ is the great antitype of Eliakim.

At His return the government of the world will be based on the promises to the House of David. Christ holds the keys to this House. It is a House of great treasure and abundance. When Christ *opens the door* during His Millennial Reign the entire earth will share in untold spiritual wealth and blessing. Unlike the other churches, Philadelphia understood the literal promises given in the Bible concerning the *Throne* and *House* of David.

- *And when thy days be fulfilled, and thou shalt sleep with thy fathers, I will set up thy seed after thee, which shall proceed out of thy bowels, and I will establish his kingdom.* **He shall build an house for my name**, *and I will stablish the throne of his kingdom for ever* (2 Sam 7:12,13).
- *The LORD hath sworn in truth unto* **David**; *he will not turn from it; Of the fruit of thy body will I set upon* **thy throne** (Psa 132:11).
- *Of the increase of his government and peace there shall be no end,* **upon the throne of David**, *and upon his kingdom, to order it, and to establish it with judgment and with justice from henceforth even for ever. The zeal of the LORD of hosts will perform this* (Isa 9:7).
- *Incline your ear, and come unto me: hear, and your soul shall live; and I will make an everlasting covenant with you, even* **the sure mercies of David** (Isa 55:3).
- *Behold, the days come, saith the LORD, that* **I will raise unto David a righteous Branch**, *and a King shall reign and prosper, and shall execute judgment and justice in the earth* (Jer 23:5).
- *In those days, and at that time, will I cause* **the Branch of righteousness to grow up unto David**; *and he shall execute judgment and righteousness in the land* (Jer 33:15).

CHAPTER 3

> • *In that day **will I raise up the tabernacle of David** that is fallen, and close up the breaches thereof; and I will raise up his ruins, and I will build it as in the days of old* (Amos 9:11).
> • *And I will pour upon **the house of David**, and upon the inhabitants of Jerusalem, the spirit of grace and of supplications: and they shall look upon me whom they have pierced, and they shall mourn for him, as one mourneth for his only son, and shall be in bitterness for him, as one that is in bitterness for his firstborn* (Zech 12:10).
> • *He shall be great, and shall be called the Son of the Highest: and the Lord God shall give unto him **the throne of his father David*** (Lk 1:32).

Today Christ opens the door of opportunity to take the Gospel to the ends of the earth. And whenever or wherever one responds to that glorious message, He opens the door and says *come ye blessed of my Father*. But also, He will shut the door of opportunity and utterance, and leave obstinate sinners shut up in the hardness of their hearts. He will also shut the door of the Millennial reign against the *foolish virgins* who have slept away their day of grace.

Today we look forward to the glad day that has so long and often been promised in Scripture. After the judgements of the Tribulation, Christ will sit upon David's ancient throne and open the hearts of the entire world to bow before His sovereign purposes and worship Him in universal adoration.

> • *Make a joyful noise unto God, **all ye lands**: Sing forth the honour of his name: make his praise glorious. Say unto God, How terrible art thou in thy works! through the greatness of thy power shall thine enemies submit themselves unto thee. **All the earth** shall worship thee, and shall sing unto thee; they shall sing to thy name. Selah* (Psa 66:1-4).

2. THE CONTENTS OF THE LETTER.
   (1) THE COMMENDATION. ***I know thy works: behold, I have set before thee an open door, and no man can shut it: for thou hast a little strength, and hast kept my word, and hast not denied my name*** (3:8). Their works which no doubt meant obedience to the Great Commission was encouraged and furthered by Christ setting before them an open door of unparalleled opportunity. Certainly God opens doors that are impossible for man to open. There is here an aspect not often realized. By the providence of God, steamships, rail, auto and air travel began during the Philadelphia era. God may view the purposes behind transport links differently than man or even many believers do. It is not just for the purpose of business or travel. Some (with *a little strength*) saw it as an opportunity to take the Gospel to the *entire world*. With street level congestion in London making travel so difficult, I have long viewed the tube system (subways) as an example of this. It is an open door to getting the Gospel to many destinations in this vast city.

The *little strength* that the Philadelphia believer has is likely to be taken in the same sense of what was said of Smyrna: *I know... thy poverty* (2:9). By the world's reckoning they were not strong or large or influential yet they were unshakeable in their testimony of Christ ***and hast kept my word, and hast not denied my name.*** Others may have wavered but Philadelphia despite her lack of worldly knowledge, strength, numbers, resources and influence did not. Her faithfulness insured an open door.

> • *Fear not, **little flock**; for it is your Father's good pleasure to give you the kingdom* (Lk 12:32).
> • *For the children of this world are in their generation **wiser than the children of light*** (Lk 16:8).

THE BOOK OF REVELATION

• *For we preach not ourselves, but Christ Jesus the Lord; and ourselves your servants for Jesus' sake. For God, who commanded the light to shine out of darkness, hath shined in our hearts, to give the light of the knowledge of the glory of God in the face of Jesus Christ. But **we have this treasure in earthen vessels**, that the excellency of the power may be of God, and not of us* (2 Cor 4:5-7).

• *For ye see your calling, brethren, how that **not many wise** men after the flesh, **not many mighty**, **not many noble**, are called: But God hath chosen the foolish things of the world to confound the wise; and God hath chosen the weak things of the world to confound the things which are mighty* (1 Cor 1:26-27).

• *For **a great door and effectual is opened** unto me, and there are many adversaries* (1 Cor 16:9).

(2) THE PROMISE.
[1] EVANGELIZATION AMONG THE JEWS. ***Behold, I will make them of the synagogue of Satan, which say they are Jews, and are not, but do lie; behold, I will make them to come and worship before thy feet, and to know that I have loved thee*** (3:9). At the time of the writing of Revelation, the Jewish nation that had rejected the Messiah, persecuted and slandered the early church, and were in effect replacing the Scriptures with the Talmud had become a vast **synagogue of Satan**. During the long centuries, Christendom did very little to bring the Gospel to the Jewish People. During the Philadelphia period that changed substantially. "Philadelphia" believers understood Bible Prophecy regarding the future of the Nation of Israel, they also understood the great imperative to bring the Gospel to the Jewish People.

Today many groups and are involved in Jewish evangelism; a brief history of one of the earlier societies is that of *Christian Witness to Israel*:

> Christian Witness to Israel (CWI) was formed by the amalgamation of two evangelical and interdenominational societies: the International Society for Evangelisation of the Jews (IJS) and the Barbican Mission to the Jews (BMJ). Both were motivated by the fact that *the gospel of Christ ... is the power of God unto salvation to every one that believeth; to the Jew first...*
>
> During the early part of the nineteenth century various gatherings were held in London and Scotland to consider what steps should be taken to reach the Jewish people with the gospel. As a result, a meeting was held in the National Scotch Church, Regent Square, London on 7 November 1842 to form the British Society for the Propagation of the Gospel among the Jews. Those present included the famous Robert Murray M'Cheyne. It was agreed to co-operate with the Church of Scotland's Mission to the Jews. The society later became the International Society for the Evangelisation of the Jews. In 1879 "an agency for gospel work among the Jews conducted by Hebrew Christians" commenced work in the Barbican district of London which, in 1891, became the Barbican Mission to the Jews.
>
> The work of both societies expanded rapidly to provincial cities and to mission stations on the Continent, particularly in Eastern Poland where many Jews responded to the gospel. Work was pioneered in Israel, Yugoslavia and Czechoslovakia. Within fifty years William Wingate, a pioneer missionary to the Jews of Budapest, could say, "Hebrew Christians are everywhere. Every class of Jewish society contributes ... professors in universities, lawyers, medical men, literary men, musicians, artists, merchants, mechanics, poor and rich are quickened by the Spirit of all grace, convinced of their sin and guilt. ***They are at the feet of Jesus*** [emphasis mine, note again verse 9] and enabled to say with every believer, 'We have redemption through the atoning blood of Jesus, even the forgiveness of our sins'."

Israel was still a scattered nation and Jewish rationalist thinkers were determined to establish a Jewish homeland. Pogroms in Russia spurred these early Zionists to return to the land of their fathers and in 1897 Theodore Herzl inaugurated the first Zionist Congress with this in view. The Balfour Declaration of 1917, which established a national home for the Jews, and the Bolshevik Revolution which closely followed, encouraged the Jews to return to the Land after an exile of eighteen centuries.

World War II with its horrific extermination of six million Jews under the Nazi regime, brought the work in Europe to a standstill. Through the efforts of Rev. I.E. Davidson, many Jewish children were rescued from certain death to be brought up, with parental permission, in England. Many came to know the Saviour and some are now serving him as ministers and full-time workers. Gospel work, closed in Europe by the war, now began to be developed in other countries. Today our ministry extends to Jewish people in Israel, France, UK, Australia, Hungary, New Zealand and Bulgaria.http://www.cwi.org.uk/whoweare/history.html#tophttp://www.cwi.org.uk/whoweare/history.html#top

[2] DELIVERANCE FROM THE TRIBULATION. *Because thou hast kept the word of my patience, I also will keep thee from the hour of temptation, which shall come upon all the world, to try them that dwell upon the earth* (3:10). It should be noted that this deliverance is not only from trial in a general sense but from a period of time in which the trial exists, *the hour of temptation*. The expression is made as strong as possible that the Philadelphian church would be delivered from this period (Walvoord).

KEPT FROM THE HOUR: EVIDENCE FOR THE PRETRIBULATION RAPTURE

One: An **hour of temptation is coming**. It is an *hour* in comparison to the *ages* of general tribulation that have fallen on parts of the earth. It is an *hour*, only a short time, yet an exceedingly intense time. It contains more tribulation than that of all the previous ages combined.

Two: It will be **upon all the earth**. It will not be in only the "trouble spots" of the earth; the entire earth will feel the full weight of its fury.

Three: Those who **kept the word of his patience** during times of *general* tribulation will be **kept** *from* the time of *great* tribulation. During these times of general tribulation, faith is exercised to wait in *patience* for His Return: *Be **patient** therefore, brethren, unto the coming of the Lord. Behold, the husbandman waiteth for the precious fruit of the earth, and hath **long patience** for it, until he receive the early and latter rain* (Jms 5:7).

Four: Believers will be **kept from** (Gr. *ek*) the terrible hour. They will not go *through* it, but will be kept *from* it. This is a key passage demonstrating that the Rapture of believers will take place before the terrible time of trouble. The coming Tribulation is one unit composed of Seven Seals containing Seven Trumpets and Seven Vials. We will not go through any part of it.

CHAPTER 4

THE TWOFOLD PURPOSE OF THE TRIBULATION: TO PURIFY ISRAEL AND PUNISH THE NATIONS. BELIEVERS HAVE NO PART IN EITHER. THE CHURCH IS NOT MENTIONED IN CHAPTERS 4-19

ISRAEL

• *When thou art in tribulation, and all these things are come upon thee, even **in the latter days**, if thou turn to the LORD thy God, and shalt be obedient unto his voice; (For the LORD thy God is a merciful God;) he will not forsake thee, neither destroy thee, nor forget the covenant of thy fathers which he sware unto them.* (Deut 4:30,31).

• ***Come, my people, enter thou into thy chambers**, and shut thy doors about thee: hide thyself as it were for a little moment, **until the indignation be overpast*** (Isa 26:20).

• *Alas! for that day is great, so that none is like it: **it is even the time of Jacob's trouble**, but he shall be saved out of it* (Jer 30:7).

• *And I will bring you out from the people, and will gather you out of the countries wherein ye are scattered, with a mighty hand, and with a stretched out arm, and **with fury poured out**. And **I will bring you into the wilderness of the people, and there will I plead with you face to face**. Like as I pleaded with your fathers in the wilderness of the land of Egypt, so will I plead with you, saith the Lord GOD* (Ezek 20:34-36).

• *And it shall come to pass **in that day, that I will seek to destroy all the nations that come against Jerusalem**. And I will pour upon the house of David, and upon the inhabitants of Jerusalem, the spirit of grace and of supplications: and **they shall look upon me whom they have pierced**, and they shall mourn for him, as one mourneth for his only son, and shall be in bitterness for him, as one that is in bitterness for his firstborn* (Zech 12:9,10).

• *And **I will bring the third part through the fire, and will refine them as silver is refined**, and will try them as gold is tried: **they shall call on my name**, and I will hear them: I will say, It is my people: and they shall say, The LORD is my God.* (Zech 13:9).

THE NATIONS

• *And **I will punish the world for their evil**, and the wicked for their iniquity; and **I will cause the arrogancy of the proud to cease**, and will lay low the haughtiness of the terrible.* (Isa 13:11).

• *With my soul have I desired thee in the night; yea, with my spirit within me will I seek thee early: for **when thy judgments are in the earth, the inhabitants of the world will learn righteousness*** (Isa 26:9).

• *For, behold, the LORD cometh out of his place **to punish the inhabitants of the earth** for their iniquity: the earth also shall disclose her blood, and shall no more cover her slain* (Isa 26:21).

• *Thus saith the LORD of hosts, Behold, **evil shall go forth from nation to nation**, and a great whirlwind shall be raised up from the coasts of the earth. And the slain of the LORD shall be at that day **from one end of the earth even unto the other end of the earth**: they shall not be lamented, neither gathered, nor buried; they shall be dung upon the ground* (Jer 25:32,33).

There will still be mercy during these awful days. God does not *leave Himself without a witness* (Acts 14:17). While the Church not mentioned nor present to carry the Gospel message; we do read about the 144,000 (Rev 7), the Two Witnesses (Rev 11), and even angelic evangelists (Rev 14). That God in those days is still *willing that none should perish* (2 Pet 3:9) is seen in the *great multitude which no man could number of all nations...which came out of great tribulation* (Rev 7:9,14). As Revelation 6-18 chronicles the Tribulation with its three-fold series of judgements (the seals, trumpets, and vials); at the beginning phase (Rev 6:17, we are given notice that *the great day of his wrath is come*. Thus from beginning to end, the Tribulation is the wrath of God. With these "final calls" there is for a while some mingling and mixture in the wrath; but from chapter 14 this will all cease, and we read only of *the wine of the wrath of God which is poured out **without mixture*** (14:10). But again, the believing Church has no part in this Seven Sealed Book of Wrath.

THE CHURCH IS RAPTURED BEFORE
THE SEVEN YEARS OF WRATH

THE RAPTURE

• *And if I go and prepare a place for you, **I will come again, and receive you unto myself**; that where I am, there ye may be also* (Jhn 14:3).

• *Behold, I shew you **a mystery**; We shall not all sleep, but **we shall all be changed, In a moment, in the twinkling of an eye**, at the last trump: for the trumpet shall sound, and the dead shall be raised incorruptible, and we shall be changed.* I Cor. 15:51,52.

• *For this we say unto you by the word of the Lord, that we which are alive and remain unto the coming of the Lord shall not prevent them which are asleep. For **the Lord himself shall descend from heaven** with a shout, with the voice of the archangel, and with the trump of God: and **the dead in Christ shall rise first: Then we which are alive and remain shall be caught up together with them in the clouds, to meet the Lord in the air**: and so shall we ever be with the Lord. Wherefore comfort one another with these words* (1 Thess 4:15-18).

• *Now we beseech you, brethren, by the **coming** of our Lord Jesus Christ, and by **our gathering together unto him*** (2 Thess. 2:1).

• *After this I looked, and, behold, a door was opened in heaven: and the first voice which I heard was as it were of a trumpet talking with me; which said, **Come up hither, and I will shew thee things which must be hereafter*** (Rev 4:1).

• *I press toward the mark for the prize of **the high calling** of God in Christ Jesus* (Phil 3:14).

• *And Enoch walked with God: and **he was not; for God took him*** (Gen 5:24).

DELIVERANCE FROM WRATH

• *Watch ye therefore, and pray always, that ye may be accounted worthy to **escape all these things** that shall come to pass, and to stand before the Son of man* (Lk 21:36).

• *Much more then, being now justified by his blood, we shall be **saved from wrath** through him* (Rom 5:9).

• *And to wait for his Son from heaven, whom he raised from the dead, even Jesus, which **delivered us from the wrath to come*** (1 Thess 1:10).

• *For **God hath not appointed us to wrath**, but to obtain salvation by our Lord Jesus Christ, Who died for us, that, whether we wake or sleep, we should live together with him* (1 Thess 5:9,10).

• *And now **ye know what withholdeth** that he might be revealed in his time. For the mystery of iniquity doth already work: only **he who now letteth will let, until he be taken out of the way**. And **then shall that Wicked be revealed**, whom the Lord shall consume with the spirit of his mouth, and shall destroy with the brightness of his* *coming* (2 Thess 2:6-8). Note: The Holy Spirit indwelt Church as salt and light is the hindering influence in the world today (Matt 5:13,16).

TEN BASIC REASONS FOR BELIEVING IN THE PRETRIIBULATION RAPTURE

1. **The Doctrine of Imminence**: Christ may come at any moment. Believers are never told to look for something to happen before the Rapture. While we may see the foreshadowing of the Tribulation, we are never told to *look first* for the Antichrist, the Seal judgements, the Mark, the Temple, the 144,000, the Two Witnesses etc. The believer today looks for Christ not Antichrist (Titus 2:13).

2. To say that *Christ will not or cannot come today*, as the mid or post-tribulationist must say, is a grievous and arrogant thing to say and places them in the category of the servant who said, *my Lord delayeth his coming* (Lk 12:45).

3. *Why have so few post and mid tribulationists not built bomb shelters* and "stocked up". If they really believe it, why have most not taken extreme measures for the extreme days coming?

4. None of the New Testament passages dealing with the Tribulation mention the church (Matt. 13:30; 39-42, 48-50; 24:15-31; 1 Thess. 1:9-10; 5:4-9; 2 Thess. 2:1-11; Rev. 4-18).

5. There are **no "Tribulation Instructions"** given to the Church in the Epistles and Revelation 2,3. Specific instructions are *not given* as to how to deal with the Antichrist, the Mark, the Seal judgements, Trumpets judgements and Vial judgements etc.

6. The Church is not mentioned in *the things which shall be hereafter* section of Revelation 4-19 (cp. Rev 1:19); whereas it is mentioned 22 times during *the things which are* section (Rev 2,3; cp.1:19). Note the absence of the oft repeated phrase *unto the churches* (Rev 2,3) in the identical statement in Revelation 13:9.

7. In an extended passage (Rev 7:9-17), there is no statement linking those saved in the Tribulation to the Church.

8. The unity of Daniel's Seventieth Week is clearly demonstrated in Scripture. By contrast, postribulationism and midtribulationists destroy the unity of Daniel's Seventieth Week and confuse Israel's program with that of the Church. The Seventy Weeks are specifically said to apply to Israel (Dan 9:24).

9. **The Seven Year Tribulation is *one unit*** composed of Seven Seals containing Seven Trumpets and Seven Vials. We will not go through any part of it. Thus, it is Chapter Six of Revelation (with the Seals) that the *wrath of the lamb begins* (Rev 5:9; 6:1), not in Chapter Eight or Nine (with the Trumpets) or Chapter Sixteen (with the Vials). Wrath intensifies with the Trumpets and the Vials, but it does not begin with them. Believers of the Church age will not go through any part of it.

10. **The believing church is not appointed to wrath** (Rom 5:9; 1Thess 5:9).

"FIFTY REASONS FOR THE PRETIBULATIONAL RAPTURE" BY JOHN WALVOORD

This well-known and classic presentation taken from the internet is from Dr. Walvoords book *The Rapture Question* (Zondervan). I have taken the liberty to enlarge and edit slightly his presentation in a number of places.

1. HISTORICAL ARGUMENT

THE BOOK OF REVELATION

"**1.** Though some as shown in 2 Thess. 2 had sought to introduce post-tribulationism into the Church, the imminency of the Lord's return, which is an essential doctrine of pretribulationism, was clearly taught and believed in the early Church.

2. The formalisation of pretribulational truth in the past two centuries does not mean that the doctrine is new or novel. Its development and elucidation from the Scriptures is similar to that of other major doctrines during the history of the Church. In the early 1800s many began to take Bible prophecy literally and break out of the mould that had existed since the 400s. Both Catholicism and the Reformers held to a replacement theology in which the church was said to take the place of Israel, that God was in fact finished with Israel as a nation, and that the Tribulation and Millennium were only in a general sense fulfilled throughout history. To them prophecies of the Tribulation and Millennium bore no immediate proximity to Christ's Return. However, the extent to which believers saw pretribulational truth during those long centuries is not the main point, the above passages show that it is not only in the Bible, but it is in the Bible substantially!

2. INTERPRETATIONAL ARGUMENT

3. Pretribulationism is the only view that allows for a literal interpretation of all Old and New Testament passages on the Great Tribulation.

4. Pretribulationism distinguishes clearly between Israel and the Church and their respective programs.

3. NATURE OF THE TRIBULATION

5. Pretribulationism maintains the Scriptural distinction between the Seven Year Tribulation which occurs in direct proximity to Christ's Second Coming and tribulation in general throughout the Church Age (Jhn 16:33).

6. The Tribulation is properly interpreted by pretribulationists as a time of preparation for Israel's restoration (Deut 4:29,30; Jer 30:4-11). It is not the purpose of the Tribulation to prepare the Church for glory.

7. None of the Old Testament passages on the Tribulation mention the Church (Deut 4:29,30; Jer 30:4-11; Dan 8:24-27; 12:1,2).

8. None of the New Testament passages on the Tribulation mention the church (Matt 13:30; 39-42, 48-50; 24:15-31; 1 Thess 1:9-10; 5:4-9; 2 Thess 2:1-11; Rev 4-18).

9. In contrast to midtribulationism, the pretribulational view provides an adequate explanation for the beginning of the Tribulation in Revelation 6. Midtribulationism teaches that the Tribulation begins with the blowing of the seventh trumpet in Revelation 11. This is refuted by the events of chapter 6 and especially verse 17.

10. The proper distinction is maintained between the prophetic trumpets of Scripture by pretribulationism. There is no proper ground for the pivotal argument of midtribulationism that the seventh trumpet of Revelation is the last trumpet of 1 Cor 15:51,52. There is no established connection between the seventh trumpet of Revelation 11, the last trumpet of 1 Corinthians 15:52, and the trumpet of Matthew 24:31. They are three distinct events.

11. The unity of Daniel's Seventieth Week is maintained by pretribulationists. By contrast, post-tribulationism and midtribulationists destroy the unity of Daniel's Seventieth Week and confuse Israel's program with that of the Church. The Seventy Weeks are specifically said to apply to Israel (Dan 9:24).

4. NATURE OF THE CHURCH

12. The Translation (Rapture) of the Church is never mentioned in any passage dealing with the Second Coming of Christ to earth after the Tribulation.

CHAPTER 4

13. The church is *saved from wrath* (Rom 5:9). It is *not appointed to wrath* (1 Thess 5:9). It is *delivered from the wrath to come* (I Thess 1:10). The Church therefore cannot enter *the great day of his wrath* (Rev 6:17).

14. Likewise the Church will not be overtaken by the Day of the Lord (1 Thess 5:1-9), which includes the Tribulation.

15. Though the Rapture is a mystery and not specifically revealed until the Epistles (1 Cor 15:51,52), the possibility of a believer escaping the Tribulation is mentioned in the Gospels (Lk 21:28,36).

16. The church of Philadelphia was promised deliverance *from the hour of temptation, which shall come upon all the world, to try them that dwell upon the earth* (Rev 3:10).

17. It is characteristic of divine dealing to deliver believers before a divine judgment is inflicted on the world as illustrated in the deliverance of Noah, Lot, Rahab, and others (2 Pet 2:5-9).

18. At the time of the Translation of the Church, all believers go to the Father's house in heaven (Jhn 14:3) and do not (as post-tribulationists teach) immediately return to the earth after meeting Christ in the air.

19. Pretribulationism does not divide the body of Christ at the Rapture on a works principle. The teaching of a partial Rapture is based on the false doctrine that the Translation of the Church is a reward for good works. It is rather a climactic consummation of salvation by grace.

20. The Scriptures clearly teach that all, not part, of the church will be raptured at the Coming of Christ for the Church (1 Cor 15:51-52; 1 Thess 4:17).

21. As opposed to a view of a partial rapture, pretribulationism is founded on the definite teaching of Scripture that the death of Christ frees from all condemnation.

22. The Godly remnant of the Tribulation are Israelites and Gentiles converted in the Tribulation, not members of the Church as maintained by post-tribulationists. The Church is not mentioned in Revelation 6-18.

23. The pretribulational view, as opposed to post-tribulationism, does not confuse general terms like elect and saints, which apply to the saved of all ages, with specific terms like Church and those *in Christ*. These latter refer only to believers of this age.

5. DOCTRINE OF IMMINENCY

24. The pretribulational interpretation teaches that the coming of Christ is imminent. While events of the Tribulation may appear on the horizon as a foreshadowing, We are to look to no other event intervening before the Rapture. We are to look for Christ rather than Antichrist (Titus 2:13).

25. The exhortation to be comforted by the Coming of the Lord (1 Thess 4:18) is very significant in the pretribulational view, and is especially contradicted by the post-tribulational. Rather than offering comfort the post-tribulationist must instead warn the Church that she faces the Antichrist, the wrath of Satan, the mark, wars, famine, pestilence, and especially the unfolding and ever increasing wrath of God in the sevenfold seal, trumpet and vial judgements.

26. The exhortation to look for *the glorious appearing of Christ* (Titus 2:13) loses its significance if the Tribulation must intervene first. Believers in that case should look for the terrible events of Revelation 6 -18.

27. The exhortation to purify ourselves in view of the Lord's return has most significance if His coming is imminent (1 Jhn 3:2,3).

28. The church is uniformly exhorted to look for the Coming of the Lord Himself, while believers in the Tribulation are directed to look for the events of that which must unfold before He returns.

THE BOOK OF REVELATION

6. THE WORK OF THE HOLY SPIRIT

29. The Holy Spirit as the restrainer of evil cannot be taken out of the world unless the Church, which the Spirit indwells, is translated at the same time. The Tribulation cannot begin until this restraint is lifted.

30. The Holy Spirit as the restrainer who indwells the Church (1 Cor 3:16) must be taken out of the world before "the man of sin," who dominates the Tribulation period, can be revealed (2 Thess 2:6-8). Yet, though the Church as salt and light is gone (cp. Matt 5:13,16), the Holy Spirit in this time will continue to work in the conversion of sinners.

31. [The expression *except there come a falling away first, and that man of sin be revealed* (2 Thess 2:3) refers to the total apostasy that must occur on earth before the *Day of Christ* takes place (2 Thess 2:2). That this *Day of Christ* refers to His actual Return to earth and not the Rapture is shown by the verses immediately before (2 Thess 1:5-10)].

7. NECESSITY OF AN INTERVAL BETWEEN THE RAPTURE AND THE RETURN

32. According to 2 Corinthians 5:10, all believers of this age must appear before the judgment seat of Christ in heaven, an event never mentioned in the detailed accounts connected with the Second Coming of Christ to the earth.

33. If the twenty-four elders of Revelation 4:1-5:14 are representatives of the Church as many expositors believe, it would necessitate the Rapture of the Church before the Tribulation, and certainly before Christ's Return to earth.

34. The coming of Christ for His Bride must take place before the Second Coming in which He returns to earth with His Bride (Rev. 19:7-10). This is in accord with the Jewish order in which the groom goes to the bride's house and takes her to his father's house for the wedding ceremony.

35. Tribulation saints are not translated at the Second Coming of Christ but carry on ordinary occupations such as farming and building houses. They will bear children during the Millennium (Isa 65:20-25). This would be impossible if the Translation had taken place at the time of the Second Coming to the earth, as post-tribulationists teach.

36. The judgment of the Gentiles following the Second Coming (Matt 25:31-46) indicates that both saved and unsaved are still in their natural bodies. This would be impossible if the Translation had taken place at the Second Coming.

37. If the Translation took place in connection with the Second Coming to the earth, there would be no need of separating the sheep from the goats as described in Matthew 25:31-46. This separation would have taken place in the very act of the Translation itself.

38. The judgment of Israel (Ezek 20:34-38), which occurs subsequent to the Second Coming, would likewise be unnecessary if the saved had previously been separated from the unsaved by a Translation at the end of the Tribulation.

8. CONTRASTS BETWEEN THE RAPTURE AND THE SECOND COMING

39. At the time of the Rapture the saints meet Christ in the air, while at the Second Coming Christ returns with His saints (Zech 14:5; Jude 14), and also to meet the Tribulation saints on earth.

40. At the time of the Rapture the Mount of Olives is unchanged, while at the Second Coming it divides and a valley is formed to the east of Jerusalem (Zech 14:4,5).

41. At the Rapture living saints are translated, while no saints are translated in connection with the Second Coming of Christ to the earth.

42. At the Rapture the saints go to heaven, while at the Second Coming the scene of activity is entirely on the earth.

CHAPTER 4

43. At the time of the Rapture the world is unjudged and continues in sin, while at the Second Coming the world is judged and righteousness is established on the earth.

44. The Translation of the Church is pictured as a deliverance before the day of wrath, while the Second Coming is followed by the deliverance of those who have believed in Christ during the wrath of the Tribulation.

45. The Rapture is described as imminent, while the Second Coming is preceded by definite signs. We cannot know the time of the Rapture, whereas time indicators are given to Tribulation saints for the Lord's Return to earth.

46. The Translation of living believers is a truth revealed only in the New Testament, while the Second Coming with its attendant events is a prominent doctrine of both Testaments.

47. The Rapture concerns only the saved, while the Second Coming deals with both saved and unsaved (cp. Rev 1:7).

48. At the Rapture Satan is not bound, while at the Second Coming Satan is bound and cast into the abyss.

49. No unfulfilled prophecy stands between the Church and the Rapture, while many signs must be fulfilled before the Second Coming.

50. No passage dealing with the resurrection of saints at the Second Coming mentions translation of living saints at that time." *John Walvoord.*

FURTHER CONSIDERATIONS ON THE PRETRIBULATIONAL RAPTURE

THE RAPTURE IS NOT TIMED; THE RETURN IS TIMED

A number of passages as Matthew 24:44 and 25:13 tell us that Christ's coming will be in *such an hour as ye think not*, and that *ye know neither the day nor the hour*. This is in striking contrast to the three and one half years (*time, times and half a time*; Rev 12:14; cp. Dan 7:25; 9:27) that will elapse from the time the Antichrist breaks his covenant with Israel until Christ Returns. The time of His Return will be marked further by –

- The Jews fleeing into the wilderness for 1260 days (Rev 12:6).
- The ministry of the Two witnesses will last for 1260 days (Rev 12:3).
- Jerusalem will be trodden down for 42 months (Rev 12:2).
- The Antichrist will reign for 42 months (Rev 13:5).

A study of these *timed* passages will show that they all occur in the second half of Daniel's Seventieth Week (cp. with Dan 9:27). It is therefore clear that believers during the Tribulation will be able to count the days and months from Antichrist setting up his image in the Jewish temple unto the Return of Christ. Therefore the Matthew 24:44; 25:13 type of passage cannot refer to the Return, and though the Rapture being a mystery is not revealed fully until the Epistles (I Cor. 15:51,52), these Gospel passages must have the Rapture in view. This leads naturally to the next point:

THE RAPTURE IS INTIMATED IN THE GOSPELS

Some ask: Why is the Rapture not seen in the Olivet Discourse (Matt 24,25; Mk 13; Lk 21). But, as the above shows: It is! It is also seen in our *being gathered* to Christ and the Father's house in John 14:1-3, and in Luke 17 it is seen in the examples of Noah and Lot. Further, Luke 21:36 shows that it will be possible to escape the coming Tribulation days. And, in Matthew 24 and 25, after describing the Tribulation and Christ's return in glory

THE BOOK OF REVELATION

(24:27-31), there are *seven illustrations to promote watchfulness*. These exhortations, without any reference to time, point to an imminent, *at any moment* return of Christ for the believer.

- The Fig Tree 24:32-35
- The Days of Noah 24:36-39.
- The One Taken, One Left 24:40,41
- The Faithful Householder 24:42-44
- The Wise Servant 24:25-51
- The Ten Virgins 25:1-13
- The Talents 25:14-30

These passages cannot apply primarily to Tribulation saints fleeing from Antichrist, for they are able to count the days from the Beast setting up his image in Jerusalem to Christ's Second Coming. They rather stress the imminency and unexpectedness of His coming as seen in the Rapture. Tribulation saints will know the hour. These are illustrations for those who must: *Watch therefore: for ye know not what hour your Lord doth come* (Matt 24:42). Thus the Rapture, as a mystery fully revealed in the Epistles (1 Cor 15:51,52), is alluded to in the Gospels.

THE RAPTURE AND THE LAST TRUMPET

The trump of God at the Rapture (1 Thess. 4:16) is called the last trump in 1 Corinthians 15:52. Some have said this refers to the last of the seven trumpets blown by angels toward the end of the Tribulation, in which each issues in a cataclysmic judgement (Rev. 8:2; 11:15). Others, that it refers to Christ's Return immediately after the tribulation of those days (Matt. 24:29), when *He shall send his angels with a great sound of a trumpet, and they shall gather together his elect from the four winds, from one end of heaven to the other* (24:31). Post-tribulationists appeal to one or the other of these as the trumpet that will be blown at the Rapture, thus indicating that the Church will go through all or most of the Tribulation.

In response there clearly seems to be a distinction between trumpets in the hands of angels and the trumpet of the Rapture which is specifically called the trump of God (1 Thess 4:16). Further, in this connection, if there is a last trumpet of God, there must also be a *first trumpet of God*. And, indeed there is.

- *And the LORD said unto Moses, Go unto the people, and sanctify them to day and tomorrow, and let them wash their clothes, And be ready against the third day: for the third day **the LORD will come down** in the sight of all the people upon mount Sinai. And thou shalt set bounds unto the people round about, saying, Take heed to yourselves, that ye go not up into the mount, or touch the border of it: whosoever toucheth the mount shall be surely put to death: There shall not an hand touch it, but he shall surely be stoned, or shot through; whether it be beast or man, it shall not live: when the trumpet soundeth long, they shall come up to the mount. And Moses went down from the mount unto the people, and sanctified the people; and they washed their clothes. And he said unto the people, Be ready against the third day: come not at your wives. And it came to pass on the third day in the morning, that there were thunders and lightnings, and a thick cloud upon the mount, and **the voice of the trumpet exceeding loud**; so that all the people that was in the camp trembled. And Moses brought forth the people out of the camp to meet with God; and they stood at the nether part of the mount. And mount Sinai was altogether on a smoke, because the LORD*

CHAPTER 4

descended upon it in fire: and the smoke thereof ascended as the smoke of a furnace, and the whole mount quaked greatly. And **when the voice of the trumpet sounded long, and waxed louder and louder**, *Moses spake, and God answered him by a voice. And* **the LORD came down upon mount Sinai**, *on the top of the mount: and the LORD called Moses up to the top of the mount;* **and Moses went up** (Exod 19:10-20).

What a tremendous Old Testament picture this is of the Rapture! It is associated with a trumpet, ***the first trumpet***! While angels were present (Acts 7:53), the trumpet is not seen to be in their hands. It is the trumpet of God. Compare: Psalms 47:5, *God is gone up with a shout, the LORD with the sound of a trumpet.* There will be trumpets sounded by angels at the end of the Tribulation and also as Christ returns to earth, but these are shown to be the trumpets of angels. The trumpet of the Rapture is the trump of God, as none bearing this description are seen again in the Scriptures, this in 1 Corinthians 15:51,52 is called ***the last trump***.

The last trump is also a military expression. In Roman warfare, guards were summoned to their posts at the sound of a trumpet. They were relieved of their watch by a second or last trumpet. So we as believers are called to our watch, and to await the Lord's Return (Acts 20:31; 1 Cor 16:13; Eph 6:18; Col 4:2; 1 Thess 5:6; 2 Tim 4:5; 1 Pet 4:7; Rev 3:2). Shortly we too will hear the last trump. Likewise in Old Testament and Roman times the last trumpet was blown to call the soldiers home (2 Sam 18:16; 20:22). Scripture describes the Christian life as a warfare (2 Tim 2:1-4). We are urged to fight the good fight of faith (1 Tim 6:12). Paul's closing testimony bore witness to this, as he spoke not only of death but primarily of the Lord's Return:

- *I have fought a good fight, I have finished my course, I have kept the faith: Henceforth there is laid up for me a crown of righteousness, which the Lord, the righteous judge, shall give me at that day: and not to me only, but unto all them also that love his appearing* (2 Tim 4:7,8).

At the Rapture, after the long warfare, after the long watch, the last trump will beckon God's soldiers home. Many also see a connection here with the Jewish Feast of Trumpets (Lev 23). The ceremony of the seventh month is marked by a series of short trumpet blasts and concluded by a long blast called the *tekiah gedolah*, the great or last trump. In the seven-feast calendar, the Feast of Trumpets is pretribulational in nature. It occurs before the Day of Atonement, Israel's day of affliction and atonement which prefigures her national salvation at Christ's Return. (See: Renald Showers, *Maranatha Our Lord, Come!* Friends of Israel Publ.).

As the Rapture will occur shortly before the commencement of the Seventieth Week of Daniel (Dan 9:24-27) this same trumpet may also be heard by Israel alerting them to that fact. Jewish people around the world will be made to know that the final stage of the long suspended program *determined upon thy people and upon thy holy city* (Dan 9:24) has now begun. Isaiah 27 elaborates upon the 70th Week and describes the purging of Israel's iniquity *in the day of the rough and east wind*. The entire 27th chapter encompasses the *Day of the Lord* and the *Time of Jacobs Trouble* (Jer 30:7). This great work of Israel's chastening and restoration is *announced by a trumpet*!

- ***Seventy weeks are determined upon thy people and upon thy holy city, to finish the transgression, and to make an end of sins***, *and to make reconciliation for iniquity, and to bring in everlasting righteousness, and to seal up the vision and prophecy, and to anoint the most Holy* (Dan 9:24).

- *In that day the LORD with his sore and great and strong sword shall punish leviathan the piercing serpent, even leviathan that crooked serpent; and he shall slay the dragon that is in the sea* (Isa 27:1).
- *Or let him take hold of my strength, that he may make peace with me; and he shall make peace with me.* **He shall cause them that come of Jacob to take root**: *Israel shall blossom and bud, and fill the face of the world with fruit. Hath he smitten him, as he smote those that smote him? or is he slain according to the slaughter of them that are slain by him* (Isa 27:5-7)?
- **Hath he smitten him**, *as he smote those that smote him? or is he slain according to the slaughter of them that are slain by him? In measure, when it shooteth forth, thou wilt debate with it*: **he stayeth his rough wind in the day of the east wind**. *By this therefore shall the iniquity of Jacob be purged* (Isa 27:7-9).
- *And it shall come to pass* **in that day**, *that the LORD shall beat off from the channel of the river unto the stream of Egypt, and ye shall be gathered one by one, O ye children of Israel. And it shall come to pass* **in that day, that the great trumpet shall be blown**, *and they shall come which were ready to perish in the land of Assyria, and the outcasts in the land of Egypt, and shall worship the LORD in the holy mount at Jerusalem* (Isa 27:12,13). Compare also Joel 2:1,15; Zeph. 1:16; Zech. 9:14.

THE RAPTURE AND *THE DAY OF CHRIST* IN II THESSALONIANS 2

2:1 *Now we beseech you, brethren, by the coming of our Lord Jesus Christ, and by* ***our gathering together unto him***,
2:2 *That ye be not soon shaken in mind, or be troubled, neither by spirit, nor by word, nor by letter as from us, as* ***that the day of Christ is at hand***.
2:3 *Let no man deceive you by any means: for* ***that day shall not come, except there come a falling away first***, *and that man of sin be revealed, the son of perdition;*

Some point to 2 Thessalonians 2:2,3 as indicating that Antichrist would be revealed before the *Day of Christ*. As it has been assumed that the term *Day of Christ* refers to the Rapture rather than the Return this would mean that the Rapture would follow rather than precede the Tribulation. Pretribulationists in seeking to answer this have made things difficult for themselves by arguing that the modern version reading, *Day of the Lord* rather than *Day of Christ* is the correct reading.

Some have further compounded the matter by suggesting the phrase, *falling away* (2:3) could refer to the Rapture rather than the apostasy that will accompany Antichrist during the Tribulation. This second proposal gives an unnatural meaning to the Greek noun *apostasia* (lit. apostasy). The word is found once else in Acts 21:21 (*to forsake* Moses). The verb form *aphisteemi* is used 15 times and in the same sense. The *apostasia* is the total and utter apostasy that will accompany the Man of Sin during the Tribulation.

Rather than go through these unwarranted contortions they should have noted that *Day of Christ* as used here is defined by the immediately preceding passage.

- *Seeing it is a righteous thing with God to recompense tribulation to them that trouble you; And to you who are troubled rest with us, when* ***the Lord Jesus shall be revealed from heaven with his mighty angels, In flaming fire taking vengeance on them that know not God, and that obey not the gospel of our Lord Jesus Christ:*** *Who shall be punished with everlasting destruction from the presence of the Lord, and from the glory* *of his power;* **When he shall come to be glorified in his saints**, *and to be admired in all them that believe (because our testimony among you was believed) in that day* (2 Thess 1:6-10).

This is the Lord Jesus coming with His saints and in flaming fire and vengeance at Armageddon. It is not the Rapture. This day in which Christ is so revealed will not come **except there come a falling away first, and that man of sin be revealed** (2 Thess 2:3). Nor for the believer will this *apostasia* come, for they will first be **gathered together unto him** (2:1). Here as in 1 Thessalonians the Rapture is described before the Tribulation. 1 Thessalonians 4:13-18 comes *before* 1 Thessalonians 5:1-11!

Returning to the *Day of Christ* question. The term is found seven times.

- *Who shall also confirm you unto the end, that ye may be blameless in* **the day of our Lord Jesus Christ** (Cor 1:8).
- *To deliver such an one unto Satan for the destruction of the flesh, that the spirit may be saved in* **the day of the Lord Jesus** (1 Cor 5:5).
- *As also ye have acknowledged us in part, that we are your rejoicing, even as ye also are our's in* **the day of the Lord Jesus** (2 Cor 1:14).
- *Being confident of this very thing, that he which hath begun a good work in you will perform it until* **the day of Jesus Christ** (Phil 1:6).
- *That ye may approve things that are excellent; that ye may be sincere and without offence till* **the day of Christ** (Phil 1:10).
- *Holding forth the word of life; that I may rejoice in* **the day of Christ**, *that I have not run in vain, neither laboured in vain* (Phil 2:16).
- *That ye be not soon shaken in mind, or be troubled, neither by spirit, nor by word, nor by letter as from us, as that* **the day of Christ** *is at hand* (2 Thess 2:2).

Pretribulationists have generally distinguished *the Day of Christ* from *the Day of the Lord* and have said that the former refers entirely to the time of blessing at the Rapture. This however poses a problem when we come to the seventh and last reference (II Thess. 2:2). In a comment on 2 Thess. 2:2, *The Scofield Reference Bible* says:

A.V. has "day of Christ" 2 Thess. 2:2, incorrectly, for "day of the LORD" (Isa. 2:12; Rev. 19:11-21). The "day of Christ" relates wholly to the reward and blessing of saints at His coming, as "day of the LORD" is connected with judgement.

On the contrary, the AV, Received Text and vast majority of Greek manuscripts are correct in reading *day of Christ* in 2 Thessalonians 2:2. The modern version *day of the Lord* reading has far less support among the total number of Greek manuscripts. And while the blessing and reward aspect is emphasised in the previous usages, the fact that *day of Christ* in 2:2,3 clearly relates back to 2 Thessalonians 1:4-10 (and also 1 Thess. 5:1-11), demonstrates that there is a clear wrath aspect in the term. To draw a sharp distinction between *the Day of Christ* and *the Day of the Lord* is unwarranted and both must be virtually synonymous. Christ *is the Lord* who comes for His Church; but He also opens the seals of wrath during the Tribulation, and returns to fight the Battle of Armageddon.

In the term *Day of Christ*, there is the blessing and reward phase, but also the wrath and Return phases. In Revelation 5,6 we clearly see the wrath phase. It is Christ who opens the seals unleashing the *wrath of God* upon the earth (5:9; 6:1). When these seals are opened there is no doubt among those on earth that they have entered **the great day of the wrath of the Lamb.**

• *And the stars of heaven fell unto the earth, even as a fig tree casteth her untimely figs, when she is shaken of a mighty wind. And the heaven departed as a scroll when it is rolled together; and every mountain and island were moved out of their places. And the kings of the earth, and the great men, and the rich men, and the chief captains, and the mighty men, and every bondman, and every free man, hid themselves in the dens and in the rocks of the mountains; And said to the mountains and rocks, Fall on us, and hide us from the face of him that sitteth on the throne, and from **the wrath of the Lamb**: For **the great day of his wrath is come**; and who shall be able to stand (Rev. 6:13-17)?*

THE RESTATED EVENTS OF II THESSALONIANS

The prophetic events of Second Thessalonians are presented in the context of what Paul had previously taught the Thessalonians in his visit and in the First Epistle.

- Believers will be ***delivered from the wrath to come*** (1 Thess 1:10).
- Christ will return ***with all his saints*** (1 Thess 3:13).
- The Rapture was described (1 Thess 4:13-18).
- The Tribulation was described (1 Thess 5:1-11).

Paul had spent only three weeks in Thessalonica (Acts 17:1-9), yet it is clear from the First Epistle and now what they are reminded of in the Second Epistle that in that short time he had thoroughly grounded them in the truths of the Second Coming. Here from the great Apostle is the principle that young believers are to be taught the basics of Bible Prophecy and to *love the Lord's Return* (2 Tim 4:8). The following points are now reinforced:

• CHRIST WILL RETURN IN FIERY JUDGEMENT
*And...the Lord Jesus shall be revealed from heaven with his mighty angels, **In flaming fire taking vengeance** on them that know not God, and that obey not the gospel of our Lord Jesus Christ: Who shall be punished with everlasting destruction from the presence of the Lord, and from the glory of his power (2 Thess 1:7-9).*

• A *GATHERING* (THE RAPTURE) COMES BEFORE THE FIERY RETURN
*Now we beseech you, brethren, by **the coming of our Lord Jesus Christ, and by our gathering together unto him,** That ye be not soon shaken in mind, or be troubled, neither by spirit, nor by word, nor by letter as from us, as **that the day of Christ is at hand** (2 Thess 2:1,2).*

• THE TIMES OF ANTICHRIST COME BEFORE CHRIST'S FIERY RETURN
*Let no man deceive you by any means: for **that day shall not come, except there come a falling away first, and that man of sin be revealed**, the son of perdition; Who opposeth and exalteth himself above all that is called God, or that is worshipped; so that he as God sitteth in the temple of God, shewing himself that he is God. **Remember ye not, that, when I was yet with you, I told you these things** (2 Thess 2:3-5)?*

• THE REMOVAL OF THE *HINDERER* (THE HOLY SPIRIT INDWELT CHURCH) IS BEFORE THE ANTICHRIST IS REVEALED AND BEFORE CHRIST DESTROYS HIM IN FIERY JUDGEMENT
*And now ye know what withholdeth that he might be revealed in his time. For the mystery of iniquity doth already work: only **he who now letteth will let, until he be taken out of the way. And then shall that Wicked be revealed**, whom the Lord shall consume with the spirit of his mouth, and shall **destroy with the brightness of his coming** (2 Thess 2:6-8).*

CHAPTER 4

- **DELUSION FOR *THEM***

*Even him, whose coming is after the working of Satan with all power and signs and lying wonders, And with all deceivableness of unrighteousness in **them** that perish; because **they** received not the love of the truth, that **they** might be saved. And for this cause God shall send **them** strong delusion, that **they** should believe a lie: That **they** all might be damned who believed not the truth, but had pleasure in unrighteousness* (2 Thess 2:9-12).

- **THANKSGIVING FOR *YOU***

*But we are bound to give thanks alway to God for **you**, brethren beloved of the Lord, because God hath from the beginning chosen **you** to salvation through sanctification of the Spirit and belief of the truth: Whereunto he called you by our gospel, to the obtaining of the glory of our Lord Jesus Christ* (2 Thess 2:13,14).

Because of erroneous letters sent to the Thessalonians and their severe trials, they were being led to believe that they were in the Tribulation. Second Thessalonians is a corrective for believers of all ages who face severe persecution. While the experience may be painful, it is not the time of wrath spoken of in the Bible. The very fact that the Thessalonians were told not to be *troubled* or shaken in *mind* (2:2), is a certain proof that believers will not have to face the time of Antichrist and the *Day of Christ* in its wrath sense.

A POST-TRIBULATION RAPTURE IS CONTRADICTORY

If Christ raptures all believers at the end of the Tribulation and slays all who have taken the mark of the beast, who will then be left in mortal bodies to populate earth during the Millennium?

If at the end of the Tribulation believers rise to meet Christ in the air, does it not seem strange that we would immediately return with Him to the earth? How can we rise to meet one who is returning to fight a war. How in such a scenario are we to be clothed in white robes and seated on white horses?

How can *the time of Jacob's Trouble* (Jer 30:7) be the time of the Church's trouble? If as stated the Sixty-nine Weeks of Daniel's prophecy applies to Israel (Dan. 9:24), how can the Seventieth Week apply to the Church?

If the Church is present on earth during the Tribulation, why after being mentioned 22 times in Rev. 1-3 is it not mentioned once in chapters 6-18? Why in Rev. 2,3 do we repeatedly read *He that hath an ear let him hear what the Spirit sayeth unto the churches*, whereas in Revelation 13:9 it is only: *If any man have an ear, let him hear*? If the Church is on earth, why is its voice so silent? Why, like the Two Witnesses or the 144,000, does it not seek to be *salt and light* (Matt 5:13,16)? How can it be so moribund?

ARGUING FOR BUT NOT PREPARING FOR
A MID OR POST-TRIBULATIONAL RAPTURE

Given the extent to which the Bible describes the absolute terror of the coming Tribulation days, and given the clear demonstration that believers will be *kept from the hour of temptation which shall come upon all the world*, it is strange that numbers of believers argue so fervently for a place on earth during that time. As Todd Stranberg writes: "You would think the desire to go through the Tribulation would be as popular as the desire to jump into a pit filled with vipers and broken glass. As illogical as it may seem....Many Christians argue strongly for the right to suffer persecution at the hands of the Antichrist and the one world government."

THE BOOK OF REVELATION

For one striking reason this attitude is completely contradictory. Post, mid, pre-wrath tribulationists are not seen making much in the way of preparation for the coming Tribulation! A scan of the Internet will show that they argue very passionately against pretribulationalism and for the right to live on earth during that time. BUT: Where are the blankets, the bottled water, the crates of canned food, electrical generators, underground bunkers, hideaways up in the hills etc.? Where is the urgency to stock up? Will they only start their survival preparations after the Tribulation begins? Their argument does not seem to go beyond the rhetorical. Have they really grasped the implications of what they teach!?

IT IS A GRIEVOUS ERROR TO SAY, "CHRIST CANNOT RETURN TODAY"!

There is and has always been a battle for the hearts and minds of professing Christians concerning the Second Coming of Jesus Christ. It seems that Satan has a number of "fall back positions". Ultimately these are designed to put the believer into the position described in Luke 12:45: *But and if that servant shall say in his heart, **My lord delayeth his coming***.

THE FALL BACK POSITIONS USED TO AVOID THE IMMINENT RAPTURE

(1) "Christ will not literally and physically return to the earth. His Coming is spiritual. He is already here. The prophetic Scriptures are to be taken symbolically. They refer to the spiritual struggles of the Church throughout history."

(2) "If one must believe in the Second Coming then by all means be an amillennialist. There is: No Millennium; No Tribulation; No Rapture. Let Christ return, but let there be only a general judgement with the saved going to Heaven and the lost going to Hell."

• Allow individual Jews to be saved, but reject any thought of Israel's national salvation in the Land of Israel at Christ's Return.

• Make the Church the recipient of the promises to Israel. In fact, replace Israel with the Church and call the Church the *New Israel* (replacement theology).

• Ignore the historical fact that the Church of the first three centuries was for the most part premillennial and believed in the *imminent* Return of Christ.

Such a teaching of course gives very little practical reality to the Blessed Hope. To treat the prophetic Scriptures in the way amillennialists do *is the height of arrogance*. Yet this view is very much in vogue today, particularly among reformed churches.

(3) "If on the other hand one comes to accept that the prophetic Scriptures are to be basically taken literally: that there is a Millennium, a Tribulation, a future for Israel, imminency must still be rejected". "A Perhaps Today hope can be avoided by resorting to the following."

• Remove any possibility of Christ coming today by projecting the Rapture into at least the middle of the Tribulation, and more preferably to its end. Life can for the most part go on as normal, and 1 John 3:3 (as one example) will not be as essential: *And every man that hath this hope in him purifieth himself, even as he is pure.*

• Ignore the huge amount of Scripture that points to the pretribulational Rapture, and concentrate instead upon the foolish notion that this doctrine had its origin in a "vision" that a fifteen year old Irish girl, Margaret MacDonald had in 1830. (This claim was made in a book by Dave Macpherson in 1973).

• Make the claim that the pretribulation Rapture was part of Jesuit plot to undermine the Protestant and reformed faith.

CHAPTER 4

- Attack the lives and writings of J.N. Darby and C.I. Scofield. Focus the attack especially against the 1917 Scofield Reference Bible. Scofield was wrong in his textual comments and the "gap theory", but otherwise the notes are sound and spiritual and have been a help *to millions*.
- Look for the opposite of Titus 2:13; look for Antichrist rather than Christ. Instead of *looking for the Blessed Hope*, look for the Beast to set up his image in Jerusalem.
- Ignore the historical fact that though they were enduring severe persecution and their statements were less than precise, the Church of the first three centuries did believe in the imminency of Christ's Return - an essential part of the pretribulational Return.

The above demonstrate that the Pretribulational Rapture is a clear Biblical truth drawn from Scripture. It is the natural conclusion of the Bible's prophetic statements. It is in harmony with its different facets and harmonizes with God's program for Israel, the Church and the nations. In contrast, insurmountable problems and contradictions are inherent within the mid, pre-wrath and post-tribulational positions. The Pretribulational Rapture is the only system that allows for Jesus Christ to come for His Church TODAY!

In his 1857 book, *The Apocalypse*, Joseph Seiss closes with the following wonderful illustration.

> Fiction has painted the picture of a maiden whose love left her for a voyage to the Holy Land, promising on his return to make her his beloved bride. Many told her that she would never see him again. But she believed his word, and evening by evening she went down to the lonely shore, and kindled there a beacon-light in the sight of the roaring waves, to hail and welcome the returning ship which was to bring again her betrothed. And by that watchfire she took her stand each night, praying to the winds to hasten on the sluggish sails, that he who was everything to her might come. Even so that blessed Lord, who has loved us unto death, has gone away to the mysterious Holy Land of heaven, promising on his return to make us his happy and eternal Bride. Some say that he has gone forever, and that here we shall never see him more. But his last word was, "Yea, I come quickly." And on the dark and misty beach sloping out into the eternal sea, each true believer stands by the love-lit fire, looking, and waiting, and praying and hoping for the fulfilment of his work, in nothing gladder than in his pledge and promise, and calling ever from the soul of sacred love, "EVEN SO, COME, LORD JESUS." And some of these nights, while the world is busy with its frivolities, and laughing at the maiden on the shore, a form shall rise over the surging waves, as once on Galilee, to vindicate forever all this watching and devotion and bring to the faithful and constant heart a joy, and glory, and triumph which nevermore shall end. *Blessed are those servants, whom the Lord when he cometh shall find watching* (Lk 12:37).

CONCLUSION OF THE PHILADELPHIA LETTER

Noting again the *Contents*, we come now to the *Appeal*:

2. THE CONTENTS OF THE LETTER.
   (1) THE COMMENDATION. ***I know thy works: behold, I have set before thee an open door, and no man can shut it: for thou hast a little strength, and hast kept my word, and hast not denied my name*** (3:8).
   (2) THE PROMISE.
      [1] EVANGELIZATION AMONG THE JEWS. ***Behold, I will make them of the synagogue of Satan, which say they are Jews, and are not, but do lie; behold, I***

will make them to come and worship before thy feet, and to know that I have loved thee (3:9).

[2] DELIVERANCE FROM THE TRIBULATION. *Because thou hast kept the word of my patience, I also will keep thee from the hour of temptation, which shall come upon all the world, to try them that dwell upon the earth* (3:10).

(3) THE APPEAL. *Behold, I come quickly: hold that fast which thou hast, that no man take thy crown* (3:11). The appeal is threefold; The Encouragement: *Behold, I come quickly*. The Exhortation: *Hold that fast which thou hast*. The Warning: *That no man take thy crown*. The encouragement at the end of the letter to this watching and Second Coming church is the same as that at the end of the Book of Revelation.

• ***Behold, I come quickly***: *blessed is he that keepeth the sayings of the prophecy of this book* (Rev 22:7).

• *And,* ***behold, I come quickly****; and my reward is with me, to give every man according as his work shall be* (Rev 22:12).

• *He which testifieth these things saith,* **Surely I come quickly**. *Amen. Even so, come, Lord Jesus* (Rev 22:20).

[1] THE ENCOURAGEMENT OF THE APPEAL. The Lord's coming for them is an imminent event. It will come suddenly without announcement. The word *quickly* is to be understood as something which is sudden and perhaps unexpected. The coming of Christ to establish a kingdom on earth is a later event following the predicted time of tribulation with its series of events. By contrast, the coming of Christ for His Church is an event which is not separated from us by any series of events, but is one of constant expectation in the daily walk of the believer. J. N. Darby wrote (quoted in Walvoord):

> That which characterizes the church of Philadelphia is its immediate connection with Himself; It is Christ Himself who is coming. It is neither knowledge nor prophecy that can satisfy the heart; but the thought that Jesus is coming to take me to Himself is the blessed hope of one who is attached to Him by grace (p. 88).

[2] THE EXHORTATION OF THE APPEAL. *Hold that fast which thou hast.* Hold fast to your Bible. Hold fast to your faith. Hold fast to your prayer life. Hold fast to your service in the local church. Hold fast to the Great Commission. Hold fast to the Second Coming of Christ.

Note: two of David's *Mighty Men* held fast and stood fast.

• *And after him was* **Eleazar** *the son of Dodo the Ahohite, one of the three mighty men with David, when they defied the Philistines that were there gathered together to battle, and the men of Israel were gone away: He arose, and* **smote the Philistines until his hand was weary, and his hand clave unto the sword**: *and the LORD wrought a great victory that day; and the people returned after him only to spoil. And after him was* **Shammah** *the son of Agee the Hararite. And the Philistines were gathered together into a troop, where was a piece of ground full of lentils: and the people fled from the Philistines. But* **he stood in the midst of the ground, and defended it**, *and slew the Philistines: and the LORD wrought a great victory* (2 Sam 23:9-12).

[3] THE WARNING OF THE APPEAL: *that no man take thy crown.* Philadelphia was a sound church, but Laodicea looms! The last stage of the church age will be in-between, lowest-common-denominator, *neither cold nor hot* (3:15). Such an influence may rob a sound believer of their reward at the Judgement Seat of Christ. As a walk through

a "Christian" book store will show, much that characterized the Philadelphia Age has been almost completely lost.

- *Look to yourselves, that we lose not those things which we have wrought, but that we receive a full reward* (2 Jhn 8).

3. THE CONCLUSION OF THE LETTER.
    (1) TO THE OVERCOMER.
        [1] MADE PILLARS. **Him that overcometh will I make a pillar in the temple of my God, and he shall go no more out** (3:12). Uzziah *intruded* into the Temple (2 Chron 26:16); Jotham *refused to enter* the Temple (2 Chron 27:2); Ahaz *desecrated* the Temple (2 Chron 28:24); Hezekiah *cleansed* the Temple (2 Chron 29:3); and here, Philadelphia believers are *made pillars* in the Temple.

The possessor of *little strength* (3:8) will be made a pillar of strength and glory in the Temple of God. Here is the result of a faith that patiently waits (3:10). On earth they were content with His Word and satisfied with His Promise. They were despised by those who claimed great pomp and authority in churches but are now made pillars in the heavenly Temple of God. and with the Names of the Great king and His City written upon them.

When John saw the New Jerusalem, *he saw no temple there* (Rev 21:22), for in the presence of Christ the entire heavenly city is a Temple. In such a Temple there will be permanence as well as position. They will stand for ever in glory when all else has fallen in a world of sin. This had peculiar significance to those of Philadelphia because of their experiences with earthquakes which frequently had destroyed their buildings and left only the pillars standing. They are assured of continuance throughout eternity because of faith in Christ as the One who enables them to overcome the world.

Believers in that day (and for lack of a better word) will be made a glorious living monument. **Him that overcometh will I make a pillar in the temple of my God.** Not a pillar to support the Temple (heaven needs no support), but a monument of the free and powerful grace of God, a monument that will never be defaced, never weathered, never worn with time, never removed. It will not be like the historical pillars seen across the world and also to this day among the ancient ruins of Philadelphia,

The great pillars of Solomon's temple also come to mind. They are described as a work of wonder and awe (1 Kng 7:13-22; 2 Chron 3:15-17). Their name were *Jachin* (He shall establish), and *Boaz* (In strength): *He shall establish in strength*. This shall be truly fulfilled on high and in resurrection for Philadelphia believers who had a *little strength*.

Observe: how the figure of a building runs through the letter to the church of Philadelphia. We have a *door*, a *temple*, a *pillar*, a *key*, a *city*.

        [2] ENSHRINED WITH NAMES. Christ declares a threefold name will be inscribed upon these living pillars.

            One. THE NAME OF GOD. **And I will write upon him the name of my God**: As the OT high priest carried on *his mitre, graven like the engraving of a signet, HOLINESS TO THE LORD* (Exod 39:30) so shall the overcomer wear the name of the God whom he had devotedly served. Note that though Christ is addressing His servants, He Himself always maintains His subordinate place to His Father. Four times in this verse He speaks of **my God**. Antichrist comes in his own name, and blasphemes the true God. Christ reverently confesses His Father Name (Jhn 5:43).

Philadelphia believers stepped through an *open door* to proclaim the Great Commission. Note how **the name** of God is described in that commission.

- *Go ye therefore, and teach all nations, baptizing them in **the name** [singular] of the Father, and of the Son, and of the Holy Ghost (Matt 28:19):*

THE BOOK OF REVELATION

Two. THE NAME OF NEW JERUSALEM. **And the name of the city of my God, which is new Jerusalem, which cometh down out of heaven from my God.** A greater name than to be called a Londoner, or New Yorker! Our city is, like Christ, as yet hid with God; but it will after the Millennial Reign be brought forth to hover over the New Earth. Thus the glories of the Thousand Years will be greatly exceeded by the glories of eternity. Like Abraham we look forward to this city that has *foundations*.

- *For he looked for **a city which hath foundations**, whose builder and maker is God* (Heb 11:10).
- *And he carried me away in the spirit to a great and high mountain, and shewed me that great city, **the holy Jerusalem, descending out of heaven** from God, Having the glory of God: and her light was like unto a stone most precious, even like a jasper stone, clear as crystal* (Rev 21:10,11).
- *And the city had no need of the sun, neither of the moon, to shine in it: for the glory of God did lighten it, and the Lamb is the light thereof. And **the nations of them which are saved shall walk in the light of it**: and the kings of the earth do bring their glory and honour into it* (Rev 21:23,24).

Three. THE NEW NAME OF CHRIST. **And I will write upon him my new name** (3:12). It will be King of kings and Lord of lords, a name that Christ has not yet borne upon the earth. This great title will be added to His many other names and titles, the Mediator, the Redeemer, the Captain of our salvation; by this it will appear under whose banner this conquering believer had enlisted, under whose conduct he acted, by whose example he was encouraged, and under whose influence he fought the good fight, and came off victorious.

The three names that the pillars bear may be summed up in the name *Jehovah Shammah*, "The Lord is there" (Ezek 48:35). To write a name on a person declared the person to be the absolute property of his owner. Such is the blissful servitude of the Christian now on earth and in New Jerusalem then. *Williams*.

(2) TO THE HEARER. **He that hath an ear, let him hear what the Spirit saith unto the churches** (3:13). Yes, this appeal has been repeated for each of the churches, but never was it more important than now. As we now are in the end time, the great question will be: What kind of Church will it be! Philadelphia or Laodecia!

He that hath an ear, let him hear what the Spirit saith unto the churches. This is a call to attention. This will be the great decision. This will be the great end time divide. Will professing Christians decide for a Philadelphia or Laodecia *lowest-common-denominator* kind of church. We now know that most have chosen the latter.

CHAPTER 4

IMAGES OF THE PHILADELPHA ERA

The Scofield Reference Bible was a Characteristic of the Philadelphia Era

That which especially characterizes the Philadelphia era was a return to the study of the Prophetic Scriptures. These great prophecies were now taken literally. Believers embraced a heighted interest in the imminent Return of Christ and the restoration of the Jewish People to the Land of Israel. Foremost in encouraging this *surely I come quickly* zeal was the 1909, 1917 publication of the *Scofield Reference Bible*. "Sale of the Scofield Reference Bible grew, and by 1930 it became the first book published by Oxford University Press to attain *the one million mark* in sales."

The Reference Bible was not his first work. *Rightly Dividing the Word of Truth* was published in 1888. In 1890 came the *Scofield Correspondence Course*, which later was turned over to Moody Bible Institute in 1914. As of 1998, over **100,000 students** had been enrolled in that program." http://www.rayofhopechurch.com/scofield.htm

The *open door* given to the Philadelphia period was seen in great city wide revivals. The Moody revivals were especially noteworthy. "In a 40-year period D.L. Moody saw *a million people profess Christ,* founded three Christian schools, launched a great Christian publishing business, established a world-renowned Christian conference center, and inspired literally thousands of preachers to win souls and conduct revivals. He travelled across the American continent and through Great Britain in some of the greatest and most successful evangelistic meetings known. His tour of the world with Sankey was considered the greatest evangelistic enterprise of the century. It was Henry Varley who said, 'It remains to be seen what God will do with a man who gives himself up wholly to Him.' And Moody endeavored to be, under God, that man; and the world did marvel to see how wonderfully God used him." http://www.nowtheendbegins.com/pages/preachers/dwight-moody.htm. Born into a poor and large Massachusetts family in 1837, Moody was converted in his uncle's Boston shoe shop on April 21st 1855. He went to be with the Lord December 22, 1899.

http://www.nowtheendbegins.com/images/preachers/dwight-moody-preaching.jpg

The D. L. Moody Revivals were Characteristic of the Philadelphia Era

THE D.L. MOODY MEETINGS IN ENGLAND, SCOTLAND AND IRELAND
By J. Wilbur Chapman (Abridged)

When Mr. Moody arrived at Liverpool, June 27, 1873, he set foot upon English soil for the third time. His former trips had been brief; now he had come with a determination "to win ten thousand souls for Christ." The first word received on landing 'was disappointing. He learned that the two friends who had invited him to England had recently died. A third invitation had been given by Mr. George Bennett, Secretary of the Young Men's Christian Association in York.

YORK

Mr. Moody telegraphed to Mr. Bennett announcing his arrival and readiness to begin work, but the reply stated that there was so little religious warmth in York that it would take at least a month to get ready for the meetings. Mr. Moody, however, was not afraid of the prevalent spiritual frost. He telegraphed to his friend, "I will be in York to-night," and at 10 o'clock arrived in that city, unheralded and unknown.

The outlook was not encouraging, but Mr. Moody sent for Mr. Sankey, who had gone from Liverpool to Manchester, and the meetings began at once. Only eight persons attended the first meeting. The other meetings on this first Sunday betrayed a

CHAPTER 4

somewhat wider interest, but during the following week the congregations were very small indeed. The second week was marked by some improvement, and before the month was over the work had made a considerable impression. The number of converts at York was in the neighbourhood of two hundred. The meetings were chiefly held in chapels, the evangelist preferring not to go to public halls for fear of seeming to neglect the regularly established worship.

SUNDERLAND

After attending some of Mr. Moody's meetings at York, the Rev. Arthur Rees, of Sunderland, invited the evangelist. Here, as at York, coldness had to be dealt with, and moreover the evangelists had been heralded from the scene of their first labours by criticism rather than by praise. Still from the first large congregations attended the meetings, although there is little doubt that the early motive of attendance was curiosity. Gradually the people of Sunderland awoke. Mr. Moody had the meetings removed to the Victoria Hall with overflow meetings conducted in various chapels. At the close of the month the results were not what he had hoped for, but the city was stirred profoundly and moved to genuine revival power.

NEWCASTLE

By invitation of the Rev. David Lowe, Mr. Moody went to Newcastle-upon-Tyne, spending a few days in Jarrow on the way. At Newcastle the fire was kindled which was to mightily move Great Britain. Ministerial opposition was overcome, five of the principal chapels of the town being offered for the services. Mr. Moody accepted the use of the Rye Hill Baptist Chapel, a large edifice, and within a fortnight crowds were turned away for want of room. All the neighbouring towns and villages felt the spiritual impulse, and in response to requests hundreds of meetings were held outside the city by multiplying assistants of the evangelist.

Mr. Moody, in order to prevent the exclusion of the unconverted by the crowds of Christians began to divide his congregations into classes, giving tickets of admission to the various services. Meetings for merchants were held in the Assembly Hall; meetings for mechanics were held at the Tyne Theatre, and in each instance the size of the crowds usually necessitated three or four overflow meetings. The name and residence of every inquirer was made a matter of record, and as a result of this month's work, hundreds of converts were received into the churches, and the whole North of England was aroused. Scores of Christian workers were sent out to carry the good tidings to the remoter districts, and the stimulus to the various churches proved unprecedented. Mr. Moody and Mr. Sankey now moved toward Scotland with brief but successful meetings in a number of small cities.

EDINBURGH

Mr. Moody's meetings commenced late in November in the Free Church Assembly Hall. From the first no place in Edinburgh could contain the crowds. Three or four of the largest halls and churches were constantly in use, and even then it was necessary to come to the place of meeting an hour or two before the appointed time in order to be sure of admittance. The converts were numbered by thousands. The awakening among the nominal church members could hardly be described. As a result of the work in Edinburgh fully 3,000 persons were received into the churches.

DUNDEE

From Edinburgh Mr. Moody went to Dundee, January 21st, and for several weeks the visitations with which the Holy Spirit had blessed other cities came to this old stronghold of Scottish faith.

GLASGOW

The meetings began at Glasgow on February 8th. Three thousand Sunday-school teachers surrounded the evangelists in the City Hall at the first meeting. An hour before the time for the services such a crowd had assembled that four large churches in the neighbourhood were filled by the overflow. Mr. Moody had been in Glasgow in 1872, when he had attracted no attention; now from the start the revival work exhibited a power almost unparalleled. The Glasgow noon prayer meeting had been commenced during the week of prayer for Scotland, was held in Edinburgh a month before the evangelists went to Glasgow. This preparation was not in vain.

At first, church-going people were affected. Then the hand of God touched the great masses of the population who were without the fold. Meetings were held in the streets and squares of the city and at the Kibble Crystal Palace. The last meetings were the greatest of all. Going to the evening service the carriage of Mr. Moody was almost blocked by the dense throngs which surrounded the Crystal Palace, and seeing the multitudes, the evangelist determined to preach from the carriage, as there were more without the building than within. Those inside the palace, learning of the change of program, immediately joined the throng outside, and the service which followed was one of wonderful effect. At the close of the discourse, Mr. Moody invited inquirers to meet him at the palace, and this great audience hall was filled. Large numbers gave themselves to Christ.

THE NORTH OF SCOTLAND

About the middle of May, Mr. Moody and Mr. Sankey, after a three days' visit to Edinburgh, went northward through Scotland, stopping in Perth, Montrose, Aberdeen, Inverness, and in some other towns. To the very end of Scotland, to John o' Groat's house, the evangelists went, meeting crowds of people at every shopping place, and holding service after service, generally in the open air. At Aberdeen 12,000 to 20,000 people attended the outdoor services; at Inverness the meetings were held at the time of the annual wool fair, and many were reached.

BELFAST

Mr. Moody and Mr. Sankey had received invitations from many different quarters, and they now decided prayerfully that the greatest opportunity before them lay in Ireland. Accordingly on September 6th, held the first meeting in Belfast, at Dougal Square Chapel. The second meeting was held in a larger church, while the evening meeting was adjourned to a still larger place of worship, with seating capacity for about two thousand persons, which was only about one-quarter of those who tried to gain admission. It became necessary here, as in Scotland, to divide the audiences, so that men's meetings, women's meetings etc., etc., were held. There were several great open air meetings. On the 15th at the final inquiry meeting at 2,150 converts' tickets were given before the close of the evening service.

DUBLIN

The difficulty of finding a place large enough for the meetings had led Mr. Moody to ask the brethren at Dublin, as a condition of his coming, the engagement of the Exhibition Palace. This condition was met, the Palace was engaged, and on October

CHAPTER 4

24th, Mr. Moody and Mr. Sankey arrived in the Irish capital.

There were in Dublin only about 40,000 Protestants, out of a population of 250,000, but the denominational line was frequently crossed by the work of the evangelists. Indeed, so deep was the encroachment of the revival upon the Roman Catholic population, that Cardinal Cullen felt himself called upon to interdict [forbid] the attendance of his flock upon the Protestant meetings. In spite of this, many Roman Catholics were converted.

Dublin was merely the centre of the revival interest. All over Ireland the effect was so powerful that the mere announcement in a village that some man who had been to the Dublin services would tell what he had seen there, was sufficient to draw a great crowd. The meetings closed on November 29th, after a conference of three days, which was attended by about 800 ministers. In Ireland, as in Scotland, the spirit which they had aroused continued to manifest itself in many increasing results. When their labours ended, Mr. Moody and Mr. Sankey went once more to England.

MANCHESTER

The first meetings of the new campaign in England, were held at Manchester. Within a week it was said, "Manchester is now on fire." The services here were not marked so much by that joyful spirit which had characterised the evangelism of Scotland and Ireland, as by a solemn earnestness, and the influence of the meetings proper was extended in a great many practical ways throughout the city and its environs.

SHEFFIELD

Meetings were held in Sheffield, beginning on the night of December 31, 1874. It was not easy to arouse the unimpressible metal workers of Sheffield, and at first considerable disappointment was felt in the results of the services, but it was not long before the power of the evangelists' message became manifest.

BIRMINGHAM

Leaving Sheffield thoroughly awakened, Mr. Moody and Mr. Sankey went to Birmingham where their meetings began on January 17th, in the Town Hall with its seating capacity for 5,000 persons. In the evening the services were held in Bingley Hall, a great enclosed area which was customarily engaged for the annual cattle show. In spite of its accommodations for 12,000 persons, the building was thronged every evening, an hour before the time of service. The conference with which the Birmingham meetings closed was attended by ministers from all parts of Britain. After the departure the work of grace continued just as it had in every city they had visited.

LIVERPOOL

Mr. Moody came to Liverpool as an old friend. As the city contained no hall large enough, an immense temporary structure, called the Victoria Hall, had been erected. It held about 10,000 persons, and the expense of building it was met by voluntary contributions, no direct solicitation being made. At the first meeting two-thirds of the congregation were young men. The noon prayer meeting was sometimes attended by 5,000 or 6,000 persons. Eighteen services were held each week in the Victoria Hall, and the Gospel was also carried into the streets and byways as well as in the open. During the month, the number of persons converted, or awakened, ran into the thousands. The inquiry rooms were invariably crowded.

LONDON

"If I come to London," Mr. Moody had said, "you will need to raise £5,000 for expenses of halls, advertising, etc." "We have £10,000 already," was the reply. This shows the spirit in which the efforts of Mr. Moody and Mr. Sankey in the Metropolis of the world were anticipated. The work of preparation had been carried on by able committees. Preliminary daily prayer meetings were crowded.

It was decided to attack the city in the four quarters. The meetings began in the north and were held in the great Agricultural Hall. The congregations in this immense structure averaged during the first week about 18,000 persons, the inquiry meetings were held in St. Mary's Hall, but so great was the curious crowd, which blocked the adjacent streets, that it was found advisable to remove these meetings to one of the galleries of the Agricultural Hall itself. The services were managed by a committee, with the assistance of seventy or eighty ushers. Interest increased weekly. Sometimes 400 or 500 persons at one time would be conversing in the inquirers galleries about the salvation of their souls.

The campaign in the East End, which began five weeks after the meetings in the North End, centred in Bow Road Hall, built especially for the services, and designed to hold an audience of 10,000 persons. Overflow meetings were held in a large tent near the building.

In the West End the services were held in the Royal Opera House, where many thousands thronged the three or four different meetings which were held each day. For several weeks Mr. Moody divided his attention between the Opera House and the Bow Road Hall.

In conducting the meetings in South London, a new hall, erected for them near Camberwell Green, was occupied by the evangelists. This structure seated about 8,000 persons. Here the chief interest centred in the inquiry room, where the spirit was as earnest and as deep as it had been in the other quarters of the city. When Mr. Moody and Mr. Sankey discontinued services in one of the four quarters of the city, the meetings were continued by others, and the fire which God had permitted the two evangelists to kindle was not suffered to die out. The final service was held July 12th, the evangelists having conducted 285 meetings in London, and having addressed fully 2,500,000 persons.

The last meeting in England was held in Liverpool, and on October 6th, attended by many loving prayers, Mr. Moody and Mr. Sankey set sail toward the West, arriving in New York eight days later.   http://biblebelievers.com/moody/index.html

STRONG PREMILLENNIAL BIBLE INSTITUTES CHARACTERIZED THE PHILADELPHIA ERA

Following upon the D. L. Moody's evangelistic work in Chicago, what became known as Moody Bible Institute was formed in 1886. Its second president was the greatly used evangelist R. A. Torrey. Torrey was later invited to become the first president of The Bible Institute of Los Angeles in 1912. On the east coast of America and arising out of their large Bible conferences, C. I. Scofield and William Pettingill established the Philadelphia School of the Bible in 1914.

CHAPTER 4

The Bible Institute of Los Angeles

During the first half of the 20th Century these three schools played an enormous role in shaping sound premillennial faith in America and other parts of the world. They spawned and became a pattern for many other Bible institutes. They stirred multitudes toward evangelism, world missions, church planting, literature outreach, Sunday school work, Jewish evangelism and rescue mission work. While not perfect; given their separation from worldliness, discernment of error, sound music, emphasis upon Romans 6 rather than psychology, their understanding of the national future of Israel, their burden to reach the lost (rather than today's overemphasis on "activities") – these schools were about as good as anything the world has seen. Note also: Their text book was the 1917 *Scofield Reference Bible*!

On most of the these points if one were to sit in the classrooms of the *same* schools today, they would *not be the same schools*. They bear faint resemblance to what was envisaged by their founders. They have travelled the road from Philadelphia to Laodicea.

THE TROJAN HORSE: A WARNING NOT HEEDED IN THE PHILADELPHIA ERA

The "Philadelphia" Era was characterised by what we have seen above. Churches and groups that could claim something of that name **kept my word, and hast not denied by name** (Rev 3:8). They stood against the rising tide of theological rationalism. They stood against Catholicism. They were sound in doctrine. But, while they stood against Darwinism and the rise of evolution, many key leaders and schools (those above) weakened by accepting the

THE BOOK OF REVELATION

"gap theory" in Genesis 1:1-3. But more subtlely, they did not recognise the catastrophic mistake of accepting a revised Greek New Testament published in 1881 that was based on two supposedly 350 AD manuscripts.

From 1611 until our generation there was only one widely used Bible in the English-speaking world. The AV became the Standard in that empire upon which the sun never set, and in that language which is the primary vehicle of international discourse. It penetrated the world's continents and brought multitudes to saving faith in Christ. It became the impetus of the great missionary movements. Through it, Christian workers heard and answered the call to world evangelisation. It was the source of the greatest revivals since the days of the Apostles. Street preachers, colporteurs, church planters, Sunday school teachers, and tract distributors took the King James Bible into teeming cities and across country lanes. It was the high water mark in the history of the Gospel's spread. But all was to change with the "discovery" of two "very old" manuscripts (Sinaiticus and Vaticanus) of which no copies are known to exist; the labours of two Cambridge professors (Brooks Westcott, Fenton Hort) and the editorial work of Eberhard Nestle followed later by Kurt Aland.

CHAPTER 4

In an unbelievably short time the professing Christian World (conservative and liberal) accepted the Westcott and Hort New Testament (**2900 fewer words**). Theological seminaries where unbelief and rationalism had taken root were only too glad to have this new bible. Sadly it was also embraced by the sound Bible Institutes. While the King James Version continued to be widely used, virtually all future translation work (English and foreign), and all study of the Greek New Testament in Bible colleges would be based upon the text of Westcott, Hort and Nestle.

John Burgon

Few took the time to see if there were significant differences. Few voices were raised in opposition. It was a *juggernaut* that swept Europe and soon crossed to America. One voice that was raised was that of the Oxford trained scholar and Dean of Chichester Cathedral, John Willian Burgon (died 1888). He argued and wrote powerfully on behalf of the Greek Text that underlies the King James Version. His three major books demonstrated the fundamental and fatal error of the text that resulted from combining Vaticanus and Sinaiticus.

- *The Revision Revised.*
- *The Last Twelve Verses of Mark Books*
- *The Causes of Corruption of the Traditional Text of the Holy Gospels*

These have long been published by and are available from The Dean Burgon Society. DBS@DeanBurgonSociety.org

FACTS THAT WERE IGNORED IN THE RUSH TO THE VATICANUS, SINAITICUS TEXT: STRIKING DIFFERENCES FROM THE RECEIVED TEXT OF THE KJV

- 8000 changes.
- 2900 fewer words, with many key doctrinal statements missing.
- 200 fewer times Names of Christ are mentioned.
- Many doctrinal passages removed or weakened.
- 86 times the Name *Jesus* is removed from association with another Name or work of Deity. This supports an ancient heresy called "adoptionism" that said Jesus was not God but was "adopted" for a while (until His death) into the Godhead.
- Vaticanus and Sinaiticus frequently disagree. They have no known copies. Why did the early church not make copies?
- There is huge variation in the forty or so manuscripts that give partial support to Vaticanus and Sinaiticus. The KJV/Received Text is based on 5500 manuscripts which are overwhelmingly cohesive.
- Vaticanus and Sinaiticus have no *provenance* (historical links demonstrating their source and supposed 350 AD date). They "suddenly became available" in the first half of the 1800s when moves were afoot for a revised Bible.
- Sinaiticus may not be a *real* manuscript (with questions also for Vaticanus). See *The Forging of Codex Sinaiticus* by Bill Cooper, and the online documentation by Chris Pinto and David Daniels. See also for the above points, *Missing in Modern Bibles* and *Early Manuscripts, Church Fathers and the AV* by J. A. Moorman.

Thankfully a significant number today understand the basics of the problem with the Modern Bibles, but amidst so much that was good in the Philadelphia Era it was a *Trojan Horse* that few recognized.

One further note: The Philadelphia Era *kept my word* (3:8). In the English speaking world and in spite of the above they continued to use the KJV, and what made the era especially remarkable was the extent that so many pastors, missionaries, evangelists and Christian workers memorized substantial portions of Scripture – and that virtually *always* from the King James Version. It soon became a fact that once they went to a modern versions, ongoing Bible memory work *stopped* ! The AV is more direct and powerful.

After the close of my 2011 debate with James White on the KJV / Modern Bible issue, he was asked by my wife Dot as to which Bible he had memorized from; his answer: *The King James Version*!

G. LAODICEA: Last Days Church – Big, wealthy, worldly, blind to Biblical truth. Its lifestyle, music etc., mixed in with that of the world 3:14-22

(3:14) *And unto the angel of the church of the Laodiceans write; These things saith the Amen, the faithful and true witness, the beginning of the creation of God;*

(3:15) *I know thy works, that thou art neither cold nor hot: I would thou wert cold or hot.* (3:16) *So then because thou art lukewarm, and neither cold nor hot, I will spue thee out of my mouth.* (3:17) *Because thou sayest, I am rich, and increased with goods, and have need of nothing; and knowest not that thou art wretched, and miserable, and poor, and blind, and naked:*

(3:18) *I counsel thee to buy of me gold tried in the fire, that thou mayest be rich; and white raiment, that thou mayest be clothed, and that the shame of thy nakedness do not appear; and anoint thine eyes with eyesalve, that thou mayest see.* (3:19) *As many as I love, I rebuke and chasten: be zealous therefore, and repent.* (3:20) *Behold, I stand at the door, and knock: if any man hear my voice, and open the door, I will come in to him, and will sup with him, and he with me.*

CHAPTER 4

(3:21) *To him that overcometh will I grant to sit with me in my throne, even as I also overcame, and am set down with my Father in his throne.* (3:22) *He that hath an ear, let him hear what the Spirit saith unto the churches.*

1. THE INSCRIPTION OF THE LETTER

(1) TO WHOM THE LETTER WAS SENT. *And unto the angel of the church of the Laodiceans write* (3:14). We now come to the last and worst of all the seven churches, the reverse of the church of Philadelphia; for as there was nothing reproved in that church, there is nothing commended in this last church and last stage of Church History, and yet this was one of *the seven golden candlesticks,* for a corrupt church may still be a church and as an era may still have a faith remnant here and there

This once famous city near the river Lycus, had a wall of vast compass and three marble theatres, and like Rome was built on seven hills. It was founded by Antiochus II in the middle of the third century before Christ and named after his wife Laodice was situated about forty miles southeast of Philadelphia on the road to Colossae. Under Roman rule Laodicea had become wealthy and had a profitable business arising from the production of wool cloth.

The Ruins of Laodecia

When destroyed by an earthquake about 60 AD, it was able to rebuild without any outside help. Its economic sufficiency tended to lull the church to sleep spiritually; and though there is mention of the church as late as the fourteenth century, the city as well as the church now is in complete ruins.

It is not known if Paul visited the church in Laodicea, but it is evident that he knew some of the Christians there from his reference in Colossians 2:1 where he speaks of his *great conflict* for the Christians both at Colossae and at Laodicea and for others whom he had not seen. Salutations are also sent to the church at Laodicea (Col 4:15). *Walvoord*.

(2) FROM WHOM THE LETTER WAS SENT. *These things saith the Amen, the faithful and true witness, the beginning of the creation of God* (3:14). The titles by which our Lord introduces Himself to this Laodicea are not those found in the vision of Him in Chapter 1. This is to warn us that He was retreating further and further from his original position and purpose for the church. As we come to the last stage of Church History we see a fallen church and something unlike its original standing.

[1] HERE IS THE UTTER FINALITY OF THE ONE DEALING WITH LAODICEA. He is the *Amen*. He is the One that is steady and unchangeable in all his

purposes and promises, *For all the promises of God in him are yea, and in him Amen* (2 Cor 1:20). The frequent use of *Amen*, meaning "so be it," is usually translated "verily," or used as an ending to a prayer. When Christ speaks, it is the final word, and His will is always effected. As *Amen* concludes a prayer, there is a finality in this Title that reflects the final stage of church before His Coming. This is His final dealing with that which calls itself a "church" and before the judgements begin to rain down upon the earth.

[2] <u>HERE IS THE UTTER VERACITY OF THE ONE DEALING WITH LAODICEA</u>. He is ***the faithful and true witness.*** He has seen all and will be swift to act in justice and righteousness against all that He has seen. And in our day it is now shortly to be done. Many, I am afraid in the Laodecian Church will find on the Sunday after the Rapture, most of the same faces in the services as on the week before. This may well represent the largely unrepentant, unconverted, Tribulation church of these last days.

* *For the time is come that judgment must begin at the house of God: and if it first begin at us, what shall the end be of them that obey not the gospel of God* (1 Pet 4:17)?

Notice that Christ is *the faithful and true witness*. It is one thing to be true and to know the truth, it is another to be *faithful* to *witness* to the truth. Christ is both.

[3] <u>HERE IS THE UTTER CONSUMMATION OF THE ONE DEALING WITH LAODICEA</u>. He is ***the beginning of the creation of God.*** He knows man from the beginning, for Christ is not only the Creator of man but He is the pattern after which man was created. Christ was always God. His *goings forth are from everlasting* (Micah 5:2). He is the Eternal Son of God. There is no beginning for His Deity or Sonship. But, in past eternity when it was decreed that man would be created, Christ took upon Himself *creature form* as the prototype after which Adam would be created. This taking of creature form was the *beginning of the creation of God*. Thus long before His Incarnation at Bethlehem we see Him in the Old Testament as the Angel of the Lord. He is described in Colossians as the *firstborn of every creature*.

* *For it came to pass, when the flame went up toward heaven from off the altar, that **the angel of the LORD ascended in the flame of the altar**. And Manoah and his wife looked on it, and fell on their faces to the ground. But the angel of the LORD did no more appear to Manoah and to his wife. Then Manoah knew that he was an angel of the LORD. And Manoah said unto his wife, We shall surely die, because <u>we have seen God</u>* (Judges 13:20-22).
* *Who is **the image of the invisible God, <u>the firstborn of every creature</u>: For by him were all things created**, that are in heaven, and that are in earth, visible and invisible, whether they be thrones, or dominions, or principalities, or powers: **all things were created by him, and for him: And he is before all things, and by him all things consist**. And he is the head of the body, the church: who is the beginning, the firstborn from the dead; that in all things he might have the pre-eminence* (Col 1:15-18).

It is also true that as to His works, all things that the Father begins, He begins in His Son. Christ is therefore the Author of Creation, He is also the Author of regeneration. As to the miserable state of the church at Laodicea, He is able to save and re-create any of *the poor and wretched and blind and naked* (3:17) that hear His voice. For their poverty He has *gold*, for their blindness *eye salve*, for their nakedness *white raiment. Williams.*

* *And he said unto me, It is done. I am Alpha and Omega, the beginning and the end. I will give unto him that is athirst of the fountain of the water of life freely* (Rev 21:6).

CHAPTER 4

2. THE CONTENTS OF THE LETTER.
   (1) THE REBUKE.
      [1] THE WEIGHTY CHARGE. *I know thy works, that thou art neither cold nor hot: I would thou wert cold or hot* (3:15). Christ addresses His message to Laodicea without a word of commendation and with the most scathing rebuke to be found in any of the seven letters. Lukewarmness or indifference by a professing Christian to Christ and the Bible is a very bad thing. If Christ and the Bible are real then they are most excellent, and to them we should be totally devoted. If one thinks Christ and the Bible are not real, then as wrong as a man may be, at least they have come out and said so. But, this refusing-to-take-a-stand, this *in between* attitude is sickening. If the faith is worth anything, it is worth everything! Indifference is inexcusable. There is no room for neutrality. Christ expects that men should declare themselves in earnest either for Him or against Him.

- *And Elijah came unto all the people, and said,* **How long halt ye between two opinions?** *if the LORD be God, follow him: but if Baal, then follow him. And the people answered him not a word* (1 King 18:21).

The indifference implied by the term *lukewarm* (only here) likely extended to conviction respecting the central doctrines of the Christian faith - repentance of sin and worldliness, the necessity of the new birth, faith in the shed blood of Christ, the great doctrines of the Atonement, a literal Hell, a sanctified life, Christ's Priesthood, His imminent Return, the full verbal inspiration of Scripture.

We ended our study of the Sixth Church Letter with the *Images that Characterized the Philadelphia Era*. We will do the same for the Laodicea Era, but will do so at the beginning rather than the end of the letter. We do not want to be distracted from the Lord's final word to this final church. Many images would come to mind: the growth of the ecumenical movement, World Council of Churches and inter- faith worship; the flashy Tele-evangelists with their opulent life styles and prosperity gospel; the mega-churches with their worldly music and "positive, non-judgemental" message; the spiritual demise of once sound Bible Colleges; dressing up for work and dressing down for church; the lack of personal holiness; a minimal, if at all, obedience to the Great Commission; the proliferation of Bible translations with an attendant fall in personal Bible study and almost complete neglect of Scripture memorization.

It does not take a great deal of discernment to see the "problem" with much of the above. They all represent Laodicea, and are all the fruit of the era but are by themselves not a primary cause. Careful students of Church History, from a Biblical perspective, know that there was something else that did much to "kick-start" this final era. It comes as a shock to many.

AN OVERRIDING CATALYST IN THE LAODECIAN ERA

There was fundamentalism and rationalism during the Philadelphia period, and it was usually one or the other. If a church or school began to depart from the faith, it frequently did not remain in limbo but descended into full blown apostasy. In the middle of the 20th Century the **neither cold nor hot neither cold nor hot** stage became a fixed position. It was not clear Biblical belief, but nor did it descend into total heresy and apostasy. It became known as **new evangelicalism**. The man most associated with its rise and who became known as the "founder of new evangelicalism" was Harold J. Ockenga of Park Street Congregational Church in Boston. Two schools in America generally associated with its beginnings in America were Fuller Theological Seminary in California (founded by Ockenga) and Wheaton College outside of Chicago.

One of major vehicle (likely *the* major vehicle) which aided the spread of new evangelicalism were the Billy Graham campaigns. These began soundly and indeed nothing like them had been seen since the D. L. Moody and Billy Sunday meetings. However as time went on it became clear that there were fundamental differences. They sought and embraced the support of liberal Protestant churches and schools and eventually also Roman Catholicism. Whatever *unequal yoke* issues arose in the Moody meetings this became endemic in the Graham campaigns. A key turning point was his 1957 New York City campaign. Billy Graham undertook this on condition that he received the support of the Protestant Council of New York, an organization that was rife with theological liberalism. The preaching in the meetings was sound and fervent and the music equally stirring. There were many salvation decisions (I have had personal friends converted in this campaign), but now the converts were sent to *both* conservative and the liberal churches that supported the meetings. This set the precedent that was to follow in *all* of his meetings. With time the message and the music was also modified.

Harold Ockenga and Billy Graham

Another major difference were the sound premillennial churches, Bible institutes and mission organizations that sprang out of the Moody meetings. This did not happen with Billy Graham. That which resulted and *was encouraged* took the lower common denominator approach. David Cloud in *New Evangelicalism: Its History, Characteristic and Fruit* writes:

> By the mid-1950s, a clear break between separatist fundamentalists and non-separatist evangelicals occurred. This was occasioned largely by the ecumenical evangelism of Billy Graham. The terms evangelicalism and fundamentalism began "to refer to two different movements" (William Martin, A Prophet with Honor, p. 224). The sons of evangelical-fundamentalist preachers determined to create a "New Evangelicalism." They would not be fighters; they would be diplomats, positive rather than militant, infiltrators rather than separatists. They would not be restricted by a separationist mentality.
>
> Harold Ockenga claimed to have coined the term "new evangelical" in 1948. Ockenga was pastor of Park Street Church in Boston, founder of the National Association of Evangelicals, co-founder and first president of Fuller Seminary, first president of the World Evangelical Fellowship, president of Gordon College and

CHAPTER 4

Gordon-Conwell Theological Seminary, a director of the Billy Graham Evangelistic Association, and chairman of the board and one-time editor of Christianity Today.

Following is how Ockenga defined New Evangelicalism in 1976 when he wrote the foreword to Harold Lindsell's *The Battle for the Bible*:

"Neo-evangelicalism was born in 1948 in connection with a convocation address which I gave in the Civic Auditorium in Pasadena. While reaffirming the theological view of fundamentalism, this address REPUDIATED ITS ECCLESIOLOGY AND ITS SOCIAL THEORY. The ringing call for A REPUDIATION OF SEPARATISM AND THE SUMMONS TO SOCIAL INVOLVEMENT received a hearty response from many evangelicals. We had no intention of launching a movement, but found that the emphasis attracted widespread support and exercised great influence. Neo-evangelicalism... DIFFERENT FROM FUNDAMENTALISM IN ITS REPUDIATION OF SEPARATISM AND ITS DETERMINATION TO ENGAGE ITSELF IN THE THEOLOGICAL DIALOGUE OF THE DAY. IT HAD A NEW EMPHASIS UPON THE APPLICATION OF THE GOSPEL TO THE SOCIOLOGICAL, POLITICAL, AND ECONOMIC AREAS OF LIFE. Neo-evangelicals emphasized the restatement of Christian theology in accordance with the need of the times,,,, THE RE-EXAMINATION OF THEOLOGICAL PROBLEMS SUCH AS THE ANTIQUITY OF MAN, THE UNIVERSALITY OF THE FLOOD, GOD'S METHOD OF CREATION, AND OTHERS" (Harold J. Ockenga, foreword to Harold Lindsell's book The Battle for the Bible. Emphasis by Cloud).

Regardless of who coined the term "New Evangelical" it is certain that it aptly described the new mood of positivism and non-militancy that was permeating that generation. Ockenga and the new generation of evangelicals, Billy Graham figuring most prominently, determined to abandon a militant Bible stance. Instead, they would pursue dialogue, intellectualism, and appeasement. They determined to stay within apostate denominations to attempt to change things from within rather than practice Biblical separation. *David Cloud.*

http://www.lacoliseum.com/wp-content/uploads/2013/07/history_billygraham_enlarged.jpg

<u>135,000 at the 1963 Billy Graham Crusade in Los Angeles</u>

THE POPULAR VIEW OF
THE BILLY GRAHAM CRUSADES (Wikipedia)

"Never in History had such vast throngs attended Gospel meetings. Beginning in 1947 Billy Graham conducted over 400 large crusades in 118 countries and on 6 continents. "According to his staff, more than **3.2 million people** have 'responded to the invitation at Crusades to accept Jesus Christ as their personal savior'. As of 2008, Graham's estimated lifetime audience, including radio and television broadcasts, topped **2.2 billion**. Because of his crusades, he has preached the gospel to more people in person than anyone in the history of Christianity. Billy Graham has repeatedly been on Gallup's list of most admired men and women. He has appeared on the list 60 times since 1955, more than any other individual in the world. Billy Graham was a spiritual adviser to American presidents; he was particularly close to Dwight D. Eisenhower, Lyndon B. Johnson (one of Graham's closest friends) and Richard Nixon.

The friendship between Graham and John Stott of London led to a further partnership in the Lausanne Movement, of which Graham was founder. It built on Graham's 1966 World Congress on Evangelism in Berlin. Graham convened what *TIME* magazine described as 'a formidable forum, possibly the widest–ranging meeting of Christians ever held 'with 2,700 participants from 150 nations gathering for the International Congress on World Evangelization. This took place in Lausanne, Switzerland (July 16–25, 1974), and the movement which ensued took its name from the host city. Its purpose was to strengthen the global church for world evangelization, and to engage ideological and sociological trends which bore on this. Graham invited Stott to be chief architect of the Lausanne Covenant, which issued from the Congress and which, according to Graham, "helped challenge and unite evangelical Christians in the great task of world evangelization. The movement remains a significant fruit of Graham's legacy, with a presence in nearly every nation".
https://en.wikipedia.org/wiki/Billy_Graham

THE OTHER VIEW: COMPLIANCE WITH
LIBERAL PROTESTANTISM AND CATHOLICISM

"Charles Haddon Spurgeon was not content to preach boldly against error, he also separated from it. Though misunderstood and misrepresented even by his own brother and some of his former students, Spurgeon did not draw back from separating from the Baptist Union of Britain because of the false doctrine that was being countenanced.

The Bible does not instruct believers to dialogue with false teachers and apostates, but rather to separate from them (Rom 16:17,18; 2 Tim 2:16-18; 3:5; Titus 3:10,11). It is not dialogue that we see in the New Testament, but preaching. The Bible does not instruct believers to dialogue with false teachers but to preach the truth to them and to rebuke their errors (2 Tim 4:1,2).

Billy Graham has worked hand-in-hand with Roman Catholics and theological modernists since the 1950s, His 1957 New York City Crusade was sponsored by the liberal Protestant Council and featured prominent theological modernists. At a preparatory banquet held the previous fall (September 17, 1956) at the Hotel Commodore in New York, Graham stated that he wanted Jews, Catholics, and Protestants to attend his meetings and then go back to their own churches. This statement was confirmed in the Sept. 18 edition of the New York Evening Journal. The New York Crusade was the catalyst for Graham's break with fundamentalists such as Bob Jones, Sr. and John R. Rice of the Sword of the Lord" (*David Cloud*).

On these points and in contrast with the great evangelistic campaigns that preceded

CHAPTER 4

him, Billy Graham took the opposite position. He *did not* warn against the apostasy that was spreading through the mainline denominations. He *did not* separate from key figures and institutions promoting the cancerous error. He *did* systematically engage the perpetrators of the apostasy in supporting his crusades. He *did* make seriously heretical statements.

Note his *unbelievable statement* in an interview with the arch-heretic Robert Schuller, then pastor of the Crystal Cathedral.

> He was a lifelong friend with Robert H. Schuller, whom Graham talked into doing his own television ministry….In a 1997 interview with Schuller, Graham said:
> "I think that everybody that loves or knows Christ, whether they are conscious of it or not, they are members of the body of Christ... [God] is calling people out of the world for his name, whether they come from the Muslim world, or the Buddhist world or the non-believing world, they are members of the Body of Christ because they have been called by God. They may not know the name of Jesus but they know in their hearts that they need something they do not have, and they turn to the only light they have, and I think that they are saved and they are going to be with us in heaven." https://en.wikipedia.org/wiki/Billy_Graham

When Billy Graham first began his ecumenical ventures, he claimed that he wanted to use ecumenism to get the gospel to more people, that the liberals and Roman Catholics needed the Gospel. After a few decades, he had changed entirely and was saying that the liberals and Roman Catholics are fine like they are. In a May 30, 1997, interview with David Frost, Graham said: "I feel I belong to all the churches. I'M EQUALLY AT HOME IN AN ANGLICAN OR BAPTIST OR A BRETHREN ASSEMBLY OR A ROMAN CATHOLIC CHURCH. ... And the bishops and archbishops and the Pope are our friends" (David Frost, *Billy Graham in Conversation*, pp. 68, 143; sourced from David Cloud).

Billy Graham with Pope John Paul II

• Of Pope John Paul II, Graham said: "I think the American people are looking for a leader, a moral and spiritual leader that believes something. And the Pope does.… Thank God, I've got somebody to quote now with some real authority." Phil Donahue Show October 11, 1979.

• Of His Esteem For The Vatican: "When I was at the Vatican I spoke at a vesper service at the North American College, which is a seminary for students from North America. I understand I was the first Protestant to speak there. It was a very inspirational and Christocentric service, with much contemporary music." Christianity Today 1981

• Of His Identification with Catholicism: "I find myself closer to Catholics than the radical Protestants. I think the Roman Catholic Church today is going through a second Reformation." *Philadelphia Evening Bulletin* 24 May, 1966

http://harpazo.proboards.com/thread/39660/billy-grahams-slide-laodicean-apostasy?page=1

A FLEETING LOOK AT WHAT IT ONCE WAS BEFORE THE BILLY GRAHAM CRUSADES DESCENDED INTO LAODECIA

The *Church Times* reported:

> "Britain's biggest religious meeting of all time" screamed the *News of the World* in Gothic type on its front page. "Billy Graham - Amazing Finale" echoed *The People*, adding: "Drama at Wembley: 10,000 converts surge forward in the rain."
> And they were right. The previous evening, Wembley Stadium was filled to overflowing with 120,000 people, some of them spilling out on to the grass. Indeed, so great was the number who wanted to be there that an extra afternoon rally was arranged at White City, attracting a further 65,000 - me among them.
> The two meetings were the culmination of the 12-week Greater London Crusade, during which, every night, thousands filled the 11,400-seat Harringay Arena, in north London, to hear the American evangelist.
> When all the numbers were counted, it was estimated that attendances exceeded 1.5 million and 38,000 people - nearly two-thirds of them under 18 - responded to the invitation to come forward at the close of the message.
> https://www.churchtimes.co.uk/articles/2014/23-may/news/uk/sixty-years-on-billy-graham-s-london-crusade

Here then, is one classic image of the Laodicea age. It is a strange, contradictory, confusing mixture, *neither hot nor cold*. It is exactly as the Bible said it would be.

The 1954 London Crusade: *If Only It Had Stayed That Way*!

CHAPTER 4

RETURN TO THE LAODICEA LETTER

1. THE INSCRIPTION OF THE LETTER
    (1) TO WHOM THE LETTER WAS SENT. *And unto the angel of the church of the Laodiceans write* (3:14).
    (2) FROM WHOM THE LETTER WAS SENT. *These things saith the Amen, the faithful and true witness, the beginning of the creation of God.*
        [1] HERE IS THE UTTER FINALITY OF THE ONE DEALING WITH LAODICEA. He is *the Amen*.
        [2] HERE IS THE UTTER VERACITY OF THE ONE DEALING WITH LAODICEA. He is *the faithful and true witness.*
        [3] HERE IS THE UTTER CONSUMMATION OF THE ONE DEALING WITH LAODICEA. He is *the beginning of the creation of God.*

2. THE CONTENTS OF THE LETTER.
    (1) THE REBUKE.
        [1] THE WEIGHTY CHARGE. *I know thy works, that thou art neither cold nor hot: I would thou wert cold or hot* (3:15). Our Lord Jesus Christ is disgusted. Here is neutrality, and no doubt under the banner of love and unity. Here is lowest common denominator kind of belief. Here is the least we can believe and still call ourselves Christians. There is no *fighting a good fight* (1 Tim 6:12), or *keeping My Word* (Rev 3:8). Here is no *light to the world* (Matt 5:16), or *salt* to counter corruption (Matt 5:13). Here is no gallant warrior bearing *the sword of the Spirit* (Eph 6:17). The last days of the church generally will be something half-hearted, soft, spongy. The end time church says, "O yes we will believe and serve, but it will be on our terms."
        [2] THE IMPENDING JUDGEMENT. *So then because thou art lukewarm, and neither cold nor hot, I will spue thee out of my mouth* (3:16). At the Rapture rather than being *caught up* (1 Thess 4:16,17) many and probably most will be *spued out*. The first Sunday after the Rapture, while a few will be missing, most of the same faces will be in the services; certainly enough to conduct the services as normal. Being lukewarm is a condition utterly intolerable to God!
        [3] THE MISGUIDED ASSESSMENT. What a difference there was between the thoughts they had of themselves and the thoughts that Christ had of them.
        First. THEIR HIGH THOUGHTS OF THEMSELVES. *Because thou sayest, I am rich, and increased with goods, and have need of nothing* (3:17). They were rich, and growing richer, and increased to such a degree as to be above all want. They were well provided for as to their bodies, and this made them overlook the need of their souls. They thought their wealth was a sign of wisdom. They were wise, but it was *worldly* wise.
        Second. CHRIST'S LOW THOUGHTS OF THEM. *And knowest not that thou art wretched, and miserable, and poor, and blind, and naked.* They were mistaken in their thoughts; Christ was not mistaken. They knew; Christ knew better.

        They were *poor*, really poor. When they said they were rich; they had no provision for their souls to live upon. Their souls were starving in the midst of abundance. They were hugely in debt to the justice of God, and had nothing to pay off the balance of that debt.

        They were *blind*, really blind. They could not see their state, nor their way, nor their danger; yet they thought they saw. The very light that was in them was darkness, and *how great was that darkness* (Matt 6:23)! They could not see the kind of road they were walking on; that it was *broad and led to destruction* (Matt 7:13). They could not see Christ by faith though He is *the light that lighteneth every man that cometh into the world*

(Jhn 1:9). They could not see death, though it was staring them in the face. They could not look into eternity, though they stood upon the very brink of it.

They were **naked**, really naked. They without clothing and without a house and harbor for their souls. They did not have *the garment of salvation and the robe of righteousness* (Isa 61:10). Their outward show of religion was but *filthy rags* (Isa 64:6). They were without house and harbor Christ is the *dwelling-place* of His people (Psa 49:11). In Christ alone the soul of man can find rest and shelter.

The riches of the body will not enrich the soul; the sight of the body will not enlighten the soul; the most fashionable house will not give rest or safety to the soul. The soul is a different thing than the body. In the midst of great physical wealth they had spiritual poverty, and were **wretched, and miserable, and poor, and blind, and naked.** This is the prophecy and the picture of the church of the last days.

LAODECIA IS WEALTHY BUT POOR: 38 RICH PREACHERS

http://myfirstclasslife.com/top-10-ludicrously-wealthy-pastors/?singlepage=1

#1 – Edir Macedo, Brazil ($1.1 Billion)
#2 – Pat Robertson ($500 Million)
#3 – George Foreman ($250 Million)
#4 – David Oyedepo, Nigeria ($150 Million)
#5 – Enoch Adeboye, Nigeria ($55 Million)
#6 – Chris Oyakhilome, Nigeria ($50 Million)
#7 – Jan Crouch ($50 Million)
#8 – Robert Tilton ($50 Million)
#9 – Benny Hinn ($42 Million)
#10 – Joel Osteen ($40 Million)
#11 – John Danforth ($30 Million)
#12 – Creflo Dollar ($27 Million)
#13 – Kenneth Copeland ($26.5 Million)
#14 – Billy Graham ($25 Million)
#15 – Rick Warren ($25 Million)
#16 – Kirk Cameron ($20 Million)
#17 – T.D. Jakes ($18 Million)
#18 – T.B. Joshua, Nigeria ($15 Million)
#19 – Cindy Trimm ($15 Million)
#20 – Ernest Angley ($15 Million)
#21 – Ed Young ($11 Million)
#22 – Juanita Bynum ($10 Million)
#23 – Matthew Ashimolowo, Britain ($10 Million)
#24 – Jesse Jackson ($10 Million)
#25 – Joyce Meyer ($10 Million)
#26 – Peter Popoff ($10 Million)
#27 – Ravi Zacharias ($7.5 Million)
#28 – Chris Okotie, Nigeria ($7.5 Million)
#29 – Noel Jones ($5 Million)
#30 – John Hagee ($5 Million)
#31 – Joseph Prince, Singapore ($5 Million)
#32 – Al Sharpton ($5 Million)
#33 – Eddie Long ($5 Million)
#34 – Kay Arthur ($5 Million)
#35 – John MacArthur ($5 Million)

CHAPTER 4

#36 – Paula White ($5 Million)
#37 – Reinhard Bonnke ($4 Million)
#38 – Tony Campolo ($4 Million)

- *Buy the truth and sell it not* (Prov 23:23).
- *And through covetousness shall they with feigned words make merchandise of you* (2 Pet 2:3).

(1) THE APPEAL
[1] HERE IS GOOD COUNSEL. *I counsel thee to buy of me gold tried in the fire, that thou mayest be rich; and white raiment, that thou mayest be clothed, and that the shame of thy nakedness do not appear; and anoint thine eyes with eyesalve, that thou mayest see* (3:18). Our Lord Jesus Christ continues to give good counsel to those who have cast His counsel behind their backs. The condition of a fallen church is never so completely desperate if the gracious calls continue to come. Our blessed Lord, the Counsellor, always gives the best advice, and that which is most suitable to the need.

First. THESE PEOPLE WERE *POOR*. Christ counsels them *to buy of me gold tried in the fire that thou mayest be rich*. He lets them know where they might have true riches and how they might have them. He tells them where they might have them—from Himself. He sends them not to a goldsmith or a gold mine, but invites them to Himself.

And how must they have this true gold from Him? They must *buy* it. But, how can those that are poor buy gold? It is as we read elsewhere:

- *Ho, every one that thirsteth, come ye to the waters, and **he that hath no money; come ye, buy**, and eat; yea, come, buy wine and milk without money and without price. 2 Wherefore do ye spend money for that which is not bread? and your labour for that which satisfieth not? hearken diligently unto me, and eat ye that which is good, and let your soul delight itself in fatness. 3 Incline your ear, and come unto me: hear, and your soul shall live; and I will make an everlasting covenant with you, even the sure mercies of David* (Isa 55:1-3).

Something indeed must be parted with, but it is nothing of a value and it is only to make room for that which is of value. Part with pride and unbelief and sin to make room for receiving true riches. Part with self-sufficiency and come to Christ with a sense of your poverty and emptiness. For such there will be hidden treasure.

Second. THESE PEOPLE WERE *NAKED*. Christ tells them where they might find the best clothing. *And white raiment, that thou mayest be clothed, and that the shame of thy nakedness do not appear.* This they must receive from Christ; and they must only put off their filthy rags that they might put on the white raiment which He had purchased and provided for them—His own imputed righteousness for justification and the garments of holiness and sanctification. This may well allude to the immodest clothing styles in the end time church.

Third. THESE PEOPLE WERE *BLIND*. *And anoint thine eyes with eyesalve, that thou mayest see.* Come to Him for *eye-salve*. Give up your own worldly philosophy and reason, and resign yourselves to His Word and Spirit, and your eyes will be opened. An arrogant "scholarolatry" has characterised the Laodecia era.

- *Woe unto them that are wise in their own eyes, and prudent in their own sight* (Isa 5:21)!

[2] HERE IS GRACIOUS ENCOURAGEMENT. *As many as I love, I rebuke and chasten: be zealous therefore, and repent* (3:19). Laodicea is still a church. It still names

THE BOOK OF REVELATION

the Name of Christ. It is *lukewarm and wretched, and miserable, and poor, and blind, and naked*; but it is still one of *the seven candlesticks*. A fallen church should take the rebukes of God's Word and the rod of His chastening as evidence of His good-will to their souls and should turn to Him in repentance.

[3] HERE IS A PERSONAL INVITATION. **Behold, I stand at the door, and knock: if any man hear my voice, and open the door, I will come in to him, and will sup with him, and he with me** (3:20). From Ephesus to Laodicea there are seven stages of Church History, but in a smaller sense *each* of these churches can be seen in *each* of these ages. Today it is Laodicea, but in such an age we want to be Philadelphia church.

To Laodicea Christ now comes to knock at the door. Here He is not even in the church. Thus it is primarily a lost church. But before all that is described in this book begins to unfold: before the Rapture; before the Tribulation, there is this *FINAL CALL*.

First. CHRIST COMES TO THE DOOR OF THE LAODICEA CHURCH. He comes by His Word and by the Holy Spirit. He draws near as the *Amen* (3:14), and as the final *Amen* is about to be pronounced upon the Church Age. He comes with a heart of mercy to **any man who will hear his voice**. Note that this is a matter that is prefaced with that very singular word, **Behold**! *Behold I stand at the door*. Despite the fallen wretched state of this church; there is Christ, the Lord of Glory standing at the door.

Second. CHRIST FINDS THE DOOR SHUT. It is shut against Him. He is no longer worshipped *in spirit and in truth* (Jhn 4:23,24). His Deity is no longer affirmed. His Scriptures are no longer believed. All has been replaced by religion and worldly show.

Third. CHRIST WAITS AT THE DOOR. When He finds the church which bears His own Name closed to Him, He does not immediately withdraw. Though the hour is late, there is still time to be gracious but He waits to be gracious, even.

Fourth. CHRIST KNOCKS AT THE DOOR. He uses all proper means to awaken those within to open to Him. He calls by His Word, He knocks by the impulses of His Spirit upon their conscience. **Behold, I stand at the door, and knock: if any man hear my voice, and open the door, I will come in to him, and will sup with him, and he with me.** This is an appeal, not to the Laodicea Church at large; it is too late for that. It is a call to individuals within a fallen church who will respond to the Scriptures in the last days. Even at this late hour there are those who have come out of modernistic Protestant and Roman Catholic churches into true faith in Christ.

Fifth. CHRIST WILL RECEIVE ALL WHO OPEN THE DOOR. Those who open to Him will enjoy His presence. He promises them a feast. They have very little to bring to the table, He will bring all. *I am come that they might have life, and that they might have it more abundantly* (Jhn 10:10).

CHAPTER 4

https://upload.wikimedia.org/wikipedia/commons/1/10/Hunt_Light_of_the_World.jpg

The Light of the World **by William Holman Hunt, St Paul's Cathedral, London**

Contrast this supper invitation to Laodicea with that given by our Lord in Luke 12:

• *Let your loins be girded about, and your lights burning; 36 And ye yourselves like unto men that wait for their lord, when he will return from the wedding; that when he cometh and knocketh, they may open unto him immediately. 37 Blessed are those servants, whom the lord when he cometh shall find watching: verily I say unto you, that he shall gird himself, and make them to sit down to meat, and will come forth and serve them. 38 And if he shall come in the second watch, or come in the third watch, and find them so, blessed are those servants. 39 And this know, that if the goodman of the house had known what hour the thief would come, he would have watched, and not have suffered his house to be broken through. 40 Be ye therefore ready also: for the Son of man cometh at an hour when ye think not* (Lk 12:35-40).

Of this supper, Robert Govett in the mid-1800s wrote:

He has knocked once and again, and waits patiently the result of the appeal. He is standing: a position of unrest. He ought to obtain a seat speedily within the house. He knocks. He will not force an entrance. He appeals to the heart of the owner.
Jesus now represents Himself as nearer than in any previous epistle. He is not *coming quickly*; He is already *at the door*.

Have we not here a hint of one of the forms of temptation, to which this wealthy Church was captive? Were they not given to worldly feasting? Were they not probably givers of expensive suppers? Were they not faring sumptuously, and collecting at entertainments the great and the rich? If they would admit Christ to their tables, He would dictate to them a better hospitality. Their own entertainments would receive their return and requital in this life. Jesus would teach them to invite the poor and the outcast, who could not recompense the : that they might be recompensed at the resurrection of the just (Lk 14:12-14). *The Apocalypse Expounded by Scripture.*

3. THE CONCLUSION OF THE LETTER AND THE CHURCH AGE.

(1) TO THE OVERCOMER. **To him that overcometh will I grant to sit with me in my throne, even as I also overcame, and am set down with my Father in his throne** (3:21). Though this church seemed to be wholly overrun and overcome with lukewarmness and self-confidence, yet it was possible that by the reproofs and counsels of Christ they (at least those included in the appeal. *if any man hear*) might be inspired with fresh zeal and vigour, and might come off conquerors in their spiritual warfare for the last days. The kingdom with its throne will be given to the Son by His Father as the result of His perfect obedience.

> • *But to which of the angels said he at any time,* **Sit on my right hand**, *until I make thine enemies thy footstool* (Heb 1:13)?
> • *But this man, after he had offered one sacrifice for sins for ever,* **sat down on the right hand of God**; *13 From henceforth expecting till his enemies be made his footstool* (Heb 10:12,13).
> • *But unto the Son he saith,* **Thy throne, O God**, *is for ever and ever: a sceptre of righteousness is the sceptre of thy kingdom. 9 Thou hast loved righteousness, and hated iniquity; therefore God, even thy God, hath anointed thee with the oil of gladness above thy fellows* (Heb 1:8,9).

There are two Thrones. The Father's Throne in Heaven, on which Christ sat after His Death and Resurrection (Heb 10:12). The second is the future Throne of the Saviour on the Millennial earth. It is the Throne of David. It is to be at Jerusalem. The overcomer during the Church Age will share with Christ in this Throne.

> • *And he said unto me, Son of man,* **the place of my throne**, *and the place of the soles of my feet, where I will dwell in the midst of the children of Israel for ever, and my holy name, shall the house of Israel no more defile ...* (Ezek 43:7).
> • *Of the increase of his government and peace there shall be no end, upon* **the throne of David**, *and upon his kingdom, to order it, and to establish it with judgment and with justice from henceforth even for ever. The zeal of the LORD of hosts will perform this* (Isa 9:7).
> • *He shall be great, and shall be called the Son of the Highest: and the Lord God shall give unto him* **the throne of his father David** (Lk 1:32).

After the Thousand Years and in the New Jerusalem, the Son no longer sits on a separate throne. Then it will be, *the throne of God and of the Lamb.*

> • *And he shewed me a pure river of water of life, clear as crystal, proceeding out of* **the throne of God and of the Lamb**....*3 And there shall be no more curse: but* **the throne of God and of the Lamb** *shall be in it; and his servants shall serve him* (Rev 22:1,3).

It is not Christ's kingdom as yet. But when Christ, after His Return, sits on, His throne of glory, and the twelve apostles sit with Him on their thrones ruling the twelve tribes of Israel (Matt 19:28), then shall the victors reign with Christ. This is the last hope set before the eye of the churches. Here again is another confirmatory witness to the truth of the Millennial Reign. The perception of the Millennial Reign is necessary to the Church's right conduct.

CHAPTER 4

Smyrna, Thyatira, and Laodicea are all three incited to holiness, by belief of our Saviour's future personal reign on earth (2:10,11; 2:25-27; 3:21).

(2) TO THE HEARER. *He that hath an ear, let him hear what the Spirit saith unto the churches* (3:22). Once again and for the last time this appeal is given to the churches. It is especially pertinent to believers today that they be not drawn into the vortex of a Laodicea kind of system. *For the time is come that judgment must begin at the house of God: and if it first begin at us,* **what shall the end be** *of them that obey not the gospel of God* (1 Pet 4:17)? We will now see what *that end* will be.

Beginning with Chapter 4 and following the divinely inspired outline of Revelation 1:19 the third major section of the book of Revelation is introduced. Note again the threefold outline of the Book.

> *Write the things*
> **(1)** *which thou hast seen* **(Chapter 1)**
> **(2)** *and the things which are* **(Chapters 2,3)**
> **(3)** *and the things which shall be hereafter* **(Chapters 4-22)**

The things which thou hast seen refer to Christ in His Glory, and as it relates to both the Church Age and His Second Coming. *The things which are* refer to the churches and the Church Age (as shown by the immanency of Christ's Return). *The things which shall be hereafter* refer to seven year Tribulation (after the believing Church is removed). This will include also: the Return of Christ, the Millennial Reign of Christ, the New Heaven, New Earth and New Jerusalem.

The major portion of third section deals with the seven year Tribulation. Note that the *things which* **shall be** *hereafter* (1:19), change to *things which* **must be** *hereafter* (4:1). This section is based on three series of judgments: The Seven Seals, Seven Trumpets, and Seven Vials. The Seals cover the entire Tribulation; the Trumpets, the latter half, and the Vials, the last months or weeks of the Tribulation.

The Seventh Seal opens up into and includes the Seven Trumpets. The Seventh Trumpet opens up into and includes the Seven Vials. Thus all of the Trumpet and Vial judgments are contained within the Seventh Seal. The following notes will demonstrate that the Seventh Seal covers the second half of the Tribulation. *Everything* in Revelation from Chapter 7 unto the Return of Christ in Chapter 19 occurs in the second half of the Tribulation.

As we come to a new epoch in the Book of Revelation, and as this next chapter gives terminology that points strongly to the Rapture, we should make a note of several other Biblical pictures of the Rapture. See http://www.spiritandtruth.org/teaching/Book_of_Revelation/commentary/htm/topics/rapture.html

(1) Noah's Flood: Enoch was raptured prior to the Flood. (Noah and his family were preserved through the flood.)

(2) Sodom and Gomorrah: Lot and his daughters were rescued prior to judgment. The angels could not destroy Sodom until Lot had been removed.

- *Haste thee, escape thither; for I cannot do anything till thou be come thither* (Gen 19:22).
- *But the same day that Lot went out of Sodom it rained fire and brimstone from heaven, and destroyed them all* (Lk 17:29).

(3) The overcomer at the church of Thyatira is promised *THE MORNING STAR*:

(Rev 2:28). The morning star is Christ (Rev 22:16). The morning star rises near the end of the long night, before the night has run its course and before the dawn. The night is the current age. The day is the Millennial Reign of Christ. The darkest part of the night lies ahead (the Tribulation). The Morning Star will appear to those who watch for Him *ere that thick darkness descend* (Joel 2:2; Zeph 1:15).

(4) And now, after Seven Periods of Church History, John hears *a voice like a trumpet* calling him up to heaven (Rev 4:1; cp. 1 Thess 4:16). Thereafter, the Church no longer appears on earth in Chapters 4-18.

CHAPTER 4 CONTINUED

III THE THINGS WHICH MUST BE HEREAFTER 4-22

A. JOHN IS CAUGHT UP: THE SCENE IN HEAVEN BEFORE THE TRIBULATION: THE THRONE, THE SEALED BOOK
1. The Throne 4

(4:1) *After this I looked, and, behold, a door was opened in heaven: and the first voice which I heard was as it were of a trumpet talking with me; which said, Come up hither, and I will shew thee things which must be hereafter.*

(4:2) *And immediately I was in the spirit: and, behold, a throne was set in heaven, and <u>one sat on the throne</u>.* (4:3) *<u>And he that sat</u> was to look upon like a jasper and a sardine stone: and there was a rainbow round about the throne, in sight like unto an emerald.* (4:4) *<u>And round about the throne</u> were four and twenty seats: and upon the seats I saw four and twenty elders sitting, clothed in white raiment; and they had on their heads crowns of gold.* (4:5) *<u>And out of the throne</u> proceeded lightnings and thunderings and voices: and there were seven lamps of fire burning <u>before the throne</u>, which are the seven Spirits of God.* (4:6) *<u>And before the throne</u> there was a sea of glass like unto crystal: and <u>in the midst of the throne, and round about the throne</u>, were four beasts full of eyes before and behind.* (4:7) *And the first beast was like a lion, and the second beast like a calf, and the third beast had a face as a man, and the fourth beast was like a flying eagle.* (4:8) *And the four beasts had each of them six wings about him; and they were full of eyes within: and they rest not day and night, saying, Holy, holy, holy, Lord God Almighty, which was, and is, and is to come.*

(4:9) *And when those beasts give glory and honour and thanks to him that sat on the throne, who liveth for ever and ever,* (4:10) *The four and twenty elders fall down before him that sat on the throne, and worship him that liveth for ever and ever, and cast their crowns before the throne, saying,* (4:11) *Thou art worthy, O Lord, to receive glory and honour and power: for thou hast created all things, and for thy pleasure they are and were created.*

As the epistles to the Seven Churches opened with a glorious vision of Christ, so now *the things which shall be hereafter* (1:19) likewise are introduced with a glorious appearance of the great God and His Throne in Heaven. Previously the scene was on earth, now it is in Heaven. Shortly we will see the terrifying judgements falling upon the earth, but now the matter is made clear: these judgement will come not from earth but from Heaven.

<u>I. THE PREPARATIONS OF THE APOSTLE</u>. *After this I looked, and, behold, a door was opened in heaven: and the first voice which I heard was as it were of a trumpet talking with me; which said, Come up hither, and I will shew thee things which must be hereafter* (4:1).

<u>1. THE TIME</u>. *After this*. We are now in the time **hereafter** (4:2). That is, not only after John had seen the vision of Christ walking in the midst of the golden candlesticks, but *after* that ministry and age on earth is completed. *After this*, the churches are no longer seen on the earth. John's vantage point will now be changed; he is no longer on the earth, and neither are the churches. John will see all that takes place on earth, but it will be from the vantage point of heaven.

There is a solemnity in the words *After this*. As God said to Joshua. *Ye have not passed this way heretofore* (Josh 3:4). We are now entering realms and events that the world has never seen nor begun to see. To take a historical view of these next chapters and seek to

THE BOOK OF REVELATION

equate them with events of past history is utterly futile. Such an attempt ignores the fact that the events here described take place in direct proximity to the Return of Christ.

2. THE SIGHT. *After this I looked, and, behold, a door was opened in heaven.* Chapter 3 ended with an open door. *Behold, I stand at the door, and knock: if any man hear my voice, and open the door, I will come in to him, and will sup with him, and he with me* (3:20). The church at Philadelphia was promised an open door of opportunity in the work of the Great Commission: *I have set before thee an open door and no man can shut it* (3:8). But those were opened doors on earth; this is an opened door in Heaven. All who open the door of their heart to Christ on earth will find a door opened for them in Heaven. The Book of Revelation describes five openings in Heaven. This is the first.

- *And **the temple of God was opened** in heaven, and there was seen in his temple the ark of his testament: and there were lightnings, and voices, and thunderings, and an earthquake, and great hail* (11:19).
- *And after that I looked, and, behold, **the temple of the tabernacle of the testimony in heaven was opened*** (15:5).
- *And I saw **heaven opened**, and behold a white horse; and he that sat upon him was called Faithful and True, and in righteousness he doth judge and make war* (19:11).
- *And I saw a new heaven and a new earth: for the first heaven and the first earth were passed away; and there was no more sea. 2 And I John saw the holy city, new Jerusalem, coming down from God **out of heaven**, prepared as a bride adorned for her husband* (21:1,2).

3. THE VOICE: *and the first voice which I heard was as it were of a trumpet talking with me.* Compare 1:10. The first and only time we heard such a trumpet was when Moses was called to the top of Mount Sinai (cp. Exod 19:13; 1 Cor 15:51,52). And so as at the Rapture, of which this is a picture, a trumpet will be sounded (1 Thess 4;16,17).

John recognized *the voice* as *that which had first addressed him,* bidding him write what he saw, and send it to the churches (1:10). The voice was loud, penetrating, metallic, rousing. It was suited to the scenes of justice, of war, of battle, of the throne of the King preparing for war. In passing through this door and now with this trumpet voice, John finds himself not at a throne of grace, but in a chamber preparing for war.

4. THE SUMMONS: *which said, Come up hither, and I will shew thee things which must be hereafter.* The Apostle, representing all believers of the church age is *caught up* to Heaven before the Tribulation begins. This was previously promised to the church at Philadelphia.

- *Because thou hast kept the word of my patience, I also will keep thee from the hour of temptation, which shall come upon all the world, to try them that dwell upon the earth (Rev 3:10).*

5. THE TRANSFORMATION. *And immediately I was in the spirit* (4:2). The Rapture will occur *in a moment, in the twinkling of an eye* (1 Cor 15:51). He was *in the spirit*, as before (1:10), *whether in the body, or out of the body, I cannot tell; God knoweth* (2 Cor 12:3). With the vivid *RAPTURE TERMINOLOGY* that describes John's translation into Heaven, we find that Chapter Four presents three demonstrations of the Pre-tribulational Rapture.

CHAPTER 4 continued

THE RAPTURE IN CHAPTER FOUR

There are in Chapter Four three distinct indications of the Rapture and the Church residing in Heaven before the Tribulation: John himself, (4:1,2); the Twenty-four Elders (4:4); the Seven Lamps of Fire (4:5).

JOHN HIMSELF IS IN HEAVEN

(4:1) *After this I looked, and, behold, a door was opened in heaven: and the first **voice** which I heard was as it were of a **trumpet** talking with me; which said, **Come up hither**, and I will shew thee things which must be hereafter. (4:2) And **immediately** I was in the spirit: and, behold, a throne was set in heaven, and one sat on the throne.*

- *For the Lord himself shall descend from heaven with **a shout**, with **the voice** of the archangel, and with **the trump** of God: and the dead in Christ shall rise first: 17 Then we which are alive and remain shall be **caught up** together with them in the clouds, to meet the Lord in the air: and so shall we ever be with the Lord* (1 Thess 4:16,17).
- *Behold, I shew you a mystery; We shall not all sleep, but we shall all be changed, **In a moment, in the twinkling of an eye**, at the **last trump**: for the trumpet shall sound, and the dead shall be raised incorruptible, and we shall be changed* (1Cor 15:51,52).
- *And if I go and prepare a place for you, I will come again, and **receive you unto myself**; that where I am, there ye may be also* (Jhn 14:3).
- *Now we beseech you, brethren, by the coming of our Lord Jesus Christ, and by **our gathering together unto him*** (2 Thess 2:1)

As with John, the saints will hear a verbal command at the Rapture (1 Thess 4:16).
As with John, a voice as a trumpet is heard by believers at the Rapture (1 Cor. 15:52; 1 Thess 4:16).
As with John, believers at the Rapture will be caught up (1 Thess 4:17).
As with John, the destination of those raptured is Heaven (Jhn 14:1-3; 1 Thess 4:17).
As with John, those raptured are transformed, in the Spirit and in Christ (1 Cor 15:51).
As with John, the Rapture occurs instantaneously (1 Cor 15:51,52).
As with John, the Rapture will occur at the end of the seven stages of the Church Age.

THE TWENTY-FOUR ELDERS ARE IN HEAVEN

(4:4) *And round about the throne were four and twenty seats: and upon the seats I saw **four and twenty elders** sitting, clothed in **white raiment**; and they had on their heads **crowns of gold**.*

The Twenty-Four Elders are a representative group, a fact made clear from the parallel in the Old Testament where the priesthood was represented by twenty-four courses of priests. There were many thousands of priests in Israel's under David and Solomon, but they all could not minister at the same time. Accordingly, they were divided into twenty-four courses or orders, each of which was represented by a priest. When these priests met together, even though there were only twenty-four, they represented the entire priesthood and at the same time the whole of the nation of Israel. In a similar way the twenty-four elders are representative of believers of the Church Age around the Throne. Like John they are seen in Heaven before the Tribulation begins.

The fact that they are Elders indicates that they may be the apostles (who will also be seen in a similar role on earth during the Millennium. Matt 19:28; cp. Eph 2:20,21) and their close associates. They are not Old Testament believers for these rise at the end of the

Tribulation (Dan 12:13). Their crowns and white raiment are a fitting emblem of their role as representative of the Church in glory.

Their representative song in Chapter Five can only refer to themselves and the Church they represent in Heaven. This great anthem of redemption is sung before the Tribulation begins.

- *And I beheld, and, lo, in the midst of the throne and of the four beasts, and in the midst of **the elders**, stood a Lamb as it had been slain, having seven horns and seven eyes, which are the seven Spirits of God sent forth into all the earth. 7 And he came and took the book out of the right hand of him that sat upon the throne. 8 And when he had taken the book, the four beasts and **four and twenty elders fell down before the Lamb**, having every one of them harps, and golden vials full of odours, which are the prayers of saints. 9 And they sung a new song, saying, Thou art worthy to take the book, and to open the seals thereof: **for thou wast slain, and hast redeemed us to God by thy blood out of every kindred, and tongue, and people, and nation** (Rev 5:6-9).*

Compare this with the later account of those saved during the Tribulation. As we will see, this account is given after the midpoint of the Tribulation.

- *After this I beheld, and, lo, **a great multitude, which no man could number**, of all nations, and kindreds, and people, and tongues, **stood before the throne**, and before the Lamb, clothed with white robes, and palms in their hands; And cried with a loud voice, saying, Salvation to our God which sitteth upon the throne, and unto the Lamb* (Rev 7:9,10).
- *And **one of the elders answered, saying unto me, What are these** which are arrayed in white robes? and whence came they? And I said unto him, Sir, thou knowest. And he said to me, **These are they which came out of great tribulation**, and have washed their robes, and made them white in the blood of the Lamb* (Rev 7:13,14).

THE SEVEN LAMPS ARE IN HEAVEN

(4:5) *And out of the throne proceeded lightnings and thunderings and voices: and there were **seven lamps of fire burning before the throne, which are the seven Spirits of God**.*

This passage shows the indivisible connection between the Holy Spirit and the seven churches. As a *lamp* and a *candlestick* are essentially the same (the purpose of both is to give light) and as that light comes from the Holy Spirit, it is likely that as the candlesticks represented the Church on earth, so the lamps represent the Church in Heaven. In both cases they are enlightened and empowered by the Holy Spirit. Therefore, the seven lamps represent the glorified Church before the throne and that before the Tribulation begins.

- *John to the seven churches which are in Asia: Grace be unto you, and peace, from him which is, and which was, and which is to come; and from **the seven Spirits which are before his throne** (Rev 1:4).*
- *And I turned to see the voice that spake with me. And being turned, I saw **seven golden candlesticks**; 13 And in the midst of the seven candlesticks one like unto the Son of man, clothed with a garment down to the foot, and girt about the paps with a golden girdle (Rev 1:12,13).*

Therefore with the total absence of any further mention of the Church on earth, and with the specific promise that the Church will be *kept from the hour of temptation which shall come upon all the world, to try them that dwell upon the earth* (Rev 3:10), and now with this

CHAPTER 4 continued

threefold representation: (1) John himself, (2) the Twenty–Four Elders, (3) the Seven Lamps before the Throne.

Note: To admit John, only a door sufficed (4:1). To give exit to the Messiah and the returning Church (*much people*, 19:1) at His Second Coming, the entire Heaven was *opened* (Rev 19:11). We have a clear picture that the Church will be in Heaven before the Tribulation begins:

- Before the Seven Seals are broken and the Four Horsemen begin their dreadful ride across the earth (Chapter 6).
- Before the Seven Trumpets are blown resulting in catastrophic judgements upon the earth (Chapters 8,9).
- Before the Antichrist takes control of the earth (Chapter 13).
- Before the Seven Vials are poured out resulting in total desolation of the earth (Chapters 15,16).

Returning now to the outline of events in Chapter four and John being caught up to Throne; we have seen:

> *I. THE PREPARATIONS OF THE APOSTLE 4:1*
> *1. THE TIME*
> *2. THE SIGHT*
> *3. THE VOICE*
> *4. THE SUMMONS*
> *5. THE TRANSFORMATION*

II. THE ASPECTS OF THE THRONE.

1. THE ONE *ON THE THRONE*. (4:2) ***And immediately I was in the spirit: and, behold, a throne was set in heaven, and <u>one sat on the throne</u>.*** (4:3) ***<u>And he that sat</u> was to look upon like a jasper and a sardine stone: and there was a rainbow round about the throne, in sight like unto an emerald.***

(1) A SET THRONE: ***and, behold, a throne was set in heaven.*** This throne is *set in Heaven.* It is firm and solid in contrast to all other thrones on earth which are constantly overturned and overthrown (Ezek 21:26,27). It is a Throne of absolute sovereignty. It is far removed from the petty struggles of earthly government. Here is the true picture of the world being made subject to the dominion of the Omnipotent God. All earthly thrones will now submit to the jurisdiction of this Throne (Rev 11:15). This is a matter to ***behold***. It is the scene that Daniel beheld (Dan 7: 9-11). As this throne rules over a guilty earth, its setting becomes, at once a time of visitation – a visitation in judgement.

- *All nations shall come and worship before thee;* ***for*** *thy judgment are made* ***manifest*** (Rev 15:4).

(2) THE COLOURS OF THE MAJESTY: ***and one sat on the throne.*** This throne was not empty; there was One in it who filled it. The Holy One who sits upon the throne is God the Father. He acts for His Son's establishment, till all is ready for Christ to Return. The LORD said unto *my Lord,* Sit thou at my right hand, until I make thy enemies, thy footstool (Psa 110:1). The Son is soon after seen *as the Lamb*; the Holy Ghost as Seven Spirits round about the Throne.

The Father is described by those things that are most precious in our world: ***And he that sat was to look upon like a jasper and a sardine stone*** (4:3). The appearance of this August Monarch is very *distantly* described. The place is holy ground. He is not described by any human features, so as to be represented by an image, but only by his transcendent brightness. The light that streamed from Him was not white, but coloured.

The *jasper* is a transparent crystalline stone, which yet offers to the eye a variety of the most vivid colours, signifying the glorious perfections of God; the **sardine-stone** is red, signifying the justice of God, that essential attribute of which He never divests himself in favour of any, but gloriously exerts it in the government of the world. This attribute is displayed in pardoning as well as in punishing, in saving as well as in destroying sinners.

Compare that which John saw with the view given to the prophet Ezekiel:

- *And the likeness of the firmament upon the heads of the living creature was as **the colour of the terrible crystal**, stretched forth over their heads above* (Ezek 1:22).
- *And above the firmament that was over their heads was the likeness of a throne, as **the appearance of a sapphire stone**: and upon the likeness of the throne was the likeness as the appearance of a man above upon it. 27 And I saw as **the colour of amber**, as the appearance of fire round about within it, from the appearance of his loins even upward, and from the appearance of his loins even downward, I saw as it were the appearance of fire, and it had brightness round about* (Ezek 1:26,27).

Note that these two stones were the first and last mentioned in breast plate worn by the Old Testament High Priest.

- *And thou shalt set in it settings of stones, even four rows of stones: the first row shall be a **sardius**, a topaz, and a carbuncle: this shall be the first row. 18 And the second row shall be an emerald, a sapphire, and a **diamond**. 19 And the third row a ligure, an agate, and an amethyst. 20 And the fourth row a beryl, and an onyx, and a **jasper**: they shall be set in gold in their inclosings* (Exod 28:17-20).

As the primary impression received by John is that of colour and as the stones are mentioned elsewhere in Scripture we may be assured that they have deep significance. The jasper stone is described in Chapter 21 as a precious stone which is clear like crystal. It is the overriding colour of New Jerusalem.

- *And he carried me away in the spirit to a great and high mountain, and shewed me that great city, the holy Jerusalem, descending out of heaven from God, 11 Having the glory of God: and **her light was like unto a stone most precious, even like a jasper stone, clear as crystal*** (Rev 21:10,11).

The Jasper is an unknown and mysteriously wonderful colour; it may be like a diamond, but is distinguished from the diamond in the breastplate of the High Priest (Exod 28:18,20). Though the jasper points to the holiness of God and the sardine stone to His redemptive work, the significance goes beyond the colours themselves. Each tribe of Israel had a representative stone and the High Priest bore these stones in his breastplate. As the sardine and the jasper stone are the first and last of these twelve stones; the sardine represented Reuben the firstborn and the jasper, Benjamin, the youngest of the sons of Jacob. As the two stones represented the first and the last, they therefore may be regarded as including all the other stones in between; that is, the whole of the covenanted people. These colours demonstrate to Israel that Jehovah is now going to restore them and fulfil the covenant that He made with Abraham.

Further, as Reuben means *behold, a son*, and Benjamin, *son of my right hand*, the restoration about to take place will be through the Son of God whom Israel rejected. Like Reuben, Christ is *the first and the only begotten son*; like Benjamin, Christ is *the son of my right hand*. The person whom John sees on the throne looking like a jasper and sardine stone

CHAPTER 4 continued

is, therefore, God in relation to the nation Israel. A primary purpose of the Tribulation now about to commence is to purify and refine Israel (Zech 13:9). It is called *the time of Jacob's trouble* (Jer 30:7).

That the scarlet sardine colour points to Christ's Redemptive Work may be seen by the fact that among the seven things that Hebrews 12:22 describes the believer *coming to* in Heaven, the seventh is the *blood of sprinkling*.

- *But ye are come unto mount Sion, and unto the city of the living God, the heavenly Jerusalem, and to an innumerable company of angels, 23 To the general assembly and church of the firstborn, which are written in heaven, and to God the Judge of all, and to the spirits of just men made perfect, 24 And to Jesus the mediator of the new covenant,* ***and to the blood of sprinkling, that speaketh better things that that of Abel*** (Heb 12:22-24).

(3) THE RAINBOW: **and there was a rainbow round about the throne, in sight like unto an emerald.** The rainbow was the seal and token of the covenant that God made with Noah and his posterity. This rainbow looked like an *emerald*; the most prevailing colour was a pleasant green, to show His faithfulness and care for His creation. As the jasper and sardine colour spoke of God's intentions for Israel, this speaks of His intentions for the world generally. Though it is now a throne of judgement and a mighty storm is about to break forth upon the earth, yet after the storm the world will know peace and beauty. Note that in this case the rainbow comes before rather than after the storm. As God is now about to send judgements upon the earth, He will do so from a Throne encircled with a rainbow like unto an emerald; for He is the gracious God who made the Covenant of Peace with Noah (Gen 9:13); and its colour (green) emphasized its relationship with the green earth, and symbolized rest.

Robert Govett writes:

A cloud is coming over the earth; yea, it is already beheld. The throne is that cloud, and from it thunders and lightnings dart. But the bow is seen in the cloud; in token, that God, while judging, means not to destroy by a flood. Accordingly, while plague after plague is rained down on men, *no inundation devastates the earth.*
Its colour was the beautiful green of the emerald, that hue which is so refreshing to the eye in the grass covered earth. It is the opposite or complementary colour to red ; and hence, *as fitly signifies mercy,* as the fiery or bloody red betokens *justice.* Thus we have an emblematic representation of the word of Habbakuk. *In wrath remember* mercy (Hab 3:3). The promises of grace encompass the throne, so that the floods of wrath shall not wholly destroy the earth. *The Apocalypse Expounded by Scripture.*

2. THE TWENTY-FOUR ELDERS *ROUND ABOUT THE THRONE.* **And round about the throne were four and twenty seats: and upon the seats I saw four and twenty elders sitting, clothed in white raiment; and they had on their heads crowns of gold** (4:4). With John being the first, the Twenty-Four Elders are the second example of the Church in Heaven before the Tribulation begins on earth. These have been thought to be the twelve Apostle and their closest companions, or perhaps they are prominent leaders of the Church Age. If they include the Apostles, then they will also reign upon the Millennial Earth.

- *Then answered Peter and said unto him, Behold, we have forsaken all, and followed thee; what shall we have therefore? 28 And Jesus said unto them, Verily I say unto you, That ye which have followed me, in the regeneration when the Son of man shall sit in the throne of his glory,* ***ye also shall sit upon twelve thrones, judging the twelve tribes of Israel*** (Matt 19:27,28).

The Twenty-Four Elders are a representative group, and represent believers of the Church Age, now raptured, glorified and before the Throne. Their sitting denotes their honour and rest. Their sitting *round about* the Throne signifies their relation to God, their nearness to Him, their sight and enjoyment they have of Him. They are near to the One who now is about to pour His wrath upon the world in which they lived.

We have seen that they are a representative group and parallel the Old Testament priesthood that was represented by twenty-four courses of priests (1 Chron 27). As the term *elder* is used frequently for the leaders of the New Testament churches it is believed that they are the representatives of believers of the Church Age after the Rapture.

- *Which also they did, and sent it to the **elders** by the hands of Barnabas and Saul* (Acts 11:30).
- *And when they had ordained them **elders** in every church, and had prayed with fasting, they commended them to the Lord, on whom they believed* (Acts 14:23).
- *When therefore Paul and Barnabas had no small dissension and disputation with them, they determined that Paul and Barnabas, and certain other of them, should go up to Jerusalem unto the apostles and **elders** about this question* (Acts 15:2).
- *And when they were come to Jerusalem, they were received of the church, and of the apostles and **elders**, and they declared all things that God had done with them* (Acts 15:4).
- *And the apostles and **elders** came together for to consider of this matter* (Acts 15:6). *Then pleased it the apostles and elders, with the whole church, to send chosen men of their own company to Antioch with Paul and Barnabas; namely, Judas surnamed Barsabas, and Silas, chief men among the brethren. And they wrote letters by them after this manner; The apostles and **elders** and brethren send greeting unto the brethren which are of the Gentiles in Antioch and Syria and Cilicia* (Acts 15:22,23).
- *And as they went through the cities, they delivered them the decrees for to keep, that were ordained of the apostles and **elders** which were at Jerusalem* (Acts 16:4).
- *And from Miletus he sent to Ephesus, and called the **elders** of the church* (20:17).
- *And the day following Paul went in with us unto James; and all the **elders** were present* (Acts 21:18).
- *As also the high priest doth bear me witness, and all the estate of the **elders**: from whom also I received letters unto the brethren, and went to Damascus, to bring them which were there bound unto Jerusalem, for to be punished* (Acts 22:5).
- *Let the **elders** that rule well be counted worthy of double honour, especially they who labour in the word and doctrine* (1 Tim 5:17).
- *For this cause left I thee in Crete, that thou shouldest set in order the things that are wanting, and ordain **elders** in every city, as I had appointed thee* (Titus 1:5).
- *Is any sick among you? let him call for the **elders** of the church; and let them pray over him, anointing him with oil in the name of the Lord* (Jms 5:14).
- *The **elders** which are among you I exhort, who am also an elder, and a witness of the sufferings of Christ, and also a partaker of the glory that shall be revealed:* (1 Pet 5:1)

This emphasis given to elders in the NT and their relation to the Church gives strong demonstration that the Twenty-Four Elders in Revelation also relate to the Church. Note also that by comparing a number of other Scriptures the terms *elder, bishop* and *pastor/shepherd* are shown to be the same offices (Acts 20:17,28; 1 Pet 5:1,2).

CHAPTER 4 continued

The Twenty-Four Elders are clothed in ***white raiment*** and have on their heads ***crowns of gold***. There are two kinds of crowns in the book of Revelation, involving two different Greek words. One is the crown of a ruler or a sovereign (*diadem*). The other is the crown of a victor (*stephanos*), such as was awarded in the Greek games when a person won a race or some contest. This crown was usually made of leaves. The word here is the crown of a victor rather than that of a sovereign. It was made of gold, indicating that the elders had been rewarded for victory accomplished.

It is significant that the passage states the Twenty-Four Elders already have their crowns of gold as victors. This is an indication that the Judgement Seat of Christ will take place shortly before the judgements of the Tribulation take place on earth. This gives further insight to 1 Peter 4:17. The Church is judged before judgement is poured out upon the earth.

- *For the time is come that **judgment must begin at the house of God**: and if it first begin at us, what shall the end be of them that obey not the gospel of God* (1 Pet 4:17)?
- *why dost thou judge thy brother? or why dost thou set at nought thy brother? for **we shall all stand before the judgment seat of Christ**. 11 For it is written, As I live, saith the Lord, every knee shall bow to me, and every tongue shall confess to God. 12 So then every one of us shall give account of himself to God* (Rom 14:10-12).
- *Every man's work shall be made manifest: for the day shall declare it, because it shall be revealed by fire; and **the fire shall try every man's work of what sort it is**. If any man's work abide which he hath built thereupon, he shall receive a reward. If any man's work shall be burned, he shall suffer loss: but he himself shall be saved; yet so as by fire* (1 Cor 3:13-15).
- *Wherefore we labour, that, whether present or absent, we may be accepted of him. For **we must all appear before the judgment seat of Christ**; that every one may receive the things done in his body, according to that he hath done, whether it be good or bad* (2 Cor 5:9,10).
- ***Henceforth there is laid up for me a crown of righteousness***, *which the Lord, the righteous judge, shall give me at that day: and not to me only, but unto all them also that love his appearing* (2 Tim 4:8).

The Church which is raptured before Chapter 4 is now complete in heaven and eligible for reward at the Judgement-Seat of Christ. This being the case, the crowns of gold on the heads of the Twenty-Four Elders are a fitting token of this and confirm the belief that they represent the Church in glory (See Walvoord). Their presence representing believers of the Church Age is the second demonstration in this chapter of the Church being raptured before the Tribulation begins.

<u>3. THE MANIFESTATIONS *PROCEEDING OUT OF THE THRONE*.</u> ***And out of the throne** proceeded lightnings and thunderings and voices* (4:5). Before the storm of wrath broke on earth John saw it breaking in heaven. They a fitting prelude and are indicative of the righteous judgment of God upon a sinful world. They are similar to the thunders, lightnings, and voice of the trumpet which mark the giving of the Law on Mount Sinai.

- *And it came to pass on the third day in the morning, that there were **thunders and lightnings**, and a thick cloud upon the mount, and **the voice of the trumpet** exceeding loud; so that all the people that was in the camp trembled* (Exod 19:16).

But now in Heaven, as the place of justice, these tokens of God's indignation were continually ***proceeding*** from the Throne. They are called forth by the enormity of the world's sin and provocation. It was a sustained but hitherto restrained activity of wrath against the sin of man, but now those restraints of grace are to be systematically removed in three great stages: *the seals, trumpets and vials.*

After the judgment is over and sinners are passed away and only the holy dwell in the New Heavens and the New Earth, the Throne of God appears; but note the great difference in the ***precedings*** from that Throne; the tokens of wrath are all in the past.

- *A And he shewed me **a pure river of water of life, clear as crystal, <u>proceeding</u>** out of the throne of God and of the Lamb (Rev 22:1).*

But now it is wrath. Note the three further times that the ***lightnings and thunderings and voices*** are mentioned:

- *And the angel took the censer, and filled it with fire of the altar, and cast it into the earth: and there were **voices, and thunderings, and lightnings**, and an earthquake (Rev 8:5).*
- *And the temple of God was opened in heaven, and there was seen in his temple the ark of his testament: and there were **lightnings, and voices, and thunderings**, and an earthquake, and great hail (Rev 11:19).*
- *And there were **voices, and thunders, and lightnings**; and there was a great earthquake, such as was not since men were upon the earth, so mighty an earthquake, and so great (Rev 16:18).*

The ***voices*** are Heaven's affirmation praising God for the judgements that He is now bringing upon earth. Compare the following and the connection in 8:3-5 and 11:13-19.

- *And when he had opened the fifth seal, I saw under the altar the souls of them that were slain for the word of God, and for the testimony which they held: 10 And **they cried with a loud voice**, saying, How long, O Lord, holy and true, dost thou not judge and avenge our blood on them that dwell on the earth (Rev 6:9,10)?*
- *And another angel came and stood at the altar, having a golden censer; and there was given unto him much incense, that he should offer it with **the prayers of all saints** upon the golden altar which was before the throne. 4 And the smoke of the incense, which came with **the prayers of the saints, ascended up before God** out of the angel's hand. 5 And the angel took the censer, and filled it with fire of the altar, and cast it into the earth: and **there were voices, and thunderings, and lightnings**, and an earthquake (Rev 8:3-5).*
- *And the seventh angel sounded; and there were **great voices in heaven**, saying, The kingdoms of this world are become the kingdoms of our Lord, and of his Christ; and he shall reign for ever and ever. 16 And the four and twenty elders, which sat before God on their seats, fell upon their faces, and worshipped God, 17 Saying, **We give thee thanks**, O LORD God Almighty, which art, and wast, and art to come; because thou hast taken to thee thy great power, and hast reigned. 18 And the nations were angry, and thy wrath is come, and the time of the dead, that they should be judged, and that thou shouldest give reward unto thy servants the prophets, and to the saints, and them that fear thy name, small and great; and shouldest destroy them which destroy the earth. 19 And the temple of God was opened in heaven, and there was seen in his temple the ark of his testament: and there were **lightnings, and voices, and thunderings**, and an earthquake, and great hail (Rev 11:15-16).*
- *And after these things I heard **a great voice of much people in heaven**, saying, Alleluia; Salvation, and glory, and honour, and power, unto the Lord our God: 2 For true and righteous are his judgments: for he hath judged the great whore, which did*

CHAPTER 4 continued

corrupt the earth with her fornication, and hath avenged the blood of his servants at her hand (Rev 19:1,2).

4. THE SEVEN LAMPS *BEFORE THE THRONE*: **and there were seven lamps of fire burning <u>before the throne</u>, which are the seven Spirits of God** (4:5). The *seven Spirits of God* (1:4; 3:1) represent the sevenfold plentitude of the Person of the Holy Spirit.

>(1) *And the* **spirit** *of the LORD shall rest upon him,*
>(2) *the* **spirit** *of wisdom*
>(3) *and understanding,*
>(4) *the* **spirit** *of counsel*
>(5) *and might,*
>(6) *the* **spirit** *of knowledge*
>(7) *and of the **fear** of the LORD* (Isa 11:2).

Ordinarily the Holy Spirit is not physically visible unless embodied in some way. Here He is represented by Seven Lamps. It is likely, as shown previously that "this passage shows the indivisible connection between the Holy Spirit and the Seven Churches. As a *lamp* and a *candlestick* are essentially the same (the purpose of both is to give light) and as that light comes from the Holy Spirit, it is likely that as the candlesticks represented the Church on earth, so the lamps represent the Church in Heaven. In both cases they are enlightened and empowered by the Holy Spirit. Therefore, the Seven Lamps represent the glorified Church before the throne and that before the Tribulation begins." The Seven candlesticks/lamps were on earth, they are now in the full effulgence of the Holy Spirit before the Throne.

There is the same indivisible connection between the Holy Spirit and the Church as there is between the Holy Spirit and the Two Witnesses.

- *And said unto me, What seest thou? And I said, I have looked, and behold **a candlestick all of gold, with a bowl upon the top of it, and his seven lamps thereon, and seven pipes to the seven lamps, which are upon the top thereof: 3 And two olive trees by it, one upon the right side of the bowl, and the other upon the left side** thereof. 4 So I answered and spake to the angel that talked with me, saying, What are these, my lord? 5 Then the angel that talked with me answered and said unto me, Knowest thou not what these be? And I said, No, my lord. 6 Then he answered and spake unto me, saying, This is the word of the LORD unto Zerubbabel, saying, **Not by might, nor by power, but by my spirit, saith the LORD** of hosts (Zech 4:2-6).*
- *And **I will give power unto my two witnesses**, and they shall prophesy a thousand two hundred and threescore days, clothed in sackcloth. 4 **These are the two olive trees, and the two candlesticks** standing before the God of the earth (Rev 11:3,4).*

The various operations of the Spirit of God that had been manifested in the churches are now to be exercised in the judgements about to fall upon the earth. These are all dispensed according to the will and pleasure of Him who sits upon the Throne. Unlike as Candlesticks on earth where the lights of the churches were shown to dim and flicker, now with the Lamps (the churches in glory), there is no danger of their going out.

The Candlesticks on earth were for light and that purpose remains, but now is added, **fire** for **burning**. The Holy Spirit descended on the Lord Jesus as a *dove*. But now He is *Spirit of judgment, and the Spirit of burning* (See Isa 4:4). Since the Rapture of the Candlesticks, it has been *night* on earth (Jhn 9:4). No part of earth now shines. The light that now descends is fire. The Churches shares in the wrath of the One who is a *flaming fire* (Heb 12:29). *The inhabitants of the earth are burned, and few men left* (Isa 24:6).

THE BOOK OF REVELATION

<u>5. THE SEA OF GLASS *BEFORE THE THRONE*.</u> ***And before the throne there was a sea of glass like unto crystal*** (4:6). As in the temple there was a great vessel of brass filled with water, in which the priests were to wash when they went to minister before the Lord (and this was called a *sea),* so there is here in Heaven, and which was the pattern for Solomon's. Here though it is crystal rather than water, for the occupants there are now eternally holy. They are *fixed* in holiness.

- *Also he made **a molten sea** of ten cubits from brim to brim, round in compass, and five cubits the height thereof; and a line of thirty cubits did compass it round about. 3 And under it was the similitude of oxen, which did compass it round about: ten in a cubit, compassing **the sea** round about. Two rows of oxen were cast, when it was cast. 4 It stood upon twelve oxen, three looking toward the north, and three looking toward the west, and three looking toward the south, and three looking toward the east: and **the sea was set above upon them**, and all their hinder parts were inward.* (2 Chron 4:2-6).
- *He made also ten lavers...**but the sea was for the priests to wash in***. (2 Chron 4:6).

This sea, like the Red Sea also speaks of judgement and will apparently be the receptacle from the vials of wrath are filled and poured upon the earth (Rev 15,16). Note the parallels between the sea the Red Sea and the Sea of Glass in Heaven.

- *And the LORD said unto Moses, **Stretch out thine hand over the sea**, that the waters may come again upon the Egyptians, upon their chariots, and upon their horsemen. 27 And **Moses stretched forth his hand over the sea**, and the sea returned to his strength when the morning appeared; and the Egyptians fled against it; and the LORD **overthrew the Egyptians in the midst of the sea**. 28 And the waters returned, and covered the chariots, and the horsemen, and all the host of Pharaoh that came into the sea after them; there remained not so much as one of them. 29 But **the children of Israel walked upon dry land** in the midst of the sea; and the waters were a wall unto them on their right hand, and on their left. 30 Thus the LORD saved Israel that day... and Israel saw the Egyptians dead upon the sea shore. 15:1 Then sang Moses and the children of Israel this song unto the LORD, and spake, saying, I will sing unto the LORD, for he hath triumphed gloriously: the horse and his rider hath he thrown into the sea (Exod 14:26-15:1).*
- *And I saw another sign in heaven, great and marvellous, seven angels having the seven last plagues; **for in them is filled up the wrath of God**. 2 And I saw as it were **a sea of glass mingled with fire**: and them that had gotten the victory over the beast, and over his image, and over his mark, and over the number of his name, **stand on the sea of glass**, having the harps of God. 3 And **they sing the song of Moses the servant of God, and the song of the Lamb**, saying, Great and marvellous are thy works, Lord God Almighty; just and true are thy ways, thou King of saints (Rev 15:1-3).*

The above may explain why there is *no more sea* in eternity, for as also in the days of Noah the sea has been a means of God's judgement.

- *And I saw a new heaven and a new earth: for the first heaven and the first earth were passed away; and **there was no more sea** (Rev 21:1).*

<u>6. THE FOUR BEASTS *IN THE MIDST OF AND AROUND THE THRONE*</u>. (4:6) ***And before the throne there was a sea of glass like unto crystal: and <u>in the midst of the throne, and round about the throne</u>, were four beasts full of eyes before and behind.*** (4:7) ***And the first beast was like a lion, and the second beast like a calf, and the third beast had***

CHAPTER 4 continued

a face as a man, and the fourth beast was like a flying eagle. (4:8) *And the four beasts had each of them six wings about him; and they were full of eyes within: and they rest not day and night, saying, Holy, holy, holy, Lord God Almighty, which was, and is, and is to come.*

John saw the living creatures (the *zoa*). A major part of Chapter Four is given to their description. They are the unfallen representatives of the four basic orders of creation upon the earth. Their proximity to the sea of glass parallels to a certain extent the oxen that were around and under the *molten sea* in the Temple of Solomon (2 Chron 4:2-6).

They are here described,

(1) BY THEIR MANY EYES: *full of eyes before and behind.* These denote their sagacity and vigilance. They are *watchers*. Compare this with the watchers in Daniel and the rings / wheels in Ezekiel:

- *I saw in the visions of my head upon my bed, and, behold,* **a watcher and an holy one** *came down from heaven* (Dan 4:13).
- *This matter is by the decree of* **the watchers**, *and the demand by the word of the holy ones: to the intent that the living may know that the most High ruleth in the kingdom of men, and giveth it to whomsoever he will, and setteth up over it the basest of men* (Dan 4:17).
- *And whereas the king saw* **a watcher and an holy one** *coming down from heaven, and saying, Hew the tree down, and destroy it; yet leave the stump of the roots thereof in the earth, even with a band of iron and brass, in the tender grass of the field; and let it be wet with the dew of heaven, and let his portion be with the beasts of the field, till seven times pass over him* (Dan 4:23).
- *As for their rings, they were so high that they were dreadful; and* **their rings were full of eyes** *round about them four* (Ezek 1:18).
- *And their whole body, and their backs, and their hands, and their wings, and* **the wheels, were full of eyes** *round about, even the wheels that they four had* (Ezek 10:12).

(2) BY THEIR FOURFOLD CHARACTER. *And the first beast was like a lion, and the second beast like a calf, and the third beast had a face as a man, and the fourth beast was like a flying eagle* (4:7). Their number is FOUR; for *four is the number of creation.* And the *four* of creation united with the Blessed *Three* of the Ruler of Creation, make up the sacred *seven.* They are seen in their lion-like courage, their great labour and diligence (in which they resemble the ox), their prudence and discretion as men, and their sublime affections and speculations, by which they mount up *with wings like eagles.*

Each of these four are supreme in their respective categories. The lion is the king of beasts and represents majesty and omnipotence. The calf or ox, representing the most important of domestic animals, signifies patience and continuous labour. Man is the greatest of all God's creatures, especially in intelligence and rational power; whereas the eagle is greatest among birds and is symbolic of sovereignty and supremacy.

This is similar to the faces of the Cherubim Ezekiel saw and which upheld the Lord's *Throne Chariot.*

- *And I looked, and, behold, a whirlwind came out of the north, a great cloud, and a fire infolding itself, and a brightness was about it, and out of the midst thereof as the colour of amber, out of the midst of the fire. 5 Also out of the midst thereof came the likeness of* **four living creatures***. And this was their appearance; they had the likeness of a man. 6 And* **every one had four faces***, and* **every one had four wings***. 7 And their feet were straight feet; and the sole of their feet was like the sole of a calf's foot: and they sparkled like the colour of burnished brass. 8 And they had the hands of a man* *under their wings on their four sides; and they four had their faces and their wings. 9 Their wings were joined one to another; they turned not when they went; they went every one straight forward. 10 As for the likeness of their faces, **they four had the face of a man, and the face of a lion, on the right side: and they four had the face of an ox on the left side; they four also had the face of an eagle**. 11 Thus were their faces: and their wings were stretched upward; two wings of every one were joined one to another, and two covered their bodies* (Ezek 1:4-11).

• *This is **the living creature that I saw under the God of Israel** by the river of Chebar; and I knew that **they were the cherubims*** (Ezek 10:20).

Comparison has also been made of the four living creatures to the four Gospels which present Christ in four major aspects of His Person. As the **Lion**, He is the *Lion of the tribe of Judah*, represented as the King in Matthew. As the **Calf**, He is the *Servant of Jehovah*, the faithful one of Mark. As **Man**, He is the human Jesus, the *Son of Man* as presented in the Gospel of Luke, and as the **Eagle**, He is the *Divine Son of God* presented in the Gospel of John.

<u>(3) BY THEIR POWERFUL ABILITIES</u>. ***And the four beasts had each of them six wings about him; and they were full of eyes within*** (4:8). They are swift to fly but only at the Lord's bidding and with deep introspection. They know and guard their hearts as those that have not fallen as the other angels.

<u>(4) BY THEIR CONTINUAL PRAISE</u>: ***and they rest not day and night, saying, Holy, holy, holy, Lord God Almighty, which was, and is, and is to come.*** While the world below has fallen into the deepest wickedness, they maintain their full submission to the holiness of God, and continue to praise His Holiness.

Note that in the number of their wings and their praise of the Lord's holiness they are as the Seraphims in Isaiah 6:

• *In the year that king Uzziah died I saw also the LORD sitting upon a throne, high and lifted up, and his train filled the temple. 2 **Above it stood the seraphims: each one had six wings**; with twain he covered his face, and with twain he covered his feet, and with twain he did fly. 3 And one cried unto another, and said, **Holy, holy, holy, is the LORD of hosts**: the whole earth is full of his glory. 4 And the posts of the door moved at the voice of him that cried, and the house was filled with smoke* (Isa 6:1-4).

<u>FIVE-FOLD PRAISE TO THE ETERNAL GOD</u>

• *John to the seven churches which are in Asia: Grace be unto you, and peace, from him **which is, and which was, and which is to come**; and from the seven Spirits which are before his throne* (1:4).

• *I am Alpha and Omega, the beginning and the ending, saith the Lord, **which is, and which was, and which is to come**, the Almighty* (1:8).

• *And the four beasts had each of them six wings about him; and they were full of eyes within: and they rest not day and night, saying, Holy, holy, holy, LORD God Almighty, **which was, and is, and is to come*** (4:8).

• *Saying, We give thee thanks, O LORD God Almighty, **which art, and wast, and art to come**; because thou hast taken to thee thy great power, and hast reigned* (11:17).

• *And I heard the angel of the waters say, Thou art righteous, O Lord, **which art, and wast, and shalt be**, because thou hast judged thus* (16:5).

George Williams in his spiritually succinct manner gives the following summary. Note, he believes the Cherubim and Seraphim refer to the same creatures.

> The four living-creatures were the Cherubim - cherubim in government (Gen 3:24); Seraphim (Isa 6:2) in worship. They formed the four sides of the Throne. The expression *full of eyes* (4:6,8) suggests perfection of intelligence, as their six wings (Isa 6:2) symbolize character, service and worship. They represented the four species of living-creatures in the ordered earth—a man, an ox, a lion and an eagle. The ancients lowered their worship from God to these beings, and tried to picture them in the huge statues that have been discovered at Nineveh. But they were the products of creative wisdom and symbolized the intelligence, the strength, the power and the vision which belong to God as Creator.
>
> The Cherubim first appear in Genesis 3:24 as guardians of the Tree of Life. They next appear in the vail of the Tabernacle and on the golden Mercy-Seat. These two objects symbolized the Messiah as Creator and Redeemer, and they correspond to Revelation 4 and 5. Creation is beautiful, but it is a vail; redemption is wonderful, it reveals what is behind the vail and is more glorious than the vail. The cherubim appear again in 1 Kings 6,7; in the Psalms, in Isaiah, in Ezekiel, and finally in Revelation 19:4.
>
> The word for *Cherubim* in Hebrew signifies fullness of knowledge. As Cherubim they are connected with creation and government; as Seraphim, with redemption and worship. Both these characters are united in the expression, *living-creature* (Ezek 10:20).
>
> They are distinguished from the angels (4:8,11). They are attached to the Throne of God and are never seen apart from it. It is impossible for the human intellect to visualize them or to declare what they are. Their connection with the Throne is a pledge of the restoration of the whole Creation (*The Students Commentary of the Holy Scriptures*).

III THE VOICES FROM THE THRONE

1. THE INITIATION OF THE BEASTS *And when those beasts give glory and honour and thanks to him that sat on the throne, who liveth for ever and ever* (4:9). The Beasts instigate this praise in Heaven, for they have been in Heaven since and before the Fall. Amidst the unspeakable ruin and depravity of man as described in Romans 1, they praise that which Romans 1:20 speaks of, and which was revealed to but rejected by fallen man. Ponder especially the praise of these Beasts in contrast to Romans 1:23.

> *For the wrath of God is revealed from heaven against all ungodliness and unrighteousness of men, who hold the truth in unrighteousness; 19 Because that which may be known of God is manifest in them; for God hath shewed it unto them. 20* ***For the invisible things of him from the creation of the world are clearly seen, being understood by the things that are made, even his eternal power and Godhead;*** *so that they are without excuse: 21 Because that, when they knew God, they glorified him not as God, neither were thankful; but became vain in their imaginations, and their foolish heart was darkened. 22 Professing themselves to be wise, they became fools, 23 And changed the glory of the uncorruptible God into an image made like to corruptible* ***man, and to birds, and fourfooted beasts, and creeping things*** (Rom 1:18-23).

Though the living creatures do not rest in their ascription of holiness to God (4:8), yet there is now notice given that periodically they give special glory and honour and praise to

God sitting on His throne. On such occasions, according to verse 10, the twenty-four elders join with them in worship.

The world today does not give much honour to the Lord God. Though men benefit from His goodness and live in a world of His creation, yet the vast majority are silent as to anything resembling true worship. One of the important purposes of Revelation is to trace the movement of this worship that has long echoed in the halls of heaven to when it is not only brought down to earth, but to *all* the earth. It is not yet as Psalm 66, but soon will be after God's terrible works in the Tribulation. This purpose of God in worship is especially related to the Son of God as shown in Philippians 2.

- ***Make a joyful noise unto God, all ye lands***: *2 Sing forth the honour of his name: make his praise glorious. 3 Say unto God,* ***How terrible art thou in thy works!*** *through the greatness of thy power shall thine enemies submit themselves unto thee. 4* ***All the earth shall worship thee, and shall sing unto thee; they shall sing to thy name****. Selah* (Psa 66:1-4).
- *Wherefore God also hath highly exalted him, and given him a name which is above every name:* ***That at the name of Jesus every knee should bow****, of things in heaven, and things in earth, and things under the earth: And that every tongue should confess that Jesus Christ is Lord, to the glory of God the Father* (Phil 2:9,10).

(1) THEY HAVE ADORED THE ONE GOD, AND ONE ONLY: **the Lord God Almighty** (4:8), the unchangeable and everlasting God.

(2) THEY HAVE ADORED THE THREE HOLIES IN THIS ONE GOD: the **Holy** *Father*, the **Holy** *Son*, and the **Holy** *Spirit* (4:8); and these are *One* infinitely holy and Eternal Being, who sits upon the throne, *and lives for ever and ever*. In this glory the prophet Isaiah saw Christ, and spoke of him (Isa 6; Jhn 12:41).

2. THE RESPONSE OF THE ELDERS. Unlike the beasts, they have only now been glorified in Heaven. They follow their lead in giving praise to God.

(1) THEIR ACTS OF ADORATION. ***The four and twenty elders fall down before him that sat on the throne, and worship him that liveth for ever and ever, and cast their crowns before the throne, saying*** (4:10). See how they bow: they fall in the most profound humility, reverence, and godly fear before Him.

See how they bestow: They gave God the glory for the grace wherewith He had crowned them. They owe all their graces and all their glories to Him, and acknowledge that his crown is infinitely more glorious than theirs, and that it is their glory to be glorifying God.

(2) THEIR WORDS OF ADORATION. ***Thou art worthy, O Lord, to receive glory and honour and power: for thou hast created all things, and for thy pleasure they are and were created*** (4:11). They do not say, *We give thee glory, and honour, and power;* for what can any creature pretend to give unto God? But they say, ***thou art worthy to receive glory***. In this they tacitly acknowledge that God is exalted far above all blessing and praise. He was worthy to receive glory, but they were not worthy to give it. The true believer is humble on earth and will remain humble in Heaven.

CHAPTER 5

2. THE LAMB AND THE SEVEN-SEALED BOOK 5

In the foregoing chapter the Apostle had a sight of God on the throne of glory and government, surrounded with His holy ones, and receiving their adorations. Now the counsels and decrees of God concerning impending judgement upon the earth are set before John. These determinations are in a book which the Father holds is His right hand. In His hand the book is sealed; placed in the hand of Christ it becomes unsealed. Here then the great principle of coming Judgement: *For the Father judgeth no man, but hath committed all judgment unto the Son* (Jhn 5:22).

The glory of Jehovah Messiah as Creator having been declared (ch. 4), His higher glory as Redeemer is now proclaimed. The first heavenly utterance asserted the holiness of His Nature (4:8); the second, the efficacy of His Atonement (5:9). Three times the one is declared (4:8), and three times the other (5:6,9,12). The importance of this thrice repeated word " slain" is emphasized by its repetition. Atonement is the great doctrine of heaven.

THE OVERALL THEME OF CHAPTER FIVE

THE BOOK IN THE HAND OF GOD THE FATHER 5:1-5
THE BOOK IN THE HAND OF THE SON OF GOD 5:6-14

<u>(5:1) *And I saw in the right hand of him that sat on the throne a book written within and on the backside, sealed with seven seals.*</u> *(5:2) And I saw a strong angel proclaiming with a loud voice, Who is worthy to open the book, and to loose the seals thereof? (5:3) And no man in heaven, nor in earth, neither under the earth, was able to open the book, neither to look thereon. (5:4) And I wept much, because no man was found worthy to open and to read the book, neither to look thereon.*

(5:5) And one of the elders saith unto me, Weep not: behold, the Lion of the tribe of Juda, the Root of David, hath prevailed to open the book, and to loose the seven seals thereof. (5:6) And I beheld, and, lo, in the midst of the throne and of the four beasts, and in the midst of the elders, stood a Lamb as it had been slain, having seven horns and seven eyes, which are the seven Spirits of God sent forth into all the earth.

<u>*(5:7) And he came and took the book out of the right hand of him that sat upon the throne.*</u> *(5:8) And when he had taken the book, the four beasts and four and twenty elders fell down before the Lamb, having every one of them harps, and golden vials full of odours, which are the prayers of saints. (5:9) And they sung a new song, saying, Thou art worthy to take the book, and to open the seals thereof: for thou wast slain, and hast redeemed us to God by thy blood out of every kindred, and tongue, and people, and nation; (5:10) And hast made us unto our God kings and priests: and we shall reign on the earth.*

(5:11) And I beheld, and I heard the voice of many angels round about the throne and the beasts and the elders: and the number of them was ten thousand times ten thousand, and thousands of thousands; (5:12) Saying with a loud voice, Worthy is the Lamb that was slain to receive power, and riches, and wisdom, and strength, and honour, and glory, and blessing.

(5:13) And every creature which is in heaven, and on the earth, and under the earth, and such as are in the sea, and all that are in them, heard I saying, Blessing, and honour, and glory, and power, be unto him that sitteth upon the throne, and unto the Lamb for ever and ever.

THE BOOK OF REVELATION

(5:14) And the four beasts said, Amen. And the four and twenty elders fell down and worshipped him that liveth for ever and ever.

I. THE BOOK IN THE HAND OF GOD THE FATHER 5:1-5

1. THE DESCRIPTION OF THE BOOK. *And I saw in the right hand of him that sat on the throne a book written within and on the backside, sealed with seven seals* (5:1).

(1) THE BOOK IS IN THE HAND OF GOD. It is in His right hand, to declare the authority of the book, and his readiness and resolution to execute all the contents, counsels and purposes therein recorded. Unlike in the Old Testament this document is not in the Ark (Deut 31:26; cp. Rev 11:19), but on the throne. That is, its provisions and powers are about to be carried out immediately.

(2) THE BOOK IS FULL: *written within and on the backside.* It is written on both sides of its pages. There are no gaps or blanks. Its subject is the judgement that is now to fall upon the earth. It will be a full judgement. The judgements are all catastrophic, but with the Seal and Trumpet judgements they are in mercy *slightly mingled*; but with the Vial judgements they are unmingled (14:10,11). Here then is a full account of the events by which God will both punish and reclaim the world unto Himself.

(3) THE BOOK IS SEALED: *sealed with seven seals*. It is known to none but to God Himself. The number of seals tells of its inscrutable secrecy. It tells of seven judgements about to fall upon the earth. This number declares that *complete* judgement is about to fall. The three especial uses of the seal, (1) to authenticate a writing, (2) to ratify a deed, and (3) to conceal from undesired eyes, all come together with these seals.

Of the nature of this document, the following is based on the comments of Williams in *The Student's Commentary of the Holy Scriptures*. It is a document that both decrees judgement and yet restores the world on the merits of Christ's Sacrificial Death:

> The vision of the chapter is the action of the Messiah, symbolized by a Lamb as having been slain in sacrifice, claiming and taking possession of the document which declared Him to be the *Goel*, the Kinsman Redeemer of the earth and of Israel particularly (Psa 59:16). Ruth 4 and Jeremiah 32 explain the vision.
>
> Boaz, as kinsman, redeemed both Ruth and the piece of ground. He did so in grace, for neither merited redemption. Jeremiah bought a piece of ground, and a sealed document recited the purchase and declared him to be the owner. No person other than Jeremiah could, therefore, claim ownership of the land; and he only as owner could break the seals on the document establishing his right as owner.
>
> The action of both Boaz and Jeremiah was Messianic in type. He, as Israel's and the World's Redeemer, *Goel*, Kinsman, at the expense of His own Precious Blood redeemed the land and the people (Jhn 1:29). The document was signed and sealed declaring the purchase and the name of the Purchaser. The necessity and importance of the price of the redemption is pressed in the triple declaration that the Divine Purchaser was slain in sacrifice. But though this purchase primarily affected Israel and the Land of Israel, its operation affects the whole world and all mankind; for, as the Scriptures abundantly declare, the salvation of Israel guarantees the salvation of all nations, so that the great purchase deed of this chapter embraces the whole world.

IS IT A SEVEN-SEALED *BOOK* OR *SCROLL*?

The Greek word *biblion* with several exceptions is translated "book" in the KJV. However, as *biblion* can mean "scroll" and as that was the ancient means of writing, nearly all modern versions and commentaries say that it was a scroll rather than a book that is presented in Revelation 5. Nevertheless there is clear evidence that the KJV, **book**, is correct.

CHAPTER 5

The Seven Seals are seen on the *outside* of the document. Thus they both *seal* and can be fully *seen*. When each seal is opened, a further section of the *biblion* is revealed. This means that not only are the seven seals visible on the outside of the document (5:1), but they are also able to bind their given portion within the document. Such an arrangement is more difficult to envisage for a scroll. Govett with many others believes that the seals are affixed to the outer edge of the scroll and that the scroll can only be read until after the last seal is broken (p. 119). This is contrary to what we read in Revelation 6.

Commentaries have gone to great length in describing the scrolls that were used in ancient times, however they ignore the simple and well documented fact that books (codices) were used by early Christians, and that the New Testament manuscripts themselves were codices and not scrolls. http://www.bible.ca/b-canon-codex-printing-press.htm.

THE USE OF *BIBLION* AND *BIBLOS* IN THE KJV
The Englishman's Greek Concordance

Biblion.
Matt 19:7. *to give a **writing** of divorcement*
Mk 10:4. *to write a **bill** of divorcement*
Lk 4:17. *delivered unto him the **book** of the prophet Esaias. And when he had opened the **book***
 4:20. *he closed the **book***
Jhn 20:30. *which are not written in this **book***
 21:25. *could not contain the **books***
Gal 3:10. *all things which are written in the **book***
2 Tim 4:13. *bring with thee, and the **books***
Heb 9:19. *sprinkled both the **book**, and all the people*
 10:7. *in the volume of the **book** it is written*
Rev 1:11. *What thou seest, write in a **book***
 5:1. *on the throne a **book** written within*
 5:2. *Who is worthy to open the **book***
 5:3. *was able to open the **book***
 5:4. *worthy to open and to read the **book***
 5:5. *hath prevailed to open the **book***
 5:7. *he came and took the **book***
 5:8. *when he had taken the **book***
 5:9. *Thou art worthy to take the **book***
 6:14. *the heaven departed as a **scroll***
 17:8. *whose names were not written in the **book***
 20:12. *the **books** were opened: and another **book** was opened*
 20:12. *which were written in the **books***
 21:27. *written in the Lamb's **book** of life*
 22:7. *sayings of the prophecy of this **book***
 22:9. *which keep the sayings of this **book***
 22:10. *sayings of the prophecy of this **book***
 22:18. *words of the prophecy of this **book***
 22:18. *plagues that are written in this **book***
 22:19. *things which are written in this **book***

Biblos
Matt 1:1. *The **book** of the generation of Jesus Christ*
Mk 12:26. *have ye not read in the **book** of Moses*

Lk 3:4. *As it is written in the **book** of the words*
20:42. *David himself saith in the **book** of Psalms*
Acts 1:20. *it is written in the **book** of Psalms*
7:42. *written in the **book** of the prophets*
19:19. *brought their **books** together, and burned*
Phil 4:3. *whose names are in the **book** of life*
Rev 3:5. *blot out his name out of the **book** of life*
13:8. *not written in the **book** of life of the Lamb*
20:15. *found written in the **book** of life*
22:19. *take away from the words of the **book***
22:19. *take away his part out of the **book** of life*

In determining whether Revelation 5 is referring to a Book or a Scroll, consideration of the above demonstrates that:

- The New Testament is a ***Book***.
- The ***Book*** of Revelation is a ***Book***.
- The Seven-sealed ***Book*** is a ***Book***.

<u>2. THE PROCLAMATION CONCERNING THE BOOK</u>. ***And I saw a strong angel proclaiming with a loud voice, Who is worthy to open the book, and to loose the seals thereof*** (5:2)?

<u>(1) THE CRIER</u>. It was ***a strong angel***. The vision opens with three notes of emphasis: a *strong angel*—only twice more is reference made to a strong angel in Revelation (10:1;18:21). The angel *proclaims*—not merely says. The word signifies *to announce as a herald*. With a *loud voice* denotes urgency and great concern (Walvoord quoting J.B Smith). There are no weak angels in Heaven; yet many angels did fall in the past in *rebellion* with Satan (Matt 25:41), and many (*strangely!*) will fall in *mortal combat* during the middle of the Tribulation (Rev 12:4). This term a ***strong angel*** alerts to the fact that there are *strong* reasons why angels will need to be *strong* in the coming days.

- *And there was war in heaven: Michael and his angels fought against the dragon; and the dragon fought and his angels* (Rev 12:7).

Who is the strong angel making the challenge? The answer is probably Gabriel, who instructed Daniel and who ordered the closing and sealing the revelation given to him (see Dan 8:16; 9:21).

- *But thou, O Daniel, **shut up the words, and seal the book**, even to the time of the end: many shall run to and fro, and knowledge shall be increased* (Dan12:4).
- *And he said, Go thy way, Daniel: for **the words are closed up and sealed till the time of the end*** (Dan 12:9).

<u>(2) THE CHALLENGE</u>. ***Who is worthy to open the book, and to loose the seals thereof.*** If there by any creature who thinks himself sufficient either to explain or execute the counsels of this book let him now stand forth and make the attempt.

God now asks, ***who*** is worthy to stand beside Himself, as chief minister and agent of the throne? ***Who*** had so glorified God, as to be worthy to be ruler over all things? ***Who*** was so trusty, as to be the fit depository of the secrets of God? ***Who*** was possessed of original intelligence, sufficient to entitle him to enter into the deep designs of God (Govett)?

<u>(3) THE SILENCE</u>. ***And no man in heaven, nor in earth, neither under the earth, was able to open the book, neither to look thereon*** (5:3). The challenge went

CHAPTER 5

unanswered. Though the cry of the strong angel pierced into all realms, none in Heaven or earth could accept the challenge.

None *in heaven*, none of the glorious holy angels, though they reside before the throne of God and the ministers of His providence (Heb 1:14); they with all their wisdom could not delve into the judgement now about to fall upon earth.

None *on earth*, no man, the wisest or the best of men, none of the magicians and soothsayers, none of the prophets of God.

Nor certainly, *none under the earth*, none of the fallen angels, none of the spirits of men departed, though they should return to our world, can open this book. Satan himself, with all his subtlety, cannot do it; the creatures cannot open it, nor look on it; they cannot read it. It is therefore completely evident that the contents of this book are of such a nature that only the power of God could bring about its revelation and execution. Only God only can do it!

But for now, the creatures' powerlessness must first be seen. All must confess: *We are unprofitable servants, we have done that* [only] *which it was our duty to do* (Lk 17:10).

(4) THE SORROW. ***And I wept much, because no man was found worthy to open and to read the book, neither to look thereon*** (5:4). John sorrows at the unmet challenge. In this court of highest and last appeal, with the Father on the throne, and an unopened book which He Himself was not prepared to open, and no one else able to open was too much for John.

The great question being the redemption of Daniel's and of John's people, both wept bitterly because no redemption was visible (Dan 10:2). It is evident from John's distress that he understood the nature of the book, and what the absence of a claimant involved.

The *I wept* is emphatic. John alone was weeping. Certainly in these last days, with so many signs abounding, there is frequently a lack of earnest zeal for the truths of Christ's Second Coming.

(5) THE CONSOLATION. ***And one of the elders saith unto me, Weep not: behold, the Lion of the tribe of Juda, the Root of David, hath prevailed to open the book, and to loose the seven seals thereof*** (5:5). John is comforted at the prospect of a *Champion*.

[1] THE ONE WHO BROUGHT THE TIDINGS. It was ***one of the elders.*** God had revealed it to His Church. What angels were not made a party to an elder of the recently raptured church was. If angels learn from the Church, how more should men. This demonstrates that he Local Church with an open Bible is the primary source of knowledge in the world here below and even in that world above.

[2] THE ONE WHO WOULD FULFILL THE CHALLENGE. The Lord Jesus Christ is ***the lion of the tribe of Judah***, according to his human nature, and alluding to Jacob's prophecy (Gen 49:10),

- ***Judah is a lion's whelp****: from the prey, my son, thou art gone up: he stooped down, he couched as a lion, and as an old lion; who shall rouse him up? 10* ***The sceptre shall not depart from Judah****, nor a lawgiver from between his feet, until Shiloh come; and unto him shall the gathering of the people be* (Gen 49:9,10).
- *The sun and the moon shall be darkened, and the stars shall withdraw their shining. 16* ***The LORD also shall roar out of Zion****, and utter his voice from Jerusalem; and the heavens and the earth shall shake: but the LORD will be the hope of his people, and the strength of the children of Israel* (Joel 3:15,16).

Christ is the ***root of David*** according to His divine nature. He, *the Mediator between God and man* (1 Tim 2:5), is fit and worthy to open and execute all the counsels of God towards men, yet as salvation is of the Jews (Jhn 4:22) it will always be done through the line of David.

THE BOOK OF REVELATION

> • *I am **Alpha and Omega**, the **beginning and the end**, the **first and the last*** (Rev 22:13).
> • *I Jesus have sent mine angel to testify unto you these things in the churches. I am the **root and the offspring of David**, and the **bright and morning star*** (Rev 22:16).
> • *And there shall come forth **a rod** out of the stem of Jesse, and **a Branch** shall grow out of his roots* (Isa 11:1).

As both these titles **the Lion of the tribe of Juda, the Root of David** present Jesus' connections with the Jew. How strange, that so many commentators should labour to exclude them from this prophecy! What can result from such an effort, but darkness and confusion? Israel's blindness was, and is, a mystery: (Rom 11:25). It is to pass away, when desolations visit the earth (Isa 6:11,12). Israel is brought into view then, when the veil is about to be taken off (Govett).

Note the words: that Christ **hath <u>prevailed</u> to open the book, and to loose the seven seals thereof**. This as is next stated refers to His Work of Redemption on the Cross.

II. THE BOOK IN THE HAND OF THE SON OF GOD 5:6-14

1. THE DESCRIPTION OF CHRIST.
And I beheld, and, lo, in the midst of the throne and of the four beasts, and in the midst of the elders, stood a Lamb as it had been slain, having seven horns and seven eyes, which are the seven Spirits of God sent forth into all the earth (5:6). On being invited to see a Lion John looked and saw a Lamb. These expressed *price* and *power*; for if the price be paid and there be no power to take possession and evict the usurper, the payment is in vain And if, on the contrary, power be used in eviction without the previous payment of redemption, the action would be unrighteous. For the redemption of a forfeited inheritance both price and power are necessary. Thus the first redemption song sings of price; the second, of power (Rev 5:9 and 12). So John saw Him in Heaven as the Lamb of God as he saw Him at the first on earth (Jhn 1:29,36).

(1) HIS PLACE: *in the midst of the throne, and of the four beasts, and of the elders*. He is on the same throne with the Father; He is nearer to Him than either the elders or beasts. He is the centre of all. Neither the cherubim, the elders, nor the angels could redeem lost man. Only the Son of Man, of the Tribe of Judah, and the Root of David was *next of kin* to fallen men. He prevailed as the slain Lamb in His First Advent, and He will prevail as the crowned Lion in His Second Advent. Rob Heaven of the doctrine of the Atonement and of the Person of the Slain Lamb and it becomes a place of tears and bitter weeping (5:4). Christ crucified is the centre of heavenly glory (Williams).

(2) HIS FORM. Before he is called *a lion;* here He **stood a Lamb as it had been slain**. He is The Lion to conquer and take up His kingly reign on earth, but a Lamb to satisfy the Divine justice for the sinner. He appears with the marks of his sufferings upon him, to show that He interceded in Heaven in the virtue of His sacrifice. He appears as a *lamb,* **having seven horns and seven eyes**, perfect power to execute all the will of God and perfect wisdom to understand it all and to do it in the most effectual manner; **for he hath the seven Spirits of God**. He has the Holy Spirit *without measure*, in all perfection of light, and life, and power. By this He will rule all parts of the earth.

> • *For he whom God hath sent speaketh the words of God: for God **giveth not the Spirit by measure unto him*** (Jhn 3:34).
> • *Hear now, O Joshua the high priest, thou, and thy fellows that sit before thee: for they are men wondered at: for, behold, I will bring forth my servant the BRANCH. 9 For behold the stone that I have laid before Joshua; **upon one stone shall be seven eyes**: behold, I will engrave the graving thereof, saith the LORD of hosts, and I will remove the iniquity of that land in one day* (Zech 3:8,9).

CHAPTER 5

- *For who hath despised the day of small things? for they shall rejoice, and shall see the plummet in the hand of Zerubbabel with **those seven; they are the eyes of the LORD, which run to and fro through the whole earth** (Zech 4:10).*

J. Vernon McGee contrasts the Lion and the Lamb characteristics of Christ:

> The Lion character refers to His Second Coming, since the Lion speaks of His majesty. As Lion He is sovereign; as Lion He is Judge. The Lion speaks of the government of God. The Lamb character refers to His First Coming, for the Lamb speaks of His meekness. As Lamb He is Saviour; as Lamb He is judged. The Lamb speaks of the grace of God. As far as the book of Revelation is concerned, however, Christ is referred to as the Lion only once (here in 5:5); this is in contrast to the many times He is identified as the Lamb. The purpose of the use of the term *Lamb* identifies the glorified Christ of Revelation with Christ the Lamb of sacrifice in His first coming. The term lamb occurs in the Apocalypse twenty-eight times (in Walvoord).

The **seven horns** speak of His fullness of power, and a power soon to be exercised in the destruction of the horns of the Antichrist:

- *After this I saw in the night visions, and behold a fourth beast, dreadful and terrible, and strong exceedingly; and it had great iron teeth: it devoured and brake in pieces, and stamped the residue with the feet of it: and it was diverse from all the beasts that were before it; and it had **ten horns** (Dan 7:7).*
- *And I stood upon the sand of the sea, and saw a beast rise up out of the sea, having seven heads and ten horns, and upon his horns **ten crowns**, and upon his heads the name of blasphemy (Rev 13:1).*

With His *eyes* and *horns* Christ is now about to come forth to remove the iniquity of the land of Israel *in one day* and of the earth itself (Isa 66:8; Psa 59:16).

Govett summarizes this appearance of Christ as the Lamb:

> He appears as the Slain Lamb. As the Lamb, He put away sin by suffering; as the Lion, He shall put it away by destruction. He is the lamb *as it had been slain* That is, the marks of sacrificial death were upon Him. So Christ rose with the scars in His hands, feet, and side ; and they identified Him to the disciples (Lk 24:39). He was not seen in Chapter 1 with any mark of His death. But the scars now appear. This is the basis of the world's redemption, but also of the vengeance that is now to fall upon it. The Throne is about to avenge His death, and the death of His martyrs.
>
> He appears as the Slain Lamb, but also with **seven horns**. The work of opening the book demands personal qualifications, of the utmost excellence. There must be the perfection of power. The strength of the animal lies in its horn: it is its weapon of offence. Power in its fullness is required to put down the force, which wickedness in both heaven and earth musters on its side. Thus Jesus is seen as the great agent about to exercise all the power of the Godhead, with the full concurrence of the Throne.
>
> He appears as the Slain Lamb, but also with **seven eyes**. In Him is full perfection of wisdom and intelligence at what must now be done. His seven eyes pierce through the seven seals of the book. The seven eyes mark Him out as the perfect *seer* and Prophet; as the seven horns as the perfect and all powerful King. David was a *seer* but the *root of David* has the Spirit without measure. The Spirit came on David: the Spirit dwells in David's Lord.

2. THE ACQUISTION OF CHRIST. *And he came and took the book out of the right hand of him that sat upon the throne* (5:7). He is described by His act and deed: He *prevailed* to do this (5:5). He prevailed by His merit and worthiness; He prevailed by His work of redemption. In the act of receiving the book from God the Father, it is made evident that judgment and power over the earth are committed to Christ the Son of God. A parallel passage to this event is given in Daniel 7:13,14. There ultimate triumph of Christ is revealed when the kingdoms of the world are given to Him.

- *I saw in the night visions, and,* **behold, one like the Son of man came with the clouds of heaven, and came to the Ancient of days**, *and they brought him near before him. And there was given him dominion, and glory, and a kingdom, that all people, nations, and languages, should serve him: his dominion is an everlasting dominion, which shall not pass away, and his kingdom that which shall not be destroyed* (Dan 7:13,14).

3. THE WORSHIP OF CHRIST. John observes the thunderous joy in song of all creation. No sooner had Christ received the book out of the Father's hand than he received the adorations of angels and men, yea, of *every creature*. And, indeed, it is a great matter of joy to all that God does not deal with men in a way of absolute power and strict justice, but in a way of grace and mercy through the Redeemer. He governs the world, not merely as a Creator and Lawgiver, but as our God and Saviour. All the world has reason to rejoice in this. The song of praise that was offered up to the Lamb on this consists of three parts.

(1) THE BEASTS AND ELDERS BEGIN THE DOXOLOGY. *And when he had taken the book, the four beasts and four and twenty elders fell down before the Lamb, having every one of them harps, and golden vials full of odours, which are the prayers of saints* (5:8).

[1] THE OBJECT OF THEIR ADORATION: *the Lamb*, the Lord Jesus Christ; all men *should honour the Son as they honour the Father* (Jhn 5:23); for he has the same nature, but it is He who within the Godhead became the Lamb.

[2] THE POSTURE OF THEIR ADORATION: They *fell down before him*. They gave Him not an inferior sort of worship, but the most profound adoration.

[3] THE INSTRUMENTS USED IN THEIR ADORATION: *harps and golden vials full of odours, which are the prayers of saints* (Rev 8:3). Prayer and praise should always go together. The golden vials filled with sacred incense represent the prayers of the saints. Here in Heaven the importance of prayer in the earthly scene is shown. Later (8:3) testimony is made to the continued witness on earth of those who trust in Christ during the time of the dreadful Tribulation. Their prayers are said to be as sweet incense before the throne of God. The role of the Elders is one of sympathetic presentation, not that of a mediator of earthly prayers.

- *And another angel came and stood at the altar, having a golden censer; and* **there was given unto him much incense, that he should offer it with the prayers of all saints** *upon the golden altar which was before the throne. 4 And the smoke of the incense, which came with the prayers of the saints, ascended up before God out of the angel's hand* (Psa 8:3,4).
- *Let my prayer be set forth before thee as incense; and the lifting up of my hands as the evening sacrifice* (Psa 141:2).

[4] THE SUBJECTS OF THEIR ADORATION. *And they sung a new song, saying, Thou art worthy to take the book, and to open the seals thereof: for thou wast slain, and hast redeemed us to God by thy blood out of every kindred, and tongue, and

CHAPTER 5

people, and nation (5:9). It was a ***new song*** suited to the new state of what was about to take place upon the earth. There will be great judgement followed by great glory. In this ***new song*** they acknowledge:

<u>One</u>. THEY PRAISE THE WORTHINESS OF THE LORD JESUS CHRIST. ***Thou art worthy to take the book, and to open the seals thereof***. He is in every way worthy and sufficient for the work and deserving the honour.

<u>Two</u>. THEY PRAISE THEIR REDEMPTION AS LOST SINNERS. Though here they do not mention the dignity of His Person as God, without which His sacrifice would have been of no avail, but they instead emphasize the merit of his sufferings. ***Thou wast slain, and hast redeemed us to God by thy blood out of every kindred, and tongue, and people, and nation.*** Though the Four Beasts and the Twenty-four Elders initiate this great doxology of praise, it is only the Elders as the representatives of the full Church in Heaven, *the general assembly and church of the firstborn* (Heb 12:23), that have experienced the words sung here. The Beasts who are Cherubim add their voice to the song, but as unfallen angelic creatures they did not participate in the Fall and were not personally redeemed. Nevertheless they sing, for all of creation (which they *do* represent!) is now about to be restored and that by ***the Blood of the Lamb***. Again note: the fact that the Elders are singing this in Heaven before the Tribulation begins is a clear demonstration that the Church is *in Heaven* before the Tribulation begins.

The song that John hears sung in Heaven contains the same message that he was inspired to write in his Gospel and Epistles.

> • *These things were done in Bethabara beyond Jordan, where John was baptizing. 29 The next day John seeth Jesus coming unto him, and saith,* **Behold the Lamb of God, which taketh away the sin of the world** *(Jhn 1:28,29).*
>
> • *Again the next day after John stood, and two of his disciples; 36 And looking upon Jesus as he walked, he saith,* **Behold the Lamb of God** *(Jhn 1:35,36)!*
>
> • *But* **one of the soldiers with a spear pierced his side, and forthwith came there out blood and water.** *35 And he that saw it bare record, and his record is true: and he knoweth that he saith true, that ye might believe. 36 For these things were done, that the scripture should be fulfilled, A bone of him shall not be broken. 37 And again another scripture saith,* **They shall look on him whom they pierced** *(Jhn 19:34-37).*
>
> • *But if we walk in the light, as he is in the light, we have fellowship one with another, and* **the blood of Jesus Christ his Son cleanseth us from all sin** *(1 Jhn 1:7).*
>
> • *And he is the propitiation for our sins: and not for our's only, but also for* **the sins of the whole world** *(1 Jhn 2:2).*
>
> • *And we have seen and do testify that the Father sent the Son to be* **the Saviour of the world** *(1 Jhn 4:14).*
>
> • *Who is he that overcometh the world, but he that believeth that Jesus is the Son of God? 6 This is he that came by water and* **blood**, *even Jesus Christ; not by water only, but by water and* **blood**. *And it is the Spirit that beareth witness, because the Spirit is truth. 7 For there are three that bear record in heaven, the Father, the Word, and the Holy Ghost: and these three are one. 8 And there are three that bear witness in earth, the Spirit, and the water, and* **the blood**: *and these three agree in one. 9 If we receive the witness of men, the witness of God is greater: for this is the witness of God which he hath testified of his Son* (1 Jhn 5:5-9).

<u>Three</u>. THEY PRAISE THEIR EXALTATION AS SAINTS. ***And hast made us unto our God kings and priests: and we shall reign on the earth*** (5:10). The raptured and glorified church in Heaven rejoice in their impending participation with

THE BOOK OF REVELATION

Christ in His Millennial Reign on earth. Heaven is so glorious, and like Peter, James and John on the Mount of Transfiguration they may perhaps not have wanted to *come down*. Yet with Christ on the earth it will be a glorious place to serve. Two further passages, at the beginning and end of Revelation, show that believers in glorified bodies will reign with Christ during the Millennium.

- *And hath made us **kings and priests** unto God and his Father; to him be glory and dominion for ever and ever. Amen* (Rev 1:6).
- *Blessed and holy is he that hath part in the first resurrection: on such the second death hath no power, but they shall be **priests** of God and of Christ, and **shall reign with him a thousand years*** (Rev 20:6).
- *But **the saints of the most High shall take the kingdom**, and possess the kingdom for ever, even for ever and ever* (Dan 7:18).

Walvoord summarizes this *new song*.

> It is declared to be a new song, that is, a song which could not have been sung prior to His redemptive act, a song over and beyond an ascription of praise to His Person or a recognition of His attributes. Here He is declared to have the right to rule, not simply in virtue of His Deity but in His victory over sin and death in His act of supreme redemption. The right to the book has been secured by conquering death and providing a complete sacrifice for sin. The act of redemption is declared to be worldwide in that every kindred, tongue, and nation has been redeemed and has transformed sinners, who once were under the wrath of God, into kings and priests who will reign with Christ on the earth.

(2) THE ANGELS ADD THEIR VOICES TO THE DOXOLOGY

[1] THEIR NUMBER. *And I beheld, and I heard the voice of many angels round about the throne and the beasts and the elders: and the number of them was ten thousand times ten thousand, and thousands of thousands* (5:11). Forty-four times in this Book John declares that he *beheld* or *saw* something and twenty-seven times he declares, *I heard*. The tremendous scene is indescribable! In concentric circles with the Lamb in the midst surrounded by the Beast and the Twenty-four Elders, the angelic hosts are seen on every side, an innumerable throng bringing forth one mighty symphony of praise. Though the angels are unfallen, yet they rejoice in the salvation of sinners, and they rejoice with the redeemed in acknowledging the infinite merits of the Lord Jesus in dying for sinners. Here is a vast expansion of that other well-known passage of angelic praise:

- *Likewise, I say unto you, there is joy in the presence of the angels of God **over one sinner** that repenteth* (Lk 15:10).

[2] THEIR PRAISE. *Saying with a loud voice, Worthy is the Lamb that was slain to receive power, and riches, and wisdom, and strength, and honour, and glory, and blessing* (5:12). The sevenfold attributes ascribed to the Lamb sum up their worship and adoration. The anthem of the angels, the cherubim and elders contained seven terms because its theme is redemption; that of the creatures in the next verse (5:13) contains four because its theme is creation. This great chorus of praise is a prelude to the mighty scenes which will unfold, when in succeeding chapters, the seven-sealed book is opened, all of which culminates in the Return of Christ to rule and reign (Rev 19-22). The Twenty-four Elders sing, and the angels chant (*saying*) their praise. Christ is worthy of all. He is worthy of all that He has done as the *slain* Redeemer. He is worthy of all the praise He shall receive as *KING OF KINGS, AND LORD OF LORDS* (Rev 19:16).

CHAPTER 5

(3) ALL OF CREATION JOINS THE DOXOLOGY. *And every creature which is in heaven, and on the earth, and under the earth, and such as are in the sea, and all that are in them, heard I saying, Blessing, and honour, and glory, and power, be unto him that sitteth upon the throne, and unto the Lamb for ever and ever* (5:13). Heaven and earth ring with the high praises of the Redeemer. The whole creation fares the better for Christ! They (in ways not yet known to us) adore that great Redeemer who delivers the creature from that bondage under which it groans through the corruption of men,

- *For I reckon that the sufferings of this present time are not worthy to be compared with the glory which shall be revealed in us. 19 For the earnest expectation of **the creature** waiteth for the manifestation of the sons of God. 20 For **the creature** was made subject to vanity, not willingly, but by reason of him who hath subjected the same in hope, 21 Because **the creature** itself also shall be delivered from the bondage of corruption into the glorious liberty of the children of God. 22 For we know that the **whole creation** groaneth and travaileth in pain together until now* (Rom 8:18-22).

Note the effect the Millennial Reign will have on the animal creation. Then as in Mark 1:13 *the wild beasts* will be *with* and not against Him.

- *And in that day will **I make a covenant for them with the beasts of the field and with the fowls of heaven, and with the creeping things of the ground**: and I will break the bow and the sword and the battle out of the earth, and will make them to lie down safely* (Hos 2:18).
- *The **wolf** also shall dwell with the **lamb**, and the **leopard** shall lie down with the **kid**; and the **calf** and the **young lion** and the **fatling** together; and a **little child** shall lead them. 7 And the **cow** and the **bear** shall feed; their young ones shall lie down together: and the **lion** shall eat straw like the **ox**. 8 And the **sucking child** shall play on the hole of the **asp**, and the weaned child shall put his hand on the cockatrice' den. 9 They shall not hurt nor destroy in all my holy mountain: for the earth shall be full of the knowledge of the LORD, as the waters cover the sea* (Isa 11: 6-9).
- *And he was there in the wilderness forty days, tempted of Satan; and was **with the wild beasts**; and the angels ministered unto him* (Mk 1:13).

(4) THE BEASTS AND ELDERS CONCLUDE THE DOXOLOGY. *And the four beasts said, Amen. And the four and twenty elders fell down and worshipped him that liveth for ever and ever* (5:14). As the great anthem of praise began so it ends, and that with the Beasts and Elders. The four Beasts say *Amen*, and the Twenty-four Elders worship in low prostration before the Throne of God. Thus we have seen this sealed book passing with great solemnity from the hand of the Father into the nail pierced hand of the Son. And, as this book is the Title Deed to a yet to be restored earth, we now see how this will be brought about.

Walvoord in making important practical applications shows this Chapter to have been the *song before the storm*!

> The beauty and wonder of the scene in chapter 5 are in startling contrast to the dark clouds of divine judgment portrayed as falling upon the earth in the tribulation as revealed in the chapters which follow. The scenes of earth are always dark in comparison to the glory of heaven. The Christian engulfed by temptation, persecution, and trial can take heart in the fact that our Lord also suffered and was tried, and that He in triumph ascended on high having completed His earthly work. Those who follow in His steps while in the world may endure many afflictions, but they are assured that they will share with the Lord His glory throughout all eternity.

THE BOOK OF REVELATION

The scene of chapter 5 can be considered as prophetic of future events in which the church of Jesus Christ bearing witness in the world today will be in the presence of the Lord in heaven. Those who have received Jesus Christ as Saviour and who have entered into the blessings of His redemptive work will be numbered among the tens of thousands pictured in chapter 5 as giving their worship and praise to the Saviour. That which John contemplated in prophetic vision will be an actual part of the future experience of the saints of God in His Kingdom.

With the introduction provided in chapters 4 and 5 which give us the heavenly side of the picture, the narrative in John's vision now turns to the earth in chapter 6. The same Lord and Redeemer who is the object of worship and praise on the part of the saints is also the righteous Judge of the wicked earth and the One by whose authority the terrible events of the tribulation unfold. In the light of these future events, how important is the decision that faces every human soul. Today is the day of grace as the Scriptures make plain. Those who hear and respond to the divine invitation have the promise of blessing throughout eternity and deliverance from the time of judgment which will fall upon those who neglect to enter into the safety of salvation in their day of opportunity.

For many Christians Heaven is an unreal place. Even Christians tend to be occupied too much with the things of this present world, which can be seen and touched and felt. Too often goals in life have little to do with eternity's values. Though to the ordinary Christian the privilege of a vision of heaven such as was given the Apostle John and the Apostle Paul is seldom granted, what they saw has been plainly written in the Word of God, and we can see through their eyes the glorious picture of the majesty which surrounds the Lord in Heaven. By comparison to the heavenly scene, earth is revealed to be temporary and transitory, and its glory and glitter are tarnished. As far as the heavens are above the earth, so far the glory of heaven transcends what the natural eye can see in this world.

Revelation puts earth and heaven in proper perspective, the scenes of earth ending in the tragic denouement of the Great Tribulation, and the scenes of heaven fulfilled both in the millennial glory and in the eternal state. The true occupation of the child of God should be one of praise and worship of the God of glory while awaiting the fulfilment of His prophetic Word.

CHAPTER 6

B. THE SEVEN YEAR TRIBULATION 6-18

1. The Seal Judgements and Other Events 6,7
a. Six Seals Opened: <u>Wrath</u> (6:17) 6
b. 144,000 Jewish Evangelists Sealed 7:1-8
c. A Multitude of Gentiles Saved 7:9-17

a. Six Seals Opened: <u>Wrath</u> (6:17) 6

The Sealed Book, the Title Deed to earth, contain the means by which the earth will be reclaimed. The Book is now in the hand of the Son of God. Without delay He enters upon the work of opening the seals, publishing the contents and sending forth the judgements. Here are seven seals, with the seventh opening into seven trumpets of ever greater judgement; and the seventh trumpet opens up seven vials containing the full unmingled wrath of God.

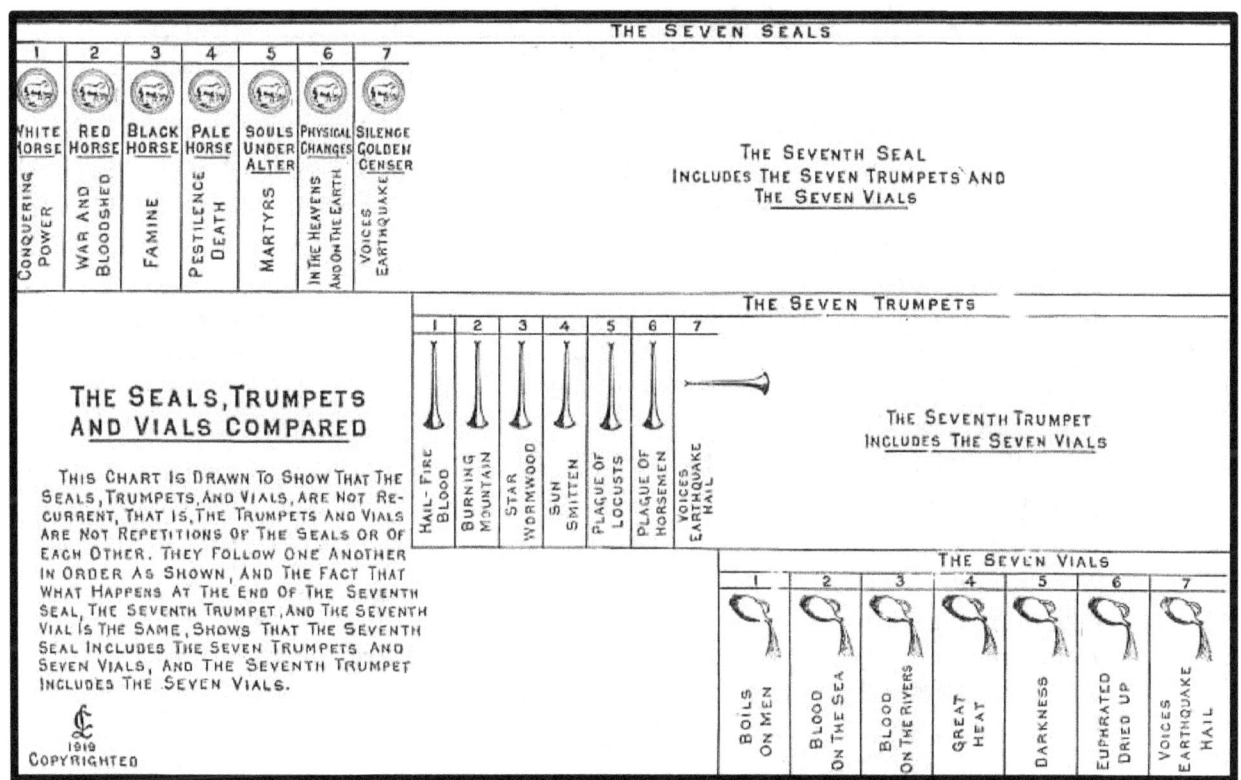

The Seven Seals, Trumpets and Vials: *Dispensational Truth* by Clarence Larken; Correct in Sequence, but Incorrect in Proportion. The Seventh Seal Containing the Seven Trumpets and Vials Occurs in the Second Half of the Tribulation.

The opening of the seals ushers in the terrible judgments to fall upon this earth after the Church has been caught up Heaven. There is a remarkable similarity between the progress of Chapter 6 as a whole and the description given by our Lord in the Olivet Discourse (Matt 24;). In both passages the order is (1) Deception; (2) War; (3) Famine; (4) Death; (5) Martyrdom; (6) Celestial Disturbances.

THE BOOK OF REVELATION

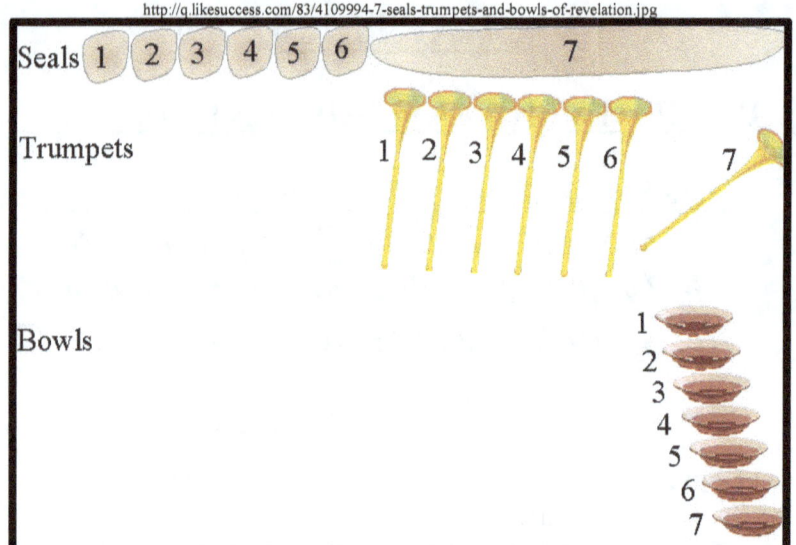

The Proportionate View: The Seventh Seal, Seven Trumpets and Seven Vials All in the Second Half of the Tribulation

THE OLIVET DISCOURSE GIVES THE SAME ORDER AS REVELATION 6

1. Deception, White Horse
• And Jesus answered and said unto them, Take heed that no man **deceive** you. 5 For many shall come in my name, saying, I am Christ; and shall **deceive** many (Matt 24:4,5).

2. War, Red Horse
• And ye shall hear of **wars and rumours of wars**: see that ye be not troubled: for all these things must come to pass, but the end is not yet. 7 For **nation shall rise against nation, and kingdom against kingdom** (Matt 24:6,7).

3. Famine, Black Horse
• and there shall be **famines** (Matt 24:7).

4. Death, Pale Horse
• and **pestilences**, and earthquakes, in divers places. 8 All these are the beginning of sorrows (Matt 24:7,8).

5. Martyrdom
• Then shall they deliver you up to be afflicted, and **shall kill you**: and ye shall be **hated of all nations** for my name's sake. 10 And then shall many be offended, and shall betray one another, and shall hate one another (Matt 24:9,10).

6. Celestial Disturbances
• Immediately after the tribulation of those days shall **the sun be darkened, and the moon shall not give her light, and the stars shall fall from heaven**, and the powers of the heavens shall be shaken (Matt 24:29).

• And there shall be **signs in the sun, and in the moon, and in the stars**; and upon the earth distress of nations, with perplexity; the sea and the waves roaring (Lk 21:25).

We will note that as we go through the Seal, Trumpet and Vial Judgements that they are each divided into two units of *four* and *three*.

CHAPTER 7

THE FIRST FOUR SEALS: THE HORSEMEN 6:1-8

(6:1) And I saw when the Lamb opened one of the seals, and I heard, as it were the noise of thunder, one of the four beasts saying, Come and see. (6:2) And I saw, and behold a white horse: and he that sat on him had a bow; and a crown was given unto him: and he went forth conquering, and to conquer.

(6:3) And when he had opened the second seal, I heard the second beast say, Come and see. (6:4) And there went out another horse that was red: and power was given to him that sat thereon to take peace from the earth, and that they should kill one another: and there was given unto him a great sword.

(6:5) And when he had opened the third seal, I heard the third beast say, Come and see. And I beheld, and lo a black horse; and he that sat on him had a pair of balances in his hand. (6:6) And I heard a voice in the midst of the four beasts say, A measure of wheat for a penny, and three measures of barley for a penny; and see thou hurt not the oil and the wine.

(6:7) And when he had opened the fourth seal, I heard the voice of the fourth beast say, Come and see. (6:8) And I looked, and behold a pale horse: and his name that sat on him was Death, and Hell followed with him. And power was given unto them over the fourth part of the earth, to kill with sword, and with hunger, and with death, and with the beasts of the earth.

<u>Four Horses of Helios</u>, **Piccadilly Circus, London, Erected 1992**

In the early 1900s the Brethren writer, George Williams, suggested the possibility that in harmony with Christ's First Coming, the events leading up to His Second Coming would cover a period of about seventy years.

It is very probable that as the First Advent covered a period of about seventy years, so also will the Second. In His First Advent He *came out of Bethlehem* (Micah 5:2) to those watching for Him, and thirty-three years later He *came unto* Jerusalem publicly (Zech 9: 9). Thirty-seven years later doom fell on Jerusalem.

THE FIRST SEAL: DECEPTION 6:1,2

(6:1) And I saw when the Lamb opened one of the seals, and I heard, as it were the noise of thunder, one of the four beasts saying, Come and see. (6:2) And I saw, and behold a

white horse: and he that sat on him had a bow; and a crown was given unto him: and he went forth conquering, and to conquer.

    1. THE FIRST SEAL IS OPENED. *And I saw when the Lamb opened one of the seals* (6:1). Having blessed and chastened the churches, Christ now begins to deal with the world.

    2. THE VOICE OF ONE OF THE BEASTS IS HEARD: *and I heard, as it were the noise of thunder, one of the four beasts saying, Come and see.* John is beckoned by a voice from one of the Angelic Beasts (likely the Lion, 4:7, cp. 6:3). The Beasts are no longer saying *holy, holy, holy.* It is now a *noise of thunder*, for judgement is coming, and that despite the seeming "peacefulness" of the rider who now appears.

    On a warm summer day one can hear thunder in the distance even though the sun is widely shining The Tribulation will begins with "assurances" of peace and safety". It will be much like *the sun that was shining* on the very day that Sodom was destroyed.

> • *For **when they shall say, Peace and safety**; then sudden destruction cometh upon them, as travail upon a woman with child; and they shall not escape* (1 Thess 5:3).
>
> • *Haste thee, escape thither; for I cannot do anything till thou be come thither. Therefore the name of the city was called Zoar. 23* **The sun was risen upon the earth** *when Lot entered into Zoar. 24 Then the LORD rained upon Sodom and upon Gomorrah brimstone and fire from the LORD out of heaven* (Gen 19:22-24).
>
> • *Likewise also as it was in the days of Lot;* **they did eat, they drank, they bought, they sold, they planted, they builded;** *29 But the same day that Lot went out of Sodom it rained fire and brimstone from heaven, and destroyed them all. 30 Even thus shall it be in the day when the Son of man is revealed* (Lk 17:28-30).

    3. THE SCENE UNFOLDS.

        (1) A WHITE HORSE GOES FORTH. *And I saw, and behold a white horse* (6:2). From the thunder that went before and the catastrophes that follow this horse and its rider cannot refer to Christ. It is a *deceptive Christ*, the Antichrist. Christ at this point, is opening the seals, He is not riding upon a horse; that will come later (Rev 19:11). The whole context and character of these seals absolutely forbid our thinking that this rider is Christ (as those taking the historical rather than the futurist believe). Christ's coming will not bring war, famine and strife in its train. Further, Christ is in Heaven opening the seals, not riding on a horse.

    Antichrist will present himself to the world as the Prince of Peace, and, therefore, riding a white horse. He will bear a crown and a bow, the insignia of imperial power. He will go forth resolving to conquer; and he will succeed for a while (Rev 13:7). But the double effect of his rule is pictured in verses 3-11—for the world, bloodshed (6:4), famine (6:5), and pestilence (6:8); and for Messiah's people, persecution (6:9).

        (2) THE RIDER IS ONLY PARTIALLY ARMED: *and he that sat on him had a bow*. He conveys the threat or the ability to go to war, but without arrows does not for now engage in war (Dan 8:25). He has a *bow* but not a *sword*, as Christ has in Revelation 19:15).

> • *And through his policy also he shall cause craft to prosper in his hand; and he shall magnify himself in his heart, and* **by peace shall destroy many***: he shall also stand up against the Prince of princes; but he shall be broken without hand* (Dan 8:25).

CHAPTER 7

Thus *The Day of the Lord* comes on gently. Its beginning is only a seal broken on high. The noise is not heard on earth. And, as its consequence, a single horseman only goes forth.

(3) <u>HE HAS A CROWN GIVEN</u>: ***and a crown was given unto him.*** But, he does not have ***many crowns***, as Christ has in Revelation 19:12. Nevertheless, for a while, the world will give this false messiah the greatest adulation and honour.

- *And **all that dwell upon the earth shall worship** him, whose names are not written in the book of life of the Lamb slain from the foundation of the world* (Rev 13:8).

(4) <u>HE IS A CONQUEROR</u>: ***and he went forth conquering, and to conquer.*** The subject now is Messiah rising up from His Father's Throne in order to resume relations with Israel, and to claim the Land and the world as His possession. The Adversary, Satan, immediately is seen in the activity of his enmity producing a counter-claimant. He will destroy all in his path for a while but will come to an ignominious end (Rev 13:4-7). He will conquer but not as Christ conquers in Revelation 19:19,20.

The rider on the white horse is the False Messiah. He will be the culmination of all false Messiahs (Matt 24:5), just as the False Prophet (Rev 13:11) will culminate all false prophets (Matt 24:24). As soon as the True Messiah arises, this False Messiah at once appears as the opponent to take the inheritance to himself. Satan from the beginning has opposed every Divine movement in regard to man and the earth. This will be his final attempt before the Return of Christ to the earth.

SIGNS OF THE COMING ANTICHRIST

We are to look for Christ rather than Antichrist (Titus 2:13). For the believer Christ will appear before Antichrist. Nevertheless as the spirit of Antichrist will be in the world before the Rapture and the beginning of the Seven Years, there will be clear indications of the stage being set for his appearance of Antichrist. Some twenty-five times, the New Testament tells believers ***to watch***. It is obvious that some of the events of the Tribulation will begin to cast a shadow before the Rapture. Nevertheless, he will not be revealed, nor will it be possible to identify him before the Rapture (2 Thess 2:7,8).

- *Little children, it is the last time: and as **ye have heard that antichrist shall come, even now are there many antichrists**; whereby we know that it is the last time* (1 Jhn 2:18).
- *And in the morning, It will be foul weather to day: for the sky is red and lowering. O ye hypocrites, **ye can discern the face of the sky; but can ye not discern the signs of the times*** (Matt 16:3)?
- *For the mystery of iniquity doth already work: only **he who now letteth will let, until he be taken out of the way. 8 And then shall that Wicked be revealed**, whom the Lord shall consume with the spirit of his mouth, and shall destroy with the brightness of his coming* (2 Thess 2:7,8).
- *Remember therefore how thou hast received and heard, and hold fast, and repent. **If therefore thou shalt not watch, I will come on thee as a thief**, and thou shalt not know what hour I will come upon thee* (Rev 3:3).
- *And **when these things begin to come to pass, then look up, and lift up your heads; for your redemption draweth nigh**. 29 And he spake to them a parable; Behold the fig tree, and all the trees; 30 When they now shoot forth, **ye see** and know of your own selves that summer is now nigh at hand. 31 So likewise ye, when **ye see** these things*

come to pass, know ye that the kingdom of God is nigh at hand. 32 Verily I say unto you, ***This generation shall not pass away, till all be fulfilled*** (Lk 21:28-32).

The following traits and actions will characterize the Antichrist in the Tribulation:

- He will be indwelt and empowered by Satan (Rev 13).
- He will rise to power first over 3 and then 10 nations likely from the old Roman Empire Europe (Dan 7:8).
- He will somehow be 'diverse from the rest' (Dan 7:7).
- He will bring 'peace', yet conquer through treaties and war (Dan 8:25).
- He will be adored by the world (Rev 13).
- He will blaspheme God (Rev 13).
- He will *not regard the desire of women* (Dan 11:37).
- He will be a great talker and speech maker (Dan 7:20).
- He will likely be charismatic and physically attractive ... like King Saul (1 Sam 10:23).
- He will receive what appears to be a fatal wound to the head (Rev 13).
- He will *appear* to be resurrected from the dead (Rev 13).
- His right eye is blinded and his arm withered (Zech 11:17).
- He will enforce a "peace" plan or upon Israel, likely a pre-existing plan (Dan 9:27).
- He will enable Israel to worship in a Temple (cp. Isa 28:15; Jhn 5:43).
- He will appear to perform miracles (Rev13).
- He will require that everybody on Earth receive a mark or identification on their forehead or hand without which no one will be able to buy or sell (Rev 13).
- He will stand in a new Jewish Temple in Jerusalem and declare he is "God" (2 Thess 2:4).
- Terror and war will then engulf Earth for *exactly* 3½ years (Rev 11-13).
- He will persecute and kill millions of Christians and Jews who come to know the Lord (cp Rev 7:13,14; Zech 13:9).
- He will lead the armies of the world into Israel . . . *Armageddon.* (Rev 16:14-16).

THE SECOND SEAL: WAR 6:3,4

(6:3) ***And when he had opened the second seal, I heard the second beast say, Come and see.*** (6:4) ***And there went out another horse that was red: and power was given to him that sat thereon to take peace from the earth, and that they should kill one another: and there was given unto him a great sword.***

The first seal was *deception*, The next three seals describe *desolation* - the desolating judgments that will follow the Rider on the White Horse. In fact these next three riders may as the first rider represent the Antichrist himself. Now his *true colours*, his full character is revealed. The Antichrist is not a man of peace but a man of war. The very fact that he is militarily dominant by the middle of the Tribulation leaves no other conclusion then that the Rider on the Red Horse refers to the Antichrist and his military prowess in the first half of the Tribulation.

- *And they worshipped the dragon which gave power unto the beast: and they worshipped the beast, saying,* ***Who is like unto the beast? who is able to make war with him*** (Rev 13:4)?

1. THE SECOND SEAL IS OPENED. ***And when he had opened the second seal*** (6:3). It is likely that the time lapse between the openings of the first two seals has been long

enough for the world's ambassadors, diplomats and the world itself to enjoy a remarkable measure of peace on the earth. Nations have taken a deep breath and stepped back from the brink. Headlines have ceased being strident and threatening. The international news is almost boring! Defence budgets have been cut, and troops brought home from the world's trouble spots. A "PEACE IN OUR TIMES" euphoria sweeps the globe.

Neville Chamberlain, 1st October 1938, *There Will Be Peace in Our Times*

- *Behold, their valiant ones shall cry without:* **the ambassadors of peace shall weep bitterly** (Isa 33:7).
- *For* **when they shall say, Peace and safety; then sudden destruction** *cometh upon them, as travail upon a woman with child; and they shall not escape* (1 Thess 5:3).

2. THE VOICE OF THE SECOND BEAST IS HEARD. *I heard the second beast say, Come and see.* If the view of the first horse leaves a question mark, that which the second presents could not be more emphatic. War is imminent! Note that as with their four faces, the Four Beasts present a fourfold picture of Christ, but also they are here presenting a fourfold view of the coming Antichrist.

3. THE SCENE UNFOLDS.

(1) A RED HORSE GOES FORTH. *And there went out another horse that was red* (6:4). The days of summer end all too soon, the world moves from *white,* apparent peace and safety, to *red* – war! No longer is it, *the earth sitteth still and is at rest*" (Zech 1:11). This horse is of the hue and colour of death. Satan is a *red dragon* (Rev 12:3). But, as Heaven is the place where these seals are opened, it is ultimately the Lord Himself who will call forth the sword during those days.

- *That all flesh may know that I the LORD have drawn forth my sword* out of his sheath: it shall not return any more (Ezek 21:5).
- *Therefore prophesy thou against them all these words, and say unto them,* **The LORD shall roar from on high**, *and utter his voice from his holy habitation; he shall mightily roar upon his habitation; he shall give a shout, as they that tread the grapes,* **against all the inhabitants of the earth**. *31 A noise shall come even* **to the ends of the earth**; *for the LORD hath a controversy with the nations, he will plead with all flesh; he will give them that are wicked to the sword, saith the LORD. 32 Thus saith the LORD of hosts, Behold,* **evil shall go forth from nation to nation**, *and a great whirlwind shall be raised up from the coasts of the earth. 33 And* **the slain of the LORD shall be at that**

day from one end of the earth even unto the other end of the earth: they shall not be lamented, neither gathered, nor buried; they shall be dung upon the ground (Jer 25:30-33).

(2) DIPLOMACY FAILS: **and power was given to him that sat thereon to take peace from the earth.** The temporary and misguided peace is broken. There is as sudden return to *wars and rumours of wars* (Matt 24:6), and then all-out war, and that on a scale unprecedented.

(3) BLOODSHED ENSUES: **and that they should kill one another.** Human passions rage to bloodshed. This horseman goes to produce war, and especially the worst form of it—civil war, This presents the spectre of civil war as well as *kingdom against kingdom* during the first half of the Tribulation.

• *And I will call for a sword against him throughout all my mountains, saith the Lord GOD:* **every man's sword shall be against his brother** (Ezek 38:21).
• *I set all men everyone against his neighbour* (Zech 8:10).
• *For* **nation shall rise against nation, and kingdom against kingdom**...*8 All these are the beginning of sorrows* (Matt 24:7,8).

(4) A GREAT SWORD IS GIVEN: **and there was given unto him a great sword.** Since Hiroshima and Nagasaki **the great sword** has been the continual upgrading of the atomic bomb. It is difficult to envisage a greater sword. Yet that is what seems to be stated here.

The First *Great Sword*

"One of the first atomic bombs detonated, the "Fat Man" was based on fission of plutonium. Sixty inches wide and 128 inches long, it struck Nagasaki, Japan with a force of 20,000 tons of TNT and destroyed seven square miles. This photograph is one of the only two pictures of the actual A-bomb ever released." https://www.livescience.com/45509-hiroshima-nagasaki-atomic-bomb.html .

Hiroshima

THE BOOK OF REVELATION

TEN WARS WITH HIGHEST DEATH TOLL, *EIGHT IN CHINA*

1. WORLD WAR II
"Although the death toll is debated till date, it was this war which saw the most number of casualties in history, with a number ranging from around **50 to 80 million** deaths. Most noted historians and most trusted sources say that the death toll, from all nations which were involved in the war, was something around 65 to 70 million, but however no official number has been considered, for the period from 1939 till 1945.

2. MONGOL CONQUESTS
Another deadly war that occurred was the Mongol conquest. The estimated death toll of people was somewhere between **30 to 60 million** deaths during the ongoing war, the war which took place from 1206 and 1324. These Mongol invasions, which however took part only during the 13th century led to the decline of the Mongol Empire in S.E Asia. It was one of the bloodiest battles in history, and took a large number of lives during that period. Most historians believe it could have exceeded that number which had not.

3. QING DYNASTY (which conquered the Ming Dynasty)
This was the dynasty which was ruling from 1644 to 1922 and was also the last imperial dynasty in the great country of China. During the course of their reign, the dynasty overtook the over powerful Ming dynasty, and also wars erupted throughout the country of China, for not only political leadership but also for land. By the Qing war's end, the estimated death toll had reached almost about **25 million** people. It also became one of the bloodiest and deadliest wars of the world.

4. TAIPING REBELLION
This revolution became the largest ever civil war to ever take place in China. It happened from 1850 to 1864, between the borders of Manchu and Qing dynasties. At least **20 million** deaths were recorded during the war, and also many of these were innocent civilians, making it again one of the deadliest wars in China. After this war, China became noted for being one of the noted nations to be encouraged with civil war and it also became the one which brought the entire nation of China against one another during the years during which the war was fought.

5. WORLD WAR I
The First war for the whole world which was known for its misery and havoc as it made countries fight against each other. This was the "global war" which lasted from the year 1914 to the year 1918 and it also involved all the world's greatest powers. Rise of imperialism was one of the main reasons the war began, in which Europe emerged and became a leading nation. The death toll during the 4 year span of the war reached almost around **17 million** people and only a fraction of the number was taken during the Second World War.

6. THE WHITE LOTUS REBELLION
Yet another deadly war which was responsible for taking **16 million** lives. This war lasted from 1794 to 1804 in the country of China. It led to the end of the powerful Qing dynasty; however the war also recorded the highest point of power during the Qing dynasty period as well. It actually initially began as a kind of tax protest in China which was led by a secret religious organization, but it however quickly emerged as a rebellion against the strong bureaucratic powers.

7. THE LUSHAN REBELLION
Yet another war remembered for its gruesome nature. This war however began in 455, when General An Lush rightfully declared himself as the powerful emperor of Northern China, and also established the Yan dynasty. Also, **13 million** deaths were recorded in this battle, which took place between the Tang and Yan dynasty. This was done to determine the strong powerhouse present in Northern China during this period.

CHAPTER 7

8. THE ERA OF WARRING STATES
This marked a slide in the warring nature of the countries. From 475 to 221 BCE, around **10 million** deaths occurred, when however the different states of China, openly declared war against one another. With Qin, Wei, Han, Zhao, and many other major powers, which were controlling different portions of China, the religious, social, political, and government powers were in these neighboring states, also led to this major era of war and powerful disunity.

9. THE DUNGAN REVOLT
This was an ethnic based war, which was done with religious underpinnings and it also took place during the early 19th century in China. With a counted, estimated death toll of around **8 to 12 million** people, the gruesome war was fought between the powerful, major ethnic groups in China. The war initially was set off mainly due to an extreme over pricing of bamboo poles, which however took place between a Hui and Han, and also this led to the years of bad fighting which took place in China during this close period.

10. THE CHINESE CIVIL WAR
Finally the major civilian war that happened for proclamation of independence was this war. Taking about **7.5 million** lives, the civil war lasted from 1927 till 1949. It was fought between the forces which were loyal to the KMT forces, and also the communist party forces that were in power during this time period. The Republic of China in Taiwan and also the powerful People's Republic (in China), were formed during this period. It showed which side these locals were loyal to, and also which religious beliefs they actually, sincerely wanted the country to follow during the entire period of the war."
https://www.toplst.com/top-10-wars-by-death-toll/

"Two major European wars, the Napoleonic and the Russian Revolution, though taking a very heavy toll, fall below the wars that took place in China. Fought between 1803 and 1815, the NAPOLEONIC WARS were a series of major conflicts pitting the French Empire, led by Napoleon Bonaparte, a French military and political leader, against an array of European powers formed into various coalitions. In his military career, Napoleon fought about 60 battles and lost just seven, mostly at the end of his reign. The European total of the wars may have reached as many as **5 million** military deaths, including diseases.

Fought between 1917 and 1922, the RUSSIAN CIVIL WAR was a multi-party war in the former Russian Empire that followed the Russian Revolutions of 1917 as many factions competed for power. The two largest combatant groups were the Bolsheviks' Red Army and the loosely allied forces known as the White Army. There were an estimated **7 – 12 million casualties** during the war, mostly civilians. The Russian Civil War has even been described as the greatest national catastrophe Europe has ever seen."
http://list25.com/25-deadliest-wars-in-human-history/

To put the terrible toll of major past wars in perspective, the highest numbers calculated each of these twelve wars would add up to about **300 million deaths**. This cannot compare with the toll that will be counted by the time the Four Horsemen finish their ride, or when the Sixth Trumpet is blown in the second series of judgements. By then the death toll from all causes will have reached **one half of the world's population**. And, as stated in Isaiah 24, after the pouring out of the Vial Judgements and the Battle of Armageddon the numbers of those living on the earth will have been decimated much further.

> • *And I looked, and behold a pale horse: and his name that sat on him was Death, and Hell followed with him. And power was given unto them over **the fourth part of the earth, to kill** with sword, and with hunger, and with death, and with the beasts of the earth* (Rev 6:8).

THE BOOK OF REVELATION

- *And thus I saw the horses in the vision, and them that sat on them, having breastplates of fire, and of jacinth, and brimstone: and the heads of the horses were as the heads of lions; and out of their mouths issued fire and smoke and brimstone. 18 By these three was **the third part of men killed**, by the fire, and by the smoke, and by the brimstone, which issued out of their mouths (Rev 9:17,18).*
- *Behold, **the LORD maketh the earth empty**, and maketh it waste, and turneth it upside down, and scattereth abroad the inhabitants thereof (Isa 24:1).*
- *The earth also is defiled under the inhabitants thereof; because they have transgressed the laws, changed the ordinance, broken the everlasting covenant. 6 Therefore hath the curse devoured the earth, and they that dwell therein are desolate: therefore **the inhabitants of the earth are burned, and few men left** (Isa 24:5,6).*

For a further discussion See "The Warfare in the Middle of the Tribulation". (Daniel 11:40-45); *Daniel: The Times of the Gentiles and the Times of Jerusalem* (J. A. Moorman).

THE THIRD SEAL: FAMINE 6:5,6

(6:5) *And when he had opened the third seal, I heard the third beast say, Come and see. And I beheld, and lo a black horse; and he that sat on him had a pair of balances in his hand.* **(6:6)** *And I heard a voice in the midst of the four beasts say, A measure of wheat for a penny, and three measures of barley for a penny; and see thou hurt not the oil and the wine.*

1. THE THIRD SEAL IS OPENED. *And when he had opened the third seal* (6:5).
2. THE VOICE OF THE THIRD BEAST IS HEARD. *I heard the third beast say, Come and see.* As the beasts are enumerated, reference should be made to their four faces. This third beast has the *face of a man*. The daily needs of *man* are now in special view. Compare also the call of God given to Elijah for a *seven year* famine.

- *And the first beast was like a **lion**, and the second beast like a **calf**, and the third beast had a face as a **man**, and the fourth beast was like a **flying eagle** (Rev 4:7).*
- *Then spake Elisha unto the woman, whose son he had restored to life, saying, Arise, and go thou and thine household, and sojourn wheresoever thou canst sojourn: for **the LORD hath called for a famine; and it shall also come upon the land seven years*** (2 Kng 8:1).

3. THE SCENE UNFOLDS.
   (1) A BLACK HORSE GOES FORTH. *And I beheld, and lo a black horse.* Famine, the natural aftermath of war. The judgements of the Tribulation like the plagues in Egypt will come hard and fast.

- ***Their visage is blacker than a coal**; they are not known in the streets: their skin cleaveth to their bones; it is withered, it is become like a stick* (Lam 4:8).
- ***Our skin was black like an oven because of the terrible famine*** (Lam 5:10).

   (2) THE SYMBOL OF FOOD SCARCITY: *and he that sat on him had a pair of balances in his hand.* Signifying that men must now eat their bread by weight: *They shall deliver your bread to you by weight* (Lev. 26:26).
   (3) THE DECREE TO RATION FOOD. *And I heard a voice in the midst of the four beasts say, A measure of wheat for a penny, and three measures of barley for a penny; and see thou hurt not the oil and the wine* (6:6). A days wage for a meal. And this famine, as all others, will fall most severely upon the poor; whereas the *oil* and the *wine*,

CHAPTER 7

which were more the luxuries of the rich, were not hurt; but if bread, the staff of life, is broken, these will not supply what wheat and barley will. When Christ the Living Bread is rejected; famine, both spiritual and physical will ensue. Williams says: "In this famine corn will be eight times its usual price."

Walvoord explains that if the *oil and wine* do not represent an absolutely basic necessity; they do nevertheless represent necessities for the perseveration of life. Their supplies must be maintained during the coming days of famine.

The silver coin designated as a penny is the Roman denarius, worth about fifteen cents. In the wage scale of that time it was common for a person to receive one denarius for an entire day's work. For such a coin, one measure of wheat or three measures of barley could be purchased.

The explanation seems to be this: A measure of wheat is approximately what a laboring man would eat in one meal. If he used his penny to buy barley, a cheaper grain, he would have enough from an entire day's wages to buy three good meals of barley. If he bought wheat, a more precious grain, he would be able to buy enough for only one meal. There would be no money left to buy other things, such as oil or wine, which were considered essential in Biblical times. To put it in ordinary language, the situation would be such that one would have to spend a day's wages for a loaf of bread with no money left to buy anything else. The symbolism therefore indicates a time of famine when life will be reduced to the barest necessities; for famine is almost always the aftermath of war.

Thus orders are given during the first half of the Tribulation for first tier and second tier necessities, and the emphasis given to preserving the former must not adversely affect the latter. This would include medicines. This is certainly how the Good Samaritan viewed *oil and wine.*

- *And went to him, and **bound up his wounds, pouring in oil and wine**, and set him on his own beast, and brought him to an inn, and took care of him* (Lk 10:34).

https://www.census.gov/population/international/data/idb/images/worldpop.png

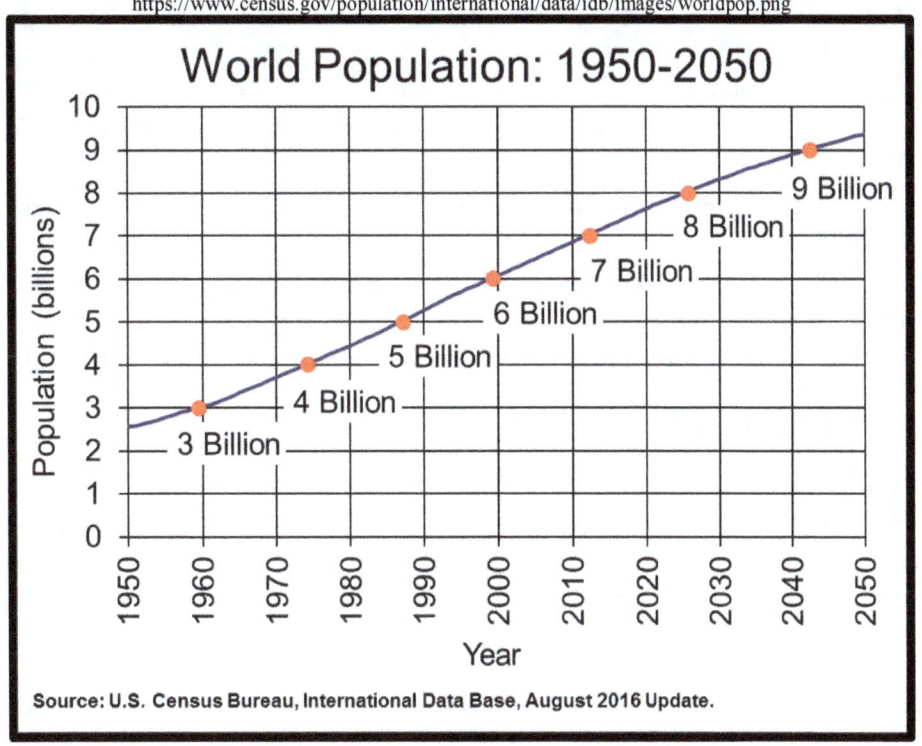

THE BOOK OF REVELATION

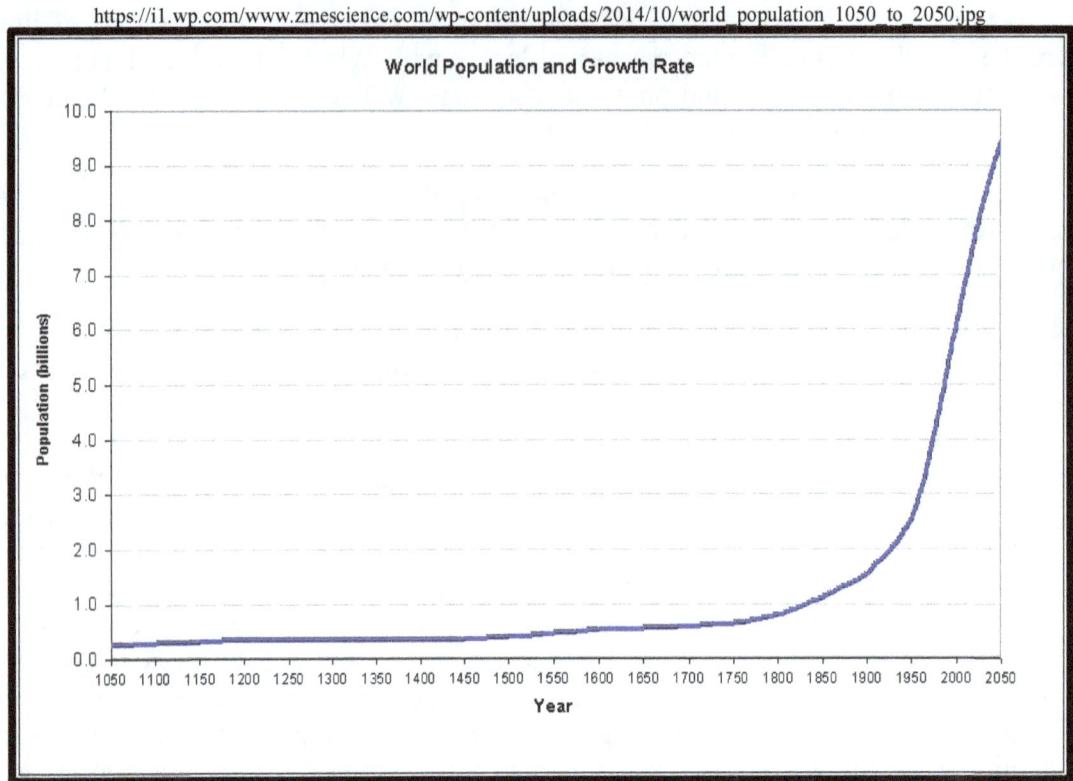

World Population 1050 - 2050

The Tribulation famine will begin suddenly, for at the beginning of the Seven Years the world will be saying *peace and safety* (1 Thess 5:2-4). This suddenness will occur against the backdrop of a huge and recent population growth.

With such vast numbers, the Great Commission to *every creature*, the night coming when no man can work, every effort must be made to enter the harvest fields.

- *And he said unto them, **Go ye into all the world, and preach the gospel to every creature*** (Mk 16:15).
- *Say not ye, There are yet four months, and then cometh harvest? behold, I say unto you, Lift up your eyes, and **look on the fields; for they are white already to harvest*** (Jhn 4:35).
- *I must work the works of him that sent me, while it is day: **the night cometh, when no man can work*** (Jhn 9:4).
- *For the love of Christ constraineth us; because we thus judge, that **if one died for all, then were all dead*** (2 Cor 5:14).
- ***The harvest is past, the summer is ended, and we are not saved*** (Jer 8:20).

THE FOURTH SEAL: GLOBAL DEATH 6:7,8

(6:7) *And when he had opened the fourth seal, I heard the voice of the fourth beast say, Come and see.* (6:8) *And I looked, and behold a pale horse: and his name that sat on him was Death, and Hell followed with him. And power was given unto them over the fourth part of the earth, to kill with sword, and with hunger, and with death, and with the beasts of the earth.*

1. THE FOURTH SEAL IS OPENED. *And when he had opened the fourth seal* (6:7). The work of judgement once begun is unrelenting.

CHAPTER 7

<u>2. THE VOICE OF THE THIRD BEAST IS HEARD</u>. *I heard the voice of the fourth beast say, Come and see.* The Fourth Beast is the Flying Eagle (4:7).

<u>3. THE SCENE UNFOLDS</u>.

<u>(1) A PALE HORSE GOES FORTH</u>. With the fourth horse, the emphatic, *behold*, is heard again. It is used with the first and fourth horses.

- *And I saw, and **behold a white horse*** (6:2).
- *And there went out another horse that was red* (6:4).
- *And I beheld, and lo a black horse* (6:5).
- *And I looked, and **behold a pale horse*** (6:7).

And I looked, and behold a pale horse (6:8). A sickly colour, but more specifically, the colour of death. The horse is an unearthly colour, literally a pale green, the same word being used to describe the colour of the grass in Mark 6:39 and Revelation 8:7; 9:4. In the context it is a sickening and alarming colour. It was the colour that in a garment or in a house marked the presence of leprosy.

- *And if the plague be **greenish** or reddish in the garment, or in the skin, either in the warp, or in the woof, or in any thing of skin; it is a plague of leprosy, and shall be showed unto the priest* (Lev 13:49).

<u>(2) THE NAME OF THE RIDER</u>: *and his name that sat on him was Death.* Death, he *king of terrors* (Job 18:14), now riding on horseback, marching across the earth, making new conquests in all places and at all times.

<u>(3) THE ATTENDANT OF THE RIDER</u>: *and Hell followed with him.* Not Death and Heaven, but Death and Hell. Here is a stark fact concerning the coming Tribulation – many on earth will die and many will go to Hell! Hell is the place of eternal misery to all who die in their sins, having rejected Christ. In times of such a general destruction, multitudes go down unprepared into that deep and terrible valley. It is an awful thought, and ought to make any reasonable person tremble, that eternal damnation immediately follows upon the death of an impenitent sinner. But as in this day and even more then, the world will be so besotted with sin and the Man of Sin, that there will be no reasoning ability.

Here we see the steep descent of the "gallant rider" on the white steed who at the beginning of the Seven Years trod out across the earth. What worldly wise excitement and anticipation he brought. At last PEACE AND SAFETY. But the colour has soon changed.

<u>4. THE RAVAGES OF THIS AND THE PREVIOUS SEALS</u>. *And power was given unto them over the fourth part of the earth, to kill with sword, and with hunger, and with death, and with the beasts of the earth.* Normally war and hunger and pestilence would not be expected to slay men on such a vast scale, but during the Tribulation they will, for then God gives these things a power to do so.

To *kill with sword* and *with hunger* we have seen, but to these now are added *death* and the *beasts to the earth*. Death refers to disease and pestilence. This is nothing new and in past centuries have taken a terrible toll. But during the first half of the Tribulation disease and pestilence will be given a force not seen before. There is much in the news today concerning diseases that have developed and antibiotic resistance. The survey of the past gives an example of what is to come.

THE BOOK OF REVELATION

FROM THE PRESENT DAY TO THE BLACK DEATH: EIGHT OF THE WORST PANDEMICS
http://www.mphonline.org/worst-pandemics-in-history/

Cholera, bubonic plague, smallpox, and influenza are some of the most brutal killers in human history. And outbreaks of these diseases across international borders, are properly defined as pandemic, especially smallpox, which throughout history, has killed between 300-500 million people in.

1. HIV/AIDS PANDEMIC (at its peak, 2005-2012)
Death Toll: **36 million.** An End Time Sign (Luke 17:29,30)
Cause: HIV/AIDS

First identified in Democratic Republic of the Congo in 1976, HIV/AIDS has proven itself as a global pandemic, killing more than 36 million people since 1981. Currently there are between 31 and 35 million people living with HIV, the vast majority of those are in Sub-Saharan Africa, where 5% of the population is infected. The annual global deaths from HIV/AIDS has dropped from 2.2 million to 1.2 million.

2. FLU PANDEMIC (1968)
Death Toll: **1 million**
Cause: Influenza

A category 2 Flu pandemic sometimes referred to as "the Hong Kong Flu," the 1968 flu pandemic was caused by the H3N2 strain of the Influenza A virus, a genetic offshoot of the H2N2 subtype. From the first reported case on July 13, 1968 in Hong Kong, it took only 17 days before outbreaks of the virus were reported in Singapore and Vietnam, and within three months had spread to The Philippines, India, Australia, Europe, and the United States. While the 1968 pandemic had a comparatively low mortality rate (.5%) it still resulted in the deaths of more than a million people, including 500,000 residents of Hong Kong,

3. ASIAN FLU (1956-1958)
Death Toll: **2 million**
Cause: Influenza

Asian Flu was a pandemic outbreak of Influenza A of the H2N2 subtype, that originated in China in 1956 and lasted until 1958. In its two-year spree, Asian Flu travelled from the Chinese province of Guizhou to Singapore, Hong Kong, and the United States. Estimates for the death toll of the Asian Flu vary depending on the source, but the World Health Organization places the final tally at approximately 2 million deaths, 69,800 of those in the US alone.

4. FLU PANDEMIC (1918)
Death Toll: **20 -50 million.** It followed the continental solar eclipse in the US.
Cause: Influenza

Between 1918 and 1920 a disturbingly deadly outbreak of influenza tore across the globe, infecting over a third of the world's population and ending the lives of 20 – 50 million people. Of the 500 million people infected in the 1918 pandemic, the mortality rate was estimated at 10% to 20%, with up to 25 million deaths in the first 25 weeks alone. What separated the 1918 flu pandemic from other influenza outbreaks was the victims; where influenza had always previously only killed juveniles and the elderly or already weakened patients, it had begun striking down hardy and completely healthy young adults, while leaving children and those with weaker immune systems still alive.

CHAPTER 7

5. SIXTH CHOLERA PANDEMIC (1910-1911)
Death Toll: **800,000+**
Cause: Cholera

Like its five previous incarnations, the Sixth Cholera Pandemic originated in India where it killed over 800,000, before spreading to the Middle East, North Africa, Eastern Europe and Russia. The Sixth Cholera Pandemic was also the source of the last American outbreak of Cholera (1910–1911). American health authorities, having learned from the past, quickly sought to isolate the infected, and in the end only 11 deaths occurred in the U.S. By 1923 Cholera cases had been cut down dramatically, although it was still a constant in India.

6. FLU PANDEMIC (1889-1890)
Death Toll: **1 million**
Cause: Influenza

Originally the "Asiatic Flu" or "Russian Flu" as it was called, this strain was thought to be an outbreak of the Influenza A virus subtype H2N2, though recent discoveries have instead found the cause to be the Influenza A virus subtype H3N8. The first cases were observed in May 1889 in three separate and distant locations, Bukhara in Central Asia (Turkestan), Athabasca in northwestern Canada, and Greenland. Rapid population growth of the 19th century, specifically in urban areas, only helped the flu spread, and before long the outbreak had spread across the globe. Though it was the first true epidemic in the era of bacteriology and much was learned from it. In the end, the 1889-1890 Flu Pandemic claimed the lives of over a million individuals.

7. THIRD CHOLERA PANDEMIC (1852–1860)
Death Toll: **1 million**
Cause: Cholera

Generally considered the most deadly of the seven cholera pandemics, the third major outbreak of Cholera in the 19th century lasted from 1852 to 1860. Like the first and second pandemics, the Third Cholera Pandemic originated in India, spreading from the Ganges River Delta before tearing through Asia, Europe, North America and Africa and ending the lives of over a million people. British physician John Snow, while working in a poor area of London, tracked cases of cholera and eventually succeeded in identifying contaminated water as the means of transmission for the disease. Unfortunately the same year as his discovery (1854) went down as the worst year of the pandemic, in which 23,000 people died in Great Britain.

8. THE BLACK DEATH (1346-1353)
Death Toll: **75 – 200 million**
Cause: Bubonic Plague

From 1346 to 1353 an outbreak of the Plague ravaged Europe, Africa, and Asia, with an estimated death toll between 75 and 200 million people. Thought to have originated in Asia, the Plague most likely jumped continents via the fleas living on the rats that so frequently lived aboard merchant ships. Ports being major urban centers at the time, were the perfect breeding ground for the rats and fleas, and thus the insidious bacterium flourished, devastating three continents in its wake.

Note that the first mentioned "pandemic" is the one *currently* in progress. It demonstrates that we have entered the Days of Lot.

- *Likewise also as it was in the days of Lot; they did eat, they drank, they bought, they sold, they planted, they builded; 29 But the same day that Lot went out of Sodom it rained fire and brimstone from heaven, and destroyed them all. 30 Even thus shall it be in the day when the Son of man is revealed* (Lk 17:28-30).

To the three great judgments of war, famine, and pestilence, is now added ***the beasts of the earth*** (Ezek 14:21). It is mentioned here as the last, because, when a nation is depopulated by the sword, famine, and pestilence, the small remnant that continue in *a waste and howling wilderness* (Deut 32:10) are vulnerable to animals of prey.

God's creatures fight on his side, whether birds or beasts. In former days, God has made use of this or a similar scourge. Upon Pharaoh and his servants He sent frogs, lice, flies and locusts. These were small creatures, but many! Against the murmuring Israelites He commissioned the fiery serpents (Num 21). On the Canaanites He sent hornets (Exod 23:28; Josh 24:12). Against the occupiers of the Land of Israel He sent lions (2 Kings 17:25,26). Against the world He will send the ***beasts of the earth***.

The mention of the ***sword*** and ***hunger*** is believed to indicate that this death toll includes those who died under the "hoofs of" the Red and Black Horses. This proposal though is not entirely certain. If it is *a fourth* in addition to these previous judgements; we can but wonder! But regardless, by any standard of comparison this is incomprehensible judgement. If one-fourth of the world population is destroyed in or by the time of the fourth seal, it would represent many times over the greatest destruction (even the *combined tolls*) of recorded history. The population of the human race in Noah's day undoubtedly was far less than the figure here cited.

If such a judgment would fall upon a world with the current (2017) population of nearly seven and one-half billion, it would mean that one billion 875 million would die. Here is something awful beyond words, a period without precedent in character and extent.

THE FIRST HALF OF THE TRIBULATION: *"NOT SO BAD"*!!

The second half of the Tribulation is indeed infinitely worse than the first half. It is described in twelve of the thirteen Tribulation Chapters of Revelation (Rev 6-18). That is, only one of the Tribulation Chapters is allocated to the first half; Chapter Six.

> • ***For then shall be great tribulation***, *such as was not since the beginning of the world to this time, no, nor ever shall be. And except those days should be shortened, there should no flesh be saved: but for the elect's sake those days shall be shortened* (Matt 24:21,22).
> • ***By these three was the third part of men killed***, *by the fire, and by the smoke, and by the brimstone, which issued out of their mouths* (Rev 9:18).
> • *Come behold the works of the LORD, what desolations he hath made in the earth* (Psa 46:9).

Because of the well-known fact that the second half is much worse than the first, many have been lulled into thinking that the first half might be "relatively manageable." IT WILL NOT BE! *IT WILL BE THE TIME OF THE FOUR HORSES*. The wars, famine and pestilence declared to take place in the first three and one half years are not unfamiliar events in the history of mankind, but never before since the time of Noah has judgment been so devastatingly consummated as to destroy one-fourth of the earth's population at one stroke.

Govett gives the terse conclusion:

> Each blow struck by the Most High has been heavier than the last, and now Pestilence on a horse goes forth. *Hades* followed after him, whether on foot or no, is not said. The place in which departed souls are gathered is personified: so great is to be

the deadliness of the plague, that Hades follows as the reaper to gather up the fallen ears. Such a scene Isaiah foretold.

• ***Therefore hell hath enlarged herself, and opened her mouth without measure***: *and their glory, and their multitude, and their pomp, and he that rejoiceth, shall descend into it. 15 And the mean man shall be brought down, and the mighty man shall be humbled, and the eyes of the lofty shall be humbled: 16 But the LORD of hosts shall be exalted in judgment, and God that is holy shall be sanctified in righteousness* (Isa 5:14-16).

• *If thou hast run with the footmen, and they have wearied thee,* ***then how canst thou contend with horses?*** *and if in the land of peace, wherein thou trustedst, they wearied thee, then how wilt thou do in the swelling of Jordan* (Jer 12:5)?

THE FIFTH SEAL: MARTYRDOM 6:9-11

(6:9) ***And when he had opened the fifth seal, I saw under the altar the souls of them that were slain for the word of God, and for the testimony which they held:*** (6:10) ***And they cried with a loud voice, saying, How long, O Lord, holy and true, dost thou not judge and avenge our blood on them that dwell on the earth?*** (6:11) ***And white robes were given unto every one of them; and it was said unto them, that they should rest yet for a little season, until their fellowservants also and their brethren, that should be killed as they were, should be fulfilled.***

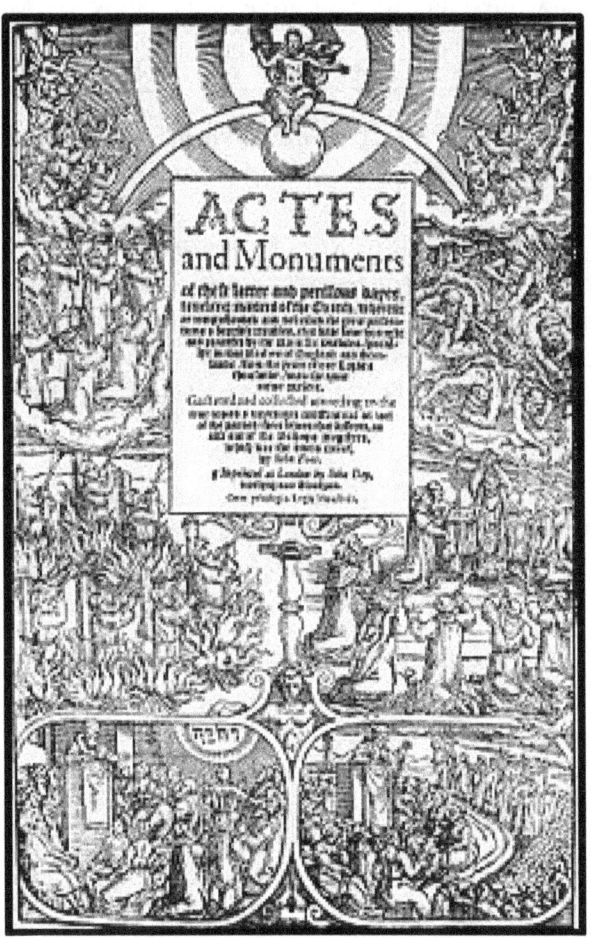

Frontispiece to the 1563 Edition of *Foxe's Book of Martyrs*

With the Fifth Seal there is no mention made of the Apostle being called to *Come and see*. The four living creatures have now discharged their responsibilities in directing John to the ravages befalling the earth. A different kind of matter is dealt with in the opening of the fifth seal. It concerns the martyrs of the Tribulation. That which took place in the past, and to a large extent under the hand of Papal Rome will occur on a much larger scale under the Beast, the final Roman Prince who will destroy Papal Rome (Dan 9:26; Rev 17:16; read Rev 13 and 17) and seek to destroy all who place faith in Christ during the Tribulation days.

The first printing of *Foxe's Book of Martyrs* was illustrated with over sixty distinctive woodcut impressions and was to that time the largest publishing project ever undertaken in England. Their product was a single volume book, "a bit over a foot long, two palms-span wide, too deep to lift with only one hand, and weighed about the same as a small infant." Foxe's own title for the first edition, is *Actes and Monuments of these Latter and Perillous Days, Touching Matters of the Church*. Long titles were conventionally expected at the time, so this title continues… *persecutions and horrible troubles that had been wrought and practiced by the Roman Prelates, speciallye in this realm of England and Scotland*. Foxe's temporal range was *from the yeare of our Lorde a thousand unto the tyme nowe present*.

The second, 1570 edition, was in two volumes and had expanded from 1,800 pages in 1563 to over 2,300 folio pages. The number of woodcuts increased from 60 to 150. The illustrations were newly cut to depict particular details, linking England's suffering back to "the primitive tyme" until, in volume I, "the reigne of King Henry VIII"; in volume two, from Henry's time to "Queen Elizabeth our gracious Lady now reigning". https://en.wikipedia.org/wiki/Foxe%27s_Book_of_Martyrs

MARTYR TIMES WILL RETURN!

1. THE FIFTH SEAL IS OPENED. *And when he had opened the fifth seal* (6:9). With this and the opening of the remaining seals, the Four Beasts no longer bid John to *come and see*.

2. THE SIGHT OF THE MARTYRS. *I saw under the altar the souls of them that were slain for the word of God, and for the testimony which they held* (6:9). In the fifth seal the scene shifts from earth to heaven and John sees a vision of those who will be martyred for their faith in Christ. They are described as being under the altar, in keeping with the fact that the blood of the sacrifices of the Old Testament was poured out under the altar (Exod 29:12). But note the two altars mentioned below.

• *And the priest shall put some of the blood upon* **the horns of the altar of sweet incense** *before the LORD, which is in the tabernacle of the congregation; and shall* **pour all the blood of the bullock at the bottom of the altar of the burnt offering**, *which is at the door of the tabernacle of the congregation (Lev 4:7).*

(1) THEIR PRESENT ABODE: *under the altar*. As the Cross of Calvary fulfills the Altar of Burnt Offering that once stood in the Tabernacle and Temple, it is unlikely that such an altar would be in Heaven.

• **We have an altar**, *whereof they have no right to eat which serve the tabernacle* (Heb 13:10).

He saw them at the foot of the altar of incense in Heaven. Persecutors can only kill the body and after that there is no more that they can do. The soul lives on awaiting the Resurrection. God has provided a good place for them, a place of worship. The form of this altar is likely pattern of which Moses copied in the construction of the Tabernacle.

CHAPTER 7

- *According to all that I shew thee, **after the pattern** of the tabernacle, and the pattern of all the instruments thereof, even so shall ye make it (Exod 25:9).*
- *And look that thou make them **after their pattern**, which was shewed thee in the mount (Exod 25:40).*
- *It was therefore necessary that **the patterns of things in the heavens** should be purified with these; but the heavenly things themselves with better sacrifices than these (Heb 9:23).*

(2) THEIR CAUSE OF DEATH. They *were slain for the word of God, and for the testimony which they held*. Never will there be a more dangerous day to be a Bible believer, and to uphold that with a firm testimony, than during the coming Tribulation.

3. THE CRY OF THE MARTYRS. *And they cried with a loud voice, saying, How long, O Lord, holy and true, dost thou not judge and avenge our blood on them that dwell on the earth* (6:10)?

(1) ITS INTENSITY. *And they cried with a loud voice.* They are anxiously aware of what is happening on earth. There is no "soul sleep" after death as some teach. With many still turning to Christ on earth (7:9-14) they are aware of a great increase of martyrdom, which like their own seems to have gone unpunished.

(2) ITS APPEAL. *How long, O Lord*? The *how long* to them was *too long*, for those who slew them were still living. Thus for the simple reason that they are not now in their resurrection bodies and that their persecutors are still living shows they are not the martyrs of the Church Age. Note that their cry is much like that which we read in Luke 18.

- *And shall not God avenge his own elect, which cry day and night unto him, though he bear long with them? 8 I tell you that he will avenge them speedily. Nevertheless when the Son of man cometh, shall he find faith on the earth (Lk 18:7,8)?*

4. THE REPOSE OF THE MARTYRS. *And white robes were given unto every one of them; and it was said unto them, that they should rest yet for a little season, until their fellowservants also and their brethren, that should be killed as they were, should be fulfilled* (6:11). They do not yet see their persecutors judged. They do not yet receive their resurrection but, but they are given a white robe. In anticipation of both. Many more will die for Christ in the Tribulation, perhaps beyond number. (See 7:14). Their position at the base of the altar of devotion—not of atonement—expresses their action in having sacrificed their lives on behalf of the One who died for them at the Alar of Atonement (Calavary's Cross).

Whether in life or in death the believer presents himself as a *living sacrifice*.

- *I beseech you therefore, brethren, by the mercies of God, that ye **present your bodies a living sacrifice**, holy, acceptable unto God, which is your reasonable service. 2 And be not conformed to this world: but be ye transformed by the renewing of your mind, that ye may prove what is that good, and acceptable, and perfect, will of God (Rom 12:1,2).*
- *By him therefore let us **offer the sacrifice of praise to God continually**, that is, the fruit of our lips giving thanks to his name (Heb 13:15).*

Despite all the martyrs of the past, Walvoord rightly asserts the view that the most severe period of martyrdom lies ahead.

> The introduction of these martyred dead in heaven at this point immediately after the Fourth Seal indicates they have come from the Tribulation scene on the earth. There have been many martyrs in every generation, and even

in the twentieth century tens of thousands have died for Christ in Asia, Africa, Central America, and South America. There are several reasons for believing that a greater period of martyrdom is yet ahead,....

From the fact that the martyrs ask for judgment upon those that dwell on the earth it is apparent that their persecutors are still living. Their cry for righteous judgment is in the same spirit as the Psalmist's call to God to vindicate His holiness and righteousness in dealing with the injustice and oppression which characterize the human race. In answer to their question as to how long it will be, the reply is given in verse 11 that there is still a little time required for the fulfillment of God's program, that other events must take place, that still additional martyrs must be added to their number. In a word, they are to wait until the time of Christ's Return in power and glory when God will deal in summary judgment with the earth.

The revelation of the Fifth Seal makes clear that in the future time of tribulation it will be most difficult to declare one's faith in the Lord Jesus. It may very well be that the majority of those who trust Christ as Saviour in that day will be put to death. This is confirmed in chapter 7 where another picture of the martyred dead of the tribulation is given, and in chapter 13 where death is inflicted on all who will not worship the beast. Martyrdom in those days will be as common as it is uncommon today. Thousands will be martyred, sealing their testimony with their own blood. Those who trust in Christ in that day will be forced to stand the test of being faithful even unto death.

AN INTERMEDIATE BODY!

With their souls in Heaven, their bodies on earth, and the resurrection still in the future, Walvoord discusses the likelihood of an "intermediate body."

In verse 11 it is revealed that the white robes given unto every one of the martyrs are symbolic of righteousness. This introduces another question, namely, what kind of a body will saints have in heaven before their own bodies are raised from the dead? If the martyred dead here pictured are those who have come from the tribulation, it is clear that they will not receive their resurrection bodies until the end of the tribulation, according to Revelation 20:4. Scholars have been divided as to whether saints who die receive temporary bodies in heaven prior to the resurrection body, or whether only their spiritual beings are in heaven before the resurrection....

The martyred dead here pictured have not been raised from the dead and have not received their resurrection bodies. Yet it is declared that they are given robes. The fact that they are given robes would almost demand that they have a body of some kind. A robe could not hang upon an immaterial soul or spirit. It is not the kind of body that Christians now have, that is, the body of earth; nor is it the resurrection body of flesh and bones of which Christ spoke after His own resurrection. It is a temporary body suited for their presence in heaven but replaced by their everlasting resurrection body given at the time of Christ's Return.

That it is a kind of *spiritual body,* yet with "substance" is indicated by the following:

• *To the general assembly and church of the firstborn, which are written in heaven, and to God the Judge of all, and to* **the spirits of just men made perfect** (Heb 12:23).

- *Furthermore we have had fathers of our flesh which corrected us, and we gave them reverence: shall we not much rather be in subjection unto **the Father of spirits**, and live* (Heb 12:9)?
- *For we know that if our earthly house of this tabernacle were dissolved, we have a building of God, an house not made with hands, eternal in the heavens. For in this we groan, earnestly desiring to be **clothed upon with our house which is from heaven**: If so be that being clothed we shall not be found naked* (2 Cor 5:1-3).

The Sixth Seal: Terrestrial and Celestial Upheaval 6:12 -17

(6:12) ***And I beheld when he had opened the sixth seal, and, lo, there was a great earthquake; and the sun became black as sackcloth of hair, and the moon became as blood;*** (6:13) ***And the stars of heaven fell unto the earth, even as a fig tree casteth her untimely figs, when she is shaken of a mighty wind.*** (6:14) ***And the heaven departed as a scroll when it is rolled together; and every mountain and island were moved out of their places.***

(6:15) ***And the kings of the earth, and the great men, and the rich men, and the chief captains, and the mighty men, and every bondman, and every free man, hid themselves in the dens and in the rocks of the mountains;*** (6:16) ***And said to the mountains and rocks, Fall on us, and hide us from the face of him that sitteth on the throne, and from the wrath of the Lamb:*** (6:17) ***For the great day of his wrath is come; and who shall be able to stand?***

With the opening of the Sixth Seal we come to the end of the first three and one half years of the Tribulation. There has been deception, war, famine, pestilence and martyrdom. At least one quarter of the world's population has died. Our Lord refers to these years and months as the Beginning of Sorrows, for that which Revelation Chapters 7 – 18 describes is much worse.

- *For **nation shall rise against nation**, and kingdom against kingdom: and there shall be **famines**, and **pestilences**, and **earthquakes**, in divers places. 8 **All these are the beginning of sorrows*** (Matt 24:7,8).

Nevertheless, the *Beginning of Sorrows* is a comparative term. The Trumpet Judgements which begin at the midpoint of the Tribulation are much worse than the Seal Judgements; and the Vial Judgements that occur near the end of the Seven Years are a great deal worse than anything that came before.

All that takes place during the Seven Years, whether directly or indirectly, is *THE WRATH OF GOD*. The Seal Judgements are directed from the Throne in Heaven, therefore they are not as some teach, *only* the wrath of man, or *only* brought by man himself. Such is sometimes taught as an argument supporting the view that the Church will go through (or some of) the Seal Judgements. God in sending these judgements has lifted the constraints of the evil heart.

There is *deception* in the First Seal, but Scripture states that this is the judgement of God upon a Christ rejecting world.

- *Even him, whose coming is after the working of Satan with all power and signs and lying wonders, 10 And with all deceivableness of unrighteousness in them that perish; because they received not the love of the truth, that they might be saved. 11 **And for this cause God shall send them strong delusion, that they should believe a lie:** 12 That* *they all might be damned who believed not the truth, but had pleasure in unrighteousness* (2 Thess 2:9-12).

There is indeed the wrath of man in the Second Seal (Red Horse), but it should be seen in the context of the Seven Sealed Book, being primarily a BOOK OF WRATH. Compare, and in this Second Seal all restraint to go to war is lifted. Compare:

- *Surely **the wrath of man shall praise thee**: the remainder of wrath shalt thou restrain* (Psa 76:10).
- *Come, behold the works of the LORD,* **what desolations he hath made in the earth** (Psa 46:8).

The opening of the Sixth Seal removes any doubt about this. The world, men great and small, have no doubt about what has taken place and is now taking place. It is *THE WRATH OF GOD*. To say that their statement in verse 17 is referring to the Trumpet and Vial Judgements is impossible; they know nothing about those judgements which are yet to come.

- *And said to the mountains and rocks, Fall on us, and hide us from the face of him that sitteth on the throne, and from **the wrath of the Lamb**:* (6:17) *For **the great day of his wrath is come**; and who shall be able to stand* (6:17,18)?

This is the WORLD'S CONCLUSION on the basis of what *had* happened, and what was *now happening*! It is not "their insight" into what is *going to happen*. Of that they have no idea. We stress this point because some teach that wrath only begins with the Trumpet or Vials. The three series of judgements are all part of the Seven Sealed Book, and their opening is here described as *the wrath of the Lamb*.

<u>1. THE SIXTH SEAL IS OPENED</u>. *And I beheld when he had opened the sixth seal* (6:12). As Walvoord writes: "It would be difficult to paint any scene more moving or more terrible than that described at the opening of the Sixth Seal. All the elements of a great catastrophic judgment of God are here present, namely, a great earthquake, the sun becoming black, the moon becoming as blood, the stars of heaven falling like ripe figs, the heaven departing as a scroll, and every mountain and island moving.

Students of Revelation have had difficulty interpreting this passage, and the tendency has been to regard these judgments as symbolic rather than real. The motive behind this interpretation has been a reluctance to accept a literal interpretation of these judgments falling on the earth at this time; hence, the disturbances of the heavens have been taken to refer to changes in human government, and disturbances in the earth as referring to the upsetting of tradition and commonly fixed ideas."

Such is not a "difficulty" for the Bible Believer. That which takes place here is just as literal and actual as the previous five seals, or the plagues of Egypt, or any other miracle or supernatural occurrence in the Bible. And of course, if this is just symbolic, then what is the entire world getting so upset about (6:15-17)? Why are they running to the rocks and the mountains? It is not likely that changes in government and human affairs would make the world do this. Even the Second Seal with its terrible wars, does not mention this kind of terrified response.

While, as Walvoord indicates, this is not the final breakup of the world and universe as described later in Revelation, it does show that beginning with the Sixth Seal, God has begun a *direct* intervention into human affairs. The judgments of deception, war, famine, pestilence, and martyrdom have to a greater or lesser extent come about by **the Divine lifting of restraint of the evil heart of man**. With the opening of the Sixth Seal **man is only a bystander**! Here is direct and unmitigated wrath upon a blasphemous world.

CHAPTER 7

Here is a shaking; First in the terrestrial and celestial sphere; and then in the hearts of men…*every man*; *every* Christ rejecting person on earth.

2. ALL OF THE EARTH AND THE HEAVENS ARE SHAKEN.

• *Whose voice then shook the earth: but now he hath promised, saying,* **Yet once more I shake not the earth only, but also heaven.** *27 And this word, Yet once more, signifieth the removing of those things that are shaken, as of things that are made, that those things which cannot be shaken may remain* (Heb 12:26,27).

Note the six-fold description; beginning and ending with the earth.

(1) THE EARTH: ***and, lo, there was a great earthquake.*** Five earthquakes are stated in Revelation to occur during the Tribulation.

During the Sixth Seal (6:12).
During the Seventh Seal (8:5).
At the end of the ministry of the Two Witnesses (11:13)
During the Seventh Trumpet (11:19)
During the Seventh Vial (16:19).

• *Though the waters thereof roar and be troubled, though* **the mountains shake** *with the swelling thereof. Selah* (Psa 46:3).

• *Thou hast made* **the earth to tremble**; *thou hast broken it: heal the breaches thereof; for* **it shaketh** (Psa 60:2).

• **To go into the clefts of the rocks, and into the tops of the ragged rocks**, *for fear of the LORD, and for the glory of his majesty, when he ariseth to* **shake terribly the earth** (Isa 2:21).

• *Therefore I will shake the heavens, and* **the earth shall remove out of her place**, *in the wrath of the LORD of hosts, and in the day of his fierce anger* (Isa 13:13).

• *And it shall come to pass, that he who fleeth from the noise of the fear shall fall into the pit; and he that cometh up out of the midst of the pit shall be taken in the snare: for the windows from on high are open, and* **the foundations of the earth do shake** (Isa 24:18).

• **The earth is moved exceedingly.** (Isa 24:19).

• **The earth shall reel to and fro like a drunkard**, *and shall be removed like a cottage; and the transgression thereof shall be heavy upon it; and it shall fall, and not rise again* (Isa 24:20).

• *For nation shall rise against nation, and kingdom against kingdom: and there shall be famines, and pestilences, and* **earthquakes, in divers places** (Matt 24:7).

(2) THE HEAVENS: ***and the sun became black as sackcloth of hair.*** The Sun is a special sign to the Gentiles. The world at large follow a solar year. This is the first of five instances where the Sun is darkened during the Tribulation

During the Sixth Seal (6:12).
During the Fourth Trumpet (8:12).
During the Fifth Trumpet (9:2).
During the Fifth Vial (16:10).
Immediately after the Tribulation at Christ's Return (Matt 24:29).

• *And it shall come to pass in that day, saith the Lord GOD, that* **I will cause the sun to go down at noon, and I will darken the earth in the clear day** (Amos 8:9)

- *Blow ye the trumpet in Zion, and sound an alarm in my holy mountain: let all the inhabitants of the land tremble: for the day of the LORD cometh, for it is nigh at hand;* **A day of darkness and of gloominess, a day of clouds and of thick darkness**, *as the morning spread upon the mountains: a great people and a strong; there hath not been ever the like, neither shall be any more after it, even to the years of many generations* (Joel 2:1,2).
- *The earth shall quake before them; the heavens shall tremble:* **the sun and the moon shall be dark, and the stars shall withdraw their shining** (Joel 2:10).

(3) THE HEAVENS: **and the moon became as blood.** The Moon is a special sign to Israel. The Jews follow a lunar-solar year. The Moon will be affected five times during the Tribulation and corresponds with the darkening of the Sun above.

- *And I will shew wonders in the heavens and in the earth, blood, and fire, and pillars of smoke.* **The sun shall be turned into darkness, and the moon into blood**, *before the great and terrible day of the LORD come (Joel 2:30,31).*
- *The sun and* **the moon shall be darkened**, *and the stars shall withdraw their* shining (Joel 3:15).

(4) THE HEAVENS. **And the stars of heaven fell unto the earth, even as a fig tree casteth her untimely figs, when she is shaken of a mighty wind** (6:13). The Greek word *atseer* is at times used in a figurative sense, as:

Christ the morning *star* (Rev 2:28);
Or of the angels as seven *stars* of the seven churches (Rev 1:16,20; 2:1; 3:1);
Or of the great *star* called Wormwood (Rev 8:10,11).
Or of the third of angels called stars cast down by Satan during the Tribulation (Rev 12:4);
Or of the *star* fall from heaven, angel of the bottomless pit (Rev 9:1,11).
Or of false teachers described as wandering *stars* (Jude 13);

Here the word is not used in this sense. It is instead the common usage in the New Testament of **the stars of heaven**. While most think verse 13 is referring to comets or a severe meteor shower; there is no clear parallel for this usage in the New Testament.

The stars were created on the Fourth Day of the Creation Week: *He made the stars also* (Gen 1:16) They are seen from earth as **points of light** with varying degrees of luminosity.

A fact not always considered: No matter how powerful the telescope, or whether it is on earth or a space telescope; no matter how large or small or far or near or how many the stars may be, it is only the light, not the disk or surface of the star that is seen. This puzzled Galileo when he first used his telescope.

That the *stars will fall* is stated further in Scripture:

- *Immediately after the tribulation of those days shall the sun be darkened, and the moon shall not give her light, and* **the stars shall fall from heaven**, *and the powers of the heavens shall be shaken:30 And then shall appear the sign of the Son of man in heaven: and then shall all the tribes of the earth mourn, and they shall see the Son of man coming in the clouds of heaven with power and great glory* (Matt 24:29,31).
- *But in those days, after that tribulation, the sun shall be darkened, and the moon shall not give her light, 25 And* **the stars of heaven shall fall**, *and the powers that are in heaven shall be shaken* (Mk 13:24,25).

CHAPTER 7

• *And all the host of heaven shall be dissolved, and the heavens **shall be rolled together as a scroll**: and **all their host shall fall down, as the leaf falleth off from the vine, and as a falling fig from the fig tree**. 5 For my sword shall be bathed in heaven: behold, it shall come down upon Idumea, and upon the people of my curse, to judgment* (Isa 34:4,5).

This dissolution of the heavens is described as both a *falling down* and a *rolling up*, This will take place initially at the opening of the Sixth Seal and more fully at the end of the Tribulation and the Return of Christ. Note that both are mention in Isaiah 34:4.

(5) THE HEAVENS. ***And the heaven departed as a scroll when it is rolled together*** (6:14). It is clear from all of this that the cosmology of the Bible is far different than that accepted by most today. The *founding* of the earth took place on the First Day. The heavenly firmament was created on the Second Day. The Sun, Moon and Stars were created and set within the firmament on the Fourth Day. This founding of the earth and *stretching out* of the heavenly firmament are frequently distinguished in the Scriptures and point clearly to a geocentric conclusion. Few have taken the time to study cosmology from a Biblical standpoint. During the Tribulation, the true nature of cosmology will become much more recognized. The world will be brought to see clearly the *works and operations* of the Creator:

• *Because **they regard not the works of the LORD, nor the operation of his hands**, he shall destroy them, and not build them up* (Psa 28:5).
• *And all the host of heaven shall be dissolved, and **the heavens shall be rolled together as a scroll**: and all their host shall fall down, as the leaf falleth off from the vine, and as a falling fig from the fig tree* (Isa 34:4).
• *And, Thou, Lord, in the beginning hast laid the foundation of the earth; and the heavens are the works of thine hands:11 They shall perish; but thou remainest; and they all shall wax old as doth a garment; 12 And **as a vesture shalt thou fold them up**, and they shall be changed: but thou art the same, and thy years shall not fail*
(Heb 1:10-12).

https://www.nasa.gov/sites/default/files/thumbnails/image/hubble_friday_06172016.jpg

Always "A Point of Light" From Even the Most Powerful Telescopes
He made the stars also. **Genesis 1:16**

THE BOOK OF REVELATION

THE WORLD DURING THE TRIBULATION WILL BE MADE TO SEE THE TRUTH REGARDING BIBLICAL COSMOLOGY

1. THEY WILL LEARN: THE EARTH WAS *FOUNDED* ON THE FIRST DAY OF THE CREATION WEEK

The term *foundation* is used for the creation of the earth. This is in contrast to the heavens that are *stretched out* on the Fourth Day. Note below the underlined statements concerning the heavens. The term *foundation* strongly implies a geocentric and non-moving earth.

- *In the beginning God created the Heaven and the Earth* (Gen 1:1).
- *For **in six days the LORD made heaven and earth**, the sea, and all that in them is, and rested the seventh day: wherefore the LORD blessed the sabbath day, and hallowed it* (Exod 20:11).
- *It is a sign between me and the children of Israel for ever: for **in six days the LORD made heaven and earth**, and on the seventh day he rested, and was refreshed* (Exod 31:17).
- *for the **pillars of the earth** are the LORD'S, and he hath set the world upon them* (1 Sam 2:8.
- *Where wast thou when I laid the foundations of the earth? declare, if thou hast understanding* (Job 38:4).
- *Whereupon are **the foundations** thereof fastened? or who **laid the corner stone** thereof.* (Job 38:6).
- *Of old hast thou **laid the foundation of the earth**: and <u>the heavens are the work of thy hands</u>* (Psa 102:25).
- *Who **laid the foundations of the earth**, that it should not be removed for ever* (Psa 104:5).
- *The LORD by wisdom hath **founded the earth**; by understanding hath he <u>established the heavens</u>* (Prov 3:19).
- *Have ye not known? have ye not heard? hath it not been told you from the beginning? have ye not understood from **the foundations of the earth**?* (Isa 40:21).
- *Mine hand also **hath laid the foundation of the earth**, and my right hand hath <u>spanned the heavens</u>* (Isa 48:13).
- *And forgettest the LORD thy maker, that hath <u>stretched forth the heavens</u>, and **laid the foundations of the earth*** (Isa 51:13).
- *the LORD, which <u>stretcheth forth the heavens</u>, and **layeth the foundation of the earth*** (Zech 12:1).
- *I will utter things which have been kept secret from **the foundation of the world**.* (Matt 13:35).
- *inherit the kingdom prepared for you from **the foundation of the world*** (Matt 25:34).
- *That the blood of all the prophets, which was shed from **the foundation of the world**.* (Lk 11:50).
- *for thou lovedst me before **the foundation of the world*** (Jhn 17:24).
- *According as he hath chosen us in him before **the foundation of the world*** (Eph 1:4).
- *And, Thou, Lord, in the beginning hast **laid the foundation of the earth**; and the heavens are the works of thine hands* (Heb 1:10).
- *although the works were finished from **the foundation of the world*** (Heb 4:3).
- *For then must he often have suffered since **the foundation of the world*** (Heb 9:26).

CHAPTER 7

- *Who verily was foreordained before **the foundation of the world*** (1Peter 1:20).
- *whose names are not written in the book of life of the Lamb slain from **the foundation of the world*** (Rev 13:8).
- *whose names were not written in the book of life from **the foundation of the world*** (Rev 17:8).

Note again: Scripture never speaks about the *foundation* of the sun, moon and stars; or of God laying their *foundation*. The concept of a foundation is contradictory with a moving object. Houses have foundations, automobiles do not. Scripture says that the sun, moon and stars are in motion (Psa 104:19; Jdg 5:20); it does not say this about the earth.

2. THEY WILL LEARN: THE FIRMAMENT WAS CREATED ON THE SECOND DAY

- *And **God made the firmament**, and divided the waters which were under the firmament from the waters which were above the firmament: and it was so. 8 And God called the firmament Heaven. And the evening and the morning were the second day* (Gen 1:7,8).
- *Praise ye him, sun and moon: praise him, all ye stars of light. 4 Praise him, ye heavens of heavens, and ye waters that be above the heavens* (Psa 148:3,4).

3. THEY WILL LEARN: THE SUN, MOON AND STARS WERE, (1) CREATED, (2) PLACED IN THE FIRMAMENT AND (3) STRETCHED OUT ON THE FOURTH DAY

- *And God said, **Let there be lights in the firmament of the heaven** to divide the day from the night; and **let them be for signs, and for seasons, and for days, and years**: 15 And let them be for lights in the firmament of the heaven to give light upon the earth: and it was so. 16 **And God made two great lights**; the greater light to rule the day, and the lesser light to rule the night: **he made the stars also**. 17 **And God set them in the firmament of the heaven to give light upon the earth**, 18 And to rule over the day and over the night, and to divide the light from the darkness: and God saw that it was good. 19 And the evening and the morning were the fourth day* (Gen 1:14-19).
- *Which alone **spreadeth out** the heavens* (Job 9:8).
- *He **stretcheth out** the north over the empty place* (Job 26:7)
- *Hast thou with him **spread out** the sky* (Job 37:18).
- *Who coverest thyself with light as with a garment: who **stretchest out** the heavens like a curtain* (Psa 104:2).
- *It is he that sitteth upon the circle of the earth, and the inhabitants thereof are as grasshoppers; **that stretcheth out the heavens as a curtain, and spreadeth them out as a tent to dwell in**.* (Isa 40:22).
- *Thus saith God the LORD, he that created the heavens, and **stretched them out*** (Isa 42:5).
- *Thus saith the LORD…that **stretcheth forth** the heavens alone* (Isa 44:24).
- *I, even my hands, have **stretched out** the heavens, and all their host have I commanded* (Isa 45:12).
- *my right hand hath **spanned** the heavens* (Isa 48:13).
- *And forgettest the LORD thy maker, that hath **stretched forth** the heavens* (Isa 51:13).
- *and hath **stretched out** the heavens by his discretion* (Jer 10:12).
- *and hath **stretched out** the heaven by his understanding* (Jer 51:15).

THE BOOK OF REVELATION

4. THEY WILL LEARN: THE BIBLE NEVER SPEAKS OF THE EARTH MOVING, EXCEPT IN TIMES OF JUDGEMENT

- *Fear before him, all the earth: the world also shall be **stable, that it be not moved*** (1 Chron 16:30).
- *Which **shaketh the earth out of her place**, and the pillars thereof tremble* (Job 9:6).
- *Let all the earth fear the LORD: let all the inhabitants of the world stand in awe of him. For he spake, and it was done; he commanded, and **it stood fast*** (Psa 33:8,9).
- *And he built his sanctuary like high palaces, like the earth which he hath **established** for ever* (Psa 78.69).
- *the world also is **stablished, that it cannot be moved**. Thy throne is **established** of old.* (Psa 93:1,2).
- *The LORD reigneth; let the people tremble: he sitteth between the cherubims; let the earth **be moved*** (Psa 99:1).
- *Who laid the foundations of the earth, that it **should not be removed for ever*** (Psa 104:5).
- *thou hast **established** the earth, and it **abideth*** (Psa 119:90).
- ***the earth shall remove out of her place*** (Isa 13:13).
- *the earth is **moved exceedingly*** (Isa 24:19)
- *The heaven is my throne, and the earth is **my footstool*** (Isa 61:1).
- *Heaven is my throne, and earth is **my footstool*** (Acts 7:49).

5. THEY WILL LEARN: THE BIBLE *ALWAYS* SPEAKS OF THE SUN MOVING

"Everyone knows the earth rotates beneath, and revolves around the Sun!" This, though, is not what our senses perceive, and Scripture in *every instance* states the opposite. To say that the following passages merely give **the language of appearance** when in fact it actually the earth in motion and not the Sun, raises the question: Why does the Bible not (at least occasionally) give **the language of actuality**? In fact on this as on all other matters, the Bible does speak in the language of actuality.

- *Sun, **stand thou still** upon Gibeon* (Josh 10:12).
- *and the sun **stood still*** (Josh 10:13).
- *Which commandeth the sun and **it riseth not*** (Job 9:7).
- *Which is **as a bridegroom coming out of his chamber*** (Psa 19:5).
- *His going forth...**his circuit*** (Psa 19:6).
- ***the sun knoweth his going down*** (Psa 104:19).
- *The sun also **ariseth**, and the sun **goeth down** and **hasteth to the place where he arose*** (Eccles 1:5).
- *the sun shall be darkened in **his going forth*** (Isa 13:10).
- *so the sun **returned ten degrees*** (Isa 38:8).
- *I will cause **the sun to go** down at noon* (Amos 8:9)
- *the sun and moon **stood still** in their habitation.* (Hab 3:11).
- *for he maketh **his sun to rise** on the evil and on the good, and **sendeth rain** on the just and on the unjust* (Matt 5:45).

These statements showing action exerted upon the sun and not the earth set a clear precedent for the **58 passages** in the Bible that speak of the Sun moving.

Note: frequently in the context of these 58 passages *something else* in addition to the Sun is said to be moving. How can motion for the one be actual and the other figurative?

CHAPTER 7

Church leaders at the beginning of the Copernican Era understood this and believed the Bible was being violated.

Martin Luther in referring to Copernicus said: "A certain new astrologer who wanted to prove that the earth moves and not the sky, the sun and the moon…I believe the Holy Scriptures, for Joshua commanded the sun to stand still and not the earth." (*Table Talks*; vol. 54; pp. 358,359).

John Owen declared the Copernican system a "delusive and arbitrary hypothesis, contrary to Scripture"; and John Wesley declared the new ideas to "tend toward infidelity". (Andrew White, *A History of the Warfare of Science with Theology in Christendom*, p.123). See *The Biblical and Observational Case for Geocentricity*.

During the Tribulation, passages of Scripture such a 1 Corinthians 1:19 will be fulfilled. Men will *learn* then what they do not *learn* now. *For it is written, I will destroy the wisdom of the wise, and will bring to nothing the understanding of the prudent.*

We now come to the Sixth Catastrophe that will befall the earth and the heavens with the opening of the Sixth Seal. All of Creation has been shaken.
To review:

1. THE SIXTH SEAL IS OPENED. *And I beheld when he had opened the sixth seal*
2. ALL OF THE EARTH AND THE HEAVENS ARE SHAKEN.
   (1) THE EARTH: *and, lo, there was a great earthquake.*
   (2) THE HEAVENS: *and the sun became black as sackcloth of hair.*
   (3) THE HEAVENS: *and the moon became as blood.*
   (4) THE HEAVENS. *And the stars of heaven fell unto the earth, even as a fig tree casteth her untimely figs, when she is shaken of a mighty wind.*
   (5) THE HEAVENS. *And the heaven departed as a scroll when it is rolled together*

   (6) THE EARTH: *and every mountain and island were moved out of their places* (6:14). It is ironic that with the mention of the *mountains* the "shelter" to which frightened men will flee in verse 15, will itself be *moved out of their places*. There will be no safe place, neither on land or sea. The mountains will provided no more protection than they did in the days of Noah. They will be *moved*! The familiar view of them on the horizon will change. No longer does the map or the road lead to their lofty, secluded, welcoming isolation.

The familiar locations will change on land and at sea. Any hopes of an "island refuge" will become problematic. All of nature will be in terrified upheaval.

• *And there shall be signs in the sun, and in the moon, and in the stars; and upon the earth distress of nations, with perplexity;* **the sea and the waves roaring***; 26 Men's hearts failing them for fear, and for looking after those things which are coming on the earth: for the powers of heaven shall be shaken* (Lk 21:26,27).

The action of the Lamb in opening the Sixth Seal has set Heaven shouting and earth shuddering (cp. 5:9 with 6:16). Its opening marks the beginning fulfilment of Bible prophecies long known to some of God's people and long ignored by the world.

• *The LORD is slow to anger, and great in power, and will not at all acquit the wicked: the LORD hath his way in the whirlwind and in the storm, and the clouds are the dust of his feet. 4* **He rebuketh the sea, and maketh it dry, and drieth up all the rivers***: Bashan languisheth, and Carmel, and the flower of Lebanon languisheth.5* **The** *mountains quake at him, and the hills melt, and the earth is burned at his presence, yea, the world, and all that dwell therein. 6 **Who can stand** before his indignation? and who can abide in the fierceness of his anger? his fury is poured out like fire, and **the rocks are thrown down** by him* (Nahum 1:3-6).

• ***And I will shake all nations***, *and the desire of all nations shall come: and I will fill this house with glory, saith the LORD of hosts* (Hag 2:7).

• ***And I will overthrow the throne of kingdoms***, *and I will destroy the strength of the kingdoms of the heathen; and I will overthrow the chariots, and those that ride in them; and the horses and their riders shall come down, every one by the sword of his brother* (Hag 2:22).

• ***The earth shall reel to and fro like a drunkard***, *and shall be removed like a cottage; and the transgression thereof shall be heavy upon it; and it shall fall, and not rise again* (Isa 24:20).

With Heaven and Earth shaking under the Sixth Seal, we now turn to man, all kinds of men. The world in that day will be paralyzed by fear.

Men's hearts failing them for fear and for looking after those things which are coming on the earth (Lk 21:26).

3. ALL OF MANKIND IS SHAKEN.

(1) THEIR STATUS. *And the kings of the earth, and the great men, and the rich men, and the chief captains, and the mighty men, and every bondman, and every free man* (6:15). The dread and terror that would seize upon all and all kinds of men in that great and awful day could not be more graphic. No authority, nor grandeur, nor riches, nor valour, nor strength, would be able to support men at that time. Those who have much of this world's glitter and glory to lose are thrown into a deadly fear. The very poorest, who, one would think, had nothing to fear, because they had nothing to lose, will likewise be in terrified amazement in that day. All levels of society are here. Some are the greatest men, others are the poorest men. In relation to judgment of the Lord Jesus Christ, however, everyone is exactly in the same impending state of doom. Success in the world does not help; no one escapes.

(2) THEIR FLIGHT. They **hid themselves in the dens and in the rocks of the mountains.** Rather than hide themselves in Christ, the *Rock* and *Stone of Israel* (Gen 49:24), they flee to something far less secure. They will do no better than those who sought to flee to the *mountains* to flee from the Flood. While the martyrs, robed in white, triumph in heaven (6:11) their persecutors tremble on earth.

• *Fear, and the pit, and the snare, are upon thee, O inhabitant of the earth. 18 And it shall come to pass, that **he who fleeth from the noise of the fear shall fall into the pit**; and he that cometh up out of the midst of the pit shall be taken in the snare: for the windows from on high are open, and the foundations of the earth do shake* (Isa 24:17,18).

(3) THEIR "PRAYER". ***And said to the mountains and rocks, Fall on us, and hide us from the face of him that sitteth on the throne, and from the wrath of the Lamb: For the great day of his wrath is come; and who shall be able to stand*** (6:16,17)?
They are no longer atheists or agnostics; they acknowledge Christ and are terrified at His wrath.

CHAPTER 7

Govett writes:

> All classes of mankind have been guilty of persecuting the saints ; and this fearful sight is sent in consequence of it. Their actions declare their fear. Their houses are no security against the earthquake; but when they flee forth into the open air to escape the falling walls, then the terrible phenomena of the troubled heavens disclose themselves to their terrified gaze. Where now shall they hide? Even kings leave their palaces in haste, and dread both the city and the open field.
>
> They flee to the rocks and caves. Even in these hiding-places, they do not esteem themselves sufficiently hid. Still the earthquake rocks them; still the sky lowers with ominous frown. The distinctions of rank and degree among men are all over-mastered by irrepressible fear. Kings and subjects, servants and freemen, all hurry to the same hiding-places. The bold soldier and the timid female are side by side. They all understand it as the act of God above; and look on it as due to no subordinate and ordinary cause.

<u>"Fleeing to the Rocks"</u>

- *And the **mean man** boweth down, and the **great man** humbleth himself: therefore forgive them not.10 **Enter into the rock, and hide thee in the dust, for fear of the LORD**, and for the glory of his majesty.11 The lofty looks of man shall be humbled, and the haughtiness of men shall be bowed down, and the LORD alone shall be exalted in that day. 12 For the day of the LORD of hosts shall be upon every one that is proud and lofty, and upon every one that is lifted up; and he shall be brought low (Isa 2:9-12).*

- *And they shall go **into the holes of the rocks**, and **into the caves of the earth**, for fear of the LORD, and for the glory of his majesty, when he ariseth to shake terribly the earth. 20 In that day a man shall cast his idols of silver, and his idols of gold, which they made each one for himself to worship, to the moles and to the bats; 21 To go **into the clefts of the rocks**, and **into the tops of the ragged rocks**, for fear of the LORD, and for the glory of his majesty, when he ariseth to shake terribly the earth.22 Cease ye* *from man, whose breath is in his nostrils: for wherein is he to be accounted of* (Isa 2:20-22) ?

The answer to the question: *Who shall be able to stand*? is given in the next chapter. In fact, they should have answered their own question. Those who are described as standing in the next chapter are the very Jewish and Gentile believers whom the fleeing men persecuted.

Despite all that we have seen under the six seal judgements, the wrath now increases *exponentially*. We now move to the wrath of the *Trumpets*, and then to the final unmingled wrath of the *Vials* (14:10,11). One chapter has been given to the wrath of the Seals; twelve chapters describe the wrath of the Trumpets and Vials.

Under the Vial Judgements the fear seen here at the midpoint of the Tribulation will give way to **angry and arrogant blasphemy** (Rev 16:9,11,21)!

B. THE SEVEN YEAR TRIBULATION 6-18
1. The Seal Judgements and Other Events 6,7
a. Six Seals Opened: Wrath (6:17) 6
b. 144,000 Jewish Evangelists Sealed 7:1-8
c. A Multitude of Gentiles Saved 7:9-17

c. A Multitude of Gentiles Saved 7:9-17

The question **who shall be able to stand** rang out at the close of the preceding chapter and the opening of the Sixth Seal. Two great multitudes now answer that question. In this Chapter we see: The restraint of the winds; the sealing of the 144,000; the singing of the Tribulation saints.

As this Chapter begins with the words, **And after these things**, and as we are now about to see a number of time designations (*time, times and half a time*; *42 months, 1260 days*) we must now come to some very important conclusions regarding the chronology of the Seven Year Tribulation.

Five matters especially are to be emphasized.

(1) As with the previous chapters of Revelation, the events are basically chronological. The Seal, Trumpet and Vial judgements are successive; they are not as some have taught parallel restatements.

(2) *Everything* from Chapter 7 to Chapter 18 takes place **during** the Second Half of the Tribulation.

(3) An *explosion of events* will take place at the Midpoint of the Seven Years. The description of these climatic events though given later (as in Chapters 11,12,13 and 17), but the enormity of what happens at the Midpoint cannot be overstated. Both Heaven and earth are in convulsion. The Book of Daniel adds further information to this *explosion of events* at the Midpoint.

(4) The Seventh Seal (8:1), Trumpet Judgements, and Vial Judgements provide the background structure to the final three and one half years. The Seventh Seal covers the entire period in the sense that it opens up into the Seven Trumpets, with the Seventh Trumpet opening into the Seven Vials.

(5) The time designations now given, each equal three and one half years and occur in the Second Half. This becomes apparent by the events with which they are associated.

CHAPTER 7

THE CHRONOLOGICAL KEY REGARDING THE SECOND HALF OF THE TRIBULATION

And after these things

1. CHAPTER SEVEN AND ALL THAT FOLLOWS ARE INTRODUCED BY: *And after these things* (7:1).

This is a unique time notation found only three times in Revelation. It is similar to John's *Rapture* statement after the Seven Ages of the Church.

> • *After this I looked, and, behold, a door was opened in heaven: and the first voice which I heard was as it were of a trumpet talking with me; which said,* **Come up hither, and I will shew thee things which must be hereafter** *(Rev 4:1).*

In its two other occurrences it is used of the fall of commercial/political Babylon at the end of the Tribulation and the Return of Christ to earth. Note that, *And after these things*, is given in the first verse of the three chapters in which it is found (7:1; 18:1; 19:1).

> • *And after these things I saw another angel come down from heaven, having great power; and the earth was lightened with his glory. 2 And he cried mightily with a strong voice, saying, Babylon the great is fallen, is fallen, and is become the habitation of devils, and the hold of every foul spirit, and a cage of every unclean and hateful bird (Rev 18:1,2).*

> • *And after these things I heard a great voice of much people in heaven, saying, Alleluia; Salvation, and glory, and honour, and power, unto the Lord our God: 2 For true and righteous are his judgments: for he hath judged the great whore, which did corrupt the earth with her fornication, and hath avenged the blood of his servants at her hand (Rev 19:1,2).*

> • *And I saw heaven opened, and behold a white horse; and he that sat upon him was called Faithful and True, and in righteousness he doth judge and make war (Rev 19:11).*

With these words we see the link between the opening of the Six Seals in Chapter 6 and the opening of the Seventh Seal in Chapter 8. The Seventh Seal (enclosing the Seven Trumpets and Seven Vials) covers the entire second half of the Tribulation. All events in these final twelve chapters of the Tribulation are *locked into* this time frame of three and one half years.

> • *And when he had opened the seventh seal, there was silence in heaven about the space of half an hour. 2 And I saw the seven angels which stood before God; and to them were given seven trumpets (Rev 8:1,2).*

THE THREE 3½ YEAR TIME DESIGNATIONS

- *a thousand two hundred and threescore days*
- *a time, and times, and half a time*
- *forty and two months*

Certain *foundational* and *interlocking* events that will occur in the Second Half of the Tribulation are described in Chapters 11, 12 and 13. They begin at the Midpoint and span (or nearly so) the 3½ years. To emphasis this fact, they are linked to one or more of the above three time designations. These are found five times in these three chapters.

1. SATAN CAST TO EARTH; THE BRINGING FORTH OF THE MAN CHILD (144,00), AND THE FLIGHT OF ISRAEL INTO THE WILDERNESS ARE LINKED BY TWO OF THE 3 ½ YEAR TIME DESIGNATIONS; THESE OCCUR AT THE BEGINNING OF THE SECOND HALF OF THE TRIBULATION.

By comparing Revelation 7, 12 and 14 with Isaiah 66, the 144,000 is (are) the Man Child brought forth by the Sun-clothed Woman (Israel, Rev 12) and after preforming their work are caught up to the Throne of God before the final Vial Judgements begin (Rev 12,14). The Man Child cannot refer to Christ (a title not given to Christ elsewhere), for the woman who begets him is seen fleeing into the wilderness and being hidden for ***1260 days*** (Rev 12:6). The context of Chapter 12 and the other passages is Israel during the Tribulation, not the times of the birth and ministry of Christ.

The 144,000 are sealed between the opening of the Sixth and Seventh Seal judgements (Rev 6:12; 7:1-8; 8:1). Comparing this with Revelation 12 will show that these events (being linked twice by the time designations) begin at about the Midpoint and extend throughout the Second Half of the Tribulation. However, they are *servants* before they receive their protective *seal*. Thus they are saved in the First Half of the Tribulation (7:3).

* *And there appeared a great wonder in heaven; **a woman clothed with the sun**, and the moon under her feet, and upon her head a crown of twelve stars: 2 And she being with child cried, **travailing in birth**, and pained to be delivered.*

  *3 And there appeared another wonder in heaven; and behold **a great red dragon**, having seven heads and ten horns, and seven crowns upon his heads. 4 And his tail drew the third part of the stars of heaven, and did cast them to the earth: and **the dragon stood before the woman which was ready to be delivered, for to devour her child as soon as it was born**.*

  *5 And **she brought forth a man child**, who was to rule all nations with a rod of iron: and **her child was caught up unto God**, and to his throne.*

  *6 And **the woman fled into the wilderness**, where she hath a place prepared of God, that they should **feed her there <u>a thousand two hundred and threescore days</u>***
  (Rev 12:1-6).

* *And when **the dragon saw that he was cast unto the earth, he persecuted the woman which brought forth the man child**. 14 And to the woman were given two wings of a great eagle, that she might **fly into the wilderness, into her place, where she is nourished for <u>a time, and times, and half a time</u>**, from the face of the serpent*
  (Rev 12:13,14).

Note verse 5: As Christ Himself *and* the resurrected Church, the Man Child (144,000) will in the Millennial Reign *rule all nations with a rod of iron*. Compare this promise with that given to the overcomers at the Church at Thyatira.

* *And **he that overcometh**, and keepeth my works unto the end, to him will I give power over the nations: 27 And he **shall rule them with a rod of iron**; as the vessels of a potter shall they be broken to shivers: even as I received of my Father (Rev 2:26,27).*

2. THE MINISTRY OF THE TWO WITNESS IS LIKEWISE LINKED TO TWO OF THE 3 ½ YEAR TIME DESIGNATION.

* *And there was given me a reed like unto a rod: and the angel stood, saying, Rise, and measure the temple of God, and the altar, and them that worship therein. 2 But the*

*court which is without the temple leave out, and measure it not; for it is given unto the Gentiles: and the holy city shall **they tread under foot <u>forty and two months</u>**. 3 And **I will give power unto my two witnesses, and they shall prophesy <u>a thousand two hundred and threescore days</u>**, clothed in sackcloth. 4 These are the two olive trees, and the two candlesticks standing before the God of the earth (Rev 11: 1-4).*

The worship of the Jews on the Temple Mount takes place during the First Half of the Tribulation (11:1), but the *treading under foot* of the Temple Mount, as well as the preaching of the Two Witnesses takes place in the Second Half. Each of these time designations occur in the Second Half.

3. THE FULL REIGN OF ANTICHRIST IN THE SECOND HALF OF THE TRIBULATION IS LINKED TO ONE OF <u>THE 3 ½ YEAR TIME DESIGNATIONS</u>

• *And there was given unto him a mouth speaking great things and blasphemies; and **power was given unto him to continue <u>forty and two months</u>*** (Rev 13:5).

Note again, the five-fold mention of the *3½ year time designations* links these foundational events and demonstrates that they all begin at the start of the Second Half of the Tribulation.

B. 144,000 JEWISH EVANGELISTS SEALED   7:1-8

*(7:1) **And after these things I saw four angels standing on the four corners of the earth, holding the four winds of the earth, that the wind should not blow on the earth, nor on the sea, nor on any tree.** (7: 2) **And I saw another angel ascending from the east, having the seal of the living God: and he cried with a loud voice to the four angels, to whom it was given to hurt the earth and the sea,** (7:3) **Saying, Hurt not the earth, neither the sea, nor the trees, till we have <u>sealed the servants of our God in their foreheads.</u>***

*(7:4) **And I heard the number of them which were sealed: and there were sealed an hundred and forty and four thousand of all the tribes of the children of Israel.** (7:5) **Of the tribe of Juda were sealed twelve thousand. Of the tribe of Reuben were sealed twelve thousand. Of the tribe of Gad were sealed twelve thousand.** (7:6) **Of the tribe of Aser were sealed twelve thousand. Of the tribe of Nepthalim were sealed twelve thousand. Of the tribe of Manasses were sealed twelve thousand.** (7:7) **Of the tribe of Simeon were sealed twelve thousand. Of the tribe of Levi were sealed twelve thousand. Of the tribe of Issachar were sealed twelve thousand.** (7:8) **Of the tribe of Zabulon were sealed twelve thousand. Of the tribe of Joseph were sealed twelve thousand. Of the tribe of Benjamin were sealed twelve thousand.***

At the close of Chapter 6 with the opening of the Sixth Seal and the fleeing of the world to the rocks and the mountains the terrified cry rang out ***the great day of his wrath is come; and who shall be able to stand*** (6:17). That many have been standing for Christ during the First Half of the Tribulation and will now continue to stand under even greater persecution during the Second Half is now fully demonstrated in this Chapter.

Regarding the conversion of sinners during the Tribulation Walvoord writes.

> The question has often been asked, "Will anyone be saved after the rapture?" The Scriptures clearly indicate that a great multitude of both Jews and Gentiles will trust in the Lord after the church is caught up to glory. Though the children of God living on earth at the time will be translated when Christ comes for His church, immediately a testimony will be raised up to the name of Christ through new converts

among Jews and Gentiles. Though these are never described by the term "church," they are constantly called saints, that is, those set apart as holy to God and saved through the sacrifice of Christ.

The presence of saved people in the world after the Rapture has puzzled some because according to 2 Thessalonians 2:7 the one who now restrains sin, often identified as the Holy Spirit, is pictured as being removed from the world. The question then is how can people be saved in the Tribulation if the Holy Spirit is taken out of the world? The answer, of course, is that the Holy Spirit is removed from the world in the same sense in which He came on the day of Pentecost. People were saved before the day of Pentecost when the Spirit of God came to indwell the church, and it should be clear from other Scriptures that the Holy Spirit is always omnipresent. He has always been in the world and always will be, in keeping with the divine attribute of omnipresence. Though the special ministries which are characteristic of the present dispensation may cease, there will be the continued ministry of the Spirit in a similar way to that which existed before Pentecost.

With greater judgements now about to fall Divine preparations are now made for a further harvest of souls in those terrible days. Here as before the truth of 2 Peter 3:9 is manifest.

- *The Lord is not slack concerning his promise, as some men count slackness; but is longsuffering to us-ward,* **not willing that any should perish, but that all should come to repentance** (2 Pet 3:9).

1. THE RESTRAINT OF THE JUDGEMENT WINDS. With the opening of the Six Seals great damage was inflicted upon earth. Now there is a brief cessation of the winds of judgement and the damage they caused. Though Satan is called *the prince of the power of the air* (Eph 2:1), and by a great wind overthrew the house of Job's eldest son (Job 1:18,19), yet here it is the angels of God that are in control of the winds.

(1) THE FOUR ANGELS HOLDING THE WINDS OF EARTH. ***And after these things I saw four angels standing on the four corners of the earth, holding the four winds of the earth, that the wind should not blow on the earth, nor on the sea, nor on any tree*** (7:1). John is so high above the earth that he sees it at once as a globe, and the angels occupying the stations of east, west, north, and south. The elements of nature keep their quiet course only during the pleasure of the Divine Throne. When let loose, the winds are destructive to the labours and habitations of men on land, and to the ships at sea. (Job 1:19; Jonah 1:4,12). Now no breath of air is to blow—the very leaves of the trees are not to rustle (Govett).

Note the other references to the *four corners* and the *four winds*. Both are terms expressing the *full extent*. The angels are for a time hold back *all* the winds of judgement upon *all* of the earth.

- *And he shall set up an ensign for the nations, and shall assemble the outcasts of Israel, and gather together the dispersed of Judah from* **the four corners of the earth** (Isa 11:12).
- *Also, thou son of man, thus saith the Lord GOD unto the land of Israel; An end, the end is come upon* **the four corners of the land** (Ezek 7:2).
- *And upon Elam will I bring* **the four winds** *from* **the four quarters of heaven**, *and will scatter them toward all those winds; and there shall be no nation whither the outcasts of Elam shall not come* (Jer 49:36).
- *Then said he unto me, Prophesy unto the wind, prophesy, son of man, and say to the wind, Thus saith the Lord GOD; Come from* **the four winds**, *O breath, and breathe*

CHAPTER 7

upon these slain, that they may live (Ezek 37:9).
- *Daniel spake and said, I saw in my vision by night, and, behold,* **the four winds of the heaven** *strove upon the great sea* (Dan 7:2).
- *Therefore the he goat waxed very great: and when he was strong, the great horn was broken; and for it came up four notable ones toward* **the four winds of heaven** (Dan 8:8).
- *And when he shall stand up, his kingdom shall be broken, and shall be divided toward* **the four winds of heaven**; *and not to his posterity, nor according to his dominion which he ruled: for his kingdom shall be plucked up, even for others beside those* (Dan 11:4).
- *Ho, ho, come forth, and flee from the land of the north, saith the LORD: for I have spread you abroad as* **the four winds of the heaven**, *saith the LORD* (Zech 2:6).
- *And he shall send his angels with a great sound of a trumpet, and they shall gather together his elect from* **the four winds, from one end of heaven to the other** (Matt 24:31).

(2) THE ANGEL HOLDING THE SEAL OF GOD. *And I saw another angel ascending from the east, having the seal of the living God: and he cried with a loud voice to the four angels, to whom it was given to hurt the earth and the sea* (7: 2).

[1] HIS REQUEST. *Saying, Hurt not the earth, neither the sea, nor the trees* (7:3). This refers to the impending Trumpet Judgements (Rev 8,9).

[2] HIS REASON: *till we have sealed the servants of our God in their foreheads.* A temporary cessation of judgement is requested to place a permanent seal upon God's servants. It is a seal on the forehead: the most visible part of the body and the most pertinent, for the seat of thought and intelligence will be affected by the seal. By this they were distinguished. By this they were set apart for mercy and safety and service in these worst of times.

2. THE SEALING OF THE 144,000.

(1) THE TIME OF THEIR SEALING. While many believe that they are sealed shortly after the Rapture; we have seen that they are not sealed until *after these things* (7:1), *after* the tumultuous events of the first Six Seals, and also just before the opening to the Seventh Seal (8:1). They are sealed near the Midpoint of the Tribulation. They have witnessed the first stage of judgement upon the earth. They know that it is far beyond anything the world has *ever* seen.

However Note! *They are already servants when they are sealed and enumerated.* This means that they were already saved during as least part of the First Half of the Tribulation and that they had immediately gone to work as *servants* in spreading the Gospel and winning the lost. They now receive a *protective seal* that enables them to withstand all of the onslaughts of the Antichrist. It will also like Israel in Goshen during the plagues of Egypt protect them from the intensification of judgement upon earth. Compare:

- *And there came out of the smoke locusts upon the earth: and unto them was given power, as the scorpions of the earth have power. 4 And it was commanded them that they should not hurt the grass of the earth, neither any green thing, neither any tree; but* **only those men which have not the seal of God in their foreheads** (Rev 9:3,4).

(2) THE SEAL ITSELF. The followers of the False Messiah will receive his name and mark in their foreheads (Rev 13:16) and these followers of the True Messiah will bear His Name in their in their foreheads (Rev 14:1). Compare also the faithful Israelites at the time of the Babylonian Captivity and the promise to the Church at Philadelphia.

• *And I looked, and, lo, a Lamb stood on the mount Sion, and with him an hundred forty and four thousand,* **having his Father's name written in their foreheads** (Rev 14:1).
• *Him that overcometh will I make a pillar in the temple of my God, and he shall go no more out: and* **I will write upon him the name of my God, and the name of the city of my God, which is new Jerusalem**, *which cometh down out of heaven from my God: and* **I will write upon him my new name** (Rev 3:12).
• *And the glory of the God of Israel was gone up from the cherub, whereupon he was, to the threshold of the house. And he called to the man clothed with linen, which had the writer's inkhorn by his side; 4 And the LORD said unto him, Go through the midst of the city, through the midst of Jerusalem, and* **set a mark upon the foreheads of the men that sigh and that cry for all the abominations that be done in the midst thereof** (Ezek 9:3,4).

Govett makes the following points concerning this seal:

The Angel has *the seal of the living God*. This manifests his dignity. He who holds the great seal of the Realm is one of its chief officers: greatly trusted by the Throne. Compare that given to Joseph by Pharaoh (Gen 41:42). That the mark left by the seal is an object of sight seems proved by the following considerations.

(1) The locusts, though animals possessed of but small intelligence, are able to see it, and respect it (Rev 9:4).

(2) The sign of the old covenant (circumcision) was a physical mark in the flesh.

(3) The sign of God's servants in Egypt was the visible mark of blood on the door.

(4) Satan imitates God: and his mark, set on the worshippers of the Beast, is assuredly visible (Rev 13).

(5) The sign set on Cain to preserve him was literal. This mark also is to preserve the receiver. The mark on Cain was to prevent anyone from assaulting him, murderer though he was. Much more is this to preserve his true servants (Gen 4:15).

(6) It is a sign to men, and to the executioners of the judgments of the Lord, not to injure the wearer.

• *He suffered no man to do them wrong: yea, he reproved kings for their sakes; 15 Saying, Touch not mine anointed, and do my prophets no harm* (Psa 105:14,15).

(7) It is the seal of *the living God*. This is the title which God usually takes, as the author of miracles, and as set in opposition to the vain gods of idolaters. By this mark, the 144,000 are constituted God's witnesses against the idolatry then abroad.

• *And the rest of the men which were not killed by these plagues yet repented not of the works of their hands, that they should not worship devils, and idols of gold, and silver, and brass, and stone, and of wood: which neither can see, nor hear, nor walk* (Rev 9:20).

<u>(3) THEIR NUMBER AND ORIGIN.</u>

[1] <u>AS TO THEIR ENUMERATION AND ETHNICITY</u>. *And I heard the number of them which were sealed: and there were sealed an hundred and forty and four thousand. of all the tribes of the children of Israel* (7:4).

[2] <u>AS TO THEIR NUMBER BY TRIBE</u>. (7:5) **Of the tribe of <u>Juda</u> were sealed twelve thousand. Of the tribe of <u>Reuben</u> were sealed twelve thousand. Of the tribe of <u>Gad</u> were sealed twelve thousand. (7:6) Of the tribe of <u>Aser</u> were sealed twelve thousand. Of the tribe of <u>Nephthalim</u> were sealed twelve thousand. Of the tribe of <u>Manasses</u> were sealed twelve thousand. (7:7) Of the tribe of <u>Simeon</u> were sealed twelve thousand. Of**

the tribe of <u>Levi</u> were sealed twelve thousand. Of the tribe of <u>Issachar</u> were sealed twelve thousand. (7:8) Of the tribe of <u>Zabulon</u> were sealed twelve thousand. Of the tribe of <u>Joseph</u> were sealed twelve thousand. Of the tribe of <u>Benjamin</u> were sealed twelve thousand. (7:5-8).

He Who in the days of Ahab and Jezebel reserved seven thousand for Himself (1 Kng 19:18) will in the days of Antichrist and the False Prophet reserve 144,000. Of these not one shall perish; just as in Numbers 31:48,49 none perished in the battle with Midian. In that battle one thousand fought out of each Tribe; in this battle twelve thousand will fight out of each Tribe (Williams).

THE ORDER OF BIRTH OF THE SONS OF JACOB WITH THEIR MOTHERS GENESIS 29,30,35

Reuben, Leah
Simeon, Leah
Levi, Leah
Judah, Leah
Dan, Bilhah maid of Rachel
Naphtali, Bilhah maid of Rachel
Gad, Zilpah maid of Leah
Asher, Zilpah maid of Leah
Zebulun, Leah
Joseph, Rachel, *Manasseh* and *Ephraim* by Pharaoh's Daughter born in Egypt
Benjamin, Rachel

Note the order of their birth in comparison to the order of their sealing. Govett shows "that the sons of the four mothers are curiously interchanged. The covenant of which these are the subjects is of grace."

Of Leah:—**Judah, Reuben**.
Of Zilpah:—**Gad, Asher**.
Of Bilhah:—**Naphthali**. But Dan, her other son, is omitted; and **Manasseh**, a son of Joseph, and descendant of Rachel's, takes his place.
Leah's earlier sons re-appear; **Simeon, Levi**.
Leah's later sons; **Issachar, Zebulon**.
Of Rachel: — **Joseph, Benjamin**.

Other Lists of the Patriarchs and Tribes are given in: Genesis 35,46,49; Exodus 1 Numbers 1,2,13,26,34; Deuteronomy 27,33; Joshua 13-22; Judges 5; 1 Chronicles 2-8,12,24,27; Ezekiel 48.

Revelation 14:9 states that the 144,000 in Chapter 7 are all men. These two chapters (Rev 7,14) demonstrates emphatically (along with the clear statements of the entire Bible) that God has and will preserve His Ancient People even to the point of (in many cases) their tribal identity.

• *And the word of the LORD came unto Jeremiah, saying, 20 Thus saith the LORD;* **If ye can break my covenant of the day, and my covenant of the night,** *and that there should not be day and night in their season; 21* **Then may also my covenant be broken** *with David my servant, that he should not have a son to reign upon his throne; and with the Levites the priests, my ministers. 22* **As the host of heaven cannot be numbered,** *neither the sand of the sea measured: so will I multiply the seed of David my servant, and the Levites that minister unto me* (Jer 33:19-22).

"There are no fewer than 29 lists of the tribes of Israel throughout the Scriptures, thus showing the prominence accorded them in the sacred page" (Walvoord quoting Swete). Here we see that the Twelve Tribes of Israel will still be in existence during the Tribulation and time of Christ's Return.

Generally in the lists, both of the sons of Joseph, Ephraim and Manasseh, are numbered as separate tribes. In this list Manasseh is mentioned but Ephraim is not, and in place of Ephraim the name of Joseph his father is given. This is perhaps to perpetuate the honour of Joseph.

There is no mention of the tribe of Dan. Early interpreters accounted for this on the theory that the Antichrist would come from the tribe of Dan (cp. Gen 49:17). Another explanation is that the tribe of Dan was one of the first to go into idolatry, and having the same mother (Bilhah) is included here with the tribe of Naphtali. Dan is listed in the allotment of Millennial Israel, and on the gates of Millennial Jerusalem (Ezek 48:1,32).

Jewish Men Gathered in New York City:
Will some of them be saved and numbered among the 144,000?

DOES *ISRAEL* EVER MEAN ANYONE OTHER THAN *ISRAEL*?

With "Replacement Theology" so common in Reformed and Catholic churches, Walvoord quoting Walter Scott and J.B. Smith makes the following points:

In the enumeration of the tribes throughout Scripture, the full representative number Twelve is always given; but as Jacob has thirteen sons, one or other is always omitted. Levi is more generally omitted than any other. In this enumeration, Dan and

Ephraim are omitted. Both these tribes were remarkable as being connected with idolatry in Israel, the probable reason for blotting out of their names here (Deut 29:18-21). But in the end grace triumphs, and Dan is named first in the future distribution of the land amongst the tribe (Ezek 48:2), but, while first named, it is the farthest removed from the Temple, being situated in the extreme north.

Though Israelites today do not normally know what tribe they belong to, in the mind of God there is no question. Here representatives for each of the twelve tribes are selected for the signal honor of being sealed by the angel.

The fact that the Twelve Tribes of Israel are singled out for special reference in the tribulation time is another evidence that the term "Israel" as used in the Bible is invariably a reference to the descendants of Jacob who was first given the name Israel. Galatians 6:16 is no exception. The prevalent idea that the church is the true Israel is not sustained by any explicit reference in the Bible, and the word Israel is never used of Gentiles and refers only to those who are racially descendants of Israel or Jacob. Though the Bible distinguishes true Israelites from those who have forsaken their heritage, the term "Israel" is never used outside the descendants of Jacob himself.

The remnant of Israel as portrayed here in the book of Revelation should not therefore be taken as meaning the church. It would be rather ridiculous to carry the typology of Israel representing the church to the extent of dividing them up into twelve tribes as was done here. The mention of the twelve tribes of Israel is likewise a refutation of the idea that the tribes of Israel are lost, as well as of the theory that the lost tribes are perpetuated in the English-speaking people of the world.

Though genealogies have been lost, a modern Jew can be assured that he belongs to the seed of Abraham; and God knows into which tribe he should be classified. In the book of James there is reference to the twelve tribes of Israel as being in existence at the time our Lord was upon earth (Jms 1:1; cp. 1 Pet 1:1).

The question has also been raised whether the "12,000" in each tribe means literally 12,000. There seems to be indication that more than 12,000 from each tribe actually will be saved. The point of this Scripture is that in any event 12,000 in each tribe are made secure. There will be other Israelites saved besides these 144,000, but many of these will die martyrs' deaths and give up their lives for their faith. The 144,000 are those who are delivered from their persecutors and brought safely through this terrible time of tribulation.

(4) THEIR IDENTITY AS *THE MANCHILD*. We have already noted that by comparing Revelation 7, 12 and 14 with Isaiah 66, the 144,000 is (are) the Man Child brought forth by the Sun-clothed Woman (Israel, Rev 12) and after performing their work are caught up to the Throne of God before the final Vial Judgements begin (Rev 12,14). A rereading of Revelation 12 in comparison with Isaiah 66 strongly supports this conclusion.

- **Revelation 12:1-6;13,14**

*1 And there appeared a great wonder in heaven; **a woman clothed with the sun**, and the moon under her feet, and upon her head a crown of twelve stars: 2 And she being with child cried, **travailing in birth**, and pained to be delivered.*

*3 And there appeared another wonder in heaven; and behold **a great red dragon**, having seven heads and ten horns, and seven crowns upon his heads. 4 And his tail drew the third part of the stars of heaven, and did cast them to the earth: and **the dragon stood before the woman which was ready to be delivered, for to devour her child as soon as it was born**.*

*5 And **she brought forth a man child**, who was to rule all nations with a rod of iron: and **her child was caught up unto God**, and to his throne.*

*6 And **the woman fled into the wilderness**, where she hath a place prepared of God, that they should **feed her there a thousand two hundred and threescore days***

*13 And when **the dragon saw that he was cast unto the earth, he persecuted the woman which brought forth the man child**. 14 And to the woman were given two wings of a great eagle, that she might **fly into the wilderness, into her place, where she is nourished for a time, and times, and half a time**, from the face of the serpent*

- **Isaiah 66:7-9**

*7 Before she travailed, she brought forth; before her pain came, **she was delivered of a man child**.*

8 Who hath heard such a thing? who hath seen such things? Shall the earth be made to bring forth in one day? or shall a nation be born at once? for as soon as Zion travailed, she brought forth her children. 9 Shall I bring to the birth, and not cause to bring forth? saith the LORD: shall I cause to bring forth, and shut the womb? saith thy God.

The importance of Isaiah 66:7-9 in detailing a twofold aspect of Israel's future *spiritual* rebirth cannot be overstated. Before her national conversion she bring forth a *Man Child*. Note the following comments from Isaiah 66.

66:7. ***Before she travailed, she brought forth; before her pain came, she was delivered of a man child.*** Before Israel gives birth, i.e. her full salvation at Christ's Return, she will deliver a *man child*. This as we have seen refers to the sudden conversion of the 144,000 during the First Half of the Tribulation, and likely early in the First Half after the Rapture. They receive their protective seal at about the Midpoint between the Sixth and Seventh Seals (Rev 6:12; 7:3; 8:1). They are caught up to Heaven before the pouring out of the Vial Judgements in Chapter 16, and are seen with the Lamb in heaven (14:1-5; cp. 12:4,5: *a man child . . . was caught up to God, and to his throne*).

As we have also shown, the context of Revelation 12:4,5 refers to the Tribulation rather than to the birth of Christ. And, as with the *overcomers* of the church age, the Man Child will have *power over the nations* during the Millennium (12:4,5 with 2:26,27; 5:10).

66:8. ***Who hath heard such a thing? who hath seen such things? Shall the earth be made to bring forth in one day? or shall a nation be born at once? for as soon as Zion travailed, she brought forth her children.*** Both the coming forth of the Man Child (the 144,00) during the early part of the Tribulation, and the conversion of Israel at Christ's Return (Zech 12:10; 13:1; Rom 11:25,26; Rev. 1:7) will be an event of the greatest wonder.

66:9. ***Shall I bring to the birth, and not cause to bring forth? saith the LORD: shall I cause to bring forth, and shut the womb? saith thy God.*** Will the Lord begin and not finish His work of restoring Israel? Will He bring to the (point of) birth, and not grant delivery (Isa 37:3)? Shall He who begets, restrain the birth (Hos 13:13; Rom. 11:1)? NO!

- *The sorrows of a travailing woman shall come upon him: he is an unwise son; for **he should not stay long in the place of the breaking forth of children** (Hos 13:13).*

c. A Multitude of Gentiles Saved 7:9-17

(7:9) ***After this I beheld, and, lo, a great multitude, which no man could number, of all nations, and kindreds, and people, and tongues, stood before the throne, and before the Lamb, clothed with white robes, and palms in their hands;*** (7:10) ***And cried with a loud voice, saying, Salvation to our God which sitteth upon the throne, and unto the Lamb.***

(7:11) ***And all the angels stood round about the throne, and about the elders and the four beasts, and fell before the throne on their faces, and worshipped God,*** (7:12)

CHAPTER 7

Saying, Amen: Blessing, and glory, and wisdom, and thanksgiving, and honour, and power, and might, be unto our God for ever and ever. Amen.
(7:13) And one of the elders answered, saying unto me, What are these which are arrayed in white robes? and whence came they? (7:14) And I said unto him, Sir, thou knowest. And he said to me, These are they which came out of great tribulation, and have washed their robes, and made them white in the blood of the Lamb.
(7:15) ***Therefore are they before the throne of God, and serve him day and night in his temple: and he that sitteth on the throne shall dwell among them.****(7:16)* ***They shall hunger no more, neither thirst any more; neither shall the sun light on them, nor any heat.*** *(7:17)* ***For the Lamb which is in the midst of the throne shall feed them, and shall lead them unto living fountains of waters: and God shall wipe away all tears from their eyes.***

We now move from one multitude to another, and the inference is inescapable that this second multitude is converted through the ministry of the 144,000. The association of the 144,000 in the first half of this chapter immediately preceding the description of the multitude of martyred dead from among the Gentiles strongly supports the contributing relationship between these two groups. The 144,000 have been a channel through which the Gospel could come to the earth. And that despite the presence of the Antichrist.

- *And this gospel of **the kingdom shall be preached in all the world for a witness unto all nations; and then shall the end come**. 15 When ye therefore shall see the abomination of desolation, spoken of by Daniel the prophet, stand in the holy place, (whoso readeth, let him understand),* (Matt 24:14,15).

The result of their ministry is a parallel expansion of the Apostolic Age when a great multitudes of Gentiles were saved through the preaching of the *Twelve* Jewish Apostles. Now a far greater host will be saved through the witness of *Twelve* times *Twelve Thousand*. This is in keeping with God's great purposes for the Jewish nation.

The following passage from Romans 11 states a Biblical principle concerning which now unfolds with the numbered multitude of Jewish believers and the unnumbered multitude of Gentile believers.

- *I say then, Have they stumbled that they should fall? God forbid: but rather through their fall salvation is come unto the Gentiles, for to provoke them to jealousy. 12 Now **if the fall of them be the riches of the world, and the diminishing of them the riches of the Gentiles; how much more their fullness*** (Rom 11:11,12)?

I. THE SIGHT OF THE GREAT MULTITUDE. ***After this I beheld, and, lo, a great multitude, which no man could number, of all nations, and kindreds, and people, and tongues, stood before the throne, and before the Lamb, clothed with white robes, and palms in their hands*** (7:9). The second half of chapter 7 of Revelation demonstrates that not only will many be saved in Israel but also many Gentiles will come to Christ in the Great Tribulation. John sees a great multitude beyond human computation coming from all nations, kindreds, people, and tongues standing before the throne, clothed with white robes, with palms in their hands, ascribing salvation to God and to the Lamb. In contrast to those coming from the Twelve Tribes, this throng comes from all nations. The white robes are those already referred to 6:11, and the palms indicate their triumph. The fact that they are martyrs is indicated from 6:11 and 7:13,14). Again, unlike the previous multitude, though vast, it could be numbered. How vast the multitude may be gathered from this, that John gives us numbers in this book amounting to two hundred millions (Rev 9:16). These then must indefinitely exceed that sum. This is beyond numbering and demonstrates that despite all, many, very many, will be saved during the Tribulation. Compare also.

THE BOOK OF REVELATION

> • *For I would not, brethren, that ye should be ignorant of this mystery, lest ye should be wise in your own conceits; that **blindness in part is happened to Israel, until the fulness of the Gentiles be come in*** (Rom 11:25).

An *Attempt* to Picture the Unnumbered Multitude in Heaven

1. THEIR NATIONALITIES: *of all nations, and kindreds, and people, and tongues.* Unlike the previous multitude which was Jewish, this is Gentile. They are from ***all*** the nations, peoples and languages of the world.

2. THEIR PLACE. They ***stood before the throne, and before the Lamb***. They are in Heaven, no longer on earth. This raises the question asked in verse 13. But for now we note they are standing before their Creator and Redeemer.

3. THEIR ADORNMENT. They are ***clothed with white robes, and palms in their hands.*** They are invested with the robes of justification, holiness, and victory. They hold palms as conquerors over the terrible afflictions they experienced on earth. They have *fought the good fight and finished their course* (2 Tim 4:7).

Of their palms and joy, Govett writes:

> They have *palms in their hands*. This sign alludes to the Feast of Tabernacles, and is a token of their joy. It appears to represent the first day of the feast, as Revelation 19 exhibits the eighth day, *the great day of the feast* (Jhn 7:37), when all the saints of every class are on high. The feast of Tabernacles took place at the natural period of rest in each year, when thou hast gathered in thy labours out of the field (Exod 23:16). It was to be a season of peculiar joy (Lev 23:40). Spontaneous joy appears upon the very face of the account. It is heard in their loud shouts of joy, attributing salvation to God.

4. THEIR PRAISE. ***And cried with a loud voice, saying, Salvation to our God which sitteth upon the throne, and unto the Lamb*** (7:10). This is their *Hosanna* and their

CHAPTER 7

Hallelujah. They give to God and the Lamb the praise of *so great salvation* (Heb 2:3). Both the Father and the Son are joined together in these praises; the Father initiated this salvation and the Son purchased it.

  5. THEIR ACCOMPANIMENT. *And all the angels stood round about the throne, and about the elders and the four beasts, and fell before the throne on their faces, and worshipped God* (7:11). They are not alone in their praise, all of Heaven gives its voice.

   (1) AS TO THEIR ASSEMBLY BEFORE THE THRONE.

    [1] THE ANGELS. *And all the angels stood round about the throne*. Though the numbers of angels are far more innumerable than that of this host they now accompany them, not one is missing. This is **all** *the angels*. Like Gabriel, they *stand in the presence of God* ready to serve (Lk 1:19).

    [2] THE ELDERS: *and about the elders*. The Twenty-four Elders who are of the Church and represent the entire glorified Church before the Throne. *the general assembly and church of the Firstborn* (Heb 12:23). They are surrounded by the angel.

    [3] THE BEASTS: *and the four beasts*. The four great angelic representatives of all of the worlds creatures, and who have for so long been crying *Holy, Holy, Holy* (Isa 6:3; Rev 4:8) are likewise before the Throne and surrounded by all the angels.

   (2) AS TO THEIR POSTURE IN WORSHIP: *and fell before the throne on their faces, and worshipped God.* Behold the most excellent of all the creatures, who never sinned, who are before Him continually, not only covering their faces, but falling down on their faces before the Lord! With what humility and reverence should we approach the Throne of grace. What humility then, and what profound reverence, become us vile frail creatures, when we come into the presence of God! We should fall down before him; there should be both a reverential frame of spirit and a humble behaviour in all our addresses to God (*Matthew Henry*).

   (3) AS TO THEIR CONSENTUAL AND ADDITIONAL PRAISES. *Saying, Amen: Blessing, and glory, and wisdom, and thanksgiving, and honour, and power, and might, be unto our God for ever and ever. Amen* (7:12). Redemption being the theme, all Heaven makes a seven-fold ascription of praise to the Atoning Lamb. They consented to the praises of the Tribulation saints, and gave their *Amen* to all their praises. And, to the praises already given, they add their own.

    [1] THEY DECLARE THE GLORIOUS ATTRIBUTES OF GOD: His *wisdom*, His *Power*, His *might*.

    [2] THEY DECLARE THE ETERNAL WORTHINESS OF HIS PRAISE: *for ever and ever. Amen.* Here we see what is the work of heaven, and here on earth we ought to begin it now.

II. THE QUESTION CONCERNING THE GREAT MULTITUDE.

  1. THE QUESTION ASKED JOHN. *And one of the elders answered, saying unto me, What are these which are arrayed in white robes? and whence came they* (7:13)?
The question the elder asked was not for his own information but for John's instruction. The question is couched in terms of admiration. *Who is this that cometh out of the wilderness* (Song 3:6).

  2. THE QUESTION RETURNED BY JOHN. *And I said unto him, Sir, thou knowest* (7:14). Nothing, no information, in this entire Book comes *from* John. All is given to John. It is as its title, the *Revelation*. Note, that as the elders represent the Church, and John also was of the Church, this interchange between John and the elder shows that the multitude represents a different body of saints. In answer to the elder, John confesses that he does not know; whereupon John is informed.

THE BOOK OF REVELATION

Walvoord makes an important point regarding the Gospel being brought to all nations at the time of the end.

> The concept sometimes advanced that the rapture cannot occur because all the world has not heard the gospel is a faulty conclusion. The requirement that all the world hear the gospel pertains not to the rapture but to the coming of Christ to set up His kingdom [Matt 24:14]. Though the church should press on with all zeal in presenting the gospel to every creature, it is not necessary for the rapture to wait until this task be completed. In spite of the difficulties, there will be worldwide preaching of the gospel during the tribulation time.

III. THE EXPLANATION CONCERNING THE GREAT MULTITUDE. *And he said to me, These are they which came out of great tribulation, and have washed their robes, and made them white in the blood of the Lamb* (7:14).

    1. THEIR FORMER HORRIFIC STATE. *And he said to me, These are they which came out of great tribulation,* (7:14). They came not from the tribulations of the Church Age for their persecutors are still living (Rev 6:10), but from the Great Tribulation. They are the ones previously mentioned who were yet to die for their faith (Rev 6:11). The prayers of the Tribulation martyrs beneath the altar has now brought a great harvest (7:9-11). They believed the preaching of the 144,000; they were saved; they refused to take the mark of the beast (Rev 13:16,17) and died as martyrs. They are those who came from that time spoken by Christ.

- *For then shall be great tribulation, such as was not since the beginning of the world to this time, no, nor ever shall be* (Matt 24:21).

    2. THEIR MEANS OF ENTERING HEAVEN: *and have washed their robes, and made them white in the blood of the Lamb.* It is not the blood of the martyrs themselves (i.e. dying as a martyr will not earn salvation), but the Blood of the Lamb that can wash away sin and make the soul pure and clean in the sight of God. The blood of others will stain; this is the only Blood that makes the robes of the saints white and clean (1:5).

Walvoord writes well concerning the Blood of Christ:

> The spiritual significance of shed blood is given prominence in both the Old and New Testaments with hundreds of references to it. According to Hebrews 9:22, *without shedding of blood is no re*mission. According to Acts 20:28, the church has been *purchased* by the blood of Christ. In Romans 3:25 Christ is declared to be the propitiation for our sins through *faith in his blood*. In Romans 5:9 we are *justified by his blood*, and therefore shall be *saved from wrath through him*. Ephesians 1:7 states that *we have redemption through his blood*. According to Colossians 1:20, Christ has *made peace through the blood of his cross*.
>
> The Apostle Peter adds his testimony in I Peter 1:18-19 when he writes, *Ye were not redeemed with corruptible things, as silver and gold, from your vain conversation received by tradition from your fathers; but with the precious blood of Christ, as of a lamb without blemish and without spot*. The frequent references to blood in the book of Revelation itself begin in chapter 1:5: *Unto him that loved us, and washed us from our sins in his own blood*. In the second advent itself in Revelation 19:13, Christ is described as *clothed with a vesture dipped in blood*.
>
> The emphasis in the Scripture upon the shed blood of sacrifice whether in the Mosaic law of the Old Testament or the sacrifice of Christ in the New Testament points to the necessity of His substitutionary death for the believer's redemption. Though a

modern world is offended by substitutionary sacrifice and especially by the reference to sacrificial blood, from God's viewpoint, like the children of Israel in Egypt, there is no safety except for those under the blood. God promised Israel in Exodus 12:13, ***When I see the blood, I will pass over you, and the plague shall not be upon you to destroy you, when I smite the land of Egypt.***

Accordingly, though not suited to the sophistication of twentieth century aesthetics, the blood of Christ is exceedingly precious in the sight of the Lord and is the only cleansing agent for sin. The blood of the Lamb is the assurance of cleansing and forgiveness for these who have been martyred for their faith in Christ. Even their own sacrificial death could not atone for their sins. They, like all others, must rest alone in that sacrifice which Christ provided for them. What is true for them is true for the saints of all ages; only the blood of Christ avails to wash away sin.

Note, as Williams says, they washed their sins away, not in the tears of penitence or the waters of baptism, but in the atoning blood of the Lamb of God.

3. THEIR PRESENT BLESSEDNESS.

(1) THEIR PLACE. ***Therefore are they before the throne of God, and serve him day and night in his temple: and he that sitteth on the throne shall dwell among them*** (7:15).

[1] BEFORE THE THRONE. ***Therefore are they before the throne of God.*** Now it is by faith that we come before the Throne (Heb 10:19); then it will be by sight.

[2] IN THE SERVICE OF THE TEMPLE: ***and serve him day and night in his temple.*** They serve God continually, and that without weakness, drowsiness, or weariness. Heaven is a place of service, though not of fatigue; it is a place of rest, but not of sloth; it is a praising, delightful, restful place.

[3] IN THE PRESENCE OF THE LORD: ***and he that sitteth on the throne shall dwell among them.*** Perhaps today we may feel we serve God "at a distance"; it will not be so then. In that presence is *fullness of joy* (Psa 16:11).

(2) THEIR FREEDOM. ***They shall hunger no more, neither thirst any more; neither shall the sun light on them, nor any heat*** (7:16). Hunger, thirst and heat were all experienced (and at a greatly *heightened* level) on earth during the Seal Judgements; now there is freedom from these ravages. Here is freedom from all *want* and all *pain*. Heat during the Tribulation will be a source of great pain (Isa 24:6; Mal 4:1).

- *Therefore hath the curse devoured the earth, and they that dwell therein are desolate: therefore **the inhabitants of the earth are burned, and few men left*** (Isa 24:6).
- *For, behold, **the day cometh, that shall burn as an oven**; and all the proud, yea, and all that do wickedly, shall be stubble: and the day that cometh shall burn them up, saith the LORD of hosts, that it shall leave them neither root nor branch* (Mal 4:1).

(3) THEIR CARE.

[1] GUIDANCE INTO ALL GOOD. ***For the Lamb which is in the midst of the throne shall feed them, and shall lead them unto living fountains of waters*** (7:17). He will put them into the possession of everything that is pleasant and refreshing to their souls.

[2] REMOVAL FROM ALL SORROW: ***and God shall wipe away all tears from their eyes.*** They have formerly had sorrows beyond measure, and shed many tears, both upon the account of sin and affliction; but God now Himself shall wipe them away and turn sorrow into joy.

THE BOOK OF REVELATION

Williams compares the song of the Tribulation saints with similar passages of Scripture:

> The beatitude of this multitude (7:15-17) corresponds to that promised to Israel. Compare Isaiah 49:8-10; 25:8 and Revelation 21:3,4. This marks relationship, as did the porch that extended from Solomon's house on the one side of the central palace to the house of Pharaoh's daughter on the other.

• *Thus saith the LORD, In an acceptable time have I heard thee, and in a day of salvation have I helped thee: and I will preserve thee, and give thee for a covenant of the people, to establish the earth, to cause to inherit the desolate heritages; 9 That thou mayest say to the prisoners, Go forth; to them that are in darkness, Shew yourselves. They shall feed in the ways, and their pastures shall be in all high places. 10* **They shall not hunger nor thirst; neither shall the heat nor sun smite them: for he that hath mercy on them shall lead them, even by the springs of water** *shall he guide them* (Isa 49:8-10).

• *He will swallow up death in victory; and* **the Lord GOD will wipe away tears from off all faces**; *and the rebuke of his people shall he take away from off all the earth: for the LORD hath spoken it* (Isa 25:8).

• *And I heard a great voice out of heaven saying, Behold, the tabernacle of God is with men, and he will dwell with them, and they shall be his people, and* **God himself shall be with them, and be their God. 4 And God shall wipe away all tears from their eyes; and there shall be no more death, neither sorrow, nor crying, neither shall there be any more pain: for the former things are passed away** (Rev 21:3,4).

CHAPTER 8

2. The Trumpet Judgements and Other Events   8-14
a. The Seventh Seal is Opened   8:1-6
b. The Six Trumpets Blown: Woeful Wrath (8:13)   8:7-9:21
c. The Herald Angel Announces the Seventh Trumpet 10 (v7)
d. The Two Witnesses   11:1-13
e. Further Announcement of the Seventh Trumpet 11:14-19
f. The Woman, The Dragon, The Manchild   12
g. The Beast and the False Prophet   13
h. The 144,000 Jewish Evangelists In Heaven   14:1-5
i. The Six Calls (The Final Call)   14

a. The Seventh Seal is Opened   8:1-6

THE PRELUDE TO THE SOUNDING OF THE TRUMPETS

The Chapter opens with the announcement that the Seventh Seal is opened. This is the last of the Seven Seals marking the prophetic judgments of God. With the opening of the Seventh Seal the judgements described in Chapter 6 now continue. Though briefly and simply introduced, the opening of the Seventh Seal is a primary event in the Seven Year Tribulation. As the Six Seals cover the First Half of the Tribulation, it covers the Second Half. Contained in the Seventh Seal are all the subsequent developments leading to the Second Coming of Christ, including the Seven Trumpet Judgements and the Seven Vial Judgments. With these judgements coming from above, the many other events on earth associated with the full power of the Antichrist are revealed.

(8:1) And when he had opened the seventh seal, there was silence in heaven about the space of half an hour. (8:2) And I saw the seven angels which stood before God; and to them were given seven trumpets.

(8:3) And another angel came and stood at the altar, having a golden censer; and there was given unto him much incense, that he should offer it with the prayers of all saints upon the golden altar which was before the throne. (8:4) And the smoke of the incense, which came with the prayers of the saints, ascended up before God out of the angel's hand. (8:5) And the angel took the censer, and filled it with fire of the altar, and cast it into the earth: and there were voices, and thunderings, and lightnings, and an earthquake.

(8:6) And the seven angels which had the seven trumpets prepared themselves to sound.

I. THE OPENING OF THE SEVENTH SEAL. *And when he had opened the seventh seal* (8:1). We have witnessed the judgements that fell on earth with the opening of six of the seals; we now come to the opening of the seventh; this will bring forth the sounding of Seven Trumpets. Each trumpet announces and brings forth judgements and catastrophe on a far greater scale.

1. THE SILENCE IS PROFOUND: *there was silence in heaven about the space of half an hour.* It is a heavy silence, a dreadful silence, though the opening of the Seventh Seal is briefly and simply stated. In fitting recognition of the enormity of what is now taking place we have this silence. An *hour* is a Hebrew idiom for a brief space of time. Compare (Dan

4:19; 5:5; Matt 26:40; Rev 17:12; 18:10). Occasionally it means a longer, but definite period (Jhn 4:21). Half an hour, therefore, signifies a very brief period. It was sufficient for the angel here (v. 3) to present the prayers and incense to the Lord. Though thirty minutes is a short time, when as here it is a time of such absolute silence, it heralds an ominous development that eclipses all that has taken place before.

- *Be silent, O all flesh, before the LORD, for he has risen up out of his holy habitation* (Zech 2:13).
- *Be still, and know that I am God: I will be exalted among the heathen, I will be exalted in the earth* (Psa 46:10).

But here, it is only in Heaven that the silence took place. It was the genuine expression of the feelings of those on high. Expectation held them mute (Govett).

2. THE TRUMPETS ARE DELIVERED. *And I saw the seven angels which stood before God; and to them were given seven trumpets* (8:2). These actions amidst the heavy silence are deliberate, considered, measured, intimidating.

3. A CENSER IS BROUGHT FORTH. *And another angel came and stood at the altar, having a golden censer* (8:3). In the Old Testament order the priests would burn incense upon the altar of incense, and the smoke would fill the Temple or the Tabernacle Incense was a picture of worship and prayer and spoke of the fact that intercession to the Lord has the character of sweet incense. The altar in heaven is referred to seven times in this Book (6:9; 8:3a, b, 5; 9:13; 14:18; 16:7).

(1) THE CENSOR IS FILLED: *and there was given unto him much incense, that he should offer it with the prayers of all saints upon the golden altar which was before the throne.* The fullness and merit of Christ's Person and Work provide the basis of this incense. It is this that makes prayer acceptable; and particularly in this case – the prayers of martyrs. The prayers of the saints themselves stand in need of the incense and intercession of Christ to make them acceptable and effectual.

The prayers are vengeance prayers and yet are now sweet to God. The Divine response is immediate. What the language of these prayers for vengeance is, will be found in the Psalms (Psalms 69 and 109 especially, and also Psalms 5, 6, 11, 12, 35, 37, 40, 52, 54, 56, 58, 69, 79, 83, 137, 139, 143). The present day of grace having closed, and the time of the wrath of the Lamb now increasing further, petitions for judgment on the persecutors of the saints and enemies of righteousness are now given their appropriate place and fulfilment. (see Williams).

(2) THE INCENSE RISES UPWARD. *And the smoke of the incense, which came with the prayers of the saints, ascended up before God out of the angel's hand* (8:4). These prayers that are now are ascending to the Throne, are about to initiate great changes on the earth.

(3) THE COALS ARE CAST DOWNWARD. *And the angel took the censer, and filled it with fire of the altar, and cast it into the earth: and there were voices, and thunderings, and lightnings, and an earthquake* (8:5). These same coals which inflamed the incense and prayers with holy devotion before the Throne, are now used to execute wrath upon the earth. The shock of the four warning sounds breaks the silence in Heaven!

Walvoord summarizes:

> Though nothing is said as to the nature of the incense, it is reasonable to suppose that it fulfils the same function as incense used in Old Testament worship, composed of the four spices mentioned in Exodus 30:34-38, and regarded as so holy that the people of Israel were forbidden to use it for any common purpose. The incense

CHAPTER 8

speaking of the perfections of Christ is inseparably bound up with any ministry of intercession, and the believer's petitions are coupled with the worthiness of Christ in their presentation at the heavenly altar, testifying at once to the necessity of praying in the name of Christ and to the efficacy of such prayer when faithfully ministered on earth.

Attention is also directed in verse 5 to the censer, corresponding to the instrument used to offer incense in the Old Testament worship. It was made of gold (Exod 37:25-28; Heb 9:4), and it was used to take fire off the altar to be carried into the Holy of Holies where the incense was added. Here the angel takes the censer filled with fire and casts it into the earth. The is followed by *voices, thunderings, lightnings, and an earthquake*. The clear implication is that the censer is here used as a symbol of judgment, in response to the intercession and prayers of the suffering saints in the midst of the great tribulation. The scene, therefore, is not set for the judgment of the seven trumpets about to sound.

And now for the second and not the last time we have that ominous phrase: ***and there were voices, and thunderings, and lightnings, and an earthquake.***

* *And out of the throne proceeded **lightnings and thunderings and voices**: and there were seven lamps of fire burning before the throne, which are the seven Spirits of God* (Rev 4:5).
* *And the seventh angel sounded; and there were **great voices** in heaven, saying, The kingdoms of this world are become the kingdoms of our Lord, and of his Christ; and he shall reign for ever and ever* (Rev 11:15).
* *And the temple of God was opened in heaven, and there was seen in his temple the ark of his testament: and there were **lightnings, and voices, and thunderings, and an earthquake**, and great hail* (Rev 11:19).
* *And there were **voices, and thunders, and lightnings; and there was a great earthquake**, such as was not since men were upon the earth, so mighty an earthquake, and so great* (Rev 16:18).

Govett writes:

Let us observe the result of this fire. Upon its descent followed *thunders and lightnings*, as it travelled through the air; then *voices* of men and angels; and when it touched earth, *earthquake*. The *thunders* and *voices* are the direct contrast to the *silence* that ensued on the seventh seal broken. After that pause in judgment, God's chariot wheels roll on again.

II. THE TRUMPETS ARE READY TO SOUND. *And the seven angels which had the seven trumpets prepared themselves to sound* (8:6). The prelude is now over. With the fearful soundings of the *voices, and thunderings, and lightnings, and an earthquake* the trumpets themselves are about *to sound*. These angels are to be distinguished from those who pour out the Seven Vials. The number *seven* is in harmony with the *seven* seals and the *seven* vials. There is a completeness in the judgements now taking place. The fact that these angels stand before God indicates a place of prominence such as is given to the angel Gabriel (Lk 1:19).

The use of trumpets is often seen in the Scriptures. They were sounded at the times of Israel's gatherings; at the time of her preparation for battle; at the signalling of import events on her calendar; at the giving of the Law; at the announcement of the New Moon and first day of her months and other important occasions (Exod 19:19; Lev 23:24; 25:9; Num 10:2-10; Joel 2:1). But here note: The Lamb opened the Seals, but angels sounded the trumpets, and proclaimed war as commanded by the law (Num 10:9). Jericho fell when the

Seven Trumpets sounded seven times on the seventh day. Note also that the Trumpet are a seven-fold answer to the petitions of verse 3 and 6:9,10.

As in the case of the seals, the first Four Trumpets are marked off from the last three. The Four Trumpets are inflicted primarily on natural objects: the earth, trees, grass, sea, rivers, lights of heaven: whereas those indicated by the two latter are expressly said to be inflicted on men (cp. 9:4,15). With the Seals we have had *Wrath*. With the Trumpets we now have *Woeful Wrath*!

B. THE SIX TRUMPETS BLOWN: WOEFUL WRATH (8:13)
8:7 - 9:21

THE FIRST FOUR TRUMPETS: DESOLATIONS ON A GREATER SCALE 8:7-13

(8:7) *The first angel sounded, and there followed hail and fire mingled with blood, and they were cast upon the earth: and the third part of trees was burnt up, and all green grass was burnt up.*

(8:8) *And the second angel sounded, and as it were a great mountain burning with fire was cast into the sea: and the third part of the sea became blood;* (8:9) *And the third part of the creatures which were in the sea, and had life, died; and the third part of the ships were destroyed.*

(8:10) *And the third angel sounded, and there fell a great star from heaven, burning as it were a lamp, and it fell upon the third part of the rivers, and upon the fountains of waters;* (8:11) *And the name of the star is called Wormwood: and the third part of the waters became wormwood; and many men died of the waters, because they were made bitter.*

(8:12) *And the fourth angel sounded, and the third part of the sun was smitten, and the third part of the moon, and the third part of the stars; so as the third part of them was darkened, and the day shone not for a third part of it, and the night likewise.* (8:13) *And I beheld, and heard an angel flying through the midst of heaven, saying with a loud voice, Woe, woe, woe, to the inhabiters of the earth by reason of the other voices of the trumpet of the three angels, which are yet to sound!*

> • *Shall a trumpet be blown in the city, and the people not be afraid?* shall there be evil in a city, and the LORD hath not done it (Amos 3:6)?

The is a great judgement; eleven times it speaks of the *third part* being destroyed. Yet under the Vial Judgements it will be *all*. Thus there is still restraint and mercy being shown. Contrast *the third* used in a blessing sense during the Millennium.

> • *In that day shall there be a highway out of Egypt to Assyria, and the Assyrian shall come into Egypt, and the Egyptian into Assyria, and the Egyptians shall serve with the Assyrians. 24 In that day shall Israel be* **the third** *with Egypt and with Assyria, even a blessing in the midst of the land. 25 Whom the LORD of hosts shall bless, saying, Blessed be Egypt my people, and Assyria the work of my hands, and Israel mine inheritance* (Isa 19:23-25).

As the trumpet at Sinai gave notice of God's descent upon the mount, so do these give proclamation of Jesus coming to judge and to reign. The seals are wrath on undeveloped rebellion: the trumpets are wrath upon those in conscious opposition to God (Govett).

CHAPTER 8

THE FIRST TRUMPET: THE STRICKEN EARTH

1. THE CATASTROPHE. *The first angel sounded, and there followed hail and fire mingled with blood, and they were cast upon the earth* (8:7). *Hail, fire, blood* : a very strange mixture. It was as actual, literal and physical as the seventh plague upon Egypt, but on a vastly greater scale. Note that the *hail, fire and blood* (It was indirectly *upon man and beast*) was also present in Egypt's plague.

• *And the LORD said unto Moses, Stretch forth thine hand toward heaven, that there may* ***be hail in all the land of Egypt, upon man, and upon beast***, *and upon every herb of the field, throughout the land of Egypt. 23 And Moses stretched forth his rod toward heaven: and the LORD* ***sent thunder and hail, and the fire ran along upon the ground****; and the LORD rained hail upon the land of Egypt. 24 So there was* ***hail, and fire mingled with the hail****, very grievous, such as there was none like it in all the land of Egypt since it became a nation* (Exod 9:22-24).

2. THE EFFECT: ***and the third part of trees was burnt up, and all green grass was burnt up.*** If limited to one area, it would be as if nearly all the forests, pastures, farm lands of Asia went up in flames. This judgment, great as it is, is only the introduction. Six more trumpets are to sound.

https://localtvktvi.files.wordpress.com/2017/09/la-me-ln-brush-fire-verdugo-20170901.jpg?quality=85&strip=all&w=770

"1000 Firefighters Battle Largest Fire in Los Angeles History" 2 Sept. 2017

ONE OF THE WORST SUMMERS IN US HISTORY FOR WILDFIRES

"A wet winter and spring in the Western U.S. brought predictions that the 2017 wildfire season would be mild. It was anything but. It ended up one of the worst in U.S. history in land burned.

The smoke, the flames, the aching lungs, the evacuations. They're summertime facts of life in the U.S. West, where every wildfire season competes with memories of previous destruction.

The foliage that sprouted from previous rain and snow has gone bone-dry in intense heat, feeding flames in places that have not seen downpours in months and strangling cities with smoke. The biggest fires came later than usual…"

http://abcnews.go.com/International/wireStory/wildfire-weary-western-us-coughs-late-season-surge-49673121

THE SECOND TRUMPET: THE STRICKEN SEAS

1. THE CATASTROPHE. *And the second angel sounded, and as it were a great mountain burning with fire was cast into the sea: and the third part of the sea became blood* (8:8). Though just as literal as the first plague of Egypt when the *life* of Egypt, the Nile turned to blood, this again, though limited, was on an infinitely greater scale. Nor was there *a great mountain* connected with Egypt.

2. THE EFFECT. *And the third part of the creatures which were in the sea, and had life, died; and the third part of the ships were destroyed* (8:9). Some think the *great mountain* is a great nation that is destroyed; but that would hardly cause the effects here described. Is the fall of this mountain the result of an earthquake which destroys nuclear power plants and contaminates the oceans? Sound familiar! Note a current forerunner to the Dying Sea of the Second Trumpet.

CLEANING UP THE FUKUSHIMA NUCLEAR PLANT IS EXPECTED TO TAKE 30 TO 40 YEARS

*Dying robots and failing hope: Fukushima clean-up falters six years after tsunami. Exploration work inside the nuclear plant's failed reactors has barely begun, with the scale of the task described as '**almost beyond comprehension**'.*

Justin McCurry at Fukushima Daiichi nuclear power plant Thursday 9 March 2017 01.23 GMT reports:

Barely a fifth of the way into their mission, the engineers monitoring the Scorpion's progress conceded defeat. With a remote-controlled snip of its cable, the latest robot sent into the bowels of one of Fukushima Daiichi's damaged reactors was cut loose, its progress stalled by lumps of fuel that overheated when the nuclear plant suffered a triple meltdown six years ago this week.

As the 60cm-long Toshiba robot, equipped with a pair of cameras and sensors to gauge radiation levels was left to its fate last month, the plant's operator, Tokyo Electric Power (Tepco), attempted to play down the failure of yet another reconnaissance mission to determine the exact location and condition of the melted fuel…The Scorpion mishap, two hours into an exploration that was supposed to last 10 hours, underlined the scale and difficulty of decommissioning Fukushima Daiichi – an unprecedented undertaking one expert has described as "almost beyond comprehension". https://www.theguardian.com/world/2017/mar/09/fukushima-nuclear-cleanup-falters-six-years-after-tsunami

In recent years there have been reports pointing to a depletion of fish stocks and marine life along the West Coast of America. While traces of radiation have been found, the main media continues to distance itself from linking this depletion with Fukushima. Time will tell.

Note the following catastrophic report regarding sea lions:

California Academy of Sciences (bioGraphic), Aug 29, 2016: Scientists Investigate a Mysterious Cancer Plaguing California Sea Lions… The disease starts in the reproductive organs… By the time they die, tumors have sometimes infiltrated their backbones and turned vertebrae to "mush," [Tenaya Norris, a scientist at The Marine

CHAPTER 8

Mammal Center] says. She describes examining one dead animal whose spine she could simply slice through. More than a quarter of the adult California sea lions that die at the Marine Mammal Center suffer from cancer, says director of veterinary science Shawn Johnson. That's one of the highest cancer rates seen in any wild animal... There's been a surge of sick animals, especially California sea lions... "Off the California coast, the ecosystem is really under stress," says Johnson. That stress is hitting California sea lions particularly hard... Over the past three years, Johnson says, 80 to 90 percent of all California sea lion pups have died... And whether or not the disease is becoming more common or simply holding steady, Johnson says he knows one thing for certain: "It's not declining." The disease rates researchers are seeing among sea lions are far from normal, and they want to know why. "Wild populations shouldn't have cancers like this," Johnson says... Inside a stricken animal, "there's just masses of yellow, cancerous tissue," says Frances Gulland, senior scientist at the Marine Mammal Center... [C]ancer-stricken sea lions have more pollutants in their blubber... "That's really important for the human health perspective as well," Gulland says. "These are contaminants the sea lions are acquiring from their prey. And the fish they eat are the same fish that we eat…"
http://enenews.com/mysterious-cancer-killing-sea-lions-along-us-west-coast-bones-turning-mush-inside-the-animals-theres-just-masses-of-yellow-cancerous-tissue-alarming-death-rates-vid

The Fukushima disaster was caused by a great earthquake and tsunami. The Second Trumpet Judgement describes a catastrophe where *a great mountain burning with fire was cast into the sea.* In addition to the marine life *the third part of the ships were destroyed.* As to its effects upon the sea and unlike Fukushima where sea life is gradually dying, this is a sudden destruction. Ships are not destroyed gradually. Noting the phrase, *as it where*, many have viewed this this *mountain* in the sense of huge asteroid crashing into the sea.

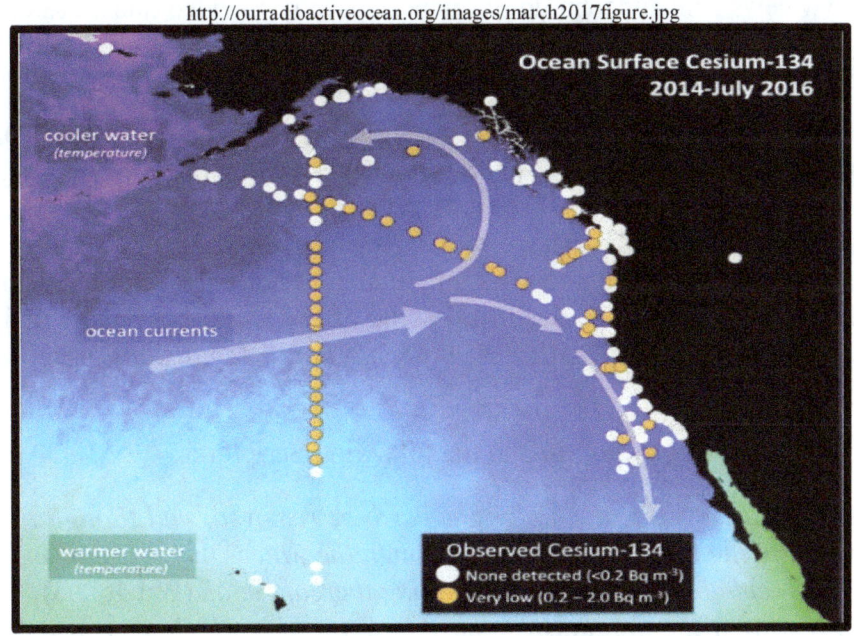

Fukushima: *Time Will Tell* !

NASA REPORTS A MAJOR INCREASE IN ASTROID ACTIVITY

In a June 2017 report, NASA documented "an unexplained increase in comet activity around earth and the discovery of new and potentially hazardous asteroids."

NASA has revealed a terrifying animation of a swarm of comets and asteroids circling our planet. The pictures come from the space agency's asteroid hunting mission, the Near-Earth Object Wide-field Infrared Survey Explorer, or Neowise for short.

NASA issued the chilling warning that 10 new "potentially hazardous" asteroids have been discovered in the past year, along with 96 other newly spotted space rocks in our midst. Scientists who have been analysing the data said they have seen an unexplained increase in comet activity, too. The risk is growing that Earth will be hit by an asteroid from a meteor stream known as the Taurids, according to astronomers from the Czech Academy of Science. They have detected a new branch with at least two asteroids measuring 200-300m in diameter. Most probably, the branch also includes many undetected asteroids which are dozens of metres in diameter or larger," the Czech Academy said in a press release. Hence, the danger of a crash with an asteroid grows markedly once every few years that the Earth encounters this stream of interplanetary material.

The new branch moves together around the sun, and the Earth encounters it once every few years for a period of about three weeks. During this period, the probability of a collision with a larger object (of about dozens of metres in diameter) is markedly higher, the Academy said. The asteroids are very fragile, but when they are this large they may penetrate deep into the atmosphere and pose a real threat of collision with Earth.

Near-Earth objects (NEOs) are comets and asteroids that have been nudged by the gravitational attraction of the planets in our solar system into orbits that allow them to enter Earth's neighbourhood. Ten of the objects discovered by Nasa's Neowise in the past year have been classified as potentially hazardous asteroids, based on their size and their orbits. It has found 693 NEOs since the mission was restarted in December 2013. Of these, 114 are new.
http://www.news.com.au/technology/science/space/nasa-video-shows-asteroids-circling-earth-after-it-spots-10-potentially-hazardous-space-rocks/news-story/c6491cbf3084b382dcd5f659ed6647c7

NEVERTHELESS! The Bible says that *as it were a great mountain* burning with *fire was cast into the sea*. When the Third Trumpet is blown *there fell a great star from heaven, burning as it were a lamp* (8:10). A *great mountain* is to be distinguished from a *great star*. Thus while it may be a huge *mountainous* asteroid, it may instead be a violent disturbance in the earth's plates that causes a mountain to not only *erupt* but also to *move*. In order for a third of the ships to be destroyed some of the world busy ports and harbors are affected. At the opening of the Sixth Seal *every mountain* and island were *moved out of their places* (6:14).

Compare the *moving mountains* in the following Scriptures:

• *Therefore will not we fear, though the earth be removed, and **though the mountains be carried into the midst of the sea**; 3 Though the waters thereof roar and be troubled, though the mountains shake with the swelling thereof. Selah* (Psa 46:2,3).
• *Which **removeth the mountains**, and they know not: which **overturneth them** in his anger* (Job 9:5).
• *He putteth forth his hand upon the rock; he **overturneth the mountains** by the roots* (Job 28:9).
• ***The mountains skipped** like rams, and the little hills like lambs* (Psa 114:4).

CHAPTER 8

- *For **the mountains shall depart**, and the hills be removed; but my kindness shall not depart from thee, neither shall the covenant of my peace be removed, saith the LORD that hath mercy on thee* (Isa 54:10).
- *When thou didst terrible things which we looked not for, thou camest down, **the mountains flowed down** at thy presence* (Isa 64:3).
- *And **the mountains shall be molten** under him, and the valleys shall be cleft, as wax before the fire, and as the waters that are poured down a steep place* (Mic 1:4).
- ***The mountains quake** at him, and the hills melt, and the earth is burned at his presence, yea, the world, and all that dwell therein* (Nah 1:5).
- *He stood, and measured the earth: he beheld, and drove asunder the nations; and **the everlasting mountains were scattered**, the perpetual hills did bow: his ways are everlasting* (Hab 3:6).
- *And Jesus said unto them, Because of your unbelief: for verily I say unto you, If ye have faith as a grain of mustard seed, ye shall **say unto this mountain, Remove hence to yonder place; and it shall remove**; and nothing shall be impossible unto you* (Matt 17:20).
- *And every island fled away, and **the mountains were not found*** (Rev 16:20).

THE THIRD TRUMPET: THE STRICKEN RIVERS

1. THE CATASTROPHE. *And the third angel sounded, and there fell a great star from heaven, burning as it were a lamp, and it fell upon the third part of the rivers, and upon the fountains of waters* (8:10). The previous judgement affected the seas, this affects the fresh water supplies. In the previous it was *as a mountain*, now it is a *star*.

2. THE EFFECT. *And the name of the star is called Wormwood: and the third part of the waters became wormwood; and many men died of the waters, because they were made bitter* (8:11). The reference to *wormwood* draws the spiritual parallel to the experience of the children of Israel at the waters of Marah. There the tree cast into the bitter waters made them sweet. Here the smoldering asteroid cast upon the fresh waters makes them bitter. Such also is the contrast between Christ on the Cross atoning for sin and making that which is bitter sweet and Christ coming in judgment which turns the vain hopes and ambitions of men into bitterness and despair. The result of this trumpet is to inflict a divine judgment directly upon men themselves (see Walvoord).

- *So Moses brought Israel from the Red sea, and they went out into the wilderness of Shur; and they went three days in the wilderness, and found no water. 23 And when they came to Marah, **they could not drink of the waters of Marah, for they were bitter**: therefore the name of it was called Marah. 24 And the people murmured against Moses, saying, What shall we drink? 25 And he cried unto the LORD; and **the LORD showed him a tree, which when he had cast into the waters, the waters were made sweet**: there he made for them a statute and an ordinance, and there he proved them* (Exod 15:23-25).

Apart from faith in Christ's Death on the Cross, life is bitter. This star is called *Wormwood*. The name describes its nature. It .communicates its bitterness to whatever it touches. But as, Govett points out, it is not only the gaseousness of the taste of that which is ordinarily tasteless, that constitutes this judgment: it produces disease and death: *many men died of the waters, because they were made bitter*. Now, for the first time in the Trumpet Judgements, the death of men is directly stated. Before, under the Second Trumpet his ships were *destroyed*: but here man himself directly said to be destroyed.

THE BOOK OF REVELATION

Not surprisingly, pollution has made scenes like this more common in recent days. The Third Trumpet will Bring Forth a Far Greater Cause and Devastation!

This kind of bitter visitation because of man's sin was described by the Prophet Jeremiah.

- *And the LORD saith, Because they have forsaken my law which I set before them, and have not obeyed my voice, neither walked therein; 14 But have walked after the imagination of their own heart, and after Baalim, which their fathers taught them: 15 Therefore thus saith the LORD of hosts, the God of Israel;* ***Behold, I will feed them, even this people, with wormwood, and give them water of gall to drink*** (Jer 9:13-15).
- *Therefore thus saith the LORD of hosts concerning the prophets; Behold,* ***I will feed them with wormwood, and make them drink the water of gall****: for from the prophets of Jerusalem is profaneness gone forth into all the land* (Jer 23:15).
- *He hath filled me with bitterness,* ***he hath made me drunken with wormwood*** (Lam 3:15).

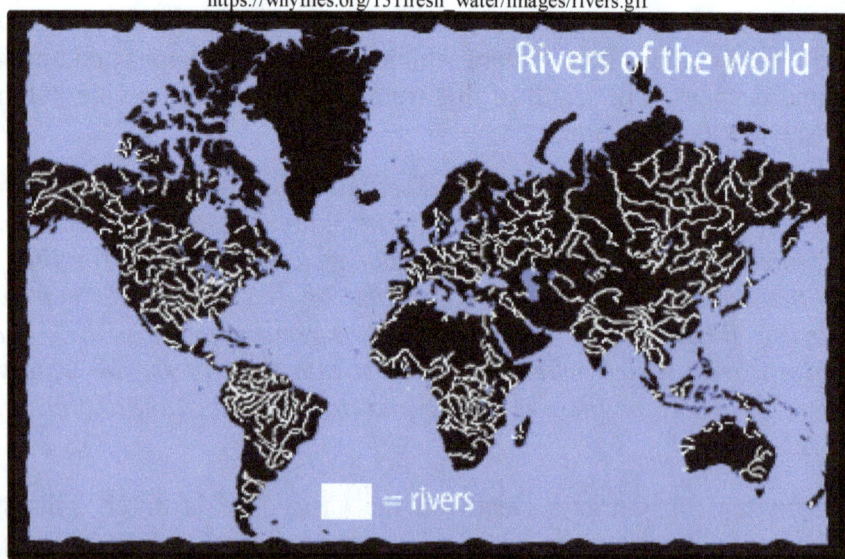

The *Wormwood Star* will strike one or more of the great river systems of the world
THE FOUTH TRUMPET: THE STICKEN UNIVERSE

CHAPTER 8

1. THE CATASTROPHE. *And the fourth angel sounded, and the third part of the sun was smitten, and the third part of the moon, and the third part of the stars; so as the third part of them was darkened* (8:12).

2. THE EFFECT: *and the day shone not for a third part of it, and the night likewise.* Note that both the day and the night are shortened by a third; both the period of light and the period of darkness – an average of four hours for each. This means that the 24 hour day is shortened to 16 hours. This is very likely the phenomena to which our Lord referred in His Olivet Discourse.

> • *For then shall be great tribulation, such as was not since the beginning of the world to this time, no, nor ever shall be. 22 And **except those days should be shortened**, there should no flesh be saved: but for the elect's sake those days shall be shortened* (Matt 24:21,22).
>
> • *For in those days shall be affliction, such as was not from the beginning of the creation which God created unto this time, neither shall be. 20 And **except that the Lord had shortened those days**, no flesh should be saved: but for the elect's sake, whom he hath chosen, he hath shortened the days* (Mk 13:19,20).

Commentators generally explain this as a shortening of the persecution: "The persecution itself will be cut short (curtailed), not the 1260 days themselves."
(*Dakes Annotated Reference Bible*). Yet, when linked with Revelation 8:12 this phenomena clearly goes beyond that. These verses state that the actual *days* themselves are shortened. There will still be 1260 days (their number will not be decreased) from the time the Antichrist sets up his image unto the Return of Christ. However, from the time of the blowing of the Fourth Trumpet and perhaps unto the Lord's Return those days will be shorter. They will be days of sixteen and not twenty-four hour.

Such is impossible to comprehend apart from a speeding up of terrestrial or celestial motion. Either the speed of earth's rotation is increased or the movement (!) of the sun, moon and stars around the earth is increased. That this latter is the Biblical view is shown in the notes on the opening of the Sixth Seal (Rev 6:12-14).

For two recent YouTube presentations of Geocentricity see:
https://www.youtube.com/watch?v=Rwx7bYEUIF4
https://www.youtube.com/watch?v=tuaB5fVr0Ao

https://c1.staticflickr.com/9/8309/8049683643_03a8b92f15_b.jpg

This Common View Would Not Reduce the Period of the Sun's Shining

Note that in so many passages such as these, action is directed against the sun, moon and stars; it is they that are *smitten*, not the earth. Likely they are smitten much like a rider strikes his horse to increase its speed. Most, however believe that verse 12 is saying that one third of the sun, moon and stars does not shine. One third of each is blackened.

The above picture may be the initial impression, but fails to account for the second half of the verse: ***and the day shone not for a third part of it, and the night likewise.*** With the above prevalent view the day would still shine for the same length of time, but with a decreased brightness. Thus the view is here proposed that the Sun, moon and stars are stricken in their daily rotation around the earth (in the sense of increasing their velocity). The resultant effect is that the 24 hour day is reduced to 16 hours. Amos 8:9 points to this.

- *And it shall come to pass in that day, saith the Lord GOD, that **I will cause the sun to go down at noon, and I will darken the earth in the clear day*** (Amos 8:9).

God and promised Noah:

- *While the earth remaineth, seedtime and harvest, and cold and heat, and summer and winter, and **day and night shall not cease*** (Gen 8:22).

All still remains, but all has been decimated. Day and Night have not *ceased*, but they have been significantly shortened, and that by a third. With the land, sea, rivers, fountains of water and now the heavens shaken; man now finds that all around him has indeed changed. All that he was used to, all the old landmarks, all of the familiar day to day experiences are now a faint memory. He finds that the availability of food is severely restricted; he finds distribution is crippled; he finds water supplies are limited; and he finds the very length of the days themselves are strangely shortened. "Surely that is enough!" "They are now told *there will be more*. It is now announced not only by the sound of trumpets but by the cries of angels.

V. THE WARNING OF GREATER CATASTROPHIES. Before the other three trumpets are sounded there is solemn warning given to the world how terrible the calamities will be that are now on their way,

1. THE MESSENGER. ***And I beheld, and heard an angel flying through the midst of heaven, saying with a loud voice*** (8:13). He comes in haste. He comes *flying*. He comes with a *loud voice*. This angel and its cry separates the first four trumpets from the last three.

2. THE MESSAGE. ***Woe, woe, woe, to the inhabiters of the earth by reason of the other voices of the trumpet of the three angels, which are yet to sound!*** He comes on an awful errand; woe and misery more than the world has yet endured are now on their way. Here are **three woes**, to show how much more these three calamities will exceed those that have just ravaged the earth.

CHAPTER 9

THE FIFTH AND SIXTH TRUMPETS: DESOLATIONS ON A WOEFUL SCALE 9

THE FIFTH TRUMPET, FIRST WOE: *THE WORLD DESIRES TO DIE* !

(9:1) And the fifth angel sounded, and I saw a star fall from heaven unto the earth: and to him was given the key of the bottomless pit. (9:2) And he opened the bottomless pit; and there arose a smoke out of the pit, as the smoke of a great furnace; and the sun and the air were darkened by reason of the smoke of the pit.

(9:3) And there came out of the smoke locusts upon the earth: and unto them was given power, as the scorpions of the earth have power. (9:4) And it was commanded them that they should not hurt the grass of the earth, neither any green thing, neither any tree; but only those men which have not the seal of God in their foreheads. (9:5) And to them it was given that they should not kill them, but that they should be tormented five months: and their torment was as the torment of a scorpion, when he striketh a man. (9:6) And in those days shall men seek death, and shall not find it; and shall desire to die, and death shall flee from them.

(9:7) And the shapes of the locusts were like unto horses prepared unto battle; and on their heads were as it were crowns like gold, and their faces were as the faces of men. (9:8) And they had hair as the hair of women, and their teeth were as the teeth of lions. (9:9) And they had breastplates, as it were breastplates of iron; and the sound of their wings was as the sound of chariots of many horses running to battle. (9:10) And they had tails like unto scorpions, and there were stings in their tails: and their power was to hurt men five months.

(9:11) And they had a king over them, which is the angel of the bottomless pit, whose name in the Hebrew tongue is Abaddon, but in the Greek tongue hath his name Apollyon. (9:12) One woe is past; and, behold, there come two woes more hereafter.

I THE FALLEN STAR. *And the fifth angel sounded, and I saw a star fall from heaven unto the earth* (9:1). In connection with the Sixth Seal (6:12-17) and the Fourth Trumpet (8:12-13), record is made of unusual disturbances in the starry heavens. In Chapter 6, *the stars of heaven fall even as a fig tree casts her untimely figs*, and heaven itself d*eparts as a scroll when it is rolled together*. In chapter 8, a great star from heaven described *as burning as it were a lamp* falls upon rivers and fountains of waters. In these instances it is material stars or asteroids or fragments of them that fall upon the earth. The star here is a person. This is clearly Satan himself; the translation of whose name is *Destroyer* in verse 11. This is the fulfilment of the *woe* pronounced in Chapter 8:13 and 12:12. It fulfils our Lord's word in Luke 10:18.

> • *And I beheld, and heard an angel flying through the midst of heaven, saying with a loud voice,* **Woe, woe, woe, to the inhabiters of the earth** *by reason of the other voices of the trumpet of the three angels, which are yet to sound (Rev 8:13).*
>
> • *Therefore rejoice, ye heavens, and ye that dwell in them.* **Woe to the inhabiters of the earth** *and of the sea! for* **the devil is come down** *unto you, having great wrath, because he knoweth that he hath but a short time (Rev 12:12).*
>
> • *And he said unto them,* **I beheld Satan as lightning fall from heaven** *(Lk 10:18).*

Note the further description in Revelation 12:4-9:

- *And there was war in heaven: Michael and his angels fought against the dragon; and the dragon fought and his angels, 8 And prevailed not; neither was their place found any more in heaven. 9 **And the great dragon was cast out, that old serpent, called the Devil, and Satan, which deceiveth the whole world**: he was cast out into the earth, and his angels were cast out with him* (Rev 12:7-9).

But in seeking with greater certainty to identify the *fallen star* in this chapter, it is proper to ask whether Satan is called a *star* elsewhere in Scripture. He is called *the great dragon, that old serpent, the Devil, and Satan*; but is he called a *star*? He is called a *star*!

- *How art thou fallen from heaven, O **Lucifer, son of the morning**! how art thou cut down to the ground, **which didst weaken the nations*** (Isa 14:12)!

The name **Lucifer** is based on the Hebrew *helel* = daystar, shining one. The English translation is further based on the Latin, *Lux* = light, and *ferre* = bearer; thus *Luxferre*. As the **son of the morning** (*shahar* = dawn), he was the greatest of the sinless angels of light and who were called *morning stars* (Job 38:7). As there will be a usurper designated and named *Antichrist*, so the name *Lucifer* is in like manner a corrupted imitation of Christ who is *the bright and morning star* (Rev. 22:16).

Note, that while it is generally assumed that Isaiah 14:12-16 refers to the fall of Satan at the time of, and or before Adam's creation, the statement, **which didst weaken the nations,** is clearly subsequent to that time (there were no nations when Adam was created). The passage in fact points to the war in Heaven that will take place during the Tribulation (see Isa 14:17).

1. THE KEY HE IS GIVEN: **and to him was given the key of the bottomless pit.** It must be *given* to him, for it is not his own key, nor does he have authority over the bottomless pit. A different and good angel uses the key to open the bottomless pit at the beginning of the Millennium (Rev 20:1,2). As Christ holds the keys it is said here that the key is **given** to Satan.

- *I am he that liveth, and was dead; and, behold, I am alive for evermore, Amen; and **have the keys of hell and of death*** (Rev 1:18).

That Satan, though cast, down should be given the key of the bottomless pit may seem strange yet it is not without precedent. As the key signifies permission; it is to be remembered that Satan was given permission to afflict Job, yet not kill him. Thus now he is given permission to severely afflict the inhabitants earth but not kill them.

- *And the LORD said unto Satan, Behold, all that he hath is in thy power; only upon himself put not forth thine hand. So Satan went forth from the presence of the LORD* (Job 1:12).

2. THE PIT HE OPENS. **And he opened the bottomless pit; and there arose a smoke out of the pit, as the smoke of a great furnace; and the sun and the air were darkened by reason of the smoke of the pit** (9:2). Certain of Satan's fallen angels/demons are loose and roam the earth, others are bound (2 Pet 2:4; Jude 6). This is the incarceration place for those who are bound. It is a place of smoke and darkness. This is also the place were Satan is bound during the Millennial Reign (Rev 20:1,2). Satan and the demons are the *powers of darkness* (Lk 22:53); hell as well as the bottomless pit is the place of darkness. The Devil carries on his designs by blinding the eyes of men, by extinguishing light and knowledge, and promoting ignorance and error. He first deceives men, and then destroys them; wretched souls follow him in the dark, (that becomes what they want). See Williams.

CHAPTER 9

In addition to the three times in this Chapter (9:1,2,11), the Greek *abussos* (abyss) is found, there are six other occurrences in the New Testament.

ABUSSOS, THE BOTTOMLESS PIT

• *And Jesus asked him, saying, What is thy name? And he said, Legion: because many devils were entered into him. 31 And they besought him that he would not command them to go out into **the deep*** (Lk 8:30,31).

• *Or, Who shall descend into **the deep**? (that is, to bring up Christ again from the dead* (Rom 10:7).

• *And when they shall have finished their testimony, the beast that ascendeth out of **the bottomless pit** shall make war against them, and shall overcome them, and kill them* (Rev 11:7).

• *The beast that thou sawest was, and is not; and shall ascend out of **the bottomless pit**, and go into perdition: and they that dwell on the earth shall wonder, whose names were not written in the book of life from the foundation of the world, when they behold the beast that was, and is not, and yet is* (Rev 17:8).

• *And I saw an angel come down from heaven, having the key of **the bottomless pit** and a great chain in his hand. 2 And he laid hold on the dragon, that old serpent, which is the Devil, and Satan, and bound him a thousand years, 3 And cast him into **the bottomless pit**, and shut him up, and set a seal upon him, that he should deceive the nations no more, till the thousand years should be fulfilled: and after that he must be loosed a little season* (Rev 20:1-3).

II. THE ASCENDING LOCUSTS. ***And there came out of the smoke locusts upon the earth: and unto them was given power, as the scorpions of the earth have power.*** (9:3). Out of this dark smoke there came a swarm of locusts, and just as literal and physical as the eighth plague upon Egypt, but very different.

Walvoord quotes Arthur Peake to this end.

> The scorpion locusts are quite literally intended; they are not heretics, or Goths, or Mohammedans, or the mendicant orders, or the Jesuits, or Protestants, or Saracens or Turks, but they are uncanny denizens of the abyss, locusts of a hellish species, animated by devilish instincts and equipped with infernal powers.

They may represent a Satanic counterfeit of the *zoon*, the four angelic beasts around the Throne (Rev 4:6). It is believed that the prophecy in Joel points to this:

THE LOCUST PLAGUE IN JOEL

• ***The word of the LORD that came to Joel*** *the son of Pethuel. 2 Hear this, ye old men, and give ear, all ye inhabitants of the land.* ***Hath this been in your days****, or even in the days of your fathers? 3 Tell ye your children of it, and let your children tell their children, and their children another generation. 4* ***That which the palmerworm hath left*** *hath the locust eaten; and* ***that which the locust hath left*** *hath the cankerworm eaten; and* ***that which the cankerworm hath left hath*** *the caterpiller eaten* (Joel 1:1-4).

• ***Blow ye the trumpet in Zion****, and sound an alarm in my holy mountain: let all the inhabitants of the land tremble: for the day of the LORD cometh, for it is nigh at hand; 2 A day of darkness and of gloominess, a day of clouds and of thick darkness, as the morning spread upon the mountains: a great people and a strong;* ***there hath not been*** *ever the like, neither shall be any more after it, even to the years of many generations. 3 A fire devoureth before them; and behind them a flame burneth:* **the land is as the garden of Eden before them, and behind them a desolate wilderness**; *yea, and nothing shall escape them. 4 The appearance of them is as* **the appearance of horses**; *and as horsemen, so shall they run. 5 Like* **the noise of chariots** *on the tops of mountains shall they leap, like* **the noise of a flame** *of fire that devoureth the stubble, as a strong people set in battle array. 6 Before their face the people shall be much pained: all faces shall gather blackness. 7* **They shall run** *like mighty men;* **they shall climb** *the wall like men of war; and* **they shall march** *every one on his ways, and* **they shall not break their ranks** (Joel 2:1-7).

1. THE DISTINCTIVE COMMAND GIVEN TO THE LOCUSTS.

(1) UNSEALED PEOPLE NOT GREENERY. *And it was commanded them that they should not hurt the grass of the earth, neither any green thing, neither any tree; but only those men which have not the seal of God in their foreheads* (9:4). They are barred from the diet of normal locusts and prey only upon people, but with the exception of the 144,000 (Rev 7:3). This indicates further that those who are converted through the ministry of the 144,000 are likewise given a seal. According to 2 Timothy 2:19, *the foundation of God standeth sure,* **having this seal**, *The Lord knoweth them that are his*. In a similar way, believers in the present age are *sealed with the Holy Spirit of promise* according to (Eph 1:13,14). While many will be martyred during this time, it seems inconceivable that any true believer in that day would be subjected to the torment of the locusts. This is a judgement upon the Christ-rejecter.

(2) TEMPORARY TORMENT NOT DEATH. *And to them it was given that they should not kill them, but that they should be tormented five months: and their torment was as the torment of a scorpion, when he striketh a man* (9:5). Satan, in leading this host would want to kill men, but as with the restraint place upon him during the time of Job, he is unable to do that. Five months is the ordinary time in the year during which locusts commit their ravages (Walvoord quoting Alford). In contrast to the pain caused by a scorpion which would pass away in a course of hours, this continues for a long period so that men shall seek death as the only means of escaping the pain.

2. THE EXTENT OF THE TORMENT CAUSED BY THE LOCUSTS. *And in those days shall men seek death, and shall not find it; and shall desire to die, and death shall flee from them* (9:6). The pain is of a scorpion is proverbial : far exceeding that of whips made by men. Note the words of King Jeroboam:

- *For whereas my father put a heavy yoke upon you, I will put more to your yoke: my father chastised you with whips, but* **I will chastise you with scorpions** (2 Chron 10:11).

Though the time of the torment is relatively short, the pain caused makes these five months far too long; they try every means possible to take their lives, but to no avail. This is a horrible picture of domination by demons to such an extent that men lose their ability of free choice and are in agony of body and soul. Satan seeks to afflict not only the righteous but also the wicked that do his bidding.

Govett describes the five months.

The article in the Greek before *men* denotes the universality of the desire. Far as the torment extends, so far does the desire reach. But men now not only desire death, as a mode of escape from the torment they suffer, but they seek it. That is, they use means to affect their purpose. Life is so weak *a thread*, that it is easily broken. The

CHAPTER 9

cord, the knife, the cup, the stream, the pistol, the fumes of deadly ingredients, offer many modes of exit from life. And ordinarily it is as easily found as sought.

But the peculiarity of those woeful five months will be, that they shall not find it. Ordinarily death comes undesired, uncalled; every means that skill can suggest is used to keep it at bay. In those five months it will be the opposite.

Here is the utter fear and anguish that parallels Joel's prophecy.

- *Before their face the people shall be **much pained**: all faces shall **gather blackness*** (Joel 2:6).

How remarkable is this future event to the connection of our Lord's word to the Seventy Disciples regarding the fall of Satan and protection from scorpions.

- *After these things **the LORD appointed other seventy also**, and sent them two and two before his face into every city and place, whither he himself would come* (Lk 10:1).
- *And the seventy returned again with joy, saying, Lord, even the devils are subject unto us through thy name. 18 And he said unto them, **I beheld Satan as lightning fall from heaven. 19 Behold, I give unto you power to tread on serpents and scorpions**, and over all the power of the enemy: and nothing shall by any means hurt you* (Lk 10:17-19).

Here, though, the plague produces not repentance, but desire for death. They seek an escape from anguish, not reconciliation with the offended Majesty of heaven.

3. THE MONSTROUS IMPRESSION CONVEYED BY THE LOCUSTS,
(1) THEIR DISPLAY OF POWER, AUTHORITY AND INTELLIGENCE.
And the shapes of the locusts were like unto horses prepared unto battle; and on their heads were as it were crowns like gold, and their faces were as the faces of men (9:7). To the unconverted during the Tribulation who reject Christ and who would save them from this plague, there is no answer. The locusts intimidate their victims with a hopelessness of unanswerable power and authority. As in Joel's prophecy they are compared with *horses* (Joel 2:4). They are horses with *crowns*, for they are assured of victory. To those who rejected the Bible, these locusts with their *faces of men* seem to give a show of wisdom and intelligence that was impossible to refute. Note that in this description he words *like* and *as* occur nine times.

"They shall keep rank. They are winged creatures: and thus height will be no security against them. They shall enter in at the windows as a thief. These infernal cherubim are like (1) horses, (2) men, (3) women. (4) lions, (5) birds, and (6) scorpions. The sound of their wings is warlike and mighty. Chariots in which many horses are driven abreast and run with speed make a terrible sound. The sound of the wings of the true cherubim was like great waters, and like the sound of an army (Ezek 1:24)". (Govett).

(2) THEIR DISPLAY OF SEDUCTIVE CHARM AND FEROCITY.
And they had hair as the hair of women, and their teeth were as the teeth of lions (9:8). They had all the allurements of seeming beauty, but at the same were completely cruel and vicious. With these teeth the locusts make their way through every obstruction and perhaps by them seize their victims, yet without devouring them.

(3) THEIR DISPLAY OF IMMOVABILITY AND SWIFTNESS.
And they had breastplates, as it were breastplates of iron; and the sound of their wings was as the sound of chariots of many horses running to battle (9:9). They must have powerful wings to make such a noise! They seemed oblivious to any counter measures and their *sounds* foretold

of a *blitzkrieg* onslaught. With this mighty noise they flew from one country to another. Compare this with the *noise of chariots* in Joel's prophecy (Joel 2:5). And also:

> • Like **the noise of chariots on the tops of mountains shall they leap**, *like the noise of a flame of fire that devoureth the stubble, as a strong people set in battle array* (Joel 2:5).
>
> • **They shall run** *like mighty men;* **they shall climb** *the wall like men of war; and* **they shall march** *every one on his ways, and* **they shall not break their ranks** (Joel 2:7).

(4) THEY DISPLAYED A TERRIBLE BUT NOT MORTAL STING. *And they had tails like unto scorpions, and there were stings in their tails: and their power was to hurt men five months* (9:10). They are as fearsome as a creature could be and their sting as great as can be imagined, but it is for five months, not eternity. May to September is the usual time for a plague of locusts. This length of time repeated twice (9:5) gives an idea of the length of the Trumpet Judgements during the last 3 and 1/2 years of the Tribulation. Men are made fearfully immortal during those months.

III. THE DESOLATING KING. *And they had a king over them, which is the angel of the bottomless pit, whose name in the Hebrew tongue is Abaddon, but in the Greek tongue hath his name Apollyon* (9:11). Ordinary locusts have no king (Prov 30:27), but these do!

1. HIS PERSON. The king and commander of this hellish squadron is here described. He is *an angel*; so he was by nature, an angel, once one of the angels of Heaven. He is an angel but *the angel of the bottomless pit*. Though now given a kind of authority over it, he will shortly become its chief occupant (Ezek 32:21).

2. HIS NAME. His true name is **Abaddon, Apollyon**—*a destroyer,* for that is his business, his design, and employment, to which he diligently attends, in which he is very successful, and takes hellish pleasure. Though Satan often appears as an angel of light in the role of that which is good and religious, here the mask is stripped away. Of our Lord it is said, *Thou shalt call his name Jesus for he shall save his people from their sins* (Matt 1:21). Here, the king of the locusts is named *Destroyer*, for he shall destroy his people *in* their sins.

> • *For such are false apostles, deceitful workers, transforming themselves into the apostles of Christ. 14 And no marvel;* **for Satan himself is transformed into an angel of light** (2 Cor 11:13,14).

The plague will not produce repentance but only a desire for death (9:6). Nor will the following plague cause men to turn from their idolatries and impurities (9:20,21). Suffering and misery apart from the Gospel are impotent to effect the New Birth.

Fearful as it is, the locusts out of the pit is only the first of three great judgments which conclude the Trumpet Period. And now we have the end of one woe; and where one ends another begins. **One woe is past; and, behold, there come two woes more hereafter** (9:12). Desperate indeed will be the situation of those who know not Christ in those tragic hours preceding Christ's Return to judge the wicked world.

Walvoord makes an important point:

> The tribulation period unmasks human wickedness and also demonstrates the true character of Satan. In our modern day while Satan is still restricted it is easy to forget the great conflict which is raging between the forces of God and the forces of Satan referred to in Ephesians 6:12. In the great tribulation, and especially in the time of the fifth trumpet, with the release of the confined demons the full character of Satan

CHAPTER 9

will be starkly manifested. For the first time in history all those who do not know the Lord Jesus Christ as Saviour will come under demonic possession and affliction.

THE SIXTH TRUMPET, SECOND WOE: *A FURTHER THIRD OF THE WORLD DIES!*

(9:13) *And the sixth angel sounded, and I heard a voice from the four horns of the golden altar which is before God,* (9:14) *Saying to the sixth angel which had the trumpet, Loose the four angels which are bound in the great river Euphrates.* (9:15) *And the four angels were loosed, which were prepared for an hour, and a day, and a month, and a year, for to slay the third part of men.*

(9:16) *And the number of the army of the horsemen were two hundred thousand thousand: and I heard the number of them.* (9:17) *And thus I saw the horses in the vision, and them that sat on them, having breastplates (of fire, and of jacinth, and brimstone: and the heads of the horses were as the heads of lions; and out of their mouths issued fire and smoke and brimstone.* (9:18) *By these three was the third part of men killed, by the fire, and by the smoke, and by the brimstone, which issued out of their mouths.* (9:19) *For their power is in their mouth, and in their tails: for their tails were like unto serpents, and had heads, and with them they do hurt.*

(9:20) *And the rest of the men which were not killed by these plagues yet repented not of the works of their hands, that they should not worship devils, and idols of gold, and silver, and brass, and stone, and of wood: which neither can see, nor hear, nor walk:* (9:21) *Neither repented they of their murders, nor of their sorceries, nor of their fornication, nor of their thefts.*

I. THE PRELUDE TO AN EASTERN INVASION.

1. THE VOICE HEARD FROM THE ALTAR. *And the sixth angel sounded, and I heard a voice from the four horns of the golden altar which is before God* (9:13). This is the place where the martyrs had prayed (6:9,10). In 8:3, this altar is the scene of the offering of incense with the prayers of saints. Here is the final mention of this altar in Revelation. This judgment like those preceding are partially an answer to the prayers of the persecuted Tribulation saints on earth. The *four horns* demonstrate that this altar provided the pattern for the altar of incense used in the Tabernacle and in the Temple (cp. Exod 25:9,40). These *horns* demonstrate that God's sovereignty is wedded to the prayers of His people; and that, as the number four represents, from around the world.

2. THE COMMAND GIVEN TO THE EPHRATEAN ANGELS. *Saying to the sixth angel which had the trumpet, Loose the four angels which are bound in the great river Euphrates* (9:14). The Euphrates has long been the dividing line between east and west. The hugely populous nations and empires to the east of this line have not generally crossed the Euphrates to invade the west. Here Scripture tells us that four angels within its waters have been restrained from leading such an invasion. This restraint is now to be removed.

THE BOOK OF REVELATION

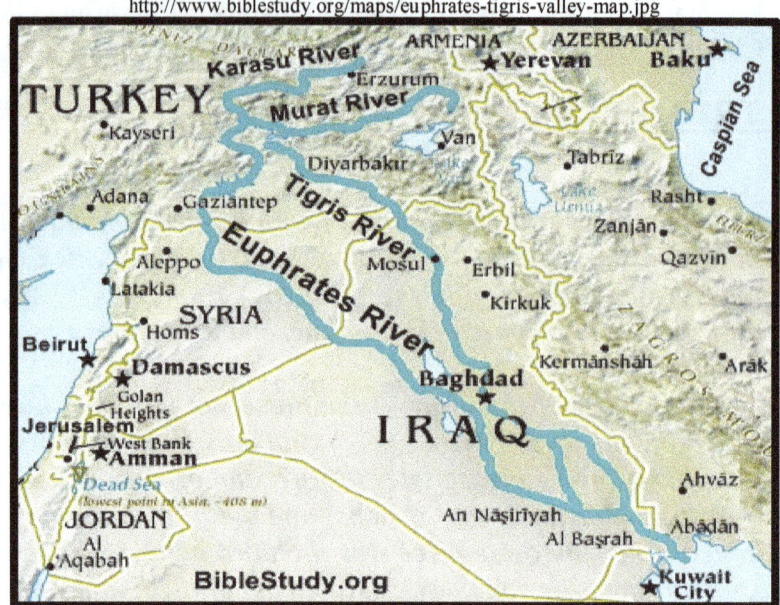

The Euphrates River

In this most unusual passage we see that these four angels are under Divine control; they cannot act without express command; and further, their presence in the Euphrates concerns an invasion from the East (the Orient). While much has *not* been revealed, we may draw the following conclusions.

(1) The angels are **bound in** and not *standing on* the Euphrates. That is, they are not "stationed" at the Euphrates. This demonstrates that they are not restraining an invasion, but if loosed will be leaders of the invasion. They are not like the four angels mentioned in 7:1, but as "opposites" do parallel them.

> • *And after these things I saw* **four angels standing on** *the four corners of the earth, holding the four winds of the earth, that the wind should not blow on the earth, nor on the sea, nor on any tree* (Rev 7:1).

These four angels as being *bound* are of a different character. There is no instance in Scripture where holy angels are bound; whereas two passages speak of evil angels as *bound and chained* (2 Pet 2:4; Jude 6).

(2) When the angels are *loosed* they seem clearly to perform a judgement that parallels that which immediately preceded – the release of the demonic locusts under the Fifth Trumpet. Thus under both the Fifth and Sixth Trumpets, satanic forces are used to bring judgement upon the earth. We may like to know more, but must be satisfied with the stark statements of the judgement given here by the Holy Spirit.

The following passage demonstrates that as the Euphrates has played a prominent role in the course of history it also do so in the judgements of the Last Days.

> • **For this is the day of the Lord GOD of hosts, a day of vengeance**, *that he may avenge him of his adversaries: and the sword shall devour, and it shall be satiate and made drunk with their blood: for the Lord GOD of hosts hath a sacrifice in the north country* **by the river Euphrates** (Jer 46:10).

As with the loosed *locust angels* who were shut up and chained in the Abyss (2 Pet 2:4; Jude 6) and loosed for a short time only to be punished in the Lake of Fire forever (Rev

19:20; 20:10,15; 21:8); so it will be for these four fallen angels in the Euphrates. They are reserved ***unto*** judgment but for a short time, reserved ***for*** judgment, i.e., to be the executors of God's wrath. Soon after they will be cast into the Lake of Fire with *the Devil and his angels* (Matt 25:41).

Note: As an eruption of Satanic and demonic activity will be permitted in connection with the Second Advent, there was also significant demonic activity at our Lord's First Advent during the Gospel and Acts period.

II. THE VISION OF THE EASTERN INVASION.

1. THE TIMING OF THE INVASION. ***And the four angels were loosed, which were prepared for an hour, and a day, and a month, and a year, for to slay the third part of men*** (9:15). The time is fixed to the hour. At this time God will *make the wrath of man praise him, and the remainder of wrath he will restrain* (Psa 76:10). They are prepared for their hour of activity much in the same way as the whale was prepared to swallow Jonah and effect divine discipline upon the prophet. These are wicked angels designated to execute the great judgment of the Sixth Trumpet but prevented from doing so until the proper moment. Though the agency of men (or even wicked angels) is used to accomplish the purposes of God, the time schedule is determined by God, not man. (see Walvoord).

Govett in contrast to most believes the four time period are to be added (to thirteen months, a day and an hour). Thus he views it as the time of the entire slaughter rather than the exact time at which the invasion begins. This we think would be too long and conflict with the chronology of the second half of the Tribulation. He also believes (likely wrongly) that it is a demonic rather than an actual army.

> I believe that the divine penman intended to define for us the duration of the plague, as in the case of the locusts, the Two Witnesses, and many others. Then we must connect the period named with the loosing, and must regard the "preparing" as subordinate and parenthetic: or else connect it with the slaughter of men. So accurately is the time determined, that it is bounded by an hour. The former plague was for five months, this is for more than thirteen. Woes deepen in dreadfulness, as men plunge deeper in sin.

Here then an additional third of the world's population will die. Earlier in the Fourth Seal, a fourth of the earth's population dies. These two judgments *alone* account for half of the world's population, and it is clear that in addition to these judgments there is widespread destruction of human life in other of the judgments contained in the Seals, Trumpets, and Vials (cp. Isa 24:6, *few men left*). Not since the Flood has such a proportion of the earth's population fallen under the righteous judgement of God. This statement of the third part of the world's people dying is repeated in verse 18.

THE BOOK OF REVELATION

China Prepares for a Military Parade

2. THE SIZE OF THE ARMY. *And the number of the army of the horsemen were two hundred thousand thousand: and I heard the number of them* (9:16). The army that will execute this great expedition is mustered, and the number found to be 200 million. Further, if this is the number of those *not on foot*; what is the number of the infantry. That would increase this great number significantly. Back in 1965 *Time Magazine* (May 21, 1965, p. 35) reported that Red China claimed to have a militia of 200 million.

Note that while Govett and others believe this is a demonic army of 200 million, it is as with the armies that are gathered to Armageddon, a human army energized by demons.

- And I saw three unclean spirits like frogs come out of the mouth of the dragon, and out of the mouth of the beast, and out of the mouth of the false prophet. For ***they are the spirits of devils, working miracles, which go forth unto the kings of the earth and of the whole world, to gather them to the battle of that great day of God Almighty*** (Rev 16:13,14).

3. THE *FIRE*-POWER OF THE ARMY. *And thus I saw the horses in the vision, and them that sat on them, having breastplates (of fire, and of jacinth, and brimstone: and the heads of the horses were as the heads of lions; and out of their mouths issued fire and smoke and brimstone* (9:17). It is *fire* that most characterises the formidable might of this eastern force. *Fire smoke and brimstone* are the foretastes of the penalties of the damned: they preview on earth the *lake which burneth with fire and brimstone, which is the second death* (Rev 21:8).

4. THE VAST CARNAGE WROUGHT BY THE ARMY. *By these three was the third part of men killed, by the fire, and by the smoke, and by the brimstone, which issued out of their mouths. For their power is in their mouth, and in their tails: for their tails were like unto serpents, and had heads, and with them they do hurt* (9:18,19) . This again is likely a picture of modern warfare rather than as some have believed – a demonic army. Once again it is stated that the magnitude of the of the numbers and the ferocity of the weapons has

brought about the deaths of one third of the world's remaining population. Before, catastrophe visited a third of earth and of the salt and fresh waters, and of the celestial bodies with their operations. Now it is ***the third of men***.

A similar judgement and likely occurring soon after is mentioned in Revelation 16. This results in the outpouring of the Sixth Vial and also depicts an invasion from the East. These are two different events, or perhaps two phases of the same event. Chronologically the time from the blowing of the Sixth Trumpet to the pouring out of the Sixth Vial will not be more than a matter of months. In the first stage under the Sixth Trumpet the Euphrates remains a hindrance to the movement of the vast army; when that hindrance is removed the ultimate destination of the eastern armies will be Israel and Armageddon!

> • *And the sixth angel poured out his vial upon **the great river Euphrates; and the water thereof was dried up**, that the way of the kings of the east might be prepared* (Rev 16:12).
>
> • *And he gathered them together into a place called in the Hebrew tongue Armageddon* (Rev 16:16).

5. THE EFFECT UPON THOSE STILL LIVING.

(1) THEY PERSISTED IN THEIR IDOLATRY. ***And the rest of the men which were not killed by these plagues yet repented not of the works of their hands, that they should not worship devils, and idols of gold, and silver, and brass, and stone, and of wood: which neither can see, nor hear, nor walk*** (9:20). In spite of the dramatic ravages inflicted by this invading military force, those who survive are declared to be unrepentant. Such is the hardness of the human heart even though faced by worldwide destruction and Divine judgment. The character of their wickedness is unfolded in these verses. They would not cast away their images, though they could do them no good: they *could not see, nor hear, nor walk*. Idolatry (9:20), immorality (9:21), and sorcery (9:21) will reach an excess never known before. All will lead up to the worship of the Beast. All will be centred upon the Antichrist and his image (likely with replicate personal images).

Note: If an idol could *see, hear and walk* it would worship man as its maker rather than receive worship! (Govett).

(2) THEY PERSISTED IN THEIR PERSONAL SINS. ***Neither repented they of their murders, nor of their sorceries, nor of their fornication, nor of their thefts*** (9:21). Verse 20 lists sins against the *First Table* of the Ten Commandments; Those in this verse are against the *Second Table*. These are the flagrant crimes of people living in the Tribulation, and after the Antichrist comes fully to power and sets up his image in Jerusalem. Though their numbers have now been *halved*, their sins have strengthened. The two closing verses of the chapter reveal an astounding picture of human depravity. Here as unlike the Sixth Seal they are not crying to the rocks and the mountains.

> • *And the kings of the earth, and the great men, and the rich men, and the chief captains, and the mighty men, and every bondman, and every free man, hid themselves in the dens and in the rocks of the mountains; And said to the mountains and rocks, Fall on us, and hide us from the face of him that sitteth on the throne, and from the wrath of the Lamb* (Rev 6:15,16).

Nor is there any crying to the mountains under the final Vial Judgements. There is instead a three-fold crescendo of blasphemy.

> • *And men were scorched with great heat, and **blasphemed the name of God**, which hath power over these plagues: and they repented not to give him glory* (Rev 16:9).

• *And **blasphemed the God of heaven** because of their pains and their sores, and repented not of their deeds* (Rev 16:11).

• *And there fell upon men a great hail out of heaven, every stone about the weight of a talent: and men **blasphemed God** because of the plague of the hail; for the plague thereof was exceeding great* (Rev 16:21).

2. The Trumpet Judgements and Other Events 8-14
a. The Seventh Seal is Opened 8:1-6
b. The Six Trumpets Blown: Woeful Wrath (8:13) 8:7-9:21
c. The Herald Angel Announces the Seventh Trumpet 10 (v7)

CHAPTER 10

C. THE HERALD ANGEL ANNOUNCES THE SEVENTH TRUMPET (VS 7)10

(10:1) *And I saw another mighty angel come down from heaven, clothed with a cloud: and a rainbow was upon his head, and his face was as it were the sun, and his feet as pillars of fire:* (10:2) *And he had in his hand a little book open: and he set his right foot upon the sea, and his left foot on the earth,* (10:3) *And cried with a loud voice, as when a lion roareth: and when he had cried, seven thunders uttered their voices.*

(10:4) *And when the seven thunders had uttered their voices, I was about to write: and I heard a voice from heaven saying unto me, Seal up those things which the seven thunders uttered, and write them not.*

(10:5) *And the angel which I saw stand upon the sea and upon the earth lifted up his hand to heaven,* (10:6) *And sware by him that liveth for ever and ever, who created heaven, and the things that therein are, and the earth, and the things that therein are, and the sea, and the things which are therein, that there should be time no longer:*

(10:7) *But in the days of the voice of the seventh angel, when he shall begin to sound, the mystery of God should be finished, as he hath declared to his servants the prophets.*

Having now witnessed the blowing of six of the Trumpet Judgements, in Chapters 10 we see the descent of a Herald Angel to announce that the blowing of the Seventh Trumpet is imminent. This Seventh Trumpet opens up the third series of judgements, the pouring out of the Seven Vials of Wrath - unmingled wrath. The Vial Judgements take place in the last weeks of the Tribulation (see 11:14). They are, however, not described until Chapters 15 and 16. In the intervening chapters we have an overview of the primary events that cover the second half of the Tribulation.

      (1) The Ministry of the Two Witnesses 11
      (2) The Flight of Israel into the Wilderness 12
      (3) The Full Power of Antichrist 13
      (4) The Final Calls before the Vial Judgements 14

I. THE HERALD ANGEL: HIS GLORY. *And I saw another mighty angel come down from heaven, clothed with a cloud: and a rainbow was upon his head, and his face was as it were the sun, and his feet as pillars of fire* (10:1). Some have thought that he is Christ. He certainly reflects some of the glory of Christ. But he is an angel - *another mighty angel.* As a created being, he *sware by him that liveth for ever and ever, who created heaven and earth* (10:6).

As this angel is mighty and holds a book, he should be compared with the strong angel in Chapter 5 who was also occupied with a *book*. It may be the same angel and it is very likely the same book.

• *And I saw* **a strong angel** *proclaiming with a loud voice,* **Who is worthy to open the book***, and to loose the seals thereof* (Rev 5:2)?

1. HIS CLOTHING. He was *clothed with a cloud.* Reflecting the glory of Christ, he veils his glory, which is too great for man to behold. That glory will not be revealed on earth until Christ Himself returns.

2. HIS HEAD-DRESS: *a rainbow was upon his head.* He reflects the glory of the One who is faithful to His covenant with His Creation. As in the days of the Flood, if judgement must fall it will be followed by mercy.

GOD'S RAINBOW VERSUS THE LGBT RAINBOW, SEVEN STIPES VERSUS SIX

From the site, *NOW THE END BEGINS*:

God's rainbow, the one that He set in the sky as a sign to Noah, has **Seven** observable colours in it – **red**, **orange**. **yellow**, **green**, **blue**, **violet**, and **indigo** [the LGBT rainbow introduces and begins with *pink*!]…

The number Seven in the Bible as well as in nature shows the completeness and perfectness of our Heavenly Father. The number Six on the other hand, does not fare so well. The number is first mentioned in connection with the flood of Noah, and last mentioned with the Mark of the Beast and the Battle of Armageddon. All judgments on sin.

How many colours in the LGBT Pride Rainbow? You guessed it – **Six**.
Gilbert Baker, a San Francisco artist and drag queen, first created the Rainbow Flag in 1978. Baker's rainbow flag actually originally had eight colours – **hot pink**, red, orange, yellow, green, turquoise, indigo/blue and violet — but it gradually lost its stripes until it became the six-colour version most commonly used today. Each of the colours has its own significance, he says: hot pink for sex, red for life, orange for healing, yellow for sunlight, green for nature, turquoise for art, indigo for harmony and violet for spirit. http://www.nowtheendbegins.com/difference-between-gods-rainbow-lgbt-pride-rainbow/#

• *And I will establish **my covenant** with you, neither shall all flesh be cut off any more by the waters of a flood; neither shall there any more be a flood to destroy the earth. 12 And God said, This is **the token of the covenant** which I make between me and you and every living creature that is with you, for perpetual generations: 13 **I do set my bow in the cloud,** and it shall be for **a token of a covenant** between me and the earth. 14 And it shall come to pass, when I bring a cloud over the earth, that **the bow shall be seen in the cloud:** 15 And I will remember **my covenant**, which is between me and you and every living creature of all flesh; and the waters shall no more become a flood to destroy all flesh. 16 And **the bow shall be in the cloud**; and I will look upon it, that I may remember **the everlasting covenant** between God and every living creature of all flesh that is upon the earth. 17 And God said unto Noah, This is **the token of the covenant**, which I have established between me and all flesh that is upon the earth* (Gen 9:11-17).

3. HIS COUNTENANCE: *and his face was as it were the sun.* In this also He reflects the glory of Christ who is the express image of His Father (Rev 1:16; Heb 1:3).

• *Who being the brightness of his glory, and the express image of his person, and upholding all things by the word of his power, when he had by himself purged our sins, sat down on the right hand of the Majesty on high* (Heb 1:3).

4. HIS FEET: *and his feet as pillars of fire.* As Christ (Rev 1:15), all his ways, both of grace and judgement, are righteous, steady and firm.

II. THE HERALD ANGEL: HIS DEMONSTRATION.

CHAPTER 10

1. AS TO FULFILLED AND YET TO BE FULFILLED REVELATION. ***And he had in his hand a little book open*** (10:2). That which was before sealed, is now opened. It is now a *little book* for much of its content has taken place. Only the final third of judgements (the Vials) along with overviews of concluding key events yet to be fulfilled. This remaining portion will be brought to pass as certainly as were the Seal and Trumpet portions. He holds the little book as the soon to be completed *Title Deed* to the earth.

Compare the *little book* with the *short work*:

- *Esaias also crieth concerning Israel, Though the number of the children of Israel be as the sand of the sea, a remnant shall be saved: 28 For he will finish the work, and cut it short in righteousness: because* **a short work will the Lord make upon the earth** (Rom 9:27,28).

2. AS TO IMPENDING DOMINION: ***and he set his right foot upon the sea, and his left foot on the earth***. Despite the Dragon, the Antichrist, the False Prophet, and Babylon the Great; Christ will shortly return and take dominion on the earth (11:15). The mighty angel as Christ's emissary now declares this. The One whom the angel represents has complete power and authority over the entire earth.

This commission is introduced here because the Ten Kings and the Antichrist, are about to be introduced on the pages of Revelation in formidable power (Rev 11,12,13,17). Despite their apparent initial success, it is Christ who will reign.

III. THE HERALD ANGEL: HIS PROCLAMATION.

1. THE PROCLAMATION BEGINS. ***And cried with a loud voice, as when a lion roareth*** (10:3). He speaks with the tones of and the representative of the *Lion of the Tribe of Judah* (Rev 5:5).

- ***The LORD also shall roar out of Zion***, *and utter his voice from Jerusalem; and the heavens and the earth shall shake: but the LORD will be the hope of his people, and the strength of the children of Israel* (Joel 3:16).

2. THE PROCLAMATION IS INTERRUPTED: ***and when he had cried, seven thunders uttered their voices. And when the seven thunders had uttered their voices, I was about to write: and I heard a voice from heaven saying unto me, Seal up those things which the seven thunders uttered, and write them not*** (10:3,4). Walter Scott (in Walvoord) relates the seven thunders to the seven times the voice of Jehovah is mentioned in Psalm 29:3-9, and states, "The seven thunders point to 'the perfection of God's intervention in judgment." However, the fact that John was commanded *from heaven* not to record the words of the seven thunders, leads us to believe that these sounds were an interruption and not *from heaven*. They are likely the response of Satan and the world under the sway of Antichrist to the proclamation of Christ's soon Return.

Note: Daniel likewise did not record the words that the Antichrist spoke: ***a mouth that spake very great things*** (Dan 7:20).

3. THE PROCLAMATION IS DELIVERED.

(1) WITH A SIGN OF SOLEMN AFFIRMATION. ***And the angel which I saw stand upon the sea and upon the earth lifted up his hand to heaven, And sware by him that liveth for ever and ever, who created heaven, and the things that therein are, and the earth, and the things that therein are, and the sea, and the things which are therein*** (10:5,6). It is in the Name and authority of the Creator of Heaven and Earth, that this declaration now is made.

THE BOOK OF REVELATION

(2) WITH A STATEMENT OF ABSOLUTE CLOSURE: *that there should be time no longer: But in the days of the voice of the seventh angel, when he shall begin to sound, the mystery of God should be finished, as he hath declared to his servants the prophets* (10:6,7). The *mystery of God* parallels with the *mystery of iniquity* (2 Thess 2:7). Satan's and sinful man's time on earth is now over. It has been a *mystery* within the counsels of God, as to why, though declared so emphatically to the Old Testament prophets, that this time should have been so long. Gods people have cried out, *How long O LORD*.

More specifically it is the Divine secret respecting the duration of the *Times of the Gentiles* (Rom 11:25) and of the judgment decreed upon Israel because of the cutting off of Messiah (Dan 9:26, 27). Compare the proclamation at the pouring out of the Seventh Vial.

- *And the seventh angel poured out his vial into the air; and there came a great voice out of the temple of heaven, from the throne, saying,* **It is done** *(Rev 16:17).*

When the Seventh Trumpet is blown the Seven Vials are poured out; Christ will Return to Earth and His Kingdom will be established on earth. There will be *no mystery* then:

- *But this shall be the covenant that I will make with the house of Israel; After those days, saith the LORD,* ***I will put my law in their inward parts****, and write it in their hearts; and will be their God, and they shall be my people. 34* ***And they shall teach no more every man his neighbour****, and every man his brother, saying, Know the LORD:* ***for they shall all know me****, from the least of them unto the greatest of them, saith the*

  LORD: *for I will forgive their iniquity, and I will remember their sin no more* (Jer 31:33,34).

This is an important chronological statement. With this and the yet to be blown Seventh Trumpet (issuing in the Vial Judgements. (cp.11:14,15) our viewpoint is brought to the end of the Tribulation and the Return of Christ. In the next three Chapters the chronology of the Book does not extend further, we are instead given an overview of the final half of the Tribulation with special emphasis upon the Two Witnesses (11); the Flight of Israel (12) and the Antichrist (13).

Note that it is after the account of the Two Witnesses and their 1260 day ministry (11:3) that the sounding of the Seventh Angel is again mentioned (11:14,15). This demonstrates that the Seventh Trumpet issuing in the Seven Vials take place very quickly at the end of the Tribulation.

- ***The second woe is past; and, behold, the third woe cometh quickly****. 15 And the* ***seventh angel sounded****; and there were great voices in heaven, saying, The kingdoms of this world are become the kingdoms of our Lord, and of his Christ; and he shall reign for ever and ever (Rev 11:14,15).*

In addition to the words, ***there should be time no longer*** (10:6), compare the following:

- *there was no more* ***sea*** (21:1)
- *there shall be no more* ***death*** (21:4)
- *neither shall there be any more* ***pain*** (21:4)
- *there shall be no more* ***curse*** (22:3)
- *there shall be no* ***night*** *there* (22:5)

CHAPTER 10

THE APOSTLE EATS THE LITTLE BOOK

(10:8) *And the voice which I heard from heaven spake unto me again, and said, Go and take the little book which is open in the hand of the angel which standeth upon the sea and upon the earth.* (10:9) *And I went unto the angel, and said unto him, Give me the little book. And he said unto me, Take it, and eat it up; and it shall make thy belly bitter, but it shall be in thy mouth sweet as honey.*

(10:10) *And I took the little book out of the angel's hand, and ate it up; and it was in my mouth sweet as honey: and as soon as I had eaten it, my belly was bitter.*

(10:11) *And he said unto me, Thou must prophesy again before many peoples, and nations, and tongues, and kings.*

I. THE CHARGE TO JOHN.

    1. TO TAKE THE BOOK. *And the voice which I heard from heaven spake unto me again, and said, Go and take the little book which is open in the hand of the angel which standeth upon the sea and upon the earth* (10:8). This charge is not given by the angel who stood upon the earth, but is the voice in heaven that in the fourth verse had told John not to write what he had heard from the seven thunders. It could well be *the voice he heard from Heaven* first heard back in 4:1.

This is the third time in this chapter that we are told that the angel stands upon *the sea and upon the earth*. In each, the sea is mentioned before earth, though the normal order in Revelation is to mention earth before sea (5:13; 7:1-3; 12:12; 14:7). This is for emphasis and demonstrates complete authority over the entire earthly scene. And, that despite Satan descending to the earth to open the abyss (Rev 9:1), and the Antichrist ascending from the earth and the abyss (Rev 11:7).

    2. TO EAT THE BOOK. *And I went unto the angel, and said unto him, Give me the little book. And he said unto me, Take it, and eat it up;* (10:9). This Book as we have shown is likely the remaining part of the Book of Revelation. John is to thoroughly digest the contents for his own good and for the good of those that will hear him.

    (1) THE EFFECT THE BOOK *WILL* HAVE: *and it shall make thy belly bitter, but it shall be in thy mouth sweet as honey.* The prophecies of Christ's Coming and Millennial Kingdom are very sweet. The prophecies of what will further take place in the Tribulation is bitter (cp. Ezek 3:3). In delivering its bitter aspect, John has known and will know what it is to be like his Master, *despised and rejected of men* (Isa 53:3). Compare the Psalmist's words:

> • *The fear of the Lord is clean, enduring for ever:* **the judgments of the Lord are true and righteous altogether.** *More to be desired are they than gold, yea, than much fine gold:* **sweeter also than honey and the honeycomb** (Psa 19:9,10).

    (2) THE EFFECT THE BOOK *DID* HAVE. *And I took the little book out of the angel's hand, and ate it up; and it was in my mouth sweet as honey: and as soon as I had eaten it, my belly was bitter* (10:10). His experience was just as was told him. So it will be with all believers who diligently study Bible prophecy. Note that eating expresses the diligent and complete reception of Scripture. It means that we deliver it fully in its positive and negative aspects.

> • *And when I looked, behold, an hand was sent unto me; and, lo,* **a roll of a book was therein; 10 And he spread it before me;** *and it was written within and without: and there was written therein lamentations, and mourning, and woe* (Ezek 2:9,10).

THE BOOK OF REVELATION

> • *Moreover he said unto me, Son of man,* ***eat that thou findest; eat this roll, and go speak unto the house of Israel****. 2 So I opened my mouth, and he caused me to eat that roll. 3 And he said unto me, Son of man, cause thy belly to eat, and fill thy bowels with this roll that I give thee.* ***Then did I eat it; and it was in my mouth as honey for sweetness****. 4 And he said unto me, Son of man, go, get thee unto the house of Israel, and speak with my words unto them (Ezek 3:1-4).*
>
> • ***Thy words were found, and I did eat them****; and thy word was unto me the joy and rejoicing of mine heart: for I am called by thy name, O LORD God of hosts (Jer 15:16).*

II. THE ONGOING COMMISSION TO JOHN. *And he said unto me, Thou must prophesy again before many peoples, and nations, and tongues, and kings* (10:11). That which he had just been given must be a subject of proclamation. It must not be added to or diminished (22:18,19). Though John is old and for a time banished on a small island, yet God is not finished with him; days of great enlargement lie ahead. As with Isaiah (Isa 6), his ministry is now renewed.

This commission emphasises the *greatness of the field*. The entire world (and as men in the world weigh up their love for a world under Antichrist and Satan) will now hear what is about to take place in the final half of the Tribulation (Rev11-18) - the Return of Christ (Rev 19), the Millennium and its judgements (Rev 20), and the Eternal Glories (Rev 21,22).

2. The Trumpet Judgements and Other Events   8-14
a. The Seventh Seal is Opened   8:1-6
b. The Six Trumpets Blown: Woeful Wrath (8:13)   8:7-9:21
c. The Herald Angel Announces the Seventh Trumpet 10 (v7)
d. The Two Witnesses   11:1-13

CHAPTER 11

D. THE TWO WITNESSES 11:1-13

THE MEASURING OF THE TRIBULATION TEMPLE

(11:1) *And there was given me a reed like unto a rod: and the angel stood, saying, Rise, and measure the temple of God, and the altar, and them that worship therein.*
(11:2) *But the court which is without the temple leave out, and measure it not; for it is given unto the Gentiles: and the holy city shall they tread under foot forty and two months.*

The three chapters now before us give an overview of the Second Half of the Tribulation, and this from three standpoints. In Chapter 11 it is from the standpoint of the 1260 day ministry of the Two Witnesses. In Chapter 12 the focus is on the 1260 day flight and refuge of Israel into the wilderness; and in Chapter 13 it is the 42 month power of the Antichrist. The chapters are unique in that times covering the same period are given for each.

In Chapter 11, the scene opens at the Temple where the Jews will be allowed to worship on the Temple Mount during the Tribulation (Dan 9:27; 12:11; Matt 24:15; 2 Thess 2:4; Rev 13:14,15). In a word: *It does not measure up!*

1. THE COMMAND TO MEASURE. *And there was given me a reed like unto a rod: and the angel stood, saying, Rise, and measure the temple of God, and the altar, and them that worship therein* (11:1). The reed was ten foot long and here represents, as in the Ten Commandments, the *Divine Standard*. John is now made a participant as well as an observer. He is called to *measure* a temple, an altar, and the worshipers. This is a place where Christ and his Finished Sacrifice have absolutely no part! Neither the temple, nor the sacrifices, nor the worshippers, *measure up*. All has *come short of the glory of God* (Rom 3:23). All is *weighed in the balances and found wanting* (Dan 5:27).

2. THE COMMAND TO EXCLUDE. *But the court which is without the temple leave out, and measure it not; for it is given unto the Gentiles: and the holy city shall they tread under foot forty and two months* (11:2). The Jewish People are allowed to have this place of worship as a key article in their covenant with the Antichrist; perhaps based on UN resolution 242. It appears that in this agreement the **outer court** was part of the complex in which they could worship but will at some later point be taken from them. From what follows, it appears that Jerusalem itself will initially be under the control of the Jewish People. However, in the midst of the seven year "treaty period" the Antichrist breaks the covenant (Dan 9:27); places his own image there; and then if not before, *the outer court and the holy city shall they tread under foot forty and two months.*

In Jerusalem, the Antichrist will have everything going his way, except for the Two Witnesses! The Jewish worshippers will flee (Matt 24:15,16). Jerusalem is under full Gentile control. The Image of the Beast is revered by the entire world. But, despite all that the Antichrist will do and attempt to do, the Two Witnesses will be witnessing from this place for the next 1260 days and the proud Man of Sin will be powerless to do anything about it.

This *treading under foot* was spoken of by our Lord in His Olivet Discourse and demonstrates that the *Times of the Gentiles* end at His Return and the conclusion of the Tribulation. This also demonstrates that Jerusalem would have alleviation from this *treading down* prior to the final forty two months. This, Jerusalem, to a greater or lesser extent has experienced since 1967.

- *And they shall fall by the edge of the sword, and shall be led away captive into all nations: and **Jerusalem shall be trodden down of the Gentiles, until the times of the Gentiles be fulfilled** (Lk 21:24).*

THE MINISTRY OF THE WITNESSES

(11:3) And I will give power unto my two witnesses, and they shall prophesy a thousand two hundred and threescore days, clothed in sackcloth. (11:4) These are the two olive trees, and the two candlesticks standing before the God of the earth.

(11:5) And if any man will hurt them, fire proceedeth out of their mouth, and devoureth their enemies: and if any man will hurt them, he must in this manner be killed. (11:6) These have power to shut heaven, that it rain not in the days of their prophecy: and have power over waters to turn them to blood, and to smite the earth with all plagues, as often as they will.

(11:7) And when they shall have finished their testimony, the beast that ascendeth out of the bottomless pit shall make war against them, and shall overcome them, and kill them. (11:8) And their dead bodies shall lie in the street of the great city, which spiritually is called Sodom and Egypt, where also our Lord was crucified. (11:9) And they of the people and kindreds and tongues and nations shall see their dead bodies three days and an half, and shall not suffer their dead bodies to be put in graves. (11:10) And they that dwell upon the earth shall rejoice over them, and make merry, and shall send gifts one to another; because these two prophets tormented them that dwelt on the earth.

(11:11) And after three days and an half the Spirit of life from God entered into them, and they stood upon their feet; and great fear fell upon them which saw them.

(11:12) And they heard a great voice from heaven saying unto them, Come up hither. And they ascended up to heaven in a cloud; and their enemies beheld them. (11:13) And the same hour was there a great earthquake, and the tenth part of the city fell, and in the earthquake were slain of men seven thousand: and the remnant were affrighted, and gave glory to the God of heaven.

In this time of the *treading down* and the *abomination of desolation* God reserves to Himself two faithful witnesses.

I. THE DESCRIPTION OF THE TWO WITNESSES. *And I will give power unto my two witnesses, and they shall prophesy a thousand two hundred and threescore days, clothed in sackcloth* (11:3).

1. THEIR AUTHORITY. *And I will give power.* Power to preach, power to perform miracles (1 Thess 1:5). This power from God will be exercised in the most hostile environment *ever* (!). They will have power to maintain an open testimony on or at least in the vicinity of the Temple Mount at the very time and from the very place that the Antichrist is presenting his Image to the world!

2. THEIR NUMBER. Their number is not great! *In the mouth of two witnesses shall every word be established* (2 Cor 13:1). They are unnamed. Some think they are Elijah and Moses who appeared on the Mount of Transfiguration, or Enoch, who with Elijah did not die and who both had *rapture* experiences. But, whoever, they will be the best of men for the worst of times.

3. THEIR TIME: *and they shall prophesy a thousand two hundred and threescore days.* In their *three and one half year* ministry every day will count. For them it will not be even, *in season and out of season* (2 Tim 4:2); every day will be *in season*. From what we have already seen, and now the fact that the Two Witnesses pour out Divine judgments upon

the earth and receive Divine protection lest they be killed, these 1260 days are clearly the Second Half of the Tribulation.

4. THEIR CLOTHING: *clothed in sackcloth*. A testimony and sign of the deepest depths to which the world has plunged (cp. Isa 37:1,2; Dan 9:3). Their general appearance and manner will be a complete opposite of what is seen today with the flashy, prosperity loving, tele-evangelists. They will directly oppose the "evangelization" promoted by the Antichrist himself.

THE 1260 DAY MINISTRY OF THE TWO WITNESSES WILL OPPOSE THE LATTER PART OF ANTICHRIST'S 2300 DAY "TELECAST" FROM THE TEMPLE MOUNT

During the 1260 days that the Two witnesses are preaching at or near the Temple Mount in Jerusalem, the Antichrist will also have been putting on *his show*. *His Show* will have begun sometime after the beginning of the Tribulation when he allows the Jewish People to worship and offer sacrifice in their own temple. His show will last for 2300 days (Dan 8:14), thus within the 2520 days of the Tribulation, and thus extending will into the Second Half. His show will be in two stages with the second beginning at the Midpoint of the Tribulation.

- *Then I heard one saint speaking, and another saint said unto that certain saint which spake, How long shall be* **(1) *the vision concerning the daily sacrifice***, *and* **(2) *the transgression of desolation***, *to give both the sanctuary and the host to be trodden under foot? And he said unto me, Unto* **two thousand and three hundred days**; *then shall the sanctuary be cleansed* (8:13,14).

The Antichrist having made the covenant with Israel and allowing them to resume sacrifices on the Temple Mount will assure that he himself receives maximum publicity for this action. A daily world-wide telecast, every morning and every evening, will present this *great man of peace* (Dan 8:25) on the Temple Mount. For the first two or three years he will appear as Israel's benefactor and will give warm "lip service" to the God of Israel. But all will change. He will unexpectedly be seen in an altogether different light; and for the remaining years he appears as the *object* of the world's worship. If interest wanes during the latter part of this 2300 day telecast, *there will be means to assure that everyone is tuned in*.

Note especially that during this time, and in reference to the Temple Mount and the Jewish sacrifices – the Antichrist will be *showing himself*.

- ***When ye therefore shall see*** *the abomination of desolation, spoken of by Daniel the prophet, stand in the holy place, (whoso readeth, let him understand:).* (Matt 24:15).
- *Who opposeth and exalteth himself above all that is called God, or that is worshipped; so that he as God sitteth in the temple of God*, ***shewing himself*** *that he is God* (2 Thess 2:4).

Daniel sees the Jewish sacrifices taking place and their abolition by the Antichrist. He also sees the catastrophic demise of this Master of Ceremonies who will be *broken without hand* (Dan 8:25). This *telecast* will also come to an abrupt end! Compare:

- *the fifth angel poured out his vial upon the seat of the beast; and **his kingdom was full of darkness**; and they gnawed their tongues for pain* (Rev 16:10).

It is against the backdrop of the Antichrist's "telecast" that the Two Witnesses will give their powerful witness.

THE IDENTITY OF THE TWO WITNESSES AND THE COMING OF ELIJAH

It is clear that the Two Witnesses will come in *the spirit and power* of Moses and Elijah and in the prophetic authority of Enoch. But, it is also a fact that they are not named and that there is no clear word in Scripture of a latter day appearing of Moses and Enoch. Many believe there is such a word concerning Elijah (Mal 4:5). On these grounds it seems best to say that the Two Witnesses are likely to be two currently unknown men whom God will raise up in that hour.

It is also believed by many that Elijah will literally come. Note, however, that his ministry seems to be distinct from the ministry of the Two Witnesses. Note also that apart from Malachi 4:5, Elijah is not mentioned in Revelation or his activity in the Tribulation seen elsewhere. Further, the Malachi prophecy may indicate that Elijah will come *before*, not during the Tribulation, a fact that points to him being equated with the ministry of John the Baptist. However, the statement likely mean Christ's actual Return (cp. Rev 16:14).

The following from Walvoord gives a summary of the primary views:

> There has been much debate on the identity of these two witnesses. J.B. Smith and others believe that they are Moses and Elijah, because of the similarity of judgment inflicted to those pronounced by Elijah and Moses, namely, fire from heaven, turning water into blood, and smiting the earth with plagues.
>
> Support for the identification of Elijah as one of the two witnesses is found in the prediction that Elijah will come *before the coming of the great and dreadful day of the Lord* (Mal 4:5). This seems to be at least partially fulfilled by the coming of John the Baptist according to the discussion of Christ with His disciples (Matt 17:10-13; Mk 9:11-13; cp. Lk 1:17).
>
> Evidence for both Moses and Elijah is found in the fact that they are related to the Second Coming and the Transfiguration (Matt 17:3). The dispute of Michael with the devil over the body of Moses (Jude 9) is mentioned preceding a prophecy of the Second Coming, but no specific connection is made between the two. All the evidence for the identification, however, is circumstantial and not clear. There are great difficulties in all points of view identifying the two witnesses with these men.
>
> Govett identifies the two witnesses as Enoch and Elijah and cites in support early tradition and apocryphal writing. The fact that Enoch and Elijah did not die but were translated is considered an argument in their favour. If Moses is included as one of the two witnesses, there is an added difficulty in that he once died. Could he die a second time?
>
> It seems far preferable to regard the Two Witnesses as two prophets who will like the 144,000 be raised up from among those who turn to Christ in the time following the Rapture.

Had Israel received Christ as their Messiah at His First Coming, the following passage from Matthew states that John the Baptist would have fulfilled the Malachi prophecy concerning Elijah. As they did not, it is believed that the prophecy remains to be fulfilled. But, as Malachi indicates that the coming of Elijah will *before* the Tribulation, it is believed by others that John did fulfil the Malachi prophecy. Thus the matter is debated.

CHAPTER 11

- ***Behold, I will send you Elijah the prophet before the coming of the great and dreadful day of the LORD***: *6 And he shall **turn the heart** of the fathers to the children, and the heart of the children to their fathers, **lest I come and smite the earth with a curse*** (Mal 4:5,6).
- *And many of the children of Israel shall he* [John the Baptist] *turn to the Lord their God. 17 And he shall go before him **in the spirit and power of Elias, to turn the hearts** of the fathers to the children, and the disobedient to the wisdom of the just; to make ready a people prepared for the Lord* (Lk 1:16,17).
- *Verily I say unto you, Among them that are born of women there hath not risen a greater than John the Baptist: notwithstanding he that is least in the kingdom of heaven is greater than he. 12 And from the days of John the Baptist until now the kingdom of heaven suffereth violence, and the violent take it by force. 13 For all the prophets and the law prophesied until John. 14 And **if ye will receive it, this is Elias, which was for to come*** (Matt 11:11-14).

A. R. Faussett (*JFB Commentary*) gives the following comments on Malachi 4:5.

> *I send you Elijah*--as a means towards your "remembering the law" (Mal 4:4). *the prophet*--emphatically; not "the Tishbite"; for it is in his official, not his personal capacity, that his coming is here predicted. In this sense, John the Baptist was *an* Elijah in spirit (Lk 1:16,17), but not *the literal* Elijah; whence when asked, "Art thou Elias?" (Jhn 1:21), He answered, "I am not." "Art thou that prophet?" "No." This implies that John, though knowing from the angel's announcement to his father that he was referred to by Malachi 4:5 (Lk 1:17), whence he wore the costume of Elijah, yet knew by inspiration that he did not exhaustively fulfil *all* that is included in this prophecy: that there is a further fulfilment (compare *Note,* see on Mal 3:1). As Moses in Malachi 4:4 represents the Law, so Elijah represents the Prophets.
>
> The Jews always understood it of the literal Elijah. Their saying is, "Messiah must be anointed by Elijah." As there is another consummating advent of Messiah Himself, so also of His forerunner Elijah; perhaps in person, as at the transfiguration (Matt 17:3; compare Matt 17:11). He in his appearance at the transfiguration in that body on which death had never passed is the forerunner of the saints who shall be found alive at the Lord's second coming. Revelation 11:3 may refer to the same witnesses as at the transfiguration, Moses and Elijah; Rev 11:6 identifies the latter (compare 1Kng 17:1; Jms 5:17). Even after the transfiguration, Jesus (Matt 17:11) speaks of Elijah's coming "to restore all things" as still future, though He adds that Elijah (in the person of John the Baptist) is come already *in a sense* (compare Acts 3:21). However... the words "before the . . . *dreadful* day of the Lord," show that John cannot be exclusively meant.

Likely the Two Witnesses are two previously unknown men and Matthew 17:11 is crucial to the actual appearance of Elijah during the Tribulation: ***Elias truly shall first come and restore all things***.

<u>II. THE PROPHETIC FULFILMENT OF THE TWO WITNESSES.</u> ***These are the two olive trees, and the two candlesticks standing before the God of the earth*** (11:4). As olive trees they possess oil; as candle sticks they communicate light in the deepest darkness the world has known. As Gabriel in Heaven, though they be on a darkened earth, they *stand in the presence of God* (Lk 1:19).

THE BOOK OF REVELATION

Yet, though identified symbolically they are not identified by name. This prophecy had an initial fulfilment in the Governor Zerubbabel and the High Priest Joshua, *the two olive-trees and candlestick* at the time of the return from Babylon. The olive oil from the olive trees in Zechariah's vision provided fuel for the two lampstands. So now the oil will continue to flow into *their lamps* until the ministry of the Two Witnesses is finished. It is, *Not by might, nor by power, but by my spirit, saith the Lord of hosts* (Zech 4:6).

The Olive Tree Symbolism of the Two Witnesses: Testimony at the Tribulation Temple and Caught Up to the Heavenly Temple

• *And said unto me, What seest thou? And I said, I have looked, and behold **a candlestick all of gold, with a bowl upon the top of it, and his seven lamps thereon, and seven pipes to the seven lamps, which are upon the top thereof: 3 And two olive trees by it, one upon the right side of the bowl, and the other upon the left side thereof**. 4 So I answered and spake to the angel that talked with me, saying, What are these, my lord? 5 Then the angel that talked with me answered and said unto me, Knowest thou not what these be? And I said, No, my lord. 6 Then he answered and spake unto me, saying, This is the word of the LORD unto Zerubbabel, saying, **Not by might, nor by power, but by my spirit, saith the LORD of hosts*** (Zech 4:2-6).

• *Then answered I, and said unto him, **What are these two olive trees upon the right side of the candlestick and upon the left side thereof**? 12 And I answered again, and said unto him, **What be these two olive branches which through the two golden pipes empty the golden oil out of themselves?** 13 And he answered me and said, Knowest thou not what these be? And I said, No, my lord. 14 Then said he, **These are the two anointed ones, that stand by the LORD of the whole earth*** (Zech 4:11-14).

III. THE MIRACLES OF THE TWO WITNESSES.

1. MIRACLES OF DEFENCE. *And if any man will hurt them, fire proceedeth out of their mouth, and devoureth their enemies: and if any man will hurt them, he must in this manner be killed* (11:5). Elijah called for the fire from heaven to consume the captains that came to seize him (2 Kng 1:12). But that was once; here there will be multiple

occurrences. Thus unlike the 144.000 whose protection was only defensive, theirs is offensive. They are empowered to deal the blows of supernatural vengeance.

2. MIRACLES OF JUDGEMENT. *These have power to shut heaven, that it rain not in the days of their prophecy: and have power over waters to turn them to blood, and to smite the earth with all plagues, as often as they will* (11:6). God will inflict plagues and judgments upon their enemies as He did on Pharaoh when He turned the river to blood (Exod 7:20) and restrained the rains of heaven in Elijah's day (1 Kng 17:1). From this it is inferred that there is a linkage between the Two Witnesses and the Trumpet Judgements.

Taking all the facts into consideration the Two Witnesses will demonstrate the greatest powers ever by mortal man. While the Antichrist is "putting on his show," it will be faint shadow of what they are doing.

IV. THE MARTYRDOM OF THE TWO WITNESSES.

1. WHEN THEY DIED. *And when they shall have finished their testimony* (11:7). They are immortal, they are invulnerable, until their work is done. The end of the ministry came when they *finished their course* (2 Tim 4:7); when the last day, and not a day earlier, of the 1260 days was finished (11:3).

2. BY WHOM THEY DIED: *the beast that ascendeth out of the bottomless pit shall make war against them, and shall overcome them, and kill them.* Though the Antichrist was satanically energized from the bottomless pit at the middle of the Tribulation; and though he *made war against them* each day thereafter, yet he did not *overcome and kill them* until the end of the Tribulation. (Thus their ministry coincided with the Trumpet and Vial Judgements).

At the Midpoint of the Tribulation the Antichrist will suffer a *deadly wound*. He will appear to experience a death and resurrection. It is at this time that he descends into and ascends from the bottomless pit. In the second half of the Tribulation he will be a virtual incarnation of Satan.

- *And I saw one of his heads as it were **wounded to death; and his deadly wound was healed**: and all the world wondered after the beast* (Rev 13:3).
- *And he exerciseth all the power of the first beast before him, and causeth the earth and them which dwell therein to worship **the first beast, whose deadly wound was healed*** (Rev 13:12).
- *And deceiveth them that dwell on the earth by the means of those miracles which he had power to do in the sight of the beast; saying to them that dwell on the earth, that they should make an image to **the beast, which had the wound by a sword, and did live*** (Rev 13:14).

This verse introduces to us to the Beast in Revelation. He is the great antagonist of the Lord Jesus, attempting to usurp His kingdom and Godhead. He is the direct moral opposite to *the Lamb*. Our Lord's character is one of mercy, patient endurance, and submission to His Father's will. The Beast portrays fierceness of passion, violent wilfulness, rebellion against all authority and blasphemous wickedness against all that is righteous and Godly.

Note that in order to overcome the Two Witnesses, the Beast must *make war against them*. A highly unusual statement regarding what it took to overcome two men! It was far more difficult for him to conquer them than to conquer the world! He does this as one who has ascended from the bottomless pit. Thus it takes all the power that he can muster on the earth and under the earth to overcome them.

> • *And they worshipped the dragon which gave power unto the beast: and they worshipped the beast, saying, Who is like unto the beast?* **who is able to make war with him** (Rev 13:4)?

It is remarkable that the Lamb is named twenty-eight times, which is equivalent to four multiplied by seven; while the Wild Beast is mentioned thirty-six times, or six times six. The sum of all the numbers from one to thirty-six equal 666 (Govett).

3. HOW THE WORLD REACTED.
(1) A DESPICABLE FUNERAL.
And their dead bodies shall lie in the street of the great city, which spiritually is called Sodom and Egypt, where also our Lord was crucified. And they of the people and kindreds and tongues and nations shall see their dead bodies three days and an half, and shall not suffer their dead bodies to be put in graves (11:8,9). The malice against them was not satisfied with their blood and death, but pursued even unto their dead bodies. They would not allow them a quiet grave; their bodies were cast out in the open streets of Jerusalem which by this time is called Sodom for monstrous wickedness (compare the annual gay pride marches now held there), and Egypt for utter worldliness. All that the world is has now descended upon Jerusalem to mock the two martyrs, and mock the crucified and risen Saviour they proclaimed. Great throngs come to witness the bodies of the Two Witnesses whom they so greatly feared in life.

(2.) A BLASPHEMOUS REJOICING.
And they that dwell upon the earth shall rejoice over them, and make merry, and shall send gifts one to another; because these two prophets tormented them that dwelt on the earth (11:10). So great is the apparent victory over the Two Witnesses and so significant their death that it is made a worldwide celebration. Their dead bodies were insulted by the inhabitants of the earth, and their death was a matter of mirth and joy. The judgements they pronounced against the background of the Trumpet Judgements are over. Gifts are exchanged; the world becomes a vast rock concert of Satanic delirium. *Happy days are here again* ! But, *The triumphing of the wicked is short* (Job 20:5).

V. THE RESURRECTION OF THE TWO WITNESSES.
And after three days and an half the Spirit of life from God entered into them, and they stood upon their feet; and great fear fell upon them which saw them (11:11). For three and one half days the two times seven torches of fire stood before the Throne of God in Heaven. They now are given leave to return to the lifeless bodies on earth. The merrymaking is cut short and *soon* cut short. They had planned a much longer celebration. It was not to be.

1. THE TIME AT WHICH THEY AROSE.
And after three days and an half. They preached three and an half years; their bodies rested *three and an half days*. Just when the party was getting in full swing, it ended.

2. THE POWER BY WHICH THEY AROSE:
the Spirit of life from God entered into them, and they stood upon their feet. They had preached the Resurrection of Christ and the resurrection of the dead; now an overwhelming confirmation is given.

3. HOW THE WORLD REACTED:
and great fear fell upon them which saw them. With the wrappings of opened gifts still fluttering in the wind, the party is suddenly broken up. Hear it again! *The triumphing of the wicked is short* (Job 20:5). Where there is guilt, there is fear; and a persecuting spirit, though cruel, is not a courageous but a cowardly spirit. *Herod feared John the Baptist* (Mk 6:20).

They have travelled far and wide to see this. They are the mockers of the Resurrection of Christ and now here is that resurrection which they denied. Their raucous delirium is turned to the greatest terror.

CHAPTER 11

VI. THE ASCENSION OF THE TWO WITNESSES.
   1. THE WELCOMING SUMMONS. *And they heard a great voice from heaven saying unto them, Come up hither. And they ascended up to heaven in a cloud* (11:12). The Apostle John had heard this same call: *Come up hither* (4:1). At the Rapture believers will be *caught up* (1 Thess 4:17). Shortly, before vials of wrath are poured upon the earth, the 144,000 will be *caught up* to heaven (Rev 14:1,3; cp. 7:1).
   2. THE FEARFUL EFFECT.
      (1) UPON THEIR ADVERSARIES: *and their enemies beheld them.* It will be no small part of the punishment of persecutors if or when they see the faithful servants of God honoured and advanced. The rich man saw Lazarus (Lk 16:23). This is a final warning to the world of God's power over man whether in life or in death.
      (2) UPON JERUSALEM. *And the same hour was there a great earthquake, and the tenth part of the city fell, and in the earthquake were slain of men seven thousand* (11:13). As when Christ Died and Arose, a mighty shock was felt in Jerusalem. A shock will be felt in that day that will begin to turn Jerusalem from its Sodom and Egypt character (11:8).

When Elijah thought that he was alone, God told him about 7,000 faithful men. Here however matters are reversed and 7000 die in the earthquake. Here, the Greek is literally seven thousand *men of name*, that is, important and distinguished men. Where is their importance now? If people will not use their "importance" for the glory of God, it will end like this.

The tenth part of the city likely refers to the Temple Mount with its false temple and Image of the Beast (*the abomination of desolation*); the subject with which the chapter began!

Under the judgments of the Seals, the Trumpets, and the Vials of Wrath, the earth will quake five times (6:12; 8:5; 11:13,19; 16:18).
      (3) UPON THE REPENTANT: *and the remnant were affrighted, and gave glory to the God of heaven.* They were convinced of their terrible error of worshipping the Antichrist and his image on the Temple Mount. In true repentance they embraced the preaching of the Two Witnesses and *gave glory to the God of heaven*. The reference to *the God of heaven* is one of two in the New Testament (Rev 16:11). It is used frequently in the Old Testament where it is used to distinguish the true God from pagan deities.

E. A FURTHER ANNOUNCEMENT OF THE SEVENTH TRUMPET
11:14-19

(11:14) *The second woe is past; and, behold, the third woe cometh quickly.* (11:15) *And the seventh angel sounded; and there were great voices in heaven, saying, The kingdoms of this world are become the kingdoms of our Lord, and of his Christ; and he shall reign for ever and ever.*

(11:16) *And the four and twenty elders, which sat before God on their seats, fell upon their faces, and worshipped God,* (11:17) *Saying, We give thee thanks, O Lord God Almighty, which art, and west, and art to come; because thou hast taken to thee thy great power, and hast reigned.* (11:18) *And the nations were angry, and thy wrath is come, and the time of the dead, that* they *should be judged, and that thou shoulders give reward unto thy servants the prophets, and to the saints, and them that fear thy name, small and great; and shouldest destroy them which destroy the earth.*

(11:19) *And the temple of God was opened in heaven, and there was seen in his temple the ark of his testament: and there were lightnings, and voices, and thunderings, and an earthquake, and great hail.*

THE BOOK OF REVELATION

I THE CONTRASTING PROCLAMATIONS.

1. THE LAST WOE WILL COME QUICKLY. *The second woe is past; and, behold, the third woe cometh quickly* (11:14). The iniquity of men against the Two Witnesses draws down the final thunderbolt. They have got rid of these two warning voices but the result will be, **the second woe is past; and, behold, the third woe cometh quickly**.

We have just had an overview of the Second Half of the Tribulation from the standpoint of the Two Witnesses. This has been the scene on earth. We now are reminded again of the judgement sequence from Heaven (the blowing of the Seven Trumpets): *The second woe is past; and, behold, the third woe cometh quickly*. This had been announced shortly before by the angel holding the little book (10:7). The Second Woe with its 200 million strong army from the east, and death of a further third of the world's population (9:18) is now over (just over!). There is no respite, the Third Woe with its Seven Vials of unmingled wrath will very shortly and in quick rapidity break forth on the earth.

2. THE SEVENTH TRUMPET BEGINS TO BLOW. *And the seventh angel sounded* (11:15). The effect on earth of the Seventh Trumpet corresponds with the effects under the Seventh Seal and the Seventh Vial. Though the Seventh Trumpet is now sounded, the judgements that it brings forth (the Vials of Wrath) are not described until Chapters 15 and 16. This will allow for the account of other things that happen during the second half of the Tribulation: the Sun-clothed Woman (ch. 12); the Beast and False Prophet (ch. 13) and the Angelic Evangelists (ch. 14).

3. THE GREAT VOICES ARE NOW HEARD: *and there were great voices in heaven, saying, The kingdoms of this world are become the kingdoms of our Lord, and of his Christ; and he shall reign for ever and ever.* At the opening of the Seventh Seal there followed a *great silence* (8:1,2): after this Seventh Trumpet come loud voices. Then there was suspense: now Heaven knows and understands the issue. The voices are apparently those of angels, the Elders, the Four Beasts and of the Great Multitude. The fullness of the time, then, for proclaiming the kingdom of God is come. With this announcement other and great voices in Heaven proclaim the absolute wonder of that which is about to take place on earth. In a word the first petition of the Lord's Prayer is to be answered: *Thy kingdom come, thy will be done, on earth as it is in heaven* (Matt 6:10). The kingdoms on earth will become the kingdoms of Christ. The Millennial Reign is not the conclusion of the reign of the Father and the Son: it extends to eternity.

Chronologically in the framework of the Book of Revelation that which verse 15 states is about to take place. With the blowing of the Seventh Trumpet, the Return of Christ and His Kingdom Rule are only weeks away. But, as there is yet much further revelation concerning the situation on earth, this is not described until Chapter 19. The fact that earthly rule will pass directly into the hands of the Lord Himself is the constant theme of Scripture. (note for example, Ezek 21:26-27; Dan 2:35,44; 4:3; 6:26; 7:14,26,27; Zech 14:9).

II. THE ELDER'S JOYFUL ACCLAMATIONS.

1. THE MANNER OF THEIR ADORATION: *And the four and twenty elders, which sat before God on their seats, fell upon their faces, and worshipped God* (11:16). All worship in Heaven is humble worship. This is the eighth time that we have seen them in this attitude of worship.

2. THE MATTERS OF THEIR ADORATIONS.

(1) THE COMMENCEMENT OF THE LORD'S REIGN. *Saying, We give thee thanks, O Lord God Almighty, which art, and wast, and art to come; because thou hast taken to thee thy great power, and hast reigned* (11:17). The three great titles, Jehovah, Elohim, and Shaddai, are here used by the Elders as by the Cherubim in 4:8. Their prayer is an acknowledgement that Scripture has stated that Christ *will reign* (their prayer points

especially to the *Second Psalm*). Their prayer is an acknowledgement that as the Eternal One, Christ has the *right* to reign. Their prayer is an acknowledgement that Christ alone *has the power* to reign.

Twice in verse 17 mention is made of the power of God; first in the word **Almighty** (*pantokrator*), and in the word **power** (*dynamin*).

(2) EVENTS MARKING THE COMMENCEMENT OF THE LORD'S REIGN. ***And the nations were angry, and thy wrath is come, and the time of the dead, that*** they ***should be judged, and that thou shouldest give reward unto thy servants the prophets, and to the saints, and them that fear thy name, small and great; and shouldest destroy them which destroy the earth*** (11:18). The wrath of men is wicked; the wrath of God is holy. The two are about to meet on the plains of Armageddon (Rev 16:14-16). Despite the world's wrath (Psa 2:1); the righteous dead will be raised and rewarded and the wicked who though their wickedness *destroyed the earth*, will themselves be destroyed (Psa 10:16).

Verse 18 is a generalized and all-inclusive statement, some of the specifics of which are dealt with in the later prophecies of Revelation. Here are fundamental issues: It is a time of Divine wrath; a time of resurrection of the dead and their reward; and a time of special dealing with those living on the earth.

The dead here are the blessed dead of 20:4. They were judged by man to be worthy of death (1 Pet 4: 6), but they shall be judged by the Messiah to be worthy of His kingdom. The wicked dead are not resurrected or judged until the end of the Millennial Reign (Rev 20:4,5).

Note: ***thou shouldest give reward unto thy servants the prophets, and to the saints, and them that fear thy name, small and great.*** Man says *great and small* (Est 1:20); God says *small and great* (Gen 19:11; 1 Sam 5:9; Psa 115:13; Acts 26:22; Rev 11:18; 13:16; 19:5, 18; 20:12). Williams.

Note: Those that ***destroy the earth***, are the masses upon earth who follow their leader Apollyon / Abaddon, the *Destroyer*.

III. THE OPENED HEAVEN.
    1. THE STEADFAST VERACITY OF HEAVEN. ***And the temple of God was opened in heaven, and there was seen in his temple the ark of his testament*** (11:19).
Though the earthly temple may have been desecrated by the Beast, its counterpart in Heaven reflects the righteousness and majesty of God. Much may change on earth but the outworkings of God from His Throne, as depicted by the Heavenly ***ark of his testament*** do not change. This is the eternal *Bureau of Standards*. There the immutable Word of God forever dwells, and there the incorruptible Blood of Christ has been sprinkled.

- *For ever, O LORD, thy word is **settled in heaven*** (Psa 119:89).
- *And to Jesus the mediator of the new covenant, and to **the blood of sprinkling**, that speaketh better things that that of Able* (Heb 12:24).

The earthly ark contained, in addition to the Law of Moses, Aaron's rod that budded (typifying Christ's Resurrection), and the golden pot that had manna representing Christ as the Sustainer of his people. This Ark in the Heavenly Temple was a pledge of the Father's Covenant with Christ, as the Ark in its earthly counterpart was a pledge of God's Covenant with Israel.

- *Now to Abraham and his seed were the promises made. He saith not, And to seeds, as of many; but as of one, And to thy seed, which is Christ. 17 And this I say, that **the covenant, that was confirmed before of God in Christ**, the law, which was four hundred and thirty years after, cannot disannul, that it should make the promise of none effect* (Gal 3:16,17).

2. THE CERTAINTY OF FURTHER JUDGEMENT UPON EARTH: *and there were lightnings, and voices, and thunderings, and an earthquake, and great hail.* The plain implication is that now God is going to deal in summary judgment with the earth. These serve to emphasize the dramatic climax of this period in the Second Coming of our Lord and Saviour, Jesus Christ.

2. The Trumpet Judgements and Other Events 8-14
   a. The Seventh Seal is Opened 8:1-6
   b. The Six Trumpets Blown: Woeful Wrath (8:13) 8:7-9:21
   c. The Herald Angel Announces the Seventh Trumpet 10 (v7)
   d. The Two Witnesses 11:1-13
   f. The Sun-clothed Woman, The Dragon, The Manchild 12

CHAPTER 12

F. THE SUN-CLOTHED WOMAN, THE DRAGON, THE MANCHILD
12

With the blowing of the Seventh Trumpet (10:7; 11:15) we have come nearly to the end of the Seven Year Tribulation. All that remains is the pouring out of the Seven Vials(covering only a few weeks) before Christ returns. As in Chapter 11, so now in Chapter 12, we have an overview of the Second Half of the Tribulation. The primary subject is the flight of Israel into the wilderness from the attack of Satan and Antichrist. As the Two Witnesses preach for 1260 days (11:3), so Israel will be sustained for 1260 days (12:6).

Here we see the link and reference to the first prophecy of the Bible in which God said he would *put enmity between the seed of the woman and the seed of the serpent* (Gen 3:15). The warfare has raged across the ages, but now it comes to a conclusion.

The Chapter is in three sections:

THE WOMAN, DRAGON AND MANCHILD INTRODUCED 12:1-6
THE DRAGON CAST OUT OF HEAVEN 12:7-12
THE FLIGHT OF THE WOMAN 12:13-17

THE WOMAN, DRAGON AND MANCHILD INTRODUCED

(12:1) *And there appeared a great wonder in heaven; a woman clothed with the sun, and the moon under her feet, and upon her head a crown of twelve stars:*
(12:2) *And she being with child cried, travailing in birth, and pained to be delivered.*
(12:3) *And there appeared another wonder in heaven; and behold a great red dragon, having seven heads and ten horns, and seven crowns upon his heads.* (12:4) *And his tail drew the third part of the stars of heaven, and did cast them to the earth: and the dragon stood before the woman which was ready to be delivered, for to devour her child as soon as it was born.*
(12:5) **And she brought forth a man child, who was to rule all nations with a rod of iron: and her child was caught up unto God, and** *to* **his throne.** (12:6) *And the woman fled into the wilderness, where she hath a place prepared of God, that they should feed her there a thousand two hundred and threescore days.*

In Chapters 12 the primary object of attention is the Sun Clothed Woman and her flight into the wilderness. In Chapter 13 the primary participant is her antagonist, the Antichrist. There are in fact a total of seven participants in these two chapters.

(1) The Sun Clothed Woman, representing Israel
(2) The Seven Headed Dragon, representing Satan and the World Powers under his dominion
(3) The Man Child, referring to the 144,000
(4) Michael, representing the Leader of the Angels
(5) The Remnant of Israel that flees to the wilderness
(6) The Beast out of the sea, the Antichrist
(7) The Beast out of the earth, the False Prophet

THE BOOK OF REVELATION

http://www.sacred-texts.com/chr/tbr/img/08900.jpg

The Sun Clothed Woman and Seven Headed Dragon
Clarence Larkin: *Dispensational Truth*

I. THE PLACE OF THE VISION. ***And there appeared a great wonder in heaven*** (12:1). Though the events take place on earth, the symbolic sign of what is to take place is seen in Heaven. Thus it is under Heavenly control and scrutiny. The word for *wonder* is *semeion*, a sign-wonder. Six further sign-wonders take place in Revelation (12:3; 13:13,14; 15:1; 16:14; 19:20). This *semeion* is distinguished by being called **great**.

II. THE THREE PERSONAGES OF THE VISION.
    1. THE WOMAN IS ISRAEL.
        (1) THE WOMAN'S DESCRIPTION IN JOSEPH'S DREAM IN GENESIS.

GENESIS 37 IS THE LINK TO GENESIS 3:15 AND REVELATION 12, THE CONFLICT AND CONSUMMATION OF THE AGES

In Genesis 37 we are given the basis of the interpretation of this *great wonder in heaven*, that John saw. Joseph has presented a prophetic dream to his brothers.

> • *And he dreamed yet another dream, and told it his brethren, and said, Behold, I have dreamed a dream more; and, behold,* **the sun and the moon and the eleven stars made obeisance to me** (Gen 37:9).
> • *And he told it to his father, and to his brethren: and his father rebuked him, and said unto him, What is this dream that thou hast dreamed?* **Shall I and thy mother and thy brethren indeed come to bow down ourselves to thee** *to the earth* (Gen 37:10)?

Jacob observed rightly that ***the sun*** referred to himself, ***the moon*** to Rachel, and ***the eleven stars*** to his sons. Jacob saw also that his family would make ***obeisance*** to Joseph. As with the first dream given to Joseph this also tells of events that will take place in Egypt during the years of famine. The dream therefore clearly refers to Jacob's family and thus to

CHAPTER 12

Israel. But the dream goes much further and provides the link to two other passages of immense prophetic importance: Genesis 3:15 and Revelation 12.

• *And the LORD God said unto the **serpent**...I will put enmity between thee and the **woman**, and between thy seed and her seed; it shall bruise thy head, and thou shalt bruise his heel* (Gen 3:14,15).

Joseph's dream provides the link and interpretational key to the *Woman and her Seed* in Genesis 3 and Revelation 12. We will now see the interpretation from two standpoints:

[1] JACOB INTERPRETED THE *MOON* AS REFERRING TO RACHEL. Joseph's mother and Jacob's beloved wife. *Rachel is Israel*. Rachel is used collectively of the Nation in Jeremiah's prophecy of the slaughter of the infants. This is but one example of the **enmity** across the ages between the *Seed of the woman* and the *seed of the serpent* as foretold in Genesis 3:15.

• *Thus saith the LORD; A voice was heard in Ramah, lamentation, and bitter weeping; **Rahel weeping for her children** refused to be comforted for her children, because they were not* (Jer 31:15).
• *Then Herod, when he saw that he was mocked of the wise men, was exceeding wroth, and sent forth, and slew all the children that were in Bethlehem, and in all the coasts thereof, from two years old and under, according to the time which he had diligently enquired of the wise men. Then was fulfilled that which was spoken by Jeremy the prophet, saying, In Rama was there a voice heard, lamentation, and weeping, and great mourning, **Rachel weeping for her children**, and would not be comforted, because they are not* (Matt 2:16-18).

[2] JACOB INTERPRETED THE *SUN* AS REFERRING TO HIMSELF. Israel was to be the one solitary nation on earth through whom *light* would come; thus Christ, the Scriptures and the Jewish People themselves are that light. Though often not their *state and condition* this representation is of Israel's in their ultimate *standing* before God.

• *Arise, shine; for thy light is come, and the glory of the LORD is risen upon thee* (Isa 60:1).

[3] JACOB INTERPRETED THE *ELEVEN STARS* AS REFERRING TO HIS ELEVEN SONS. Thus the Tribes of Israel. Joseph would be the *twelfth*, but in this instance as a Type of Christ he is pictured as the one to whom the homage described in the dream is given.

Now compare the second description of this same basic vision:

(2) THE WOMAN'S DESCRIPTION IN REVELATION 12: ***a woman clothed with the sun, and the moon under her feet, and upon her head a crown of twelve stars*** (12:1).

[1] AS A *WOMAN*. She is the restored Daughter of Zion and Wife of Jehovah. Israel in the Old Testament frequently is represented symbolically as a woman related to the Lord as her husband but often as being unfaithful (Isa 54:3-6; Jer 3:6-10; 31:32; Ezek 16:32; Hos 2:14-16; 3:1).

The Woman of Revelation 12 pictures Israel during the Tribulation. It is the *Time of Jacob's Trouble* (Jer 30:7). It describes the *end* of the conflict begun in Genesis 3:15. It does not refer to the time of Christ's Incarnation and First Coming. *Every statement* in the chapter including the coming forth of *the Manchild* is in immediate proximity to the Second Coming of Christ.

Jerusalem in particular is the *Daughter of Zion*. The designation is given 25 times in the Old Testament. We have listed them here to demonstrate this city's centrality to the purposes of God (2 Chron 6:6). There during the days of Abraham, Melchisedec was priest (Gen 14); there under the Law the Temple stood (1 Kng 7); there on the Day of Pentecost the Church was formed (Acts 2) and to Jerusalem Christ will return and reign *unto the ends of the earth* (Psa 59:13).

- *This is the word that the LORD hath spoken concerning him; The virgin* **the daughter of Zion** *hath despised thee, and laughed thee to scorn; the daughter of Jerusalem hath shaken her head at thee* (2 Kng 19:21).
- *That I may shew forth all thy praise in the gates of* **the daughter of Zion**...(Psa 9:14).
- *And* **the daughter of Zion** *is left as a cottage in a vineyard, as a lodge in a garden of cucumbers, as a besieged city* (Isa 1:8).
- *As yet shall he remain at Nob that day: he shall shake his hand against the mount of* **the daughter of Zion**, *the hill of Jerusalem* (Isa 10:32).
- *Send ye the lamb to the ruler of the land from Sela to the wilderness, unto the mount of* **the daughter of Zion** (Isa 16:1).
- *The virgin,* **the daughter of Zion**, *hath despised thee, and laughed thee to scorn; the daughter of Jerusalem hath shaken her head at thee* (Isa 37:22).
- *Shake thyself from the dust; arise, and sit down, O Jerusalem: loose thyself from the bands of thy neck,* **O captive daughter of Zion** (Isa 52:2).
- *Behold, the LORD hath proclaimed unto the end of the world, Say ye to* **the daughter of Zion**, *Behold, thy salvation cometh*...Isa 62:11).
- *For I have heard a voice as of a woman in travail, and the anguish as of her that bringeth forth her first child, the voice of* **the daughter of Zion** ...(Jer 4:31).
- *I have likened* **the daughter of Zion** *to a comely and delicate woman* (Jer 6:2).
- *...they ride upon horses, set in array as men for war against thee,* **O daughter of Zion** (Jer 6:23).
- *And from* **the daughter of Zion** *all her beauty is departed*...(Lam 1:6).
- *How hath the Lord covered* **the daughter of Zion** *with a cloud in his anger*...(Lam 2:1)!
- *He hath bent his bow like an enemy...and slew all that were pleasant to the eye in the tabernacle of* **the daughter of Zion**: *he poured out his fury like fire* (Lam 2:4).
- *The LORD hath purposed to destroy the wall of* **the daughter of Zion**: *he hath stretched out a line, he hath not withdrawn his hand from destroying...* (Lam 2:8).
- *The elders of* **the daughter of Zion** *sit upon the ground...* (Lam 2:10).
- *What thing shall I take to witness for thee? what thing shall I liken to thee, O daughter of Jerusalem? what shall I equal to thee, that I may comfort thee,* **O virgin daughter of Zion**? *for thy breach is great like the sea: who can heal thee* (Lam 2:13)?
- *Their heart cried unto the Lord, O wall of* **the daughter of Zion**...(Lam 2:18).
- *The punishment of thine iniquity is accomplished,* **O daughter of Zion**... (Lam 4:22).
- *O thou inhabitant of Lachish, bind the chariot to the swift beast: she is the beginning of the sin to* **the daughter of Zion**...Micah 1:13).
- *And thou, O tower of the flock, the strong hold of* **the daughter of Zion**, *unto thee shall it come, even the first dominion; the kingdom shall come to the daughter of Jerusalem* (Micah 4:8).
- *Be in pain, and labour to bring forth,* **O daughter of Zion**, *like a woman in travail:*

CHAPTER 12

for now shalt thou go forth out of the city, and thou shalt dwell in the field, and thou shalt go even to Babylon; there shalt thou be delivered; there the LORD shall redeem thee from the hand of thine enemies (Micah 4:10).
- *Arise and thresh,* ***O daughter of Zion****: for I will make thine horn iron, and I will make thy hoofs brass: and thou shalt beat in pieces many people...* (Micah 4:13).
- *Sing,* ***O daughter of Zion****; shout, O Israel; be glad and rejoice with all the heart, O daughter of Jerusalem* (Zeph 3:14).
Sing and rejoice, ***O daughter of Zion****: for, lo, I come, and I will dwell in the midst of thee, saith the LORD* (Zech 2:10).
- *Rejoice greatly,* ***O daughter of Zion****; shout, O daughter of Jerusalem: behold, thy King cometh unto thee: he is just, and having salvation; lowly, and riding upon an ass, and upon a colt the foal of an ass* (Zech 9:9).

[2] AS *CLOTHED WITH THE* SUN. Her identification with Jacob and Rachel demonstrate that she is a recipient of the Abrahamic Covenant. She has, or will shortly have, the imputed righteousness of Christ, *the Sun of righteousness* (Mal 4:2).

[3] AS HAVING *THE MOON UNDER HER FEET*. She finds her prophetic fulfilment in the Seven Feasts, the Calendar of the Messiah; which is lunar by computation. These are described in Leviticus 23. They cover a period of seven *lunar* rather than solar months. While the computation of Israel's years over an extended period are of solar years; her Seven Feasts coincide with her lunar months. Beginning with the Passover and ending with Tabernacles. The Seven Feasts are the *Calendar of the Messiah*. They portray Christ in His Death and Resurrection, the formation of the Church at Pentecost and the Second Coming. Israel long missed the significance of these feasts, but during the Tribulation *her every step* will be in accordance with them.

[4] AS HAVING *A CROWN OF TWELVE STARS*. Her Twelve Tribes are now, or shortly to be, exalted in glory. The Gospel preached by the Twelve Apostles provides a crown of glory to all true believers.

There are other representative women mentioned in Revelation: *Jezebel* (2:20), representative of false and persecuting religion; the *Harlot* (17:1-7, 15-18), the apostate church of the end times; *the Bride, the Lamb's Wife* (19:7), the glorified Church joined to Christ.

(2) HER TRAVAIL. ***And she being with child cried, travailing in birth, and pained to be delivered*** (12:2). Though, historically, the nation gave birth to Christ through the Virgin Mary, this was not the period of her *travail*. Verse 2 points to the travail (birth pangs) of Israel during the Tribulation. As described below, this refers to Israel bringing forth the 144,000 during the Time of Jacobs Trouble (Jer 30:7), and before the general conversion of the nation at Christ's Return (Rom 11:26). The *entire* chapter and events are in the context of the future Seven Years. They do not refer to Christ's birth at Bethlehem.

- ***Before she travailed, she*** *brought forth; before her pain came,* ***she was delivered of a man child****. Who hath heard such a thing? who hath seen such things? Shall the earth be made to bring forth in one day? or shall a nation be born at once? for as soon as Zion travailed, she brought forth her children. Shall I bring to the birth, and not cause to bring forth? saith the LORD: shall I cause to bring forth, and shut the womb? saith thy God* (Isa 66:7-9).
- ***Therefore will he give them up, until the time that she which travaileth hath brought forth***: *then the remnant of his brethren shall return unto the children of Israel* (Micah 5:3).

2. THE DRAGON IS SATAN.

(1) HIS DESCRIPTION. *And there appeared another wonder in heaven; and behold a great red dragon, having seven heads and ten horns, and seven crowns upon his heads* (12:3).

[1] AS A *GREAT RED DRAGON*. A *dragon* for strength and terror; a *red* dragon for murderous cruelty; *a murderer from the beginning* (Jhn 8:44). Satan is again called the *Dragon* in 12:9, and it is clear that he the Dragon both in his own person and in the nations through which he works. In the Garden of Eden he was the Serpent, now he is the Dragon. From him will flow all of his power to the Beast.

[2] AS *HAVING SEVEN HEADS*. Commonly believed to represent seven stages of historical world empires: Egypt, Assyria, Babylon, Persia, Greece, Rome, Revived Rome. It is through these governments and culminating in their final stage under the Beast that Satan has made himself *the god of this world* (2 Cor 4:4).

[3] AS HAVING *TEN HORNS*. Ten powerful nations of the end time that will support the rise of Revived Rome.

[4] AS HAVING *SEVEN CROWNS UPON HIS HEADS*. In addition to the Ten Horns, it is suggested that the nations representing the previous empires will give their support to the Revived Roman Empire (cp. also the *seven kings*, 17:10).

AN ALTERNATIVE AND LIKELY CORRECT VIEW OF THE SEVEN CROWNED HEADSAND THE TEN CROWNED HORNS

The above presents the common view, however, as Chapter 12 appears to refer *entirely* to the future Tribulation it would mean that the seven empires of the past with Revived Rome will be the Seven **Crowned** Heads during the second half of the Tribulation. While Egypt, Babylon (Iraq), Persia (Iran), Greece and Italy are active today, they are certainly not strong and are but the faintest shadow of their empire days. It is also difficult to see how they would relate to the Ten Horns. Note that Persia (Iran) cannot be one of the *crowned heads* for it joins with Russia's attack on Israel (Ezek 38:5).

Walvoord offers an alternative view in which he appears to equate the seven heads with the horn each one bears. That is, with reference to Daniel 7, there were ten heads with each having a horn. Three of the head-horns were defeated by the Antichrist. Nevertheless the three horns of the conquered regions remained influential under the authority of the Antichrist and also received a crown (Rev 13:1). Walvoord says:

> From the similar description given in 13:1 and the parallel reference in Daniel 7:7,8, 24, it is clear that the revived Roman Empire is in view. The seven heads and ten horns refer to the original ten kingdoms of which three were subdued by the little horn of Daniel 7:8, who is to be identified with the world ruler of the great tribulation who reigns over the revived Roman Empire.

• *After this I saw in the night visions, and behold a fourth beast, dreadful and terrible, and strong exceedingly; and it had great iron teeth: it devoured and brake in pieces, and stamped the residue with the feet of it: and it was diverse from all the beasts that were before it; and **it had ten horns**. 8 I considered the horns, and, behold, there came up among them another little horn, before whom **there were three of the first horns plucked up by the roots**: and, behold, in this horn were eyes like the eyes of man, and a mouth speaking great things* (Dan 7:7,8).

• *Thus he said, The fourth beast shall be the fourth kingdom upon earth, which shall be diverse from all kingdoms, and shall devour the whole earth, and shall tread it down,*

CHAPTER 12

and break it in pieces. 24 And **the ten horns out of this kingdom are ten kings that shall arise:** *and another shall rise after them; and he shall be diverse from the first, and he* **shall subdue three kings** (Dan 7:23,24).

• *And I stood upon the sand of the sea, and saw a beast rise up out of the sea, having* **seven heads** *and* **ten horns**, *and* **upon his horns ten crowns**, *and upon his heads the name of blasphemy* (Rev 13:1).

(2) HIS CONQUEST. ***And his tail drew the third part of the stars of heaven, and did cast them to the earth*** (12:4). This refers to angelic warfare during the Tribulation as described in Daniel 8:10. This does not refer to the fall of angels at the time of or before the Creation. This angelic warfare will be in two stages: In the first there will be defeat the Angels of God; in the second stage of the conflict (shortly after) there will be victory.

• *And out of one of them came forth a little horn, which waxed exceeding great, toward the south, and toward the east, and toward the pleasant land. 10 And* ***it waxed great, even to the host of heaven; and it cast down some of the host and of the stars to the ground, and stamped upon them*** (Dan 8:9,10).

• *And there was* ***war in heaven: Michael and his angels fought against the dragon; and the dragon fought and his angels***, *8 And prevailed not; neither was their place found any more in heaven. 9 And the great dragon was cast out, that old serpent, called the Devil, and Satan, which deceiveth the whole world: he was cast out into the earth, and* ***his angels were cast out with him*** (Rev 12:7-9).

(3) HIS THREAT: ***and the dragon stood before the woman which was ready to be delivered, for to devour her child as soon as it was born.*** He will seek to prevent the conversion and rise of the 144,000 Jewish evangelists. As today and especially in the Tribulation days Satan seeks to supress any attempt to spread the Gospel. Though this passage is commonly thought to refer Herod's attempt to prevent the birth of Christ, that which precedes and follows shows clearly that it is an event of the Tribulation.

3. THE MANCHILD IS THE 144,000 (cp. 12:2,4,5,13).

Though several statements in the chapter may seem to point to Christ and His birth, there is simply too much in the chapter that conflicts with this view. Scripture elsewhere never refers to Christ by this name. The Manchild refers to the 144,000 of the Tribes of Israel described in Revelation 7 and 14. They are all *males* (Rev 14:4); they are converted *suddenly* (much like Saul of Tarsus, cp. 1 Cor 15:8), and they begin to *serve immediately* (Rev 7:3,4,9). They do a man's work though young in the faith. Thus they are called the ***manchild***.

They are saved near the beginning of the Tribulation and are the first fruits of Israel's general conversion at the time of Christ's Return to earth (Isa 66:7-9; cp. Rom 11:25,26). They are given a protective seal during Midpoint of the Tribulation (Rev 7:3). Note that they are brought forth at the time of Israel's ***travail***. This is a term used of the Second Coming. Compare, *beginning of sorrows* (lit. *birth pangs*, Matt 24:8). ***Travail*** does not describe Israel's state at the time of Christ's birth.

Compare once again the crucial passage from Isaiah. *Before* Israel's general birth pangs resulting in the conversion of the nation at Christ's Return (Rom 11:26) she is delivered of a Manchild.

• *And she* ***being with child cried, travailing in birth***, *and pained to be delivered.... And* ***she brought forth a man child*** (Rev 12:2,5),

• ***Before she travailed, she brought forth; before her pain came, she was delivered of a man child***. *Who hath heard such a thing? who hath seen such things? Shall the earth* *be made to bring forth in one day? or shall a nation be born at once? for as soon as Zion travailed, she brought forth her children. Shall I bring to the birth, and not cause to bring forth? saith the LORD: shall I cause to bring forth, and shut the womb? saith thy God* (Isa 66:7-9).

(1) THEIR DESTINY ON EARTH. ***And she brought forth a man child, who was to rule all nations with a rod of iron*** (12:5). As this is said of Christ, most believe the Manchild must be Christ. This *rule of iron* is used of Christ on two occasions (Psa 2:9; Rev 19:15); and on two other occasions it refers to the overcomers at Thyatira (Rev 2:27) and here to the **manchild** (Rev 12:5). Along with believers from the Church Age (Rev 2:26,27) the 144,000 will reign with Christ during the Millennial Reign.

• *But that which ye have already* **hold fast till I come**. *26 And he that overcometh, and keepeth my works unto the end,* **to him will I give power over the nations: 27 And he shall rule them with a rod of iron; as the vessels of a potter shall they be broken to shivers**: *even as I received of my Father* (Rev 2:25-27).

(2) THEIR RAPTURE TO HEAVEN: ***and her child was caught up unto God, and to his throne.*** The 144,000 are on earth in Chapter 7, and are before the Throne in Heaven in 14:1-4. They were protected during the Trumpet Judgements (9:4) but will be evacuated before the pouring out of the Vials of Wrath (chs. 15,16).

As in 1 Thessalonians 4:17, **caught up** (*harpazo*) is a Rapture term. It is sudden and contrasts with the words used of Christ's Ascension. In the four different accounts (Mark, Luke, John and Acts), our Lord was *carried up, received up, ascended up, taken up*.

III. THE FLIGHT OF THE WOMAN.
1. HER PLACE. ***And the woman fled into the wilderness, where she hath a place prepared of God*** (12:6). Christ Himself warned of this flight during the days of Antichrist (Matt 24:15-21).

• *When ye therefore shall see the abomination of desolation, spoken of by Daniel the prophet, stand in the holy place, (whoso readeth, let him understand:) 16* **Then let them which be in Judaea flee into the mountains** (Matt 24:15,16*)*.

2. HER TIME: ***that they should feed her there a thousand two hundred and threescore days.*** This is three and one half years, but stated thusly to show that she will have *daily bread* (Matt 6:11). She will be sustained for each day.

THE DRAGON CAST OUT OF HEAVEN

(12:7) ***And there was war in heaven: Michael and his angels fought against the dragon; and the dragon fought and his angels,*** (12:8) ***And prevailed not; neither was their place found any more in heaven.*** (12:9 ***And the great dragon was cast out, that old serpent, called the Devil, and Satan, which deceiveth the whole world: he was cast out into the earth, and his angels were cast out with him.***

(12:10) ***And I heard a loud voice saying in heaven, Now is come salvation, and strength, and the kingdom of our God, and the power of his Christ: for the accuser of our brethren is cast down, which accused them before our God day and night.*** (12:11) ***And they overcame him by the blood of the Lamb, and by the word of their testimony; and they loved not their lives unto the death.***

(12:12) ***Therefore rejoice, ye heavens, and ye that dwell in them. Woe to the***

CHAPTER 12

inhabiters of the earth and of the sea! for the devil is come down unto you, having great wrath, because he knoweth that he hath but a short time.

Satan was cast from his residence in Heaven in past eternity yet he was still allowed access to Heaven. In Job 1 Satan along with other angels presents himself before God and accuses Job of fearing God because of God's goodness to him (Job 1:8-11). Thus along with the account in Eden, Satan from the beginning of human history is revealed as an accuser.

- ***Thou art the anointed cherub that covereth****; and I have set thee so: thou wast upon the holy mountain of God; thou hast walked up and down in the midst of the stones of fire. 15 **Thou wast perfect in thy ways from the day that thou wast created, till iniquity was found in thee*** (Ezek 28:14,15).
- *Now there was a day when the sons of God came to present themselves before the LORD, and Satan came also among them. 7 And the LORD said unto Satan, Whence comest thou? Then Satan answered the LORD, and said, From going to and fro in the earth, and from walking up and down in it* (Job 1:6,7).

Satan is now excluded from any further access to Heaven and with his activity limited to the earth, the earth becomes a virtual prison house for his wickedness and violence.

1. THE PLACE OF THE WAR. ***And there was war in heaven*** (12:7). A first battle had been waged shortly before which resulted in the angels of God being defeated (12:4; Dan 8:10); now it continues with a far better outcome.

2. THE PARTICIPANTS IN THE WAR. ***Michael and his angels fought against the dragon; and the dragon fought and his angels.*** With Gabriel, one of the two named angels in Scripture, and a host of other angels, the Lord is indeed the LORD of hosts (1 Sam 1:3; first reference) Satan also has angels. In this battle fought in the angelic sphere; righteousness will be shown to be the victor over wickedness.

- *And at that time **shall Michael stand up**, the great prince which standeth for the children of thy people: and there shall be a time of trouble, such as never was since there was a nation even to that same time* (Dan 12:1).
- *Then shall he say also unto them on the left hand, Depart from me, ye cursed, into everlasting fire, prepared for **the devil and his angels*** (Matt 25:41):

3. THE OUTCOME OF THE WAR. ***And prevailed not; neither was their place found any more in heaven. And the great dragon was cast out, that old serpent, called the Devil, and Satan, which deceiveth the whole world: he was cast out into the earth, and his angels were cast out with him*** (12:8,9). There was a great struggle but the victory fell to Michael and his angels. Satan and his angel would no longer have access to heaven.

Here, each of Satan's important titles are given. These, with the extent of his conquest demonstrate the greatness of his defeat. He is **the great dragon**, a term speaking of his murderous ruthlessness and also to his seven-headed empire during the Tribulation. He is **that old serpent**, a reference to his subtility and first conquest on earth in the Garden of Eden. He is **the Devil**, from the Greek *diabolos*, and the verb *diaballo*, which means to defame or slander. He is **Satan,** from Hebrew, and means "adversary. This name is found fourteen times in Job, and also in other OT passages (1 Chron 21:1; Psa 109:6; Zech 3:1-2).

As **Satan** he is seen in three characterizations. As *the accuser of the brethren* (12:10), he is in opposition to Christ as Priest; as the one who brings forth the Beast, he is in opposition to Christ as King; as bringing forth the False Prophet (Rev 13:11-18), he is opposed to Christ as Prophet. (from Walvoord quoting Coates).

THE BOOK OF REVELATION

Here is what has been his success, starkly stated: *which deceiveth the whole world* (*oikoumene*)! Thus six times in the New Testament, he is called *the prince* and *the god of this world* (cp. Jhn 14:30; 2 Cor 4:4).

4. THE TRIUMPHAL SONG THAT FOLLOWED THE WAR.
(1) HOW THE LORD IS ADORED.
And I heard a loud voice saying in heaven, Now is come salvation, and strength, and the kingdom of our God, and the power of his Christ (12:10). The *loud voice* is not identified. It is not the Lord himself or the angels for the loud voice mentions *the accuser of our brethren*. It may be the Twenty four Elders or the martyred saints. This latter had previously *cried with a loud voice* (6:10). Though the conflict was won by the angels, all the glory is given to the God of the Angels.

Now God has shown himself to be a mighty God. Now Christ has shown himself to be a strong and mighty Saviour. His own arm has brought salvation, and now His kingdom will be seen on earth in power (Matt 6:13; Rev 11:15).

The first of the four great things that have *come* is *salvation*. This is the deliverance and completion of God's Divine program. The second is *strength* (*dynamis*). The Lord is going to show His mighty arm as never before. The third is the proclamation that *the kingdom of our God* is now about to come. This leads us to the fourth, *and the power of his Christ*. The world has seen the power of evil in the world's governments and kingdoms; now they will see *the power* (*exousia*) *of his Christ*. *His Christ* parallels *His Anointed* in Psalm 2:2.

(2) HOW THE CONQUERED FOE IS DESCRIBED.
[1] BY HIS MALICE:
for the accuser of our brethren is cast down, which accused them before our God day and night. It is a mystery, but he has continually appeared before God as an adversary to believers; ever bringing indictments and accusations, whether true or false. Thus he accused Job, and thus he accused Joshua the high priest (Zech 3:1). Though he hates the presence of God, yet he is willing to appear there to accuse the people of God. Let us therefore ever bring this oppressive onslaught to Christ our High Priest and Advocate (Heb 4:14-16). Note that as Satan had accused believers before God *day and night*, so the Four Beasts, the cherubim, the living creatures cease not *day or night* to praise and ascribe holiness to the Lord (Rev 4:8).

[2] BY HIS DEFEAT.
And they overcame him by the blood of the Lamb, and by the word of their testimony; and they loved not their lives unto the death (12:11). The conflict is both defensive and offensive; trusting fully in the Shed Blood of Christ and carrying out diligently the Great Commission. The accusations of Satan are nullified by the Blood of the Lamb which renders the believer pure (1 Jhn 1:7-9). And, when the love of life stood in competition with their loyalty to Christ; they clung to Christ rather than life. The martyrs of 6:10 are especially in view here. The foundation of all victory and the only title of inheritance is the Atonement (Rom 5:11).

(3) HOW THERE IS A GREAT DIVIDE OF REJOICING AND WAILING.
[1] IN HEAVEN.
Therefore rejoice, ye heavens, and ye that dwell in them (12:12). This call is made poignant by the likelihood that it was made by either the Twenty four Elders or the martyrs – two recent dwellers on earth.

[2] ON EARTH.
Woe to the inhabiters of the earth and of the sea! for the devil is come down unto you, having great wrath, because he knoweth that he hath but a short time. It was bad without Satan dwelling directly upon earth, and more so as *the prince of the power of the air* (Eph 2:2); how much then will it be when he is confined to the earth. Earth is not only now facing the wrath of God (Rev 14:10,11), but also the wrath of Satan. For, though his malice is chiefly bent against the servants of God, yet he is an enemy

CHAPTER 12

and hater of all mankind and all that the Creator has made. He will now seek to destroy every vestige of the Creator's handwork.

The rage of Satan grows so much the greater as he is now limited in both place and time. He now especially turns his gaze to the *wilderness* where the *woman* has fled. Contrast: When Satan comes to earth it is *Woe to the inhabiters of the earth*. When Christ came to earth it was: *Peace, good will toward men* (Lk 2:14).

Note: The word for the **wrath** of Satan here is *thymos*. The word for God's wrath in Revelation is *orge*. This is the stronger of the two words. That for Satan means a strong passion or emotion. It is an emotional rather than a rational state of mind and stems from Satan's awareness that his days are numbered. (see Walvoord).

THE FLIGHT OF THE WOMAN

(12:13) *And when the dragon saw that he was cast unto the earth, he persecuted the woman which brought forth the man child.* (12:14) *And to the woman were given two wings of a great eagle, that she might fly into the wilderness, into her place, where she is nourished for a time, and times, and half a time, from the face of the serpent.*

(12:15) *And the serpent cast out of his mouth water as a flood after the woman, that he might cause her to be carried away of the flood.* (12:16) *And the earth helped the woman, and the earth opened her mouth, and swallowed up the flood which the dragon cast out of his mouth.*

(12:17) *And the dragon was wroth with the woman, and went to make war with the remnant of her seed, which keep the commandments of God, and have the testimony of Jesus Christ.*

1. SATAN PURSUES THE WOMAN, THE SOURCE OF ANTISEMITISM. *And when the dragon saw that he was cast unto the earth, he persecuted the woman which brought forth the man child* (12:13). First on the agenda after Satan is cast out of Heaven; *Destroy the Jewish People*! Here is the source and conclusion of Antisemitism. This coincides with the Antichrist setting up his image at middle of the Tribulation. As we have seen, our Lord warned of this time (Matt 24:15-22).

* *When ye therefore shall see the abomination of desolation, spoken of by Daniel the prophet, stand in the holy place, (whoso readeth, let him understand:) 16* **Then let them which be in Judaea flee into the mountains** *(Matt 24:15-22).*

(1) AN ESCAPE IS PROVIDED. *And to the woman were given two wings of a great eagle, that she might fly into the wilderness, into her place, where she is nourished for a time, and times, and half a time, from the face of the serpent* (12:14). God conveys the Jewish people as on *eagles' wings* (Exod 19:4; Deut 32:10,11), into a place of safety. Many have thought it is Petra, but we do not know. It is a strange inaccessible place, for she will be there for three and one half years *from the face of the serpent*; yet the serpent will soon know the place.

* *Ye have seen what I did unto the Egyptians, and how* **I bare you on eagles' wings**, *and brought you unto myself* (Exod 19:4).
* *He found him in a desert land, and in the waste howling wilderness; he led him about, he instructed him, he kept him as the apple of his eye.11 As an eagle stirreth up her nest, fluttereth over her young, spreadeth abroad her wings, taketh them,* **beareth them on her wings** (Deut 32:10,11).

THE BOOK OF REVELATION

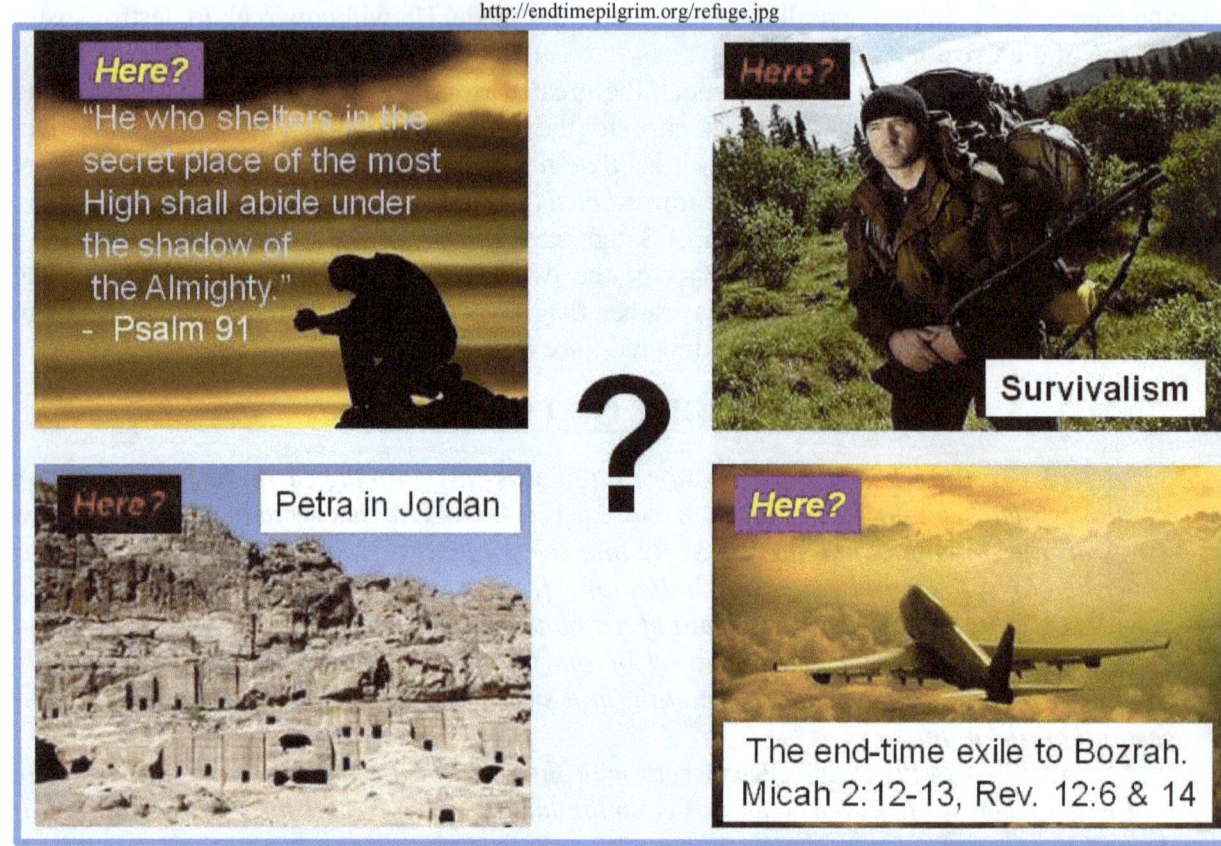

The Flight and Hiding Place of Israel During the Tribulation

There may be an airlift or other means of ferrying out the fleeing Jews. This will be provided by Gentiles converted through the preaching of the 144,000. The first question that Christ as Judge will ask the survivors of the Tribulation in the Judgement of the Nations will concern their *kindness shown toward the Jewish People* during the Tribulation. Then many more will help the fleeing Jews than helped when they sought to escape Nazi Germany!

> • ***And before him shall be gathered all nations***: *and he shall separate them one from another, as a shepherd divideth his sheep from the goats: 33 And he shall set the sheep on his right hand, but the goats on the left.*
> *34* ***Then shall the King say unto them on his right hand****, Come, ye blessed of my Father, inherit the kingdom prepared for you from the foundation of the world: 35 For I was an hungred, and ye gave me meat: I was thirsty, and ye gave me drink: I was a stranger, and ye took me in: 36 Naked, and ye clothed me: I was sick, and ye visited me: I was in prison, and ye came unto me.*
> *37* ***Then shall the righteous answer him****, saying, Lord, when saw we thee an hungred, and fed thee? or thirsty, and gave thee drink? 38 When saw we thee a stranger, and took thee in? or naked, and clothed thee? 39 Or when saw we thee sick, or in prison, and came unto thee?*
> *40* ***And the King shall answer and say unto them****, Verily I say unto you,* ***Inasmuch as ye have done it unto one of the least of these my brethren, ye have done it unto me*** *(Matt 25:32-40).*

(2) AN ENTRAPMENT IS CONTRIVED.

[1] HOW IT COMES. *And the serpent cast out of his mouth water as a flood after the woman, that he might cause her to be carried away of the flood* (12:15). *The enemy shall come as a flood* (Isa 59:19). However, this is flood of *water*. Satan is *the*

CHAPTER 12

prince of the power of the air (Eph 2:2). On two occasions it was likely Satan who raised the *tempest* when the disciples were crossing the Sea of Galilee (Matt 8:23-25; 14:22-24). In this passage before us Satan seeks to destroy the Jews fleeing Judea with a violent tempest of storm and prolonged torrential rain.

For Israel *the end thereof shall be with a flood* (Dan 9:26). Note that this *flood* occurs at Midpoint of the Tribulation. This is when the seven year treaty with Antichrist is broken and when Satan is cast out of Heaven. From the passage below one might wonder if, *poured upon the desolate* (Dan 9:27) has any relation to, *the end thereof shall be with a flood* (9:26).

- *And after threescore and two weeks shall Messiah be cut off, but not for himself: and the people of **the prince that shall come** shall destroy the city and the sanctuary; and **the end thereof shall be with a flood**, and unto the end of the war desolations are determined. 27 And **he shall confirm the covenant with many for one week**: and **in the midst of the week** he shall cause the sacrifice and the oblation to cease, and for the overspreading of abominations he shall make it desolate, even until the consummation, and that determined shall be **poured upon the desolate*** (Dan 9:26,27).

[2] HOW IT IS NULLIFIED. **And the earth helped the woman, and the earth opened her mouth, and swallowed up the flood which the dragon cast out of his mouth** (12:16). It will happen just as stated. The ground will open to receive the flood waters. Satan's attempt at a *final solution* regarding the Jewish People has been thwarted. Thus like Elijah at the brook Cherith, or Israel in the wilderness (perhaps in part *this same wilderness*) living on manna (cp. 12:14) the nation has been spared.

2. SATAN PURSUES THE WOMAN'S SEED.

(1) THE DRAGON'S RAGE. **And the dragon was wroth with the woman, and went to make war with the remnant of her seed** (12:17). This appears to be scattered Jewish believers not geographically with this main group just described. They will also become the object of Satan's wrath.

(2) THE REMNANT'S FAITH: **which keep the commandments of God, and have the testimony of Jesus Christ.** As Israel is brought through the *fires* (Zech 13:9) during the *Time of Jacob's Trouble* (Jer 30:7), her faith will become increasingly purified (Job 23:10). The extent of her fires are described further at the close of Zechariah 13.

- *And it shall come to pass, that in all the land, saith the LORD, **two parts therein shall be cut off and die**; but the third shall be left therein. 9 And **I will bring the third part through the fire**, and will refine them as silver is refined, and will try them as gold is tried: they shall call on my name, and I will hear them: I will say, It is my people: and they shall say, The LORD is my God* (Zech 13:8,9).

Thus the Chapter ends with the great fact of the ages: Satan hates and make war against those who believe and hold to the Bible; and that especially when God's Ancient People do. This Chapter has demonstrated a final stage in Satan's warfare before the Return of Christ. The events recorded are entirely in the future. For comparison, note some of the key stages of his warfare before the First Coming of Christ.

So Satan from the first sought to make impossible the birth of the promised Redeemer. His action explains the corruption that necessitated the destruction of the human race in the Flood; the hindered birth of Isaac; the murderous animosity of Ishmael and Esau; the edict of Pharaoh; the rebellions in the Wilderness; the idolatry of Solomon; the murder of the Royal family by Athaliah; the curse upon Jehoiachim; and the slaughter of the Bethlehem children by Herod. (Williams).

2. The Trumpet Judgements and Other Events   8-14
   a. *The Seventh Seal is Opened   8:1-6*
   b. *The Six Trumpets Blown: Woeful Wrath (8:13)   8:7-9:21*
   c. *The Herald Angel Announces the Seventh Trumpet 10 (v7)*
   d. *The Two Witnesses   11:1-13*
   f. *The Sun-clothed Woman, The Dragon, The Manchild   12*
   g. *The Beast and the False Prophet   13*

g. The Beast and the False Prophet   13

CHAPTER 13

THE BEAST

(13:1) And I stood upon the sand of the sea, and saw a beast rise up out of the sea, having seven heads and ten horns, and upon his horns ten crowns, and upon his heads the name of blasphemy. (13:2) And the beast which I saw was like unto a leopard, and his feet were as the feet of a bear, and his mouth as the mouth of a lion: and the dragon gave him his power, and his seat, and great authority.

(13:3) And I saw one of his heads as it were wounded to death; and his deadly wound was healed: and all the world wondered after the beast. (13:4) And they worshipped the dragon which gave power unto the beast: and they worshipped the beast, saying, Who is like unto the beast? who is able to make war with him?

(13:5) And there was given unto him a mouth speaking great things and blasphemies; and power was given unto him to continue forty and two months.
(13:6) And he opened his mouth in blasphemy against God, to blaspheme his name, and his tabernacle, and them that dwell in heaven. (13:7) And it was given unto him to make war with the saints, and to overcome them: and power was given him over all kindreds, and tongues, and nations.

(13:8) And all that dwell upon the earth shall worship him, whose names are not written in the book of life of the Lamb slain from the foundation of the world. (13:9) If any man have an ear, let him hear. (13:10) He that leadeth into captivity shall go into captivity: he that killeth with the sword must be killed with the sword. Here is the patience and the faith of the saints.

Christ came to save the world, we are now introduced to that one who during the Tribulation will seek to destroy the world. He is perhaps best known as the Antichrist, and everything about him is opposed to Christ. Here, however, whatever the world thinks of him, he is called the *Beast*. Both his empire, and he himself are here interlocked as one and the same. His empire is the revived Roman Empire. Both the man and the empire are energized by Satan.

I. THE ORIGIN OF THE BEAST. *And I stood upon the sand of the sea, and saw a beast rise up out of the sea* (13:1). The *sea* may refer to *peoples, and multitudes, and nations and tongues* (17:15). In this chapter *the sea* clearly parallels the *earth* from which the False Prophet arises (13:11). In our study of the *little horn* in Daniel 7 and 8 we saw the likelihood of the Antichrist's inauspicious origin from one of the lesser Gentile nation. Virtually everywhere else in Scripture *the sea* refers to the Mediterranean Sea. Perhaps he will come from the Southern European area bordering on the Mediterranean where Alexander arose. But also, he will bear a relationship to strong nations who in the latter days exercise power in the Mediterranean. The island of Patmos was in Grecian waters. John sees both the man and his empire rise out of the sea.

THE BOOK OF REVELATION

**The Beast Empire: Seven Heads, Ten Horns, Ten Crowns
Appearance of a Leopard, Feet of a Bear, Mouth of a Lion**

II. THE SYMBOLIC DESCRIPTION OF THE BEAST: *having <u>seven heads</u> and <u>ten horns,</u> and upon his horns ten crowns, and upon his heads the name of blasphemy. And the beast which I saw was <u>like unto a leopard</u>, and his feet were as <u>the feet of a bear</u>, and his mouth as <u>the mouth of a lion</u>: and the dragon gave him his power, and his seat, and great authority.* (13:1,2). Note that these same symbols appear in Daniel 7 and Revelation 12.

> • (7:3) *And **four great beasts came up from the sea**, diverse one from another. (7:4) The first was like **a lion**, and had eagle's wings: I beheld till the wings thereof were plucked, and it was lifted up from the earth, and made stand upon the feet as a man, and a man's heart was given to it. (7:5) And behold another beast, a second, like to **a bear**, and it raised up itself on one side, and it had three ribs in the mouth of it between the teeth of it: and they said thus unto it, Arise, devour much flesh. (7:6) After this I beheld, and lo another, like **a leopard**, which had upon the back of it four wings of a fowl; the beast had also four heads; and dominion was given to it. (7:7) After this I saw in the night visions, and behold **a fourth beast**, dreadful and terrible, and strong exceedingly; and it had great iron teeth: it devoured and brake in pieces, and stamped the residue with the feet of it: and it was diverse from all the beasts that were before it; and it had **ten horns**. (7:8) I considered the horns, and, behold, there came up among them another **little horn**, before whom there were three of the first horns plucked up by*

CHAPTER 13

the roots: and, behold, in this horn were eyes like the eyes of man, and a mouth speaking great things (Dan 7:3-8).

• *And there appeared another wonder in heaven; and behold a great red dragon, having **seven heads** and **ten horns**, and **seven crowns upon his heads*** (Rev 12:3).

The Beast (Antichrist) will accept *the kingdoms of the world* which the True Messiah refused (Lk 4: 5). Therefore as Satan previously controlled these Seven Heads and Ten Horns (Rev 12:3) they now have been received by the Beast

1. HIS *SEVEN HEADS*: **having seven heads.** The Antichrist will be a Roman (Dan 9:26), and his empire will be the revived Roman Empire (Dan 2:40-45) but from what we see here and in Daniel he (his empire also) will be *utterly* a COMPOSITE MAN ! He bears the marks of the of the **Lion**, **Bear** and **Leopard**, and he (with his empire) has **Seven Heads** and **Ten Horns**. The *Seven Heads* are generally thought to be the seven great empires of the past: Egypt, Assyria, Babylon, Persia, Greece, Rome and Revived Rome revived Rome of the last days. For example, he appears to be linked with Assyria and Greece (Micah 5:5; Zech 9:13). Nevertheless, as shown in the notes on 12:3, there is a fundamental problem with this view. The Seven Heads are not past history! They are not the great empires of the past but seven powerful nations that give total support to the Antichrist and form the core of his Revived Roman Empire during the Tribulation. Through them he will have worldwide dominion.

2. HIS *TEN HORNS*: **and ten horns.** A horn has to have a head! The general view is to separate the Ten Horns from the Seven Heads, or (usually) view the Seventh Head (Revived Rome) as bearing the Ten Horns. This means that that the Six Heads bear a *historical* (six empires of the past beginning with ancient Egypt) rather than a *current* link to the Seventh Head. When the Red Dragon (12:3) is cast to earth at the middle of the Tribulation, he has *then and there* Seven Heads. Further, they are **crowned** Heads! They are current. *All* that takes place in Revelation 12 is in the future Tribulation. The great historical empires lost their crowns long ago. What now encompasses the earth is Revived Rome whose core power has developed into and is composed of Seven Heads (cp. *ten toes*: Dan 2:40-45).

Concerning the relationship of the Heads to the Horns, note again what was said in the comments on Revelation 12:3.

Walvoord offers an alternative view in which he appears to equate the seven heads with the horn each one bears (they are not separated). That is, with reference to Daniel 7, there were ten heads originally with each having a horn. Three of the head-horns were defeated by the Antichrist (Dan 7:8). Nevertheless the three horns of the conquered regions remained influential under the authority of the Antichrist and also received a crown (Rev 13:1). Walvoord says:

"From the similar description given in 13:1 and the parallel reference in Daniel 7:7,8, 24, it is clear that the revived Roman Empire is in view. The seven heads and ten horns refer to the original ten kingdoms of which three were subdued by the little horn of Daniel 7:8, who is to be identified with the world ruler of the great tribulation who reigns over the revived Roman Empire."

3. HIS *NAME OF BLASPHEMY*: **and upon his heads the name of blasphemy.** Here is blasphemy and here is also unity. There will be no "multi-faith". Upon the Seven Heads that support the Antichrist, there is but one name of blasphemy. We do not know that name, nor do we need to know.

4. HIS THREEFOLD APPEARANCE. ***And the beast which I saw was like unto a leopard, and his feet were as the feet of a bear, and his mouth as the mouth of a lion*** (13:2).

The Lion, Bear and Leopard in Daniel 7 represent latter day nations that will be dominant in the Mediterranean (the *middle of the earth* sea). Here in Revelation 13, we see them as they become *composite* in the kingdom of the Beast.

As a *Leopard*: ***And the beast which I saw was like unto a leopard*** (13:2). Though many believe the leopard represents Germany; in the Daniel 7 notes reasons were given for a Muslim identification. The Antichrist will not be a Muslim but a Roman. He will assimilate the Muslims and to an extent be characterised by their ferocity.

As a *Bear*: ***and his feet were as the feet of a bear.*** The bear in Daniel 7 were the Russian and Slavic peoples. He will not be Russian, but will have the crushing military might of Russia's nuclear arsenal (this will be after Russia's defeat, Ezek 38,39).

As a *Lion*: ***and his mouth as the mouth of a lion.*** As he has dominated the Muslim and Slavic peoples, he will dominate the English speaking peoples. English will be the *lingua franca*.

His Power from the *Dragon*: ***and the dragon gave him his power, and his seat, and great authority.*** In order to supress *the world* the Beast will be empowered by *the god of this world* (2 Cor 4:4).

COMPARING BEAST'S DESCRIPTION IN REVELATION 12,13 AND DANIEL 7, 8: A DEVELOPING AND COMPLEMENTARY PICTURE OF THE SAME PERSON AND EMPIRE

DANIEL 7
Preceded by the Lion, Bear, Leopard
One Head and Ten Horns, Three Horns Plucked (no crowns)

DANIEL 8
Symbolism from a different standpoint
The Antichrist arises out of one of the four divisions of Alexander's empire; i.e. the eastern side of the Roman Empire

REVELATION 12
No mention of the Lion, Bear, Leopard
Seven Crowned Heads and Ten Horns

REVELATION 13
Composite with the Leopard, Bear, Lion
Seven Heads and Ten Crowned Horns ("carries" Papal Rome for a while, Rev 17:7 ,16)

III, THE DEADLY WOUND OF THE BEAST. ***And I saw one of his heads as it were wounded to death; and his deadly wound was healed: and all the world wondered after the beast*** (13:3).

1. HIS COUNTRY OF ORIGIN MAY SUFFER A DEATH WOUND. ***And I saw <u>one of his heads</u> as it were wounded to death.*** Some have speculated that Germany which had suffered such a catastrophic defeat in WWII would be an example of this.

2. HE HIMSELF WILL SUFFER A DEATH WOUND: ***and <u>his</u> deadly wound was healed.*** Having suffered an assassination attempt, as the Antichrist he will seek to emulate the Slain Lamb (Rev 5:6).

- *whose deadly wound was healed* (13:12).
- *which had the wound by a sword, and did live* (13:14).

CHAPTER 13

3. HIS RECOVERY WILL BE A WONDER TO THE WORLD: *and all the world wondered after the beast.* To say as some have that the world's wonder is caused by the reviving of the Roman Empire after it was dissolved 1453 is highly unlikely. This *deadly wound* is as current as todays newspaper; it will not make the world think back to the distant past.

IV. THE RELIGION OF THE BEAST.
1. HE WILL BE THE OBJECT OF WORSHIP. *And they worshipped the dragon which gave power unto the beast: and they worshipped the beast, saying, Who is like unto the beast? who is able to make war with him*(13:4)? What the Bible calls a *beast* will be so attractive that he will be universally accepted as the promised Prince of Peace and restorer of humanity. He will claim to be *God*, and the world will accept the claim and worship him Here and then beginning at verse 11, we find a *Satanic trinity*: the Dragon, Beast and False Prophet.

Now "at last" Satan as *the god of this world* (2 Cor 4:4), is worshipped by the world as *god*. The final form of apostasy is the worship of Satan himself who from the beginning set out a program in which he seeks to be *like God* (Isa 14:14). What a terrible place the earth will be when it gathers to give homage to the Dragon and the Beast.

Note: In Eden, the Serpent was believed but not worshipped, now the Dragon is both believed and worshipped (Govett).

2. HE WILL LEAD A GREAT PROCLAMATION OF BLASPHEMY. *And there was given unto him a mouth speaking great things and blasphemies; and power was given unto him to continue forty and two months. And he opened his mouth in blasphemy against God, to blaspheme his name, and his tabernacle, and them that dwell in heaven* (13:5,6). When their tongues are not worshipping the Beast, they turn their energies toward Heaven. Here blasphemy thunders from across the earth toward the God of Heaven and toward the inhabitants of Heaven. Blasphemy is not an incidental feature of the Beast's kingdom but *its feature*. As Satan's mouthpiece he utters the ultimate in vile blasphemy.

* *I considered the horns, and, behold, there came up among them another little horn, before whom there were three of the first horns plucked up by the roots: and, behold, in this horn were eyes like the eyes of man, and **a mouth speaking great things** (Dan 7:8).*
* *I beheld then because of **the voice of the great words** which the horn spake: I beheld even till the beast was slain, and his body destroyed, and given to the burning flame* (Dan 7:11).
* *And **he shall speak great words against the most High**, and shall wear out the saints of the most High, and think to change times and laws: and they shall be given into his hand until a time and times and the dividing of time* (Dan 7:25).

The fact that we are told that they do it is bad enough; we can be thankful that the Scriptures do not reveal what they say. We are thankful that we are told how long this "religious service" will last - *forty and two months*. That is *too long*, but not very long in comparison with *the eternal worship* in which the righteous are engaged (cp. 5:13). The saints in Heaven are far above the reach of the blasphemous clatter on earth. All that Satan can do is blaspheme, but the saints on earth are *more exposed* as we now see.

3. HE WILL SUPPRESS ALL WHO RESIST. *And it was given unto him to make war with the saints, and to overcome them: and power was given him over all kindreds, and tongues, and nations* (13:7). The Beast rages at Heaven, with no effect except to record the fact, but now ominously he seeks a *final solution* against believers on earth. Daniel records that the Little horn will *devour the whole earth, and shall tread it down, and break it in*

pieces (Dan 7:23). This has been the dream of countless rulers in the past; with the Beast now empowered by Satan it will be accomplished.

4. HIS WORSHIP WILL LEAD TO PERDITION. *And all that dwell upon the earth shall worship him, whose names are not written in the book of life of the Lamb slain from the foundation of the world* (13:8). The oppression is dire, but not nearly so dire as for those who surrender to the Beast's worship. The Book of Life enrols the names of all believers (cp. Rev 3:5; 17:8; 20:12,15; 21:27; 22:19; cp. Lk 10:20; Phil 4:3). *For Jesus knew from the beginning who they were that believed not* (Jhn 6:63). They are: Redeemed by His Blood, Recorded in His Book, Sealed by His Spirit.

Note: It is believed correct to distinguish between the *Lambs Book of Life* (Rev 21:27) and the *Book of Life* in general. The Book of Life contains the names of all who will live on the earth; their names are *blotted out* when they die without being saved. Thus there are "gaps" in this book (Rev 3:5; 22:19). The *Lamb's Book of Life* contains only the names of the saved.

V. THE EXHORTATION TO HEAR. *If any man have an ear, let him hear. He that leadeth into captivity shall go into captivity: he that killeth with the sword must be killed with the sword. Here is the patience and the faith of the saints* (13:9,10). Despite the universal warfare against believers during the Tribulation, it will come to a conclusion; and unlike our day they will be able to count the days to that glorious consummation when Christ returns in glory (13:5).

At this crisis is heard for the last time the solemn words that all who hear these revelations will be held responsible. The invitation, *If any man have an ear, let him hear*, is an added emphasis to take careful heed to what has just been said. It is an invitation to now make a decision (I Kng 18:21). These words are found frequently in the Gospels (Matt 11:15; 13:9,43; Mk 4:9,23; 7:16; Lk 8:8; 14:35). They are found in the invitation to the Seven Churches (Rev 2,3). There we find the additional words to *hear what the Spirit says unto the churches*. The omission of the phrase **unto the churches** in 13:9 demonstrates the truth that the Church, the Body of Christ is not on earth at this time and has been raptured. There is now no Church to invite.

To the suffering saints on earth verse 10 represents the principle of divine retribution. Those who persecute the saints and lead them into captivity must in turn suffer the righteous wrath of God. (Gen 9:6 Matt 5:38; 26:52; Rom 12:19; Gal 6:7). The same truth which serves as an encouragement to the saints acts as a warning to the persecutors. Their ultimate doom is assured after their brief period of power under reign of the Beast (Rev 13:5; 16:6; 18:2,3,5-8, 20; 19:20). Their choice has been very, very foolish.

THE FALSE PROPHET

(13:11) *And I beheld another beast coming up out of the earth; and he had two horns like a lamb, and he spake as a dragon.*

(13:12) *And he exerciseth all the power of the first beast before him, and causeth the earth and them which dwell therein to worship the first beast, whose deadly wound was healed.* (13:13) *And he doeth great wonders, so that he maketh fire come down from heaven on the earth in the sight of men,*

(13:14) *And deceiveth them that dwell on the earth by the means of those miracles which he had power to do in the sight of the beast; saying to them that dwell on the earth, that they should make an image to the beast, which had the wound by a sword, and did live.* (13:15) *And he had power to give life unto the image of the beast, that the image of the beast should both speak, and cause that as many as would not worship the image of the beast should be killed.*

CHAPTER 13

(13:16) *And he causeth all, both small and great, rich and poor, free and bond, to receive a mark in their right hand, or in their foreheads: (13:17) And that no man might buy or sell, save he that had the mark, or the name of the beast, or the number of his name. (13:18) Here is wisdom. Let him that hath understanding count the number of the beast: for it is the number of a man; and his number is Six hundred threescore and six.*

We have seen the first two members of the Satanic trinity, we now have the third described, who as the Holy Spirit to Christ, directs the world's attention to the Antichrist.

I. THE PEDIGREE THAT *INTRODUCES* THE FALSE PROPHET.

1. HIS ENIGMATIC ORIGIN. *And I beheld another beast coming up out of the earth* (13:11). This False Prophet appears four times (13:11; 16:13; 19:20; 20:10). He will be the great Priest of the future. The worship he will introduce will be based on the resurrection of the First Beast and he will accredit this worship by great miracles. Man is superstitious. He demands miracles rather than truth from the Bible.

He is called *another beast*. He is destructive to the true flock of God. He shares something of the same nature as the First Beast. He is called *the false prophet* (19:20; 20:10). He may be the head of the apostate and *left behind* church during the first half of the Tribulation. With the rise of the First Beast, the apostate church is destroyed (Rev 17:16), and the worship of the world is directed to him. The Second Beast survives the destruction and he now promotes the Antichrist in this transition.

He also is seen coming up *out of the earth*. This parallels and contrasts with *the sea* from which the Antichrist comes (13:1). Does he come from the *Land* of Israel? Certainly that would give him a "religious edge". However, it far from certain and would seem unlikely as both beasts will seek to exterminate the Jewish People. One thing is certain, he does not come from *above*. Compare Christ's words, and the words of the *Witch of Endor* to King Saul, and the four latter day powers of Daniel 7.

- *He that cometh from above is above all:* **he that is of the earth is earthly, and speaketh of the earth:** *he that cometh from heaven is above all* (Jhn 3:31).
- *And the king said unto her, Be not afraid: for what sawest thou? And the woman said unto Saul,* **I saw gods ascending out of the earth** (1 Sam 28:13).
- *These great beasts, which are four, are four kings, which shall* **arise out of the earth** (Dan 7:17).

Note: Messiah in the person of His angelic deputy, planted His feet *upon the sea and upon the earth* (Rev 10:2). Satan must also claim both realms. This in the view of Williams is why the Beasts are seen coming out of the sea and the land (13:1,11). It therefore an attempt to claim *total dominion*.

2. HIS SYMBOLIC APPEARANCE: *and he had two horns like a lamb.* "At first sight" he will seem to be a kind, endearing man, yet also with his horns he has undeniable authority. Do his two horns represent the eastern (Orthodox) and western side (Roman) of the Catholic Church? He will not like the first beast have *a look more stout than his fellows* (Dan 7:20).

3. HIS FORMIDABLE SPEECH: *and he spake as a dragon.* Any pretence or doubt as to his true nature is removed as soon as he speaks. He is *of his father the devil* (Jhn 8:44).

II. THE MIRACLES *PERFORMED* BY THE FALSE PROPHET.

1. THEIR FIRST PURPOSE. *And he exerciseth all the power of the first beast before him, and causeth the earth and them which dwell therein to worship the first beast, whose deadly wound was healed* (13:12). He has the same demonic power of the Beast, but all is for and in behalf of the Beast's *person* and *work*. As the Holy Spirit exalts the Person

and Work of Christ on the Cross, so he will do likewise for this one *whose deadly wound was healed.* He will be like Johannes and Jambres the magicians of Pharaoh who withstood Moses with their satanic miracles (cp. 2 Tim 3:8).

2. THEIR SECOND PURPOSE. *And he doeth great wonders, so that he maketh fire come down from heaven on the earth in the sight of men* (13:13). As the magicians replicated the miracles of Moses and Aaron, he will replicate the miracles of the Two Witnesses (11:5). These may seek to be an imitation of Pentecost (Acts 2:3), or of Elijah's miracles (2 Kng 1:10-12), or especially that of the two witnesses (Rev 11:5). The Scriptures indicate that the devil does have power to perform miracles and that by their use he deceives people into worshiping the Beast. (Walvoord).

The False Prophet and Two Witnesses will be in constant conflict on or near the Temple Mount for the entire second half of the Tribulation. This now brings us to the third purpose for his miracles.

III. THE IMAGE *PROPAGATED* BY THE FALSE PROPHET.

1. IT WILL BE BUILT BY THE ENTIRE WORLD. *And deceiveth them that dwell on the earth by the means of those miracles which he had power to do in the sight of the beast saying to them that dwell on the earth, that they should make an image to the beast, which had the wound by a sword, and did live* (13:14). On the basis of the impression the previous miracles have made makes on *them that dwell on the earth* an image to the Beast will be made. And for the third time in this chapter we are told it will be to him which *had the wound by a sword and did live.*

The world will be whipped into a fever pitch for this project. All the world will likely participate by being taxed to bring about the construction of this new "wonder". Highly trained workmen will be swiftly gathered to insure its rapid completion. We can only wonder what it will be and look like! The image that Nebuchadnezzar set up at the beginning of the *Times of the Gentiles* is a forerunner (Dan 3). This will be the final act of blasphemy in the Times of the Gentiles (Lk 21:24). The image is mentioned three times in this chapter and seven further times in Revelation (14:9,11; 15:2; 16:2; 19:20; 20:4). As Walvoord says, "The image is the center of the false worship and the focal point of the final state of apostasy, the acme of the idolatry which has been the false religion of so many generations." Perhaps this is the image that the Psalmist is speaking of:

- *Thou shalt despise their image* (Psa 73:20).

2. IT WILL BE ENLIVENED BY SATANIC POWER. *And he had power to give life unto the image of the beast, that the image of the beast should both speak.* (13:15). In this it will contrast with all other idolatry and that which was previously mentioned.

- *And the rest of the men which were not killed by these plagues yet repented not of the works of their hands, that they should not worship devils, and **idols of gold, and silver, and brass, and stone, and of wood: which neither can see, nor hear, nor walk*** (Rev 9:20).

3. IT WILL BE WORSHIPPED UNDER CRUEL DURESS: *and cause that as many as would not worship the image of the beast should be killed.* The events on the Plain of Dura in Daniel 3 at the beginning of the *Times of the Gentiles* (Lk 21:24) were a foreshadowing of how the *Times of the Gentiles* will end. But there is a second thing that the False Prophet will *cause*. In fact, note the strange way it is stated: the Image of the will *both speak and cause....*

CHAPTER 13

IV. THE PAYMENT SYSTEM *ENFORCED* BY THE FALSE PROPHET.

    1. THE MARK. *And he causeth all, both small and great, rich and poor, free and bond, to receive a mark in their right hand, or in their foreheads* (13:16). The need for security will me the initial means by which *he causeth all*... In this current day great effort is being made to find a more secure way of paying for daily purchases. It is a foregone conclusion that soon there will be the widespread use of a tiny electronic implant on the hand. The security benefits of such a step seem almost overwhelmingly reasonable. *A more onerous means of compliance will follow*!

    2. THE TRAP. *And that no man might buy or sell, save he that had the mark, or the name of the beast, or the number of his name* (13:17). For a considerable time there has been more than enough technology in place to enable immediate implementation.

    3. THE NUMBER. *Here is wisdom. Let him that hath understanding count the number of the beast: for it is the number of a man; and his number is Six hundred threescore and six* (13:18). Six in the Scripture is man's number. He was created on the sixth day (Gen 1). He was to work six days and rest the seventh. Six is the best man can do in his own strength, but whether it is six, or six six or six six six, it will always fall short of seven.

- With the beginning of the Times of the Gentiles and the setting up of Nebuchadnezzar's image we see this number: The image was *sixty cubits high* and *six cubits broad* and orchestrated by *six musical instruments*,
- It is the number that appears on the armament of Goliath in his battle against David. Goliath was *six cubits in height*, his *spear's head weighed six shekels* and he had *six pieces of armour*. (1 Sam 17:4-7).
- It is remarkable that as Scripture points strongly to the Antichrist being a Roman (see authors' notes on Daniel 7) *the first six Roman Numerals* **add up to 666**.

$$I, V, X, L, C, D = 666$$

- It is also remarkable that as this chapter calls the Antichrist the *Beast*, and the name Beast when referring to Antichrist is found *36 times* in Revelation, *the numerals 1 to 36 when added up equal 666*!

$$1+2+3+4+5+6+7+8+9+10+11+12+13+14+15+16+17+18+19+20+21+22+23+24+25+26+27+28+29+30+31+32+33+34+35+36 = 666$$

The means of computing the number of the Beast would have to be accessible to the world at large during the time of the end. It would not be a highly complex calculation. It would have to be based on a language known to most in the world. This seemingly rules out Biblical Greek and Hebrew, or Latin. As the identity of the Antichrist will not be revealed until after the Rapture (2 Thess 2:7,8), it is certainly obvious that his number or perhaps even the specific means of computing the number may remain unknown until then. Nevertheless there is a simple approach that has received considerable attention.

For many years students of Bible Prophecy have noted that if English is used and if A is made to equal 6, and if each of the following letters is increased by 6 the results can be interesting. If valuations derived from A=6 B=12 C=18....X=144 Y=150 Z=156 are applied to a number of words the following will equal 666.

THE BOOK OF REVELATION

666 WORDS DERIVED BY INCREASING EACH LETTER IN THE ALPHABET BY SIX

PEOPLE SIN = 666 (Rom 3:23)

MARK OF BEAST = 666 (Rev 13:16-18, 14:9-11, 16:2, 19:20)

COMPUTER = 666 (Rev 13:14-18)

MONETARY = 666 (Rev 13:17: *And that no man might buy or sell, save he that had the mark, or the name of the beast, or the number of his name.*

CALCULATION = 666 (Rev 13:18: *...count* [calculate] *the number of the beast...*

NEW YORK = 666 (Rev 18)

WITCHCRAFT = 666

NECROMANCY = 666

SORCERIES = 666

LUSTFUL = 666 (1 Jhn 2:16,17)

ILLUSION = 666 (2 Thess 2:8-12)

LUCIFER HELL = 666 (Isaiah 14:12-15)

LUCIFER HADES = 666 (See Note 1)

DEVIL SHEOL = 666 (See Note 2)

888 WORD VALUES

THE TRINITY = 888 (1 John 5:7)

MESSIAH JESUS = 888 (In Koine Greek the name "JESUS" also equals 888)

THE KING JESUS = 888 (1 Tim 6:15; Rev 17:14, 19:16)

FINISHED CROSS = 888 (John 19:30)

THE LION OF JUDAH = 888 (Rev 5:5)

THE LORD'S TIME = 888

THE HOUSE OF GOD = 888 (1 Tim 3:15)

SCRIPTURES = 888
    From http://www.angelfire.com/nt/baptist/Prophecy/666Calculator.html

In Chapter Thirteen (a number which in its first use in Scripture speaks of *rebellion*, Gen 14:4) we have the ultimate rebellion and wickedness that will reside on earth during the second half of the Tribulation: the Dragon, Beast and False Prophet - the *Satanic Trinity*.

2. *The Trumpet Judgements and Other Events   8-14*
a. The Seventh Seal is Opened   8:1-6

CHAPTER 13

b. The Six Trumpets Blown: Woeful Wrath (8:13)   8:7-9:21
c. The Herald Angel Announces the Seventh Trumpet 10 (v7)
d. The Two Witnesses   11:1-13
f. The Sun-clothed Woman, The Dragon, The Manchild   12
g. The Beast and the False Prophet   13
h. The 144,000 Jewish Men In Heaven   14:1-5
i. The Six Calls (The Final Call)   14:6-20

CHAPTER 14

H. THE 144,000 JEWISH EVANGELISTS IN HEAVEN 14:1-5

The 144,000 are the first fruits of Israel's greater conversion (Rev 14:4). They are the Manchild brought forth by the Sun Clothed Woman (Isa 66:7,8; Rev 12:2,5). They are saved (become *servants*, 7:3) in the First Half of the Tribulation. They are sealed at the Midpoint before the Trumpet Judgements begin (Rev 7:1-4). They are the instrument in bringing a large number of Gentiles to faith in Christ during the Tribulation years (Rev 7:8,9). They are protected during the Trumpet Judgements (Rev 9:4). They are caught up to Heaven before the pouring out of the Vials of Wrath (Rev 12:5). They are now seen before the Throne of God in Heaven, the Heavenly Mount Zion (Rev 14:1-5).

(14:1) And I looked, and, lo, a Lamb stood on the mount Sion, and with him an hundred forty and four thousand, having his Father's name written in their foreheads.

(14:2) And I heard a voice from heaven, as the voice of many waters, and as the voice of a great thunder: and I heard the voice of harpers harping with their harps: (14:3) And they sung as it were a new song before the throne, and before the four beasts, and the elders: and no man could learn that song but the hundred and forty and four thousand, which were redeemed from the earth.

(14:4) These are they which were not defiled with women; for they are virgins. These are they which follow the Lamb whithersoever he goeth. These were redeemed from among men, being the firstfruits unto God and to the Lamb. (14:5) And in their mouth was found no guile: for they are without fault before the throne of God.

1. THEIR TRIUMPH. *And I looked, and, lo, a Lamb stood on the mount Sion, and with him an hundred forty and four thousand, having his Father's name written in their foreheads* (14:1).

(1) THEY ARE WITH CHRIST. *And I looked, and, lo, a Lamb.* They followed Him *by faith* on earth, they are now with Him *by sight* in Heaven. As Jewish believers they know him as *a Lamb, the Passover Lamb, the Lamb of God*. A counterfeit lamb had appeared on earth (13:11), but they believed in Christ as the fulfilment of the Old Testament prophecies of the true Paschal Lamb.

(2) THEY ARE IN THE HEAVENLY SION: *on the mount Sion.* Zion or Mount Zion (Sion in NT, seven times) but here as in Hebrews 12:24 it refers to the Heavenly Zion. This name gives emphasis to the special link between Heaven and Jerusalem where God placed His Name (2 Chron 6:6). They are with the Lamb *before the Throne* (14:3; cp. Heb 12:22-24). There were on earth where they served as *servants* (7:3), very fruitful servants (7:9); but now before the Vials are poured out they have *been caught up unto God, and his throne* (12:5).

(3) THEIR NUMBER IS STILL THE SAME. It is still **an hundred forty and four thousand.** Not one has been lost since they were saved to be servants and then sealed as servants during the grim days of the Tribulation (7:3,4).

(4) THEIR SEAL IS UNDIMINISHED: *having his Father's name written in their foreheads.* They bore it faithfully on earth while most others had a *different seal* (Rev 13:16,17; cp. 9:4).

> • *And I saw another angel ascending from the east,* **having the seal of the living God***: and he cried with a loud voice to the four angels, to whom it was given to hurt the earth and the sea, 3 Saying, Hurt not the earth, neither the sea, nor the trees,* **till we have sealed the servants of our God in their foreheads** (Rev 7:2,3).

THE BOOK OF REVELATION

Note: As Satan and the Beast are *counterfeiters*, it is likely that the 144,000 are sealed *before* the Beast requires all be given his mark (Rev 13:16-18). The 144,000 with their seal so plainly displayed will have made such an impression on the world that that the Beast must respond by requiring his own "seal". (see William R. Newell, *The Book of Revelation*).

2. THEIR SONG.

(1) THE MAGNITUDE OF THE ACCOMPANIMENT. *And I heard a voice from heaven, as the voice of many waters, and as the voice of a great thunder: and I heard the voice of harpers harping with their harps* (14:2). This vast accompaniment introduces the song to be sung, but must then step back while the song is sung.

(2) THE UNIQUENESS OF THE LYRICS. *And they sung as it were a new song before the throne, and before the four beasts, and the elders: and no man could learn that song but the hundred and forty and four thousand, which were redeemed from the earth* (14:3). Heaven will be a place of *new songs* to mark unique events (as when the Lamb opened the seals, 5:9,10) and so here to commemorate the unique experience of the 144,000 during the Tribulation. As this is a Jewish company, their song is likely to be that which is mentioned at the beginning of the next chapter and which parallels the song Moses sang on the banks of the Red Sea (Exod 15:1-21).

- *And* ***they sing the song of Moses the servant of God, and the song of the Lamb****, saying, Great and marvellous are thy works, Lord God Almighty; just and true are thy ways, thou King of saints* (Rev 15:3).

3. THEIR STANDING AND STATE. *These are they which were not defiled with women; for they are virgins. These are they which follow the Lamb whithersoever he goeth. These were redeemed from among men, being the firstfruits unto God and to the Lamb. And in their mouth was found no guile: for they are without fault before the throne of God* (14:4,5).

(1) THEIR STATE.

[1] MORAL PURITY. *These are they which were not defiled with women; for they are virgins* (14:4). they are not defiled by love of the world or compromise with evil (1 Jhn 2:15,16), but keep themselves pure in a world situation which is morally filthy under the reign of *the man of sin* (2 Thess 2:3). In like manner Israel is referred to frequently in the Bible as *the virgin the daughter of Zion* (2 Kng 19:21; Isa 37:22), They will fulfil that term better than Israel in the past did.

[2] UNSWERVING DEVOTION. *These are they which follow the Lamb whithersoever he goeth.* The ministry of the Two Witnesses appears to have been limited to Jerusalem (Rev 11), but the 144,000 followed a path directed by their Lord that circumvented the entire earth. How else could the following be said of the fruit of their labours.

- *After this I beheld, and, lo,* ***a great multitude, which no man could number, of all nations, and kindreds, and people, and tongues****, stood before the throne, and before the Lamb, clothed with white robes, and palms in their hands* (Rev 7:9).

(2) THEIR STANDING.

[1] REDEEMED FROM THE EARTH. *These were redeemed from among men.* The redemption of the 144,000 coming as it did after the Rapture and in the early months of the Tribulation was sudden and unexpected. Yet it was the common redemption, the only redemption provided for the sons of men.

- *Forasmuch as ye know that ye were **not redeemed with corruptible things**, as silver and gold, from your vain conversation received by tradition from your fathers; 19 **But with the precious blood of Christ, as of a lamb without blemish and without spot*** (1 Pet 1:18,19).

[2] FIRSTFRUITS FROM AMONG ISRAEL: *the firstfruits unto God and to the Lamb.* Before Israel's general conversion at the end of the Tribulation and Return of Christ, the conversion of the 144,000 (the Manchild) will be near the beginning of these terrible years. This is an utterly unique occurrence and with unparalleled results.

- ***Before she travailed**, she brought forth; before her pain came, **she was delivered of a man child*** (Isa 66:7).

(3) THEIR STATE.

[1] IN SPEECH. *And in their mouth was found no guile* (14:5). The world will believe and speak a lie. The days of Antichrist will be days of utter falsehood (cp, Rom 3:4; 2 Thess 2:9). Like the Saviour they follow they will speak the truth.

- *Never man spake like this man* (Jhn 7:46).
- *Hast professed **a good profession** before many witnesses* (1 Tim 6:12).
- ***Sound speech**, that cannot be condemned* (Titus 2:8).

[2] IN RIGHTEOUSNESS: *for they are without fault before the throne of God.* Believers in the present age are exhorted to be *without blame before him* (Eph 1:4); *without blemish* (Eph 5:27; 1 Pet 1:19); *unblameable* (Col 1:22); *without spot* (Heb 9:14); *faultless* (Jude 24).

I. THE SIX CALLS (THE FINAL CALL) 14:6-20

With neither the Two Witnesses or the 144,000 any longer on earth, we have now through the mediation of angels, earth's final call before the Vials of undiluted wrath are poured out. These will be followed in a few weeks by the Return of Jesus Christ.

THE FIRST CALL: THE EVERLASTING GOSPEL

(14:6) *And I saw another angel fly in the midst of heaven, having the everlasting gospel to preach unto them that dwell on the earth, and to every nation, and kindred, and tongue, and people,* (14:7) *Saying with a loud voice, Fear God, and give glory to him; for the hour of his judgment is come: and worship him that made heaven, and earth, and the sea, and the fountains of waters.*

1. THE MESSENGER. *And I saw another angel fly in the midst of heaven* (14:6). It is astonishing that some should think that the Church is still on earth during these Tribulation days. Certainly not here, nor at any point can the Church be found during these seven terrible years. Here even at this last hour is an evidence that *God is willing that none should perish* (2 Pet 3:9). With the 144,000, their martyred converts (7:9) and the Two Witnesses all safely in Heaven, God now sends angels with the final call.

2. THE MESSAGE: *having the everlasting gospel to preach.* Everlasting in its Person, content and consequences. Christ is the eternal Creator and Redeemer; the message of repentance and faith in Him does not change; nor do the consequences: eternal life to the believer, eternal damnation to the unbeliever. Though *all flesh be grass, the word of the Lord endureth for ever* (Isa 40:8).

The Gospel is everlasting in the sense that it is ageless, and for all ages. It may be presented from different standpoints and against the background of different ages and circumstances, but at its heart it will always contain the Death, Burial and Resurrection of Jesus Christ. For example, those truths were presented by type and prophecy in the Old Testament. Likewise the Gospel of the Kingdom, the Millennial Reign has at its basis the Sacrificial Work of Christ. While allowing for the latitude of attendant truths, the term *Gospel* is reserved for the Death, Burial and Resurrection of Christ.

- *Moreover, brethren,* ***I declare unto you the gospel*** *which I preached unto you, which also ye have received, and wherein ye stand; 2 By which also ye are saved, if ye keep in memory what I preached unto you, unless ye have believed in vain. 3 For I delivered unto you first of all that which I also received, how that* ***Christ died for our sins according to the scriptures; 4 And that he was buried, and that he rose again the third day according to the scriptures*** (1 Cor 15:1-4).
- *And* ***this gospel of the kingdom shall be preached in all the world*** *for a witness unto all nations; and then shall the end come* (Matt 24:14).

3. THE RECIPIENTS: ***unto them that dwell on the earth, and to every nation, and kindred, and tongue, and people***. No place, no one, is to be excluded. Wherever there are people, whether many or few they will be told. Now is the time for decision; "neutral you cannot be". Men will have to decide between the worship of the True Christ or the false.

4. THE CURRENT EMPHASIS.

(1) FEAR GOD FOR THE HOUR IS LATE. ***Saying with a loud voice, Fear God, and give glory to him; for the hour of his judgment is come*** (14:7).

(2) WORSHIP GOD FOR HE IS THE CREATOR: ***and worship him that made heaven, and earth, and the sea, and the fountains of waters***. God has given these things and now in the judgements that have just taken place He has taken them away.

Note: God created man in his own image and that on the sixth day (Gen 1:26,27); and is therefore to be worshipped. Six times in Revelation the worship of the Beast is described as directed to *his image*. (Newell).

THE SECOND CALL: THE FALL OF BABLYON

(14:8) ***And there followed another angel, saying, Babylon is fallen, is fallen, that great city, because she made all nations drink of the wine of the wrath of her fornication.***

1. BABYLON'S TWOFOLD FALL. ***Babylon is fallen, is fallen.*** This is the first mention of Babylon in Revelation. Her judgment (Chs. 17,18) is here anticipated, for she will be the great city of the false Messiah, the place of his throne and the center of his religion. That religion will be the full grown fruit of the idolatry introduced by Nimrod (Gen 10:8). All nations have drunk of the maddening wine of that system of abominations. From the very beginning, the Babylonian spirit is that which so intoxicates the minds of men.

Beginning with Nebuchadnezzar it is the chief characteristic of *The Times of the Gentiles* (Lk 21:24). It has both a religious and commercial capital and has been thought to be represented in the end time by Rome and New York (Chapters 17,18). This passage is the second of three times that the *two-fold fall* of Babylon is mentioned.

- *And, behold, here cometh a chariot of men, with a couple of horsemen. And he answered and said,* ***Babylon is fallen***, *is fallen; and all the graven images of her gods he hath broken unto the ground* (Isa 21:9).

CHAPTER 14

• *And he cried mightily with a strong voice, saying,* ***Babylon the great is fallen, is fallen****, and is become the habitation of devils, and the hold of every foul spirit, and a cage of every unclean and hateful bird* (Rev 18:2).

Religious Babylon as a system is destroyed by the Beast at the Midpoint of the Tribulation. It is an open question as to whether its chief city, Rome, will remain and be given to the Beast as one of his capitals – only to be destroyed with the commercial capital at the end of the Tribulation. Note the Midpoint destruction of the religions system and its capital.

• *And* ***the ten horns which thou sawest upon the beast, these shall hate the whore, and shall make her desolate and naked, and shall eat her flesh, and burn her with fire****. 17 For God hath put in their hearts to fulfil his will, and to agree, and give their kingdom unto the beast, until the words of God shall be fulfilled. 18 And* ***the woman which thou sawest is that great city, which reigneth over the kings of the earth*** (Rev 17:16-18).

2. BABYLON THE GREAT CITY: *that great city.* While the Babylonian spirit pervades the entire world, it is here clearly an actual end time city. The fall of commercial Babylon, here announced, may be New York (18:8-10). See the notes on Daniel 4:10-18. The fact that Rome, the city, may share in this fall with commercial Babylon at the end of the Tribulation is indicated by the last verse of Chapter 18.

• *And in her was found the blood of prophets, and of saints, and of all that were slain upon the earth* (Rev 18:24).

3. BABYLON'S OVERSPREADING MATERIALISM: *because she made all nations drink of the wine of the wrath of her fornication.* When the Bible says: *Love not the world, neither the* ***things*** *that are in the world* (1 Jhn 2:15), it is speaking of Babylon. The corrupting, debauching, intoxicating and spreading love of things will end with Babylon's final fall.

THE THIRD CALL: THE DOOM OF BEAST WORSHIPPERS

(14:9) *And the third angel followed them, saying with a loud voice, If any man worship the beast and his image, and receive his mark in his forehead, or in his hand,* (14:10) *The same shall drink of the wine of the wrath of God, which is poured out without mixture into the cup of his indignation; and he shall be tormented with fire and brimstone in the presence of the holy angels, and in the presence of the Lamb:* (14:11) *And the smoke of their torment ascendeth up for ever and ever: and they have no rest day nor night, who worship the beast and his image, and whosoever receiveth the mark of his name.*

(14:12) *Here is the patience of the saints: here are they that keep the commandments of God, and the faith of Jesus.*

1. THE URGENCY OF THE WARNING. *And the third angel followed them, saying with a loud voice, If any man worship the beast and his image, and receive his mark in his forehead, or in his hand* (14:9). As with the offer of grace with first angel, so here with the warning of doom, it is with *a loud voice*. With the Beast's "marking clinics" and *marking vans* traversing the earth, the angel warns those waiting in the long lines. *Don't do it!*

2. THE CERTAINTY OF JUDGEMENT.

(1) IN THE VIAL JUDGEMENTS. *The same shall drink of the wine of the wrath of God, which is poured out without mixture into the cup of his indignation; and he*

shall be tormented with fire and brimstone in the presence of the holy angels, and in the presence of the Lamb (14:10). This is imminent. The next Chapter sees the preparation (15:6).

Compare the *Two Drinks*:

- *Babylon is fallen, is fallen, that great city, because* **she made all nations drink of the wine of the wrath of her fornication** (14:8).
- **The same shall drink of the wine of the wrath of God**, *which is poured out without mixture into the cup of his indignation* (14:10).

Compare the *Ascending Wrath* in the Seal, Trumpet and Vial Judgements:

- The Seals: Wrath (6:17)
- The Trumpets: Woeful Wrath (8:13)
- The Vials: Unmingled Wrath (14:10)

Note: The Vial Judgements described in the next two chapters will be poured out *in the presence of the holy angels, and in the presence of the Lamb.* Heaven has watched in horror at the fearful choice that a world of men and women have made. Where has there ever been such a sight. Heaven now looks on "in deep, awful and holy approval of the divine sentence", (Newell).

(2) IN ETERNAL JUDGEMENT. *And the smoke of their torment ascendeth up for ever and ever: and they have no rest day nor night, who worship the beast and his image, and whosoever receiveth the mark of his name* (14:11). *Fleeting* respite with the Beast, but with the certain prospect of eternal torment. Their torment is not as some vainly teach "a momentary one", for it is literally, *unto the ages of ages*, the strongest expression of eternity of which the Greek language is capable. And that, without ever any **rest day nor night.** "Anyone disposed to discredit the Biblical teaching on the eternal destiny of the wicked should be reminded that Jesus and His beloved disciple said more in regard to this doctrine than all the remaining contributors to the New Testament record." (Walvoord quoting J.B. Smith). "Christ referred to hell (*gehenna*) eleven out of the twelve occurrences, and made twelve out of nineteen references to *hell fire*, and used other similar expressions more than any other in the New Testament. How dangerous it is for men to trifle with false religions, which dishonour the incarnate Word and contradict the written Word."

We are now in the realm of the final call. Year after year in these Tribulation years they have spurned the testimony of the 144,000 and the powerful entreaties of the Two Witnesses. They are now plunging with ever more determination to their doom.

3. THE HEARTENING ALTERNATIVE. *Here is the patience of the saints: here are they that keep the commandments of God, and the faith of Jesus* (14:12). Here is the proper link between works emanating from true faith in Christ. Here is how a Tribulation saint during this late dark hour is characterized. With the enforcers of the Beast's decree getting closer and bearing down upon them, they may know that the Lord's Coming is near and *getting nearer*.

THE FOURTH CALL: THE BLESSED MARTYRS

(14:13) *And I heard a voice from heaven saying unto me, Write, Blessed are the dead which die in the Lord from henceforth: Yea, saith the Spirit, that they may rest from their labours; and their works do follow them.*

CHAPTER 14

Never before could such a word be spoken! Always before it had been better, despite all the trials, for the believer to live out the full time of his pilgrimage on earth. But not in the Tribulation days! Then it will be better; then it will be blessed to die! The Beast *will wear out the saints of the most High* (Dan 7:27; see Newell).

1. THE MEANS OF THE ANNOUNCEMENT. ***And I heard a voice from heaven saying unto me.*** Unlike the previous calls which came from Heaven through a mediating angel, this came directly from Heaven. Four times previously there is a record of *a voice from heaven* (10:4,8; 11:12; 14:2). Again in 18:4 and 21:3 a voice is heard, a direct communication from God as contrasted with communication through an angel. The implication is that this is unusually important and a direct Divine pronouncement. (Walvoord).

2. THE EMPHASIS OF THE ANNOUNCEMENT. ***Write.*** The entire Book of Revelation was to be written (1:11), but here for emphasis it is again so stated.

3. THE SUBJECT OF THE ANNOUNCEMENT. ***Blessed are the dead which die in the Lord.*** There is a great gulf between the blessedness and misery of dying in union with the Lord and dying in your sins separated from the Lord (Jhn 8:24). Here especially it is infinitely better to be dead at the hand of the Beast than to have favour for a few days as his worshipper.

(1) THE DISTINCTIVENESS OF THEIR BLESSEDNESS: ***from henceforth: Yea, saith the Spirit.*** It is always and in every age a blessing to die in the Lord, but for these Great Tribulation martyrs special notice is given. All this is ratified and confirmed by the testimony of the Spirit witnessing with their spirits and with the written Word.

(2) THE NATURE OF THEIR BLESSEDNESS.

[1] BLESSED IN THEIR REST: ***that they may rest from their labours.*** These are the labours in serving Christ in the unbelievably oppressive days of the Tribulation.

[2] BLESSED IN THEIR RECOMPENSE: ***and their works do follow them.*** They will be rewarded by the Lord; and the souls won by them will follow them into His presence. If their works were not appreciated or recognized when they were performed, they will be now.

This verse is the second of *Seven Beatitudes* in Revelation (1:3; 16:15; 19:9; 20:6; 22:7,14).

• ***Blessed*** *is he that readeth, and they that hear the words of this prophecy, and keep those things which are written therein: for the time is at hand* (Rev 1:3).

THE FIFTH CALL: THE REAPING OF THE EVIL HARVEST

(14:14) ***And I looked, and behold a white cloud, and upon the cloud one sat like unto the Son of man, having on his head a golden crown, and in his hand a sharp sickle.***
(14:15) ***And another angel came out of the temple, crying with a loud voice to him that sat on the cloud, Thrust in thy sickle, and reap: for the time is come for thee to reap; for the harvest of the earth is ripe.*** (14:16) ***And he that sat on the cloud thrust in his sickle on the earth; and the earth was reaped.***

The enormity of the subject now requires two announcements, the fifth and the sixth. Both deal with reaping. The first deals with the reaping *of* the entire earth, *of* a dry harvest, *of* an overripe crop. It deals with the lost generally. The second concerns the reaping of the clusters of fully ripe grapes and gathering them to Armageddon. It deals with the armies of the earth (cp Rev 16:14-16; 19:11-21). That both deal with the lost can be seen in the following passage. Both the *harvest* and the *press* is for the lost.

THE BOOK OF REVELATION

> • *Put ye in the sickle, for **the harvest is ripe**: come, get you down; for **the press is full**, the fats overflow; for their wickedness is great. 14 Multitudes, multitudes in the valley of decision: for the day of the LORD is near in the valley of decision* (Joel 3:13,14).

1. THE LORD OF THE REAPING. ***And I looked, and behold a white cloud, and upon the cloud one sat like unto the Son of man,*** (14:14). One so *like unto the Son of man* that it is in fact the Son of man. It *is* the Lord Jesus Christ who is so described. This is a statement of wonder and contemplation. The **Son of Man** is Christ's Judgement Name (Jhn 5:22,27).

(1) HIS CHARIOT: ***a white cloud.*** A cloud that had a brightness of grace to the redeemed, but a blinding brightness of judgement to the wicked.

(2) HIS ENSIGN: ***having on his head a golden crown.*** The emblem of authority declaring His reign upon the earth. By the reaping now described, all of the wicked will be removed from the earth.

> • *The LORD is King for ever and ever: **the heathen are perished out of his land*** (Psa 10:16).

In the first mention of the *Son of Man* in the New Testament (Matt 8:20), He *had not where to lay His head.* His head is now crowned with gold, as promised in Psalm 21:3.

> • *For thou preventest him with the blessings of goodness: **thou settest a crown of pure gold on his head**.*

(3) HIS INSTRUMENT: ***and in his hand a sharp sickle.*** The word *sickle* occurs only twelve times in the Scriptures of which seven are in the verses of this section. Also the word *sharp* occurs seven times in Revelation and four times in this chapter.

2. THE ENTREATY TO PROCEED WITH THE REAPING. ***And another angel came out of the temple, crying with a loud voice to him that sat on the cloud, Thrust in thy sickle, and reap*** (14:15). As the martyrs pray for God to intervene against the wickedness on earth (Rev 6:9), so now a holy angel implores Christ to intervene directly on the basis of His authority as the Judge of men.

> • *For **the Father judgeth no man, but hath committed all judgment unto the Son**: 23 That all men should honour the Son, even as they honour the Father. He that honoureth not the Son honoureth not the Father which hath sent him* (Jhn 5:22,23).
> • ***And hath given him authority to execute judgment also, because he is the Son of man*** (Jhn 5:27).
> • *Because he hath appointed a day, in the which he will judge the world in righteousness **by that man whom he hath ordained**; whereof he hath given assurance unto all men, in that he hath raised him from the dead* (Acts 17:31).

The sickle is the sword of God's judgement; the field is the world; the reaping is the cutting down of the inhabitants of the earth and gathering them to judgement.

3. THE TIME OF THE REAPING: ***for the time is come for thee to reap; for the harvest of the earth is ripe*** (14:15). The measure of the sin of men is filled up, and they are ripe for destruction, ripe for ruin. He will spare them no longer; he will thrust in his sickle, and *the earth shall be reaped.*

Note: The verb, ***is ripe*** (*exeranthe* = to become dry or withered), has a bad connotation (Matt 21:19,20; Mk 3:1,3; 11:20; Lk 8:6; Rev 16:12). The picture is of fruit or vegetables that have become so ripe that it has begun to dry up and wither. Man has gone too

CHAPTER 14

far. The *time has come* that rotten moral condition of the world must be dealt with *now*; and that with a sharp sickle.

4. THE EXECUTION OF THE REAPING. *And he that sat on the cloud thrust in his sickle on the earth; and the earth was reaped* (14:16). Say it again! ... *and the earth was reaped.* That is the end of all things of which man boasts!

Note: Several operations will be involved when Christ returns; but before the Millennial Reign begins there will not be a single lost person left on the earth! The earth has been *reaped*.

- *Let both grow together until the harvest: and* **in the time of harvest I will say to the reapers, Gather ye together first the tares, and bind them in bundles to burn them**: *but gather the wheat into my barn* (Matt 13:30).
- *The Son of man shall send forth his angels, and* **they shall gather out of his kingdom all things that offend, and them which do iniquity** (Matt 13:41).
- *When* **the Son of man** *shall come in his glory, and all the holy angels with him, then shall he sit upon the throne of his glory: 32 And* **before him shall be gathered all nations**: *and* **he shall separate them one from another**, *as a shepherd divideth his sheep from the goats* (Matt 25:31,32).
- *Then shall he say also unto them on the left hand,* **Depart from me, ye cursed, into everlasting fire, prepared for the devil and his angels** *(Matt 25:41).*

THE SIXTH CALL: THE VINTAGE OF ARMAGEDDON

(14:17) *And another angel came out of the temple which is in heaven, he also having a sharp sickle.*

(14:18) *And another angel came out from the altar, which had power over fire; and cried with a loud cry to him that had the sharp sickle, saying, Thrust in thy sharp sickle, and gather the clusters of the vine of the earth; for her grapes are fully ripe.*

(14:19) *And the angel thrust in his sickle into the earth, and gathered the vine of the earth, and cast it into the great winepress of the wrath of God.* (14:20) *And the winepress was trodden without the city, and blood came out of the winepress, even unto the horse bridles, by the space of a thousand and six hundred furlongs.*

1. THE ONE PERFORMING THE VINTAGE. *And another angel came out of the temple which is in heaven, he also having a sharp sickle* (14:17). Though not as in the previous case, the Son of Man; yet with His authority for he comes *out of the temple*. Like the Son of man he has a sharp sickle telling of the severity of the judgment.

2. THE ONE CALLING FOR THE VINTAGE.

(1) HIS DISTINCTIONS. *And another angel came out from the altar, which had power over fire* (14:18). He comes from the altar where the prayers of martyrs were heard (6:9). He has power over fire, and was perhaps the one who set one third of the earth on fire with the blowing of the First Trumpet (8:7).

(2) HIS ENTREATY: *and cried with a loud cry to him that had the sharp sickle, saying, Thrust in thy sharp sickle, and gather the clusters of the vine of the earth; for her grapes are fully ripe* (14:18). The statements of Divine judgement are enlarged. With the prospect that *her grapes are fully ripe*, for the second time *the sharp sickle* is mentioned.

The expression *fully ripe* (*ekmasan*) is different than the word for *ripe* (*exeranthe*) used in the previous description of the harvest (14:15). Here it pictures grapes fully grown and almost bursting. The figure is different but the meaning is the same. The time has come for the final harvest. While the figure of the vine is used of Israel and the believers relationship with Christ, this is not the subject now. Here it is *the grapes of wrath*. The fullness of the worlds sin now demands the unmingled wrath of God.

3. THE WORK OF THE VINTAGE.

(1) THE GATHERING. ***And the angel thrust in his sickle into the earth, and gathered the vine of the earth, and cast it into the great winepress of the wrath of God*** (14:19). This final action is a consistent theme of Scripture.

> • *Proclaim ye this among the Gentiles;* **Prepare war***, wake up the mighty men, let all the men of war draw near; let them come up: 10* **Beat your plowshares into swords** *and your pruninghooks into spears: let the weak say, I am strong. 11* **Assemble yourselves***, and come, all ye heathen, and* **gather yourselves together round about***: thither cause thy mighty ones to come down, O LORD. 12* **Let the heathen be wakened***, and come up to the valley of Jehoshaphat: for there will I sit to judge all the heathen round about. 13* **Put ye in the sickle, for the harvest is ripe***: come, get you down; for the press is full, the fats overflow; for their wickedness is great. 14* **Multitudes, multitudes in the valley of decision***: for the day of the LORD is near in the valley of decision. 15 The sun and the moon shall be darkened, and the stars shall withdraw their shining. 16 The LORD also shall roar out of Zion, and utter his voice from Jerusalem; and the heavens and the earth shall shake: but the LORD will be the hope of his people, and the strength of the children of Israel* (Joel 3:9-16).
>
> • *And I saw the beast, and* **the kings of the earth, and their armies, gathered** *together to make war against him that sat on the horse, and against his army* (Rev 19:19).
>
> • *Therefore wait ye upon me, saith the LORD, until the day that I rise up to the prey: for* **my determination is to gather the nations***, that I may assemble the kingdoms, to pour upon them mine indignation, even all my fierce anger: for* **all the earth shall be devoured with the fire of my jealousy** (Zeph 3:8).

(2) THE TRAMPLING. ***And the winepress was trodden without the city, and blood came out of the winepress, even unto the horse bridles, by the space of a thousand and six hundred furlongs*** (14:20).

> • *And out of his mouth goeth a sharp sword, that with it he should smite the nations: and he shall rule them with a rod of iron: and* **he treadeth the winepress** *of the fierceness and wrath of Almighty God* (Rev 19:15).

CHAPTER 14

The Diameter and Depth of the *Winepress*
Where the Sin and Arrogance of Man Will Soon End

This is the first of three times that Armageddon in mentioned in Revelation (16:14-16; 19:11-21).

• *For they are **the spirits of devils, working miracles, which go forth unto the kings of the earth and of the whole world, to gather them to the battle of that great day of God Almighty**. 15 Behold, I come as a thief. Blessed is he that watcheth, and keepeth his garments, lest he walk naked, and they see his shame. 16 And **he gathered them together into a place called in the Hebrew tongue Armageddon*** (Rev 16:14-16).

The carnage will extend to Edom in the south and east. It is indeed *the day of the LORD'S vengeance, and the year of his recompence for the controversy of Zion* (Isa 34:8). We have already had seas of blood and will shortly have seas and rivers of blood on an ever larger extent (8:8; 16:3,4); yet what we have here is something deeper and infinitely greater.

• *Who is this that cometh from Edom, with dyed garments from Bozrah? this that is glorious in his apparel, travelling in the greatness of his strength? I that speak in righteousness, mighty to save. 2 Wherefore art thou **red in thine apparel, and thy garments like him that treadeth in the winefat? 3 I have trodden the winepress alone**; and of the people there was none with me: for **I will tread them in mine anger, and trample them in my fury; and their blood shall be sprinkled upon my garments, and I will stain all my raiment**. 4 For the day of vengeance is in mine heart, and the year of my redeemed is come. 5 And I looked, and there was none to help; and I wondered that there was none to uphold: therefore mine own arm brought salvation unto me; and my* *fury, it upheld me. 6 And **I will tread down the people in mine anger**, and make them drunk in my fury, and I will bring down their strength to the earth* (Isa 63:1-6).

• ***Come near, ye nations**, to hear; and hearken, ye people: let the earth hear, and all that is therein; the world, and all things that come forth of it. 2 For **the indignation of the LORD is upon all nations, and his fury upon all their armies**: he hath utterly destroyed them, **he hath delivered them to the slaughter**. 3 Their slain also shall be cast out, and **their stink shall come up out of their carcases, and the mountains shall be melted with their blood** (Isa 34:1-3).

3. The Vial Judgements and Other Events   15-18
a. The Preparation   15
b. The Seven Vials Poured Out: <u>Unmingled, Full Wrath</u>   16
c. Judgement on Religious Babylon   17
d. Judgement on Commercial-Political Babylon   18

CHAPTER 15

A. THE PREPARATION FOR THE VIAL JUDGEMENTS 15

(15:1) And I saw another sign in heaven, great and marvellous, seven angels having the seven last plagues; for in them is filled up the wrath of God.

(15:2) And I saw as it were a sea of glass mingled with fire: and them that had gotten the victory over the beast, and over his image, and over his mark, and over the number of his name, stand on the sea of glass, having the harps of God. (15:3) And they sing the song of Moses the servant of God, and the song of the Lamb, saying, Great and marvellous are thy works, Lord God Almighty; just and true are thy ways, thou King of saints. (15:4) Who shall not fear thee, O Lord, and glorify thy name? for thou only art holy: for all nations shall come and worship before thee; for thy judgments are made manifest.

(15:5) And after that I looked, and, behold, the temple of the tabernacle of the testimony in heaven was opened: (15:6) And the seven angels came out of the temple, having the seven plagues, clothed in pure and white linen, and having their breasts girded with golden girdles. (15:7) And one of the four beasts gave unto the seven angels seven golden vials full of the wrath of God, who liveth for ever and ever.

(15:8) And the temple was filled with smoke from the glory of God, and from his power; and no man was able to enter into the temple, till the seven plagues of the seven angels were fulfilled.

The Chapter before us contains the solemn preparation for the pouring out of the Vials of Wrath upon the earth. There was wrath before in the Seal Judgements(6:17), and woeful wrath with the Trumpet Judgements, but now it is without respite. It is *full* wrath (15:1). It is *without mixture* (14:10). The Vials of Wrath constitute the *Third Woe*, the *Seventh Trumpet Judgement*. As the Seventh Seal contained the Seven Trumpets, so the Seventh Trumpet contains the Seven Vials. The Vials are poured out in the weeks before Christ's Return and Battle of Armageddon (14:19,20; 16:14-16). This is the final pouring out of wrath before Christ comes *IN PERSON* to tread *alone* the winepress of wrath (Isa 63:3-5; Rev 14:18-20).

- *The second woe is past; and, behold, **the third woe cometh quickly. And the seventh angel sounded**; and there were great voices in heaven, saying, The kingdoms of this world are become the kingdoms of our Lord, and of his Christ; and he shall reign for ever and ever* (11:15,16).

I. THE SIGHT OF THE ANGELS. *And I saw another sign in heaven, great and marvellous, seven angels having the seven last plagues; for in them is filled up the wrath of God* (15:1). The final series of judgements is introduced by the words, **another sign in heaven**. This word refers to the two previous *signs* of Chapter 12, The Sun Clothed Woman and the Great Red Dragon. The three signs taken together represent (1) Israel as the woman, (2) the final Seven-headed World Empire under Satan and the Beast, and (3) the Seven brief but catastrophic judgements upon the political power of the Beast.

The sign here is called **great and marvellous** (*mega kai thaumaston*). These words appear together only here and in verse 3 in the entire New Testament.

The sight of the angels is the **sign** of the unparalleled wrath about to fall. Before the first of the Trumpet Judgements there was a brief time given to prepare and a *silence for a half hour* (7:1; 8:1); no such time is given here.

THE BOOK OF REVELATION

<u>1. THE SPECTATORS: THEIR STANDING</u>. *And I saw as it were a sea of glass mingled with fire: and them that had gotten the victory over the beast, and over his image, and over his mark, and over the number of his name, stand on the sea of glass, having the harps of God* (15:2). Before judgement proceeds (cp. Rev 7:1,3,9), the triumph of Grace is shown (Newell). The harp and the trumpet are the only musical instruments mentioned in the book of Revelation, but they are used to the full. Back at the end of Chapter 6 a question was asked.

- *For the great day of his wrath is come; and* **who shall be able to stand** (Rev 6:17)?

These in Chapter 15 stood on earth against the Antichrist and all his satanic power. They are now standing in Heaven. They stand on **the sea of glass** (cp. Rev 4:6) which was the pattern for the great laver in the Old Testament Temple. It was also called *a sea* and there the priests washed.

- *And he made* **a molten sea**, *ten cubits from the one brim to the other: it was round all about, and his height was five cubits: and a line of thirty cubits did compass it round about* (1 Kng 7:23).
- *And before the throne there was* **a sea of glass like unto crystal**: *and in the midst of the throne, and round about the throne, were four beasts full of eyes before and behind* (Rev 4:6).

Now its waters are fixed, crystalized, glassy. The righteousness of those in Heaven is not only declared but actual. But righteousness spurned brings wrath; thus it is **mingled with fire**. As they sing the song of Moses, the scene is also reminiscent of Israel at the Red Sea and the wrath that fell upon Pharaoh.

<u>2. THE SPECTATORS: THEIR SONG.</u>

<u>(1) THEY EXTOL THE GREATNESS OF GOD</u>. *And they sing the song of Moses the servant of God, and the song of the Lamb, saying, Great and marvellous are thy works, Lord God Almighty; just and true are thy ways, thou King of saints* (15:3). They sing, not of their bravery and fidelity, but of the perfections and glories of the Lamb as *Jehovah, Elohim, Shaddai, King of saint*; and from verse 4, *Lord Most Holy* and *the only Lord*. The fact that the word *song* is repeated and with a definite article in both cases indicates that two songs are in view. The former recounts the faithfulness of God to Israel at the Red Sea and her victory over Pharaoh (Exod 15). Such would especially be a song that the 144,000 would sing (Rev 14:3). Others point to Deuteronomy 32 as the song that is meant, a song to the children of Israel by Moses shortly before his death. It is an overview of God's faithfulness to Israel and His ultimate purpose to defeat their enemies.

The **song of the Lamb** speaks of redemption from sin made possible by the Sacrifice of the Lamb of God (Jhn 1:29). Yet the two songs are combined, and by that fact these great Old Testament titles are applied to Jesus Christ, the Lamb of God.

- **Then sang Moses** *and the children of Israel this song unto the LORD, and spake, saying, I will sing unto the LORD, for he hath triumphed gloriously: the horse and his rider hath he thrown into the sea* (Exod 15:1....22).
- *And Moses spake in the ears of all the congregation of Israel the words of this song, until they were ended* (Deut 31:30....32:45).

By singing the Song of Moses reference is made to the promise to Moses concerning the unparalleled judgements which would one day fall upon earth. It is noteworthy that this promise was made after the terrible breach of the golden calf.

CHAPTER 15

> • *And he said, Behold, I make a covenant: before all thy people **I will do marvels, such as have not been done in all the earth**, nor in any nation: and all the people among which thou art shall see the work of the LORD: **for it is a terrible thing that I will do with thee*** (Exod 34:10).

(2) THEY CALL THE NATIONS TO EXTOL THE GREATNESS OF GOD. *Who shall not fear thee, O Lord, and glorify thy name? for thou only art holy: for all nations shall come and worship before thee; for thy judgments are made manifest* (15:4). His judgements have indeed been manifest in the opening of the Seals and blowing of the Trumpets; now before the final stroke the question is asked: *Who shall not fear thee?* Though the nations neither fear God nor glorify Him in their mad unbelief, the day will soon come when they will be forced to bow beneath His wrath. A similar question is found in Jeremiah 10:7: *Who would not fear thee, O King of nations?* (cp. also Rev. 14:7).

The prospect of all nations worshiping the Lord during the Millennial Reign, frequently stated in the OT, is brought out in the words: *For thou only art holy: for all nations shall come and worship before thee* (cp. Psa 2:8-9; 24:1-10; 66:1-4; 72:8-11; 86:9; Isa 2:2-4; 9:6-7; 66:18-23; Dan 7:14; Zeph 2:11; Zech 14:9).

II. THE COMING FORTH OF THE ANGELS.
 1. HOW THEY APPEARED. *And after that I looked, and, behold, the temple of the tabernacle of the testimony in heaven was opened* (15:5). Our attention is arrested by the phrase *I looked, and, behold*. This expression always introduces something dramatically new. As John observes, the Holy of Holies in the heavenly Tabernacle is opened. The scene of these angels coming forth is shortly after the previous scene of the opened Temple. However, there the Temple is portrayed as the place of God's unchangeable, immutable sovereignty. Here, the only message conveyed is that of wrath.

> • *And the temple of God was **opened** in heaven, and there was seen in his temple **the ark of his testament**: and there were lightnings, and voices, and thunderings, and an earthquake, and great hail* (11:19).

 2. HOW THEY WERE EQUIPPED.
  (1) THEIR VESTMENTS OF AUTHORITY. *And the seven angels came out of the temple, having the seven plagues, clothed in pure and white linen, and having their breasts girded with golden girdles* (15:6). These were the garments of the high priests when they went in to enquire of God, and came out with an answer. This showed that these angels were acting in all things under the Divine appointment and direction. They are the ministers of divine justice, and they do everything in a pure and holy manner.
  (2) THEIR VESSELS OF WRATH. *And one of the four beasts gave unto the seven angels seven golden vials full of the wrath of God, who liveth for ever and ever* (15:7). Here is their artillery and the means by which to perform this great execution. In the two previous series of judgements it was Seals that were opened and Trumpets that were blown; now they are given the actual means of the judgement. They are armed with *seven golden vials full of the wrath of God*. It was full wrath, and if we dare inquire into its fullness it is *the wrath of God, who liveth for ever and ever*. It has been building up against the sin of man for a long time.

From whom do they receive these vials? From one of the four living creatures, one of the cherubim who have has been speaking out his *holy, holy, holy*, while the sin of man raged on the earth (Isa 6:3; Rev 4:8).

III. THE *SMOKE* IN HEAVEN. *And the temple was filled with smoke from the glory of God, and from his power; and no man was able to enter into the temple, till the seven*

plagues of the seven angels were fulfilled (15:8). The scene is often compared to the cloud that filled the Tabernacle after its construction in Exodus 40:34,35. But there it was *glory*. Here it is *glory* and *wrath*. Heaven itself is made to feel something of that which is now to fall upon the earth. It is an ominous sign of impending doom for those who persist in their blasphemous rebellion against a *Holy* God.

Newell writes: "God will so turn to *anger* at last, that all else ceases, even in Heaven! Wrath will be the only business."

- *Thou, even thou, art to be feared: and* **who may stand in thy sight when once thou art angry** (Psa 76:7)?

CHAPTER 16

B. THE SEVEN VIALS POURED OUT: UNMINGLED, FULL WRATH (14:10; 15:1)   16

THE FIRST VIAL: THE MALIGNITY OF THE MARK

(16:1) *And I heard a great voice out of the temple saying to the seven angels, Go your ways, and pour out the vials of the wrath of God upon the earth.*

In this chapter we have the account of the pouring forth of the Vials that are filled with the wrath of God. It is *concentrated* wrath; it is *full* (15:1); it is *without mixture* (14:10). In the foregoing chapter we had the preparation, the great and solemn preparation; now we have the performance. Though everything was made ready, yet nothing was to be put in execution without an immediate command from God. No sooner was the word of command given than it was immediately obeyed; no delay, no objection made. We find that some of the best men, as Moses and Jeremiah, did not so readily come and comply with the call of God; but the angels of God excel not only in strength, but in a readiness. God says, *Go your ways, and pour out the vials,* and immediately the work is done.

We have parallels here to five of the Ten Plagues of Egypt: boils, blood, darkness, frogs and hail, but this goes further, much further. There is also a parallel resemblance to the Seven Trumpets.

SIMILARITIES OF THE TRUMPETS AND THE VIALS

The First in both series deals with **the earth**
The Second with **the sea**
The Third with **rivers and fountains of water**
The Fourth with **the sun**
The Fifth with **darkness**
The Sixth with **the Euphrates River**
The Seventh with **lightnings, thunders, and a great earthquake**

The differences between the two series of Judgements are numerous and significant. The chief difference is the intensity and magnitude of the Vials. The first four Trumpet Judgments deal with one-third of the earth; the Vial Judgments cover the earth and that with greater force. They devastate the entire earth. Everyone and everything that aided the Beast and was at war with the God of Heaven is under attack. Their land, their atmosphere, their sea, their rivers, their cities are all consigned to ruin.

REVELATION SIXTEEN IS THE *GREAT* CHAPTER

- *a **great** voice* (v. 1)
- ***great** heat* (v. 9)
- *the **great** river Euphrates* (v. 12)
- *that **great** day of God Almighty* (v. 14)
- *a **great** voice* (v. 17)
- *a **great** earthquake* (v. 18)
- *so mighty an earthquake, and so **great*** (v. 18)
- *the **great** city* (v. 19)

- ***great** Babylon* (v. 19)
- *a **great** hail* (v. 21)
- *the plague thereof was exceeding **great*** (v. 21)

(16:2) ***And the first went, and poured out his vial upon the earth; and there fell a noisome and grievous sore upon the men which had the mark of the beast, and upon them which worshipped his image.***

1. WHERE IT FELL: **upon the earth**. Not part of the earth: the earth! More specifically it fell upon all on the earth who had taken the mark. No matter where they lived or what their station was in life. This is a notable contrast with the First Trumpet that burns up *a third part of the trees and all the green grass* (8:7). Here the judgment is specifically upon people and is directed to those who took the mark.

2. WHAT IT PRODUCED: **a noisome and grievous sores on all who had the mark of the beast**. The Mark that was supposed to protect them became the lightning rod for this plague. It is likely that it was on the mark itself that the plague fell. It is described as a **sore** (*helkos*) which is **noisome**, offensive to the senses, repulsive, bad, causing the *noise* of pain (*kakos*) and **grievous**, malignant and spreading (*poneros*).

The only ones who escape are those who have refused in those evil days to take the Mark and follow Christ. From 13:8 it is clear that at this end stage of the Tribulation their numbers will be small. The warning given in Revelation 14:9-11 against the Beast worshipers is now reinforced and points to their imminent doom.

Note: That the period of the Vials is brief is evident with the *pain* of the First Vial still being felt in the *darkness* of the Sixth (16:11). They will crowd in on the earth.

THE SECOND VIAL: *OCEANS OF BLOOD*

(16:3) ***And the second angel poured out his vial upon the sea; and it became as the blood of a dead man: and every living soul died in the sea.***

1. WHERE IT FELL: **upon the sea**. As in the Second Trumpet (one third of the seas, 8:8), there is a parallel to the First Plagues in Egypt (Exod 7:20-25) which made the waters blood and killed all the fish in the Nile. But that is a faint glimmering of what we now have. The first two vials demonstrate the vast compass – *earth and sea*. As with the single word *earth*, **sea** means all the seas.

2. WHAT IT PRODUCED: It turned the sea into blood, **as the blood of a dead man, and every living soul died in the sea**. The vast oceans are here described as the clotting blood of a dead man. The beautiful rolling seas became a cesspool of death, and that upon the entire earth, for most of the earth is covered by water. *The wages of sin is death* (Rom 6:23). The blood of a vast number of Tribulation martyrs will now be avenged.

THE THIRD VIAL: *RIVERS OF BLOOD*

(16:4) ***And the third angel poured out his vial upon the rivers and fountains of waters; and they became blood.***

(16:5) ***And I heard the angel of the waters say, Thou art righteous, O Lord, which art, and wast, and shalt be, because thou hast judged thus.*** **(16:6)** ***For they have shed the blood of saints and prophets, and thou hast given them blood to drink; for they are worthy.***

(16:7) ***And I heard another out of the altar say, Even so, Lord God Almighty, true and righteous are thy judgments.***

CHAPTER 16

1. WHERE IT FELL: *upon the rivers, and upon the fountains of waters*. As with the Third Trumpet, judgement upon the waters is extended from oceans to the fresh waters. There it was a third, now it is the world wide networks of rivers and streams.

2. WHAT IT PRODUCED: *the rivers and fountains of waters…became blood*. Salt water for cleansing the earth, now fresh water for sustaining the dwellers on earth – *all blood*.

3. THE JUSTICE IT PROCLAIMED.

(1) THE VERDICT OF THE ANGEL. *And I heard the angel of the waters say, Thou art righteous, O Lord, which art, and wast, and shalt be, because thou hast judged thus. 6 For they have shed the blood of saints and prophets, and thou hast given them blood to drink; for they are worthy* (16:5,6). The bloodletting during the Tribulation, as believers practically beyond number have been slaughtered is without precedent. Now a hitherto unknown angel stands up to declare the absolute justice of what has now taken place.

(2) THE VERDICT OF THE MARTYRS. *And I heard another out of the altar say, Even so, Lord God Almighty, true and righteous are thy judgments* (16:7). Another angel follows with the same pronouncement. This twofold intervention of angels is a testimony to the enormity of a world waking up to find all the water has turned to blood. Again, God will avenge His martyred saints.

- *And when he had opened the fifth seal,* **I saw under the altar the souls of them that were slain for the word of God,** *and for the testimony which they held: And they cried with a loud voice, saying, How long, O Lord, holy and true, dost thou not judge and avenge our blood on them that dwell on the earth* (6:9,10)?

THE FOURTH VIAL: *THE SCORCHING SUN*

(16:8) *And the fourth angel poured out his vial upon the sun; and power was given unto him to scorch men with fire.* (16:9) *And men were scorched with great heat, and blasphemed the name of God, which hath power over these plagues: and they repented not to give him glory.*

Under the fourth trumpet (8:12) the sun's light decreased, but now it burns hot against the dwellers on earth. Already, in the Tribulation something of its unusual heat had been felt and even the righteous suffered under it. Now the sun goes beyond all bounds. Yet, as with *the angel of the waters* (16:5), here there is an angel who controls the sun's scorching heat and deflects its rays so as to discriminate between the worshippers of the Beast and the worshippers of the Lamb (cp. 16:2).

- *They shall hunger no more, neither thirst any more;* **neither shall the sun light on them, nor any heat** (7:16).
- *For, behold, the day cometh, that shall burn as an oven; and all the proud, yea, and all that do wickedly, shall be* **stubble***: and the day that cometh shall* **burn them up***, saith the LORD of hosts, that it shall leave them neither root nor branch* (Mal 4:1).

The Fourth Plague brings forth the first chorus of blasphemy in this chapter. It does not bring men to repentance but only increases their wicked profanity against God. We are now entering that zone where it is too late to repent

THE FIFTH VIAL: DARKNESS UPON THE BEAST'S COMMAND POST

(16:10) *And the fifth angel poured out his vial upon the seat of the beast; and his kingdom was full of darkness; and they gnawed their tongues for pain,* (16:11) *And blasphemed the God of heaven because of their pains and their sores, and repented not of their deeds.*

THE BOOK OF REVELATION

    1. WHERE IT FELL: **upon the seat of the beast** (16:10). This likely fails upon Commercial Babylon as described in Chapter 18, after Ecclesiastical Babylon (Ch. 17) is destroyed.
    2. WHAT IT PRODUCED:
    (1) DARKNESS: **and his kingdom was full of darkness.** That very city which was the seat of the Antichrist's policies and dictates is plunged into darkness, and the world gropes about in that same darkness as it looks in vain for any to lead.
    (2) PAIN: **and they gnawed their tongues for pain.** In the Ninth Plague it was a darkness that *may be felt* (Exod 10:21), now it is felt also in an agonizing way. It was a unbearable darkness and further magnified the pains of the earlier vials. Shut up in the darkness with their sores! Sores that are *still sore* since the First Vial; *grievous* then, *gnawing their tongues* now.
    (3) BLASPHEMY. **And blasphemed the God of heaven because of their pains and their sores, and repented not of their deeds.** The wicked gnaw their tongues rather than call out for mercy. And, when they do call out it is a second explosion of blasphemy (16:9). The Scriptures plainly refute the idea that wicked men will repent when faced with catastrophic judgement. Only the Gospel message of the Death, Burial and Resurrection of Christ saves the sinner.

THE SIXTH VIAL: THE STAMPEDE TO ARMAGEDDON

(16:12) *And the sixth angel poured out his vial upon the great river Euphrates; and the water thereof was dried up, that the way of the kings of the east might be prepared.*

(16:13) *And I saw three unclean spirits like frogs come out of the mouth of the dragon, and out of the mouth of the beast, and out of the mouth of the false prophet.*

(16:14) *For they are the spirits of devils, working miracles, which go forth unto the kings of the earth and of the whole world, to gather them to the battle of that great day of God Almighty.*

(16:15) *Behold, I come as a thief. Blessed is he that watcheth, and keepeth his garments, lest he walk naked, and they see his shame.*

(16:16) *And he gathered them together into a place called in the Hebrew tongue Armageddon.*

The Euphrates River "Downstream from Eden"

CHAPTER 16

1. THE WORK OF THE ANGEL: OPENING THE WAY FOR THE EASTERN ARMIES. *And the sixth angel poured out his vial upon the great river Euphrates; and the water thereof was dried up, that the way of the kings of the east might be prepared* (16:12). Compare this with the advance of the eastern army not long before at the blowing of the Sixth Trumpet (9:13-21). Then there was an army of 200 million that crossed the Euphrates and which resulted in the death of a third of the world's population (9:15). That was the initial stage in the *stampede* to Armageddon. Now the remaining hindrance of the 1780 mile long river itself has been removed.

Note: The army of 200 million that we saw in Chapter 9 is only a "drop in the bucket" when compared to the population of China, India and the heavily populated adjacent nations. Now the westward movement of soldiers and military hardware is without number.

2. THE WORK OF SATAN: INCITEMENT OF THE WORLD'S ARMIES.

(1) THE NATURE OF THE INCITEMENT. *And I saw three unclean spirits like frogs come out of the mouth of the dragon, and out of the mouth of the beast, and out of the mouth of the false prophet* (16:14). Satan may appear as *an angel of light* (2 Cor 11:14) but here he appears as a *frog, three frogs*, and the world follows. Base little creatures, illustrating the baseness of the men who will follow them! "Go to a marsh at night, when one frog starts croaking, you can hear nothing else" (Newell quoting Alford). Compare the frogs of the Second Plague in Egypt (Exod 8:1-14). Even then the frogs were far more than a nuisance!

- *He sent divers sorts of flies among them, which devoured them;* **and frogs, which destroyed them** (Psa 78:45).

(2) THE PURPOSE OF THE INCITEMENT. *For they are the spirits of devils, working miracles, which go forth unto the kings of the earth and of the whole world, to gather them to the battle of that great day of God Almighty* (16:14). Here is blind fury. Nations that hate each other and hate God will be filled with the insane compulsion to get there armies into armies into the Land of Israel. And why Israel and Jerusalem? This is where Christ will return (Zech 14:1-4). This is the final attempt of Satan and the Satanic Trinity to prevent the Return of Christ. Compare the following example of the inflaming and inciting power of Satan and the Beast.

- *Even him whose coming is after the working of Satan, with all power, and signs, and lying wonders, and with all deceivableness of unrighteousness,* (2 Thess 2:9,10).

3. THE WORK OF CHRIST:

(1) HIS ANNOUNCEMENT. *Behold, I come as a thief. Blessed is he that watcheth, and keepeth his garments, lest he walk naked, and they see his shame* (16:15). Here at the Sixth Vial as with the Sixth Trumpet (likely), the voice of the Lord Himself is heard. This is the Third of Seven Benedictions thus far (1:3; 14:13). The Benediction is coupled with an insight into the degradation to which the Man of Sin (2 Thess 2:3) will bring the world and to which the world will be only too willing to follow. For believers in all ages, *Garments* symbolize conduct. When it does not accord with profession the "nakedness" of that profession is seen by all and the unwatchful Christian is covered with shame(Williams).

The seven year Tribulation will descend upon the lost world as *a thief* (1 Thess 5:2,3; 2 Pet 3:10). It will be unexpected. As the world that died in the flood *they knew not until the flood came* (Matt 24:39). Once in the Tribulation and to any one listening to Elijah or the Two witnesses or reading Revelation (cp. Rev 11:2,3), the time of Christ's Return will become known. Otherwise it will be as a *thief* (Rev 16:15).

THE BOOK OF REVELATION

Believers awaiting the Rapture do not look for Christ as a thief, that is a term for the unconverted, yet in one instance for the unprepared believer His *is* said to return as a thief (Rev 3:3).

(2) HIS GATHERING. ***And he gathered them together into a place called in the Hebrew tongue Armageddon*** (16:16). It was here that Barak overcame Sisera, and all the kings in alliance with him (Jdg 5:19). And here also Josiah was slain (2 Kng 23:29). Thus in Biblical times the place was famous for two events of a very different nature. But now it shall be the field of the last battle, and that with a very good outcome.

- *Therefore wait ye upon me, saith the LORD, until the day that I rise up to the prey: for my determination is to **gather the nations**, that I may **assemble the kingdoms**, to pour upon them mine indignation, even all my fierce anger: for all the earth shall be devoured with the fire of my jealousy (Zeph 3:8).*

Concerning Armageddon Walvoord writes;

> There has been considerable discussion concerning the meaning of the term "Armageddon," taken by some to mean "Mount of Slaughter." Geographically, it relates to the Mount of Megiddo located adjacent to the plain of Megiddo to the west and the large plain of Esdraelon to the northeast. Megiddo is the Hebrew word corresponding to the Greek word Armageddon. This area was the scene of many of the great battles of the Old Testament such as that of Barak and the Canaanites in Judges 4 and the victory of Gideon over the Midianites in Judges 7. Here also occurred the deaths of Saul and Josiah. The area, though it is a large one, is not sufficient for the armies of all the world, though the valley of Esdraelon is fourteen miles wide and twenty miles long. What this Scripture seems to indicate is that this area is the central point for the military conflict which ensues. Actually the armies are deployed over a 200-mile area up and down from this central location (cp. 14:20). At the time of the Second Coming, some of the armies are in Jerusalem itself (Zech 14:1-3).

http://static.panoramio.com/photos/large/6704022.jpg

The Plain of Armageddon

CHAPTER 16

THE SEVENTH VIAL: WORLD WIDE DEVASTATION

(16:17) And the seventh angel poured out his vial into the air; and there came a great voice out of the temple of heaven, from the throne, saying, It is done. (16:18) And there were voices, and thunders, and lightnings; and there was a great earthquake, such as was not since men were upon the earth, so mighty an earthquake, and so great.

(16:19) And the great city was divided into three parts, and the cities of the nations fell: and great Babylon came in remembrance before God, to give unto her the cup of the wine of the fierceness of his wrath. (16:20) And every island fled away, and the mountains were not found.

(16:21) And there fell upon men a great hail out of heaven, every stone about the weight of a talent: and men blasphemed God because of the plague of the hail; for the plague thereof was exceeding great.

1. WHERE THE SEVENTH VIAL WAS POURED. *And the seventh angel poured out his vial into the air; and there came a great voice out of the temple of heaven, from the throne, saying, It is done* (16:17). Though barred from any further access to heaven and cast down to the earth (12:7-9), Satan as *the prince of the power of the air* (Eph 2:2) still retained power in the atmospheric heavens. This last outpost now comes under attack and with it the confirmation, **It is done.** All that is done in the future is based on our Lord's **It in finished** on the Cross (Jhn 19:30). Here the word is *gegonen*, in the perfect tense, indicating action accomplished. It is the final act of God leading up to the Second Coming. Men and women who will not have the Saviour's *IT IS FINISHED* at Calvary, must have the *IT IS DONE* at Armageddon.

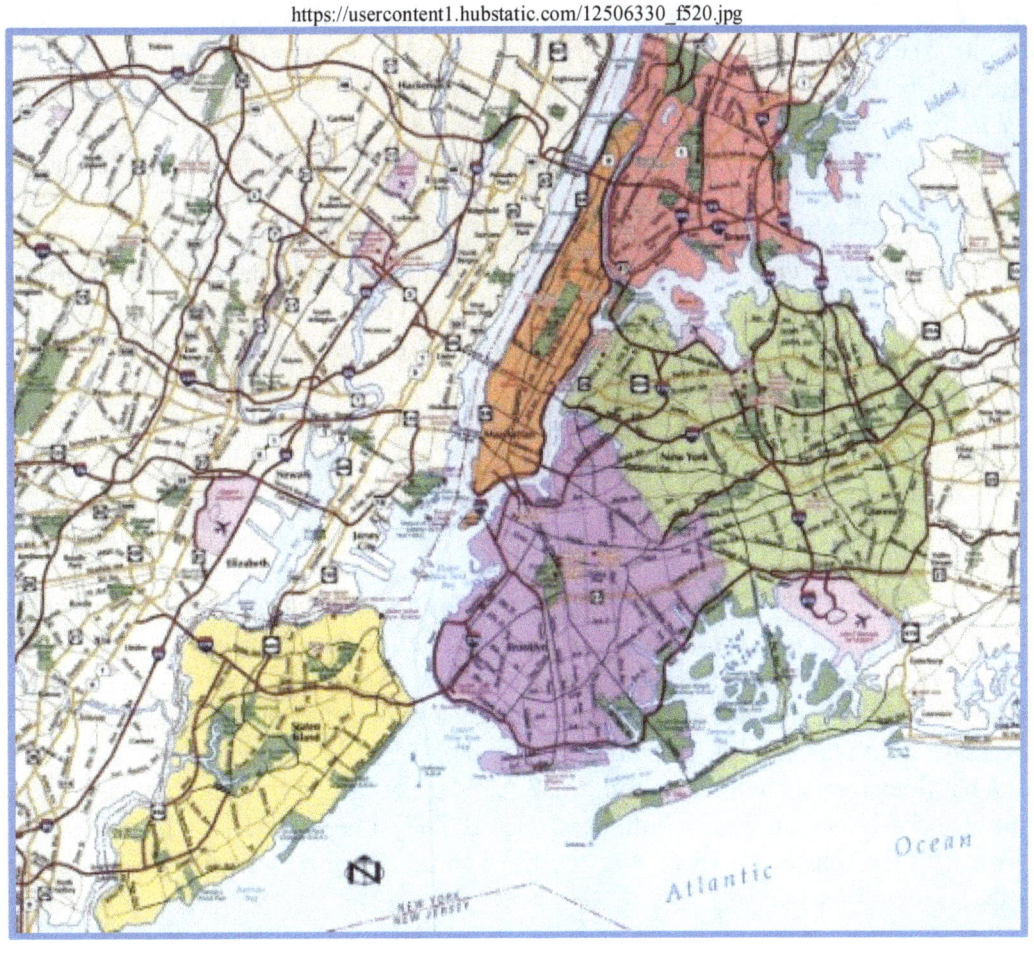

Is NYC the *Great City Divided Into Three Parts*? Its Three Main Sections Already Are! (1) Manhattan, (2) The Bronx to the North, (3) Brooklyn – Queens to the East

    2. WHAT IT PRODUCED.

        (1) IN THE HEAVENS. *And there were voices, and thunders, and lightnings* (16:18). All is in convulsion as the Times of the Gentiles comes to an end and the Lord Jesus Christ returns to reign on earth.

        (2) UPON THE CITIES: *and there was a great earthquake, such as was not since men were upon the earth, so mighty an earthquake, and so great. 19 And the great city was divided into three parts, and the cities of the nations fell: and great Babylon came in remembrance before God, to give unto her the cup of the wine of the fierceness of his wrath* (16:18,19). A mighty convulsion takes place. All monuments of men's ingenuity and grandeur are now ruins. Great changes take place in the topography of the earth. It has changed beyond recognition. Unlike all previous earthquakes which were localized, this will be worldwide.

    Students of prophecy are not agreed on the question of *the great city divided into three parts* (16:19). Jerusalem is call *the great city* in 11:8. Zechariah 13:8,9 speak of a threefold division of Jewish People who die *in all the land* during the Tribulation. Many feel this points to Jerusalem as being the divided city. But, Jerusalem has already had an earthquake at the end of the Tribulation with *a tenth part* of the city falling (Rev 11:13). And, as the words *divided into three parts* point to a substantial destruction of the city, this cannot refer to Jerusalem for Jerusalem will not be destroyed. Most therefore believe this is latter day Babylon with New York the more likely of several possibilities.

    Wherever there is a nation and wherever there is a city within that nation, they will fall. The *cities of the nations fell* is a statement of utter and worldwide devastation. The greatest city, the central city, the seat of the Beast (16:10), commercial Babylon is especially singled out (Ch. 18). Though her destruction was a long time coming and as her *sins have reached unto heaven* (18:5) some may have thought that God forgot; He has not; she now comes into **remembrance.** This is the subject of the final two chapters of Revelation before the Return of Christ.

        (3) UPON THE NATURAL WORLD. *And every island fled away, and the mountains were not found* (16:20). In 6:14 the mountains and islands were *moved*. Here they *flee*. After the Millennium the whole earth and heaven will be *driven away and no place be found for them* (Rev 20:11). Here under the Sixth Vial we have a statement of total devastation! The islands and mountains cannot be found. The world that men knew the day before has perished. The movement of the islands and mountains under the Sixth Seal (6:14) is now brought to a ferocious conclusion with the entire earth radically changed. Such a judgment undoubtedly causes great loss of life and disruption of all the order and organization that the world has depended upon. This is the concentrated, unmingled, full wrath of God.

        (4) UPON THE UNREPENTANT. *And there fell upon men a great hail out of heaven, every stone about the weight of a talent: and men blasphemed God because of the plague of the hail; for the plague thereof was exceeding great* (16:21). The talent weighed about 100 pounds and represented all that a man could normally carry. Such a hail will devastate what was still left after the earthquake.

    What does man have to say about this? Amidst the falling masonry, steel, ruined cities and rubble there is not an atheist left upon earth. They know exactly where these plagues come from and the reason for them. For the third time, the only word we hear is blasphemy (16:9,11).

CHAPTER 16

This has been called the *GREAT CHAPTER*, for that word is found 11 times, the judgements are great and on a level never seen before. The hardness of men's hearts is also great. God's judgement has the final word. There is no escape except for those who avail themselves of the grace of God by faith in Jesus Christ.

3. The Vial Judgements and Other Events   15-18
a. The Preparation   15
b. The Seven Vials Poured Out: <u>Unmingled, Full Wrath</u>   16
c. Judgement on Religious Babylon   17

CHAPTER 17

C. JUDGEMENT ON RELIGIOUS BABYLON 17

**Religious Babylon, the Great City that has *reigned over the kings of the earth*
Revelation 17:18**

This Chapter and the next describe the final destruction of Babylon in both its ecclesiastical and political – commercial forms. Chapter 17 shows that the fall of religious Babylon will take place at the middle of the Tribulation: All worship will then be transferred to the Beast. It is also clear that Babylon in its commercial and political aspect is destroyed at the end of the Tribulation with the pouring out of the Sixth Vial (16:19) and the Return of the Lord Jesus Christ.

A further conclusion must also be made: rather than a complete end of religious Babylon in Chapter 17, and solely a description of commercial Babylon in Chapter 18; there is in Chapter 18 a kind of merging of the two systems. Religious Babylon under the Papacy has given way to religious Babylon under the Beast. He is now the final head of both civil and religious Babylon.

This explains why *Babylon is called Babylon* in both chapters. It also explains why reference is made to religious Babylon at the end of Chapter 18, and at beginning of Chapter 19, when Christ returns. It is also significant that an angel who likely poured his Vial over Babylon is the one now speaking to John (Rev 16:17-19; 17:1).

- *And **in her was found the blood of prophets, and of saints, and of all that were slain upon the earth*** (Rev 18:24).
- *And after these things I heard a great voice of much people in heaven, saying, Alleluia; Salvation, and glory, and honour, and power, unto the Lord our God: 2 For true and righteous are his judgments: for **he hath judged the great whore, which did***

*corrupt the earth with her fornication, and hath avenged the blood of his servants at her hand. 3 And again they said, Alleluia And **her smoke rose up for ever and ever*** (Rev 19:1-3).

THE DESCRIPTION OF THE WOMAN AND THE BEAST

(17:1) *And there came one of the seven angels which had the seven vials, and talked with me, saying unto me, Come hither; I will shew unto thee the judgment of the great whore that sitteth upon many waters:* **(17:2)** *With whom the kings of the earth have committed fornication, and the inhabitants of the earth have been made drunk with the wine of her fornication.*

(17:3) *So he carried me away in the spirit into the wilderness: and I saw a woman sit upon a scarlet coloured beast, full of names of blasphemy, having seven heads and ten horns.* **(17:4)** *And the woman was arrayed in purple and scarlet colour, and decked with gold and precious stones and pearls, having a golden cup in her hand full of abominations and filthiness of her fornication:* **(17:5)** *And upon her forehead was a name written, MYSTERY, BABYLON THE GREAT, THE MOTHER OF HARLOTS AND ABOMINATIONS OF THE EARTH.*

(17:6) *And I saw the woman drunken with the blood of the saints, and with the blood of the martyrs of Jesus: and when I saw her, I wondered with great admiration.*

1. THE APOSTLE IS ALERTED CONCERNING THE WOMAN.

(1) THE ONE ISSUING THE CALL: AN ANGEL OF WRATH. *And there came one of the seven angels which had the seven vials, and talked with me, saying unto me; Come hither;* (17:1). This angel has seen religious Babylon destroyed under both the Papacy in the middle of the Tribulation and under the Beast at the end. Of this latter he was likely the participant; the one who poured out the Vial upon commercial Babylon (16:17-21).

(2) THE SUBJECT OF THE CALL: A WOMAN OF GREAT WICKEDNESS.

[1] HER EPITHET OF INFAMY: *I will shew unto thee the judgment of the great whore.* It is exceedingly rare that one who bore this label should be call **great**. A harlot may be alluring, treacherous and wicked, but never *great*. She professes the Name of Christ but is unfaithful to that Name. The symbolism of spiritual adultery is not used of those who do not know God, but always of people who profess His Name. It is a term used of the apostasy of Israel (Ezek. 16; 23 and all of Hosea; cp. Isa 54:1-8; Jer. 3:14; 31:32). In the New Testament the church is viewed as a virgin destined to be joined to her husband in the future (2 Cor 11:2), but she is warned against spiritual adultery (Jms 4:4).

[2] HER VAST INFLUENCE: *that sitteth upon many waters.* As far as the oceans extend so is her authority and power. The waters are interpreted as *peoples, and multitudes, and nations, and tongues* (Rev 17:15).

[3] HER REGAL ALLIANCES: *With whom the kings of the earth have committed fornication, and the inhabitants of the earth have been made drunk with the wine of her fornication* (17:2). In an unholy union with civil authority she draws from their wealth and authority and then shares with them her favours – but always to extend her own ends. Kings and nations come and go, but Roman Catholicism prevailed across the ages. Until now!

2. THE APOSTLE IS TRANSPORTED TO SEE THE WOMAN. *So he carried me away in the spirit into the wilderness* (17:3). Despite the extent of her domain and influence, everywhere she gains a foothold, it becomes a *wilderness*! Nevertheless for many she is an object of awe and devotion.

CHAPTER 17

(1) HER SITTING: *and I saw a woman sit upon a scarlet coloured beast, full of names of blasphemy, having seven heads and ten horns.* "The fact that the woman, representing the apostate church, is in such close association with the Beast, which is guilty of utter blasphemy, indicates the depth to which apostasy will ultimately descend. The only form of a world church recognized in the Bible is this apostate world church destined to come into power after the true church has been raptured." (Walvoord).

This is the same Beast that was described in Revelation 13:1.

- *And I stood upon the sand of the sea, and saw a beast rise up out of the sea, having **seven heads and ten horns, and upon his horns ten crowns**, and upon his heads the name of blasphemy* (Rev 13:1).

As indicated below, there *may* be a secondary reference to the seven great empires of the past upon which false religion has sat (the mother and child religion of Mystery Babylon). There *may* also be an allusion to the seven hills of Rome. Nevertheless the PRIMARY INTERPRETATION is that Seven Powerful Nations will support the Babylonian religions system, first under the Papacy (represented by the woman) and then under the Beast and his worship. As Walvoord says: "While such a relationship has many parallels in the past history of the Roman church in relation to political power, the inference is that this is a future situation which will take place in the end time." Note again: These are Seven Heads that are "then and there" during the Tribulation. John does not see them coming up one after another.

As we saw in Chapters 12 and 13, each of the Seven Nations will have a *Horn* and *Crown* on their horn. Originally there were Ten Heads (each with a horn) but as the Beast rises to power three are defeated, yet the influence as represented by their horns and crowns remains (Dan 7:8).

(2) HER ALLUREMENTS. *And the woman was arrayed in purple and scarlet colour, and decked with gold and precious stones and pearls, having a golden cup in her hand full of abominations and filthiness of her fornication* (17:4). Here are all of the allurements of worldly honour and riches, pomp and pride, suited to sensual and worldly minds. But as with the cup she holds, her visual splendour hides great wickedness. It may be a golden cup but it contains great depths of evil. "The description of the woman as arrayed in purple and scarlet and decked with gold, precious stones, and pearls is all too familiar to one acquainted with the trappings of ecclesiastical pomp today and especially of high officials in the Roman Catholic and Greek Orthodox churches. Purple and scarlet, symbolically so rich in their meaning when connected with true spiritual values, are here prostituted to this false religious system and designed to glorify it with religious garb in contrast to the simplicity of pious adornment (cp. 1 Tim. 2:9-10)." (Walvoord).

Walvoord says further:

> The most striking aspect of her presentation, however, is that she has *a golden cup* in her hand described as "full of abomination and filthiness of her fornication." The Word of God does not spare words in describing the utter filthiness of this adulterous relationship in the sight of God. Few crimes in Scripture are spoken of in more unsparing terms than the crime of spiritual adultery of which this woman is the epitome.

(3) HER NAME. *And upon her forehead was a name written, MYSTERY, BABYLON THE GREAT, THE MOTHER OF HARLOTS AND ABOMINATIONS OF THE EARTH* (17:5). This use of large capital letters is found twenty-five times in the King James Version. Though not occurring in the underlying text or in previous versions, it is

believed that the AV Translators were, and in consent with each other, providentially impressed to give this emphasis. This is one of two occurrences in Revelation. They span a great extremity!

- *And he hath on his vesture and on his thigh a name written,* **KING OF KINGS, AND LORD OF LORDS** (Rev 19:16).

It was the custom of harlots to hang out signs with their names, that all might know where they were. Thus here the name is emblazoned in capital letters for all to see. And as with a harlot generally, one will not have to look hard to find her. Not now; not in past history.

- *Thou hadst a whore's forehead, thou refusedst to be ashamed* (Jet 3:3).

She is named from her original place of residence—**BABYLON THE GREAT**. But that we might not limit it to ancient Babylon, we are told that there is **MYSTERY** in this name. It has been replicated across the centuries and now to its final end. She is a **MOTHER OF HARLOTS**, breeding up heresies and teachings which like herself are unfaithful to Christ. She is the parent and nurse of false religion and wicked behaviour associated with religion. These mysteries began with Nimrod and Babel in Genesis 10. For a full discussion of the Babylonian Mystery Religion, see the account given of Pergamos and *Satan's Seat* (2:12-17).

(4) HER DRUNKENESS: *And I saw the woman drunken with the blood of the saints, and with the blood of the martyrs of Jesus: and when I saw her, I wondered with great admiration* (17:6). She satiated herself with *the blood of the saints and martyrs of Jesus*. She drank their blood with such greediness that she intoxicated herself; it was so pleasant to her that she could not tell when she had enough. She was satiated, but never satisfied. See Chapter 2:18-29 for a historical account of Roman Catholic persecution. Those martyr days will return during the Tribulation and with vengeance far exceeding the terrible atrocities of the past.

THE INTERPRETATION OF THE *BEAST*

(17:7) *And the angel said unto me, Wherefore didst thou marvel? I will tell thee the mystery of the woman, and of the beast that carrieth her, which hath the seven heads and ten horns.*
(17:8) *The beast that thou sawest was, and is not; and shall ascend out of the bottomless pit, and go into perdition: and they that dwell on the earth shall wonder, whose names were not written in the book of life from the foundation of the world, when they behold the beast that was, and is not, and yet is.*
(17:9) *And here is the mind which hath wisdom. The seven heads are seven mountains, on which the woman sitteth.* (17:10) *And there are seven kings: five are fallen, and one is, and the other is not yet come; and when he cometh, he must continue a short space.* (17:11) *And the beast that was, and is not, even he is the eighth, and is of the seven, and goeth into perdition.*

1. THE APOSTLE IS SHOWN THE INTERPRETATION. *And the angel said unto me, Wherefore didst thou marvel? I will tell thee the mystery of the woman, and of the beast that carrieth her, which hath the seven heads and ten horns* (17:7). The interpreting angel, the one who poured out one of the final Vials (and likely upon the final state of Babylon; 16:17-21) comes now to give the interpretation to John. That is, he steps directly out of the end of Chapter 16, (and at the end of the Tribulation), directly into the events of

CHAPTER 17

Chapter 17. Note carefully that at this point he can speak of the Beast *which **HATH** the seven heads and ten horns.*

As seen in 12:2 and 13:1 both Satan and the Beast ***HAVE** the Seven Heads then and there* during the Tribulation; they are *not* seven successive empires from the past to the present. Therefore the verses that now follow (17:8-11) must be interpreted on the basis of this fact. It is true that from what follows, *the woman* (Papal Rome) will indeed have lost her "perch" 3 and 1/2 years earlier, but the Seven Heads and Ten Horns will together remain intact until the end of the Tribulation.

HEREAFTER IN CHAPTER 17 THE EMPHASIS IS INCREASINGLY ON INDIVIDUAL LEADERS RATHER THAN THE NATIONS OVER WHICH THEY RULED

- The Beast Himself
- The Seven Kings of the Seven Heads (Seven Mountains)
- The Ten Kings of the Ten Horns

(1) THE EMPOWERMENT OF THE BEAST. *The beast that thou sawest was, and is not; and shall ascend out of the bottomless pit, and go into perdition: and they that dwell on the earth shall wonder, whose names were not written in the book of life from the foundation of the world, when they behold the beast that was, and is not, and yet is* (17:8). This is the second time *the Book of life* is mentioned and in connection with those who follow the Beast. See the notes on 13:8. At the Midpoint of the Tribulation, the Antichrist and his kingdom will be energized from the *bottomless pit*. This will coincide with the Antichrist's *death wound*. It is the Beast as an individual that is especially emphasised.

It is the Beast as an <u>individual</u> that is said to **ascend out of the bottomless pit**. Certainly the entire revived Roman Empire will not ascend out of the bottomless pit!

- *And when they shall have finished their testimony,* ***the beast that ascendeth out of the bottomless pit*** *shall make war against them, and shall overcome them, and kill them* (Rev 11:7).

This ascension out of the Abyss is associated with the death wound that he incurs as an <u>individual</u>.

- *And I saw one of his heads as it were **wounded to death**; and **his deadly wound was healed**: and all the world wondered after the beast* (Rev 13:3).
- *And he exerciseth all the power of the first beast before him, and causeth the earth and them which dwell therein to worship the first beast,* ***whose deadly wound was healed*** (Rev 13:12).
- *And deceiveth them that dwell on the earth by the means of those miracles which he had power to do in the sight of the beast; saying to them that dwell on the earth, that they should make an image to the beast,* ***which had the wound by a sword, and did live*** (Rev 13:14).

Therefore:

- It is the Beast as <u>individual</u> that had **the deadly wound that was healed** (13:3,12).
- It is to the Beast as an <u>individual</u> that **the world wonders** (13:3).
- It is to the Beast as an <u>individual</u> that the world **worships** (13:4,12).
- It is to the Beast as an <u>individual</u> that the world **makes an image** (13:14).

THE BOOK OF REVELATION

• It is the Beast as an *individual* that was, and is not, and yet is (17:8,11).

With the greatest amazement the world will **behold the beast that was, and is not, and yet is** (17:8). This is a Biblical expression for death and is the term given to the "death and resurrection "of the Beast. To say that this refers to the revival of the Roman Empire misses the point that what happens to the Beast is **sudden**, dramatic and resulting in worldwide wonderment and surprise. It will be an event of a few days at most. Rome's restoration will be a process over one or two years. "Rome wasn't built in a day," and it will not be restored in a day.

• *And he returned unto his brethren, and said,* **The child is not***; and I, whither shall I go* (Gen 37:30)?
• *And they said, Thy servants are twelve brethren, the sons of one man in the land of Canaan; and, behold, the youngest is this day with our father, and* **one is not** (Gen 42:13).

(2) THE HEADS OF THE BEAST. *And here is the mind which hath wisdom. The seven heads are seven mountains, on which the woman sitteth* (17:9).

[1] THE *SUCCESSION OF SEVEN WORLD EMPIRES* VIEW.
False religion (the woman), and with a strongly Babylonian emphasis, is seen here seated on the back of seven successive world empires: 1. Egypt, 2. Assyria, 3. Babylon, 4. Persia, 5. Greece, 6. Rome, 7. Revived Rome. Though different names are used for the false religious system that has *sat* upon the great empires of the past, there is the common source in Nimrod and the Babel of Genesis 10. It is Mystery Babylon the Great the Mother of Harlots (17:5). This is a fact of history. However, in harmony with Revelation 12:3; 13:1 and Daniel 7: the woman at the time of her destruction will be sitting on a Beast having Seven **Simultaneous** Heads.

Capitoline is the Only Distinct Hill Today

[2] THE *SEVEN HILLS ROME* VIEW. Rome sits on seven hills to signify that she is the heir and final resting place of the Babylonian mysteries which resided

on the previous empires. This is an attractive suggestion but like the above does not fulfil the requirement for Seven Simultaneous Powers. The Seven Hills of Rome are not *mountains*. The ravines between the hills were filled long ago. Only one of the Seven is clearly discernible as a *hill* today.

[3] THE ENDTIME *SEVEN NATION* VIEW.

And here is the mind which hath wisdom.
The <u>seven heads are seven mountains</u>, on which the woman sitteth (17:9).
And there are <u>seven kings</u>:
(5)   *<u>five</u> are fallen,*
(6th) *and <u>one is</u>,*
(7th) *and <u>the other is not yet come</u>;*
         and when he cometh, he must continue a short space (17:10).
(8th) *And the beast that was, and is not, even he is the eighth, and is of the seven,*
         and goeth into perdition (17:11).

Walvoord rightly says: "The explanation of the beast introduced by the unusual phrase, *here is the mind which hath wisdom,* anticipates the difficulty and complexity of the revelation to follow. The reader is warned that spiritual wisdom is required to understand that which is unfolded."

Key to understanding these pivotal verses begins with the primary facts that have been stressed before:

(1) The Woman (Papal Rome) rides a Beast that has Seven Heads and Ten Horns.

(2) Each Beast has a horn, but three horns are the remains of three defeated heads. Thus the Beast though having Seven Heads has a total of Ten Horns (Dan 7:8).

(4) The Seven *Heads* are also called Seven *Mountains* (seven powerful nations) that support the Woman until the middle of the Tribulation. Papal Rome is then destroyed by the Seven Nations (*Heads-Mountains*) and the *Ten Horns* (17:16).

(5) One of the Heads is the nation from which the Antichrist comes. This nation has had a succession of Five Previous Kings (before the Tribulation begins). This Sixth King, *one is,* is also likely to be before the Tribulation. The term of the Seventh King is cut short at the beginning of the Tribulation (the Seventieth Week), The Antichrist is the eighth and *is of the seven* (a natural heir of the previous kings). The following passage is especially relative:

- *And I saw **one of his heads as it were wounded to death**; and his deadly wound was healed: and all the world wondered after the beast* (Rev 13:3).

Note: The Rapture is imminent! We look first for Christ, not Antichrist; nor do we look for kings who might precede Antichrist. The fact that this scenario might tend toward that, demonstrates that the actual start of the Tribulation with the confirming of the seven year treaty with Israel (Dan 9:26,27) seems likely to occur sometime after the Rapture. For the Rapture to be a *mystery*, such would have to be the case (1 Cor 15:51). The prospect of a Psalm 83 war may also point to such a gap between the Rapture and start of the Tribulation.

THE FINAL SEVEN NATIONS AND THE CURRENT GROUP OF SEVEN (G 7)

"The Group of 7 (G7) is a group consisting of **Canada**, **France**, **Germany**, **Italy**, **Japan**, the **United Kingdom** and the **United States**. These countries, with the 7 largest advanced economies in the world, represent more than 64% of the net global wealth ($263 trillion). The G7 countries also represent 46% of the global nominal GDP evaluated at market exchange rates and 32% of the global purchasing power parity GDP. The European Union is also represented within the G7 summit.

The G7 originates with the Group of Six. It was founded ad hoc in 1975, consisting of finance ministers and central bank governors from France, West Germany, Italy, Japan, the United Kingdom and the United States, when Giscard d'Estaing invited them for an "informal gathering at the chateau of Rambouillet, near Paris …Canada became the seventh member to begin attending the summits in 1976 after which the name 'Group 7' or G7 Summit was used.

Following 1994's G7 summit in Naples, Russian officials held separate meetings with leaders of the G7 after the group's summits….After the 1997 meeting Russia was formally invited to the next meeting and formally joined the group in 1998, resulting in a new governmental political forum, the Group of Eight, or G8. However Russia was ejected from the G8 political forum in March 2014 following the Russian annexation of Crimea." (Wikipedia).

During the first half of the Tribulation, the *Woman* (Papal Rome) will be supported by Seven Nations (*Heads, Mountains*). With the exception of Japan and Russia, six of the others give strong support to the Roman Catholic Church. Time will tell which of the above will be in the Final Seven. Certainly on the basis of Revelation 17, each of the Seven would have a substantial Roman Catholic population. That might rule out Britain.

THE INTERPRETATION OF THE *HORNS*

(17:12) *And the ten horns which thou sawest are ten kings, which have received no kingdom as yet; but receive power as kings one hour with the beast.* (17:13) *These have one mind, and shall give their power and strength unto the beast.* (17:14) *These shall make war with the Lamb, and the Lamb shall overcome them: for he is Lord of lords, and King of kings: and they that are with him are called, and chosen, and faithful.*

**The Beast Empire: Seven Heads, Ten Horns, Ten Crowns
Appearance of a Leopard, Feet of a Bear, Mouth of a Lion**

CHAPTER 17

As we have seen, each of the Seven Heads has a horn, and the three additional horns are the remains of three defeated heads (Dan 7:8). Note again the picture by Michael Defazio. This gives the best representation that I have seen.

1. THE SHORT REIGN OF THE HORNS. *And the ten horns which thou sawest are ten kings, which have received no kingdom as yet; but receive power as kings one hour with the beast. 13 These have one mind, and shall give their power and strength unto the beast* (17:12,13). The Ten Horns are the ten end time kings who receive their status as *Horns* (with *crowns*, Rev 13:1) from the Antichrist. They will provide the powerbase for his world domination. Their horn status will not last long; only **one hour**.

2. THE FOOLISH WAR OF THE HORNS. *These shall make war with the Lamb, and* (17:14). Their foolish wicked and short-lived support of the Beast will be brought to a catastrophic end by the **Lord of lords, and King of kings.** One hour with the Beast on earth, an eternity with the Beast in the Lake of fire (19:20; 20:10). This is the third time in recent chapters that the impending Battle of Armageddon has been mentioned (14:18-20; 16:12-14).

3. THE GROUND OF VICTORY OVER THE HORNS: *the Lamb shall overcome them for he is Lord of lords, and King of kings: and they that are with him are called, and chosen, and faithful.*

(1) THE CHARACTER OF THE LAMB: *He is King of kings and Lord of lords*. He has, both by nature and by office, supreme dominion and power over all things; all the powers of earth and hell are subject to His control.

(2) THE CHARACTER OF HIS FOLLOWERS. *They are called, and chosen, and faithful.* They are called out by commission to this warfare; they are chosen and fitted for it, and they will be faithful in it. Such an army, under such a Commander, will overcome all that the world would wage against them.

THE INTERPRETATION OF THE *WOMAN SITTING ON THE BEAST*

(17:15) *And he saith unto me, The waters which thou sawest, where the whore sitteth, are peoples, and multitudes, and nations, and tongues.*

(17:16) *And the ten horns which thou sawest upon the beast, these shall hate the whore, and shall make her desolate and naked, and shall eat her flesh, and burn her with fire.* (17:17) *For God hath put in their hearts to fulfil his will, and to agree, and give their kingdom unto the beast, until the words of God shall be fulfilled.*

(17:18) *And the woman which thou sawest is that great city, which reigneth over the kings of the earth.*

1. THE EXTENT OF THE *WOMAN'S* POWER. *And he saith unto me, The waters which thou sawest, where the whore sitteth, are peoples, and multitudes, and nations, and tongues* (17:16). Here is the vast multitude who paid homage to Roman Catholicism and the apostate Protestant churches who followed her. Here is the final stage of the Ecumenical Movement presided over by Rome during the last days. She is seen sitting upon **waters, many** waters (17:1). The *waters* are the multitudes of the earth. They are *waters*, unstable, changeable, easily influenced. The woman *sits* on them; she rules with oppressive force over them.

2. THE MAGNITUDE OF THE *WOMAN'S* DESTRUCTION.

(1) THE MEANS OF HER DESTRUCTION. *And the ten horns which thou sawest upon the beast, these shall hate the whore, and shall make her desolate and naked, and shall eat her flesh, and burn her with fire* (17:16). They at last shall see their folly, and how they have been bewitched and enslaved by the Papacy and in just resentment will

THE BOOK OF REVELATION

destroy her and all her trappings. They, though worshipping the Beast, are made the instruments of God's wrath in Rome's destruction. Likely the rampant child abuse among the Roman clergy will be an incentive toward this.

(2) THE INDUCEMENT TO HER DESTRUCTION. *For God hath put in their hearts to fulfil his will, and to agree, and give their kingdom unto the beast, until the words of God shall be fulfilled* (17:17).

- *Surely the wrath of man shall praise thee: the remainder of wrath shalt thou restrain* (Psalm 76:10).

3. THE DOMINION OF THE *WOMAN'S* CITY. *And the woman which thou sawest is that great city, which reigneth over the kings of the earth* (17:18). Not only does Rome rule over vast multitudes, but no city on earth has reigned over kings as she has. Frequently they have been her tributaries and vassals. This means also that she *had* great influence over the Ten Kings of the Ten Nations who were her *destroyers*!

CHAPTER 18

D. JUDGEMENT ON POLITICAL-COMMERCIAL BABYLON 18

The first Babylon (Babel) of Genesis 10 was both Religious and Political. By being Political, it was also Commercial. In latter day Babylon, there is also the fall of both the Religious and the Political-Commercial. But, unlike Nimrod's or Nebuchadnezzar's Babylon this is represented by the fall of two cities. Both are great cities. Both fall. And, both are linked at the end of Chapter to receive the same final condemnation.

- *And the woman which thou sawest is **that great city**, which reigneth over the kings of the earth* (Rev 17:18).
- *Standing afar off for the fear of her torment, saying, Alas, alas **that great city Babylon, that mighty city! for in one hour is thy judgment come** (Rev 18:10).*
- *And cried when they saw the smoke of her burning, saying, **What city is like unto this great city** (Rev 18:18)!*
- ***Rejoice over her, thou heaven, and ye holy apostles and prophets; for God hath avenged you on her*** *(Rev 18:20).*
- *And **in her was found the blood of prophets**, and of saints, and of all that were slain upon the earth* (Rev 18:24).
- *And after these things I heard a great voice of much people in heaven, saying, Alleluia; Salvation, and glory, and honour, and power, unto the Lord our God: 2 For true and righteous are his judgments: for **he hath judged the great whore, which did corrupt the earth with her fornication, and hath avenged the blood of his servants** at her hand. 3 And again they said, Alleluia And her smoke rose up for ever and ever* (Rev 19:1-3).

Chapter 18 begins with the words *after these things*. After the fall of Religious Babylon (which is Rome, shortly after the midpoint of the Tribulation), we have here the fall of Commercial and Political Babylon (often thought to be New York). Thus Babylon *is fallen, is fallen* (Isa 21:9; Rev 18:2). Religious Babylon is hated, the fall of Commercial Babylon causes the world to lament. This is a sombre chapter and reflects the Fifth Vial which brought darkness to the Beast's capital city and the Seventh Vial which brought Babylon *in remembrance before God* (Rev 16:10,19).

Students of Bible Prophecy have for nearly a century been convinced that New York City is the prime candidate to partner with Rome as the commercial side of latter day Babylon. It is huge, though several cities are larger. Tourists flock there, but more come to London. It is a center of world commerce, but other cities are challenging her dominance. Yet the one thing that makes New York different is that the rest of the world perceives her to be the *Big Apple*. The world does not say this about Tokyo or London or Paris or Shanghai. That title belongs to New York. New York has three place names that make it the world's byword for consumerism, finance and entertainment. For commerce and consumerism it has Fifth Avenue; for finance, Wall Street and for entertainment, Broadway and Times Square.

The NYC area has a larger Roman Catholic population than Rome; a larger Irish population than Dublin; a huge Spanish population. It has Harlem. It has almost as many Jewish people as Israel. New York is the world! It is the home of the United Nations. It is the world as to its philosophy. It is big business; big money; big entertainment. It also has had *big crime*. It has been a stronghold for the Mafia and organised crime.

THE BOOK OF REVELATION

New York is the world's ultimate *love of the world city* (1 Jhn 2:15). The city is notable for being *a bastion against the Gospel*. My wife's mother was born in New York. We lived there for a short time. Our eldest son was born there. There is not a mission field on the entire earth with a greater need.

For another Babylon candidate one might consider London. *It was a Roman city* and the virtual capital of a large part of the world when the British Empire was at its height. It issued the 1917 Balfour Declaration. Its financial importance equals New York and yearly receives a third more tourists. New York, though, has a third larger metro population, a much larger port (cp.18:17-19) and a much larger Jewish population (cp. 18:4). From Revelation 13:18 it is shown that by a common computation, the name New York equals 666.

Times Square

BABYLON'S DESTRUCTION DECLARED

(18:1) *And after these things I saw another angel come down from heaven, having great power; and the earth was lightened with his glory.* (18:2) *And he cried mightily with a strong voice, saying, Babylon the great is fallen, is fallen, and is become the habitation of devils, and the hold of every foul spirit, and a cage of every unclean and hateful bird.* (18:3) *For all nations have drunk of the wine of the wrath of her fornication, and the kings of the earth have committed fornication with her, and the merchants of the earth are waxed rich through the abundance of her delicacies.*

(18:4) *And I heard another voice from heaven, saying, Come out of her, my people, that ye be not partakers of her sins, and that ye receive not of her plagues.* (18:5) *For her sins have reached unto heaven, and God hath remembered her iniquities.* (18:6) *Reward her even as she rewarded you, and double unto her double according to her works: in the cup which she hath filled fill to her double.* (18:7) *How much she hath glorified herself, and lived deliciously, so much torment and sorrow give her: for she saith in her heart, I sit a queen, and am no widow, and shall see no sorrow.* (18:8) *Therefore shall her plagues come in one day, death, and mourning, and famine; and she shall be utterly burned with fire: for strong is the Lord God who judgeth her.*

THE FIRST CALL 18:1-3.
<u>1. THE ONE MAKING THE CALL</u>. *And after these things I saw another angel come down from heaven, having great power; and the earth was lightened with his glory*

CHAPTER 18

(18:1). Another angel sent from heaven, attended with great power and brightness descends upon the darkened earth (cp. 16:10).

2. THE SUBJECT OF THE ANNOUNCEMENT.

(1) BABYLON'S TWO-FOLD FALL. *And he cried mightily with a strong voice, saying, Babylon the great is fallen, is fallen* (18:2). The angel announces that the fall of Babylon is so fully determined in the counsels of God that no doubt must be left that it has been destroyed in both of its parts; religious and political-commercial. This two-fold fall was the subject of Isaiah's prophecy, and shortly before the Vial Judgements fell a similar angelic announcement was made.

- *And, behold, here cometh a chariot of men, with a couple of horsemen. And he answered and said,* **Babylon is fallen, is fallen**; *and all the graven images of her gods he hath broken unto the ground* (Isa 21:9).
- *And there followed another angel, saying,* **Babylon is fallen, is fallen**, *that great city, because she made all nations drink of the wine of the wrath of her fornication* (Rev 14:8).

(2) BABYLON'S WICKEDNESS: *and is become the habitation of devils, and the hold of every foul spirit, and a cage of every unclean and hateful bird.* The devils of the city are symbolized by birds and are as common as the birds on the city's tree lined streets. Nor do they fly elsewhere for this great city is their *habitation, hold* and *cage*. The city was a chattering madhouse of demons!

Compare:

- *And when* **the fowls came down** *upon the carcasses, Abram drove them away* (Gen 15:11).
- *Which indeed is the least of all seeds: but when it is grown, it is the greatest among herbs, and becometh a tree, so that* **the birds of the air come and lodge** *in the branches thereof* (Matt 13:32).

It is striking to note that birds were also mentioned in the prophecy of the fall of Nebuchadnezzar's Babylon. Here, the birds illustrate the absolute desolation that would come to the city. But, in both cases Babylon has been *abandoned to the birds*!

- *But the* **cormorant** *and the* **bittern** *shall possess it; the* **owl** *also and the* **raven** *shall dwell in it: and he shall stretch out upon it the line of confusion, and the stones of emptiness* (Isa 34:11).
- *There shall the* **great owl** *make her nest, and lay, and hatch, and gather under her shadow: there shall the* **vultures** *also be gathered, every one with her mate* (Isa 34:15).

(3) BABYLON'S INCITEMENT. *For all nations have drunk of the wine of the wrath of her fornication, and the kings of the earth have committed fornication with her, and the merchants of the earth are waxed rich through the abundance of her delicacies* (18:3). The nations, kings and merchants did not wax as rich through the city of Rome, they were, if anything, impoverished by her. It is rather though *the abundance of…delicacies* of a great market place like New York or London that wealth is made. These delicacies incite a desire for the material rather than the things of Christ. Babylon has drawn all sorts of men into the love of the world and has kept them close with interest.

- *Covetousness, which is idolatry* (Col 3:5).
- *For* **the love of money is the root of all evil**: *which while some coveted after, they have erred from the faith, and pierced themselves through with many sorrows* (1 Tim 6:10).

THE SECOND CALL 18:4-8. *And I heard another voice from heaven, saying* (18:4).

1. FLEE THE CITY. *Come out of her, my people, that ye be not partakers of her sins, and that ye receive not of her plagues* (18:4). In a similar way the people of God were urged to leave Babylon after the Captivity (Jer 51:45); and also as Lot was warned to leave Sodom (Gen 19:15-22). In the case of New York this would especially be a call to the millions of Jewish People who live there. The *plagues* refer to the Vials of chapter 16, and especially the Seventh Vial which falls upon Babylon itself (16:17-21).

(1) THE ENORMITY OF HER SINS. *For her sins have reached unto heaven* (18:5). The word for *reached* is *kollao*; literally "glued" or "welded together." The picture is that of her sins piled one on another as bricks in a building. It is an allusion to the beginning of Babylon at the Tower of Babel (Gen 11:5-9). It may also allude to the skyscrapers of New York

(2) THE KNOWLEDGE OF HER SINS: *and God hath remembered her iniquities.* When the sins of a city reach up to Heaven, the wrath of God will reach down to the city.

2. "REWARD" THE CITY. *Reward her even as she rewarded you, and double unto her double according to her works: in the cup which she hath filled fill to her double* (18:6). This is similar to Israel at the command of the Lord to *spoil the Egyptians* when they left Egypt (Exod 3:22; 12:36). This was for unpaid wages. The word for *reward* (*apodidomi*) means literally "to pay a debt" or "to give back that which is due." The normal law of retribution is now doubled because of the enormity of the sin of Babylon.

(1) BECAUSE OF HER AGGRANDISEMENT. *How much she hath glorified herself, and lived deliciously, so much torment and sorrow give her: for she saith in her heart, I sit a queen, and am no widow, and shall see no sorrow* (18:7). The wealthy church at Laodicea also boasted of these things.

- *Because thou sayest,* **I am rich, and increased with goods, and have need of nothing**; *and knowest not that thou art wretched, and miserable, and poor, and blind, and naked (Rev 3:17).*

- *Go to now, ye rich men, weep and howl for your miseries that shall come upon you. Your riches are corrupted, and your garments are motheaten. Your gold and silver is cankered; and the rust of them shall be a witness against you, and shall eat your flesh as it were fire.* **Ye have heaped treasure together for the last days**. *Behold, the hire of the labourers who have reaped down your fields, which is of you kept back by fraud, crieth: and the cries of them which have reaped are entered into the ears of the Lord of sabaoth (Jms 5:1-4).*

(2) BECAUSE OF HER IMMINENT DESTRUCTION. *Therefore shall her plagues come in one day, death, and mourning, and famine; and she shall be utterly burned with fire: for strong is the Lord God who judgeth her* (18:8). Verse 7 was all wishful thinking. It was a *sunny day* when God reigned fire upon Sodom (Gen 19:22-24). It was *party time* when Belshazzar feasted in Babylon. It was *build new barns time* for the farmer in Luke 12.

- *And thou his son, O Belshazzar, hast not humbled thine heart, though thou knewest all this: 23 But hast lifted up thyself against the Lord of heaven; and they have brought the vessels of his house before thee, and thou, and thy lords, thy wives, and thy concubines, have drunk wine in them; and thou hast praised the gods of silver, and gold, of brass, iron, wood, and stone, which see not, nor hear, nor know: and the God in whose hand thy breath is, and whose are all thy ways, hast thou not glorified (Dan 5:22,23).*

CHAPTER 18

- *In that night was Belshazzar the king of the Chaldeans slain* (Dan 5:30).
- *And I will say to my soul, Soul, thou hast much goods laid up for many years; take thine ease, eat, drink, and be merry.* **20 But God said unto him, Thou fool, this night thy soul shall be required of thee**: *then whose shall those things be, which thou hast provided* (Lk 12:19,20)?

BABYLON'S DESTRUCTION LAMENTED

(18:9) *And the kings of the earth, who have committed fornication and lived deliciously with her, shall bewail her, and lament for her, when they shall see the smoke of her burning,* (18:10) *Standing afar off for the fear of her torment, saying, Alas, alas, that great city Babylon, that mighty city! for in one hour is thy judgment come.*

(18:11) *And the merchants of the earth shall weep and mourn over her; for no man buyeth their merchandise any more:* (18:12) *The merchandise of gold, and silver, and precious stones, and of pearls, and fine linen, and purple, and silk, and scarlet, and all thyine wood, and all manner vessels of ivory, and all manner vessels of most precious wood, and of brass, and iron, and marble,* (18:13) *And cinnamon, and odours, and ointments, and frankincense, and wine, and oil, and fine flour, and wheat, and beasts, and sheep, and horses, and chariots, and slaves, and souls of men.* (18:14) *And the fruits that thy soul lusted after are departed from thee, and all things which were dainty and goodly are departed from thee, and thou shalt find them no more at all.* (18:15) *The merchants of these things, which were made rich by her, shall stand afar off for the fear of her torment, weeping and wailing,*

(18:16) *And saying, Alas, alas, that great city, that was clothed in fine linen, and purple, and scarlet, and decked with gold, and precious stones, and pearls!* (18:17) *For in one hour so great riches is come to nought. And every shipmaster, and all the company in ships, and sailors, and as many as trade by sea, stood afar off,* (18:18) *And cried when they saw the smoke of her burning, saying, What city is like unto this great city!* (18:19) *And they cast dust on their heads, and cried, weeping and wailing, saying, Alas, alas, that great city, wherein were made rich all that had ships in the sea by reason of her costliness! for in one hour is she made desolate.*

<u>1. THE GOVERNMENTAL WORLD LAMENTS</u>. *And the kings of the earth, who have committed fornication and lived deliciously with her, shall bewail her, and lament for her, when they shall see the smoke of her burning, 10 Standing afar off for the fear of her torment, saying, Alas, alas, that great city Babylon, that mighty city! for in one hour is thy judgment come* (18:9,10).These kings are a wider designation than the Ten Kings of 17:12,16, and who participated in the destruction of Papal Babylon. Here there is lament over the destruction of Commercial Babylon. The very kings who participated in the wickedness and wealth of Babylon now mourn her passing. It is a fiery passing.

<u>(1) THEIR TWO-FOLD INVOLVEMENT WITH BABYLON</u>.

[1] *who have committed fornication.* There is both religious and materialistic *fornication* (Rev 17:2; Col 3:10). This sin was committed with both Religious and Commercial Babylon.

- *With whom the kings of the earth have committed **fornication**, and the inhabitants of the earth have been made drunk with the wine of her fornication* (Rev 17:2).
- *Covetousness, which is idolatry* (Col 3:10).

[2] *and lived deliciously with her.* The feast may have seemed delicious, but it did not last long.

(2) THEIR FOUR-FOLD LAMENTATION.

[1] *shall bewail her.* They did not bewail Religious Babylon (17:16).

[2] *and lament for her, when they shall see the smoke of her burning.* They are not said to be lamenting theirs sins that have brought them to this terrible hour.

[3] ***Standing afar off for the fear of her torment*** (18:10). Babylon's friends will stand at a distance from her fall. Though they had been partakers with her in her sins, and in her sinful pleasures and profits, they were not willing to bear a share in her plagues. There is fear but no help. They are not seen attempting to put out the fire.

[4] ***saying, Alas, alas, that great city Babylon, that mighty city! for in one hour is thy judgment come.*** The lament of the kings over Babylon is most emphatic in the Greek by the repetition of the article: literally "***the*** city ***the*** great, Babylon ***the*** city ***the*** mighty". In spite of Babylon's greatness and strength it was all over in ***one hour*** (see 18:19).

2. THE COMMERCIAL WORLD LAMENTS 18:11-16.

(1) THEY LAMENT THE TWENTY EIGHT-FOLD LOSS OF BUSINESS.
And the merchants of the earth shall weep and mourn over her; for no man buyeth their merchandise any more (18:11). The fall of the world's greatest marketplace will affect all the other centers of commerce on earth. Here are 28 items. With *four* the number of the world and *seven* the number of completeness; this is 4 x 7, a complete inventory of what the world has to offer.

[1-4] JEWELLERY. ***The merchandise of gold, and silver, and precious stones, and of pearls.*** Precious stones and costly metals, characteristic of wealth and luxury; and characteristic of the *display* of wealth.

[5-8] CLOTHING: ***and fine linen, and purple, and silk, and scarlet.*** Fine fabrics and luxurious colours used in their clothing. To see and be seen.

[9-14] FURNITURE: ***and all thyine wood, and all manner vessels of ivory, and all manner vessels of most precious wood, and of brass, and iron, and marble*** (18:12). From this marketplace the luxury of the apparel for sale is matched by the opulence of the furnishings on offer. ***Thyine*** was a fragrant wood similar to cypress and was used for expensive furniture.

[15-18] AROMATICS. ***And cinnamon, and odours, and ointments, and frankincense*** (18:13). Expensive perfumes and spices are abundantly displayed. All are for the wealthy.

[19-24] EDIBLES: ***and wine, and oil, and fine flour, and wheat, and beasts, and sheep.*** Both the accompaniments and the "mains" for the lavish feasts of latter day Babylon.

[25-26] CONVEYANCES: ***and horses, and chariots.*** Every means of transport is available for purchase.

[27-28] MANPOWER: ***and slaves, and souls of men.*** Commercial Babylon under the Beast will drive a hard bargain with the masses whom she employs. Given also the plagues descending on the earth, it will be *starvation wages*. Both body and soul will be under the complete dominance of the employer (contrast 1 Cor 7:23).

THE SUMMARY: ***And the fruits that thy soul lusted after are departed from thee, and all things which were dainty and goodly are departed from thee, and thou shalt find them no more at all*** (18:14). The combined picture is one of complete abandonment to the wealth of this world and total disregard of God who gave it. We have here a large inventory of the wealth and merchandise of Commercial Babylon of the last days, all which was suddenly lost and all lost irrecoverably. There is here a sweeping removal of everything

CHAPTER 18

thy soul lusted after. Compare this with Ancient Tyre another great market place that points to the maddening desire for "thing" in the Last Days (Ezek 27).

New York and "The World's Largest Store"

(2) THEY LAMENT THE DESTRUCTION OF THE CITY.

[1] HOW THEY LAMENT. *The merchants of these things, which were made rich by her, shall stand afar off for the fear of her torment, weeping and wailing* (18:15). Like the kings who *stood far off* (18:9,10), the wealthy merchants now get their view of the burning city.

[2] WHAT THEY SAY. *And saying, Alas, alas, that great city, that was clothed in fine linen, and purple, and scarlet, and decked with gold, and precious stones, and pearls* (18:16)! They did not lament their sins, but their loss of business and wealth; the loss of their marketplace where deals were made. The spirit of Antichrist is a worldly spirit, and their sorrow is worldly sorrow; they did not lament that the anger of God had now fallen upon them, but for the loss of their enjoyment of the world. They now know how transient and fleeting it all is.

3. THE MARITIME WORLD LAMENTS 18:17-19.

(1) HOW SOON THE DESTRUCTION CAME. *For in one hour so great riches is come to nought. And every shipmaster, and all the company in ships, and sailors, and as many as trade by sea, stood afar off* (18:17). Thus, as New York is, latter day Babylon is here a great sea port. This passages likely rules out either London or Rome.

(2) HOW WOEFUL WAS THE WAILING.

[1] WHAT THEY SAW. *And cried when they saw the smoke of her burning, saying, What city is like unto this great city* (18:18)! For over a century it has been New York that draws forth the exclamation: *What City is like this Great City!*

[2] WHAT THEY REMEMBERED. *And they cast dust on their heads, and cried, weeping and wailing, saying, Alas, alas, that great city, wherein were made rich all that had ships in the sea by reason of her costliness! for in one hour is she made desolate* (18:19). For the third time the wailing cry is heard. Mere worldly sorrow only

adds to the calamity! It happened fast! It happened forever! Here is *the sorrow of the world that worketh death* (2 Cor 7:10). The Lord Jesus Christ warned against coveting the wealth of this world:

> • *Lay not up for yourselves treasures upon earth, where moth and rust doth corrupt, and where thieves break through and steal: But lay up for yourselves treasures in heaven, where neither moth nor rust doth corrupt, and where thieves do not break through nor steal: For where your treasure is, there will your heart be also* (Matt 6:19-21).

Latter day, commercial Babylon will fall in *one hour*; Nebuchadnezzar's Babylon declined gradually. Therefore the Babylon of Revelation 18 is the primary fulfilment of the Jeremiah prophecy.

> • ***As God overthrew Sodom and Gomorrah*** *and the neighbour cities thereof, saith the LORD; so shall no man abide there, neither shall any son of man dwell therein* (Jer 50:40).

BABYLON'S DESTRUCTION EFFECTED

(18:20) ***Rejoice over her, thou heaven, and ye holy apostles and prophets; for God hath avenged you on her.***
(18:21) ***And a mighty angel took up a stone like a great millstone, and cast it into the sea, saying, Thus with violence shall that great city Babylon be thrown down, and shall be found no more at all.*** (18:22) ***And the voice of harpers, and musicians, and of pipers, and trumpeters, shall be heard no more at all in thee; and no craftsman, of whatsoever craft he be, shall be found any more in thee; and the sound of a millstone shall be heard no more at all in thee;*** (18:23) ***And the light of a candle shall shine no more at all in thee; and the voice of the bridegroom and of the bride shall be heard no more at all in thee: for thy merchants were the great men of the earth; for by thy sorceries were all nations deceived.*** (18:24) ***And in her was found the blood of prophets, and of saints, and of all that were slain upon the earth.***

1. THE REJOICING IN HEAVEN. ***Rejoice over her, thou heaven, and ye holy apostles and prophets; for God hath avenged you on her*** (18:20). In verse 6 the call was to *reward her*, now it rises to *rejoice over her*. While her own people were bewailing her, the servants of God are called to *rejoice*. There is a world (or should we say *Babylon*) of difference between a man who is saved, and a *man of the world whose portion is in this world* (Psa17:14). The mention of the Apostles and prophets shows that as we come to the end of this chapter there is a merging of latter day Babylon in both its ecclesiastical and commercial sense (cp. 18:24; 19:1-4).

2. THE SIGN IN THE SEA. (18:21) ***And a mighty angel took up a stone like a great millstone, and cast it into the sea, saying, Thus with violence shall that great city Babylon be thrown down, and shall be found <u>no more at all</u>.*** As an assurance that Babylon's fall would be an irreversible ruin, and that she would never rise again to *fall* again (18:2), this sign is given. This was also the prophecy of Jeremiah. Thus Babylon will not only *burn* but also *drown* (18:8,9).

> • *And Jeremiah said to Seraiah, When thou comest to Babylon, and shalt see, and shalt read all these words; Then shalt thou say, O LORD, thou hast spoken against this place, to cut it off, that none shall remain in it, neither man nor beast, but that it shall be desolate for ever. And it shall be, when thou hast made an end of reading this book,*

*that **thou shalt bind a stone to it, and cast it into the midst of Euphrates: And thou shalt say, Thus shall Babylon sink, and shall not rise from the evil that I will bring upon her**: and they shall be weary. Thus far are the words of Jeremiah* (Jer 51:61-64)..

3. THE SILENCE IN THE CITY. Of the nine different features mentioned, seven are described as ***the voice of*** (*phone*, literally "sound") of *harpers, musicians, pipers, trumpeters, millstone* (the word ***sound*** is the same as "voice" in Greek), *bridegroom*, and *bride*. The silence of the city testifies to the finality of God's judgment.

(1) NO MORE MUSIC: ***And the voice of harpers, and musicians, and of pipers, and trumpeters, shall be heard no more at all in thee*** (18:22). The second of the seven ***no more at all*** cadences (cp. 18:21). The party with the blaring, throbbing music is over.

(2) NO MORE WORK: ***and no craftsman, of whatsoever craft he be, shall be found any more in thee; and the sound of a millstone shall be heard no more at all in thee***: All the time, effort and money spent building this great city has now come to end. In its last hour it is shown to have been built on sand. The believer looks forward to a city that has *foundations* (Heb 11:10; Rev 21:14).

(3) NO MORE LIGHT: ***And the light of a candle shall shine no more at all in thee*** (18:23). Rejecting the light of Christ and the Light of Scripture (Jhn 8:12; Psa 119:130), they now find they have no light of their own.

(4) NO MORE LIFE: ***and the voice of the bridegroom and of the bride shall be heard no more at all in thee***: No more marriages; no more births.

[1] DESPITE THE GREATNESS OF HER RESIDENTS: ***for thy merchants were the great men of the earth.*** They gained the world and lost their soul (Mk 8:36).

[2] BECAUSE OF THE GREATNESS OF HER SINS: ***for by thy sorceries were all nations deceived.*** The love of money is the root of all evil (1 Tim 6:10).

4. THE REMEMBRANCE OF THE MARTYRS. ***And in her was found the blood of prophets, and of saints, and of all that were slain upon the earth*** (18:24). This is a summary statement of Babylon from the beginning (Genesis 10) to end (the Great Tribulation). It combines both the religious and commercial side of what Babylon has always been. It especially shows that New York City which has been so hard against the Gospel, will be an especially dangerous city to those who come to Christ during the Tribulation.

The great city will be no longer a dwelling place for man. No work shall be done there, no comfort enjoyed, no light seen. All is utter darkness and desolation, the reward of her great wickedness; first in *deceiving the nations with her sorceries,* and secondly in destroying and murdering those whom she could not deceive. Such abominable sins deserved so great a ruin. *Matthew Henry.*

As Babylon began with *a tower, whose top may reach unto heaven* (Gen 11:4), it will end with towers; likely the skyscrapers of New York.

THE BABYLON AND ISRAEL PARALLELS IN JEREMIAH 50, 51

In the two extended Jeremiah 50,51 Chapters, a series of prophecies are given concerning Babylon and Israel. They are coupled together. They contain prophecies for the nearer future – the ***gradual*** destruction of Babylon and Judah's deliverance from captivity. They also foresee latter day ***sudden*** destruction of Babylon and the future restoration of Israel. With respect to latter day Babylon, they have a direct bearing upon what is said in Revelation 18 (and often using the same language).

THE BOOK OF REVELATION

BABYLON: FIRST PROPHECY

50:1 The word that the LORD spake against Babylon *and* against the land of the Chaldeans by Jeremiah the prophet. **2** Declare ye among the nations, and publish, and set up a standard; publish, *and* conceal not: say, Babylon is taken, Bel is confounded, Merodach is broken in pieces; her idols are confounded, her images are broken in pieces. **3** For out of the north there cometh up a nation against her, which shall make her land desolate, and none shall dwell therein: they shall remove, they shall depart, both man and beast.

ISRAEL

4 In those days, and in that time, saith the LORD, the children of Israel shall come, they and the children of Judah together, going and weeping: they shall go, and seek the LORD their God. **5 They shall ask the way to Zion** with their faces thitherward, *saying*, Come, and let us join ourselves to the LORD in a perpetual covenant *that* shall not be forgotten. **6** My people hath been lost sheep: their shepherds have caused them to go astray, they have turned them away *on* the mountains: they have gone from mountain to hill, they have forgotten their restingplace. **7** All that found them have devoured them: and their adversaries said, We offend not, because they have sinned against the LORD, the habitation of justice, even the LORD, the hope of their fathers.

BABYLON: SECOND PROPHECY

8 Remove out of the midst of Babylon (Rev 18:4), and go forth out of the land of the Chaldeans, and be as the he goats before the flocks. **9** For, lo, I will raise and cause to come up against Babylon an assembly of great nations from the north country: and they shall set themselves in array against her; from thence she shall be taken: their arrows *shall be* as of a mighty expert man; none shall return in vain. **10** And Chaldea shall be a spoil: all that spoil her shall be satisfied, saith the LORD. **11** Because ye were glad, because ye rejoiced, O ye destroyers of mine heritage, because ye are grown fat as the heifer at grass, and bellow as bulls; **12 Your mother shall be sore confounded**; she that bare you shall be ashamed: behold, **the hindermost of the nations** *shall be* a wilderness, a dry land, and a desert. **13** Because of the wrath of the LORD it shall not be inhabited, but it shall be wholly desolate: every one that goeth by Babylon shall be astonished, and hiss at all her plagues. **14** Put yourselves in array against Babylon round about: all ye that bend the bow, shoot at her, spare no arrows: for she hath sinned against the LORD. **15** Shout against her round about: she hath given her hand: her foundations are fallen, her walls are thrown down: for **it is the vengeance of the LORD**: take vengeance upon her; as she hath done, do unto her. **16** Cut off the sower from Babylon, and him that handleth the sickle in the time of harvest: for fear of the oppressing sword they shall turn every one to his people, and they shall flee every one to his own land.

ISRAEL

17 Israel *is* a scattered sheep; the lions have driven *him* away: first the king of Assyria hath devoured him; and last this Nebuchadrezzar king of Babylon hath broken his bones. **18** Therefore thus saith the LORD of hosts, the God of Israel; Behold, I will punish the king of Babylon and his land, as I have punished the king of Assyria. **19 And I will bring Israel again to his habitation**, and he shall feed on Carmel and Bashan, and his soul shall be satisfied upon mount Ephraim and Gilead. **20 In those days**, and in that time, saith the LORD, **the iniquity of Israel shall be sought for, and** *there shall be* **none**; and the sins of Judah, and they shall not be found: for I will pardon them whom I reserve.

BABYLON: THIRD PROPHECY

21 Go up against the land of Merathaim, *even* against it, and against the inhabitants of Pekod: waste and utterly destroy after them, saith the LORD, and do according to all that I

CHAPTER 18

have commanded thee. **22** A sound of battle *is* in the land, and of great destruction. **23 How is the hammer of the whole earth cut asunder** and broken! how is Babylon become a desolation among the nations! **24** I have laid a snare for thee, and thou art also taken, O Babylon, and thou wast not aware: thou art found, and also caught, because thou hast striven against the LORD. **25** The LORD hath opened his armoury, and hath brought forth the weapons of his indignation: for this *is* the work of the Lord GOD of hosts in the land of the Chaldeans. **26** Come against her from the utmost border, open her storehouses: cast her up as heaps, and destroy her utterly: let nothing of her be left. **27** Slay all her bullocks; let them go down to the slaughter: woe unto them! for their day is come, the time of their visitation. **28** The voice of them that flee and escape out of the land of Babylon, **to declare in Zion the vengeance of the LORD** our God, the vengeance of his temple. **29** Call together the archers against Babylon: all ye that bend the bow, camp against it round about; let none thereof escape: recompense her according to her work; according to all that she hath done, do unto her: for **she hath been proud against the LORD**, against the Holy One of Israel. **30** Therefore shall her young men fall in the streets, and all her men of war shall be cut off in that day, saith the LORD. **31** Behold, I *am* against thee, *O thou* most proud, saith the Lord GOD of hosts: for **thy day is come (Rev 18:10)**, the time *that* I will visit thee. **32** And the most proud shall stumble and fall, and none shall raise him up: and **I will kindle a fire in his cities, and it shall devour all round about him (Rev 18:8)**.

ISRAEL

33 Thus saith the LORD of hosts; The children of Israel and the children of Judah *were* oppressed together: and all that took them captives held them fast; they refused to let them go. **34 Their Redeemer *is* strong**; the LORD of hosts *is* his name: he shall throughly plead their cause, that he may give rest to the land, and disquiet the inhabitants of Babylon.

BABYLON: FOURTH PROPHECY

35 A sword *is* upon the Chaldeans, saith the LORD, and upon the inhabitants of Babylon, and upon her princes, and upon her wise *men*. **36** A sword *is* upon the liars; and they shall dote: a sword *is* upon her mighty men; and they shall be dismayed. **37** A sword *is* upon their horses, and upon their chariots, and upon all the mingled people that *are* in the midst of her; and they shall become as women: a sword *is* upon her treasures; and they shall be robbed. **38** A drought *is* upon her waters; and they shall be dried up: for it *is* the land of graven images, and they are mad upon *their* idols. **39** Therefore the wild beasts of the desert with the wild beasts of the islands shall dwell *there*, and the owls shall dwell therein: and it shall be no more inhabited for ever; neither shall it be dwelt in from generation to generation. **40 As God overthrew Sodom and Gomorrah (Rev 18:21)** and the neighbour *cities* thereof, saith the LORD; *so* shall no man abide there, neither shall any son of man dwell therein. **41** Behold, a people shall come from the north, and a great nation, and many kings shall be raised up from the coasts of the earth. **42** They shall hold the bow and the lance: they *are* cruel, and will not shew mercy: their voice shall roar like the sea, and they shall ride upon horses, *every one* put in array, like a man to the battle, against thee, O daughter of Babylon. **43** The king of Babylon hath heard the report of them, and his hands waxed feeble: anguish took hold of him, *and* pangs as of a woman in travail. **44** Behold, he shall come up like a lion from the swelling of Jordan unto the habitation of the strong: but **I will make them suddenly run away from her (Rev 18:10,17)**: and who *is* a chosen *man, that* I may appoint over her? for who *is* like me? and who will appoint me the time? and who *is* that shepherd that will stand before me? **45** Therefore hear ye the counsel of the LORD, that he hath taken against Babylon; and his purposes, that he hath purposed against the land of the Chaldeans: Surely the least of the flock shall draw them out: surely he shall make *their* habitation desolate with them. **46 At the noise of the taking of Babylon the earth is moved, and the cry is heard among the**

THE BOOK OF REVELATION

nations (Rev 18:9).

51:1 Thus saith the LORD; Behold, I will raise up against Babylon, and against them that dwell in the midst of them that rise up against me, **a destroying wind**; **2** And will send unto Babylon fanners, that shall fan her, and shall empty her land: for **in the day of trouble** they shall be against her round about. **3** Against *him that* bendeth let the archer bend his bow, and against *him that* lifteth himself up in his brigandine: and spare ye not her young men; destroy ye utterly all her host. **4** Thus the slain shall fall in the land of the Chaldeans, and *they that are* thrust through in her streets.

ISRAEL

5 For Israel *hath* not *been* forsaken, nor Judah of his God, of the LORD of hosts; though their land was filled with sin against the Holy One of Israel.

BABYLON: FIFTH PROPHECY

6 Flee out of the midst of Babylon (Rev 18:4), and deliver every man his soul: be not cut off in her iniquity; for **this *is* the time of the LORD'S vengeance**; he will render unto her a recompence. **7 Babylon *hath been* a golden cup in the LORD'S hand, that made all the earth drunken: the nations have drunken of her wine (Rev 18:3)**; therefore the nations are mad. **8 Babylon is suddenly fallen and destroyed (Rev 18:10,17,19)**: howl for her; take balm for her pain, if so be she may be healed. **9** We would have healed Babylon, but she is not healed: forsake her, and let us go every one into his own country: for **her judgment reacheth unto heaven (Rev 18:5)**, and is lifted up *even* to the skies. **10** The LORD hath brought forth our righteousness: come, and let us declare in Zion the work of the LORD our God. **11** Make bright the arrows; gather the shields: the LORD hath raised up the spirit of the kings of the Medes: for his device *is* against Babylon, to destroy it; because it *is* the vengeance of the LORD, the vengeance of his temple. **12** Set up the standard upon the walls of Babylon, make the watch strong, set up the watchmen, prepare the ambushes: for the LORD hath both devised and done that which he spake against the inhabitants of Babylon. **13 O thou that dwellest upon many waters, abundant in treasures, thine end is come (Rev 18:17,18,21)**, *and* the measure of thy covetousness. **14** The LORD of hosts hath sworn by himself, *saying*, Surely I will fill thee with men, as with caterpillers; and they shall lift up a shout against thee. **15** He hath made the earth by his power, he hath established the world by his wisdom, and hath stretched out the heaven by his understanding. **16** When he uttereth *his* voice, *there is* a multitude of waters in the heavens; and he causeth the vapours to ascend from the ends of the earth: he maketh lightnings with rain, and bringeth forth the wind out of his treasures. **17** Every man is brutish by *his* knowledge; every founder is confounded by the graven image: for his molten image *is* falsehood, and *there is* no breath in them. **18** They *are* vanity, the work of errors: in the time of their visitation they shall perish.

ISRAEL

19 The portion of Jacob *is* not like them; for he *is* the former of all things: and *Israel is* the rod of his inheritance: the LORD of hosts *is* his name.

BABYLON: SIXTH PROPHECY

20 Thou *art* my battle axe *and* weapons of war: for with thee will I break in pieces the nations, and with thee will I destroy kingdoms; **21** And with thee will I break in pieces the horse and his rider; and with thee will I break in pieces the chariot and his rider; **22** With thee also will I break in pieces man and woman; and with thee will I break in pieces old and young; and with thee will I break in pieces the young man and the maid; **23** I will also break in pieces with thee the shepherd and his flock; and with thee will I break in pieces the husbandman and his yoke of oxen; and with thee will I break in pieces captains and rulers. **24** And I will render unto Babylon and to all the inhabitants of Chaldea all their evil that they

CHAPTER 18

have done in Zion in your sight, saith the LORD. **25** Behold, **I *am* against thee, O destroying mountain**, saith the LORD, which destroyest all the earth: and I will stretch out mine hand upon thee, and roll thee down from the rocks, and will make thee a burnt mountain. **26** And they shall not take of thee a stone for a corner, nor a stone for foundations; but thou shalt be desolate for ever, saith the LORD. **27** Set ye up a standard in the land, blow the trumpet among the nations, prepare the nations against her, call together against her the kingdoms of Ararat, Minni, and Ashchenaz; appoint a captain against her; cause the horses to come up as the rough caterpillers. **28** Prepare against her the nations with the kings of the Medes, the captains thereof, and all the rulers thereof, and all the land of his dominion. **29** And the land shall tremble and sorrow: for every purpose of the LORD shall be performed against Babylon, to make the land of Babylon a desolation without an inhabitant. **30** The mighty men of Babylon have forborn to fight, they have remained in *their* holds: their might hath failed; they became as women: they have burned her dwellingplaces; her bars are broken. **31** One post shall run to meet another, and one messenger to meet another, to shew the king of Babylon that his city is taken at *one* end, **32** And that the passages are stopped, and the reeds they have burned with fire, and the men of war are affrighted. **33** For thus saith the LORD of hosts, the God of Israel; The daughter of Babylon *is* like a threshingfloor, *it is* time to thresh her: yet a little while, and the time of her harvest shall come.

ISRAEL

34 Nebuchadrezzar the king of Babylon hath devoured me, he hath crushed me, he hath made me an empty vessel, he hath swallowed me up like a dragon, he hath filled his belly with my delicates, he hath cast me out. **35** The violence done to me and to my flesh *be* upon Babylon, shall the inhabitant of Zion say; and my blood upon the inhabitants of Chaldea, shall Jerusalem say.

BABYLON: SEVENTH PROPHECY

36 Therefore thus saith the LORD; Behold, I will plead thy cause, and take vengeance for thee; and I will dry up her sea, and make her springs dry. **37** And Babylon shall become heaps, a dwellingplace for dragons, an astonishment, and an hissing, without an inhabitant. **38** They shall roar together like lions: they shall yell as lions' whelps. **39** In their heat I will make their feasts, and I will make them drunken, that they may rejoice, and sleep a perpetual sleep, and not wake, saith the LORD. **40** I will bring them down like lambs to the slaughter, like rams with he goats. **41** How is Sheshach taken! and **how is the praise of the whole earth surprised! how is Babylon become an astonishment among the nations! 42 The sea is come up upon Babylon (Rev 18:21)**: she is covered with the multitude of the waves thereof. **43** Her cities are a desolation, a dry land, and a wilderness, a land wherein no man dwelleth, neither doth *any* son of man pass thereby. **44** And I will punish Bel in Babylon, and I will bring forth out of his mouth that which he hath swallowed up: and the nations shall not flow together any more unto him: yea, the wall of Babylon shall fall.

ISRAEL

45 My people, go ye out of the midst of her (Rev 18:4), and deliver ye every man his soul from the fierce anger of the LORD. **46** And lest your heart faint, and ye fear for the rumour that shall be heard in the land; a rumour shall both come *one* year, and after that in *another* year *shall come* a rumour, and violence in the land, ruler against ruler.

BABYLON: EIGHTH PROPHECY

47 Therefore, **behold, the days come**, that I will do judgment upon the graven images of Babylon: and her whole land shall be confounded, and all her slain shall fall in the midst of her. **48 Then the heaven and the earth, and all that *is* therein, shall sing for Babylon (Rev 18:20)**: for the spoilers shall come unto her from the north, saith the LORD. **49** As

Babylon *hath caused* **the slain of Israel to fall, so at Babylon shall fall the slain of all the earth (Rev 18:24)**. **50** Ye that have escaped the sword, go away, stand not still: remember the LORD afar off, and **let Jerusalem come into your mind**. **51** We are confounded, because we have heard reproach: shame hath covered our faces: for strangers are come into the sanctuaries of the LORD'S house. **52** Wherefore, **behold, the days come**, saith the LORD, that I will do judgment upon her graven images: and through all her land the wounded shall groan. **53 Though Babylon should mount up to heaven (Rev 18:5)**, and though she should fortify the height of her strength, *yet* from me shall spoilers come unto her, saith the LORD. **54** A sound of a cry *cometh* **from Babylon, and great destruction from the land of the Chaldeans: 55 Because the LORD hath spoiled Babylon, and destroyed out of her the great voice; when her waves do roar like great waters (Rev 18:21)**, a noise of their voice is uttered: **56** Because the spoiler is come upon her, *even* upon Babylon, and her mighty men are taken, every one of their bows is broken: for **the LORD God of recompences shall surely requite**. **57** And I will make drunk her princes, and her wise *men*, her captains, and her rulers, and her mighty men: and they shall sleep a perpetual sleep, and not wake, saith the King, whose name *is* the LORD of hosts. **58** Thus saith the LORD of hosts; The broad walls of Babylon shall be utterly broken, and her high gates shall be burned with fire; and the people shall labour in vain, and the folk in the fire, and they shall be weary.

BABYLON: CONCLUDING PROPHECY

59 The word which Jeremiah the prophet commanded Seraiah the son of Neriah, the son of Maaseiah, when he went with Zedekiah the king of Judah into Babylon in the fourth year of his reign. And *this* Seraiah *was* a quiet prince. **60** So Jeremiah wrote in a book all the evil that should come upon Babylon, *even* all these words that are written against Babylon. **61** And Jeremiah said to Seraiah, When thou comest to Babylon, and shalt see, and shalt read all these words; **62** Then shalt thou say, O LORD, thou hast spoken against this place, to cut it off, that none shall remain in it, neither man nor beast, but that it shall be desolate for ever. **63** And it shall be, when thou hast made an end of reading this book, *that* **thou shalt bind a stone to it, and cast it into the midst of Euphrates**: **64** And thou shalt say, **Thus shall Babylon sink, and shall not rise from the evil that I will bring upon her (Rev 18:21)**: and they shall be weary. Thus far *are* the words of Jeremiah.

CHAPTER 19

C. THE SECOND COMING OF THE LORD JESUS CHRIST   19
1. The Rejoicing   1-10
2. The Return of Jesus Christ   11-16
3. Armageddon   17-21

1. The Rejoicing   19:1-10

"Chapter 19 marks the dramatic change in the tone of Revelation. The destruction of Babylon, the capital of the Beast's kingdom, marks the end of the Great Tribulation. The somber gives way to song. The transfer is from darkness to light, from dreary days of judgment to bright days of blessing. This chapter makes a definite division in Revelation, and ushers in the greatest event for this earth— the Second Coming of Christ. It is the bridge between the Great Tribulation and the Millennium." (J. Vernon McGee).

With Babylon in her two cities having *fallen* and *fallen* (18:2), and both engulfed in flames (17:16; 18:18), the call is echoed from Heaven to *rejoice*.

- *Rejoice over her, thou heaven, and ye holy apostles and prophets; for God hath avenged you on her* (18:20).

In verse 1 they rejoice over the destruction of the Harlot, and in verse 6 they rejoice because of the blessing and glory of the true Wife. That call to rejoice is now answered with a thunderous and fourfold ***Alleluia***. It is also answered with the most thunderous event – the Return of the Lord Jesus Christ to the earth. Chapter 19 describes two great subjects of rejoicing that will immediately precede the Return of Christ: Rejoicing over the fall of Babylon which corrupted the earth, and rejoicing over the Marriage Supper of the Lamb which will bring praise to the earth.

CHRIST'S RETURN: PRECEDED BY REJOICING FOR THE FALL OF BABYLON

(19:1) *And after these things I heard a great voice of much people in heaven, saying, Alleluia; Salvation, and glory, and honour, and power, unto the Lord our God:* (19:2) *For true and righteous are his judgments: for he hath judged the great whore, which did corrupt the earth with her fornication, and hath avenged the blood of his servants at her hand.*

(19:3) *And again they said, Alleluia. And her smoke rose up for ever and ever.*

(19:4) *And the four and twenty elders and the four beasts fell down and worshipped God that sat on the throne, saying, Amen; Alleluia.*

(19:5) *And a voice came out of the throne, saying, Praise our God, all ye his servants, and ye that fear him, both small and great.* (19:6) *And I heard as it were the voice of a great multitude, and as the voice of many waters, and as the voice of mighty thunderings, saying, Alleluia: for the Lord God omnipotent reigneth.*

1. THE FIRST ALLELUIA.
    (1) THE MANNER OF THE PRAISE. *And after these things I heard a great voice of much people in heaven, saying, Alleluia; Salvation, and glory, and honour, and power, unto the Lord our God* (19:1). The *much people* is thought to mean "everyone in Heaven", but because the word seems to delineate, and because of the emphasis on Babylon

and distinction from the 24 Elders, it is likely that it refers to the Tribulation saints (6:9,10; 7:9-14). See verse 4.

Here we have that most comprehensive word, *Alleluia, praise to Jehovah*. With this they begin; with this they continue on and with this they conclude (19:6). Their prayers are now turned into praises and their hosannas to hallelujahs. ***Alleluia*** is a transliteration of *allelouia*, the Greek equivalent for Hebrew *hallelujah*. The four instances of *alleluia* in the New Testament are in 19:1-6. As the short doxology, *Praise ye the LORD* (it does not appear as *hallelujah*), it appears twenty-four times in the Old Testament. Its first occurrence (Psa 104:35) corresponds with its final occurrences here, the Lords destruction of sinners out of the earth. That over which earth laments (18:10), Heaven rejoices (19:1).

- *Let the sinners be consumed out of the earth, and let the wicked be no more. Bless thou the LORD, O my soul.* **Praise ye the LORD** (Psa 104:35).

The saints express praise to the Lord for what He has done and is about to do in three great words: **salvation** (*soteria*), **glory** (*dox*a), and **power** (*dynamis*).

(2) THE PROCLAMATION OF THE PRAISE. ***For true and righteous are his judgments: for he hath judged the great whore, which did corrupt the earth with her fornication, and hath avenged the blood of his servants at her hand*** (19:2). They rejoice over the ruin of Babylon, which had been a mother, nurse, and nest of demonic evil and cruelty. It was all that was the opposite of and opposed against *the salvation, and glory, and honour, and power unto God* of the previous verse. Note that it is particularly Religious Babylon that slew God's *servants* (cp. note on 18:24). Yet, as Chapter 18:24 shows it is also Commercial Babylon.

2. THE SECOND ALLELUIA. ***And again they said, Alleluia. And her smoke rose up for ever and ever*** (19:3). Heaven's moral judgment of sin and sinners is different from earth's. The reason why the great multitude shout ***Alleluia*** is because Babylon is judged, and the reason why they repeat the ***Alleluia*** is because the judgment is irrevocable and eternal. The cry of 6:10 is now answered and the blood of the martyrs avenged. The ascending fires of judgement bring forth ascending praise to God. Babylon will *for ever and ever* be the kindling in the Lake of Fire (Rev 20:10). This is the verdict of Heaven upon the love of the world (1 Jhn 2:15,16). There is also here the stark reminder that those who chose Babylon rather than Christ will suffer in that fire forever.

- *And **the smoke of their torment ascendeth up for ever and ever: and they have no rest day nor night**, who worship the beast and his image, and whosoever receiveth the mark of his name* (Rev 14:11).

3. THE THIRD ALLELUIA. ***And the four and twenty elders and the four beasts fell down and worshipped God that sat on the throne, saying, Amen; Alleluia*** (19:4). Here is the blessed harmony of the Elders and the Cherubim in this praise. Though their number is small (24 elders and four beasts) yet they add their voice in perfect harmony to the thunderous worship of the *much people* (19:1). This is the last time the Four Beasts (the Cherubim) appear. While sin reigned in earth they continued their long *Holy, Holy, Holy*; now that judgment is accomplished they withdraw—adding their significant *Amen*.

The fact that there is a distinction between the worship of the 24 Elders and the *much people*, indicates further that this great multitude of Tribulation martyrs (6:9,10; 7:9-14), who suffered so recently at the hands of Babylon and the Beast. The 24 Elders as representatives of the Church have much to praise also, but their experience is different.

CHAPTER 19

4. THE FOURTH ALLELUIA.

(1) THE CALL TO THOSE REMAINING ON EARTH. *And a voice came out of the throne, saying, Praise our God, all ye his servants, and ye that fear him, both small and great* (19:5). This may mean " all the rest in Heaven". There is also the view that the first three Alleluias came from Heaven, this call goes to the earth, where the redeemed, still alive after the horrors of the Tribulation, are called to add their voices to the Heavenly Choirs. Thus, when Christ Returns, there will be a host greeting him with joyful praises. However, as the following passage shows this appeal would be a call to *turn wailing to rejoicing*!

- *Behold, he cometh with clouds; and **every eye shall see him**, and they also which pierced him: and **all kindreds of the earth shall wail because of him**. Even so, Amen* (Rev 1:7).

(2) THE RESPONSE OF A MULTITUDE. *And I heard as it were the voice of a great multitude, and as the voice of many waters, and as the voice of mighty thunderings, saying, Alleluia: for the Lord God omnipotent reigneth* (19:6). To the *much people* (19:1) is added this *great multitude*. There were *many waters* of people who were deceived by Religious Babylon (17:1,15), but these who were not deceived praise Him with a voice as *many waters*. The proclamation of their praise is that *the Lord God omnipotent reigneth,* not Babylon!

CHRIST'S RETURN: PRECEDED BY REJOICING FOR THE MARRIAGE OF THE LAMB

(19:7) *Let us be glad and rejoice, and give honour to him: for the marriage of the Lamb is come, and his wife hath made herself ready.* (19:8) *And to her was granted that she should be arrayed in fine linen, clean and white: for the fine linen is the righteousness of saints.*

(19:9) *And he saith unto me, Write, Blessed are they which are called unto the marriage supper of the Lamb. And he saith unto me, These are the true sayings of God.*

(19:10) *And I fell at his feet to worship him. And he said unto me, See thou do it not: I am thy fellowservant, and of thy brethren that have the testimony of Jesus: worship God: for the testimony of Jesus is the spirit of prophecy.*

1. THE MARRIAGE (SUPPER) OF THE LAMB IS ANNOUNCED.

(1) THE WIFE IS PREPARED. *Let us be glad and rejoice, and give honour to him: for the marriage of the Lamb is come, and his wife hath made herself ready* (19:7). The verb "to marry" is *gameo*. The equivalent noun used here for *marriage* is *gamos*. This same word *gamos* is translated *marriage feast* is 19:9. *Gamos* is used 16 times is the NT, and with the exception of Hebrews 13:4 were it refers to the married state, appears always to refer to the Marriage Supper and the invitation of guests. As this is nearly always assumed the word "supper" is not affixed to the word except in in 19:9. Thus in Revelation 19:7,9, when the marriage (supper) of the Lamb is come, the wife is already the wife. It is not the one getting married who makes herself ready, it is the one who is already the wife. She was glorified at the Rapture (1 Cor 15:51,52; 1 Thess 4:16,17). She has given an account of herself at the Judgement Seat of Christ (Rom 14:10; 1Cor 3:10-15; 2 Cor 5:9,10). She is now ready for the Marriage Supper.

From this it clear that among the many other titles and names given to believers, and though stated in a collective sense, we become the Bride and Wife of Christ at conversion. It is then that we are made *complete in Him* and become *bone of His bone and flesh of His flesh*.

THE BOOK OF REVELATION

- *For I am jealous over you with godly jealousy: for **I have espoused you to one husband, that I may present you as a chaste virgin to Christ*** (2 Cor 11:2).

- *And **ye are complete in him**, which is the head of all principality and power* (Col 2:10).
- *For **the husband is the head of the wife, even as Christ is the head of the church**: and he is the saviour of the body* (Eph 5:23).
- ***Husbands, love your wives, even as Christ also loved the church**, and gave himself for it; 26 That he might sanctify and cleanse it with the washing of water by the word, 27 That he might present it to himself a glorious church, not having spot, or wrinkle, or any such thing; but that it should be holy and without blemish* (Eph 5:25-27).
- *For **we are members of his body, of his flesh, and of his bones*** (Eph 5:30).
- *Know ye not that **your bodies are the members of Christ**? shall I then take the members of Christ, and make them the members of an harlot? God forbid.16 What? know ye not that he which is joined to an harlot is one body? for two, saith he, shall be one flesh. 17 But **he that is joined unto the Lord is one spirit*** (1 Cor 6:15-17).

The believing church is both the Bride and Wife of Christ. The bliss of the Bride will never cease. One Thousand Years later in New Jerusalem she is still called *the Bride*.

- *Come hither, I will shew thee **the bride, the Lamb's wife*** (Rev 21:9).

(2) THE BRIDE IS ADORNED. *And to her was granted that she should be arrayed in fine linen, clean and white: for the fine linen is the righteousness of saints* (19:8). She does not appear in the dress of the *Mother of Harlots* (17:4,5). "She appears in the robes of Christ's righteousness, both imputed for justification and imparted for sanctification—the *stola*, the *white robe* of absolution, adoption, and enfranchisement, and the white robe of purity and holiness. She had *washed her robes and made them white in the blood of the Lamb* (7:14). and these her nuptial ornaments she did not purchase by any price of her own, but received them as the gift and grant of her blessed Lord." (Matthew Henry).

The pure and spotless raiment of the Wife contrasts with the purple and scarlet clothing of the Harlot (17:4). The one was *arrayed* in the gaudy raiment that befitted her, and the other was *arrayed* in the spotless clothing suitable to her. Their raiment is like the Saviour's on the Mount of Transfiguration – *white and glistering* (Lk 9:29). This will be their clothing when they follow Christ in His Return (19:14).

- *I will greatly rejoice in the LORD, my soul shall be joyful in my God; for **he hath clothed me with the garments of salvation, he hath covered me with the robe of righteousness**, as a bridegroom decketh himself with ornaments, and as a bride adorneth herself with her jewels* (Isa 61:10).

2. THE MARRIAGE SUPPER OF THE LAMB IS ANNOUNCED FURTHER.
(1) THE BLESSEDNESS OF IT. *And he saith unto me, Write, Blessed are they which are called unto the marriage supper of the Lamb* (19:9). The *blessing* here is the *Fourth Beatitude* of Revelation (1:3; 14:13; 16:15; 19:9). The entire Millennial Reign will be a Wedding Feast.

- ***Blessed is he that shall eat bread in the kingdom of God*** (Lk 14:15).
- *And they shall come from the east, and from the west, and from the north, and from the south, **and shall sit down in the kingdom of God*** (Lk 13:29).

CHAPTER 19

- *And **in this mountain shall the LORD of hosts make unto all people a feast of fat things**, a feast of wines on the lees, of fat things full of marrow, of wines on the lees well refined* (Isa 25:6).

(2) THE TRUTH OF IT. *These are the true sayings of God.* This event along with all other events of the Second Coming of Christ are true in the most absolute sense and will be fulfilled as literally as the events of our Lord's First Coming. Even though the events of Revelation startle the senses, they will all be fulfilled literally.

Note further: *These are the true sayings of God* (19:9), forms an epilogue to all that has gone before in Revelation, and an introduction to that which is to follow.... *THE SECOND COMING OF JESUS CHRIST.*

3. THE OVERWHELMED APOSTLE. *And I fell at his feet to worship him. And he said unto me, See thou do it not: I am thy fellowservant, and of thy brethren that have the testimony of Jesus: worship God: for the testimony of Jesus is the spirit of prophecy.* (19:10). This error was immediately corrected. The angel, and though an angel, was a creature, a created being, as was John. *Worship God* not angels. "That the Apostle John should have twice so acted (22:8) is a proof of the incurable religious blindness of the natural mind, and of its idolatrous bent." (Williams).

The testimony of Jesus is the spirit of prophecy. Christ has testified fully to His absolute Deity. Thus prophecy at its very heart is designed to unfold the beauty and loveliness of our Lord and Saviour Jesus Christ. In the present age the Spirit of God is not only to glorify Christ but to show believers *things to come* as they relate to His Person and Majesty (cp. John 16:13-15).

- *And, behold, I come quickly; and my reward is with me, to give every man according as his work shall be. I am Alpha and Omega, the beginning and the end, the first and the last* (Rev 22:12,13).

Note: "It is most significant and in keeping with the concept of a pretribulational Rapture that those in the great multitude composed of tribulation saints should thus regard the wife of the Lamb as an entity other than themselves." (Walvoord).

2. THE RETURN OF JESUS CHRIST 19:11-16

(19:11) *And I saw heaven opened, and behold a white horse; and he that sat upon him was called Faithful and True, and in righteousness he doth judge and make war.*
(19:12) *His eyes were as a flame of fire, and on his head were many crowns; and he had a name written, that no man knew, but he himself.*
(19:13) *And he was clothed with a vesture dipped in blood: and his name is called The Word of God.*
(19:14) *And the armies which were in heaven followed him upon white horses, clothed in fine linen, white and clean.*
(19:15) *And out of his mouth goeth a sharp sword, that with it he should smite the nations: and he shall rule them with a rod of iron: and he treadeth the winepress of the fierceness and wrath of Almighty God.*
(19:16) *And he hath on his vesture and on his thigh a name written, KING OF KINGS, AND LORD OF LORDS.*

The final prophetic hour is now reached and the True Messiah appears in all His power and glory—faithful to His promises and true to His judgments.

THE BOOK OF REVELATION

> • *Lift up your heads, O ye gates; and be ye lift up, ye everlasting doors; and **the King of glory shall come in**. 8 **Who is this King of glory?** The LORD strong and mighty, the LORD mighty in battle. 9 Lift up your heads, O ye gates; even lift them up, ye everlasting doors; and **the King of glory shall come in**. 10 **Who is this King of glory? The LORD of hosts, he is the King of glory**. Selah* (Psa 24:7-10).

As soon as the Marriage Supper is announced, ***heaven is opened*** (cp. 4:11; 11:19; 15:5). Thus, as the context shows, He comes not only to destroy the legions of Satan and the Beast, but also to prepare for the Marriage Supper. Nevertheless, the subject now turns to the Beast and his armies gathering to make war. From above the long awaited expedition toward the earth begins… and is soon completed.

1. THE DESCRIPTION OF THE GREAT COMMANDER.

(1) HIS THRONE. ***And I saw heaven opened*** (19:11). *He that cometh from above is above all* (Jhn 3:31). His Throne is in Heaven. He will rule on the earth, but it will be a rule in complete harmony with Heaven. This is the Kingdom of Heaven so often spoken of in the Gospel of Matthew. And, of which Daniel foresaw: *The heavens do rule* (Dan 4:26).

(2) HIS MOUNT: ***and behold a white horse.*** This demonstrates the equity of His cause, and certainty of His success. It is no longer a donkey (Lk 19:30); nor the white horse of a false rider (Rev 6:2).

(3) HIS ATTRIBUTES: ***and he that sat upon him was called Faithful and True, and in righteousness he doth judge and make war.*** He is *faithful and true* to his covenant and promise. He is *righteous* in all his judicial and military proceedings. Faith knew Him as *faithful and true*: and His appearing now in judgment will be a demonstration of His faithfulness and truth.

His eyes were as a flame of fire (19:12). He has penetrating insight into all the strength and stratagems of His enemies. He sees into all depths, and behind all masks. He knows perfectly what must be done and is to be done. We read of His flaming eyes at the beginning of Revelation.

> • *His head and his hairs were white like wool, as white as snow; and **his eyes were as a flame of fire*** (Rev 1:14).

And on his head were many crowns. The Beast had ten crowns (13:1); but they were usurped. Christ has all the crowns and that by right (Jhn 18:37; Rev 11:15). He is *King of kings, and Lord of lords* (19:16).

And he had a name written, that no man knew, but he himself. The depths of His Being are imperceptible. *Great is the mystery of godliness: God was manifest in the flesh* (1 Tim 3:16). *No man knoweth the Son but the Father* (Matt 11:27).

Williams seeks to comment on the *unknowable*:

> Though thus revealed, He has a glory no man can penetrate into. That Name of glory is written so that it is not to be unknown but yet it will be unknowable; for *no man knows the Son but the Father*. In His humiliation that glory was hidden from man in the unsounded depths of His Person, but it was written there and read by the Father. When revealed in glory that Name will remain unsearchable to man. His revealed Name was the Word of God, for He revealed God in His grace and power so as to make Him known, and so the believer can say *I know Him*.

(4) HIS VESTURE. ***And he was clothed with a vesture dipped in blood*** (19:13). This is in anticipation of what is about to happen, His vesture was also dyed with the

blood of His enemies in the past. He is the veteran of past conflicts. Fighting on behalf of Israel he slew 185,000 Assyrian soldiers (Isa 37:36). He comes now to *tread the winepress* (14:20; 19:15).

> • *Then shall the LORD go forth, and fight against those nations,* **as when he fought** *in the day of battle* (Zech 14:3).
> • *Who is this that cometh from Edom, with* **dyed garments** *from Bozrah? this that is glorious in his apparel, travelling in the greatness of his strength? I that speak in righteousness, mighty to save. 2 Wherefore art thou* **red in thine apparel**, *and* **thy garments like him that treadeth in the winefat**? *3 I have trodden the winepress alone; and of the people there was none with me: for I will tread them in mine anger, and trample them in my fury; and* **their blood shall be sprinkled upon my garments, and I will stain all my raiment** (Isa 63:1-6).

(5) HIS NAME: ***and his name is called The Word of God.*** Though imperceptible as above (19:12), yet here it is given. He as the Word, is *the Alpha and the Omega* (Rev 22:13). He is the fount of all wisdom and knowledge. On the eve of *the* Battle He knows all that is to be done.

2. THE ARMY HE COMMANDS. ***And the armies which were in heaven followed him upon white horses, clothed in fine linen, white and clean*** (19:14). This is the same *fine linen, clean and white* given in verse 8. The army is vast, and in their bearing they resemble their Commander. But they accompany Him, not to participate but to witness.

> • *The LORD my God shall come, and* **all the saints with thee** (Zech 14:5).
> • *And Enoch also, the seventh from Adam, prophesied of these, saying, Behold,* **the Lord cometh with ten thousands of his saints** (Jude 14).

3. THE ARMAMENTS OF HIS WARFARE.
(1) THE SWORD. ***And out of his mouth goeth a sharp sword, that with it he should smite the nations*** (19:15). His spoken word is the sword (cp. Heb 4:12).

> • *But with righteousness shall he judge the poor, and reprove with equity for the meek of the earth: and he shall smite the earth with* **the rod of his mouth**, *and with* **the breath of his lips** *shall he slay the wicked* (Isa 11:4).

(2) THE ROD: ***and he shall rule them with a rod of iron.*** Those who do not fall to the sword of his mouth, will be governed righteously with the rod of iron and with no allowance *at all* for disobedience. This is the persistently stated characteristic of His reign in the Millennium (Psa 2:9; Rev 2:27; 12:5). Unlike today when *the law is slacked and judgement doth never go forth* (Hab 1:4), there will be strict justice.

(3) THE TREADING: ***and he treadeth the winepress of the fierceness and wrath of Almighty God.*** The world makes its choice, *white unto harvest* or *red unto vintage* (Jhn 4:35: Rev 14:18-20). The nations will be smitten by sword of His mouth. The armies that march into Israel will be cast into the wine press of Armageddon.

> • *I have trodden the winepress alone; and of the people there was none with me: for* **I will tread them in mine anger**, *and trample them in my fury; and their blood shall be sprinkled upon my garments, and I will stain all my raiment* (Isa 63:3)
> • *And the angel thrust in his sickle into the earth, and gathered the vine of the earth, and cast it into* **the great winepress of the wrath of God**. *20 And the winepress was*

*trodden without the city, and **blood came out of the winepress, even unto the horse bridles, by the space of a thousand and six hundred furlongs*** (Rev 14:19,20).

• ***And he gathered them together into a place called in the Hebrew tongue Armageddon*** (Rev 16:16)..

4. THE INSIGNIA OF HIS AUTHORITY. ***And he hath on his vesture and on his thigh a name written, KING OF KINGS, AND LORD OF LORDS*** (19:16)**.** The second of two capitalized descriptions in Revelation, and, with an eternity of difference between them (17:5). He bears this as His coat of arms. The *Name* is *on the thigh*, the place normally for the sword.

In these verses, the Divine titles of *Elohim, Jehovah, Shaddai,* the *Lamb,* the *Word of God*, and *King of Kings and Lord of Lords* are here heaped together and given to Him. All judgment is committed unto Him, just as all creation was formed by Him and all redemption accomplished by Him. The faith that trusted Him through the long intervening years will now acclaim Him as **KING OF KINGS, AND LORD OF LORDS.** All will be in contrast to the impotency of the false king and his prophet.

3. ARMAGEDDON   19:17-21

> And it shall come to pass in that day, that the light shall not be clear, nor dark:
> — Zechariah 14:6 (KJV)

http://bibleencyclopedia.com/kjvsmall/KJV_Zechariah_14-6.jpg

THE SUPPER OF THE GREAT GOD 19:17-21

(19:17) ***And I saw an angel standing in the sun; and he cried with a loud voice, saying to all the fowls that fly in the midst of heaven, Come and gather yourselves together unto the supper of the great God;*** (19:18) ***That ye may eat the flesh of kings, and the flesh of captains, and the flesh of mighty men, and the flesh of horses, and of them that sit on them, and the flesh of all men, both free and bond, both small and great.***

(19:19) ***And I saw the beast, and the kings of the earth, and their armies, gathered together to make war against him that sat on the horse, and against his army.***

(19:20) ***And the beast was taken, and with him the false prophet that wrought miracles before him, with which he deceived them that had received the mark of the beast, and them that worshipped his image. These both were cast alive into a lake of fire burning***

CHAPTER 19

with brimstone.(19:21) *And the remnant were slain with the sword of him that sat upon the horse, which sword proceeded out of his mouth: and all the fowls were filled with their flesh.*

1. THE CALL IS GIVEN.

(1) THE PROCLAMATION OF THE GREAT SUPPER. *And I saw an angel standing in the sun; and he cried with a loud voice, saying to all the fowls that fly in the midst of heaven, Come and gather yourselves together unto the supper of the great God* (19:17). For the angel to be seen standing in the sun will mean that his brilliance is greater than that of the sun. By this display the angel prepares the way for the One who will outshine the sun (Isa 24:23).

"Foul demons" (Rev 16:14) gathered these armies together but a holy angel summons the fowls of the heaven to devour them, for they are but men, and hence the word *flesh* is repeated five times in verse 18. This will be Supper of a different sort than the Marriage Supper (19:9). The world has made its choice as to which of the two it attends.

(2) THE *MENU* OF THE GREAT SUPPER. *That ye may eat the flesh of kings, and the flesh of captains, and the flesh of mighty men, and the flesh of horses, and of them that sit on them, and the flesh of all men, both free and bond, both small and great* (19:18). The Battle of Armageddon (cp. 16:14,16) is marked first by an invitation to spoil. As the Beast at the head of the armies of earth draws closer to Israel, the skies overhead darkened by vast hosts of circling birds of prey could not but paralyze the approaching armies with fear.

The world of kings and armies has already seen one terrible supper. Three and one half years earlier the Land of Israel became the slaughter house for the legions of Gog and Magog. They should have considered this venture to the same field of battle more carefully. Note the similarity.

- *And, thou son of man, thus saith the Lord GOD;* **Speak unto every feathered fowl**, *and to every beast of the field, Assemble yourselves, and come; gather yourselves on every side to* **my sacrifice** *that I do sacrifice for you, even* **a great sacrifice upon the mountains of Israel**, *that ye may* **eat** *flesh, and* **drink** *blood. 18 Ye shall* **eat** *the flesh of the mighty, and* **drink** *the blood of the princes of the earth, of rams, of lambs, and of goats, of bullocks, all of them fatlings of Bashan. 19 And ye shall* **eat** *fat till ye be full, and* **drink** *blood till ye be drunken, of* **my sacrifice** *which I have sacrificed for you. 20 Thus* **ye shall be filled at my table** *with horses and chariots, with mighty men, and with all men of war, saith the Lord GOD* (Ezek 39:17-20).

The actual parallel to the scene in Revelation 19 is found in Matthew 24:27,28.

- *For as the lightning cometh out of the east, and shineth even unto the west; so shall also the coming of the Son of man be. 28 For* **wheresoever the carcase is, there will the eagles be gathered together** *(Matt 24:27,28).*

2. THE BATTLE IS JOINED. *And I saw the beast, and the kings of the earth, and their armies, gathered together to make war against him that sat on the horse, and against his army* (19:19). How vast is the army; how brazen the attempt. Their *armies* are plural: many nations, uniforms, weapons, outlooks and purposes. Our Lord's *armies* are one; *one in Him* (19:14).

The enemy with great fury, headed by *the beast, and the kings of the earth*, have now made this the *largest* assemblage for warfare in history. It will also be the *shortest*. Their commander is the one of whom they said: *Who is like unto the beast? who is able to make war with him* (Rev 13:4)? They will soon be able to answer that question.

- *Why do the heathen rage, and the people imagine a vain thing? The kings of the earth set themselves, and the rulers take counsel together, against the LORD, and against his anointed, saying, Let us break their bands asunder, and cast away their cords from us* (Psa 2:1-3).

3. THE VICTORY IS IMMEDIATELY GAINED.

(1) OVER THE DECEIVERS.
And the beast was taken, and with him the false prophet that wrought miracles before him, with which he deceived them that had received the mark of the beast, and them that worshipped his image. These both were cast alive into a lake of fire burning with brimstone (19:20). John in his vision sees not only the carnage but also the Beast and his helper. The leaders of the army, are taken prisoners, both he who led them by power and he who led them by deception. They are cast but not burnt up in the Lake of Fire (20:10). As they refused burial to the Two Witnesses (Rev 11:9) and likely the many martyrs of the Tribulation, so will burial be refused them.

There are different stages of descent into the Lake of Fire. Walvoord explains:

> The doom of the Beast and the False Prophet culminates in their being cast alive into the Lake of Fire burning with brimstone. The Lake of Fire thus introduced is mentioned again in 20:15. By comparison with other Scriptures, the Beast and the False Prophet are the first to inhabit the Lake of Fire. Unsaved who die prior to this time are cast into Hades, a place of torment, but not into the Lake of Fire, which is reserved for those who have been finally judged as unworthy of eternal life.
>
> Alford observes: "These only, and not the Lord's human enemies yet, are cast into eternal punishment. The latter await the final judgment (20:11)." These who were Satan's masterpieces precede Satan himself to this final place of everlasting punishment into which he is cast a thousand years later (20:10). The rest of the wicked dead after being judged at the great white throne will follow the beast, the false prophet, and the devil into this eternal doom.

H.A. Ironside, quoted by Walvoord, points out further: "Two men, be it noted, are taken alive. They are the two arch-conspirators who have bulked so largely in this book—the Beast and the False Prophet, the civil and religious leaders of the last league of nations, which will be Satan-inspired in its origin and Satan-directed until its doom. These two men are *cast alive into the lake burning with fire and brimstone*, where a thousand years later they are still said to be *suffering the vengeance of eternal fire*, thus incidentally proving that the Lake of Fire is not annihilation, and that it is not purgatorial either, for it neither annihilates nor purifies these two fallen foes of God and man after a thousand years under judgment.

(2) OVER THE DECEIVED.
And the remnant were slain with the sword of him that sat upon the horse, which sword proceeded out of his mouth: and all the fowls were filled with their flesh (19:21). Whether officers or common soldiers, they are given up to military execution, and made a feast for *the fowls of heaven*! Though their numbers were beyond number, the largest army ever assembled, yet they are only called, the remnant. In view of the all-consuming power of the Coming One it is pertinent that the kings of earth heed the invitation first given long ago.

- ***Be wise now therefore, O ye kings: be instructed, ye judges of the earth****. 11 Serve the LORD with fear, and rejoice with trembling. 12 Kiss the Son, lest he be angry, and ye perish from the way, when his wrath is kindled but a little. Blessed are all they that put their trust in him* (Psa 2:10-12).

CHAPTER 20

D. THE THOUSAND YEAR REIGN OF JESUS CHRIST   20
  1. Satan is Bound   1-3
  2. The Saints Reign   4-6
  3. Sinners Rebel   7-9
  4. Satan is Doomed   10
  5. The Great White Throne Judgement   11-15

1. SATAN IS BOUND   20:1-3

(20:1) *And I saw an angel come down from heaven, having the key of the bottomless pit and a great chain in his hand.*
(20:2) *And he laid hold on the dragon, that old serpent, which is the Devil, and Satan, and bound him a thousand years,* (20:3) *And cast him into the bottomless pit, and shut him up, and set a seal upon him, that he should deceive the nations no more, till the thousand years should be fulfilled: and after that he must be loosed a little season.*

The foundation for the fall of Satan is Christ's substitutionary work on the Cross, and that for the sins that Satan brought into the world. His power has been further diminished for the past 2000 years by the preaching of the Gospel. It has now been further broken by the twofold fall of Babylon; and further still by the casting out of Antichrist at the Return of Christ and Battle of Armageddon. Now, awaiting his complete overthrow (20:10) there is one further diminution of his power; Satan will be bound for a thousand years.

1. TO WHOM THE WORK IS COMMITTED. *And I saw an angel come down from heaven* (20:1). Christ Himself could do this but it is delegated to an angel. Note: There are angels that are stronger than Satan. Here, as so frequently in Revelation, we see the work of an angel (cp. 7:2; 8:1; 10:1; 14:6,8,9,15,17,18; 17:1; 18:1; 19:17).

2. THE MEANS FOR PERFORMING THE WORK: *having the key of the bottomless pit and a great chain in his hand.* The bottomless pit (*abussos*) is the temporary prison of fallen angels before their final abode in the Lake of Fire (Matt 25:41; see 9:1-11). Compare the following passages.

- *I am he that liveth, and was dead; and, behold, I am alive for evermore, Amen; and have **the keys of hell and of death*** (Rev 1:18).
- *And the fifth angel sounded, and I saw a star fall from heaven unto the earth: and to him was given **the key of the bottomless pit*** (Rev 9:1).

The angel has a *key* and a *chain*. The **chain** (*halysis*) is the word used of the man possessed by demons in Mark 5:3. It is also used for the *chains* which fell off Peter (Acts 12:7) and for Paul's *chains* (Acts 28:20; 2 Tim 1:16). A different word (*seiros*) is used for *chains of darkness* in 2 Peter 2:4. The fact that Satan is bound for a thousand years is confirmed by the multitude of passages dealing with the kingdom period in which Satan is never found working in the world. (see Walvoord).

Note: As the angels whom Satan corrupted are bound in the abyss with chains (2 Pet 2:4; Jude 6), so will Satan himself be bound (20:2).

3. THE EXECUTION OF THE WORK.

(1) THE CLAMPING. *And he laid hold on the dragon, that old serpent, which is the Devil, and Satan, and bound him a thousand years* (20:2). Neither his strength as the *dragon*, nor his subtlety as the *serpent*, was sufficient to rescue Satan out of the hands of the angel; the strong angel caught hold, and kept his hold.

This verse for the first time in Scripture gives the exact length of the visible Kingdom Reign of Christ on earth. The *Thousand Years* are stated six times in verses 1-6. Like so many other Scripture statements concerning the Return of Christ, amillennialists say it is "only figurative language". They are wrong.

(2) THE CASTING: *And cast him into the bottomless pit* (20:3). He cast him down with force and with a just vengeance to his own special place and prison (cp. the *chains* in 2 Pet 2:4; Jude 6).

(3) THE SHUTTING: *and shut him up, and set a seal upon him, that he should deceive the nations no more*. In the authority of Christ, this angel shuts and none can open; he shuts by his power and seals by his authority. His lock and seal neither the Devil nor the demons cannot break open.

(4) The Termination: *till the thousand years should be fulfilled: and after that he must be loosed a little season.* This is the last dispensation before Eternity. It will demonstrate that while Satan may incite, there is also something in man that allows him to be incited. Within the terrible word *must* lies a Divine secret. Jennings below seeks to inquire into it. If the abyss is such a place of horror that the legion of devils besought the Lord not to dismiss them thither (Mk 5:12), how much more terrible must be the horror of the Lake of Fire (Williams).

2. THE SAINTS REIGN   20:4-6

(20:4) *And I saw thrones, and they sat upon them, and judgment was given unto them: and I saw the souls of them that were beheaded for the witness of Jesus, and for the word of God, and which had not worshipped the beast, neither his image, neither had received his mark upon their foreheads, or in their hands; and they lived and reigned with Christ a thousand years.*

(20:5) *But the rest of the dead lived not again until the thousand years were finished. This is the first resurrection.*

(20:6) *Blessed and holy is he that hath part in the first resurrection: on such the second death hath no power, but they shall be priests of God and of Christ, and shall reign with him a thousand years.*

1. THE JUSTICE OF THE MARTYR'S JUDGEMENT. *And I saw thrones, and they sat upon them, and judgment was given unto them* (20:4). When Christ returns to set up His Kingdom, He will first be the Judge of *the quick and the dead* (2 Tim 4:1).

- *I charge thee therefore before God, and **the Lord Jesus Christ, who shall judge the quick and the dead at his appearing and his kingdom** (2 Tim 4:1).*

Among those still living at the end of the Tribulation Christ (Jhn 5:22) will in separate judgements judge Israel and the Nations. The Apostles who may be included among the Twenty-four Elders (cp. Rev 5:10) will participate in judgement and government of Israel.

- *As I live, saith the Lord GOD, surely with a mighty hand, and with a stretched out arm, and with fury poured out, will I rule over you: 34 And **I will bring you out from the people**, and will gather you out of the countries wherein ye are scattered, with a*

CHAPTER 20

*mighty hand, and with a stretched out arm, and with fury poured out. 35 And **I will bring you into the wilderness of the people, and there will I plead with you face to face**. 36 Like as I pleaded with your fathers in the wilderness of the land of Egypt, so will I plead with you, saith the Lord GOD. 37 And **I will cause you to pass under the rod, and I will bring you into the bond of the covenant**: 38 And **I will purge out from among you the rebels**, and them that transgress against me: I will bring them forth out of the country where they sojourn, and **they shall not enter into the land of Israel**: and ye shall know that I am the LORD* (Ezek 20:33-38).

• *And I appoint unto you a kingdom, as my Father hath appointed unto me; That ye may eat and drink at my table in my kingdom, and sit on thrones **judging the twelve tribes of Israel*** (Lk 22:29,30).

• ***When the Son of man shall come in his glory**, and all the holy angels with him, then shall he sit upon the throne of his glory: 32 And **before him shall be gathered all nations**: and he shall separate them one from another, as a shepherd divideth his sheep from the goats: 33 And he shall set the sheep on his right hand, but the goats on the left. 34 Then shall the King say unto them on his right hand, Come, ye blessed of my Father, inherit the kingdom prepared for you from the foundation of the world....* (Matt 25:31,46).

Here, however, it is not the *quick*, but the *dead* to whom judgement is given; the Tribulation martyrs. At last, after the years of the Beast there is a just judgement upon the earth and behalf of them (cp. Hab 1:4). These beleaguered Tribulation martyrs whom the world condemned to death are now resurrected to hear a righteous verdict. The ones participating are likely the Twenty-four elders (Rev 5:10) and the apostles (Lk 22:29,30; Matt 19:28).

2. THE RIGHTEOUSNESS OF THE MARTYR'S CHARACTER:
(1) THEIR POSITIVE WITNESS: *and I saw the souls of them that were beheaded for the witness of Jesus, and for the word of God* (20:4). This detailed description fits only one class of saints, those of the Tribulation, who in refusing to worship the Beast are martyred. Here we learn that they are beheaded! Among the different groups special mention is made of the Tribulation martyrs. They have suffered and have been subjected to a level of public humiliation that far exceeds that experienced by previous groups of believers. God now selects them for special honour at the beginning of His Kingdom Reign.

(2) THEIR NEGATIVE WITNESS: *and which had not worshipped the beast, neither his image, neither had received his mark upon their foreheads, or in their hands.* They were the special objects of Satan's hatred. The "roaming and beheading squads" did not terrify them into submission.

3. THE EXTENT OF THE MARTYR'S REIGN: *and they lived and reigned with Christ a thousand years.* Thus both those with natural and glorified bodies will reign together with Christ on the Millennial Earth.

4. THE CONTRAST OF THE MARTYR'S RESURRECTION.
(1) THE FIRST RESURRECTION CONTRASTED WITH THE 1000 YEAR INTERNMENT OF THE LOST. *But the rest of the dead lived not again until the thousand years were finished. This is the first resurrection* (20:5). A further honour given the Tribulation martyrs, is that among the other participants of the *first resurrection*, it is concerning them that this term is first given.

Concerning the first resurrection, Walvoord makes the following points:

> In what sense can the tribulation saints in their resurrection be labelled "the first resurrection? It is obvious that Christ was the first one raised from the dead with a

resurrection body as He was *the firstfruit from the dead* (1 Cor 15:20). On the occasion of the resurrection of Christ, Matthew mentions that at the death of Christ, *the graves were opened*, and that later, *many bodies of the saints which slept arose, And came out of the graves after his resurrection, and went into the holy city, and appeared unto many* (Matt 27:52,53). This is best explained as an actual resurrection of a token number of saints in keeping with the symbolism of the feast of the firstfruits, when a handful of grain, not just one stalk, was presented to the priest. There is no evidence that the resurrection of Matthew 27 included all the righteous saints up to that time. Daniel 12:2 places the resurrection of the Old Testament saints immediately after the Great Tribulation (Dan 12:1).

At the Rapture of the Church the dead in Christ will be raised (1 Thess 4:17). And at the end of the Tribulation, the martyrs seen above will be raised from the dead. From these facts it is clear that the term, *the first resurrection* is not a single event but an order of resurrections of all the righteous who are raised from the dead before the Millennial Kingdom begins. They are *first* in contrast to those who are raised last, after the Millennium, when the wicked dead are raised and judged. Just as there are two kinds of physical death, namely, the *first death* which results in burial, and the *second death* which is described as being cast into the Lake of Fire (20:14), so there are two kinds of resurrection, a first resurrection having to do with the resurrection of the righteous, and a second resurrection having to do with the wicked. They are separated by at least one thousand years. Just as the first death did not occur to all in one moment but is experienced individually by those who die over a long period of time, so the first resurrection is fulfilled according to the groups that are in view.

(2) THE FIRST RESURRECTION CONTRASTED WITH THE SECOND DEATH. ***Blessed and holy is he that hath part in the first resurrection: on such the second death hath no power, but they shall be priests of God and of Christ, and shall reign with him a thousand years*** (20:6). Continually in this Book, God and Christ are presented as One in the Unity of the Godhead. The blessedness of those who take part in the first resurrection regardless of classification are summarized in this verse. Thus there are five stages of the first resurrection:

(1) Christ Himself (1 Cor 15:20)
(2) Those who rose at Christ's Resurrection (Matt 27:52,53)
(3) The Church at the Rapture before the Tribulation (1 Thess 4:16)
(4) The Tribulation martyrs at the end of the Tribulation (Rev 20:4)
(5) The Old Testament saints at the end of the Tribulation (Dan 12)

• *And he said, Go thy way, Daniel: for the words are closed up and sealed till **the time of the end*** (Dan 12:9).
• *But go thou thy way till the end be: for **thou shalt rest, and stand in thy lot at the end of the days*** (Dan 12:13).

The saved of Israel and the *sheep* among the nations will live during the Millennium in their natural bodies. The Church, Old Testament and Tribulation Saints will dwell in their glorified bodies. With Christ reigning in Jerusalem, such is the wonderful prospect for final stage of human history!

CHAPTER 20

THE CHARACTER OF THE MILLENNIAL KINGDOM
(Edited from Bible Study Tools)

Attribute	Description	Scriptures
Duration	One thousand years.	Rev. 20:2-7
Theocratic Rule	The Lord Jesus Christ reigns on the Throne of David. David himself may reign as a Prince under Christ.	2 Sam. 7:16; Psa. 89:20-37; Isa. 24:23; Jer. 30:9; 33:15-17; Ezek. 34:23-24; 37:24-25; 45:22; Dan. 7:13-14; Hos. 3:5; Luke 1:30-33
Governmental Rule	Under Christ, the Twelve Apostles will govern the twelve tribes of Israel. Church-age and Tribulation saints will govern the Gentiles.	Isa. 32:1; Dan. 7:17-18, 7:21-22, 27; Matt. 19:28; Luke 22:30; Rev. 3:21; 5:10.
Worldwide Rule	Christ's rule will extend both spiritually and literally over the entire earth.	Psa. 2:6-9; 72:8; Dan. 2:44; 4:34; 7:14,27; Mic. 4:1-2; Zech. 9:10
Seat of Government	The earthly Jerusalem will be restored, blessed, and greatly expanded to serve as the seat of government and worship.	Isa. 62:1; 65:18-19; Ezek. 48:15-19; Luke 21:24
Global Conditions	The heavens and earth will be renewed to restore the creation to Eden-like conditions and repair the damage from man's long reign of sin and the judgments of the Tribulation period.	Isa. 65:17-25; Matt. 19:28
Populace	Resurrected and glorified saints will rule in the midst of Christ's "brothers" (the faithful Jewish remnant), and the "sheep" (faithful Gentiles) who survive the Tribulation and enter the kingdom to form its initial population. Children will be born to those who enter the kingdom in their natural bodies.	Dan. 12:2; Isa. 26:19; 65:20,23; Matt. 25:31; Rev. 20:4
The Curse	Many aspects of the curse (Gen. 3:15-19) will be reversed. People will live to a great age, but death will still occur. As before the flood, animals will revert to vegetarianism and will no longer fear man. Living waters will flow from beneath the sanctuary of the Millennial Temple bringing life to the regions they water.	Isa. 11:6-9; 65:20,25; Ezek. 47:8-12; Zech. 8:4; 14:8
Fruitfulness	The earth will be fruitful and men will enjoy the fruit of their labours.	Psa. 67:6-7; 72:16; Isa. 35:1; 55:13; 65:22; Joel 2:24-26; 3:18; Amos 9:13-14

Mount Zion	The region of Mount Zion will be lifted up to form the Mountain of the Lord's House.	Isa. 2:2; 56:7; Ezek. 20:40; 40:2; Zech. 14:4, 10-11; Micah. 4:1
Israel	Israel will finally inhabit the Promised Land permanently. She will serve as the focal point of the nations because Jesus will reign from Jerusalem.	Gen. 13:15; 17:8; 1Chron. 17:9; Psa. 105:8-11; Isa. 60:21; Jer. 3:18; 7:7; 30:3; 31:8-9; Ezek. 37:25; 39:25-29; Amos 9:11-15
Peace	All implements of war will be destroyed in favor of implements of productivity. Nations will no longer go to war. Disagreements between nations will be judged by Christ from Jerusalem.	Psa. 72:3-7; Isa. 2:5; 9:7; Ezek. 37:26; Micah. 4:3
Worship	A temple will stand in Jerusalem and all the nations will go up to Jerusalem to the Feast of Tabernacles. Sacrificial offerings memorializing Calvary will be resumed.	Isa. 2:3; 56:6-7; 66:20-23; Ezek. 43:20,26; 45:15,17,20; Jer. 33:18; Dan. 9:24; Joel 3:18; Hag. 2:7-9; Zech. 6:12-15; 8:20-23; 14:16-21; Mal. 3:3-4.
Satan	Satan and his demons will be removed from the earth.	Rev. 20:3
Language	The curse of Babel (Gen. 11), the introduction of varied languages, will be reversed. All the earth will have one language.	Zeph. 3:8-10

https://www.biblestudytools.com/commentaries/revelation/related-topics/summary-of-the-millennial-kingdom.html

To the above we add Walvoord's excellent summary of the Kingdom Age:

The character of Christ's reign on earth is fully described in many Old Testament passages such as Isaiah 2:2-4; 11:4-9; Psalm 72, and many others. From these Scriptures it may be seen that Jerusalem will be the capital of the Millennial Kingdom (Isa 2:3) and that *war will be no more* (Isa 2:4).

Isaiah 11 describes the righteous reign of Christ and the peace and tranquillity of His Kingdom. There will be justice for all, the wicked will be punished, and even the natural ferocity of beasts will be abated. The character and extent of the kingdom are summarized in Isaiah 11:9: *They shall not hurt nor destroy in all my holy mountain: for the earth shall be full of the knowledge of the Lord, as the waters cover the sea.* In the latter portion of Isaiah 11, Israel is revealed to be regathered from the various parts of the earth and brought back to her ancient land rejoicing in the fulfilment of God's Prophetic Word.

Psalm 72 gives a similar picture of the righteous reign of Christ, describing righteousness as flourishing and *abundance of peace as continuing as long as the moon endures*. The dominion of Christ is stated to be from sea to sea with all kings bowing down before Him, all nations serving Him, and the earth being filled with the glory of the Lord. Then will be fulfilled the desire of the nations for peace and righteousness, for the knowledge of the Lord, for economic justice, for deliverance from satanic oppression and evil.

For the whole period of one thousand years the earth will revel in the immediate presence of the Lord and His perfect divine government. Israel will be exalted and Gentiles also will be blessed. The major factors of the millennium, therefore, include a perfect and righteous government with Christ reigning in absolute power over the entire earth. Every nation will be under His sway, and God's purpose in originally placing man in charge of the Garden of Eden will have its ultimate fulfilment in the Last Adam, the Lord Jesus Christ, who will reign over the earth.

The prominence of Israel in the millennial scene is evidenced in many passages of the Old Testament. After the purging experience of the Great Tribulation, those who survive become the citizens of the kingdom after the rebels are purged out (Ezek 20:34-38). Israel then is re-joined to God in the symbol of marriage, being transformed from an unfaithful wife to one who reciprocates the love of Jehovah.

Gentiles who share in the kingdom blessings have unparalleled spiritual and economic benefits, and the thousand-year reign of Christ is a time of joy, peace, and blessing for the entire earth. Though problems in understanding this period persist due to the fact that there is not a complete revelation on all details, the major facts are sufficiently clear for anyone who is willing to accept the authority and accuracy of Scripture and interpret language in its ordinary sense.

The length of the Millennial Reign the glory of which is so emphasized in Psalms and Isaiah to Malachi is only mentioned in Revelation 20. ***They lived and reigned with Christ a thousand years*** (20:4). The Bible thus closes with a description, not of *time*, but *eternity*. Sadly and in fact incomprehensibly the Millennium will *not* have a good ending for many of the world's inhabitants.

Note: Righteousness will ***reign*** during that Millennium, but it will ***dwell*** in the New earth (Rev 21:1; 2 Pet 3:13; Williams).

3. SINNERS REBEL   20:7-9

(20:7)***And when the thousand years are expired, Satan shall be loosed out of his prison,*** (20:8) ***And shall go out to deceive the nations which are in the four quarters of the earth, Gog and Magog, to gather them together to battle: the number of whom is as the sand of the sea.*** (20:9) ***And they went up on the breadth of the earth, and compassed the camp of the saints about, and the beloved city: and fire came down from God out of heaven, and devoured them.***

The final dispensation before the eternal ages is now concluded. A thousand years in the most terrible confinement will be shown ***not*** to have changed the character of the Devil; nor will a thousand years of unspeakable bliss and in the visible presence of Christ have changed the fallen nature of man. In fact Satan seems to have gone further, and with more followers, and in a shorter time than ever before. His final effort is to be his greatest! Nevertheless for all his trouble the result is as short and sharp as before.

THE CATASTROPHIC SHOCK AT THE CLOSE OF THE MILLENNIUM

At first reading this event seems inconceivable. J. Dwight Pentecost in *Things to Come* (pp. 348-351), with quotations, gives the following assessment.

"Man has been tried and tested under every possible condition, in every possible way – goodness, government, law, grace, and now under glory" (Walter Scott). The purpose for which Satan was released, then, was to demonstrate that, even when tested under the reign of the King and the revelation of His holiness, man is a failure. While those going into the millennium were saved, they were not perfected. The progeny born to them during the millennial age were born with the same fallen sin nature with which their parents were born and consequently needed regeneration. During the administration of the King, in which He ruled with a *rod of iron*, outward conformity to His law was necessary. The binding of Satan, the removal of external sources of temptation, the fullness of knowledge, the bountiful provision from the King, caused many, whose hearts had not been regenerated, to give this required conformity to the law of the King. There must be a test to determine the true heart condition of the individuals in the age."

F.C. Jennings writes:

Has human nature changed, at least apart from sovereign grace? Is the carnal mind at last in friendship with God? Have a thousand years of absolute power and absolute benevolence, both in unchecked activity, done away with all war forever and forever? These questions must be marked by a practical test. Let Satan be loosed once more from his prison. Let him range once more over earth's smiling fields that he knew of old. He saw them last soaked with blood and flooded with tears, the evidence and accompaniments of his own reign, he sees them now "laughing with abundance." . . .
But as he pursues his way further from Jerusalem, the center of this blessedness, these tokens become fainter; until, in the far-off corner of the earth, they cease altogether, for he finds myriads who have instinctively shrunk from close contact with that holy center, and are not unprepared once more to be deceived (*Studies in Revelation*).

The results of this test are set forth by Ford C Ottman:

But even such a sovereignty over the earth does not change the heart of man. A righteous reign, together with all the blessings associated with it, and the full enjoyment of a world redeemed from the curse, does not avail to make man other than he is naturally and the testing and proving of this is accomplished by the loosing of Satan after the thousand years are finished. A thousand years in prison has wrought no moral change in the nature of this evil spirit. He comes up out of his dungeon with his heart filled with the smouldering fire of hate, which immediately flames forth and kindles a revolution among the nations that are in the four corners of the earth (*The Unfolding of the Ages*).

1. SATAN IS RELEASED. *And when the thousand years are expired, Satan shall be loosed out of his prison* (20:7). The restraints laid for a long time on Satan are at length taken off, and with no visible effect except that he is more angry than when cast upon the earth during the Tribulation (Rev 12:12). He loses no time in resuming the work that he is so accustomed to and plunges into his campaign to deceive the nations of the entire earth.
These who are tempted are the descendants of the Tribulation saints who survive the Tribulation and enter the Millennium in their natural bodies. The children of those born after the Millennium begins far outnumber their ancestors who first entered that glorious time. Likely with earth's favoured conditions there will be a far greater population than now. Outwardly all have been required to make a profession of obedience, but in many cases it will only be outward conformity without inward change of heart.

William Hoste explains:

The golden age of the kingdom will last a thousand years, during which righteousness will reign, and peace, prosperity, and the knowledge of God be universally enjoyed. But this will not entail universal conversion, and all profession must be tested… Will not a thousand years under the beneficent sway of Christ and the manifested glory of God suffice to render men immune to his [Satan's] temptations, will they not have radically changed for the better, and become by the altered conditions of life and the absence of Satanic temptations, children of God and lovers of His will? Alas! It will be proved once more that man whatever his advantages and environment, apart from the grace of God and the new birth, remains at heart only evil and at enmity with God (*The Vision of John the Divine*; quoted from Walvoord).

Robert Govett gives four reasons why Satan must be loosed after the Millennium:

(1) To demonstrate that man even under the most favorable circumstances will fall into sin if left to his own choice; (2) to demonstrate the foreknowledge of God who foretells the acts of men as well as His own acts; (3) to demonstrate the incurable wickedness of Satan; (4) to justify eternal punishment, that is, to show the unchanged character of wicked people even under divine jurisdiction for a long period of time (quoted in Walvoord).

George Williams summarizes:

So incurably diseased is the natural heart (Jer 17:9) that a thousand years of perfect happiness and absolutely just government, together with exemption from all forms of suffering, will fail to win man's heart to God; and he will at the close choose Satan and the depthless miseries of his government rather than Emmanuel and His righteousness.

The counsel of God as revealed in the Scriptures decreed an exhaustive test of man as a moral creature in order to demonstrate his inability to stand in his own strength, and thus illustrate the great lesson of the Bible that, apart from Christ, no creature and no created thing can stand. He created all things; and only in Him do, and can all things continue to exist. Hence man was tested under Innocence, Conscience, Law, Grace and will be tested in the future under Righteousness. Revelation 20 foretells that he will fail under it as he failed under the previous tests. This final test explains the word **must** in verse 3 (*The Student's Commentary of the Holy Scriptures*).

The Feast of Tabernacles may give a prophetic fore view of the Millennial decline. In this feast there was to be a systematic reduction of the animals sacrificed during its eight days of observation (see Num 29:12-40). Regarding this feast, as Govett observes, "Zechariah 14:16-19 teaches us, in general, the nations will be disinclined for the long yearly pilgrimage to Jerusalem, in order to keep the Feast of Tabernacles."

And it shall come to pass, that every one that is left of all the nations which came against Jerusalem shall even go up from year to year to worship the King, the LORD of hosts, and to keep the feast of tabernacles. 17 And it shall be, that whoso will not come up of all the families of the earth unto Jerusalem to worship the King, the LORD of hosts, even upon them shall be no rain. 18 And if the family of Egypt go not up, and come not, that have no rain; there shall be the plague, wherewith the LORD will smite the heathen that come not up to keep the feast of tabernacles. 19 This shall be the punishment of Egypt, and the punishment of all nations that come not up to keep the feast of tabernacles (Zech 14:16-19).

<u>2. SATAN GOES FORTH.</u>

THE BOOK OF REVELATION

(1) THE GEOGRAPHICAL EXTENT OF HIS EXPEDITION. *And shall go out to deceive the nations which are in the four quarters of the earth, Gog and Magog, to gather them together to battle* (20:8). No sooner is Satan let loose than he returns to his old work, *deceiving the nations* (making them think it is a good cause), and stirring them against the people of God. He covers a vast area, *the nations* in *the four quarters of the earth*, thus the entire earth. But as he did during the Tribulation he finds his deceptive work especially fruitful in Gog and Magog (Russia: Ezek 38,39).

Gog and Magog are here used in a far wider sense than in Ezekiel, and their invasion differs in time and details, though it agrees precisely in character and object: *an attack upon Jerusalem*. The former was from the north; this latter is from all directions, from the four quarters of the earth. Russia has long been synonymous with antisemitism. In that future day, Satan will incite anti-Semitic, Gog and Magog venom in the four quarters of the earth. An attack against Israel is an attack against Christ and the Bible; and that in every age.

**The Gog and Magog Philosophy:
"In Russia, an Old Anti-Semitic Blood Libel Gains Political Traction"**

"A bishop close to Putin claims Czar Nicholas II may have been killed in a ritual slaying, a century-old canard blaming the Jews for regicide.

On Monday (13 Nov. 2017), flanked by the patriarch of the Russian Orthodox Church at a press conference in Moscow, the influential Russian Orthodox Church Bishop Tikhon Shevkunov—who is closely linked to Vladimir Putin and serves as the titular chair of the commission charged with investigating the execution of the last Czar, his family, and retinue—called for an investigation into the circumstances surrounding the death of Nicholas II in Yekaterinburg. He was particularly interested in finding out whether the slain monarch was killed in a ritual murder, reviving a widely held belief in the former Soviet Union that the Jews assassinated the Czar in a dark religious ceremony essential to ushering in Bolshevism." http://www.tabletmag.com/scroll/250701/in-russia-an-old-anti-semitic-blood-libel-gains-political-traction

As in Ezekiel 38 where Gog refers to the ruler and Magog to the people so at the end of the Millennium the nations of the world will follow Satan with Russia and its leader at the helm in this last attack against Jerusalem.

(2) THE NUMERICAL EXTENT OF HIS EXPEDITION: *the number of whom is as the sand of the sea.* As stated this is a description indicating a much greater number than a thousand years previously.

CHAPTER 20

3, SATAN IS DEFEATED.

(1) THE SCALE OF HIS ONSLAUGHT. *And they went up on the breadth of the earth* (20:9). An army that covers *the breadth of the earth* indicates the largest army in history. But soon it narrows its focus.

(2) THE FOCUS OF HIS ONSLAUGHT: *and compassed the camp of the saints about, and the beloved city.* Jerusalem as before and as always is the center of the conflict.

(3) THE CONFLAGRATION UPON HIS ONSLAUGHT: *and fire came down from God out of heaven, and devoured them.* This is the end of the road for the nations who rebel against God as well as for the career of Satan. Thus as before, the fire from the Lord immediately consumes Gog and Magog.

- *I will rain upon him and upon his bands an overflowing rain, and great hailstones, and fire and brim*stone (Ezek 38:22).

4. SATAN IS DOOMED   20:10

(20:10) *And the devil that deceived them was cast into the lake of fire and brimstone, where the beast and the false prophet are, and shall be tormented day and night for ever and ever.*

The doom and final punishment of the great enemy is now accomplished. He is cast into the Lake of Fire, with his two lieutenants, *the beast and the false prophet.* They are still there after a thousand years. They are not annihilated. They will soon be joined by many others in this place *prepared for the devil and his angels* (Matt 25:41; Rev 20:15). They will **be tormented night and day, for ever and ever**.

In this final act of Satan's doom, there are many names and accounts of his actions that could be mentioned. But here the stark statement is made that he is **the devil that deceived them**. Walvoord points out, "Satan, who was first self-deceived in launching his career to be like God (Isa 14:14) and then began his career by deceiving Eve in the garden, is still the same character at the time of his final judgment." Satan is the deceiver. The big thing about deception is the simple fact that the deceived do not know they are being deceived!

5. THE GREAT WHITE THRONE JUDGEMENT   20:11-15

(20:11) *And I saw a great white throne, and him that sat on it, from whose face the earth and the heaven fled away; and there was found no place for them.*

(20:12) *And I saw the dead, small and great, stand before God; and the books were opened: and another book was opened, which is the book of life: and the dead were judged out of those things which were written in the books, according to their works.*

(20:13) *And the sea gave up the dead which were in it; and death and hell delivered up the dead which were in them: and they were judged every man according to their works.*

(20:14) *And death and hell were cast into the lake of fire. This is the second death.*

(20:15) *And whosoever was not found written in the book of life was cast into the lake of fire.*

The utter destruction of the devil's kingdom leads directly to an account of the judgement of those who despite all of the Gospel appeals were only too willing to be deceived by him. *The prince of this world is judged* (Jhn 16:11), now the judgement upon his followers. This is the judgement that made the governor Félix *tremble* (Acts 24:25).

THE BOOK OF REVELATION

1. THE SIGHT OF THE THRONE. *And I saw a great white throne* (20:11). Behold *the throne,* and tribunal of judgment, *great* and *white,* very glorious and perfectly just and righteous. Contrast, *the throne of iniquity* (Psa 94:20). John saw a Throne in 4:2, and thereafter the Throne is mentioned more than thirty times. Revelation is pre-eminently the Book of the Throne! But the Throne here is different; it is one set entirely for judgement.

2. THE APPEARANCE OF THE JUDGE: *and him that sat on it, from whose face the earth and the heaven fled away; and there was found no place for them.* The One on the Throne is the Lord Jesus Christ.

• *For as the Father raiseth up the dead, and quickeneth them; even so the Son quickeneth whom he will. 22* **For the Father judgeth no man, but hath committed all judgment unto the Son**: *23 That all men should honour the Son, even as they honour the Father. He that honoureth not the Son honoureth not the Father which hath sent him* (Jhn 5:21-23).

All of the old order now flees in terror. Because of the proceedings now to take place there is a dissolution of the whole frame of nature (cp. 2 Pet 3:10). The earth and the starry heavens fled from this site, but for the multitudes standing there, escape will not be possible.

• *Heaven and earth shall pass away, but my words shall not pass away* (Matt 24:35).
• *And it is easier for heaven and earth to pass, than one tittle of the law to fail* (Lk 16:17).
• *But the day of the Lord will come as a thief in the night; in the which* **the heavens shall pass away with a great noise**, *and the elements shall melt with fervent heat,* **the earth also and the works that are therein shall be burned up** (2 Pet 3:10).

3. THE PERSONS TO BE JUDGED. *And I saw the dead, small and great, stand before God* (20:12). Young and old, low and high, poor and rich. None are so lowly that they have nothing of which to give an account. None are so great that they can avoid the jurisdiction of this court. All are *dead* at this judgement; *dead in trespasses and sins* (Eph 2:1). These are *the rest of the dead* (20:5), and thus entirely separated from the righteous.

Their standing posture means that they are now about to be sentenced. There is no period of deliberation. The One who is all-knowing has made an immediate decision. This is a fulfilment of the principle of Hebrews 9:27, *It is appointed unto men once to die, but after this the judgment.*

That dead people are to stand is one of the most dreadful statements of prophecy. Whether devoured by the fish of the sea or the worms of the land, they shall rise from their graves and shall be "shaken out" of death and the grave into the Lake of Fire. Not one shall by any possibility find a hiding place (see Williams).

4. THE SETTLED RULE OF THE JUDGMENT: *and the books were opened: and another book was opened, which is the book of life: and the dead were judged out of those things which were written in the books, according to their works.*

• *And I intreat thee also, true yokefellow, help those women which laboured with me in the gospel, with Clement also, and with other my fellowlabourers, whose names are in* **the book of life** (Phil 4:3).
• *He that overcometh, the same shall be clothed in white raiment; and* **I will not blot out his name out of the book of life**, *but I will confess his name before my Father, and before his angels* (Rev 3:5).

CHAPTER 20

• *And all that dwell upon the earth shall worship him, whose names are not written in **the book of life of the Lamb** slain from the foundation of the world* (Rev 13:8).

• *The beast that thou sawest was, and is not; and shall ascend out of the bottomless pit, and go into perdition: and they that dwell on the earth shall wonder, whose names were not written in **the book of life** from the foundation of the world, when they behold the beast that was, and is not, and yet is* (Rev 17:8).

• *And there shall in no wise enter into it any thing that defileth, neither whatsoever worketh abomination, or maketh a lie: but they which are written in **the Lamb's book of life*** (Rev 21:27).

• *And if any man shall take away from the words of the book of this prophecy, God shall take away his part out of **the book of life**, and out of the holy city, and from the things which are written in this book* (Rev 22:19).

The ***Books of Works***, the ***Book of Life***; all is recorded for all to see. The Book of Life will have contained the names of all who lived, but their names will be blotted out if they die without receiving Christ (Rev 3:5). Thus at the Great White Throne this book will be a book of gaps. None of those standing there will be able to find their name.

The Book of Works describes the life, character and actions of the lost. Everything is recorded (acts both secret and open; Rom 2:16; 1 Tim 5:24). Many of the works recorded are quite grim, but a considerable number may be good. None of those standing there will find works recorded that sprang out of faith in Christ (Eph 2:10) and therefore none of their works will avail (Isa 64:6).

Note what was said previously in 3:5 concerning names that were *blotted out* of the Book of Life.

He that overcometh, the same shall be clothed in white raiment; and <u>I will not blot out his name out of the book of life</u>, but I will confess his name before my Father, and before his angels (3:5). This relates directly to those who had or were seeking *a name* at Sardis (3:1). Men may be enrolled in the registers of the church but in the rolls of Heaven that name may come to be blotted out when it appears that it was only a name, without evidence of spiritual life. There were many at Sardis that ***had a name that they lived but were dead*** (3:1). This verse indicates that when they lived on earth, their names were for a time recorded in the Book in Heaven (they could have been saved!), but when they died without receiving eternal life in Christ, their names were blotted out.

Relating this passage to true believers: the world may have ignored or misrepresented or even sought to blot out their names. While others were seeking a *name*, they simply went on their way serving Christ (cp. Jhn 3:30). Any notice of them many have been forgotten, but that will not be the case in Heaven. It will not happen in Christ's Book or in the day He declares their ***name*** *before His angels*.

<u>5. THE SUMMONS OF THOSE WHO DIED PREVIOUSLY.</u> ***And the sea gave up the dead which were in it; and death and hell delivered up the dead which were in them: and they were judged every man according to their works. And death and hell were cast into the lake of fire. This is the second death*** (20:13,14). It is not only those who are alive physically that now appear, but all who have died before and died in their sins (Jhn 8:24); the grave shall surrender the bodies of the lost and hell shall surrender their souls. The sea shall surrender the many who were lost at sea. If they can be delivered from the sea, they will be delivered from every other place.

Note that ***hell*** (*hades*) is the intermediate state of the souls of the lost in which the unsaved suffer prior to the judgment of the Great White Throne at which time both soul and body are cast into the Lake of Fire. A second Greek word translated **hell** is *gehenna*. Both soul **and body** are said to be cast into *gehenna* and therefore it must refer to the eternal state of the lost in the Lake of Fire (Matt 5:22, 29,30; 10:28; 18:9; Mk 9:43,45,47).

Note also that the body and soul of the lost are named after the abodes that held them. Death, and in whatever place, held the body; and hell (*hades*) held the soul. It is in this sense that ***death and hell were cast into the lake of fire***.

The resurrection of the wicked dead is in sharp contrast to the resurrection of the righteous dead. They are separated by at least a thousand years. The righteous are given bodies like the holy, immortal, and incorruptible body of Christ in His resurrection. The wicked dead are given resurrection bodies suited for eternal punishment.

- *And have hope toward God, which they themselves also allow, that **there shall be a resurrection of the dead, both of the just and unjust*** (Acts 24:15).

Works are emphasised in this judgement, for they demonstrate the true state of the soul. As Walvoord writes; "When ***every man is judged according to his works***, he thus becomes subject to the perfect righteousness of God. The peculiar construction of the closing clause of verse 13, "they were judged every man," uses a third person plural for the verb, but a first person singular in the masculine for the term "every man" or "each" (*ekastos*). The meaning is that while they are judged as a group, the resulting judgment, nevertheless, is individual."

<u>6. THE EXECUTION OF THE SENTENCE</u>. ***And whosoever was not found written in the book of life was cast into the lake of fire*** (20:15). Each in that vast multitude will be able to see that their name does not appear. Salvation and damnation is a personal not a corporate matter. The name does not appear and they are ***cast into the lake of fire.*** There is no opportunity for appeal. Many Gospel appeals were made to them (Jhn 1:9; Ron 10:18; Titus 2:11). Many tracts were given but there are none to be given out at the Great White Throne or in the Lake of Fire.

Walvoord writes concerning this most stark of statements.

> If the point of view be adopted that the book of life was originally the book of all living from which have been expunged the names of those who departed from life on earth without salvation, it presents a sad picture of a blank space where their names could have been written for all eternity as the objects of divine grace. Though they are judged by their works, it is evident that their destiny is determined primarily by their lack of spiritual life. When the fact is contemplated that Jesus Christ in His death reconciled the world to Himself (2 Cor 5:19) and that He died for the reprobate as well as for the elect, it is all the more poignant that these now raised from the dead are cast into the lake of fire. Their ultimate destiny of eternal punishment is not, in the last analysis, because God wished it but because they would not come to God for the grace which He freely offered.

The only revelation that has been given concerning the eternal state recognizes two destinies and two only: one of blessedness in the presence of the Lord, the other of eternal punishment.

- *And shall cast them into a furnace of fire: there shall be **wailing and gnashing of teeth*** (Matt 13:42).
- *Then shall he say also unto them on the left hand, Depart from me, ye cursed, into **everlasting fire**, prepared for the devil and his angels* (Matt 25:41).

- *And these shall go away into **everlasting punishment**: but the righteous into life eternal* (Matt 25:46).
- *But the fearful, and unbelieving, and the abominable, and murderers, and whoremongers, and sorcerers, and idolaters, and all liars, **shall have their part in the lake which burneth with fire and brimstone**: which is the second death* (Rev 21:8).

With this the Bible concludes the history of the earth and the celestial heavens. With this we see the following significant fact.

CREATION IN SEVEN DAYS POINTS TO EARTH'S HISTORY COMPLETED IN SEVEN THOUSAND YEARS

Prior to the sixfold announcement by the Apostle John that the Kingdom would last for a thousand years, there was also the prevalent view in Jewish that this would be the length of the Messiah's Kingdom. Walvoord writes:

> The idea that the future millennium would be 1,000 years has been suggested by apocalyptic writers before Christ. In the Book of the Secrets of Enoch, 32:2; 33:1-2 Enoch holds the idea that the history of man will run for seven thousand years, the last millennium of which will be one of great blessedness and will precede the eighth millennium, which is eternity. According to R. H. Charles, Enoch's view can be explained as follows:
> "As the world was made in six days, so its history will be accomplished in 6,000 years, and as the six days of creation were followed by one of rest, so the 6,000 years of the world's history would be followed by a rest of 1,000 years. On its close would begin the eighth eternal day of blessedness when time should be no more, 32:2-33:2."

Nevertheless, though the BC third century Book of Enoch may reflect Jewish opinion, it is not (as its contents will soon show) Inspired Scripture. There is a far more direct and better line of evidence. Based on *inspired* Biblical Chronology it is now known to be about 6000 years since the creation of Adam. Based on the prophecy of Revelation 20; the Reign of Christ on earth will last for one thousand years. Based on Bible Prophecy and the reestablishment of the Nation of Israel we are clearly in the last days. With this in mind, 2 Peter 3:8 supports the likelihood of linking the Seven Days of Genesis One with Seven Thousand Years of human history culminating in the New Heavens and New Earth.

- *But, beloved, be not ignorant of this one thing, that **one day is with the Lord as a thousand years**, and a thousand years as one day* (2 Pet 3:8).

There are some things we can be *ignorant of*, but *we must not be ignorant of **this one thing***.

ETERNAL GENERATIONS AS THE SAND OF THE SEA AND THE STARS OF HEAVEN !

Extraordinary promises are made concerning the extent of Abraham's offspring.

- *And I will make thy seed as the dust of the earth: so that **if a man can number the dust of the earth, then shall thy seed also be numbered*** (Gen 13:16).

- *And he brought him forth abroad, and said,* **Look now toward heaven, and tell the stars, if thou be able to number them**: *and he said unto him,* **So shall thy seed be** (Gen 15:5).
- *That in blessing I will bless thee, and in multiplying* **I will multiply thy seed as the stars of the heaven, and as the sand which is upon the sea shore**; *and thy seed shall possess the gate of his enemies* (Gen 22:17).
- *And they blessed Rebekah, and said unto her, Thou art our sister,* **be thou the mother of thousands of millions**, *and let thy seed possess the gate of those which hate them.* (Gen 24:60).
- *And* **I will make thy seed to multiply as the stars of heaven**, *and will give unto thy seed all these countries; and in thy seed shall all the nations of the earth be blessed* (Gen 26:4).
- *And* **thy seed shall be as the dust of the earth**, *and thou shalt spread abroad to the west, and to the east, and to the north, and to the south: and in thee and in thy seed shall all the families of the earth be blessed* (Gen 28:14).
- *And thou saidst, I will surely do thee good, and* **make thy seed as the sand of the sea, which cannot be numbered for multitude** (Gen 32:12).
- *Remember Abraham, Isaac, and Israel, thy servants, to whom thou swarest by thine own self, and saidst unto them,* **I will multiply your seed as the stars of heaven**, *and all this land that I have spoken of will I give unto your seed, and they shall inherit it for ever* (Exod 32:13).

Though the numbers become great during the Millennium the promise to Abraham, Isaac and Jacob could hardly said to be fulfilled during the Millennium if they were so drastically reduced at the end of that time. In fact they were reduced by a *sand of the sea* number.

- *And shall go out to deceive the nations which are in the four quarters of the earth, Gog and Magog, to gather them together to battle:* **the number of whom is as the sand of the sea** (20:8).

The question therefore must be asked; what is the state of the righteous who in their natural bodies have lived to the end of the Millennial Reign and are now entering the New Heavens and the New Earth (21:1). There is no Scripture that indicates that they will be glorified and live in New Jerusalem with the *fixed number* of Church, Old Testament and martyred Tribulation saints. We conclude that as Satan and the curse of sin is now removed and as the righteous nations will partake of the Tree of Life for their healing, that these who enter Eternity will be confirmed in holiness (as before the Fall) and will multiply in righteousness from the New Earth to the New Heavens *FOREVER*. Thus where sin abounded, grace did much more abound (Rom 5:20). The Lord's purpose for Eden is fulfilled and on a vastly greater level.

- *And God blessed them, and God said unto them,* **Be fruitful, and multiply, and replenish the earth** (Gen 1:28).
- **And there shall be no more curse**: *but the throne of God and of the Lamb shall be in it; and his servants shall serve him* (Rev 22:3).

Note several further passages that point to eternal and increasing generations.

- ***A little one shall become a thousand, and a small one a strong nation***: *I the LORD will hasten it in his time* (Isa 60:22).

CHAPTER 20

- ***Of the increase of his government and peace there shall be no end***, *upon the throne of David, and upon his kingdom, to order it, and to establish it with judgment and with justice from henceforth even for ever. The zeal of the LORD of hosts will perform this* (Isa 9:7).
- *And the city had no need of the sun, neither of the moon, to shine in it: for the glory of God did lighten it, and the Lamb is the light thereof. 24 And **the nations of them which are saved shall walk in the light of it**: and the kings of the earth do bring their glory and honour into it* (Rev 21:23,24).
- *And he shewed me a pure river of water of life, clear as crystal, proceeding out of the throne of God and of the Lamb. 2 In the midst of the street of it, and on either side of the river, was there the tree of life, which bare twelve manner of fruits, and yielded her fruit every month: **and the leaves of the tree were for the healing of the nations*** (Rev 22:1,2).

CHAPTER 21 & 22

E. THE ETERNAL AGES   21,22
1. Eternity: Joy or Sorrow Forever   21:1-8
2. New Jerusalem: Its Exterior   21:9-27
3. New Jerusalem: Its Interior   22:1-5
4. The Bible's Final Call   22:6-21

1. ETERNITY: JOY OR SORROW FOREVER   21:1-8

(21:1) *And I saw a new heaven and a new earth: for the first heaven and the first earth were passed away; and there was no more sea.*

(21:2) *And I John saw the holy city, new Jerusalem, coming down from God out of heaven, prepared as a bride adorned for her husband.*

(21:3) *And I heard a great voice out of heaven saying, Behold, the tabernacle of God is with men, and he will dwell with them, and they shall be his people, and God himself shall be with them, and be their God.* (21:4) *And God shall wipe away all tears from their eyes; and there shall be no more death, neither sorrow, nor crying, neither shall there be any more pain: for the former things are passed away.*

(21:5) *And he that sat upon the throne said, Behold, I make all things new. And he said unto me, Write: for these words are true and faithful.* (21:6) *And he said unto me, It is done. I am Alpha and Omega, the beginning and the end. I will give unto him that is athirst of the fountain of the water of life freely.* (21:7) *He that overcometh shall inherit all things; and I will be his God, and he shall be my son.*

(21:8) *But the fearful, and unbelieving, and the abominable, and murderers, and whoremongers, and sorcerers, and idolaters, and all liars, shall have their part in the lake which burneth with fire and brimstone: which is the second death.*

"Paradise is always presented in Scripture as a definite place. It was Planted in Genesis 2; Lost in Genesis 3; Reappears in Luke 23:43; Visited in 2 Corinthians 12:2-4; Promised in Revelation 2:7; and Regained in Revelation 22:1-5,14,17. Its first inhabitants bid themselves from the face of God. Its future occupants shall see the face of God (22:4)." George Williams.

1. THE NEW HEAVEN AND NEW EARTH APPEAR. *And I saw a new heaven and a new earth: for the first heaven and the first earth were passed away; and there was no more sea* (21:1). The expression, *And I saw,* is stated three times in 21:1,2, 22. *And I heard* is also added (21:3). These repetitions displace imagination and assert reality.

Life lived beyond the Millennium will be confirmed in holiness and *extend* and likely *expand* throughout eternity upon the New Earth and ultimately to the New Heavens. With the curse removed and in a state of absolute holiness, God's original purpose in an unfallen Eden will be fulfilled. The heavens today, void of life (unless angelic, cp. Neh 9:6), are a wasteland; that will not be the case of the New Heavens in that day. In Eternity the *sand of the sea* and *stars of the heaven* prophecies will be fulfilled literally.

- *Of the* **increase** *of his government and peace* **there shall be no end** (Isa 9:7).
- *For, behold, I create new heavens and a new earth: and the former shall not be remembered, nor come into mind* (Isa 65:17).

THE BOOK OF REVELATION

The old world, with all its troubles and commotions likened to the troubled sea has *passed away* forever. While this and the next chapter describe New Jerusalem, with one exception no description is given of the New Heavens or the New Earth except that the nations will dwell on the New Earth and that it will hover beneath or exist beside the New Jerusalem (21:24).

Concerning the New Earth we are told that there will be **no more sea**. As seventy-one percent of the present earth is covered with water, this is a very significant difference. There will no doubt be rivers and large lakes, but as the New Earth will be *perfect* there will be no need for the saline *purification* provided by the present oceans. Nor will there be oceans to *separate* the expanding population (cp. Gen 11:4-9). Nor will there be the storms and the perils of the sea. Nor will the seas be a means of judgement as in Noah's day. Nor in judgement will the New Earth ever experience *the sea and the waves roaring* (Lk 21:25). This New Earth does not arise out of the waters (Gen 1:2); nor will it be covered by the waters (Gen 7:19).

2. THE CITY, NEW JERUSALEM APPEARS.

(21:2) *And I John saw the holy city, new Jerusalem, coming down from God out of heaven, prepared as a bride adorned for her husband* (21:2). This is the *prepared* city that our Lord has *gone to prepare* (Jhn 14:2). This will be the home of the redeemed with resurrected bodies. Thus it has a fixed population. It will hover above or rest beside the New Earth throughout Eternity.

> • *And the city had no need of the sun, neither of the moon, to shine in it: for the glory of God did lighten it, and the Lamb is the light thereof.* **And the nations of them which are saved shall walk in the light of it**: *and the kings of the earth do bring their glory and honour into it* (Rev 21:23,24).

Long before John saw this city, Abraham *by faith* in revelation given to him began to look for it.

> • ***By faith*** *he sojourned in the land of promise, as in a strange country, dwelling in tabernacles with Isaac and Jacob, the heirs with him of the same promise:* **For he looked for a city which hath foundations, whose builder and maker is God**
> (Heb 11:9,10).

The New Jerusalem was in existence in Heaven long before John saw it. Following the example of the Tabernacle and Temple of Solomon which were patterned after the Heavenly Sanctuary (cp. Exod 25:9,40), the earthly Jerusalem and certainly the Millennial Jerusalem were to a certain extent patterned after the Heavenly City (cp. Ezek 48:30-35).
It is likely that it was to this City that our Lord referred when He said, *In my Father's house are many mansions ... I go to prepare a place for you* (Jhn 14:2). Though New Jerusalem did not appear and was not directly mentioned in relation to the millennial earth, yet it seems clear that the Church and other glorified saints had access to both it and the earth during the Thousand Years.

As verse 2 speaks of New Jerusalem, *prepared as a bride adorned for her husband,* and as the Church is called both the *bride* and *wife* in Revelation 19:7,9; 21:2,9; some believe that the Church alone will dwell in New Jerusalem. (Note: the Church is not directly called the *bride* in the Epistles; cp. 2 Cor 11:2; Eph 5:24-33). However, on the basis of Abraham's foreview of New Jerusalem (Heb 11:10,16), it seems clear that the fixed company of all glorified believers will be residents of the New Jerusalem (saints of the Old Testament, the Church and Tribulation martyrs). As Jennings says: "Every child of God through all the ages, whose earthly tabernacle has been dissolved, shall be at this time in his heavenly house, and thus together form the heavenly city."

CHAPTER 21 & 22

(1) IT IS THE CITY OF THE LORD'S IMMEDIATE PRESENCE. *And I heard a great voice out of heaven saying, Behold, the tabernacle of God is with men, and he will dwell with them, and they shall be his people, and God himself shall be with them, and be their God* (21:3). There are a total of twenty-one great or loud voices in Revelation; this is the last. It is matter of wonder that a holy God would ever dwell in this closest proximity with any of the children of men, yet because of the infinite merit of Christ's Work on the Cross such is now the case.

(2) IT IS THE CITY FREE FROM ALL SORROW.

[1] ALL THE EFFECTS OF PAST TROUBLE ARE FINISHED. *And God shall wipe away all tears from their eyes; and there shall be no more death, neither sorrow, nor crying* (21:4). There has been overwhelming sin, affliction and calamity that has brought a flood of tears. It and the tears are now gone. There will be no sign nor remembrance of any of it. God reaches down removes the remembrance and wipes the tears away. There were many tears on earth and in the earthly Jerusalem, but none on New Earth or in the New Jerusalem.

[2] ALL THE CAUSES OF FUTURE SORROW ARE FOREVER REMOVED: *neither shall there be any more pain: for the former things are passed away.* Those things were there *before*, but now they are *former things* and *former things have passed away.*

(3] IT IS THE CITY OF "BLESSED ASSURANCE".

[1) IT IS ASSURED BY THE NEW BEGINNING. *And he that sat upon the throne said, Behold, I make all things new* (21:5). All is made new for man and in God's dealings with man. With no more sin, Satan and the curse, this great pronouncement can now be made (Rev 22:3).

[2] IT IS ASSURED BY WRITTEN DECLARATION. *And he said unto me, Write: for these words are true and faithful.* John has been writing continually, but now once again for emphasis, he is told to write. This is the last of twelve times John is told to *write*.

> • *Saying, I am Alpha and Omega, the first and the last: and, What thou seest,* **write** *in a book, and send it unto the seven churches which are in Asia; unto Ephesus, and unto Smyrna, and unto Pergamos, and unto Thyatira, and unto Sardis, and unto Philadelphia, and unto Laodicea* (Rev 1:11).
>
> • **Writ**e *the things which thou hast seen, and the things which are, and the things which shall be hereafter* (Rev 1:19).
>
> • *Unto the angel of the church of Ephesus* **write***; These things saith he that holdeth the seven stars in his right hand, who walketh in the midst of the seven golden candlesticks* (Rev 2:1).
>
> • *And unto the angel of the church in Smyrna* **write***; These things saith the first and the last, which was dead, and is alive* (Rev 2:8).
>
> • *And to the angel of the church in Pergamos* **write***; These things saith he which hath the sharp sword with two edges* (Rev 2:12).
>
> • *And unto the angel of the church in Thyatira* **write***; These things saith the Son of God, who hath his eyes like unto a flame of fire, and his feet are like fine brass* (Rev 2:18).
>
> • *And unto the angel of the church in Sardis* **write***; These things saith he that hath the seven Spirits of God, and the seven stars; I know thy works, that thou hast a name that thou livest, and art dead* (Rev 3:1).
>
> • *And to the angel of the church in Philadelphia* **write***; These things saith he that is holy, he that is true, he that hath the key of David, he that openeth, and no man shutteth; and shutteth, and no man openeth* (Rev 3:7).

THE BOOK OF REVELATION

  • *And unto the angel of the church of the Laodiceans* **write**; *These things saith the Amen, the faithful and true witness, the beginning of the creation of God* (Rev 3:14).
  • *And I heard a voice from heaven saying unto me,* **Write***, Blessed are the dead which die in the Lord from henceforth: Yea, saith the Spirit, that they may rest from their labours; and their works do follow them* (Rev 14:13).
  • *And he saith unto me,* **Write***, Blessed are they which are called unto the marriage supper of the Lamb. And he saith unto me, These are the true sayings of God* (Rev 19:9)
  • *And he that sat upon the throne said, Behold, I make all things new. And he said unto me,* **Write***: for these words are true and faithful* (Rev 21:5).

[3] IT IS ASSURED BY ABSOLUTE FINALITY. **And he said unto me, It is done** (21:6). We may take God's promise as present payment. If He has said that He *makes all things new, it is done. He spake and it was done* (Psa 33:9). This is the great conclusion of the declaration at Calvary's Cross: ***It is finished*** (Jhn 19:30).

As Williams says, "The mighty declaration **Finished** heard in the morn of creation (Gen 2:1), and at Calvary, and now here repeated for the last time, closes all prophecy. He Who as the *Alpha* created the old heavens and the earth will as the *Omega* establish the New Heavens and Earth, and so once more in His love He invites all who thirst for eternal life to accept it from Him as a gift."

[4] IT IS ASSURED BY THE GUARANTOR'S ETERNAL BEING. ***I am Alpha and Omega, the beginning and the end.*** As it was *He* that created the world, so it is *His* greater glory to bring everything to this grand perfection. It is by this Title that Christ is introduced in 1:8 and again in 22:13. This Book is the Revelation of Jesus Christ, all things from above whether at its beginning or ending proceed from Him.

With the appearance of our Lord here, Christ appears eight times in Revelation (1:13; 4:3,11; 5:6; 7:9; 14:1; 14:14; 19:11; 21:6). There are four appearings of the Resurrected Christ in John 20 and 21. (see Williams).

[5] IT IS ASSURED BY REVITALIZING EXPERIENCE. ***I will give unto him that is athirst of the fountain of the water of life freely.*** The people of God will dwell at the fountain-head of all blessedness. This promise was also given to the Tribulation martyrs (Rev 7:17). Beside it being a literal promise and especially to those on the New Earth, it expresses the abundant spiritual experience of the redeemed in Eternity.

3. THE GREAT CONTRAST REAPPEARS.
(1) A SURPASSING INHERITANCE. **He that overcometh shall inherit all things; and I will be his God, and he shall be my son** (21:7). It would be impossible to set out a more surpassing inheritance to this given those who overcome by faith (1 Jhn 4:4: 5:4). Frequently in Scripture, particular promises are given those who triumph in faith. Here the extraordinary provision is announced that they *shall inherit all things* rather than some particular aspect of the divine provision. (see Walvoord). But the greatest provision is the full realization and experience of sonship.

(2) A WRETCHED DOMICILE.
[1] THE INHABITANTS. **But the fearful, and unbelieving, and the abominable, and murderers, and whoremongers, and sorcerers, and idolaters, and all liars** (21:8). In contrast to the abundant blessings of those who exercise faith in the Lord Jesus Christ is the terrible inheritance of unbelief. The unbelievers are described by those characteristics which stem from a life that has not found refuge in Christ. A similar list is found in 21:27 and in 22:15. This is a bad list, but at its head are *the fearful*. They are afraid to receive Christ because of what family, friend, and enemy might think! Williams says, It is

of arresting solemnity that the *fearful*, i.e., the cowardly, are here placed with murderers and idolaters,"

Some of the saved were guilty of the same offenses but turned in repentant faith to Christ. Another similar list is given in I Corinthians 6:9-11, but it has a blessed conclusion.

- ***Know ye not that the unrighteous shall not inherit the kingdom of God?*** *Be not deceived: neither fornicators, nor idolaters, nor adulterers, nor effeminate, nor abusers of themselves with mankind, 10 Nor thieves, nor covetous, nor drunkards, nor revilers, nor extortioners, shall inherit the kingdom of God. 11* ***And such were some of you: but ye are washed, but ye are sanctified, but ye are justified in the name of the Lord Jesus, and by the Spirit of our God*** (1 Cor 6:9-11).

[2] THE TORMENT. ***shall have their part in the lake which burneth with fire and brimstone: which is the second death.*** A lake, but one of fire. Death, but always dying. This is the great divide. This is the difference between being saved and being lost. Revelation opens with the washing of Calvary (1:5) and closes with the Lake of Fire.

2. NEW JERUSALEM: ITS EXTERIOR 21:9-27

A. THE VISTA OF THE CITY 21:9-11

*(21:9) **And there came unto me one of the seven angels which had the seven vials full of the seven last plagues, and talked with me, saying, Come hither, I will shew thee the bride, the Lamb's wife.***

*(21:10) **And he carried me away in the spirit to a great and high mountain, and shewed me that great city, the holy Jerusalem, descending out of heaven from God,***
*(21:11) **Having the glory of God: and her light was like unto a stone most precious, even like a jasper stone, clear as crystal;***

1. THE GUIDE.

(1) HIS APPROACH. ***And there came unto me one of the seven angels which had the seven vials full of the seven last plagues*** (21:9). This may be the same angel that showed Religious Babylon to John, *the Harlot* (17:1). The contrast could not be greater as he shows him *the Bride*. Note here how he angels readily execute every commission they receive from God.

(2) HIS INVITATION: ***and talked with me, saying, Come hither, I will shew thee the bride, the Lamb's wife.*** In keeping with the earlier revelation, see comments on Revelation 19:7-9 and 21:2, the city is named after her inhabitants. the new Jerusalem. It is here characterized as *the bride, the Lamb's wife*. The Church is both the Bride and the Wife. Yet as we have seen the Old Testament saints and Tribulation martyrs will also dwell there. As with, *he shall be by son* (21:7), *bride* and *wife* will further characterize the inhabitants of New Jerusalem. Further, the city itself is to be compared to a *bride* for beauty and a *wife* for perpetuity.

2. THE VANTAGE POINT. ***And he carried me away in the spirit to a great and high mountain*** (21:10). A similar experience was afforded in 17:3. But in every other respect the experience is different. There John was *carried away in the spirit into the wilderness* to see a harlot. This mountain is likely on the New Earth, and over which the New Jerusalem will hover (21:24). It was from the top of Mount Pisgah that Moses saw the Promised Land. This vista is far better (Deut 34:1).

THE BOOK OF REVELATION

3. THE PROSPECT: *and shewed me that great city, the holy Jerusalem, descending out of heaven from God, Having the glory of God: and her light was like unto a stone most precious, even like a jasper stone, clear as crystal* (21:10,11). The city has a four-fold glory. It is:

- *great*
- *from God,*
- *having the glory of God,*
- *her light was like unto a stone most precious.*

"The city is said to have the glory of God, and to have a brilliant light. As the glory of God is the sum of His infinite perfections in their manifestations, so the New Jerusalem reflects all that God is.

The city is ablaze with light compared to the brightness of a precious stone such as jasper (*clear as crystal*). The stone here described as a jasper has its name transliterated from a similar word in the original (*iaspis*), a name used for stones of various colours, but here specifying the qualities *precious* and *clear as crystal*. The mention of this stone which is costly to men but used lavishly in the new Jerusalem (21:19) is designed to manifest the glory of God. Later in the passage (21:23), the fact is revealed that the city does not originate its light or radiance, but all illumination comes from the Lamb. The believer in Christ does not generate the light of Christ, but he should both reflect and transmit its glory without blurring the beauty and loveliness of Christ." (Walvoord).

B. THE WALL, GATES AND FOUNDATIONS 21:12-22

(21:12) *And had a wall great and high, and had twelve gates, and at the gates twelve angels, and names written thereon, which are the names of the twelve tribes of the children of Israel:* (21:13) *On the east three gates; on the north three gates; on the south three gates; and on the west three gates.*

(21:14) *And the wall of the city had twelve foundations, and in them the names of the twelve apostles of the Lamb.*

(21:15) *And he that talked with me had a golden reed to measure the city, and the gates thereof, and the wall thereof.* (21:16) *And the city lieth foursquare, and the length is as large as the breadth: and he measured the city with the reed, twelve thousand furlongs. The length and the breadth and the height of it are equal.* (21:17) *And he measured the wall thereof, an hundred and forty and four cubits, according to the measure of a man, that is, of the angel.*

(21:18) *And the building of the wall of it was of jasper: and the city was pure gold, like unto clear glass.* (21:19) *And the foundations of the wall of the city were garnished with all manner of precious stones. The first foundation was jasper; the second, sapphire; the third, a chalcedony; the fourth, an emerald;* (21:20) *The fifth, sardonyx; the sixth, sardius; the seventh, chrysolite; the eighth, beryl; the ninth, a topaz; the tenth, a chrysoprasus; the eleventh, a jacinth; the twelfth, an amethyst.* (21:21) *And the twelve gates were twelve pearls; every several gate was of one pearl: and the street of the city was pure gold, as it were transparent glass.*

NUMBER TWELVE IN NEW JERUSALEM

After viewing the overall vista of New Jerusalem we are now presented with a number of the specific details. In these we see that the number twelve is prominent:

CHAPTER 21 & 22

- Twelve gates,
    Twelve angels, the names of the twelve tribes of Israel (21:12)
    Twelve pearls (21:21)
- Twelve foundations (21:14)
    The names of the twelve apostles (21:14)
    Twelve thousand furlongs (1,342 miles) for the height, length, and width (21:16)
- 144 cubits, twelve times twelve cubits for the height of the wall (over 200 feet (21:17)
- Twelve kinds of fruit (22:2).

1. THE WALL OF THE CITY. ***And had a wall great and high*** (21:12). The description begins with the wall. New Jerusalem is a safe city, nevertheless it is enclosed with a wall and signifies the security of the city. No one will ever fall out of this city. It is a high wall, upwards of 70 metres, yet in comparison to the rest to the city, it is small. It will accentuate rather than hide the glory of New Jerusalem.

This reminds us also that only those who have come by the *Door* (Christ is the Door, Jhn 10:9) may enter this city. The wall is too high for those who *would climb up some other way* (Jhn 10:9).

2. THE GATES OF THE CITY: ***and had twelve gates, and at the gates twelve angels, and names written thereon, which are the names of the twelve tribes of the children of Israel: On the east three gates; on the north three gates; on the south three gates; and on the west three gates*** (21:12,13). The gates are for entrance. New Jerusalem will be an accessible city. There will be a constant flow of the redeemed through these gates from the New Earth below.

Their number is twelve and their names are of the twelve tribes of Israel. They will ever remind of the covenant with Abraham and that *salvation is of the Jews* (Jhn 4:22).

Twelve angels stand at these gates as honour guards, and to remind the inhabitants of the New Earth that they are passing from the earthly to the Heavenly.

Three gates are on each side of the city with the names of the Tribes of Israel, answers to the same arrangement in the Millennial Jerusalem as recorded in Ezekiel (Ezek 48:30-35). However unlike Ezekiel the placement of the names are not stated in Revelation. These names of the tribes demonstrate further the inclusion of Old Testament saints in the Heavenly City.

3. THE NAMES ON THE TWELVE FOUNDATIONS OF THE CITY. ***And the wall of the city had twelve foundations, and in them the names of the twelve apostles of the Lamb*** (21:14). As with the Twelve Tribes, the Twelve Apostles are also inscribed on the city. They too are all of Israel! The Scriptures inspired through and taught by the Twelve Apostles are the doctrines upon which New Jerusalem is founded. In this we see the principle that as far as Biblical revelation is concerned, *Salvation is of the Jews* (Jhn 4:22).

- *And are built upon the foundation of the apostles and prophets, Jesus Christ himself being the chief corner stone* (Eph 2:20).

4. THE MEASUREMENTS OF THE CITY.
    (1) THE UNIT OF MEASUREMENT. ***And he that talked with me had a golden reed to measure the city, and the gates thereof, and the wall thereof*** (21:15). The reed to measure is about ten feet in length. These are literal measurements. One does not measure symbols.
    (2) THE CITY ITSELF. (21:16) ***And the city lieth foursquare, and the length is as large as the breadth: and he measured the city with the reed, twelve thousand***

furlongs. The length and the breadth and the height of it are equal. The form of it is *uniform*: *It was four-square, the length and breadth as large as the height*. In the New Jerusalem all shall be equal in purity and perfection. There shall be an absolute unity there and no discord at all there. That which was not achieved among believers in this day will be experienced then.

As it would be easier to visualize, some have noted that the measurements would allow for a pyramid. But this as J. B. Smith observes would reduce it to dimensions far inferior to those indicated by a cube. We shall have to wait before we can comprehend how a city can be foursquare. However, the precedent for a cube is the Old Testament Tabernacle and Temple where the inner Holy of Holies was foursquare. The entire New Jerusalem will be a *Holy of Holies*!

The measure of it was great. A furlong is equal to 582 feet, the measured distance is equivalent to 1,342 miles, often spoken of roughly as 1,500 miles. Here is room sufficient for all the people of God with resurrected bodies. There are *many mansions in the Father's house* (Jhn 14:1).

(3) THE WALL. *And he measured the wall thereof, an hundred and forty and four cubits, according to the measure of a man, that is, of the angel* (21:17). Though measured by an angel, a human standard was employed. Thus the measurements are to be taken in an absolutely literal sense. The height of the wall is *great and high* (21:12), and that it is in comparison to any wall known today. But at about 216 feet it is not so high as to obscure the city. Yet, as we have said, it is too high to enter by any other way than the Door.

While, as we have stated and as it is commonly believed, the city is viewed as hovering above the New Earth (21:24). Walvoord believes it will rest on the New Earth.

> The city taken as a whole is pictured as descending from heaven to the new earth, and the fact that it has foundations and comes from heaven to the earth seems to imply that it rests on the new earth itself. This also is implied in the fact that people go in and out of the gates, which fact is difficult to visualize unless the gates themselves rest upon the earth.

5. THE MATERIALS OF THE CITY.

(1) OF THE WALL AND CITY ITSELF. *And the building of the wall of it was of jasper: and the city was pure gold, like unto clear glass* (21:18). The jasper stone is described in verse 11 as being *clear as crystal*. The city will have the radiance of a diamond. As we proceed to the next description - *pure gold, like unto clear glass* – we are reminded that we are dealing with subjects far beyond what we imagine on earth. The transparency of some of the materials lets us know that the city will transmit the light of God's presence without hindrance.

(2) OF THE FOUNDATIONS OF THE WALL. *And the foundations of the wall of the city were garnished with all manner of precious stones* (21:19). There are twelve sorts of precious stones, denoting the variety and excellency of the doctrines of the Gospel, the graces of the Holy Spirit and the personal excellences of the Lord Jesus Christ. "The colours reflect the glory of God in a spectrum of brilliant colour. The light of the city within shining through these various colours in the foundation of the wall topped by the wall itself composed of the crystal-clear jasper forms a scene of dazzling beauty in keeping with the glory of God and the beauty of His holiness." (Walvoord).

> ***The first foundation was jasper***; *clear as crystal* and mentioned also as describing the overall appearance of the city and the wall (21:11,18).
> ***the second, sapphire***; similar to a diamond in hardness and blue in colour.

CHAPTER 21 & 22

the third, a chalcedony; from Chalcedon (in Turkey), thought to be sky-blue with stripes of other colours.
the fourth, an emerald (21:19); bright green.
The fifth, sardonyx; red and white.
the sixth, sardius; a reddish colour. The sardius is used with the jasper in Revelation 4:3 to describe the glory of God on the Throne.
the seventh, chrysolite; a transparent stone golden in colour, thought to be different from the modern pale-green chrysolyte stone.
the eighth, beryl; sea-green.
the ninth, a topaz; yellow-green and transparent.
the tenth, a chrysoprasus; another shade of green.
the eleventh, a jacinth; a violet colour.
the twelfth, an amethyst (21:20); purple.

(3) OF THE GATES. *And the twelve gates were twelve pearls; every several gate was of one pearl:* (21:21). By the hearing we recognize the materials used, but upon further notice all is different – from a small pearl down here to a huge gate composed of a single pearl. The pearls we know are formed around an irritant or injury sustained by an oyster. Thus in that city it will not be the dazzling brightness of a diamond that greets the traveller, but the soft radiance of a pearl. It is grace, *great* grace that welcomes, and that because an injury was sustained (1 Pet 3:18).

- *For as by one man's disobedience many were made sinners, so by the obedience of one shall many be made righteous. Moreover the law entered, that the offence might abound. But* **where sin abounded, grace did much more abound** *(Rom 5:19,20).*

(4) OF THE STREET: *and the street of the city was pure gold, as it were transparent glass.* The grandest boulevards on earth are made of tarmac and concrete; it is not so there. The saints in heaven walk upon gold. The experiences in heaven, in even its most basic parts (the *street*), are glorious. They walk with Christ. They have communion with one another; and all their steps are firm and righteous.

C. THE APPROACHES TO THE CITY 21:22-27

(21:22) *And I saw no temple therein: for the Lord God Almighty and the Lamb are the temple of it.*
(21:23) *And the city had no need of the sun, neither of the moon, to shine in it: for the glory of God did lighten it, and the Lamb is the light thereof.*
(21:24) *And the nations of them which are saved shall walk in the light of it: and the kings of the earth do bring their glory and honour into it.*
(21:25) *And the gates of it shall not be shut at all by day: for there shall be no night there.* (21:26) *And they shall bring the glory and honour of the nations into it.* (21:27) *And there shall in no wise enter into it any thing that defileth, neither whatsoever worketh abomination, or maketh a lie: but they which are written in the Lamb's book of life.*

1. THE TEMPLE OF THE CITY. *And I saw no temple therein: for the Lord God Almighty and the Lamb are the temple of it* (21:22). The familiar clause *And I saw*, alerts the reader to an important phase in the description now given. But unlike the previous usage of the term, where he saw some something, here he does not. The Church has had its buildings; Israel had its Tabernacle and Temple. The Millennial earth will have a great Temple (Ezek 40-48). Thus unlike the approach to a large European City where a Cathedral dominates the horizon, this will not be the case in New Jerusalem. Rather than a Temple

THE BOOK OF REVELATION

housing the Lord (cp. 1 Kng 8:27), the Lord Himself will be the Temple. There will be no *path* to God, but rather perfect and immediate communion with Him. That is difficult to visualize, but that will be the glorious reality of those times.

The word for **temple** is *naos* and refers to the Holy of Holies rather than the entire Temple complex. This further demonstrates that the city is a cube. It is the Holy of Holies for all eternity.

2. THE LIGHT OF THE CITY. *And the city had no need of the sun, neither of the moon, to shine in it: for the glory of God did lighten it, and the Lamb is the light thereof* (21:23). Heaven is *the inheritance of the saints in light* (Col 1:12). And that light is the Lord Himself. Christ the Lamb will be *the light* of that *world* (Jhn 8:12). What a contrast are the everlasting days of New Jerusalem with the last days of Babylon.

- *And the light of a candle shall shine no more at all in thee* (18:23).

The new Jerusalem is distinguished by the things that are missing. There will be no Temple, no sun, no darkness, no sin, no curse, no opening of gates.

3. THE TRAVEL TO THE CITY.

(1) FROM THE NEW EARTH. *And the nations of them which are saved shall walk in the light of it: and the kings of the earth do bring their glory and honour into it* (21:24). The expanding nations will not only walk in the light of the City, but will be drawn to that light. Produce from the furthest reaches of the New Earth, and the New Heavens will be brought to the New Jerusalem. How different this is from the terrible situation that arose at the end of the Millennium (20:7-9).

The question is an open one as to whether the New Jerusalem with its foundations actually rests upon the New Earth. Twice it is seen coming down, but we are not told specifically that it touches the earth. Nevertheless the nations bring their glory and honour *into it*, and **the tabernacle of God is with men**. Note again the three passages from this chapter that touch upon this question

- *And **I John saw the holy city, new Jerusalem, coming down from God out of heaven**, prepared as a bride adorned for her husband. 3 And I heard a great voice out of heaven saying, Behold, **the tabernacle of God is with men, and he will dwell with them**, and they shall be his people, and God himself shall be with them, and be their God* (21:2,3).
- *And he carried me away in the spirit to a great and high mountain, and shewed me that great city, **the holy Jerusalem, descending out of heaven from God*** (21:10).
- *And **the nations of them which are saved shall walk in the light of it: and the kings of the earth do bring their glory and honour into it*** (21:24).

(2) THROUGH OPEN GATES. *And the gates of it shall not be shut at all by day: for there shall be no night there. And they shall bring the glory and honour of the nations into it* (21:25,26). There is continual accession and entrance into this City. There is never any need to shut the gates. Vast multitudes coming at every hour and moment, always find the gates open; they have *an abundant entrance into the kingdom*.

- *For so **an entrance shall be ministered unto you abundantly** into the everlasting kingdom of our Lord and Saviour Jesus Christ* (2 Pet 1:11).

(3) WITH NO DISQUIET. *And there shall in no wise enter into it any thing that defileth, neither whatsoever worketh abomination, or maketh a lie: but they which are*

written in the Lamb's book of life (21:27). Border controls are a time-consuming necessity today; there will not be that need in New Jerusalem. The inhabitants of the city and travellers to the city will be characterized by eternal life and absolute moral purity.

3. NEW JERUSALEM: ITS INTERIOR   22:1-5

(22:1) *And he shewed me a pure river of water of life, clear as crystal, proceeding out of the throne of God and of the Lamb.*
(22:2) *In the midst of the street of it, and on either side of the river, was there the tree of life, which bare twelve manner of fruits, and yielded her fruit every month: and the leaves of the tree were for the healing of the nations.*
(22:3) *And there shall be no more curse: but the throne of God and of the Lamb shall be in it; and his servants shall serve him:*
(22:4) *And they shall see his face; and his name shall be in their foreheads.*
(22:5) *And there shall be no night there; and they need no candle, neither light of the sun; for the Lord God giveth them light: and they shall reign for ever and ever.*

The heavenly New Jerusalem is a Paradise in the fullest sense. It alludes to the first paradise which was lost by the sin of the first Adam. Here is another paradise restored by the Second Adam. A Paradise in a city, or a whole city in a Paradise! In the first paradise there were only two persons to behold the beauty and taste the pleasures of it; but in this second great multitudes will find abundant delight there.

1. THE RIVER OF THE CITY. *And he shewed me a pure river of water of life, clear as crystal, proceeding out of the throne of God and of the Lamb* (22:1). The earthly paradise was well watered: no place can be pleasant or fruitful that is not so. The Millennial Temple will also have the outflow of a miraculous stream (Ezek 47:1-2; Joel 3:18; Zech 14:8). Today, eternal life (Jhn 4:14), and the outflow of the Gospel though the believer is likened to living water (Jhn 7:38). All of this anticipates the River of Life in New Jerusalem.

(1) BY ITS FOUNTAIN-HEAD: *the throne of God and the Lamb*. All our springs of grace, comfort, and glory, are in God; and all our streams from him are through the mediation of the Lamb. All of our streams in this day and in that day are from the Throne.

(2) BY ITS QUALITY: *pure river of life, clear as crystal*. All the streams of earthly comfort are muddy; but these are clear, productive and refreshing; giving life and preserving life. Far beyond our ability to articulate, standing on the banks of that *RIVER* in that day will be to the worshipper a full experience of the Holy Spirit.

- *There is a river, the streams whereof* **shall make glad** *the city of God, the holy place of the tabernacles of the most High* (Psa 46:4).

2. THE TREE OF THE CITY. *In the midst of the street of it, and on either side of the river, was there the tree of life, which bare twelve manner of fruits, and yielded her fruit every month: and the leaves of the tree were for the healing of the nations* (22:2). Such a tree there was in the earthly paradise (Gen 2:9). This far excels it.

(1) THE SITUATION OF THE TREE: *in the midst of the street, and on either side the river*. The river runs in the midst of the grand boulevard with the tree(s) of life on both sides of the river. The Tree of Life is singular as to its *species*, and plural as to its *number*.

Walvoord writes further on the two views regarding the placement of the Tree in relation to the River.

The visual picture presented is that the river of life flows down through the middle of the city, and the tree is large enough to span the river, so that the river is in the midst of the street, and the tree is on both sides of the river. It would appear that the pure river of the water of life is not a broad body but a clear stream sufficiently narrow to allow for this arrangement. Swete offers a possible solution to the problem of this description by saying, "The picture presented is that of a river flowing through the broad street which intersects the city, a row of trees being on either side. Swete interprets the word tree as a collective reference and finds a parallel situation in Ezekiel 47:12.

(2) THE FRUITFULNESS OF THE TREE.

[1] IT HAS GREAT VARIETY: *which bare twelve manner of fruits.* Though their taste and nature differ, each has the life giving or sustaining essence of the tree - *life. twelve kinds,* suited to the refined taste of all the saints in glory.

[2] IT HAS GREAT FRUITFULNESS: *and yielded her fruit every month*. This tree is never empty, never barren; there is always fruit upon it. In heaven there is not only a variety of pure and satisfying pleasures, but a continuance of them, and always fresh.

[3] IT IS THERAPEUTIC: *and the leaves of the tree were for the healing of the nations.* At the beginning of Eternity the Millennial saints in non-resurrected bodies will be *healed* by the leaves of this tree. As regarding the fruit, it will be eaten for pleasure.

3. THE ABOLITION OF THE CURSE. *And there shall be no more curse: but the throne of God and of the Lamb shall be in it; and his servants shall serve him* (22:3). In the Millennium there will be great joy and a lifting of the curse but not a total removal, for it will still be possible for the sinner to be *accursed*.

- *And I will rejoice in Jerusalem, and joy in my people: and the voice of weeping shall be no more heard in her, nor the voice of crying. 20 There shall be no more thence an infant of days, nor an old man that hath not filled his days: for the child shall die an hundred years old;* ***but the sinner being an hundred years old shall be accursed*** (Isa 65:19,20).

Here is the great excellency of the New Jerusalem, the New Earth and the New Heavens; Satan and fallen human nature have absolutely no presence there. Nor is there any residual effect from the Fall. Because of Christ's Work on the Cross *there shall be no more curse*. On the contrary *the throne of God and of the Lamb* is there! And, in joyful adoration *his servants shall serve him*.

4. THE SUPREME JOY OF THE CITY. *And they shall see his face; and his name shall be in their foreheads* (22:4). There, the saints shall see the face of God, which was not possible before (Jhn 1:18). Immediate access to the glory of God will be the constant experience. There, God will own them to the extent of having His seal and Name on their foreheads. Thus man in that day will be brought into perfect harmony with the Lord Himself.

- *Him that overcometh will I make a pillar in the temple of my God, and he shall go no more out: and **I will write** upon him the name of my God, and the name of the city of my God, which is new Jerusalem, which cometh down out of heaven from my God: and **I will write** upon him my new name* (Rev 3:12).

CHAPTER 21 & 22

5. THE ABSENCE OF ANY DISTRACTION OR SHADOW IN THE CITY. *And there shall be no night there; and they need no candle, neither light of the sun; for the Lord God giveth them light: and they shall reign for ever and ever* (22:5). They shall be full of wisdom and comfort, continually walking in the light of the Lord; and this not for a time, *but for ever and ever.* In joyful harmony they shall reign over the ever expanding peoples of the New Heaven and the New Earth.

A.T. Pearson summarizes verses 3-5:

- *There shall be no more curse*—perfect restoration.
- *But the throne of God and of the Lamb shall be in it*—perfect administration.
- *His servants shall serve him*—perfect subordination.
- *And they shall see his face*—perfect transformation.
- *And his name shall be in their foreheads*—perfect identification.
- *And there shall be no night there; and they need no candle, neither light of the sun; for the Lord giveth them light*—perfect illumination.
- *And they shall reign forever and ever*—perfect exultation. (from Walvoord).

4. THE FINAL CALL   22:6-21

A. THE FIRST TESTIMONY 22:6,7

THE FINAL CONFIRMATIONS

(22:6) *And he said unto me, These sayings are faithful and true: and the Lord God of the holy prophets sent his angel to shew unto his servants the things which must shortly be done.* (22:7) *Behold, I come quickly: blessed is he that keepeth the sayings of the prophecy of this book.*

We have here a solemn ratification of the contents of this book, and coming as it does at the end of the Bible of the Bible itself. The final four testimonies assure of the imminence of the Lord's Return and the blessing reserved for all who love and watch for it.

1. IT IS CONFIRMED BY THE LORD HIMSELF. *And he said unto me, These sayings are faithful and true* (22:6). The *Lord God* is *faithful and true,* and so are all His pronouncements.

2. IT IS CONFIRMED BY THE MESSENGERS HE CHOSE: *and the Lord God of the holy prophets sent his angel.* God chose the best through whom He inspired the words of the Book of Revelation, and the entire Bible. *Holy men of God spake as they were moved by the Holy Ghost* (2 Pet 1:21).

3. IT IS CONFIRMED BY THE SOON AND IMMINENT ACCOMPLISHMENT: *the things which must shortly be done. Behold, I come quickly.* (22:7). *Yet, a little while* (Heb 10:37), is always the word that describes the immediacy of the Lord's Return. T*hough it tarry wait for it* (Hab 2:3). And, when it comes *it will be suddenly*!

Here the promise of His Coming is especially to those to whom it was first addressed in the Book of Revelation – The Churches (Chapters 1-3)! That is, addressed to those living in the period before the end time events, so fully described in Revelation, begin to unfold.

- *Behold, I come quickly: hold that fast which thou hast, that no man take thy crown* (Rev 3:11).

THE BOOK OF REVELATION

4. IT IS CONFIRMED BY PRESENT AND FUTURE BLESSEDNESS: *blessed is he that keepeth the sayings of the prophecy of this book.* Thus the Book of Revelation begins and ends with a special promise of blessedness to those who take its contents seriously (Rev 1:3). They will soon be confirmed by their accomplishment: they are things that *must shortly come* (Rev 1:1). Christ will make haste, *he will come quickly,* and put all things out of doubt; and then those will prove to be the wise and happy men who have believed and kept his words. The *blessed* in this verse is the sixth of the seven beatitudes in Revelation.

Note: "The certain accomplishment of the prophecies of this Book is three times declared (19:9; 21:5; 22:6). In the Introduction and Conclusion it is three times affirmed that these are Divine predictions and not mere human imaginations (1:1; 22:6 and 22:16). At the opening and close of the Book a blessing is pronounced on its readers and observers (1:3 and 22:7)." Williams.

B. THE SECOND TESTIMONY 22: 8-15

THE FINAL CHOICES

(22:8) *And I John saw these things, and heard them. And when I had heard and seen, I fell down to worship before the feet of the angel which shewed me these things.* (22:9) *Then saith he unto me, See thou do it not: for I am thy fellowservant, and of thy brethren the prophets, and of them which keep the sayings of this book: worship God.*

(22:10) *And he saith unto me, Seal not the sayings of the prophecy of this book: for the time is at hand.*

(22:11) *He that is unjust, let him be unjust still: and he which is filthy, let him be filthy still: and he that is righteous, let him be righteous still: and he that is holy, let him be holy still.*

(22:12) *And, behold, I come quickly; and my reward is with me, to give every man according as his work shall be.*

(22:13) *I am Alpha and Omega, the beginning and the end, the first and the last.* (22:14) *Blessed are they that do his commandments, that they may have right to the tree of life, and may enter in through the gates into the city.* (22:15) *For without are dogs, and sorcerers, and whoremongers, and murderers, and idolaters, and whosoever loveth and maketh a lie.*

1. THE CHOICE IN WORSHIP. *And I John saw these things, and heard them. And when I had heard and seen, I fell down to worship before the feet of the angel which shewed me these things. Then saith he unto me, See thou do it not: for I am thy fellowservant, and of thy brethren the prophets, and of them which keep the sayings of this book: worship God* (22:8,9). John for the second time is overwhelmed (19:10). The angel who had been the apostle's guide and interpreter in these visions immediately corrects his error. As great as angels are they are not to be worshipped. Multitudes have had objects of worship that were a lot less than angels. Shortly the world will worship the Beast (13:8). A choice must be made in worship. This relapse, left as a perpetual entry at the close of Scripture, demonstrates that in this work of inspiration John was a faithful and an impartial writer. It also demonstrates that snares can beset a believer at the very end of their work.

2. THE CHOICE IN STUDY. *And he saith unto me, Seal not the sayings of the prophecy of this book: for the time is at hand* (22:10). The order is given to leave this Book of Divine Prophecy open and to study it continually. The Book of Revelation is literally *the Apocalypse* (*apo kalupto* = to take away the covering). It is now unsealed. It is now open. Do not reseal it! Do not close it! Do not ignore it! This is the exactly what many professing

Christians have done. John Calvin did not comment on Revelation. This is in effect a prophecy that many by purpose or neglect will *seal the book*.

Daniel was told that Divine purposes had to intervene prior to the commencement of the prophecies shown to him (Dan 12:9,13); but John was assured that *the time was at hand*, that is, that this future period of human history beginning in Chapter 4 was *at hand*, imminent, next in order for fulfilment. See Williams.

3. THE CHOICE IN CHARACTER. *He that is unjust, let him be unjust still: and he which is filthy, let him be filthy still: and he that is righteous, let him be righteous still: and he that is holy, let him be holy still* (22:11). The *effect* of the Book of Revelation kept open or shut is the *effect* that such a choice has on the character. Heed or ignore what is in this capstone of the Bible and this is the result! Present choices fix character. Present choices unless readily repented of will become permanent in character.

4. THE CHOICE IN WATCHING. *And, behold, I come quickly; and my reward is with me, to give every man according as his work shall be.* (22:12). Here in these concluding verses is the second announcement of our Lords imminent Return (22:7), again introduced by behold (it is something to *be beholden of*). Note how from the following how *watching* for the Lord's Return can decline.

- *Blessed are those servants, whom the lord when he cometh **shall find watching*** (Lk 12:37).
- *But and if that servant say in his heart, **My lord delayeth his coming**; and shall begin to beat the menservants and maidens, and to eat and drink, and to be drunken* (Lk 12:45).
- *If therefore thou **shalt not watch**, I will come on thee as a thief, and thou shalt not know what hour I will come upon thee* (Rev 3:3).

Here is added the promise that the Lord is bringing His reward. This looks forward to the Judgement Seat of Christ for the saved (Rom 14:10;1 Cor 3:13: 2 Cor. 5:10). "It is noteworthy, however, that all final judgments relate to *works* whether they are in connection with Christians who are being rewarded or unsaved who are being punished. God, the righteous judge, will deal with all men's works in the proper time and order." (Walvoord). Works demonstrate whether faith is a *resident* or is absent from the heart.

5. THE CHOICE OF WITHIN OR WITHOUT.
(1) FROM WHOM THE DECREE COMES. *I am Alpha and Omega, the beginning and the end, the first and the last* (22:13). Here is the majesty of the everlasting Saviour. Three great pairs of titles declaring His eternality are now given. Christ again repeats that He is *the Alpha and Omega* (see 1:8,11,17; 2:8; 21:6). It is the Word of Him who is the author, finisher, and rewarder of the faith and holiness of his people. He is *the first and the last*, and the same from first to last, and thus so is His Word also. *Forever, O LORD, thy word is settled in heaven* (Psa 119:89).

Note: There could be no more decisive and conclusive assertion of absolute Godhead and Deity than for Christ to claim to be *the Alpha and the Omega*. Williams.

(2) FOR WHOM THE DECREE IS MADE.
[1] THOSE WHO MAY ENTER. *Blessed are they that do his commandments, that they may have right to the tree of life, and may enter in through the gates into the city* (22:14). At the beginning of Eternity the Millennial saints in non-resurrected bodies will be *healed* by the leaves of this tree (22:2). All who thus enter will have demonstrated their faith by their adherence to the Lord's word and commandments (Matt 7:20; 1 Jhn 3:22).

With this *blessed* we have the seventh and last beatitude of Revelation. (1:3; 14:13; 16:15; 19:9; 20:6; 22:7). It is a blessing to those who though they reside outside of the New Jerusalem, they may freely come and share of the blessings within the city, including the inestimable blessing of partaking of the Tree of Life.

[2] THOSE WHO ARE BARRED. *For without are dogs, and sorcerers, and whoremongers, and murderers, and idolaters, and whosoever loveth and maketh a lie* (22:15). There will be no sin the New Earth or New Heavens. The Lake of Fire is *without* and these seven categories of sin describe its inhabitants. Note, that by this statement they have not been *annihilated* in the Lake of Fire. What they were when they entered, they still are.

- *Then shall he say also unto them on the left hand, Depart from me, ye cursed, into everlasting fire, prepared for the devil and his angels (Matt 25:41).*

C. THE THIRD TESTIMONY 22:16,17

THE FINAL INVITATIONS

(22:16) *I Jesus have sent mine angel to testify unto you these things in the churches. I am the root and the offspring of David, and the bright and morning star.* (22:17) *And the Spirit and the bride say, Come. And let him that heareth say, Come. And let him that is athirst come. And whosoever will, let him take the water of life freely.*

1. THE LORD'S CONFIRMATION OF THE BOOK. *I Jesus have sent mine angel to testify unto you these things in the churches. I am the root and the offspring of David, and the bright and morning star* (22:16). This Book is the testimony of *I Jesus*. And this Jesus, as God, is *the root of David*, though, as man, He is *the offspring of David* - a Person in whom all *uncreated* and *created* excellences meet (cp. Isa 11:1). He is the fountain of all light, *the bright and morning star* (Num 24:17; Rev 2:28). He heralds the coming day as the One who comes for His Church at the Rapture and by opening the Seals (Rev 5,6) prepares the world for the Millennial Day.

This is the first times *churches* have been mentioned since Chapter 3. With that mention, the conclusion of the Book is similar to the beginning.

Joseph Seiss notes the points of similarity between the introduction and conclusion:

> Its derivation from God, the signifying of it by the angel, the seeing, hearing, and writing of it by John, the blessing upon those who give due attention to it, the nearness of the time for fulfilment of what is described, the solemn authentication from Christ, the titles by which he describes himself, and even the personal expressions of John, recur in the Epilogue, almost the same as in the Prologue. (from Walvoord).

Note: "The Messiah assures John that the angel was His messenger. He calls Himself *Jesus*, but John addresses Him as *Lord Jesus* (22:20); and all Christians should be similarly reverent." Williams.

2. THE JOINT INVITATION TO *WHOSOEVER WILL*. *And the Spirit and the bride say, Come. And let him that heareth say, Come. And let him that is athirst come. And whosoever will, let him take the water of life freely* (22:17). The Spirit of God working through all true believers sends out this Gospel invitation. All who have felt in their souls a thirst which nothing in this world can quench and have received these waters add their voices to the great invitation.

CHAPTER 21 & 22

Note: The threefold invitation is addressed first to the one that **hereth**, then to the one who is **athirst** and then to **whosoever will**.

- **Ho, every one that thirsteth, come ye to the waters**, *and he that hath no money; come ye, buy, and eat; yea, come, buy wine and milk without money and without price* (Isa 55:1).

D. THE FOURTH TESTIMONY 22:18-21
THE FINAL WARNINGS

(22:18) *For I testify unto every man that heareth the words of the prophecy of this book, If any man shall add unto these things, God shall add unto him the plagues that are written in this book:* (22:19) *And if any man shall take away from the words of the book of this prophecy, God shall take away his part out of the book of life, and out of the holy city, and from the things which are written in this book.*

(22:20) *He which testifieth these things saith,* Surely I come quickly. *Amen. Even so, come, Lord Jesus.* (22:21) *The grace of our Lord Jesus Christ be with you all. Amen.*

1. THE BOOK OF REVELATION CLOSES WITH A SOLEMN WARNING. This warning goes to all who should dare to corrupt or change the Words of God.

(1) BY ADDING TO THE SCRIPTURES. *For I testify unto every man that heareth the words of the prophecy of this book, If any man shall add unto these things, God shall add unto him the plagues that are written in this book* (22:18). The sufficiency of the Holy Scriptures as a full and final revelation from God, is here asserted. The Bible ends with a warning against tampering with the Bible (cp. Deut. 4:2; 12:32; Prov. 30:6). He that adds to the Words of God draws down upon himself *all the plagues written in this book*. As the plagues in this Book are Tribulation plagues, this is an end time warning when so much corruption has been brought into the Bible through the Modern Versions.

(2) BY TAKING FROM THE SCRIPTURES. *And if any man shall take away from the words of the book of this prophecy, God shall take away his part out of the book of life, and out of the holy city, and from the things which are written in this book* (22:19). Nearly 2900 Greek words have been deleted from the Aleph-B (Sinaiticus-Vaticanus) text of modern New Testaments. Those who knowingly and with determination support this will have no place in either the Book of Life or the New Jerusalem. He who takes anything away from the Bible cuts himself off from all the promises and privileges of the Bible. This sanction is like a flaming sword, to guard the Text and Canon of the Scriptures from profane hands. Such a fence as this God set about the Law (Deut 4:2), and the whole Old Testament (Mal 4:4), and now in the most solemn manner places around the entire Bible.

For a recent example of how weak the manuscript evidence is for the modern editions of the New Testament, see *The Forging of Codex Sinaiticus* by Bill Cooper.

2. THE BOOK OF REVELATION CLOSES WITH A WONDERFUL PROMISE.

(1) THE PROMISE OF HIS COMING. *He which testifieth these things saith,* Surely I come quickly. *Amen. Even so, come, Lord Jesus* (22:20). Once more Christ speaks, and for the last time His voice is heard saying, **Surely I come quickly**. As when He ascended into heaven, He parted with a promise of His gracious presence, so here he parts with a promise of a swift return. This is the third time the promise is given in the closing chapter (20:7,12,20).

If any say, *Where is the promise of his coming*, when so many ages have passed since this was written? Let them know He is *not slack* to his people, but *longsuffering* to the lost (2 Pet 3:9). His Coming will be sooner than they are aware, sooner than they are prepared, sooner than they desire; and to his people it will be seasonable. The vision is for an appointed time, and will not tarry. *He will come quickly;* let this word be always sounding in our ear, and let us give all diligence that we may be found of him in peace, *without spot and blameless. Matthew Henry.*

The believer gives a hearty echo to Christ's promise. **Amen. Even so, come, Lord Jesus.** Here is a firm belief. Here is a firm desire. May both be in our hearts in these closing days. What comes from Heaven in a promise should be sent back to heaven in a prayer.

(2) THE PROMISE OF HIS GRACE. **The grace of our Lord Jesus Christ be with you all. Amen** (22:21). Nothing should be more desired by us than that the grace of Christ may be with us as we serve Him in this world and as we await His Return to take us to the upper world.

"This final book of the Scriptures which began with the revelation of Jesus Christ ends with a prayer that His grace might be with those who have witnessed the scene through John's pen. Probably no book in the Bible presents in more stark contrast the grace of God as seen in the lives and destinies of the saints as compared to the righteous judgment of God on the wicked. In no other book are the issues made more specific. The book of Revelation is the presentation in the Word of God of what the saints will witness and experience in the glorious consummation of the ages. With John we can pray, *Even so, come, Lord Jesus.*" (John Walvoord).

THE SEVEN BEATITUDES OF THE BOOK OF REVELATION

- ***Blessed** is he that readeth, and they that hear the words of this prophecy, and keep those things which are written therein: for the time is at hand* (1:3).
- *And I heard a voice from heaven saying unto me, Write, **Blessed** are the dead which die in the Lord from henceforth: Yea, saith the Spirit, that they may rest from their labours; and their works do follow them* (14:13).
- *Behold, I come as a thief. **Blessed** is he that watcheth, and keepeth his garments, lest he walk naked, and they see his shame* (16:15).
- *And he saith unto me, Write, **Blessed** are they which are called unto the marriage supper of the Lamb. And he saith unto me, These are the true sayings of God* (19:9).
- ***Blessed** and holy is he that hath part in the first resurrection: on such the second death hath no power, but they shall be priests of God and of Christ, and shall reign with him a thousand years* (20:6).
- *Behold, I come quickly: **blessed** is he that keepeth the sayings of the prophecy of this book* (22:7).
- ***Blessed** are they that do his commandments, that they may have right to the tree of life, and may enter in through the gates into the city* (22:14).

Once again! The final words that our Lord spoke as the Bible closes:

Surely I come quickly

ABOUT THE AUTHOR

Dr. J. A. Moorman and his wife, Dot. 2017

Jack A. Moorman studied for a while at the Indianapolis campus of Purdue University, attended briefly Indiana Bible College, and graduated from Tennessee Temple Bible School. He has been with Baptist International Missions Inc. (BIMI) since 1967 and has been involved in church planting, Bible Institute teaching and extensive distribution of Scriptures and gospel tracts in Johannesburg, South Africa from 1968 – 1988, and in England and London since 1988. He married his wife, Dot, on November 22 1963.

J.A. Moorman has written the following scholarly books defending the King James Bible and the Hebrew, Aramaic and Greek words that underlie it:

1. When the KJV Departs from the "Majority Text".
2. Early Manuscripts, Church Fathers, and the Authorized Version.
3. Forever Settled
4. Missing in Modern Bibles—The Old Heresy Revived.
5. Samuel P. Tregelles—The Man Who Made the Critical Text Acceptable to Bible Believers.
6. 8,000 Differences Between the Textus Receptus and the Critical Text.
7. Bible Chronology: The Two Great Divides.
8. The Biblical and Observational Case for Geocentricity.
9. Genesis to the Exodus
10. Daniel, The Times of the Gentiles & The Times of Jerusalem

These well-documented works and are replete with evidence which he has gleaned from his own resources as well as references found in the British Museum, British Library and other libraries in South Africa and the United Kingdom.

He has been the pastor of Bethel Baptist Church in London, England since 1993. A great deal of his time, and on a nearly daily basis, is spent in distributing Gospel Literature on the crowded streets of London and beyond. May God bless his unfailing service to the Lord Jesus Christ.

www.ingramcontent.com/pod-product-compliance
Lightning Source LLC
Chambersburg PA
CBHW080804010526
44113CB00013B/2323